Guide to Biosimilars Litigation and Regulation in the U.S.

2019–2020 Edition

THOMSON REUTERS®

For Customer Assistance Call 1-800-328-4880

Mat #42647197

For authorization to photocopy, please contact the **Copyright Clearance Center** at 222 Rosewood Drive, Danvers, MA 01923, USA (978) 750-8400; fax (978) 646-8600 or **West's Copyright Services** at 610 Opperman Drive, Eagan, MN 55123, fax (651) 687-7551. Please outline the specific material involved, the number of copies you wish to distribute and the purpose or format of the use.

ISBN 978-1-539-28672-1

Senior Editors

Robert V. Cerwinski
Michael B. Cottler
Alexandra D. Valenti
Lindsey A. Wanner

Contributors

Christine Armellino
Beth Ashbridge
Naomi Birbach
Elaine Herrmann Blais
Jacqueline Genovese Bova
James Breen
Brian Burgess
Cindy Chang
Linnea P. Cipriano
Jane Cullis
Natasha E. Daughtrey
Kevin J. DeJong
Brian T. Drummond
Samantha M. Flener
Sarah K. Frederick
Christopher T. Holding
Zachariah Holmes
Nilda M. Isidro
William G. James
William M. Jay
Glenn S. Kerner
Scott Lassman
Ira J. Levy
Alexandra Lu
Daniel Margolis
Nicholas K. Mitrokostas
Elizabeth Mulkey
Khurram Naik
Emily L. Rapalino
Alison Siedor
Steven S. Tjoe
Vi Tran
Josh Weinger
Joshua A. Whitehill
Daryl L. Wiesen
Huiya Wu
Jenny J. Zhang
Keith A. Zullow

Goodwin

Goodwin is an *AmLaw* 50 law firm with more than 1,200 lawyers across the United States, Europe, and Asia. We excel at complex transactions, high stakes litigation, and world class advisory services in the life sciences, private equity, real estate, and technology industries.

Goodwin's IP Litigation team has made serving the needs of the biopharmaceutical industry a strategic priority for more than two decades. As evidenced by our significant trial and appellate victories, our deep bench of experienced trial lawyers, and our numerous awards and recognitions, Goodwin has one of the premier Hatch-Waxman and Biosimilars practices in the United States. We have successfully represented both innovators and generic companies in some of the most significant litigations brought over the past decades. These victories have come not only after trial, but at the pretrial stage, on appeal, and through favorable settlements.

We have significant experience before the Patent Trial and Appeal Board, the United States International Trade Commission, and the United States Supreme Court. At the PTAB, Goodwin has substantial experience representing both patent owners and challengers in IPR and CBM proceedings. We have counseled dozens of companies regarding filing strategies and have successfully achieved institution of multiple IPR trials and defended multiple patent owners facing reexamination, IPR, and CBM petitions.

Our IP litigation team has been recognized as a leader among law firms, having been named "IP Practice of the Year" for four consecutive years. We have also been recognized as a five-time winner of Biotech Law Firm of the Year by *U.S. News - Best Lawyers*. We have received consistent honors from *LMG Life Sciences* including the prestigious "Life Cycle Firm of the Year" and "Hatch-Waxman Firm of the Year."

To keep up-to-date on legal developments in the biosimilars space, subscribe to our award-winning blog, Big Molecule Watch,[1] or our companion blog, Big Molecule Watch China.[2]

---

[1] www.bigmoleculewatch.com.

[2] https://www.bigmoleculewatch.cn/.

Guide to Biosimilars Litigation and Regulation in the U.S.

I. INTRODUCTION

The statute that created a regulatory pathway for the approval of biosimilar products in the U.S. is known as the Biologics Price, Competition and Innovation Act of 2009 ("BPCIA" for short). While the BPCIA has been praised for its policy goal of expanding patient access to biologic medicines, few have lauded it as a model of legislative clarity. In the landmark case *Amgen v. Sandoz*, in which the U.S. Court of Appeals for the Federal Circuit first attempted to clarify the BPCIA's labyrinthine patent infringement resolution scheme commonly referred to as "the patent dance," Judge Lourie (channeling Winston Churchill) declared the statute "a riddle wrapped in a mystery inside an enigma."[1] After wrestling with fundamental ambiguities in the statute, such as whether the patent dance is mandatory and whether its steps are enforceable by a reference product sponsor or biosimilar applicant, Judge Lourie appended a footnote to the court's opinion that suggested more than a little judicial frustration with the statute's lack of clarity: "[i]n these opinions, we do our best to unravel the riddle, solve the mystery, and comprehend the enigma."[2]

The *Amgen v. Sandoz* opinion issued in 2015, at a time when the biosimilar industry had very limited experience with the BPCIA. Only one biosimilar had been approved by the U.S. Food & Drug Administration (Sandoz's Zarxio® (filgrastim-sndz)) and only two patent infringement litigations had been brought under the BPCIA (against Zarxio® and Celltrion's Inflectra® (infliximab-dyyb)). In the four years that have elapsed since then, much has happened to clarify the BPCIA and regulatory pathway for biosimilars.

---

[1] *Amgen Inc. v. Sandoz Inc.*, 794 F.3d 1347, 1351 n.1 (Fed. Cir. 2015), *rev'd in part, vacated in part*, 137 S. Ct. 1664 (2017).

[2] *Amgen*, 794 F.3d at 1351 n.1. Given that the U.S. Supreme Court ultimately disagreed with the way in which Judge Lourie and the Federal Circuit resolved some of the statutory ambiguities, Judge Lourie's frustration was not misplaced.

The initial trickle of applications into the U.S. Food & Drug Administration ("FDA") has become a vigorous stream, and the FDA has gotten increasingly comfortable and efficient in approving products that meet the BPCIA's threshold requirements for biosimilarity. As of the date of this edition, FDA has approved over twenty biosimilar products. Unsurprisingly, reference product sponsors have defended their markets aggressively and brought patent infringement litigations against every single one of these products, and indeed every single biosimilar manufacturer that has submitted an application to FDA for review. The U.S. Supreme Court has also issued an opinion to clarify the mechanics of the patent dance, including—crucially—whether the steps of the dance are enforceable, the penalties for not dancing, and when notice of first commercial marketing to initiate the second wave of the dance may be given.[3] This means that courts and litigants have become at least somewhat familiar with how the dance works in practice, as well as the benefits and drawbacks of dancing.

And yet while four years of litigation and FDA review have clarified certain provisions of the patent dance and much of the regulatory pathway for establishing biosimilarity, other aspects of the BPCIA remain unclear. For example, not a single applicant has sought an interchangeable designation from FDA, and thus the requirements—and costs—for establishing interchangeability remain uncertain. Perhaps even more importantly, the relative dearth of biosimilar launches in the U.S., as well as the effectiveness of strategies designed to forestall biosimilar competition (including patent "thickets" and exclusionary contracting practices by reference product sponsors), have raised vitally important questions about how effective the BPCIA ultimately will be in facilitating biosimilar market entry in the U.S.

Given the number of biosimilar applications and litigations pending at the moment, as well as the number of commercial launches expected in 2020–2023 from publicly-announced litigation settlements, we expect many of these legal and market uncertainties to be clarified over the next few years. In particular, as multiple biosimilar versions of biologics such as rituximab, trastuzumab and adalimumab enter the U.S. market, it will be revealing to see whether biosimilar uptake in the U.S. is as robust as in Europe and

---

[3] *Sandoz Inc. v. Amgen Inc.*, 137 S. Ct. 1664 (2017).

elsewhere, or whether commercial tactics such as those that have effectively defended the market for Remicade® against biosimilar infliximab products will end up becoming commonplace. It will also be interesting to see whether any biosimilar applicant invests in the higher-powered—and higher cost—clinical trials needed to obtain an interchangeable designation, and whether the market dynamics for that interchangeable approximate those seen with small molecule generic drugs approved under the Hatch Waxman Act. Indeed, if biosimilar manufacturers continue to turn their backs on the automatic pharmacy substitution available for interchangeable biosimilars in most states, which is intended to drive the kind of rapid market conversion seen with small molecule generic drugs, Congress may ultimately need to go back to the drawing board and amend the BPCIA to make interchangeability more economically attractive.

What we can be sure of is that legal, regulatory and market developments in the world of biosimilars will continue at a rapid pace. For the past four years, the authors of this Guide have tracked those developments on a daily basis at www.bigmoleculewatch.com, the award-winning biosimilar blog published by Goodwin Procter LLC. What has been missing from this and other coverage of the biosimilars industry is a publication that guides readers with specific questions about particular statutory requirements, litigations or regulatory requirements to the statutory sections, court opinions and FDA guidances that answer those questions. This Guide is intended to fill that need. We hope it will serve both as a reference tool for veterans in the biosimilar industry and a useful guide for those new to biosimilars.

— [the Editorial Staff]

Summary of Contents

Chapter 1. Overview of the U.S. Biosimilar Market

Chapter 2. Overview of BPCIA Litigation

Chapter 3. The FDA Approval Process for Biosimilar and Interchangeable Biological Products

Chapter 4. BPCIA Patent Litigation

Chapter 5. Post-Grant Proceedings and BPCIA Litigations

Chapter 6. ITC Section 337 Actions

Chapter 7. Discovery in the United States for Use in Foreign Litigation

Chapter 8. Antitrust Actions

Chapter 9. Product Liability Claims Against Biosimilars

Appendices

Appendix A. Compilation of Relevant Statutes (42 USC 262 and 35 USC 271)

Appendix B. Compilation of Relevant Regulations (21 CFR 10.115, 21 CFR Part 600, 37 CFR 42)

Appendix C1. Scientific Considerations in Demonstrating Biosimilarity to a Reference Product

Appendix C2. Clinical Pharmacology Data to Support a Demonstration of Biosimilarity to a Reference Product

Appendix C3. Assessing User Fees Under the Biosimilar User Fee Amendments of 2017

Appendix C4. Labeling for Biosimilar Products Guidance

Appendix C5. Interpretation of the "Deemed to be a License" Provision of the Biologics Price Competition and Innovation Act of 2009

Appendix C6. Questions and Answers on Biosimilar Development and the BPCI Act

Appendix C7.   Considerations in Demonstrating Interchangeability With a Reference Product

Appendix D1.   Guidance for Industry Reference Product Exclusivity for Biological Products Filed Under Section 351(a) of the PHS Act

Appendix D2.   Citizen Petitions and Petitions for Stay of Action Subject to Section 505(q) of the Federal Food, Drug, and Cosmetic Act

Appendix D3.   Formal Meetings Between the FDA and Sponsors or Applicants of BsUFA Products

Appendix D4.   New and Revised Draft Q&As on Biosimilar Development and the BPCI Act (Revision 2)

Appendix D5.   Development of Therapeutic Protein Biosimilars: Comparative Analytical Assessment and Other Quality-Related Considerations

Appendix E.   FDA Approvals and U.S. Launches of Biosimilars

Appendix F.   BPCIA Litigations

Table of Laws and Rules

Table of Cases

Index

Table of Contents

CHAPTER 1. OVERVIEW OF THE U.S. BIOSIMILAR MARKET

§ 1:1   U.S. biosimilars market generally

CHAPTER 2. OVERVIEW OF BPCIA LITIGATION

§ 2:1   BPCIA litigation generally

CHAPTER 3. THE FDA APPROVAL PROCESS FOR BIOSIMILAR AND INTERCHANGEABLE BIOLOGICAL PRODUCTS

I. GENERALLY

§ 3:1   Approval process overview

II. APPLICATION TYPES

§ 3:2   Biologics License Applications (BLAs)
§ 3:3   Abbreviated Biologics License Applications (aBLAs)
§ 3:4   Drug products not regulated as biological products
§ 3:5   Converting NDAs to BLAs in 2020

III. ABBREVIATED BIOLOGICS LICENSE APPLICATIONS

§ 3:6   Requirements for demonstrating biosimilarity
§ 3:7   —Manufacturing information
§ 3:8   —Clinical trials
§ 3:9   —Proving biosimilarity
§ 3:10 —Consequences of being better or worse than a Reference Product
§ 3:11 —Labeling requirements
§ 3:12 Additional requirements for demonstrating interchangeability
§ 3:13 —Benefits: Interchangeable product exclusivity
§ 3:14 No Patent Linkage

IV. BIOBETTERS

§ 3:15   Biobetters generally

V. THE FDA APPROVAL PROCESS

§ 3:16   The FDA review timeline
§ 3:17   —Exclusivity provisions impacting biosimilars
§ 3:18   — —Reference product exclusivity
§ 3:19   — —Pediatric exclusivity
§ 3:20   — —Orphan drug exclusivity
§ 3:21   Naming
§ 3:22   Citizen petitions
§ 3:23   Complete response letters

VI. POST-LICENSURE REQUIREMENTS

§ 3:24   Post-Licensure establishment inspection
§ 3:25   Additional post-licensure requirements

CHAPTER 4. BPCIA PATENT LITIGATION

I. JURISDICTION BEFORE SUBMISSION OF THE ABLA

§ 4:1   Pre-submission jurisdiction

II. THE PATENT DANCE

§ 4:2   Patent dance overview
§ 4:3   The Biosimilar applicant discloses information
          regarding its product to the RPS
§ 4:4   The biosimilar applicant discloses information
          regarding its product to the RPS—Providing a
          Copy of the aBLA
§ 4:5   —Providing "Such Other Information"
§ 4:6   —Consequences (or Lack Thereof) for failing to
          "Provide"
§ 4:7   —Providing additional requested information
§ 4:8   Protection of confidential information
§ 4:9   —Recipients of confidential information
§ 4:10   — —Prosecution bar
§ 4:11   — —Regulatory bar
§ 4:12   —Use of confidential information during and after
          the patent dance
§ 4:13   —Enforceability

§ 4:14 The RPS provides the "3(A) statement"—the list of patents it believes would be infringed

§ 4:15 3(B) statement by the biosimilar applicant

§ 4:16 —Biosimilar applicant's 3(B) list

§ 4:17 —Biosimilar applicant's detailed statement

§ 4:18 3(C) statement by the RPS

§ 4:19 Negotiation of patents to be litigated and the first wave litigation

§ 4:20 —Initiation of first-wave suit after negotiations

III. NEWLY-ISSUED OR LICENSED PATENTS

§ 4:21 Newly issued or licensed patents generally

IV. NOTICE OF COMMERCIAL MARKETING

§ 4:22 Overview

§ 4:23 The Statute governing NCM

§ 4:24 —Timing of NCM

§ 4:25 —Requirements for providing NCM

§ 4:26 The statute governing NCM—Enforcement of NCM provisions

§ 4:27 The Statute governing NCM—Some open NCM-related questions

§ 4:28 Second wave litigation

§ 4:29 —Who can bring suit after the applicant provides NCM?

§ 4:30 —Factors that could impact bringing suit after providing NCM

§ 4:31 —What will second wave litigation look like?

V. COMMENCEMENT OF SUIT

§ 4:32 Venue for biosimilar litigation

§ 4:33 —Venue in patent-infringement actions generally

§ 4:34 — —Venue based on defendant's residence

§ 4:35 — —Venue based on infringement and place of business

§ 4:36 — — —Foreign defendants

§ 4:37 —Venue in actions for a declaratory judgment

§ 4:38 —Venue in patent-infringement actions generally—Is a declaratory-judgment action ever "For Patent Infringement"?

§ 4:39 — —Where can a declaratory judgment action be brought?

§ 4:40 Subject matter jurisdiction

§ 4:41 Personal jurisdiction

§ 4:42   Standing
§ 4:43   The right of an RPS to bring a declaratory
          judgment action
§ 4:44   —RPS declaratory judgment suits based on
          section 262(*l*)(9)(C)
§ 4:45   — —RPS declaratory judgment suits based on
          section 262(*l*)(9)(B)
§ 4:46   — —Restrictions on the timing of an RPS
          declaratory judgment suit under section
          262(*l*)(9)(A)
§ 4:47   —Limits on the ability of biosimilar applicants to
          seek declaratory relief
§ 4:48   —Courts have treated the BPCIA's limits on
          declaratory judgment actions as
          non-jurisdictional
§ 4:49   —Whether the BPCIA's restrictions on
          declaratory judgment actions apply to
          counterclaims
§ 4:50   —The exercise of declaratory judgment
          jurisdiction is discretionary
§ 4:51   Limitation on claims
§ 4:52   —Applicant who fails to provide notice under
          § 262(*l*)(2)(A)
§ 4:53   —Scope-limiting ability of applicant in first wave
          litigation
§ 4:54   —Second wave litigation
§ 4:55   Right to a jury trial—General overview
§ 4:56   — —Right to jury trial in BPCIA cases
§ 4:57   — —Right to jury trial in biosimilar v. biosimilar
          patent cases

VI. PRELIMINARY INJUNCTIONS

§ 4:58   Preliminary injunctions

VII. SCHEDULING AND STAGING

§ 4:59   General scheduling & staging
§ 4:60   BPCIA scheduling issues

VIII. DISCOVERY ISSUES IN BPCIA LITIGATIONS

§ 4:61   General scope of discovery
§ 4:62   Discovery of manufacturing information
§ 4:63   Discovery of information from litigations
          concerning the same biological product or one or
          more overlapping patents-in-suit

§ 4:64   Expedited discovery in advance of a preliminary
          injunction
§ 4:65   Protective orders
§ 4:66   —Prosecution bars
§ 4:67   —Regulatory bars
§ 4:68   —Confidentiality tiers

IX. LIABILITY

§ 4:69   Patent infringement
§ 4:70   —Claim construction
§ 4:71   —Literal direct infringement
§ 4:72   —direct infringement under the doctrine of
          equivalents
§ 4:73   — —prosecution history estoppel
§ 4:74   — —Ensnarement
§ 4:75   —Indirect infringement
§ 4:76   — —Induced infringement
§ 4:77   — —Contributory infringement
§ 4:78   —Products manufactured abroad using a
          domestically patented process
§ 4:79   —Safe harbor under section 271(e)
§ 4:80   Patent validity
§ 4:81   —Ineligible subject matter (Section 101)
§ 4:82   —Anticipation (Section 102)
§ 4:83   —Obviousness (Section 103)
§ 4:84   —Lack of written description, lack of enablement,
          and indefiniteness (section 112)
§ 4:85   —Obviousness-Type double patenting
§ 4:86   Patent enforceability
§ 4:87   —Unclean hands
§ 4:88   —Inequitable conduct
§ 4:89   —Unenforceability allegations in the BPCIA
          patent dance

X. POTENTIAL REMEDIES FOR INFRINGEMENT

§ 4:90   Infringement remedies generally
§ 4:91   The BPCIA's conforming amendments to 35
          U.S.C.A. § 271(e)(4)
§ 4:92   Delaying the effective date of FDA approval
§ 4:93   Awarding monetary relief
§ 4:94   Patent enforceability—Monetary damages where
          safe harbor provision does not protect pre-
          market activity

§ 4:95   —Monetary damages for an at-risk launch
§ 4:96   —Attorneys' fees
§ 4:97   Awarding permanent injunctive relief
§ 4:98   Limitations on remedies Under 35 U.S.C.A.
          § 271(e)(6)

CHAPTER 5. POST-GRANT PROCEEDINGS AND BPCIA LITIGATIONS

§ 5:1   Introduction
§ 5:2   Background on Post-Grant Proceedings
§ 5:3   Parallel post-grant proceedings and BPCIA
          litigations
§ 5:4   Stays
§ 5:5   —The stage of the litigation
§ 5:6   —Simplification of issues
§ 5:7   —Undue prejudice
§ 5:8   — —Timing of review request
§ 5:9   — —Timing of stay request
§ 5:10   — —Status of review proceedings
§ 5:11   — —Relationship of the parties
§ 5:12   Motions to stay in BPCIA litigation
§ 5:13   Estoppel generally
§ 5:14   Real parties in interest & privity
§ 5:15   Scope of estoppel
§ 5:16   Patent owner estoppel
§ 5:17   Settlement
§ 5:18   Joinder
§ 5:19   Serial petitions
§ 5:20   Appeals

CHAPTER 6. ITC SECTION 337 ACTIONS

§ 6:1   ITC Section 337 actions generally
§ 6:2   Elements of a section 337 violation
§ 6:3   ITC remedies
§ 6:4   Comparison between section 337 investigations
          and district court litigations

CHAPTER 7. DISCOVERY IN THE UNITED STATES FOR USE IN FOREIGN LITIGATION

§ 7:1   The use of U.S. discovery in foreign litigation
          generally

§ 7:2   Procedures for a Section 1782 Action
§ 7:3   —The Ex Parte application
§ 7:4   —discretion under section 1782

CHAPTER 8. ANTITRUST ACTIONS

§ 8:1   Antitrust actions generally
§ 8:2   Challenges to patent settlement agreements
§ 8:3   Filing agreements with the government
§ 8:4   Intellectual property acquisition and
       enforcement—Sham litigation and walker process
       fraud
§ 8:5   —Patent thickets
§ 8:6   Exclusionary contracting and rebating strategies

CHAPTER 9. PRODUCT LIABILITY CLAIMS AGAINST BIOSIMILARS

§ 9:1   Failure to warn claims
§ 9:2   FDA biosimilar labeling
§ 9:3   Manufacturing defect claims
§ 9:4   Product design defect claims
§ 9:5   Field preemption and primary jurisdiction

APPENDICES

Appendix A.   Compilation of Relevant Statutes (42 USC
       262 and 35 USC 271)

Appendix B.   Compilation of Relevant Regulations (21
       CFR 10.115, 21 CFR Part 600, 37 CFR
       42)

Appendix C1.   Scientific Considerations in
       Demonstrating Biosimilarity to a
       Reference Product

Appendix C2.   Clinical Pharmacology Data to Support a
       Demonstration of Biosimilarity to a
       Reference Product

Appendix C3.   Assessing User Fees Under the Biosimilar
       User Fee Amendments of 2017

Appendix C4.   Labeling for Biosimilar Products Guidance

Appendix C5.   Interpretation of the "Deemed to be a
       License" Provision of the Biologics Price
       Competition and Innovation Act of 2009

Appendix C6.   Questions and Answers on Biosimilar
       Development and the BPCI Act

Appendix C7.   Considerations in Demonstrating
               Interchangeability With a Reference
               Product

Appendix D1.   Guidance for Industry Reference Product
               Exclusivity for Biological Products Filed
               Under Section 351(a) of the PHS Act

Appendix D2.   Citizen Petitions and Petitions for Stay of
               Action Subject to Section 505(q) of the
               Federal Food, Drug, and Cosmetic Act

Appendix D3.   Formal Meetings Between the FDA and
               Sponsors or Applicants of BsUFA
               Products

Appendix D4.   New and Revised Draft Q&As on
               Biosimilar Development and the BPCI
               Act (Revision 2)

Appendix D5.   Development of Therapeutic Protein
               Biosimilars: Comparative Analytical
               Assessment and Other Quality-Related
               Considerations

Appendix E.   FDA Approvals and U.S. Launches of
               Biosimilars

Appendix F.   BPCIA Litigations

Table of Laws and Rules

Table of Cases

Index

Chapter 1

Overview of the U.S. Biosimilar Market

> **KeyCite®:** Cases and other legal materials listed in KeyCite Scope can be researched through the KeyCite service on Westlaw®. Use KeyCite to check citations for form, parallel references, prior and later history, and comprehensive citator information, including citations to other decisions and secondary materials.

§ 1:1 U.S. biosimilars market generally

The potential for biosimilars to significantly increase patient access to biologic medicines and drive the costs of such therapies down has been widely studied and commented upon. According to a 2017 report by the RAND Corporation,[1] the increasing use of biologics (and other specialty drugs) is a primary reason why U.S. prescription drug spending continues to rise each year.[2] While less than 1-2 percent of the U.S. population is treated with a biologic each year, biologics constitute about 40% of U.S. pharmaceutical spending, and 70% of drug spending growth.[3] After analyzing the literature and public data regarding biologic pricing and market dynamics, the RAND report concluded that biosimilars have the potential to reduce U.S. pharmaceutical spending by $54 billion from 2017 to 2026.[4]

[Section 1:1]

[1]Biosimilar Cost Savings in the United States: Initial Experience and Future Potential, available at https://www.rand.org/content/dam/rand/pubs/perspectives/PE200/PE264/RAND_PE264.pdf.

[2]Biosimilar Cost Savings in the United States: Initial Experience and Future Potential, p. 2, available at https://www.rand.org/content/dam/rand/pubs/perspectives/PE200/PE264/RAND_PE264.pdf.

[3]Biosimilar Cost Savings in the United States: Initial Experience and Future Potential, p. 2, available at https://www.rand.org/content/dam/rand/pubs/perspectives/PE200/PE264/RAND_PE264.pdf.

[4]Biosimilar Cost Savings in the United States: Initial Experience and Future Potential, p. 1, available at https://www.rand.org/content/dam/

And yet as of the writing of this Guide, the U.S. is off to a slow start in realizing these cost savings. The BPCIA became law in 2010, but the FDA has approved only 23 biosimilar products for marketing in the U.S. to date. When one considers that just two-and-a-half years ago the FDA had approved only five biosimilars, this figure is encouraging in that it suggests that the FDA is now receiving and approving biosimilar applications at an accelerating rate. However, the U.S. remains substantially behind Europe. The European Medicines Agency (EMA) has approved over 60 biosimilar products, and over 20 have reached the market.

Moreover, even though the FDA has approved 23 biosimilars, the number of approved *molecules* is quite a bit smaller, and is limited to older, first-generation biologics. As can be seen from Appendix E, all of the approved U.S. biosimilars are versions of the same eight biologics, all of which were originally approved decades ago: filgrastim (in native and longer-acting pegylated forms), etanercept, adalimumab, infliximab, bevacizumab, trastuzumab, epoetin alfa and rituximab. The dearth and vintage of these reference products is due almost exclusively to the fact that the BPCIA gives reference product sponsors 12 years of market exclusivity against biosimilar competition. This is far longer than the five years of market exclusivity given to most new small-molecule drugs in the U.S. under the Hatch-Waxman laws that govern generic drug approvals.[5] This protracted period of exclusivity for new biologics has been a substantial barrier to biosimilar entry.

The number of approved biosimilars that have actually reached the U.S. market is also quite modest. Only nine biosimilars products have launched to date, and they constitute versions of only five biologic active ingredients: filgrastim (and pegfilgrastim), infliximab, epoetin alfa, trastuzumab, and bevacizumab. (*See* Appendix E). And while market uptake of the three filgrastim and two pegfilgrastim biosimilars has been relatively robust, the uptake of the two infliximab biosimilars that have launched in the U.S. has suggested that biosimilar manufacturers may face a panoply of creative, aggressive marketing tactics by reference prod-

---

rand/pubs/perspectives/PE200/PE264/RAND_PE264.pdf.

[5]However, it is not much different than the "8+2+1" exclusivity scheme for new biologics applied in Europe. The EMA grants new biologics eight years of data exclusivity, two years of market exclusivity and a one-year extension for new indications.

uct sponsors seeking to defend their markets. Johnson & Johnson's subsidiary Janssen Biotech, which markets the infliximab product referenced by all the biosimilars under the brand name Remicade, has adopted exclusive contracts with the clinical pharmacies that dispense infliximab and other injectable biologics that have, to date, effectively thwarted competition from multiple, lower-priced biosimilars. As described in detail below, Janssen's contracting methods have attracted private antitrust lawsuits from biosimilar manufacturers and prescription drug payors, and scrutiny from Congress and the Federal Trade Commission. If Janssen's contracts are ultimately found to be lawful, however, it is likely that other reference product sponsors will follow suit. Widespread use of such tactics could deal a serious, even crippling, blow to the fledgling biosimilar industry in the U.S.

The rate of biosimilar uptake in the U.S. has also been hampered by the complex and uncertain approval pathway in the BPCIA for interchangeable biosimilars. Interchangeable biosimilars were intended to be similar to generic small molecule drugs in that pharmacies could automatically substitute them for the reference product without doctor or patient involvement. Most U.S. states have enacted laws permitting such automatic substitutability. In theory, these laws should be potent drivers of market uptake and thus induce manufacturers to invest in the higher-powered clinical studies required for an interchangeability designation. To date, however, no manufacturer has sought an interchangeable designation from FDA. Although the FDA has published a guidance document to clarify the approval pathway for interchangeables, the cost of the additional clinical trial(s) required, as well as the risks associated with navigating uncharted regulatory waters, appear to have chilled interest in the pathway. Thus, a provision of the BPCIA that was intended to be a linchpin of biosimilar competition sits largely unused. It is unclear at this point whether biosimilar manufacturers are waiting for a pioneer to trailblaze the pathway for them, or whether they are unconvinced that the interchangeability study is worth the investment. What is clear is that a robust, competitive market dominated by interchangeable biosimilars is a long way off in the U.S.

Chapter 2

Overview of BPCIA Litigation

> **KeyCite®:** Cases and other legal materials listed in KeyCite Scope can be researched through the KeyCite service on Westlaw®. Use KeyCite to check citations for form, parallel references, prior and later history, and comprehensive citator information, including citations to other decisions and secondary materials.

§ 2:1 BPCIA litigation generally

The core policy goal behind the BPCIA is essentially the same as that of the Hatch Waxman laws that govern generic small molecule drugs: to facilitate the approval and market entry of lower-cost versions of older, previously-approved medicines. Both sets of laws arose out of a desire to create price competition—and achieve cost savings—for popular, expensive medicines that were nearing the end of market exclusivity created by patent protection.

But the ways in which the BPCIA seeks to achieve this policy goal are very different than the Hatch-Waxman laws. Most importantly, as mentioned, the 12-year exclusivity afforded new biologics in exchange for the obligation to permit biosimilar manufacturers to reference the brand manufacturer's safety and efficacy data is much longer than the five years afforded new small molecule drugs.

Equally important is that the tried-and-true "Orange Book" patent linkage system has been abandoned for the BPCIA's convoluted "patent dance." In the Orange Book scheme, the reference product sponsor (RPS) must provide a list of patents to the FDA for each approved product that the RPS believes cover the product or a method of using the product. The FDA publishes those lists in the Orange Book.[1] A generic manufacturer hoping to receive FDA approval earlier than the expiry of the listed patents must provide a

---

[Section 2:1]

[1]The Orange Book's official title is *Approved Drug Products with Therapeutic Equivalence Evaluations*.

5

detailed statement to the RPS describing why the generic product and its use for the indications sought will not infringe any of the listed patents, or why the listed patents are invalid. The generic manufacturer may also provide an offer of confidential access to its FDA application. Thereafter, the RPS may sue the generic manufacturer for patent infringement. In the BPCIA's patent dance, as described in detail below, there is no FDA-administered list of patents covering each product. Instead, the biosimilar applicant first discloses its aBLA and manufacturing method to the RPS, and only then does the RPS disclose a list of patents that it believes may be asserted against the biosimilar. Thereafter, the parties exchange detailed statements concerning infringement and validity, and then negotiate which patents to litigate and whether the litigation will proceed in one wave on all patents, or two waves in which a narrow set of key patents is litigated first. This pre-litigation patent dance takes around eight months to complete, which is far longer than the 45-day period of pre-suit exchanges that is typical in the Orange Book scheme. In contrast to the Orange Book scheme, however, the RPS's list of patents must contain all patents that may cover the biosimilar product, including manufacturing process patents, and patents omitted from the list may not be asserted against the biosimilar.

Further, while in the Orange Book scheme a lawsuit brought by the RPS on one or more of the listed patents will trigger an automatic 30-month stay of FDA approval of the generic, during which the parties litigate patent infringement, the BPCIA provides no such automatic stay. Instead, the biosimilar applicant must give 180 days' notice to the RPS before it may market its product, with the expectation that the RPS will bring a motion for preliminary injunction on one or more of the listed patents if it wants to keep the biosimilar off the market while the parties litigate.

And while the Orange Book scheme provides generic drug manufacturers with a six-month period of generic market exclusivity as an inducement to be the "first to file" an application that challenges the listed patents in litigation, there is no similar period of exclusivity in the BPCIA. Instead, the first applicant to obtain an interchangeable designation for its biosimilar gets a limited period of exclusivity vis-à-vis other interchangeable biosimilars. The BPCIA does not provide the first biosimilar filer any exclusivity with respect to later-filed biosimilars.

In practice, the BPCIA has not streamlined litigation or

facilitated market uptake of biosimilars as effectively as the Hatch-Waxman laws did for generic drugs. First, RPS's generally have acquired much larger patent estates in connection with their biologic reference products than what is typically listed in the Orange Book, and, indeed, in some cases have listed forty or more patents during the patent dance. This strategy, known as "patent thicketing," has made litigation under the BPCIA more expensive, less predictable, and more difficult for courts and biosimilar manufacturers to streamline. As a result, many biologics manufacturers have sat on the sidelines, unwilling to undertake the considerable financial risk of being among the first to develop biosimilars to reference products covered by patent thickets.

The interchangeability scheme and exclusivities in the BPCIA have also been far less effective in promoting switching from the reference product to the biosimilar. While generic drug makers eagerly search for and exploit any first-to-file opportunities in the Hatch Waxman world, biosimilar manufacturers have so far largely shunned the interchangeable pathway in the BPCIA. This means that biosimilar manufacturers are often caught up in a race to be the first to get FDA approval and a settlement of patent litigation, so they can obtain the first-mover advantage. This settlement race can, as seen in the case of Humira, lead to a series of settlements in which biosimilar makers who are late to file or settle have to wait behind their more aggressive competitors.

On the plus side, the fact that there is no automatic 30-month stay of FDA approval in the BPCIA, and that an RPS must move for a preliminary injunction if it wishes to preserve its market exclusivity during litigation, has meant that cases have settled earlier than they might otherwise have. Courts faced with the prospect of a complex evidentiary hearing in support of a preliminary injunction motion have sometimes required the RPS to streamline its case and pick only its best patents, or decided to have an early trial in lieu of a preliminary injunction hearing. The risk for both sides from the prospect of an early adjudication on the merits has facilitated early settlements.

Finally, the patent dance itself has been unwieldy and confusing in comparison to the Hatch-Waxman scheme. The patent dance is effectively "optional" in the sense that while the statute says the parties "shall" comply with the provisions. An applicant that wants to avoid the eight-month dance may simply refuse to initiate it, as long as it is willing to suffer the penalties provided by the BPCIA for not dancing. The applicant also may decline to proceed with two separate waves of litigation by providing its 180-day notice of commercial marketing at the outset of the dance. The value of dancing versus not dancing has been the subject of much debate. While the data defy any clear trends, in general where an RPS has a large number of patents and there is uncertainty about which may be applicable to a given biosimilar, the applicant has usually engaged in all steps of the patent dance. When an RPS only has a few well known patents and prior litigation has reduced uncertainty, applicants have been willing to forego the dance and avoid the resulting eight-month delay. It also appears that applicants have eschewed two-wave litigation in favor of one-wave litigation where all potentially applicable patent claims get adjudicated at the same time. Only in the case of Humira, where AbbVie's patent thicket was unusually large, did the applicants use a first wave of litigation to focus on certain key patents.

In sum, biosimilar applicants have been fickle when it comes to the BPCIA. Some important provisions like two-wave litigation and interchangeability have gone largely unused, while others such as the requirement to provide 180 days' notice of commercial launch have been leveraged in creative ways to obtain early decisions on the merits (or the threat thereof) and settlements. No doubt as courts and litigants become more experienced with the pros and cons of certain litigation strategies, litigation under the BPCIA will become more straightforward and predictable, much as litigation under the Hatch-Waxman laws has become more predictable since enactment of those laws in 1984. Until then, we will continue to see RPSs and applicants test and stretch the language of the BPCIA in order to obtain a litigation or market advantage.

Chapter 3

The FDA Approval Process for Biosimilar and Interchangeable Biological Products

I. GENERALLY

§ 3:1   Approval process overview

II. APPLICATION TYPES

§ 3:2   Biologics License Applications (BLAs)
§ 3:3   Abbreviated Biologics License Applications (aBLAs)
§ 3:4   Drug products not regulated as biological products
§ 3:5   Converting NDAs to BLAs in 2020

III. ABBREVIATED BIOLOGICS LICENSE APPLICATIONS

§ 3:6   Requirements for demonstrating biosimilarity
§ 3:7   —Manufacturing information
§ 3:8   —Clinical trials
§ 3:9   —Proving biosimilarity
§ 3:10   —Consequences of being better or worse than a
          Reference Product
§ 3:11   —Labeling requirements
§ 3:12   Additional requirements for demonstrating
          interchangeability
§ 3:13   —Benefits: Interchangeable product exclusivity
§ 3:14   No Patent Linkage

IV. BIOBETTERS

§ 3:15   Biobetters generally

V. THE FDA APPROVAL PROCESS

§ 3:16   The FDA review timeline
§ 3:17   —Exclusivity provisions impacting biosimilars
§ 3:18   — —Reference product exclusivity

§ 3:19 — —Pediatric exclusivity
§ 3:20 — —Orphan drug exclusivity
§ 3:21 Naming
§ 3:22 Citizen petitions
§ 3:23 Complete response letters

VI. POST-LICENSURE REQUIREMENTS

§ 3:24 Post-Licensure establishment inspection
§ 3:25 Additional post-licensure requirements

KeyCite®: Cases and other legal materials listed in KeyCite Scope can be researched through the KeyCite service on Westlaw®. Use KeyCite to check citations for form, parallel references, prior and later history, and comprehensive citator information, including citations to other decisions and secondary materials.

I. GENERALLY

§ 3:1 Approval process overview

On March 23, 2010, President Obama signed into law the Patient Protection and Affordable Care Act ("Affordable Care Act"),[1] which upon enactment, amended the Public Health Service Act (the "PHSA")[2] and other statutes to create an abbreviated licensure pathway for biological products that are demonstrated to be "highly similar" (biosimilar) to or "interchangeable" with a U.S. Food and Drug Administration ("the FDA") approved biological product. These statutory provisions are commonly referred to as the Biologics Price Competition and Innovation Act of 2009 (the "BPCIA").[3]

Immediately following enactment of the BPCIA, the FDA formed a working group to plan the Agency's approach to implementation of the statute.[4] The FDA also began to develop and issue "guidance" documents about demonstrat-

---

[Section 3:1]

[1]Pub. L. No. 111-148, 124 Stat. 119 (2010) (codified as amended in scattered sections of the Internal Revenue Code and 42 U.S.C.).

[2]Ch. 373, 58 Stat. 682 (1944) (codified as amended in scattered section of 42 U.S.C.).

[3]Pub. L. No. 111-148, §§ 7001–7003, 124 Stat. 119, 804–21 (2010) (codified principally at 42 U.S.C.A. § 262).

[4]See FDA Implementation of the Biologics Price Competition and Innovation Act of 2009, available at https://www.FDA.gov/drugs/guidance-compliance-regulatory-information/implementation-biologics-price-competiti

ing biosimilarity and interchangeability. Guidance documents are documents prepared for the FDA staff, applicants/ sponsors, and the public that describe the FDA's interpretation of the Agency's policy on a regulatory issue and reflect the Agency's current thinking at the time of publication.[5] As of October 2019, 10 guidance documents specific to biosimilar products and interchangeable biological products have been issued, four of which remain in draft form and six of which have been finalized.[6] The FDA has indicated that the Agency's biosimilar program "will continue to put in place the foundational regulations and guidance . . . to provide regulatory certainty with respect to the approval pathway for biosimilar and interchangeable products."[7] On March 6, 2015, approximately five years from the date of enactment of the BPCIA, the FDA approved the first biosimilar product in the U.S., Zarxio® (filgrastimsndz).[8] As of October 2019, the FDA had approved 23 biosimilar products[9] and has not approved any interchangeable biological product.

II. APPLICATION TYPES

§ 3:2   Biologics License Applications (BLAs)

Under the BPCIA, all biological products, including biosimilars and interchangeable biological products, are required to be licensed under section 351 of the PHSA, via a Biologics License Application (BLA) or an abbreviated BLA (aBLA),[1] as applicable. A full BLA requires the sponsor to provide the FDA with a complete data set, including clinical trials and non-clinical studies, demonstrating that the

---

on-and-innovation-act-2009.

[5]21 C.F.R. § 10.115. Guidance documents do not establish legally enforceable rights or responsibilities and do not legally bind the public or the FDA; however, guidance documents, when finalized, represent the FDA's current thinking.

[6]This excludes withdrawn guidance documents.

[7]See FDA Biosimilar Action Plan: Balancing Innovation and Competition, July 2018, p. 9, available at https://www.FDA.gov/media/114574/download.

[8]Zarxio is a registered trademark of Novartis AG Corporation.

[9]See FDA Biosimilar Product Information, available at https://www.FDA.gov/drugs/biosimilars/biosimilar-product-information.

[Section 3:2]

[1]BPCIA § 7002(e)(1), 124 Stat. 817 (2010).

biological product is safe, pure and potent (which the FDA generally interprets to mean safe and effective). A full BLA is intended to be used primarily for novel biological products.

Section 351(i)(1) of the PHSA defines "biological product" as "a virus, therapeutic serum, toxin, antitoxin, vaccine, blood, blood component or derivative, allergenic product, protein (except any chemically synthesized polypeptide), or analogous product, or arsphenamine or derivative of arsphenamine (or any other trivalent organic arsenic compound), applicable to the prevention, treatment, or cure of a disease or condition of human beings."[2] However, the FDA regulations at 21 C.F.R. § 600.3, which are the Agency's rules governing the definition of a "biological product," are based upon the law that existed prior to the enactment of the BPCIA and do not conform with it.[3] The regulation defines a "biological product" as "any virus, therapeutic serum, toxin, antitoxin, or analogous product applicable to the prevention, treatment or cure of diseases or injuries of man."[4]

On December 12, 2018, the FDA proposed an amendment to this regulation to conform to the statutory definition enacted in the BPCIA.[5] In an effort to enhance regulatory clarity, the FDA has proposed interpreting the BPCIA definition of "biological product" to define "protein" as "any alpha amino acid polymer with a specific defined sequence that is greater than 40 amino acids in size."[6] The FDA has proposed this "bright-line" approach for differentiating proteins from peptides, based on review of scientific literature and alignment with current regulatory practice. Amino acid polymers that meet this 40 amino acid threshold are generally more complex, while peptides are "smaller, perform fewer functions, contain less three-dimensional structure, are less likely to be post-translationally modified, and, therefore, are generally characterized more easily than proteins."[7] Thus, unless a peptide otherwise meets the statutory definition of

---

[2]42 U.S.C.A. § 262(i)(1).

[3]Congress enacts statutes such as the BPCIA, which become the laws that govern the U.S. Congress has also authorized the FDA and other federal agencies to implement statutes by creating and enforcing agency regulations. An agency regulation must be consistent with the governing statute.

[4]21 C.F.R. § 600.3(h).

[5]83 Fed. Reg. 63817, December 12, 2018.

[6]83 Fed. Reg. 63817, December 12, 2018.

[7]83 Fed. Reg. 63817, December 12, 2018.

a "biological product," it would be regulated as a drug, and not as a biologic. As explained below, new drugs must be licensed via a New Drug Application ("NDA"). Generic versions of approved drugs must be licensed via an abbreviated NDA ("ANDA") or 505(b)(2) NDA.

As part of the same proposed rule, the FDA has proposed defining a "chemically synthesized polypeptide" as "any alpha amino acid polymer that is made entirely by chemical synthesis and is greater than 40 amino acids but less than 100 amino acids in size."[8] Such chemically synthesized polypeptides would be excluded from the definition of "protein," and thus excluded from the definition of "biological product."

Peptides and chemically synthesized polypeptides would be regulated as drugs unless the molecule in question otherwise meets the statutory definition of "biological product." Vaccines, for example, are specifically identified in the definition of "biological product," regardless of their size, content, or method of manufacture. Thus, a vaccine might be an amino acid chain of 40 or fewer amino acids, or a chemically synthesized polypeptide composed of greater than 40 amino acids but less than 100 amino acids, but the vaccine would otherwise meet the definition of a "biological product." Because vaccines are expressly identified as "biological product[s]" they will continue to be regulated as such, even with the FDA's proposed revisions to its regulatory definitions.

§ 3:3   Abbreviated Biologics License Applications (aBLAs)

An aBLA, by contrast, is intended to be used for follow-on biological products that are either biosimilar to or interchangeable with a previously-approved biological product (known as a reference product[1] or "RP"). An aBLA is generally regarded as a streamlined approval pathway because it can rely upon the safety and effectiveness data supporting approval of the reference product. The aBLA pathway allows

---

[8]83 Fed. Reg. 63817, December 12, 2018.

[Section 3:3]

[1]A reference product is the "single biological product licensed under subsection (a) [of Section 351 of the PHSA] against which a biological product is evaluated in an application submitted under subsection (k) [of Section 351 of the PHSA]." 42 U.S.C.A. § 262(i)(4).

a biological product to be licensed based on less than a full complement of product-specific preclinical and clinical data.[2] The approval process for a biosimilar may require "analyti-cal studies and at least one clinical PK [pharmacokinetic] study and, if appropriate, at least one PD [pharmacodynamic] study" in order to provide an adequate comparison to the reference product.[3] The FDA will evaluate biosimilar ap-plications on an individual basis to determine whether any data elements can be waived, if scientifically appropriate. The FDA may evaluate the strength of the comparative stud-ies between the reference product and the proposed biosimi-lar, as well as the similarity of the pharmacokinetic and pharmacodynamic profiles of the two products, and the safety profile of the reference product when determining the precise data needed to make a determination of biosimilarity.[4]

§ 3:4   Drug products not regulated as biological products

Products that are not considered to be biological products, such as peptides and chemically synthesized polypeptides, are regulated and approved under the Federal Food, Drug, and Cosmetic Act (FFDCA).[1] In addition, some protein products that are now considered to be "biological products," such as human growth hormone and insulin, historically have been regulated by the FDA as "drugs" rather than as "biological products" and thus received approval under the FFDCA rather than the PHSA. As discussed further below,[2] these protein products can continue to be approved under the FFDCA until March 23, 2020.

There are three main application types under the FFDCA

---

[2]*See* Leah Christl, FDA's Overview of the Regulatory Guidance for the Development and Approval of Biosimilar Products in the U.S., p. 5, available at https://www. FDA.gov/media/90496/download.

[3]*See* FDA Guidance for Industry: Scientific Considerations in Dem-onstrating Biosimilarity to a Reference Product (Apr. 2015), p. 6, available at https://www.FDA.gov/media/82647/download; *see infra* Sections 3:6 to 3:12.

[4]*See* FDA Biosimilar Development, Review, and Approval, available at https://www.FDA.gov/drugs/biosimilars/biosimilar-development-review-and-approval.

[Section 3:4]

[1]Ch. 675, 52 Stat. 1040 (1938) (codified as amended in scattered sec-tion of 21 U.S.C.).

[2]*See infra* Section 3:5.

for traditional drug products that are not biological products: full New Drug Applications (NDAs), 505(b)(2) applications, and Abbreviated New Drug Applications (ANDAs). Novel drug products typically are approved via full NDAs, which are very similar to full BLAs and require the applicant to submit a full data set supporting the safety and effectiveness of the drug product. Follow-on products can be approved via either 505(b)(2) applications or ANDAs, both of which allow reliance on data contained in a previously approved application (referred to as a "listed drug" or "reference listed drug"). Thus, 505(b)(2) applications and ANDAs are considered to be abbreviated approval pathways for drugs regulated under the FFDCA.

An ANDA typically is used to obtain approval of a duplicate of a previously approved drug, meaning a drug with the same active ingredient, dosage form, strength and route of administration, also called a "generic" drug. Because the variations permitted for generic drugs are minimal (and limited primarily to excipients), ANDA approval typically is based primarily on bioequivalence studies. An ANDA, in fact, cannot be submitted if safety or effectiveness data are required for approval.

A 505(b)(2) application, by contrast, typically is submitted for a drug product that incorporates certain novel changes from a previously approved drug, such as a new dosage form, new dosing schedule or even a new indication. A 505(b)(2) application also can be used for a "duplicate" if clinical trials are necessary to support the safety and effectiveness of the duplicate (such as when a novel excipient is used). This is because a 505(b)(2) application can contain new safety and effectiveness information, such as data from a Phase III clinical trial, to support approval of the novel features.

Because peptides, chemically synthesized polypeptides, and proteins (such as insulin) that are regulated as drugs are more complex than small-molecule drugs typically approved under the FFDCA, the FDA historically has been hesitant to approve follow-on versions of complex products via the ANDA route. In most cases, the FDA has deemed an ANDA to be inappropriate because of difficulties demonstrating that the active ingredient in the follow-on and reference products are the "same." Accordingly, many follow-on products for peptides, polypeptides, proteins, or mixtures of the foregoing have been approved via the 505(b)(2) pathway based on a finding that their active ingredient is "highly similar" to the active ingredient in the reference product. In some cases, however, the FDA has approved a "duplicate" version of a complex product via an ANDA, such as with menotropins, enoxaparin and glatiramer acetate.

§ 3:5   Converting NDAs to BLAs in 2020

As noted above, the BPCIA now requires all biological products to be approved under the PHSA via BLAs or aBLAs, except for certain protein products, such as human growth hormone and insulin, that historically were regulated and approved as drugs (rather than biological products) under the FFDCA. The BPCIA provides that NDAs, 505(b)(2) applications and ANDAs can continue to be submitted for approval of these products, known as "transitional biologics," until March 23, 2020.[1] The BPCIA further provides that on March 23, 2020, all approved NDAs, 505(b)(2) applications and ANDAs for such products willed be "deemed" to be BLAs licensed under the PHSA.[2]

The FDA has issued a final guidance document[3] explaining how it intends to implement the BPCIA's transition provision. According to the FDA, an *approved* application for such a product under the FFDCA will be deemed to be a BLA on March 23, 2020, and will cease to exist as an NDA, 505(b)(2) application or ANDA. The FDA intends to convert all approved NDAs and 505(b)(2) applications to full BLAs, rather than aBLAs, on the transition date. Moreover, if there are pending supplements for any such application, the FDA will administratively convert them to pending supplements to the deemed BLA and review them under applicable standards for BLAs.

The FDA has stated that it will not administratively convert pending NDAs and 505(b)(2) applications to pending BLAs or aBLAs on the transition date. According to the FDA, if a pending application is not approved on the transition date, it will never be approved by the FDA. To obtain approval, the sponsor would need to withdraw the application and re-submit it as a BLA or an aBLA. If re-submitted as an

---

[Section 3:5]

[1]BPCIA § 7002(e)(2), 124 Stat. 817 (2010).

[2]BPCIA § 7002(e)(4), 124 Stat. 817 (2010).

[3]*See* FDA Guidance for Industry: Interpretation of the "Deemed to be a License" Provision of the Biologics Price Competition and Innovation Act of 2009 (Dec. 2018), available at https://www.FDA.gov/media/119272/d ownload.

aBLA, the sponsor would need to pay additional user fees under the Biosimilar User Fee Act (BsUFA), but no additional user fees would be required to re-submit the application as a full BLA.

The FDA has indicated that a biological product whose application is deemed to be a BLA on March 23, 2020, will not be eligible for four or 12-year reference product exclusivity, which are more thoroughly discussed below.[4] Moreover, such a product would lose any unexpired exclusivity protecting its NDA or 505(b)(2) application, other than orphan drug exclusivity and pediatric exclusivity, on and after the transition date. The FDA has stated that it intends to remove biological products subject to deemed BLAs from the Orange Book[5] on March 23, 2020.

III. ABBREVIATED BIOLOGICS LICENSE APPLICATIONS

§ 3:6 Requirements for demonstrating biosimilarity

An application for a biosimilar product must include data demonstrating biosimilarity to the reference product. There is no requirement in an aBLA to demonstrate that the proposed biological product contains the "same" active ingredient as the RP. This is due, in part, to the recognition that it is virtually impossible to demonstrate "sameness" for two biological products, which typically are much larger and more complex than small-molecule active ingredients and have much more inherent variability. Accordingly, the BPCIA instead requires aBLA applicants to demonstrate that the proposed biological product is "biosimilar" to the RP. In order to be determined "biosimilar," the product must be "highly similar to the reference product notwithstanding minor differences in clinically inactive components," and have "no clinically meaningful differences [from] the reference product in terms of . . . safety, purity, and potency."[1]

An aBLA must contain, among other things, information demonstrating that the biological product is biosimilar to a reference product based upon data derived from—

---

[4]*See infra* at Section 3:13.

[5]*See* FDA Approved Drug Products with Therapeutic Equivalence Evaluations (Orange Book), available at https://www.FDA.gov/drug-approvals-and-databases/approved-drug-products-therapeutic-equivalence-evaluations-orange-book.

[Section 3:6]

[1]42 U.S.C.A. § 262(i)(2).

- analytical studies that demonstrate that the proposed biosimilar product is highly similar to the reference product notwithstanding minor differences in clinically inactive components;
- animal studies (including an assessment of toxicity); and
- a clinical study or studies (including an assessment of immunogenicity and pharmacokinetics or pharmacodynamics) that are sufficient to demonstrate the safety, purity, and potency of the biological product in one or more appropriate conditions of use for which the reference product is licensed.[2]

An aBLA must contain information demonstrating that the route of administration, dosage form, and strength of the proposed biological product are the same as those of the RP. An applicant must also demonstrate that, to the extent the mechanism(s) of action are known for the reference product, the proposed biosimilar product uses the same mechanism(s) of action for the condition(s) of use prescribed, recommended, or suggested in the proposed labeling.[3] The condition(s) of use in the labeling proposed for the biological product must have been previously approved for the reference product, and the route of administration, dosage form, and strength of the biological product must be the same as those of the reference product.[4] The applicant must also demonstrate that the facility in which the biological product is manufactured, processed, packed, or held meets standards designed to assure that the biological product continues to be safe, pure, and potent.[5]

Consistent with the FDA's longstanding approach to evaluating scientific evidence, the Agency will consider the "totality of the evidence" a sponsor provides when assessing the sponsor's demonstration of biosimilarity.[6] Such evidence includes "structural and functional characterization, nonclinical evaluation, human PK and PD data, clinical im-

---

[2]42 U.S.C.A. § 262(k)(2)(A)(i)(I)(aa) to (cc).

[3]42 U.S.C.A. § 262(k)(2)(A)(i)(II).

[4]42 U.S.C.A. § 262(k)(2)(A)(i)(III) to (IV).

[5]42 U.S.C.A. § 262(k)(2)(A)(i)(V).

[6]*See* FDA Guidance for Industry: Scientific Considerations in Demonstrating Biosimilarity to a Reference Product (Apr. 2015), p. 7, available at https://www.FDA.gov/media/82647/download.

munogenicity data, and comparative clinical study(ies) data."[7] Thus, even if there are minor structural differences between the proposed biosimilar and the reference product, the sponsor may be able to demonstrate biosimilarity, provided that the totality of evidence demonstrates that there are no clinically meaningful differences.

The FDA also recommends a "stepwise approach" when developing the evidence required to support a demonstration of biosimilarity. At each step of the development process, beginning with structural and functional characterization of the proposed product and the reference product, the sponsor should evaluate the residual uncertainty about the biosimilarity of the proposed product.[8] More comprehensive and rigorous studies can be useful in determining what additional studies are needed.

A sponsor must demonstrate biosimilarity to a "single reference product that previously has been licensed by the FDA."[9] However, a sponsor may use data generated from studies comparing the proposed biosimilar to a non-U.S.-licensed comparator to address some of the requirements of section 351(k) of the PHSA.[10] If the sponsor uses this data as part of the biosimilar application, the sponsor must also demonstrate the scientific justification for making this comparison and "bridge" the non-U.S. licensed comparator data to the U.S.-licensed comparator. Thus, while a non-U.S.-licensed comparator may not be the reference product, a sponsor can utilize a non-U.S.-licensed comparator in generating data required to demonstrate biosimilarity.

Finally, the FDA has issued draft guidance on the applicability of pediatric testing requirements under the

---

[7]*See* FDA Guidance for Industry: Scientific Considerations in Demonstrating Biosimilarity to a Reference Product (Apr. 2015), p. 7, available at https://www.FDA.gov/media/82647/download.

[8]*See* FDA Guidance for Industry: Scientific Considerations in Demonstrating Biosimilarity to a Reference Product (Apr. 2015), p. 7, available at https://www.FDA.gov/media/82647/download.

[9]*See* FDA Guidance for Industry: Scientific Considerations in Demonstrating Biosimilarity to a Reference Product (Apr. 2015), p. 6, available at https://www. FDA.gov/media/82647/download.

[10]*See* FDA Guidance for Industry: Questions and Answers on Biosimilar Development and the BPCI Act (Dec. 2018), p. 8, available at https://www.FDA.gov/media/119258/download.

Pediatric Research Equity Act ("PREA")[11] to aBLAs. According to the FDA's guidance:

> PREA requirements are applicable to proposed biosimilar products that have not been determined to be interchangeable with a reference product only to the extent that compliance with PREA would not result in: (1) a condition of use that has not been previously approved for the reference product; or (2) a dosage form, strength, or route of administration that differs from that of the reference product.[12]

Under the BPCIA, biosimilars are considered to have a different active ingredient than the RP for purposes of PREA and thus typically would be required to conduct pediatric testing unless deferred or exempted. However, according to the FDA, if the RP does not include adequate pediatric information in its labeling, a biosimilar applicant is not required to conduct pediatric testing and/or develop a new pediatric formulation under PREA because of the limitation in the BPCIA that an aBLA cannot be approved for a condition of use for which the RP was not previously approved. If the RP labeling does include pediatric information, the biosimilar applicant can seek to include such information in its labeling via extrapolation. If extrapolation is not justified, then (and only then) would a biosimilar applicant be required to conduct pediatric tests under PREA.[13] Because interchangeable biologics are considered to have the same active ingredient as the RP, interchangeable biologics are not subject to the PREA requirements.[14]

§ 3:7   Requirements for demonstrating biosimilarity—Manufacturing information

Biologics are often defined by their manufacturing processes, due to the limited ability to identify with certainty the identity of the clinically active component(s) of a complex

---

[11]Pub. L. No. 108-155, 117 Stat. 1936, codified as 21 U.S.C.A. § 355c (2003).

[12]*See* FDA Draft Guidance: New and Revised Draft Q&As on Biosimilar Development and the BPCI Act (Revision 2) (Dec. 2018), p. 8, available at https://www.FDA.gov/media/119278/download.

[13]*See* FDA Draft Guidance: New and Revised Draft Q&As on Biosimilar Development and the BPCI Act (Revision 2) (Dec. 2018), pp. 6-7, available at https://www.FDA.gov/media/119278/download.

[14]*See* FDA Guidance for Industry: Questions and Answers on Biosimilar Development and the BPCI Act (Dec. 2018), p. 13, available at https://www.FDA.gov/media/119258/download.

biological product.[1] Thus, the PHSA provides for controls over all aspects of the manufacturing process. The manufacturer of a proposed biosimilar product will generally have a different manufacturing process (e.g., different cell line, raw materials, equipment, processes, process controls, and acceptance criteria), than the manufacturer of the RP.[2] In a recent draft guidance, the FDA has provided recommendations on the scientific and technical information needed for the chemistry, manufacturing, and controls (CMC) section of a biosimilar application to sponsors of proposed biosimilars.[3] The FDA's draft guidance focuses on therapeutic proteins, noting that because "therapeutic proteins are made in living systems, there may be heterogeneity in certain quality attributes of these products."[4] Thus, comprehensive analytical procedures are necessary to identify and characterize the product, product-related substances, and product—and process—related impurities in order to ultimately demonstrate biosimilarity to the RP. The FDA recommends in-depth chemical, physical, and bioactivity comparisons with side-by-side analyses of an appropriate number of lots of the proposed product and the reference product, and a comparison with a reference standard for suitable attributes (e.g., potency) where available and appropriate.[5] The manufacturer of a proposed biosimilar will have no direct knowledge of the

---

[Section 3:7]

[1]*See* FDA Frequently Asked Questions About Therapeutic Biological Products (July 2015), available at https://www.FDA.gov/drugs/therapeutic-biologics-applications-bla/frequently-asked-questions-about-therapeutic-biological-products.

[2]*See* FDA Guidance for Industry: Scientific Considerations in Demonstrating Biosimilarity to a Reference Product (Apr. 2015), p. 6, available at https://www.FDA.gov/media/82647/download.

[3]*See* FDA Draft Guidance: Development of Therapeutic Protein Biosimilars: Comparative Analytical Assessment and Other Quality-Related Considerations (May 2019), available at https://www.FDA.gov/media/125484/download.

[4]*See* FDA Draft Guidance: Development of Therapeutic Protein Biosimilars: Comparative Analytical Assessment and Other Quality-Related Considerations (May 2019), p. 8, available at https://www.FDA.gov/media/125484/download.

[5]*See* FDA Draft Guidance: Development of Therapeutic Protein Biosimilars: Comparative Analytical Assessment and Other Quality-Related Considerations (May 2019), p. 9, available at https://www.FDA.gov/media/125484/download.

manufacturing process for the RP and must instead develop its own manufacturing process.[6]

§ 3:8   Requirements for demonstrating biosimilarity—Clinical trials

To establish biosimilarity, the sponsor of a proposed product must submit data and information in its aBLA demonstrating that there are no "clinically meaningful differences" between its proposed product and the RP in terms of safety, purity and potency of the product. The nature and scope of any clinical trials required in an aBLA thus will depend on the nature and extent of any "residual uncertainty" about biosimilarity after the structural and functional characterization data have been analyzed. At a minimum, however, the FDA generally expects all aBLAs to contain data and information from comparative pharmacokinetic ("PK") and (where available) pharmacodynamic ("PD") clinical trials as well as a clinical immunogenicity assessment.[1] If residual uncertainty remains after conducting these studies, additional comparative clinical trials with safety and efficacy endpoints may be required.

§ 3:9   Requirements for demonstrating biosimilarity—Proving biosimilarity

As noted above, the FDA recommends that sponsors use a "stepwise approach" when developing the evidence required to support a demonstration of biosimilarity. At each step, the FDA directs sponsors to evaluate the extent to which there is residual uncertainty about the biosimilarity of the proposed product. Based on this evaluation, the sponsor (with FDA guidance) can then identify the appropriate next steps and testing necessary to address that uncertainty. Because of the iterative nature of this process, the FDA recommends that companies meet early and often with the

---

[6]*See* FDA Draft Guidance: Development of Therapeutic Protein Biosimilars: Comparative Analytical Assessment and Other Quality-Related Considerations (May 2019), p. 4, available at https://www.FDA.go v/media/125484/download.

[Section 3:8]

[1]For additional information concerning the FDA's current thinking on the use of clinical pharmacology studies to support demonstration of biosimilarity, *see* FDA Guidance for Industry: Clinical Pharmacology Data to Support a Demonstration of Biosimilarity to a Reference Product (Dec. 2016), available at https://www.FDA.gov/media/88622/download.

Agency to discuss the development process and plans for future studies.

The first step in demonstrating biosimilarity generally involves conducting analytical studies that demonstrate that the proposed biosimilar product is highly similar to the reference product notwithstanding minor differences in clinically inactive components. This involves extensive structural and functional characterization of both the proposed biosimilar product and the RP. The importance of this step cannot be overstated, as the FDA has described it as the "foundation" of the biosimilar development program. A comprehensive and robust characterization program can reduce residual uncertainty and thus lead to a "more selective and targeted approach to animal and/or clinical testing."[1]

The next step often involves animal studies. These typically include animal toxicity studies, animal PK and PD tests, and animal immunogenicity studies. The need for and scope of any of these animal studies will depend on the information obtained from the structural and functional characterization of the products.

Finally, biosimilarity generally must be supported by data from one or more clinical studies (including an assessment of immunogenicity and pharmacokinetics or pharmacodynamics) that are sufficient to demonstrate the safety, purity, and potency of the biological product in one or more appropriate conditions of use for which the reference product is licensed.[2] Here, again, the nature and scope of the clinical study or studies will depend on the nature and extent of residual uncertainty about biosimilarity after conducting structural and functional characterization and, where relevant, animal studies. The safety risks associated with the RP may also affect the scope and design or required clinical studies.

As noted above, the FDA expects companies, at a minimum, to conduct comparative human PK and PD studies (where available) and a clinical immunogenicity assessment. The FDA has stated that in certain cases, these studies alone may provide sufficient clinical data to support a finding that

---

[Section 3:9]

[1]For additional information, see FDA Draft Guidance: Development of Therapeutic Protein Biosimilars: Comparative Analytical Assessment and Other Quality-Related Considerations (May 2019), available at http s://www.FDA.gov/media/125484/download.

[2]42 U.S.C.A. § 262(k)(2)(A)(i)(I)(aa) to (cc).

there are no clinically meaningful differences between the proposed biosimilar product and the RP. In other cases, the sponsor will be required to conduct one or more comparative efficacy studies because of residual uncertainty regarding whether the proposed product is biosimilar to the RP. The need for comparative clinical studies can be affected by a number of factors, including the nature and complexity of the RP and the extent of structural and functional characterization; the extent to which differences in structure, function, nonclinical pharmacology or toxicology predict differences in clinical outcome; and the extent of any clinical experience with the reference product or proposed biosimilar (e.g., foreign experience).

If the RP is approved for multiple indications, a proposed biosimilar need not be studied in all indications. Rather, the FDA has indicated that a biosimilar applicant can seek licensure for any indication for which the RP is approved by extrapolating from data gathered in a different indication. Such extrapolation can be scientifically justified based upon a number of factors, including whether the mode of action is known and the same in each indication, whether there are PK and/or PD differences in the different patient populations, whether the immunogenicity risks are different in different patient populations, and any other factor that may affect the safety or efficacy of the product in each indication and patient population for which licensure is sought.

Consistent with the FDA's longstanding approach to evaluating scientific evidence, the Agency will consider the "totality of the evidence" provided by the sponsor when assessing the sponsor's demonstration of biosimilarity.[3] This means that even if there are minor structural differences between the proposed biosimilar and the reference product, the sponsor may still be able to demonstrate biosimilarity if the totality of the evidence demonstrates that there are no clinically meaningful differences.

§ 3:10   Requirements for demonstrating biosimilarity—Consequences of being better or worse than a Reference Product

A "biosimilar" is defined as a biological product that is

---

[3]*See* FDA Guidance for Industry: Scientific Considerations in Demonstrating Biosimilarity to a Reference Product (Apr. 2015), p. 7, available at https://www.FDA.gov/media/82647/download.

"highly similar" to the RP (notwithstanding minor differences in clinically inactive components) and for which there are "no clinically meaningful differences" compared to the RP.[1] Consequently, if clinical or other testing demonstrates that the proposed biological product differs from the RP in terms of safety or effectiveness, it will not satisfy the requirements of "biosimilarity" because it will have "clinically meaningful differences." Importantly, this applies even if the proposed biological product is *safer or more effective* than the RP. A biological product that is safer or more effective has "clinically meaningful differences" compared to the RP and thus would not qualify as a "biosimilar." Accordingly, such a product could not be approved via an aBLA but instead would be required to submit a full BLA to obtain marketing approval.

§ 3:11 Requirements for demonstrating biosimilarity—Labeling requirements

There is no "same labeling" requirement for biosimilars under the BPCIA. This is in sharp contrast to generic drugs approved via ANDAs, which must use the same labeling (with minor exceptions) as the reference product. Thus, at least in theory, biosimilars have more latitude to adopt labeling that differs from the RP than their generic drug counterparts.[1]

In practice, however, the FDA has strongly encouraged biosimilar applicants to use the RP labeling as a template[2] and to make changes only when necessary and adequately justified. Typically, such changes have been allowed when necessary to carve out an indication or other condition of use that is protected by exclusivity (*e.g.*, orphan drug exclusivity) or patents. Because biosimilars can differ from the RP in certain ways, such as presentation (e.g., pen injector versus vial), the FDA also has allowed labeling changes to reflect

---

[Section 3:10]

[1]42 U.S.C.A. § 262(i)(2).

[Section 3:11]

[1]As explained in Section 9:1, this may spawn debate over whether biosimilar products will enjoy the same scope of immunity from so-called "failure to adequately warn" product liability lawsuits as small-molecule generic drugs.

[2]*See* FDA Guidance for Industry: Labeling for Biosimilar Products (July 2018), available at https://www.FDA.gov/media/96894/download.

these differences. But by and large, the FDA has not permitted significant revisions to biosimilar labeling even though it arguably has the authority to do.

§ 3:12   Additional requirements for demonstrating interchangeability

As of the date of June 2019, the FDA has not yet licensed any interchangeable biological products, so it is somewhat speculative to discuss how an aBLA applicant can demonstrate interchangeability. Nevertheless, the FDA recently finalized its guidance on demonstrating interchangeability, and the final guidance provides useful insights into how the Agency will review evidence of interchangeability.[1]

Under the BPCIA, to obtain licensure as an interchangeable biologic product, an aBLA applicant must demonstrate that its proposed product is both biosimilar to the RP and "can be expected to produce the same clinical result as the reference product in any given patient."[2] If a biological product is initially licensed as a biosimilar, this licensure can be referenced to satisfy the first requirement.[3] If the aBLA applicant is seeking initial licensure as an interchangeable biological product, it must provide data and information (as described above) to satisfy the statutory requirements of biosimilarity.

The data necessary to demonstrate that the proposed interchangeable biological product "can be expected to produce the same clinical result as the reference product in any given patient" will vary depending on the nature of the proposed interchangeable product. Generally, it will involve a number of different analyses, including analyzing the mechanism or mechanisms of action in each condition of use; analyzing any differences in the expected pharmacokinetics and biodistribution of the product in different patient populations; and analyzing any differences in expected immunogenicity risk of the product in different patient populations.

[Section 3:12]

[1]*See* FDA Guidance for Industry: Considerations in Demonstrating Interchangeability with a Reference Product (May 2019), available at http s://www.FDA.gov/media/124907/download.

[2]42 U.S.C.A. §§ 262(k)(4)(A)(i)-(ii).

[3]*See* FDA Guidance for Industry: Considerations in Demonstrating Interchangeability with a Reference Product (May 2019), p. 3, available at https://www.FDA.gov/media/124907/download.

The data and information may also include a scientific rationale to justify extrapolation. The FDA, however, has indicated that it does not expect to require additional clinical studies (other than those necessary to support other aspects of interchangeability, such as switching) to support a finding that the proposed interchangeable biological product "can be expected to produce the same clinical result as the reference product in any given patient."[4]

For products that are used more than once, the BPCIA requires a demonstration that there is no enhanced safety risk or diminished efficacy from alternating or switching between the proposed interchangeable biological product and the RP. The FDA generally expects this demonstration to be supported by one or more switching studies. The FDA has explained that "a switching study is typically designed to assess whether switching between the reference product and the proposed interchangeable product will present risk in terms of safety or diminished efficacy that is greater than using the reference product without such switching."[5] The FDA recommends that switching studies measure PK and/or PD endpoints, which are viewed as more sensitive than efficacy endpoints, and include an assessment of immunogenicity.[6] The FDA also recommends a study design that includes multiple switches between the proposed interchangeable product and the RP.[7]

The FDA also strongly recommends that aBLA applicants seek licensure of an interchangeable biological product for all conditions of use for which the RP is licensed.[8] As with biosimilarity, however, the FDA will allow extrapolation of data from one condition of use to another (when scientifically

---

[4]*See* FDA Guidance for Industry: Considerations in Demonstrating Interchangeability with a Reference Product (May 2019), p. 5, available at https://www.FDA.gov/media/124907/download.

[5]*See* FDA Guidance for Industry: Considerations in Demonstrating Interchangeability with a Reference Product (May 2019), p. 9, available at https://www.FDA.gov/media/124907/download.

[6]*See* FDA Guidance for Industry: Considerations in Demonstrating Interchangeability with a Reference Product (May 2019), pp. 9-10, available at https://www.FDA.gov/media/124907/download.

[7]*See* FDA Guidance for Industry: Considerations in Demonstrating Interchangeability with a Reference Product (May 2019), p. 9, available at https://www.FDA.gov/media/124907/download.

[8]*See* FDA Guidance for Industry: Considerations in Demonstrating Interchangeability with a Reference Product (May 2019), p. 5, available at https://www.FDA.gov/media/124907/download.

justified) to support an interchangeability determination. Generally, the same factors that would support extrapolation of data in the context of biosimilarity would also support extrapolation in the context of an interchangeability determination.

§ 3:13   Additional requirements for demonstrating interchangeability—Benefits: Interchangeable product exclusivity

The BPCIA created a period of market exclusivity for the first interchangeable version of a reference product licensed under Section 351(a). This interchangeable product exclusivity applies until the earlier of:

- 1 year after the first commercial marketing of the first interchangeable biological product to be approved;
- 18 months after a "final court decision" or the dismissal with or without prejudice of a patent infringement action brought against the first interchangeable biological product applicant; or
- 42 months after approval of the first interchangeable biological product if the patent infringement action brought against the first interchangeable biological product applicant is still ongoing; or
- 18 months after approval of the first interchangeable biological product if no patent infringement suit has been brought against the first interchangeable biological product applicant.[1]

The exclusivity granted to the first interchangeable product is quite limited. It only prohibits the FDA from making any interchangeability determination for a later-filed product for any condition of use until expiration of the interchangeable product exclusivity period.[2] The exclusivity does not prevent licensure of a subsequent product that is biosimilar to the same reference product.

§ 3:14   No Patent Linkage

Patent linkage refers to the relationship between the marketing approval of a generic drug by a regulatory authority and the status of any patent on its branded equivalent.

[Section 3:13]

   [1]42 U.S.C.A. §§ 262(k)(6)(A) to (C).

   [2]42 U.S.C.A. § 262(k)(6).

In general, patent linkage laws tie marketing approval of a generic drug product with the expiration of patents protecting the equivalent branded product or to an adjudication by a relevant authority that such patents are invalid or will not be infringed by the generic product. Various countries have enacted patent linkage systems where, e.g., a generic drug product cannot be approved (1) prior to the expiration of patent protection for the branded equivalent, (2) until the relevant authority has determined that the patents covering the branded equivalent's patent are invalid or will not be infringed, (3) until the applicable statutorily established periods staying approval of the generic have expired, or (4) unless the patent owner consents to the marketing approval.

In the United States, for biosimilar and interchangeable biosimilar products, there is no patent linkage. While the BPCIA sets forth a procedure for resolving patent disputes,[1] the FDA's approval of a biosimilar or interchangeable biological product application is not affected by the patent status of the reference product. This significantly differs from that established by the Hatch-Waxman Amendments.[2]

IV. BIOBETTERS

§ 3:15 Biobetters generally

Whereas a biosimilar is a biological product that is highly

[Section 3:14]

[1]*See infra* Chapter 4.

[2]Drug Price Competition and Patent Term Restoration Act of 1984, Pub. L. No. 98-417, 98 Stat. 1585 (1984) (codified at 21 U.S.C.A. §§ 301 et. seq.) (the "Hatch-Waxman Amendments"). Under the framework established by the Hatch-Waxman Amendments, branded drugs are listed in the FDA's Orange Book, along with patents that cover the drugs and methods of using them. When a company files an abbreviated new drug application (ANDA) or 505(b)(2) application, the company generally must certify that each listed patent (a) has expired (a "paragraph II certification"), (b) will expire before the drug is marketed (a "paragraph III certification"), or (c) is invalid, unenforceable, or will not be infringed by the drug (a "paragraph IV certification"). Alternatively, a "paragraph I certification" may be filed if the Orange Book does not list a patent that the company believes claims the drug or method of using it. When a company files a paragraph IV certification, the company must notify the new drug application (NDA) holder for the branded drug and all patent owners. If the patent owner sues the generic drug company for patent infringement within 45 days of that notice, a "30-month" stay of regulatory approval is triggered. If no suit is initiated within the 45-day period, there is no 30-month stay preventing the FDA from approving the drug.

similar to and has no clinically meaningful difference from an existing FDA-approved reference product, and an interchangeable biological product is expected to produce the same clinical result as the reference product in any given patient, a "biobetter" is generally understood[1] to be biological product that is structurally altered to be superior to the originator molecule, by for example, providing substantial differences in clinical efficacy or decreasing side effects or immunogenicity.

Biobetters thus do not qualify for the abbreviated approval pathway created by the BPCIA. Instead, biobetters require the submission of full BLAs under Section 351(a) of the PHSA, including a full complement of pre-clinical and clinical data for licensure. Further, just as for any new biological products, biobetters are not subject to the patent litigation provisions of the BPCIA, are not blocked by reference product exclusivity, and may receive their own 12-year period of reference product exclusivity.

V.   THE FDA APPROVAL PROCESS

§ 3:16   The FDA review timeline

Under the Biosimilar User Fee Act (BsUFA) reauthorization for fiscal years 2018–2022 (BsUFA II),[1] the FDA is authorized to assess and collect fees in connection with its review of biosimilar biological product applications. BsUFA sets performance and procedural goals for the timeline of this review.[2] Currently, the FDA's review goals are to:

- Review and act on 90 percent of original biosimilar

[Section 3:15]

[1]The term "biobetter" is not a term that appears in the FFDCA, the PHSA, or the FDA's regulations implementing its statutory authorities.

[Section 3:16]

[1]Formally known as the FDA Reauthorization Act of 2017, Pub. L. No. 115-52, 131 Stat. 1005 (2017).

[2]For additional information, see FDA Guidance for Industry: Assessing User Fees Under the Biosimilar User Fee Amendments of 2017 (June 2018), available at https://www.FDA.gov/media/109054/download. BsUFA II similarly set meeting management goals for formal meetings that occur between the FDA and sponsors or applicants of biosimilar or interchangeable biological products. For additional information, see FDA Guidance for Industry: Formal Meetings Between the FDA and Sponsors or Applicants of BsUFA Products (June 2018), available at https://www.FDA.gov/media/113913/download.

biological product application submissions within 10 months of the 60 day filing date[3]

- Review and act on 90 percent of resubmitted original biosimilar biological product applications within six months of receipt
- Review and act on 90 percent of original supplements with clinical data within 10 months of receipt
- Review and act on 90 percent of resubmitted supplements with clinical data within six months of receipt

The FDA has also set increasing goals for review and action on biosimilar manufacturing process supplements requiring prior approval (75% within four months in 2019, 80% in 2020, 85% in 2020, and 90% in 2022).[4] A major amendment to an original application, a supplement containing clinical data, or the resubmission of an application submitted during the original application review cycle may extend the goal date by three months.

The FDA encourages applicants to discuss the content of a planned application during a pre-submission 351(k) BLA (BPD Type 4) meeting.[5] The FDA has stated that it wants to communicate with applicants throughout the review process, including through mid-and late-cycle meetings. The FDA has set further goals to keep applicants informed of the planned review timeline, and to inform applicants of significant deficiencies in an application no later than its target date.

§ 3:17 The FDA review timeline—Exclusivity provisions impacting biosimilars

At the same time the BPCIA amended the PHSA and other statutes to create an abbreviated licensure pathway for biosimilar and interchangeable biosimilar products, the BPCIA added marketing protections for reference products through the addition of statutory limitations on the period

---

[3]*See* FDA Biosimilar Biological Product Reauthorization Performance Goals and Procedures Fiscal Years 2018 Through 2022, p. 4, available at https://www.FDA.gov/media/100573/download.

[4]*See* FDA Biosimilar Biological Product Reauthorization Performance Goals and Procedures Fiscal Years 2018 Through 2022, p. 5, available at https://www.FDA.gov/media/100573/download.

[5]*See* FDA Biosimilar Biological Product Reauthorization Performance Goals and Procedures Fiscal Years 2018 Through 2022, p. 4, available at https://www.FDA.gov/media/100573/download.

during which the FDA's could accept for review or approve applications for such products. These provisions confer what is generally known as "exclusivity" or "non-patent exclusivity" to reference products. The types of exclusivities governing the FDA review and approval of applications for biosimilar and interchangeable biological products are discussed in turn below.

§ 3:18   The FDA review timeline—Exclusivity provisions impacting biosimilars—Reference product exclusivity

As amended by the BPCIA, Section 351(k)(7)(A) of the PHSA provides that the FDA may not approve an application for a biosimilar or interchangeable product under Section 351(k) until the date that is 12 years after the date on which the reference product referred to in such 351(k) application was first licensed under Section 351(a).[1] Further, a 351(k) application may not be submitted to the FDA for review until 4 years after the date of first licensure of the reference product.[2] This 12-year period of exclusivity is known as "reference product exclusivity."[3]

Generally, the date of first licensure for purposes of reference product exclusivity will be the initial date the original version of the reference product was licensed in the United States. In order to deter "evergreening" of lengthy 12-year exclusivity periods, the PHSA limits the availability of reference product exclusivity in two respects. Section 351(k)(7)(C) of the PHSA provides that the 12-year and four-year periods shall not apply to a license for or approval of—

(i)   a supplement for the biological product that is the reference product; or

(ii)   a subsequent application filed by the same sponsor or manufacturer of the biological product that is the reference product (or a licensor, predecessor in interest, or other related entity) for—

[Section 3:18]

[1] 42 U.S.C.A. § 262(k)(7)(A).

[2] Section 351(k)(7)(B) of the PHSA; codified as 42 U.S.C.A. § 262(k)(7)(B).

[3] *See e.g.*, FDA Draft Guidance for Industry: Reference Product Exclusivity for Biological Products Filed Under Section 351(a) of the PHS Act (Aug. 2014), p. 1, available at https://www.FDA.gov/media/89049/download.

(I)   a change (not including a modification to the structure of the biological product) that is a new indication, route of administration, dosing schedule, dosage form, delivery system, delivery device, or strength; or

(II) a modification to the structure of the biological product that does not result in a change in safety, purity, and potency.[4]

Given these exclusions, most modifications to a previously licensed biologic—even significant changes such as new indications—will not be eligible for a separate period of reference product exclusivity, unless made by an unrelated company. Instead, for each product licensed under Section 351(a) of the PHSA that may serve as a reference product for a 351(k) application, the FDA must make a case-by-case determination of the date of first licensure. For example, the FDA will determine whether a full BLA should be considered a "subsequent application filed by the same sponsor or manufacturer of the biological product (or a licensor, predecessor in interest, or other related entity)."[5] For such applications, the FDA will determine whether the application is for a "modification to the structure" of a biological product previously licensed by such an entity. Further, for such structural modifications, the FDA will determine whether such modification would result in a "change in safety, purity, or potency."

Determination of the date of first licensure of a reference product, and whether a reference product qualifies for a period of reference product exclusivity or is subject to an exclusion, requires consideration of both scientific and legal concepts. The FDA's determination of the date of first licensure and of eligibility for exclusivity may not always be made at the time of licensure. When such decisions are made, they generally are published in the FDA's "Purple Book," which is a list of approved biologic products.[6] The FDA has issued draft guidance on how the Agency intends to interpret

---

[4]Section 351(k)(7)(C) of the PHSA; codified as 42 U.S.C.A. § 262(k)(7)(C).

[5]*See* FDA Draft Guidance for Industry: Reference Product Exclusivity for Biological Products Filed Under Section 351(a) of the PHS Act (Aug. 2014), p. 6, available at https://www. FDA.gov/media/89049/downl oad.

[6]*See* FDA Background Information: Lists of Licensed Biological Products with Reference Product Exclusivity and Biosimilarity or

and apply some of the statutory terms under the second exclusion described above, as well as suggested information for Section 351(a) applicants to provide to the FDA to assist the Agency in its evaluation of the date of first licensure and the applicability of the exclusions.[7]

§ 3:19   The FDA review timeline—Exclusivity provisions impacting biosimilars—Pediatric exclusivity

Section 351(m) of the PHSA provides that an additional 6-month period of pediatric exclusivity will extend the 12-year and four-year reference product exclusivity periods[1] if the sponsor conducts pediatric studies that meet the requirements for pediatric exclusivity pursuant to Section 505A of the FFDCA.[2]

The pediatric exclusivity period may stem from pediatric studies requested by the FDA before or after licensure of a reference product; however, for the pediatric exclusivity period to apply, the FDA must grant the exclusivity not later than nine (9) months prior to the expiration of the period of reference product exclusivity.[3]

§ 3:20   The FDA review timeline—Exclusivity provisions impacting biosimilars—Orphan drug exclusivity

Licensure of a biosimilar or interchangeable biological product may also be delayed by "orphan drug exclusivity" granted to the reference product. Under the Orphan Drug

---

Interchangeability Evaluations (Purple Book), available at https://www.F DA.gov/drugs/biosimilars/background-information-lists-licensed-biological-products-reference-product-exclusivity-and.

[7]*See* FDA Draft Guidance for Industry: Reference Product Exclusivity for Biological Products Filed Under Section 351(a) of the PHS Act (Aug. 2014), available at https://www.FDA.gov/media/89049/download.

[Section 3:19]

[1]Unlike drugs approved under the FFDCA (e.g., NDA), pediatric exclusivity does not attach to patents covering the reference product.

[2]*See e.g.,* FDA Draft Guidance for Industry: Reference Product Exclusivity for Biological Products Filed Under Section 351(a) of the PHS Act (Aug. 2014), p. 2, available at https://www.FDA.gov/media/89049/down load.

[3]Section 351(m)(4) of the PHSA; codified as 42 U.S.C.A. § 262(m)(4).

Act,[1] the FDA may grant "orphan designation" to a biological product intended to treat a rare disease or condition, which is defined to be any disease or condition which affects less than 200,000 individuals in the United States, or affects more than 200,000 individuals in the United States and for which there is no reasonable expectation that the cost of developing and making the product available in the United States for this type of disease or condition will be recovered from sales of the product.[2]

If a product that has orphan designation subsequently receives the first FDA approval for the disease or condition for which it has such designation, the product is entitled to "orphan drug exclusivity." A biosimilar or interchangeable biosimilar of a reference product indicated for a rare disease or condition and subject to the seven-year period of orphan drug exclusivity may not be licensed for the protected orphan indication until the later of the expiration of that seven-year period or the 12-year reference product exclusivity period.[3] An aBLA applicant may submit data and information to support licensure of a proposed biosimilar or interchangeable product for one or more indications for which the reference product has unexpired orphan exclusivity; however, the FDA will not approve the proposed biosimilar or interchangeable product for the protected indication(s) until the orphan drug exclusivity expires. The orphan drug exclusivity period may be extended by six-months by pediatric exclusivity.[4]

There are two exceptions to this seven-year exclusivity period: (1) if the FDA determines, after providing the holder of the orphan drug exclusivity with notice and an opportunity to be heard, that the holder cannot ensure the availability of sufficient quantities of the product to meet the needs of persons with the disease or condition for which the product was designated; or (2) the holder provides written consent

---

[Section 3:20]

[1]Pub. L. No. 97-414; 96 Stat. 2049; codified principally as 21 U.S.C.A. §§ 360aa to 360ee.

[2]21 U.S.C.A. § 360ee(b)(2).

[3]BPCIA § 7002(h), 124 Stat. 821 (2010).

[4]*See* 21 U.S.C.A. § 355a(b)(1)(A)(ii); *see also* 21 U.S.C.A. § 355a(c)(1)(A)(ii).

for the approval of other applications or licenses before the expiration of the seven-year period.[5]

§ 3:21   Naming

Many licensed biologics, including biosimilars and interchangeable biosimilars, are marketed under a proprietary name, also known as a brand name. This name is different from the nonproprietary or "proper" name designated by the FDA in the license for the biological product.[1] The proper name "reflects certain scientific characteristics of the product, such as chemical structure and pharmacological properties."[2] As part of its effort to provide consistency among biologics and facilitate pharmacovigilance, the FDA has implemented a special nonproprietary naming system for biological products, including both reference products and biosimilars/interchangeables. Under this system, the proper name of a biological product will consist of a "core" name followed a meaningless, four-letter suffix. The "core" name is shared by the reference product and any licensed biosimilar and interchangeable products, while the suffix is intended to distinguish between and among the reference product, biosimilars and interchangeables.

In March 2019, the FDA issued an updated guidance to clarify the implementation of the naming system and seek guidance from stakeholders. According to that guidance, the FDA does not intend to add a suffix to the proper names of biological products that were previously licensed or approved without an FDA-designated suffix in their proper names.[3] The FDA will, however, incorporate a unique four-letter suffix to all other biological products to distinguish between reference products, biosimilars, and interchangeable products that share a core name.

---

[5]21 U.S.C.A. § 360cc(b).

[Section 3:21]

[1]*See* 21 C.F.R. § 600.3(k).

[2]*See* FDA Draft Guidance for Industry: Nonproprietary Naming of Biological Products: Update (March 2019), available at https://www.FDA.gov/media/121316/download.

[3]*See* Statement from former FDA Commissioner Scott Gottlieb, M.D., on FDA's steps on naming of biological medicines to balance competition and safety for patients receiving these products, released March 7, 2019, available at https://www.FDA.gov/news-events/press-announcements/statement-FDA-commissioner-scott-gottlieb-md-FDAs-steps-naming-biological-medicines-balance.

§ 3:22 Citizen petitions

The citizen petition process allows stakeholders to request that the FDA take or refrain from taking virtually any Agency action. In the biosimilar context, a party may use a citizen petition to request that the FDA take a particular action relating to a pending application under Section 262(k). Citizen petitions concerning pending biosimilar or interchangeable applications are governed by Section 505(q) of the FFDCA, which provides that the FDA will not delay approval of such applications unless the FDA determines that a delay of approval would be necessary to protect the public health.[1] Under Section 505(q)(1)(E), the FDA may deny a petition that was submitted primarily to delay approval of a pending biosimilar application and does not, on its face, raise valid scientific or regulatory issues.[2] If the FDA determines that a delay of approval is necessary to protect the public health, the FDA will delay approval of a pending application until the issues raised in the petition are resolved. When a citizen petition is received while a biosimilar application is under review, and the goal date for the review falls within the next 150 days, the guidance states that the FDA would expect to respond to the petition within 150 days.[3]

§ 3:23 Complete response letters

When the FDA declines to approve an application to market a drug, including a biosimilar or interchangeable product, the FDA informs the applicant in a "complete response letter."[1] A complete response letter describes all of the deficiencies that the FDA had identified in the application,

---

[Section 3:22]

[1]21 U.S.C.A. § 355(q). The review process set forth in Section 505(q) of the FFDCA does not apply to a pending application for a full BLA.

[2]See FDA Guidance for Industry: Citizen Petitions and Petitions for Stay of Action Subject to Section 505(q) of the Federal Food, Drug, and Cosmetic Act (Sept. 2019), p. 4, available at https://www.fda.gov/media/130878/download.

[3]See Statement from former FDA Commissioner Scott Gottlieb, M.D., on new agency actions to further deter "gaming" of the generic drug approval process by the use of citizen petitions, Oct. 2, 2018, available at https://www.FDA.gov/news-events/press-announcements/statement-FDA-commissioner-scott-gottlieb-md-new-agency-actions-further-deter-gaming-generic-drug.

[Section 3:23]

[1]21 C.F.R. § 601.3(a).

except if the FDA determines after an application is filed that the data submitted are inadequate to support approval, the FDA may issue a complete response letter without first conducting required inspections, testing submitted products lots, or reviewing proposed product labeling.[2] Additionally, a complete response letter will, when possible, include recommended actions that the applicant might take to place the application in condition for approval.[3] Deficiencies the FDA may identify span concerns related to efficacy, safety, clinical pharmacology, non-clinical studies, chemistry, manufacturing and controls (CMC), labeling, and more general concerns (e.g., deficiency in the conduct of a trial).

Following receipt of a complete response letter, an applicant may either resubmit the application and address all deficiencies identified in the complete response letter or voluntarily withdraw the application without prejudice to a subsequent submission.[4] Should the applicant fail to act within one year after issuance of a complete response letter, the FDA will generally consider the application to be withdrawn.[5] Should an applicant resubmit the application, the FDA will set a goal date to review and act on the application within six months of receipt of the application.[6] By contrast, the FDA sets a goal date of 10 months of the 60 day filing date to review and act on an original biological product application submission.[7]

VI. POST-LICENSURE REQUIREMENTS

§ 3:24   Post-Licensure establishment inspection

Following licensure of a biological product, the FDA is authorized to inspect establishments that propagate, manufac-

---

[2]21 C.F.R. §§ 601.3(a)(1) to (2).

[3]21 C.F.R. § 601.3(a)(3).

[4]21 C.F.R. § 601.3(b).

[5]21 C.F.R. § 601.3(c).

[6]*See* Biosimilar Biological Product Reauthorization Performance Goals and Procedures Fiscal Years 2018 Through 2022, p. 4, available at https://www.fda.gov/media/100573/download.

[7]*See* Biosimilar Biological Product Reauthorization Performance Goals and Procedures Fiscal Years 2018 Through 2022, p. 4, available at https://www.fda.gov/media/100573/download.

ture, or prepare the biological product.[1] The FDA is required by statute to inspect such establishments in accordance with a risk-based schedule established by the FDA.[2] In establishing such a risk-based schedule, the FDA inspects establishments in accordance with the known safety risks of such establishments, which is based upon the compliance history of the establishment, the record, history, and nature of recalls linked to the establishment, the inherent risk of the product manufactured at the establishment, the inspection frequency and history of the establishment, whether the establishment has been inspected by a foreign government or a recognized agency of a foreign government, and other criterion the FDA deems necessary and appropriate for purposes of allocating inspection resources.[3]

Establishment inspections are utilized by the FDA to determine compliance with the laws and regulations administered by the FDA, including compliance with the FDA's current good manufacturing practice (cGMP) regulations. Inspections may be used to collect evidence to document violations and support regulatory action. Upon completion of an inspection and before leaving the premises, an FDA inspector provides the inspectional findings in writing ("the FDA Form 483") to the company. The FDA Form 483 notifies the company's management of any conditions that in their judgment may constitute violations of the FFDCA, the PHSA, and related Acts. Observations are made when in the investigator's judgment, conditions or practices observed would indicate that the biological product has been adulterated or is being prepared, packed, or held under conditions whereby the product may become adulterated or rendered injurious to health.[4]

The issuance of an FDA Form 483 does not mean that the FDA has made a final determination of whether any condition is in violation of the FFDCA, PHSA or any relevant regulations. The FDA considers the FDA Form 483 along with a written report called an Establishment Inspection Report ("EIR"), all evidence or documentation collected onsite, and any responses provided by the company. After

---

[Section 3:24]

[1]See 21 U.S.C.A. § 374; see also 42 U.S.C. 262(c).

[2]21 U.S.C.A. § 360(h)(3).

[3]21 U.S.C.A. § 360(h)(4).

[4]21 U.S.C.A. § 374(b).

consideration of all this information, the FDA determines whether to take any further regulatory action or whether to consider the inspection closed.

§ 3:25   Additional post-licensure requirements

Following licensure of a biosimilar or interchangeable biological product, the manufacturer of the licensed product is subject to continuing post-licensure requirements. Such requirements include ongoing compliance with the terms of any Risk Evaluation and Mitigation Strategy (REMS).[1] Further, such requirements include, among other requirements, establishment registration and drug product listing,[2] reporting of adverse events,[3] and compliance with the FDA's promotion and advertising requirements, which include restrictions on promoting products for unapproved uses or patient populations.[4] Manufacturers must continue to comply with the FDA's current good manufacturing practice (cGMP) regulations at all times, including ensuring appropriate quality control, maintenance of records and documentation, and investigation and correction of any deviations from cGMP.[5] The discovery of violative conditions could result in the FDA taking enforcement action, and the discovery of problems with the product post-licensure may result in restrictions being placed on the product, manufacturer, or holder of the license.

[Section 3:25]

[1]*See supra.*
[2]21 C.F.R. Part 207.
[3]21 C.F.R. Part 600, Subpart D.
[4]21 C.F.R. Parts 202 and 203.
[5]21 C.F.R. Part 211.

Chapter 4

BPCIA Patent Litigation

I. JURISDICTION BEFORE SUBMISSION OF THE ABLA

§ 4:1   Pre-submission jurisdiction

II. THE PATENT DANCE

§ 4:2   Patent dance overview
§ 4:3   The Biosimilar applicant discloses information regarding its product to the RPS
§ 4:4   The biosimilar applicant discloses information regarding its product to the RPS—Providing a Copy of the aBLA
§ 4:5   —Providing "Such Other Information"
§ 4:6   —Consequences (or Lack Thereof) for failing to "Provide"
§ 4:7   —Providing additional requested information
§ 4:8   Protection of confidential information
§ 4:9   —Recipients of confidential information
§ 4:10   — —Prosecution bar
§ 4:11   — —Regulatory bar
§ 4:12   —Use of confidential information during and after the patent dance
§ 4:13   —Enforceability
§ 4:14   The RPS provides the "3(A) statement"—the list of patents it believes would be infringed
§ 4:15   3(B) statement by the biosimilar applicant
§ 4:16   —Biosimilar applicant's 3(B) list
§ 4:17   —Biosimilar applicant's detailed statement
§ 4:18   3(C) statement by the RPS
§ 4:19   Negotiation of patents to be litigated and the first wave litigation
§ 4:20   —Initiation of first-wave suit after negotiations

III. NEWLY-ISSUED OR LICENSED PATENTS

§ 4:21   Newly issued or licensed patents generally

IV. NOTICE OF COMMERCIAL MARKETING

§ 4:22   Overview
§ 4:23   The Statute governing NCM
§ 4:24   —Timing of NCM
§ 4:25   —Requirements for providing NCM
§ 4:26   The statute governing NCM—Enforcement of
          NCM provisions
§ 4:27   The Statute governing NCM—Some open NCM-
          related questions
§ 4:28   Second wave litigation
§ 4:29   —Who can bring suit after the applicant provides
          NCM?
§ 4:30   —Factors that could impact bringing suit after
          providing NCM
§ 4:31   —What will second wave litigation look like?

V. COMMENCEMENT OF SUIT

§ 4:32   Venue for biosimilar litigation
§ 4:33   —Venue in patent-infringement actions generally
§ 4:34   — —Venue based on defendant's residence
§ 4:35   — —Venue based on infringement and place of
          business
§ 4:36   — — —Foreign defendants
§ 4:37   —Venue in actions for a declaratory judgment
§ 4:38   —Venue in patent-infringement actions
          generally—Is a declaratory-judgment action ever
          "For Patent Infringement"?
§ 4:39   — —Where can a declaratory judgment action be
          brought?
§ 4:40   Subject matter jurisdiction
§ 4:41   Personal jurisdiction
§ 4:42   Standing
§ 4:43   The right of an RPS to bring a declaratory
          judgment action
§ 4:44   —RPS declaratory judgment suits based on
          section 262(l)(9)(C)
§ 4:45   — —RPS declaratory judgment suits based on
          section 262(l)(9)(B)
§ 4:46   — —Restrictions on the timing of an RPS
          declaratory judgment suit under section
          262(l)(9)(A)
§ 4:47   —Limits on the ability of biosimilar applicants to
          seek declaratory relief
§ 4:48   —Courts have treated the BPCIA's limits on

declaratory judgment actions as non-jurisdictional
§ 4:49 —Whether the BPCIA's restrictions on declaratory judgment actions apply to counterclaims
§ 4:50 —The exercise of declaratory judgment jurisdiction is discretionary
§ 4:51 Limitation on claims
§ 4:52 —Applicant who fails to provide notice under § 262(*l*)(2)(A)
§ 4:53 —Scope-limiting ability of applicant in first wave litigation
§ 4:54 —Second wave litigation
§ 4:55 Right to a jury trial—General overview
§ 4:56 — —Right to jury trial in BPCIA cases
§ 4:57 — —Right to jury trial in biosimilar v. biosimilar patent cases

VI. PRELIMINARY INJUNCTIONS

§ 4:58 Preliminary injunctions

VII. SCHEDULING AND STAGING

§ 4:59 General scheduling & staging
§ 4:60 BPCIA scheduling issues

VIII. DISCOVERY ISSUES IN BPCIA LITIGATIONS

§ 4:61 General scope of discovery
§ 4:62 Discovery of manufacturing information
§ 4:63 Discovery of information from litigations concerning the same biological product or one or more overlapping patents-in-suit
§ 4:64 Expedited discovery in advance of a preliminary injunction
§ 4:65 Protective orders
§ 4:66 —Prosecution bars
§ 4:67 —Regulatory bars
§ 4:68 —Confidentiality tiers

IX. LIABILITY

§ 4:69 Patent infringement
§ 4:70 —Claim construction
§ 4:71 —Literal direct infringement

§ 4:72   —direct infringement under the doctrine of
         equivalents
§ 4:73   — —prosecution history estoppel
§ 4:74   — —Ensnarement
§ 4:75   —Indirect infringement
§ 4:76   — —Induced infringement
§ 4:77   — —Contributory infringement
§ 4:78   —Products manufactured abroad using a
         domestically patented process
§ 4:79   —Safe harbor under section 271(e)
§ 4:80   Patent validity
§ 4:81   —Ineligible subject matter (Section 101)
§ 4:82   —Anticipation (Section 102)
§ 4:83   —Obviousness (Section 103)
§ 4:84   —Lack of written description, lack of enablement,
         and indefiniteness (section 112)
§ 4:85   —Obviousness-Type double patenting
§ 4:86   Patent enforceability
§ 4:87   —Unclean hands
§ 4:88   —Inequitable conduct
§ 4:89   —Unenforceability allegations in the BPCIA
         patent dance

X. POTENTIAL REMEDIES FOR INFRINGEMENT

§ 4:90   Infringement remedies generally
§ 4:91   The BPCIA's conforming amendments to 35
         U.S.C.A. § 271(e)(4)
§ 4:92   Delaying the effective date of FDA approval
§ 4:93   Awarding monetary relief
§ 4:94   Patent enforceability—Monetary damages where
         safe harbor provision does not protect pre-
         market activity
§ 4:95   —Monetary damages for an at-risk launch
§ 4:96   —Attorneys' fees
§ 4:97   Awarding permanent injunctive relief
§ 4:98   Limitations on remedies Under 35 U.S.C.A.
         § 271(e)(6)

I. JURISDICTION BEFORE SUBMISSION OF THE ABLA

§ 4:1 Pre-submission jurisdiction

A biosimilar manufacturer that has not yet submitted an aBLA for its proposed biosimilar product typically lacks an "injury of sufficient immediacy and reality to create subject matter jurisdiction" over a declaratory judgment action challenging infringement, enforceability, or validity of patents that may be asserted against the proposed product.[1] In this pre-submission context, there usually remains "significant uncertainties" over whether the manufacturer will submit an aBLA and whether the proposed biosimilar product will be materially modified before any aBLA is submitted.[2] As such, the biosimilar manufacturer's declaratory judgment claims are typically insufficient to support a "case or controversy" under Article III of the United States Constitution because "the events exposing [the manufacturer] to infringement liability 'may not occur as anticipated, or indeed may not occur at all.' "[3]

II. THE PATENT DANCE

§ 4:2 Patent dance overview

Section 262(*l*) of chapter 42 of the U.S.C. lays out a process for exchanging information and materials prior to the

---

[Section 4:1]

[1]*Sandoz Inc. v. Amgen Inc.*, 773 F.3d 1274, 1275, 112 U.S.P.Q.2d 2004 (Fed. Cir. 2014) (holding that Sandoz had not alleged an injury supporting subject matter jurisdiction over its declaratory judgment action against Amgen's patents when Sandoz had not yet submitted its aBLA for approval of a biosimilar version of Amgen's Embrel® (etanercept)); *see also Celltrion Healthcare Co., Ltd. v. Kennedy Trust for Rheumatology Research*, 2014 WL 6765996, *3–4, 6 (S.D. N.Y. 2014) (dismissing for lack of subject matter jurisdiction Celltrion's pre-aBLA suit challenging the enforceability of patents directed to Remicade® (infliximab)).

[2]*Sandoz Inc.*, 773 F.3d at 1280.

[3]*Sandoz Inc.*, 773 F.3d at 1281 (citing *Texas v. U.S.*, 523 U.S. 296, 300, 118 S. Ct. 1257, 140 L. Ed. 2d 406, 124 Ed. Law Rep. 28 (1998)).

initiation of litigation arising out of the submission of an aBLA under the BPCIA. This information exchange is often referred to informally as the "patent dance." In short, the patent dance requires the applicant to disclose the aBLA and manufacturing process information to the RPS, the RPS to list all patents it may assert against the applicant based on the applicant's disclosure of information, the parties to exchange patent infringement and validity contentions regarding the listed patents, and then to negotiate which (if any) patents they want to litigate in a first-wave litigation. The parties may agree to litigate all the listed patents in the first-wave litigation; otherwise, the remaining patents may be asserted in a second-wave litigation once the biosimilar applicant provides notice no later than 180 days prior to commercial launch—the notice of commercial marketing ("NCM"). This procedure allows the applicant to retain some control of the patents litigated in the first-wave case. Moreover, an applicant can decide not to dance at all, by choosing not to provide its aBLA and manufacturing information. If it makes this choice, the RPS is authorized to immediately bring a declaratory judgment action of infringement, validity, and enforceability with respect to all the patents that can be reasonably asserted against the applicant.[1]

The patent dance can be broken down into the following steps:

Step 1: Within 20 days of the FDA's acceptance of the aBLA for review,[2] the applicant "shall provide" its application and "such other manufacturing information that describes the process or processes used to manufacture the . . . product" to the RPS.[3] The applicant may also provide "additional information requested by. . . the reference product sponsor."[4] The statute further allows the applicant to designate any information produced during the patent dance as "confidential," and the RPS's outside counsel, in-house counsel, and experts, to have

---

[Section 4:2]

[1]42 U.S.C.A. § 262(*l*)(9)(C); *infra* Section 4:43 to 4:50, regarding the RPS's ability to bring a declaratory judgment action when the biosimilar applicant does not dance.

[2]This usually happens within 60 days of the date on which the aBLA is submitted to FDA.

[3]42 U.S.C.A. § 262(*l*)(2)(A); *infra* Sections 4:4 to 4:6, regarding Section 262(*l*)(2)(A) disclosures.

[4]42 U.S.C.A. § 262(*l*)(2)(B); *infra* Section 4:7, regarding Section 262(*l*)(2)(B) disclosures.

access to such information, subject to various restrictions on use and disclosure.[5]

Step 2: The RPS "shall provide" a list of patents it believes "could reasonably be asserted" for patent infringement no later than 60 days from the receipt of the application.[6] This is often referred to as the "3(A)" list, from the section of the BPCIA that requires it. Further, the RPS may identify which of these patents they are willing to license to the applicant.

Step 3: Within 60 days of receipt of the patent list from the RPS, the applicant "may provide" a list of patents it believes "could reasonably be asserted" by the RPS for patent infringement.[7] In addition, the applicant "shall provide" either a detailed statement describing the non-infringement, invalidity, and unenforceability contentions of the patents listed by the RPS on a claim-by-claim basis or a statement that commercial marketing of the biological product will not begin until the expiration of the RPS's patent.[8] These are often referred to as the "3(B)" disclosures, from the section of the BPCIA that requires them. If the RPS identified patents they would be willing to license, the applicant "shall provide" a response at this time.[9]

Step 4: Within 60 days of receipt of the patent list and detailed statement from the applicant, the RPS "shall provide" a detailed statement of the "factual and legal basis of the opinion" that such patents will be infringed by the commercial marketing of the biological product on a claim-by-claim basis, in addition to a response to the applicant's statement concerning the validity and enforceability of the patents on the 3(A) list.[10] These are often referred to as the "3(C)" disclosures, from the section of the BPCIA that requires them.

Step 5: The applicant and RPS shall negotiate in good faith which patents will be litigated in the first phase.[11] There are two possible outcomes:

---

[5]42 U.S.C.A. § 262(*l*)(1); *infra* Sections 4:8 to 4:13, regarding Section 262(*l*)(1) confidentiality provisions.

[6]42 U.S.C.A. § 262(*l*)(3)(A); *infra* Section 4:14, regarding RPS's Section 262(*l*)(3)(A) statement.

[7]42 U.S.C.A. § 262(*l*)(3)(B); *infra* Sections 4:15 to 4:17, regarding Applicant's Section 262(*l*)(3)(B) statement.

[8]42 U.S.C.A. § 262(*l*)(3)(B); *infra* Sections 4:15 to 4:17, regarding Applicant's Section 262(*l*)(3)(B) statement.

[9]42 U.S.C.A. § 262(*l*)(3)(B); *infra* Sections 4:15 to 4:17, regarding Applicant's Section 262(*l*)(3)(B) statement.

[10]42 U.S.C.A. § 262(*l*)(3)(C); *infra* Section 4:18, regarding RPS's Section 262(*l*)(3)(C) statement.

[11]42 U.S.C.A. § 262(*l*)(4) to (5); *infra* Sections 4:19 to 4:20, regarding Section 262(*l*)(4) to (5) negotiations.

- Step 5a: The RPS and applicant agree on the list of patents to be litigated for patent infringement.[12]
- Step 5b: If the RPS and applicant do not agree on the list of patents to be litigated within 15 days of the start of negotiations, the applicant "shall notify" the RPS "of the number of patents that such applicant will provide to the [RPS]."[13] No later than five days after the applicant's notification, the applicant and RPS "shall simultaneously exchange" lists of patents they believe should be the subject of immediate patent infringement action.[14] The number of patents believed to be the subject of patent infringement action by the RPS may not exceed the number of patents listed by the applicant; the RPS may, however, list one patent if the applicant does not list any patent.[15]

Step 6: The RPS "shall" bring an action for patent infringement either (A) for the patents mutually agreed upon within 30 days of the agreement or, (B), in the case of disagreement between the applicant and the RPS, for the patents included on the exchanged lists within 30 days of the simultaneous exchange.[16]

Although the first wave of infringement litigation can be restricted in scope by the applicant, the RPS can assert the remainder of the patents on the 3(A) list once the applicant provides NCM.[17] This is known as a "second-wave" litigation. The patent dance further provides a series of exchanges concerning patents that issue, or were licensed to the RPS, after the RPS's service of its patent list: the RPS "shall provide" the applicant the newly issued or licensed patents within 30 days of their issuance or licensing; in response, the applicant "shall provide" the RPS with a statement describing the non-infringement, invalidity, and unenforceability contentions of the patents on a claim-by-claim basis or a statement that commercial marketing of the biological product will not begin until the expiration of the RPS' patent.[18] These later-issued or -licensed patents may be as-

---

[12]42 U.S.C.A. § 262(*l*)(4)(A).

[13]42 U.S.C.A. § 262(*l*)(4)(B) to (5)(B)(i).

[14]42 U.S.C.A. § 262(*l*)(5)(B)(i).

[15]42 U.S.C.A. § 262(*l*)(5)(B)(ii).

[16]42 U.S.C.A. § 262(*l*)(6)(A) to (B); *infra* Section 4:20, regarding initiation of patent litigation under Section 262(*l*)(6)(A)–(B).

[17]42 U.S.C.A. § 262(*l*)(8)(B); *infra* Sections 4:28 to 4:31, regarding initiation of second wave litigation under Section 262(*l*)(8)(B).

[18]42 U.S.C.A. § 262(*l*)(7)(A) to (B); *infra* Section 4:21, regarding newly

serted only after the applicant provides an NCM.[19] Moreover, upon receipt of the NCM, the RPS may seek a preliminary injunction against the applicant prohibiting the manufacture or sale of the biologic product until the courts have ruled on the infringement, invalidity, and enforcement of the patents at issue.[20]

Applicants may comply to varying degrees with the provisions of the patent dance. If the applicant does not participate in the patent dance, the RPS may "bring an action under section 2201 of title 28 for a declaration of infringement, validity, or enforceability of any patent that claims the biological product or a use of the biological product."[21] The RPS may also seek a declaratory judgment if the applicant fails to engage in subsequent steps of the patent dance.[22] To date, applicants have used different strategies in navigating the patent dance. For example, applicants have:

- opted out of the dance entirely by not producing the aBLA and manufacturing information.[23]

- opted to dance, but limited their Section 262(l)(2)(A) disclosures to their aBLAs—in other words, they do not produce any manufacturing information beyond what is included in the aBLA.[24]

- filed an NCM after dancing most of the way until the end, and immediately thereafter sought declaratory

---

issued or licensed patents.

[19]42 U.S.C.A. § 262(l)(8)(B)(i); *infra* Sections 4:28 to 4:31, regarding initiation of second wave litigation under Section 262(l)(8).

[20]42 U.S.C.A. § 262(l)(8)(B); *infra* Section 4:58, regarding preliminary injunctions sought under Section 262(l)(8)(B).

[21]42 U.S.C.A. § 262(l)(9)(C); *infra* Sections 4:43 to 4:57, regarding RPS's ability to bring a declaratory judgment action when the biosimilar applicant does not dance.

[22]42 U.S.C.A. § 262(l)(9)(B).

[23]*See, e.g., Sandoz Inc. v. Amgen Inc.*, 137 S. Ct. 1664, 198 L. Ed. 2d 114, 122 U.S.P.Q.2d 1685 (2017). In that case, Sandoz refused to provide a copy of its aBLA for a filgrastim biosimilar or any manufacturing information. The Supreme Court held that Sandoz's failure to dance allowed Amgen to bring an immediate declaratory judgment action under 42 U.S.C.A. § 262(l)(9)(C). *Id.* at 1675.

[24]*See, e.g., Amgen Inc. v. Hospira, Inc.*, 866 F.3d 1355, 123 U.S.P.Q.2d 1697 (Fed. Cir. 2017); *Genentech, Inc. v. Amgen Inc.*, 1:17-cv-00165-GMS (D. Del.), D.I. 1 ¶ 26. In cases in which the applicant does not produce manufacturing information beyond its aBLA, the RPS will typically contend that the applicant violated Section 262(l)(2)(A). *Infra* Section 4:6. To date, no court has ruled on this issue.

judgment actions regarding non-infringement, invalidity, and unenforceability regarding the patents identified during the patent dance.[25]

- served an NCM after the RPS serves its Section 262(*l*)(3)(A) patent list, and after the RPS filed a complaint asserting all patents on that list, the parties continued to dance.[26]

§ 4:3 The Biosimilar applicant discloses information regarding its product to the RPS

The biosimilar applicant may initiate the patent dance by disclosing to the Reference Product Sponsor ("RPS"), within 20 days of the FDA accepting the aBLA for filing, the information described in Section 262(*l*)(2) of the BPCIA:

(2) Subsection (k) application information

Not later than 20 days after the Secretary notifies the subsection (k) applicant that the application has been accepted for review, the subsection (k) applicant—

(A) shall provide to the reference product sponsor a copy of the application submitted to the Secretary under subsection (k), and such other information that describes the process or processes used to manufacture the biological product that is the subject of such application; and

(B) may provide to the reference product sponsor additional information requested by or on behalf of the reference product sponsor.[1]

Section 262(*l*)(2)(A) states that not later than 20 days after the FDA notifies the biosimilar applicant that its subsection (k) application has been accepted for review, the applicant "shall provide" to the RPS "a copy" of the aBLA and "such other information that describes the process or processes used to manufacture the biological product that is the subject of such application."[2]

Although compliance with this provision is required under the BPCIA, the questions of whether compliance is "mandatory," and whether failure to comply is "unlawful," are

---

[25]*See, e.g., Genentech, Inc. v. Amgen Inc.*, 1:17-cv-00165-GMS (D. Del.), D.I. 16. Ultimately, the court dismissed Genentech's declaratory judgment action.

[26]*See, e.g., Genentech v. Pfizer*, 1:17-cv-01672-CFC (D. Del).

[Section 4:3]

[1]42 U.S.C.A. § 262(*l*)(2).

[2]42 U.S.C.A. § 262(*l*)(2)(A).

unresolved, and will probably remain so: "The BPCIA, standing alone, does not require a court to decide whether § 262(*l*)(2)(A) is mandatory or conditional; the court need only determine whether the applicant supplied the sponsor with the information required under § 262(*l*)(2)(A)."[3] Under federal law, if an applicant declines to comply with Section 262(*l*)(2)(A), the RPS may not bring an action to compel compliance with the statute.[4] Rather, under Section 262(*l*)(9)(C), an RPS's sole remedy for a biosimilar applicant's failure to comply with Section 262(*l*)(2)(A) is to bring an action for declaratory judgment of patent infringement, validity, or enforceability of any patent that claims the biological product or a use of the biological product.[5] This, in effect, permits the biosimilar applicant to "opt out" of the patent

---

[3]*Sandoz Inc. v. Amgen Inc.*, 137 S. Ct. 1664, 1676, 198 L. Ed. 2d 114, 122 U.S.P.Q.2d 1685 (2017). In *Sandoz*, Sandoz did not provide a copy of its aBLA pursuant to Section 262(*l*)(2)(A). Amgen filed a suit for patent infringement and also asserted two state law claims under California's unfair competition law, under which a business act or practice is unlawful if it violates a rule contained in a state or Federal Statute. Amgen alleged that Sandoz engaged in "unlawful" conduct by, among other things, failing to provide its application and manufacturing information under Section 262(*l*)(2)(A). *See Sandoz*, 137 S. Ct. at 1673. Sandoz counterclaimed for, *inter alia*, a declaratory judgment that it had not violated Section 262(*l*)(2)(A). *See Sandoz*, 137 S. Ct. at 1673. The district court issued judgment to Sandoz on its Section 262(*l*)(2)(A) counterclaim and dismissed Amgen's unfair competition state law claim, based on violation of Section 262(*l*)(2)(A), with prejudice. *Amgen Inc., et al v. Sandoz Inc., et al, 3:14-cv-04741-RS*, 2015 WL 1264756, *10-11 (N.D. Cal., Mar. 19, 2015). Appeals, regarding this issue, and regarding a separate issue concerning Sandoz's notice of commercial marketing (*see infra* §§ 4:23 to 4:31), were then heard by the Federal Circuit (*Amgen Inc. v. Sandoz, Inc.*, 794 F.3d 1347 (Fed. Cir. 2015)) and the Supreme Court (*Sandoz Inc. v. Amgen Inc.*, 137 S. Ct. 1664, 198 L. Ed. 2d 114, 122 U.S.P.Q.2d 1685 (2017)). The Supreme Court remanded to the Federal Circuit to determine whether California law would treat noncompliance with Section 262(*l*)(2)(A) as unlawful. See *Amgen Inc. v. Sandoz Inc.*, 877 F.3d 1315, 125 U.S.P.Q.2d 1001 (Fed. Cir. 2017).

[4]*Sandoz*, 137 S. Ct. at 1667-68.

[5]42 U.S.C.A. § 262(l)(9)(C): "If a subsection (k) applicant fails to provide the application and information required under paragraph (2)(A), the reference product sponsor, but not the subsection (k) applicant, may bring an action under section 2201 of title 28 for a declaration of infringement, validity, or enforceability of any patent that claims the biological product or a use of the biological product." *See also Sandoz*, 137 S. Ct. at 1674-75. In *Sandoz*, the Supreme Court affirmed the Federal Circuit's holding that an injunction under federal law is not available to enforce Section 262(*l*)(2)(A), but based on different reasoning. The Federal Circuit had held that 42 U.S.C.A. § 262(l)(9)(C) and 35 U.S.C.A. § 271(e) provide

dance, and invites the RPS to commence a patent infringement suit immediately. The mandatory or conditional nature of the BPCIA's requirements matters *only* for purposes of state laws that penalize "unlawful" conduct, and therefore only state law *could* be used to determine whether a party's failure to comply with Section 262(*l*)(2)(A) is unlawful.[6] Any state law claim that an applicant's failure to dance is unlawful, however, is likely preempted by the BPCIA because (1) biosimilar patent litigation is a field occupied exclusively by federal law (field preemption), and (2) any state-law remedies would conflict with the framework of remedies laid out by Congress in the BPCIA (conflict preemption).[7]

§ 4:4   The biosimilar applicant discloses information regarding its product to the RPS—Providing a Copy of the aBLA

The requirement under Section 262(*l*)(2)(A) that the applicant provide the RPS with a copy of the aBLA has been relatively uncontroversial. That is to say, where a biosimilar applicant has engaged in the patent dance, the RPS and the applicant have rarely debated whether the applicant had in fact provided a copy of the aBLA.[1] Nevertheless, while it has not been resolved by a court, questions remain about what it

---

the only remedies for a violation of Section 262(*l*)(2)(A). According to the Supreme Court, the Federal Circuit mistakenly held that the Section 271(e)(4) remedies do not apply because there has been no artificial act of infringement if the biosimilar applicant does not comply with Section 262(*l*)(2)(A). The Supreme Court explained that under Section 271(e)(2)(C), the filing of an aBLA is an artificial act of infringement, but that Section 262(*l*)(9)(C) provides the only remedy for violation of Section 262(*l*)(2)(A), and the Section 262(*l*)(9)(C) remedy does not include an injunction to enforce Section 262(*l*)(2)(A). *See infra* Sections 4:43 to 4:50, discussing regarding the RPS's ability to bring a declaratory judgment action when the biosimilar applicant does not dance.

[6]*Sandoz*, 137 S. Ct. at 1676.

[7]*See Amgen*, 877 F.3d at 1325–1330. In *Sandoz*, the Supreme Court remanded to the Federal Circuit to determine whether California law would treat noncompliance with Section (*l*)(2)(A) as unlawful. *Sandoz*, 137 S. Ct. at 1676–77. On remand, the Federal Circuit found that Amgen's state law claims were preempted by the BPCIA, and therefore declined to consider the parties' arguments relating to whether failure to comply with Section 262(*l*)(2)(A) is "unlawful" under California law. *See Amgen*, 877 F.3d at 1325–1330.

[Section 4:4]

[1]One exception is *Genentech, Inc. et al. v. Pfizer, Inc.*, 1:19-cv-00638-CFC (D. Del. April 5, 2019), where Genentech alleged in its complaint that

means to provide "a copy of the application." For example, must the applicant provide every single page of the aBLA?[2] Moreover, must the applicant provide an electronic copy of the application as provided to the FDA, or will a paper copy do? Furthermore, is it enough to provide a copy of the application as it existed when accepted by the FDA, or does the applicant have a continuing duty to provide correspondence to and from the FDA regarding the application?

§ 4:5 The biosimilar applicant discloses information regarding its product to the RPS—Providing "Such Other Information"

The requirement under Section 262(*l*)(2)(A) that an applicant "shall provide . . . a copy of the application . . . *and such other information* that describes the process or processes used to manufacture the biological product that is the subject of such application"[1] has been hotly contested—albeit without any final court resolution. In many instances, applicants have declined or refused to provide manufacturing process information beyond the (usually) extensive process information contained in the aBLA itself,[2] and RPSs have challenged such withholding as a violation of the BPCIA.[3] In those cases, the parties disagreed as to whether applicants can satisfy their obligations under Section 262(*l*)(2)(A) to

---

Pfizer produced only portions of its aBLA (D.I. 1 at ¶ 8). In its answer, Pfizer stated that "[t]o the extent that portions of Pfizer's aBLA were not produced, those portions are not relevant or necessary for Genentech to understand the process or processes used to manufacture Pfizer's product." *Genentech*, D.I. 14 at ¶ 8. *See also infra*, Section 4:5, regarding production of the biosimilar applicant's manufacturing information.

[2]*See Genentech*, 1:19-cv-00638-CFC (D. Del.); *see also infra*, Section 4:6, addressing consequences for failure to comply with Section 262(*l*)(2)(A).

[Section 4:5]

[1]42 U.S.C.A. § 262(*l*)(2)(A) (emphasis added).

[2]*Infra* Section 3:7, describing, *inter alia*, manufacturing information required in an aBLA.

[3]*See, e.g., Amgen Inc. v. Hospira, Inc.*, 866 F.3d 1355, 123 U.S.P.Q.2d 1697 (Fed. Cir. 2017) (on appeal from 1:15-cv-00839-RGA (D. Del.)), *Janssen Biotech, Inc. et al v. Celltrion Healthcare Co., Ltd. et al*, 1:15-cv-10698-MLW (D. Mass.); *AbbVie Inc. et al v. Sandoz Inc. et al*, 3:18-cv-12668-FLW-LHG (D.N.J.); *Genentech, Inc. v. Amgen, Inc.*, 1:17-cv-00165-GMS (D. Del.) ("*Genentech I*"); *Amgen Inc. v. Genentech, Inc. et al*, 2:17-cv-07349-GW-AGR (C.D. Cal.) ("*Genentech II*"); *Genentech, Inc. et al v. Amgen, Inc.*, 1:17-cv-01407-CFC (D. Del.) ("*Genentech III*"). *See also infra* Section 4:6, addressing consequences for failure to comply with Section 262(*l*)(2)(A).

produce "such other information" by producing manufacturing process information from their aBLAs, without any additional manufacturing information from outside of the aBLA. No court has ruled on how to interpret the "and such other information" clause of Section 262(*l*)(2)(A), leaving open whether complying with the statute requires a biosimilar applicant to provide manufacturing information beyond what is included in the aBLA. One court, however, suggested that it was leaning toward an interpretation of Section 262(*l*)(2)(A) that required production of manufacturing information beyond the aBLA, but for the issue at hand, the issue was moot and the court never ruled on it.[4] Further, even if it was settled that information in the aBLA alone cannot satisfy an applicant's obligations under Section 262(*l*)(2)(A), it would still be unclear as to what additional manufacturing information the applicant would need to provide. Neither the BPCIA nor any court has set forth a legal standard for making that determination.

---

[4]*See Genentech I*, 1:17-cv-00165-GMS (D. Del.) (the court's comments were made during an oral argument). In that case, the biosimilar applicant, Amgen, did not produce any manufacturing information beyond the aBLA during the patent dance. Plaintiffs immediately sought a declaratory judgment that Amgen violated Section 262(*l*)(2)(A) by only producing its aBLA. Amgen, in response, moved to dismiss the action as procedurally improper in light of *Amgen Inc. v. Sandoz, Inc.*, 794 F.3d 1347 (Fed. Cir. 2015). At an oral argument, the court suggested that it was leaning toward an interpretation of Section 262(*l*)(2)(A) that required production of manufacturing information beyond the aBLA, telling Amgen that "you don't get to constrain the flow of information to just the application, the statute does not permit that." See *Genentech II*, D.I. 35-1, Ex. 1 at 23-25 (C.D. Cal. Nov. 15, 2017) Ultimately, the court did not need to rule on the issue, because it agreed with Amgen that the lawsuit was procedurally improper. The proper interpretation of the disputed language was, in other words, moot. In the related cases *Genentech II*, which is now dismissed, and in *Genentech III*, which is still pending, the parties continued to dispute the requirements of Section 262(*l*)(2)(A), but the issue remains unresolved. In *Genentech II*, the RPS moved to dismiss Amgen's declaratory judgment action in light of the fact that, *inter alia*, Amgen did not produce any manufacturing information outside the aBLA. *Infra* Section 4:5. The court, however, dismissed Amgen's action on other grounds. And in *Genentech III*, Plaintiffs have moved to dismiss Amgen's counterclaims and certain affirmative defenses again because Amgen did not produce any manufacturing information outside the aBLA. The court has not yet resolved this issue.

§ 4:6 The biosimilar applicant discloses information regarding its product to the RPS—Consequences (or Lack Thereof) for failing to "Provide"

While there is some ambiguity about an applicant's disclosure requirements under Section 262(*l*)(2)(A), courts have shed some light on the consequences of non-compliance.

To date, it is settled that if an applicant fails to comply with Section 262(*l*)(2)(A), an RPS can bring a declaratory judgment action pursuant to Section 262(*l*)(9)(C), which states that an applicant's failure to comply with Section 262(*l*)(2)(A) entitles the RPS to immediately seek a "declaration of infringement, validity, or enforceability of any patent that claims the biological product or a use of the biological product."[1] If, for example, Section 262(*l*)(2)(A) requires an applicant to provide a complete copy of the aBLA and not a portion, the failure to provide a complete copy would allow that RPS to immediately bring an action under Section 262(*l*)(9)(C)—just as if the biosimilar applicant had not danced at all.[2]

It is also settled that certain remedies are not available to an RPS in the event that the applicant does not comply with Section (*l*)(2)(A). First, an RPS may not seek an injunction under federal law to force compliance with the patent dance,

---

[Section 4:6]

[1]42 U.S.C.A. § 262(*l*)(9)(C); *see Sandoz Inc. v. Amgen Inc.*, 137 S. Ct. 1664, 1675, 198 L. Ed. 2d 114, 122 U.S.P.Q.2d 1685 (2017). In this case, the applicant did not dance at all. The Supreme Court explained that "a separate provision of § 262 . . . does provide a remedy for an applicant's failure to turn over its application and manufacturing information. When an applicant fails to comply with § 262(l)(2)(A), § 262(l)(9)(C) authorizes the sponsor, but not the applicant, to bring an immediate declaratory-judgment action for artificial infringement as defined in § 271(e)(2)(C)(ii). Section 262(l)(9)(C) thus vests in the sponsor the control that the applicant would otherwise have exercised over the scope and timing of the patent litigation. It also deprives the applicant of the certainty that it could have obtained by bringing a declaratory-judgment action prior to marketing its product."

[2]For example, in *Genentech*, 1:19-cv-00638-CFC (D. Del.), after Pfizer allegedly only provided a portion of the aBLA and the parties otherwise continued to dance, Genentech included in its complaint a count for declaratory judgment under Section 262(*l*)(9)(C) in view of Pfizer's alleged failure to comply Section 262(*l*)(2)(A). The Court there, however, has yet to determine whether Pfizer complied with the statute.

including the provisions of Section 262(*l*)(2)(A).[3] Further, due to preemption, there is also likely no state law theory pursuant to which an RPS can obtain an injunction to enforce compliance with the federal statute.[4] Second, if, *e.g.*, the applicant only produces part of its aBLA and in response the RPS does not include certain patents in its 3(A) list, the RPS cannot obtain discovery during a BPCIA litigation to determine whether the unlisted patents are infringed.[5] Section 3(A) is a "list or lose" provision and unlisted patents

---

[3]*Sandoz*, 137 S. Ct. at 1674. In *Sandoz*, the Supreme Court held that "an injunction under federal law is not available to enforce § 262(*l*)(2)(A)." *Sandoz*, 137 S. Ct. at 1674. The Supreme Court came to this conclusion in agreement with the Federal Circuit in *Amgen Inc. v. Sandoz Inc.*, 794 F.3d 1347 (Fed. Cir. 2015), cert. granted, 137 S. Ct. 808, 196 L. Ed. 2d 594 (2017) and cert. granted, 137 S. Ct. 808, 196 L. Ed. 2d 594 (2017) and rev'd in part, vacated in part, 137 S. Ct. 1664, 198 L. Ed. 2d 114, 122 U.S.P.Q.2d 1685 (2017), "though for slightly different reasons." *Sandoz*, 137 S. Ct. at 1674. *See also supra* Sections 4:3 to 4:7. After the Federal Circuit issued its ruling in *Amgen v. Sandoz*, RPSs tried, but were ultimately not successful, to bring claims against applicants seeking to enforce compliance with Section 262(*l*)(2)(A) after applicants refused to produce manufacturing process information beyond that in the aBLA. See *Genentech I* (granting motion to dismiss declaratory judgment action seeking to enforce compliance with Section 262(*l*)(2)(A) in light of the Federal Circuit's holding in *Amgen v. Sandoz*); *Amgen v. Hospira*, Case No. 1:15-cv-00839-RGA (D. Del.) (RPS withdrew a claim seeking a declaration that Hospira's withholding of additional manufacturing information violated Section 262(*l*)(2)(A), as well as injunctive relief to compel Hospira's compliance with the statute); *Janssen v. Celltrion*, 1:15-cv-10698-MLW (D. Mass.) ("[T]he BPCIA does not confer a private right of action to enforce allegations of non-compliance with the statutory requirements, and there is no case or controversy to enforce the remedy in 42 U.S.C.A. § 262(l)(9)(C).").

[4]In *Sandoz v. Amgen*, the Supreme Court expressly reserved the question of whether an RPS could seek an injunction to enforce Section 262(*l*)(2)(A) under a state law theory. On remand, the Federal Circuit held that no injunction was available under California state law due to preemption. *Amgen Inc. v. Sandoz Inc.*, 877 F.3d 1315, 125 U.S.P.Q.2d 1001 (Fed. Cir. 2017). Based on the Federal Circuit's reasoning, the same outcome is likely regardless of the state law under which such an injunction is sought. *See also supra* Sections 4:3 and 4:6.

[5]*See Amgen Inc. v. Hospira, Inc.*, 866 F.3d 1355, 123 U.S.P.Q.2d 1697 (Fed. Cir. 2017) (appeal from 1:15-cv-00839-RGA (D. Del.)). In that case, Hospira produced only its aBLA. In its Section 262(*l*)(3)(A) list, Amgen omitted certain cell-culture medium patents because it allegedly could not assess the reasonableness of asserting infringement of the omitted patents without first reviewing requested, but unproduced "other information." In litigation, Amgen sought discovery on the processes claimed in the unlisted, unasserted patents. The district court denied the discovery because it lacked relevance to the patents-in-suit. Amgen filed an interlocutory appeal to the Federal Circuit, which found that it lacked jurisdiction

may not be asserted against the aBLA product. As in any federal case, in a BPCIA litigation, the Federal Rules of Civil Procedure limit discovery to "relevant" information, and discovery concerning an un-asserted patent is not relevant.[6] Instead, if the RPS believes a patent *may* reasonably be asserted, the RPS should include the patent on its Section 262(*l*)(3)(A) list. The BPCIA "provides no sanction for holding or asserting a mistaken belief in good faith."[7]

It remains unsettled, however, whether RPSs are correct that failure to provide "such other [manufacturing] information" precludes an applicant (a) from proceeding with a declaratory judgment action of non-infringement, invalidity, and/or unenforceability against the RPS if the parties continue to dance after the applicant's Section 262(*l*)(2)(A) production and the applicant serves a notice of commercial marketing,[8] or (b) from maintaining counterclaims in a litigation that ensues.[9] Under Section 262(*l*)(9)(C), when an applicant has not complied with Section 262(*l*)(2)(A), "the refer-

---

over the lower court's "run-of-the-mill" discovery ruling. Nevertheless, it suggested that if a RPS does not list a patent, it cannot seek discovery during litigation directed solely to determining whether the unlisted patent could be asserted.

[6]*Amgen Inc. v. Hospira, Inc.*, 866 F.3d 1355, 123 U.S.P.Q.2d 1697 (Fed. Cir. 2017).

[7]*Amgen*, 866 F.3d at 1362.

[8]In *Amgen, Inc. v. Genentech, Inc.*, 2:17-cv-07349-GW-AGR (C.D. Cal.), Amgen provided Genentech with a notice of commercial marketing pursuant to Section 262(*l*)(8)(A) and Amgen immediately filed a declaratory judgment action against Genentech seeking a declaration of noninfringement, invalidity, and/or unenforceability. Genentech moved to dismiss, arguing, *inter alia*, that Amgen's withholding of additional manufacturing process information violated Section 262(*l*)(2)(A) and barred Amgen from bringing a declaratory judgment action. The California court granted Genentech's motion to dismiss, but for reasons unrelated to—and therefore without interpreting—Section (*l*)(2)(A). Instead, the court dismissed the declaratory judgment action pursuant to the discretion granted to it by the Declaratory Judgment Act to decline declaratory judgment jurisdiction.

[9]In *Amgen Inc. v. Sandoz Inc.*, 2015 WL 1264756, *9 (N.D. Cal. 2015), aff'd in part, vacated in part, remanded, 794 F.3d 1347 (Fed. Cir. 2015), and cert. granted, 137 S. Ct. 808, 196 L. Ed. 2d 594 (2017) and rev'd in part, vacated in part, 137 S. Ct. 1664, 198 L. Ed. 2d 114, 122 U.S.P.Q.2d 1685 (2017) and aff'd, 877 F.3d 1315, 125 U.S.P.Q.2d 1001 (Fed. Cir. 2017), Amgen moved to dismiss Sandoz's counterclaims on summary judgment under Section 262(*l*)(9)(C) because Sandoz did not comply with Section 262(*l*)(2)(A). The Court denied Amgen's motion because Section 262(*l*)(9)(C) addresses the biosimilar applicant's ability to "bring" a declaratory judgment action, but not the biosimilar applicant's ability to assert a

ence product sponsor, but not the subsection (k) applicant, may bring an action under section 2201 of title 28, United States Code, for a declaration of infringement, validity, or enforceability of any patent that claims the biological product or a use of the biological product." This provision, RPSs have argued, prohibits applicants from filing declaratory judgment actions or filing counterclaims. No court has resolved the former issue, although one court has suggested—without ruling—that an applicant who did not comply with Section 262(*l*)(2)(A) might not be permitted to bring a declaratory judgment action in view of Section 262(*l*)(9)(C).[10] Another court also distinguished "bringing" or commencing a suit, from bringing a counterclaim, and ruled that Section 262(*l*)(9)(C) did not prohibit an applicant from bringing a counterclaim.[11] Neither the Federal Circuit or the Supreme Court have weighed in on this issue.

§ 4:7   The biosimilar applicant discloses information regarding its product to the RPS—Providing additional requested information

The BPCIA also provides that the applicant "may provide to the reference product sponsor additional information requested by or on behalf of the reference product sponsor" under Section 262(*l*)(2)(B). This section of the statute has not yet been litigated, and therefore open questions remain. First, under what circumstances would an RPS request additional information? Second, what is the permitted scope of such a request? And third, if the aBLA filer refuses to provide additional information requested under Section 262(*l*)(2)(B), are there any consequences? The BPCIA is silent as to the consequences, if any, for an applicant's fail-

---

counterclaim to defend against an infringement suit. This aspect of the Court's decision was never addressed on appeal.

[10]*Amgen Inc. v. Genentech, Inc. et al*, 2:17-cv-07349-GW-AGR, D.I. 56 at 5 (C.D. Cal., Jan. 11, 2018).

[11]*Amgen Inc. v. Sandoz Inc.*, 2015 WL 1264756, *9 (N.D. Cal. 2015), aff'd in part, vacated in part, remanded, 794 F.3d 1347 (Fed. Cir. 2015), cert. granted, 137 S. Ct. 808, 196 L. Ed. 2d 594 (2017) and cert. granted, 137 S. Ct. 808, 196 L. Ed. 2d 594 (2017) and rev'd in part, vacated in part, 137 S. Ct. 1664, 198 L. Ed. 2d 114, 122 U.S.P.Q.2d 1685 (2017) and aff'd, 877 F.3d 1315, 125 U.S.P.Q.2d 1001 (Fed. Cir. 2017).

ure to respond to requests by the RPS under Section 262(*l*)(2)(B).¹

§ 4:8 Protection of confidential information

The biosimilar applicant initiates the patent dance by disclosing the information described in Section 262(*l*)(2) of the BPCIA to the Reference Product Sponsor ("RPS") within 20 days of the FDA accepting the aBLA for filing. To protect the disclosure of such confidential information to unauthorized individuals or entities, the BPCIA provides a default protective order, which is described in Section 262(*l*)(1). The provisions of this default protective order specify the recipients and use of this confidential information.

(B)(i) Provision of confidential information:
When a subsection (k) applicant submits an application under subsection (k), such applicant shall provide to the persons described in clause (ii), subject to the terms of this paragraph, confidential access to the information required to be produced pursuant to paragraph (2) and any other information that the subsection (k) applicant determines, in its sole discretion, to be appropriate (referred to in this subsection as the "confidential information").¹

The provisions of Section 262(*l*)(1)(B) apply to the exchange of confidential information unless otherwise agreed to by the applicant and RPS.²

§ 4:9 Protection of confidential information— Recipients of confidential information

Section 262(*l*)(1)(B)(ii) provides that during the patent dance, the applicant's confidential information can be accessed by one or more outside counsel designated by the RPS

[Section 4:7]

¹Notably, Section 262(*l*)(9)(C), the only provision of the BPCIA which provides a remedy for an applicant's failure to comply with Section 262(*l*)(9)(A)—that is the RPS can immediately seek a "declaration of infringement, validity, or enforceability of any patent that claims the biological product or a use of the biological product"—is silent as to Section (l)(2)(B).

[Section 4:8]

¹42 U.S.C.A. § 262(*l*)(1)(B)(i).

²42 U.S.C.A. § 262(*l*)(1)(A). For example, in Immunex Corp. v. Sandoz Inc., No. 4:16-CV-01118-CCC-MF (D.N.J.), the parties entered into a pre-litigation Confidentiality Agreement in place of the default provisions.

and one in-house counsel of the RPS. The statute defines "outside counsel" as attorneys "who are employees of an entity other than the reference product sponsor" and defines "in-house counsel" as an "attorney that represents the reference product sponsor who is an employee of the reference product sponsor."[1] The parties can agree to allow access to the confidential information to additional individuals, such as additional in-house counsel for the RPS or staff of the outside or in-house counsel.[2]

Section 262(*l*)(1)(B)(iii) further provides that a representative of an owner of an exclusively licensed patent covering the reference product who has retained a right to assert the patent or participate in litigation concerning the patent may be provided with the confidential information, provided that the representative agrees to be subject to the confidentiality provisions set forth in this paragraph.[3]

The recipients of the confidential information cannot "disclose the confidential information to any other person or entity, including the reference product sponsor employees, outside scientific consultants, or other outside counsel retained by the reference product sponsor, without the prior written consent of the subsection (k) applicant, which shall not be unreasonably withheld."[4]

§ 4:10   Protection of confidential information— Recipients of confidential information— Prosecution bar

Section 262(*l*)(1)(B)(ii) provides a "prosecution bar" that prevents the recipients of the applicant's confidential information from "engag[ing], formally or informally, in patent

---

[Section 4:9]

[1]42 U.S.C.A. § 262(*l*)(1)(B)(ii).

[2]For example, in *Immunex v. Sandoz*, the parties additionally agreed that the staff of the outside counsel engaged by the RPS "including paralegal, secretarial, and clerical personnel who assist such counsel," technical consultants, three-designated in-house counsel of the RPS and their staff could access the confidential information exchanged under the agreement. No. 4:16-CV-01118-CCC-MF (D.N.J.), ECF No. 79, Ex. B at 1.

[3]42 U.S.C.A. § 262(*l*)(1)(B)(iii).

[4]42 U.S.C.A. § 262(*l*)(1)(C).

prosecution" relevant to the reference product.[1] The default protective order does not define "patent prosecution" and is silent as to the duration of the bar. Although no court has interpreted Section 262(*l*)(1)(B)(ii) specifically,[2] prosecution bars are common in patent litigations as courts have recognized the risk of the strategic use of confidential information in patent prosecution.[3] Federal Circuit law controls disputes regarding patent prosecution bars.[4]

§4:11 Protection of confidential information— Recipients of confidential information— Regulatory bar

The BPCIA default protective order is silent as to whether recipients of the applicant's confidential information are barred from the preparation of regulatory submissions to or communications with the Food and Drug Administration ("the FDA") regarding the reference product. The parties can, however, enter into a confidentiality agreement in lieu of the default provisions that includes such a regulatory bar.[1]

[Section 4:10]

[1]42 U.S.C.A. § 262(*l*)(1)(B)(ii).

[2]Parties have, however, disputed the terms and duration of prosecution bars when negotiating protective orders during BPCIA litigations. One issue that often arises is whether counsel subject to a prosecution bar can participate in reissues, reexaminations, *inter partes* reviews and/or post-grant review proceedings. *See, e.g.*, Amgen Inc. v. Sandoz Inc., Case No. 14-cv-4741, ECF No. 48 at 5, 12–13 (N.D. Cal.).

[3]*In re Deutsche Bank Trust Co. Americas*, 605 F.3d 1373, 1378, 95 U.S.P.Q.2d 1399 (Fed. Cir. 2010).

[4]*In re Deutsche Bank Trust Co. Americas*, 605 F.3d 1373, 1378, 95 U.S.P.Q.2d 1399 (Fed. Cir. 2010).

[Section 4:11]

[1]Immunex Corp. v. Sandoz Inc., No. 4:16-CV-01118-CCC-MF, ECF No. 79, Ex. B (D.N.J. July 11, 2016) (barring in-house counsel who access the confidential information from "patent prosecution, the preparation of regulatory submissions, or participation in any regulatory proceedings relevant to or relating to" the reference product.). Moreover, in BPCIA litigations, parties have disputed the necessity, terms, and duration of regulatory bars when negotiating protective orders. *See also infra* Section 4:65.

§ 4:12   Protection of confidential information—Use of confidential information during and after the patent dance

The BPCIA provides limitations concerning the use of confidential information produced during the patent dance. In particular, the RPS cannot use the biosimilar applicant's confidential information for any purpose other than "determining, with respect to each patent assigned to or exclusively licensed by the reference product sponsor, whether a claim of patent infringement could reasonably be asserted" against the applicant.[1] If the RPS files a patent infringement suit, the confidentiality provisions of Section 262(*l*)(1) remain in effect, and the previously produced documents remain confidential, until a court enters a protective order in a patent infringement suit between the BPCIA parties.[2] Once the protective order is entered, the applicant may re-designate confidential information in accordance with its terms. However, "[n]o confidential information shall be included in any publicly-available complaint or other pleading."[3] If the RPS does not file a patent infringement suit within the time frame specified under Section 262(*l*)(6), the RPS must return or destroy the confidential information it received from the applicant.[4] The default protective order does not provide a timeframe for the return or destruction of such confidential information.[5]

§ 4:13   Protection of confidential information—Enforceability

Section 262(*l*)(H) provides that the disclosure of confidential information in violation of these provisions "shall be deemed to cause the subsection (k) applicant to suffer irreparable harm for which there is no adequate legal remedy

---

[Section 4:12]

[1]42 U.S.C.A. § 262(*l*)(1)(D).

[2]42 U.S.C.A. § 262(*l*)(1)(F).

[3]42 U.S.C.A. § 262(*l*)(1)(F).

[4]42 U.S.C.A. § 262(*l*)(1)(F).

[5]*See* Immunex v. Sandoz, ECF No. 79, Ex. B at 3. The default protective order also does not provide guidance for situations where a suit is filed, but some of the confidential information is not relevant to the suit. One such example would be where an applicant produces confidential manufacturing information and a patent infringement suit is subsequently filed without asserting manufacturing related patents.

and the court shall consider immediate injunctive relief to be an appropriate and necessary remedy for any violation or threatened violation of this paragraph."[1] Because this default protective order applies to the exchange of confidential information pre-litigation, a party would need to bring an action to seek injunctive relief for violation of this agreement. Parties can also agree to provisions protecting the accidental disclosure of confidential information.[2]

§ 4:14 The RPS provides the "3(A) statement"—the list of patents it believes would be infringed

Section 262(*l*)(3)(A) provides that the RPS shall, within 60 days of receiving a copy of the aBLA from the aBLA applicant, provide to the applicant a list of patents the RPS believes would be infringed by the aBLA and identify which of those patents the RPS would be willing to license.

(3) **List and description of patents**
(A) Not later than 60 days after the receipt of the application and information under paragraph (2), the reference product sponsor shall provide to the subsection (k) applicant—
(i) a list of patents for which the reference product sponsor believes a claim of patent infringement could reasonably be asserted by the reference product sponsor, or by a patent owner that has granted an exclusive license to the reference product sponsor with respect to the reference product, if a person not licensed by the reference product sponsor engaged in the making, using, offering to sell, selling, or importing into the United States of the biological product that is the subject of the subsection (k) application; and
(ii) an identification of the patents on such list that the reference product sponsor would be prepared to license to the subsection (k) applicant.[1]

Thus far, there have been no disputes about the suffi-

[Section 4:13]

[1]42 U.S.C.A. § 262(*l*)(1)(H).

[2]For example, in *Immunex v. Sandoz,* the parties agreed that in the event of the inadvertent disclosure of the biosimilar applicant's confidential information, the RPS would contact the biosimilar applicant to identify "(i) what has been disclosed; (ii) the individuals by whom such information was disclosed; (iii) the individuals to whom such information has been disclosed; and (iv) steps taken by [the RPS] and Authorized Evaluators to ensure the information in and/or derived from [the applicant's] Confidential Information is not further disseminated." ECF No. 79, Ex. B at 3.

[Section 4:14]

[1]42 U.S.C.A. § 262(*l*)(3)(A)(i) to (ii).

ciency, or timeliness, of an RPS's 3(A) statement. Rather, many disputes have centered on whether the RPS had sufficient information from the applicant, for example, where the applicant only provided its aBLA, for the RPS to provide a comprehensive list of patents.[2]

Crucially, an RPS's failure to list in the 3(A) statement a patent that it owns or has licensed bars the RPS from thereafter asserting that patent under 35 U.S.C.A. § 271 against the product described in the aBLA.[3] In some cases, an RPS has challenged whether this bar applies when the applicant allegedly did not disclose certain allegedly relevant manufacturing information in step one of the dance, but the RPS nevertheless chose to continue to dance.[4]

Even where the RPS believes it does not have all of the

---

[2]*See Amgen Inc. v. Hospira, Inc.*, 866 F.3d 1355, 123 U.S.P.Q.2d 1697 (Fed. Cir. 2017); *see also supra* Section 4:3 to 4:5, addressing the information the applicant is required to provide at the beginning of the patent dance.

[3]35 U.S.C.A. § 271 (e)(6)(C): "The owner of a patent that should have been included in the list described in section 351(l)(3)(A) of the Public Health Service Act, including as provided under section 351(*l*)(7) of such Act for a biological product, but was not timely included in such list, may not bring an action under this section for infringement of the patent with respect to the biological product." Under section 351 (*l*)(7), the RPS may only add to its 3(A) statement newly issued or licensed patents. *See* 42 U.S.C.A. § 262 (l)(7); *see also Amgen Inc. v. Apotex Inc.*, 827 F.3d 1052, 1057–59, 119 U.S.P.Q.2d 1318 (Fed. Cir. 2016) ("While the reference product sponsor may later supplement its (3)(A) list under paragraph (7), it is the original lists under (3) that form the basis of the next steps in the process leading to immediate litigation under paragraph 6.").

[4]This situation arose in *Amgen Inc. v. Hospira, Inc.*, 866 F.3d 1355, 123 U.S.P.Q.2d 1697 (Fed. Cir. 2017), where Hospira produced only its aBLA, omitting any additional information. As a result, Amgen failed to list certain cell-culture medium patents on its 3(A) statement. According to Amgen, because Hospira failed to produce sufficient "other information," *Amgen*, 866 F.3d. at 1357, Amgen could not fully evaluate what patents could "reasonably be asserted" against Hospira. *Amgen*, 866 F.3d. at 1357. Amgen sought discovery related to the unlisted, unasserted cell-culture patents and the district court denied the discovery because it lacked relevance. On appeal, Amgen argued that Hospira was "gam[ing] the system," affecting which patents were in the (*l*)(6) lawsuit by failing to provide complete information under (*l*)(2)(A). *Amgen*, 866 F.3d. at 1361. While the Federal Circuit dismissed for lack of jurisdiction, the Court did indicate that if a patent was not on the 3(A) statement, the RPS could not seek discovery during litigation directed towards assessing whether that additional patent could be asserted. *Amgen*, 866 F.3d. at 1361–62. In *Genentech Inc. v. Amgen Inc.*, Amgen provided only its aBLA, and no additional manufacturing information. The Court made clear on the record that it did not read the statute to permit Amgen to produce *only* the infor-

manufacturing information from the applicant at the time the 3(A) statement is due, the RPS will likely be barred from adding patents to its 3(A) list later on. Section 262(*l*)(3)(A) states that a patent should be listed when it "could reasonably be asserted by the reference product sponsor." Courts have interpreted this language to mean that the RPS must list all potentially relevant patents, regardless of any alleged deficiencies in the applicant's disclosure.[5] If, based on the information (even if incomplete) provided by the aBLA, the RPS believes the patent could be reasonably asserted—*i.e.*, nothing in what the applicant provided indicates that a claim for patent infringement cannot reasonably be brought—the patent should be included in the 3(A) statement.[6] Under those circumstances, the RPS is deemed to have satisfied Rule 11 and is at no risk of being sanctioned, since the BPCIA "provides no sanction for holding or asserting a mistaken belief in good faith."[7] In the alternative, if the RPS believes that the applicant has not complied with the first step of the patent dance, the RPS has the option of filing an immediate declaratory judgment action of infringement, validity, and enforceability under 42 U.S.C. § 262 (1)(9)(C), instead of continuing to dance and serving its 3(A) statement.

While the statute provides that the RPS may later supplement the 3(A) statement under paragraph (*l*)(7), the original 3(A) statement forms the basis for the immediate litigation. The supplementation permitted under paragraph (*l*)(7) is limited to "patents that were issued to or exclusively licensed by the reference product sponsor after it gave the applicant its 3(A) list."[8]

Disputes over the exchange of information under paragraph 2 may also affect the scope of later discovery. If the

---

mation in the application. *See* Genentech Inc. v. Amgen Inc., 17-cv-165, D.I. 12 (Feb. 27, 2017) ("[Amgen] seem[s] to believe that [it has] satisfied [its] obligations under the statute. That's not the way I read the statute."). However, the Court here did not have the benefit of the Federal Circuit's decision in *Amgen Inc. v. Hospira Inc.*

[5]*Amgen Inc. v. Hospira, Inc.*, 866 F.3d 1355, 1362, 123 U.S.P.Q.2d 1697 (Fed. Cir. 2017).

[6]*Amgen*, 866 F.3d at 1362–63 (The Court in *Amgen v. Hospira* stated that Amgen misunderstood paragraph (*l*)(3)(A) and that it only requires the sponsor to list patents that it "believes . . . *could* reasonably be asserted.").

[7]*Amgen, Inc. v. Hospira Inc.*, 866 F.3d at 1362.

[8]*Amgen, Inc. v. Apotex, Inc.*, 827 F.3d at 1057; *see also infra* Section 4:21, addressing supplementation under Section 262(*l*)(7).

aBLA applicant allegedly fails to complete step 2 by producing less than all of the information required, but the RPS nevertheless proceeds to participate in the patent dance by providing its 3(A) statement, the RPS will likely not be permitted to argue that the applicant's noncompliance with (l)(2)(A) justifies discovery relating solely to unlisted, unasserted patents.

§ 4:15   3(B) statement by the biosimilar applicant

After the patent dance is initiated under Section 262(l)(2), the biosimilar applicant "may provide" to the RPS a list of patents the biosimilar applicant believes could reasonably be asserted and "shall provide" the RPS with a detailed statement explaining why each patent listed by the RPS under Section 262(l)(3)(A) is invalid, unenforceable, or will not be infringed by the proposed biosimilar.

> (B) List and description by subsection (k) applicant
>
> Not later than 60 days after receipt of the list under subparagraph (A), the subsection (k) applicant—
>
>> (i) may provide to the reference product sponsor a list of patents to which the subsection (k) applicant believes a claim of patent infringement could reasonably be asserted by the reference product sponsor if a person not licensed by the reference product sponsor engaged in the making, using, offering to sell, selling, or importing into the United States of the biological product that is the subject of the subsection (k) application;
>>
>> (ii) shall provide to the reference product sponsor, with respect to each patent listed by the reference product sponsor under subparagraph (A) or listed by the subsection (k) applicant under clause (i)—
>>
>>> (I) a detailed statement that describes, on a claim by claim basis, the factual and legal basis of the opinion of the subsection (k) applicant that such patent is invalid, unenforceable, or will not be infringed by the commercial marketing of the biological product that is the subject of the subsection (k) application; or
>>>
>>> (II) a statement that the subsection (k) applicant does not intend to begin commercial marketing of the biological product before the date that such patent expires.

§ 4:16   3(B) statement by the biosimilar applicant— Biosimilar applicant's 3(B) list

The biosimilar applicant "may provide" the RPS a list of patents the biosimilar applicant believes could reasonably be asserted by the RPS.[1] The plain language of the statute confirms that this is an optional step for the biosimilar applicant. Indeed, no publicly available documents from BPCIA litigations have referred to an applicant providing a list of patents to the RPS under this section.

§4:17 3(B) statement by the biosimilar applicant— Biosimilar applicant's detailed statement

Unlike the permissive requirements of Section 262(*l*)(3)(B)(i), 262(*l*)(3)(B)(ii) requires that the biosimilar applicant "shall provide" the RPS a detailed statement describing the applicant's basis for its opinion that each patent listed by the RPS under Section 262(*l*)(3)(A) is invalid, unenforceable, or will not be infringed by the biosimilar product. This exchange is often referred to as a "3(B) statement." While a biosimilar applicant is required by the statute to provide the 3(B) statement, it must do so only if the patent dance exchanges under 42 U.S.C. § 262 have commenced. If the applicant elects not to begin the patent dance at all by refusing to provide a copy of the aBLA under Section 262(*l*)(2)(A), it can avoid having to provide a 3(B) statement,[1] and the RPS may not bring an action to compel the patent dance disclosures under federal[2] or state law.[3] Instead, the RPS's sole remedy is to file a declaratory judgment action for patent infringement pursuant to Section 262(*l*)(9)(C).[4]

The BPCIA does not specify the content of the 3(B) statement. In general, however, its purpose is somewhat analogous to the "detailed statement" provided by an ANDA filer under the Hatch-Waxman Act when it seeks to chal-

---

[Section 4:16]

[1]42 U.S.C.A. § 262(*l*)(3)(B)(i).

[Section 4:17]

[1]*Supra* Section 4:5, regarding applicant's production of manufacturing information during patent dance.

[2]*Sandoz Inc. v. Amgen Inc.*, 137 S. Ct. 1664, 198 L. Ed. 2d 114, 122 U.S.P.Q.2d 1685 (2017).

[3]*Amgen Inc. v. Sandoz Inc.*, 877 F.3d 1315, 125 U.S.P.Q.2d 1001 (Fed. Cir. 2017).

[4]42 U.S.C.A. § 262(*l*)(2)(A); *Sandoz Inc. v. Amgen Inc.*, 137 S. Ct. 1664, 198 L. Ed. 2d 114, 122 U.S.P.Q.2d 1685 (2017); *Amgen Inc. v. Sandoz Inc.*, 877 F.3d 1315, 125 U.S.P.Q.2d 1001 (Fed. Cir. 2017).

lenge a patent identified in the Orange Book[5] as covering the reference product.[6] A Paragraph IV notice letter must include "a detailed statement of the factual and legal basis of the opinion of the applicant that the patent is invalid or will not be infringed,"[7] but the Hatch-Waxman Act does not specify the level of detail required. 3(B) statements, like Paragraph IV detailed statements, typically contain a summary of one or more defenses to a claim of patent infringement, but like the Hatch-Waxman Act, the BPCIA does not specify the level of detail required. 3(B) statements can sometimes be very lengthy (numbering in the thousands of pages), likely due in part to the large number of patents often identified by the RPS in its 3(A) list.[8]

3(B) statements made by the biosimilar applicant, while not binding, may be considered party admissions.[9] While the 3(B) statement may be used as a party admission, there is no statutory prohibition against a biosimilar applicant modifying the positions taken in the 3(B) statements throughout the litigation. However, in at least one instance, the RPS moved to dismiss invalidity counterclaims that it alleged exceeded the scope of the 3(B) statement.[10] Similar to what often happens in Hatch-Waxman litigation, a party

---

[5]FDA, *Orange Book: Approved Drug Products with Therapeutic Equivalence Evaluations*, available at https://www.accessdata.fda.gov/scripts/cder/ob/index.cfm.

[6]21 U.S.C.A. § 355(b)(2)(iv).

[7]21 U.S.C.A. § 355(b)(3)(D)(ii).

[8]*Abbvie, Inc. et al. v. Amgen Inc. et al.*, 1:16-cv-00666-MSG, D.I. 13 (D. Del. Sept. 13, 2016) (Amgen's 3(B) statement totaled over 2,750 pages).

[9]*See Amgen Inc. v. Apotex Inc.*, 712 Fed. Appx. 985, 989 (Fed. Cir. 2017) ("[W]e agree that a district court cannot ignore letters sent during the BPCIA's information exchange if properly offered into evidence. Indeed, the pre-litigation information exchange is part of the BPCIA's 'carefully calibrated scheme for preparing to adjudicate, and then adjudicating, claims of infringement.' . . . The statements in the pre-litigation letters are party admissions and therefore have some probative weight.") (internal citations omitted).

[10]*See Genentech, Inc. v. Amgen Inc.*, 2019 WL 4058929 (D. Del. 2019). Genentech moved to dismiss Amgen's invalidity counterclaims, arguing that Amgen's invalidity counterclaims improperly exceed the scope of Amgen's detailed statements under subsection (*l*)(3)(B) during the patent dance. Genentech argued that it would defeat the objectives of the BPCIA if the "parties' contention became non-binding once the BPCIA ligation started" and "if the contentions exchanged during the 'patent dance' do not define the scope of the litigation, what purpose do they serve?" *Genentech*, D.I. 149 at 6–8. Amgen, in its Answering brief argued that, *inter alia*, it should be allowed to raise invalidity defenses not raised in

may want to modify its legal theories or defenses as a result of information gathered during discovery. Claim construction positions put forward by the parties, or the court's claim construction order, can also cause the parties to change the theories or defenses in the case.

3(B) statements may also have an impact on invalidity contentions exchanged during the ensuing patent infringement litigation. Invalidity and non-infringement contentions exchanged during litigation may incorporate in whole, or in part, the 3(B) statement. However, RPS's have sometimes attempted to challenge invalidity contentions during litigation that differ from those provided in the 3(B) statements.[11]

Taking guidance from the Hatch-Waxman context, arguments should have legal and factual support. Courts have found that ANDA filers challenging patents under the Hatch-Waxman Act have a duty of care.[12] "Baseless certifications" made by an ANDA filer that a patent is not valid or not infringed may form part of the basis for an exceptional case under 35 U.S.C.A. § 285 and entitle the RPS to an award of attorneys' fees. A biosimilar applicant may similarly be accused of making "baseless" arguments when challenging patents in the BPCIA patent dance if they lack factual or legal support. This could potentially be used as evidence supporting a finding of an exceptional case under 35 U.S.C.A. § 285.

There are often multiple BPCIA litigations involving different aBLAs and biosimilar applicants for any given reference biologic product. 3(B) statements and other patent

---

the patent dance since Genentech had the opportunity to supplement their infringement contentions. *Genentech*, D.I. 149 at 2–3. The court has not entered an order on the motion.

[11]*See supra* § 3:2.

[12]*See Takeda Chemical Industries, Ltd. v. Mylan Laboratories, Inc.*, 459 F. Supp. 2d 227 (S.D. N.Y. 2006), subsequent determination, 2007 WL 840368 (S.D. N.Y. 2007), aff'd, 549 F.3d 1381, 89 U.S.P.Q.2d 1218 (Fed. Cir. 2008) and aff'd, 549 F.3d 1381, 89 U.S.P.Q.2d 1218 (Fed. Cir. 2008); *see also Yamanouchi Pharmaceutical Co., Ltd. v. Danbury Pharmacal, Inc.*, 231 F.3d 1339, 1347, 56 U.S.P.Q.2d 1641, 180 A.L.R. Fed. 743 (Fed. Cir. 2000) ("The joint operation of §§ 271(e) and 285 require the [ANDA filer] to display care and regard for the strict standards of the Hatch-Waxman Act when challenging patent validity. . . . The Hatch-Waxman Act thus imposes a duty of care on an ANDA certifier. Thus, a case initiated by a [ANDA] filing, like any other form of infringement litigation may become exceptional if the ANDA filer makes baseless certifications.").

dance disclosures may be discoverable in other litigations concerning the same product or same patents.[13]

For patents in the RPS's 3(A) list that expire before the commercial marketing of the proposed biosimilar product, the biosimilar applicant may provide a statement indicating that it does not intend to begin commercial marketing of its product until the expiration of the patent(s).[14] This statement is analogous to a so-called "Paragraph III" statement in Hatch-Waxman cases where an ANDA filer states that it will not sell its generic drug until the patents expire, except that the statement does not limit when the FDA may approve the aBLA.[15] There have been several instances where biosimilar applicants have provided notice under this provision that they would not begin commercial marketing before the expiration of certain 3(A) list patents.[16]

§ 4:18   3(C) statement by the RPS

After the biosimilar applicant provides its 3(B) detailed statement, the RPS must then provide a responsive detailed statement explaining why the 3(A)-listed patents will be infringed and responding to any invalidity or unenforceability contentions in the applicant's 3(B) statement. This exchange is often referred to as a "3(C) statement."

(C) Description by reference product sponsor
Not later than 60 days after receipt of the list and statement under subparagraph (B), the reference product sponsor shall provide to the subsection (k) applicant a detailed statement that describes, with respect to each patent described in subparagraph (B)(ii)(I), on a claim by claim basis, the factual and legal basis of the opinion of the reference product sponsor

---

[13]*Supra* Section 4:63.

[14]35 U.S.C.A. § 262(*l*)(3)(B)(ii)(II).

[15]21 U.S.C.A. § 355(b)(2)(A)(iii).

[16]*See Abbvie Inc et al. v. Amgen Inc et al.*, 1:16-cv-00666-MSG, D I. 62 (D. Del Apr. 27, 2017); *Genentech Inc. et al. v. Celltrion, Inc. et al.*, 1:18-cv-01025-CFC, D.I. 11 (D. Del. Aug. 24, 2018); *Genentech, Inc. et al. v. Amgen, Inc.*, 1:17-cv-01471-CFC, D.I. 122 (D. Del. Jun. 12, 2018); *Genentech, Inc. et al. v. Amgen, Inc.*, 1:17-cv-01407-CFC, D.I. 120 (D. Del. Jun. 5, 2018); *Celltrion, Inc. et al. v. Genentech, Inc. et al.*, 4:18-cv-00274-JSW, D I. 38 (N.D. Cal. Feb. 8, 2018); *Celltrion, Inc. et al. v. Genentech, Inc. et al.*, 4:18-cv-00276-JSW, D.I. 38 (N.D. Cal. Feb. 8, 2018); *Amgen Inc. v. Genentech, Inc. et al.*, 2:17-cv-07349-GW-AGR, D.I. 1 (C.D. Cal. Oct. 6, 2017); *Amgen Inc. et al. v. Hospira, Inc.*, 1:15-cv-00839-RGA, D.I. 82, (D. Del. Aug. 26, 2016); *Amgen Inc. et al. v. Apotex Inc. et al.*, 0:15-cv-61631-JIC, D.I. 48 (S.D. Fla. Oct. 29, 2015).

that such patent will be infringed by the commercial marketing of the biological product that is the subject of the subsection (k) application and a response to the statement concerning validity and enforceability provided under subparagraph (B)(ii)(I).

The RPS must serve the 3(C) statement on the biosimilar applicant "not later than 60 days" after the RPS receives the 3(B) statement. At least one biosimilar applicant has alleged that a delay in serving the 3(C) statement weighed in favor of staying the litigation pending a motion to dismiss.[1]

Once the RPS receives the 3(B) statement, the plain language of the statute ("shall provide") indicates that the RPS must provide a 3(C) statement.[2] The 3(C) statement must address at least all of the patents included in the 3(B) statement that the RPS wishes to assert in litigation.[3]

In at least one instance, a biosimilar applicant has sought to "waive" the requirement for the RPS to provide a 3(C) (and further BPCIA exchanges) in an attempt to force the RPS to file an immediate infringement action.[4] However, in

---

[Section 4:18]

[1]*Amgen Inc. v, Coherus Biosciences, Inc.*, 1:17-cv-00546-LPS, D.I. 25 (D. Del. July 25, 2017). In that case the applicant argued that the RPS "drag[ged] its feet during the patent dance" by serving the 3(C) statement on the "second to last day possible." However, the applicant had served its 3(B) statement three weeks earlier than was required by the statute. The motion to stay was subsequently withdrawn without any decision from the court. *Amgen*, D.I. 32.

[2]*Sandoz Inc. v. Amgen Inc.*, 137 S. Ct. 1664, 1671, 198 L. Ed. 2d 114, 122 U.S.P.Q.2d 1685 (2017) ("Then, within 60 days of receiving the applicant's responses, the sponsor 'shall provide' to the applicant its own arguments concerning infringement, enforceability, and validity as to each relevant patent. § 262(*l*)(3)(C).").

[3]*Abbvie Inc. v. Amgen, Inc.*, 1:16-cv-00666-MSG, D.I. 1, ¶ 43 (D. Del. Aug. 5, 2016). Amgen's answer stated that Abbvie "reserve[d] the right to assert [the omitted patents and claims] and seek any and all remedies, including lost profits and injunctive relief" in its 3(C) statement. *Abbvie.* at D.I. 13, ¶ 21.

[4]*Amgen Inc. et al v. Sandoz Inc. et al.*, 2:16-cv-01276-SRC-CLW, D.I. 1 (D.N.J. Mar. 7, 2016) (complaint for declaratory judgment related to Sandoz's pegfilgrastim biosimilar). At the time of the pegfilgrastim complaint, Amgen and Sandoz were already involved in BPCIA litigation related to Sandoz's filgrastim product that concerned the same patents which were identified in Amgen's 3(A) list and were the subject of Sandoz's 3(B) statement in the pegfilgrastim patent dance. When Sandoz provided its 3(B) statement, it stated that since it already had Amgen's 3(C) notice on those patents, that it was waiving its right to receive them in the

most of the litigations to date, once an applicant provided the 3(B) statement, the RPS has provided the 3(C) statement.

Applicants have repeatedly challenged [the] adequacy of 3(C) statements that allegedly did not contain sufficient explanation or detail,[5] but no Court has yet rendered a decision elucidating what level of detailed is required for a 3(C)statement. As with 3(B) statements, 3(C) statements have been incorporated by reference into subsequent complaints,[6] and parties have relied on the allegations in 3(C) statements to withstand motions to dismiss infringement actions.[7]

---

pegfilgrastim patent dance. After Amgen filed its declaratory judgment action seeking, *inter alia*, an order compelling Sandoz's compliance with the remaining steps in the patent dance, the parties agreed to restart the patent dance exchanges. Amgen ultimately provided Sandoz with a 3(C) statement, and Amgen's declaratory judgment complaint was dismissed. *Amgen*, D.I. 52.

[5]*See, e.g., Abbvie v. Amgen*, 1:16-cv-00666-MSG16, D.I. 13 (D. Del. Sept. 13, 2016) (noting that AbbVie's 3(C) letter did not provide a response for six of the patents from Amgen's 3(B) statement, and did not provide infringement arguments for all claims in the other 59 patents contained in the 3(C) statement); *Genentech, Inc. et al. v. Celltrion, Inc. et al.*, 1:18-cv-00095-CFC, D.I. 1, (D. Del. Jan. 16, 2018) (referring to 3(C) statement in infringement allegations); *Amgen Inc. v. Hospira, Inc.*, 1:18-cv-01064-CFC, D.I. 1 (D. Del. July 19, 2018) (referring to Amgen's 3(C) statement as describing the factual and legal bases for infringement, and noting that because it contains confidential information Amgen will not repeat it in the Complaint).

[6]*Genentech, Inc. v. Amgen, Inc.*, 1:17-cv-01407-CFC, D.I. 19 (D. Del.) (incorporating by reference the 3(C) statement).

[7]In *Amgen Inc. et al v. Mylan Inc. et al.*, 2:17-cv-01235-MRH (W.D. Pa.), Mylan filed a motion for judgment on the pleadings regarding infringement of one patent related to producing a biosimilar pegfilgrastim. *Amgen*, D.I. 80. In opposition, Amgen argued that the allegations in its 3(C) statement should be considered because Mylan cited to an excerpt of the 3(C) statement in its motion. *Amgen*, D.I. 90 at 1. Amgen argued that while "Amgen's Contentions are not part of the complaint," to the extent the Court considered them, the allegations in the 3(C) statement in addition to those in the Complaint sufficiently alleged infringement to satisfy the pleading standards. *Amgen*, D.I. 90 at 1. ("Thus, the dispositive question here is whether Amgen has alleged facts in its Complaint and 3(C) Statement that are sufficient to show a plausible claim for relief for infringement of the '707 Patent."). The Court denied Mylan's motion without prejudice, holding that there were claim construction disputes between the parties that were not appropriate for resolution at the pleading stage. *Amgen*, D.I. 171 at n. 1. The Court did not address whether Amgen's 3(C) statement was properly considered as part of the factual allegations of the Complaint in opposing a motion to dismiss.

The 3(C) statement, like the 3(B) statement,[8] may be considered a party admission. Also, like the 3(B) statement, the 3(C) statement can form the basis for invalidity and non-infringement contentions exchanged during litigation and may be discoverable in other litigations related to the same product or patents.

§ 4:19 Negotiation of patents to be litigated and the first wave litigation

After the steps outlined above have taken place, negotiations begin to determine which patents will be included in an immediate "first wave" of patent infringement litigation. This may include all of the patents on the 3(A) list, or fewer than all of the patents. The process by which the biosimilar applicant and RPS identify and negotiate a list of patents for first wave litigation is outlined in Sections 262(*l*)(4) and 262(*l*)(5).[1]

While the RPS may in certain instances later supplement its list under 262(*l*)(3)(A) as provided for under 262(*l*)(7), the original list under Section 262(*l*)(3)(A) is the foundations for the negotiation process. The negotiations for the first-wave litigation provide the applicant significant ability to limit the scope of the litigation.[2]

The negotiation process starts with Section 262(*l*)(4), which provides:

(A) In general
After receipt by the subsection (k) applicant of the statement under paragraph 3(C), the reference product sponsor and the subsection (k) applicant shall engage in good faith negotiations to agree on which, if any, patents listed under paragraph (3) by the subsection (k) applicant or the reference product sponsor shall be the subject of an action for patent infringement under paragraph (6).

(B) Failure to Reach Agreement
If, within 15 days of beginning negotiations under subpara-

---

[8]*See Amgen Inc. v. Apotex Inc.*, 712 Fed. Appx. 985, 989 (Fed. Cir. 2017).

[Section 4:19]

[1]*Sandoz Inc. v. Amgen Inc.*, 137 S. Ct. 1664, 1666, 198 L. Ed. 2d 114, 122 U.S.P.Q.2d 1685 (2017).

[2]*Amgen Inc. v. Apotex Inc.*, 827 F.3d 1052, 1062, 119 U.S.P.Q.2d 1318 (Fed. Cir. 2016) (Section 262(*l*) "gives the applicant substantial authority to force such a limitation on the scope of the first-stage litigation.").

graph (A), the subsection (k) applicant and the reference product sponsor fail to agree on a final and complete list of which, if any, patents listed under paragraph (3) by the subsection (k) applicant or the reference product sponsor shall be the subject of an action for patent infringement under paragraph (6), the provisions of paragraph (5) shall apply to the parties.

The applicant and RPS first "shall engage in good faith negotiations" under subsection (A) to determine the list of patents for the immediate litigation after receipt by the applicant of the Section 262(*l*)(3)(C) statement.[3] If the applicant and RPS attempt in good faith but fail to reach an agreement on the list of patents to be included in the immediate litigation within 15 days, Section 262(*l*)(5) will then apply as dictated by 262(*l*)(4)(B).[4] Section 262(*l*)(5) provides:

(A) Number of patents
The subsection (k) applicant shall notify the reference product sponsor of the number of patents that such applicant will provide to the reference product sponsor under subparagraph (B)(i)(I).

(B) Exchange of patent lists
(i) In general
On a date agreed to by the subsection (k) applicant and the reference product sponsor, but in no case later than 5 days after the subsection (k) applicant notifies the reference product sponsor under subparagraph (A), the subsection (k) applicant and the reference product sponsor shall simultaneously exchange—

(I) the list of patents that the subsection (k) applicant believes should be the subject of an action for patent infringement under paragraph (6); and

(II) the list of patents, in accordance with clause (ii), that the reference product sponsor believes should be the subject of an action for patent infringement under paragraph (6).

(ii) Number of patents listed by reference product sponsor
(I) In general
Subject to subclause (II), the number of patents listed by the reference product sponsor under clause (i)(II) may not exceed the number of patents listed by the subsection (k) applicant under clause (i)(I).

(II) Exception
If a subsection (k) applicant does not list any patent under clause (i)(I), the reference product sponsor may list 1 patent under clause (i)(II).

---

[3]42 U.S.C.A. § 262(*l*)(4).
[4]42 U.S.C.A. § 262(*l*)(4).

Under 262(*l*)(5), the applicant must first provide to the RPS under subsection (A) the number of patents (e.g., one, two, etc.) that it asserts are the proper subject of the patent litigation.[5] No later than five days after the RPS receives the number of patents provided by the applicant, the parties must simultaneously exchange lists of patents that each contends should be the subject of the first wave of patent litigation.[6] The number of patents listed by the RPS may not exceed the number of patents provided by the applicant, with the sole exception that if the applicant listed none, the RPS may list one.[7]

The consequences of a failure to negotiate in good faith or exchange the patent lists in accordance with the procedures outlined in Section 262(*l*)(4) and Section 262(*l*)(5) remain an unsettled issue. One district court found that (under the particular facts of the case at issue) an applicant's alleged failure to participate in good faith negotiations meant that the RPS would not be limited to a reasonable royalty for damages regardless of whether its claim for patent infringement was filed more than 30 days after the patent dance concluded (i.e., the 30-day clock of Section 271(e)(6)(B) was not triggered).[8]

If the applicant fails to notify the RPS of the number of patents that the applicant will list or does not exchange the list of patents under Section 262(*l*)(5), the RPS may bring a declaratory judgment action asserting any patent listed by the RPS under Section 262(*l*)(3) or Section 262(*l*)(7).[9] One court noted that "the BPCIA expects the applicant to either agree or disagree with the reference product sponsor's proposed list of patents before the reference product sponsor files it 'immediate patent infringement action.' "[10]

---

[5]42 U.S.C.A. § 262(*l*)(5)(A).

[6]42 U.S.C.A. § 262(*l*)(5)(B)(i).

[7]42 U.S.C.A. § 262(*l*)(5)(B)(ii).

[8]*See Janssen Biotech, Inc. v. Celltrion Healthcare Co. Inc.*, 239 F. Supp. 3d 328 (D. Mass. 2017). The court found that "shall" as used in §§ 262(*l*)(4) and (5) indicates a statutory requirement of following the complete process in order to receive the statutory benefit of limited damages.

[9]*See* 42 U.S.C.A. § 262(*l*)(9)(B).

[10]*Genentech, Inc. v. Amgen Inc.*, 2018 WL 503253, at *2 (D. Del. 2018).

§ 4:20 Negotiation of patents to be litigated and the first wave litigation—Initiation of first-wave suit after negotiations

Under Section 262(*l*)(6), the RPS has 30 days to bring suit on the subset of patents identified by the parties and either agreed upon under Section 262(*l*)(4) or as exchanged in the lists under Section 262(*l*)(5).[1] Section 262(*l*)(6) provides:

> (A) Action if agreement on patent list
> If the subsection (k) applicant and the reference product sponsor agree on patents as described in paragraph (4), not later than 30 days after such agreement, the reference product sponsor shall bring an action for patent infringement with respect to each such patent.
> (B) Action if no agreement on patent list
> If the provisions of paragraph (5) apply to the parties as described in paragraph 4(B), not later than 30 days after the exchange of lists under paragraph 5(B), the reference product sponsor shall bring an action for patent infringement with respect to each patent that is included on such lists.

If the RPS fails to sue within 30 days after the scope of the litigation has been negotiated under Section 262(*l*)(4) or Section 262(*l*)(5), the "sole and exclusive" remedy for infringement of a listed patent is a reasonable royalty.[2]

The applicant must provide notice to the U.S. Department of Health and Human Services (HHS) of the lawsuit no later than 30 days after the complaint is served.[3] The applicant's failure to provide notice to the secretary within 30 days after the complaint is served permits the RPS to bring a declaratory judgment action asserting any patent listed by the RPS under either Section 262(*l*)(3) or Section 262(*l*)(7).[4] Upon receipt of notice from the applicant, the HHS will publish a notice of the complaint in the Federal Register.[5]

III. NEWLY-ISSUED OR LICENSED PATENTS

§ 4:21 Newly issued or licensed patents generally

Patents that issue or are newly licensed by the RPS after

[Section 4:20]

[1] 42 U.S.C.A. § 262(*l*)(5).
[2] 35 U.S.C.A. 271(e)(6)(A), (B).
[3] 42 U.S.C.A. § 262(*l*)(6)(C)(i).
[4] 42 U.S.C.A. § 262(*l*)(9)(B).
[5] 42 U.S.C.A. § 262(*l*)(6)(C)(ii).

initiation of the patent dance are also subject to the provisions of the BPCIA.

262(l)(7) Newly issued or licensed patents

In the case of a patent that

(A) is issued to, or exclusively licensed by, the reference product sponsor after the date that the reference product sponsor provided the list to the subsection (k) applicant under paragraph (3)(A); and

(B) the reference product sponsor reasonably believes that, due to the issuance of such patent, a claim of patent infringement could reasonably be asserted by the reference product sponsor if a person not licensed by the reference product sponsor engaged in the making, using, offering to sell, selling, or importing into the United States of the biological product that is the subject of the subsection (k) application, not later than 30 days after such issuance or licensing, the reference product sponsor shall provide to the subsection (k) applicant a supplement to the list provided by the reference product sponsor under paragraph (3)(A) that includes such patent, not later than 30 days after such supplement is provided, the subsection (k) applicant shall provide a statement to the reference product sponsor in accordance with paragraph (3)(B), and such patent shall be subject to paragraph (8).[1]

For a patent that issues or is newly licensed by the RPS after the RPS provides its 3(A) list during the patent dance, the RPS must supplement its 3(A) list to add the newly issued or licensed patent within 30 days of issuance or licensure. Within 30 days of receipt of the (3)(A) list, the biosimilar applicant must provide its supplemental response under Section 262(l)(3)(B), including a detailed statement that describes why the newly issued or licensed patent is not infringed, is invalid or unenforceable, and whether the biosimilar applicant believes a claim for patent infringement could reasonably be asserted.

Newly issued or licensed patents are also subject to the provisions regarding notice of commercial marketing. If a biosimilar applicant provides notice of commercial marketing, an RPS may assert the newly-issued or -licensed patents in any motion seeking to enjoin the launch of the biosimilar

---

[Section 4:21]

[1]42 U.S.C.A. § 262(l)(7).

until the court rules on any issues of patent validity, enforcement, and infringement.[2]

In several cases, the RPS has supplemented its Section (*l*)(3)(A) list with newly issued patents, and the biosimilar applicant has, in turn, revised its Section(*l*)(3)(B) list without any dispute about compliance with Section 262(*l*)(7) of the statute.[3] In one case, however, the parties disputed compliance with Section 262(*l*)(7).[4] In that case the RPS alleged that the applicant's failure to provide its application and manufacturing information pursuant to 262(*l*)(2)(A) prevented the RPS from complying with the requirements of 262(*l*)(7)(A) with respect to a newly issued patent.[5] Nonetheless, the RPS sued for infringement of the newly issued patent and the district court granted summary judgment of non-infringement on the merits without addressing any failure to comply with Section (7)(A).

---

[2]42 U.S.C.A. § 262(*l*)(8).

[3]*AbbVie Inc. et al. v. Boehringer Ingelheim Int'l GmbH et al.*, No. 1:17-cv-01065-MSG-RL, D.I. 1 at ¶¶ 54-55, 60 (D. Del, Aug. 2, 2017); *Amgen Inc. et al. v. Mylan Inc. et al.*, No. 2:17-cv-01235-MRH, D.I. 1 at ¶¶ 70-71, 74-75 (W.D. Pa., Sept. 22, 2017); *Genentech, Inc. et al. v. Amgen, Inc.*, No. 1:17-cv-01471-CFC, D.I. 17 at ¶¶ 4-6 (D. Del. Oct. 26, 2017); *Amgen Inc. et al v. Hospira, Inc. et al.*, No. 1:18-cv-01064-CFC, D.I. 1 at ¶¶ 44-48 (D. Del. Jul. 18, 2018); *Amgen Inc. et al. v. Apotex Inc. et al.*, No. 0:18-cv-61828-WPD, D.I. 1 at ¶ 43 (S.D. Fla. Aug. 07, 2018); *Genentech, Inc. et al. v. Samsung Bioepis Co., Ltd.*, No. 1:18-cv-01363-CFC, D.I. 1 at ¶¶ 26-32 (D. Del. Sep. 04, 2018); *Genentech, Inc. et al. v. Amgen Inc.*, No. 1:18-cv-00924-CFC, D.I. 10 at ¶¶ 25-36 (D. Del. Jul. 02, 2018).

[4]*Amgen Inc. et al v. Sandoz Inc. et al.*, No. 3:14-cv-04741-RS (N.D. Cal.).

[5]Sandoz did not dispute that it did not provide its BLA or manufacturing information to Amgen, and further included in its answer counterclaims of noninfringement and invalidity of the newly-issued patent. *Amgen Inc. et al v. Sandoz Inc. et al.*, No. 3:14-cv-04741-RS, D.I. 22 (N.D. Cal. Nov. 20, 2014). On July 21, 2015, the Federal Circuit held that Sandoz did not violate the BPCIA by not providing its application and manufacturing information. On appeal, the Supreme Court affirmed that the disclosure requirements of Section 262(*l*)(2)(A) are not subject to enforcement by injunction under federal law, and remanded to determine if they are unlawful under state law. On remand, the Federal Circuit on December 14, 2017 affirmed dismissal of Amgen's state law claims for preemption. Following remand, the district court granted summary judgment of noninfringement as to the newly issued Amgen patent. The district court's grant of summary judgment was based on the merits, not on compliance with Section 262(*l*)(7). *Amgen Inc. et al v. Sandoz Inc. et al.*, No. 3:14-cv-04741-RS, D.I. 346 (Dec. 19, 2017).

IV. NOTICE OF COMMERCIAL MARKETING

§ 4:22 Overview

The first wave of litigation may not include all patents that the RPS identified in its Section (*l*)(3)(A) list. These patents, however, can be part of a second wave of litigation that can be triggered by the biosimilar applicant providing to the RPS a notice of commercial marketing ("NCM") as described in Section (*l*)(8)(A). The biosimilar applicant must provide this notice at least 180 days before the date of the first commercial marketing of its biosimilar product. Once the biosimilar applicant provides NCM, the RPS may seek a preliminary injunction prohibiting the biosimilar applicant from engaging in commercial manufacture or sale of the biosimilar product before the court decides issues of validity, enforcement and infringement with respect to patents included in the Section (*l*)(3)(A) or (*l*)(3)(B) list that are or were not part of the first wave litigation. In this phase, pursuant to Section (*l*)(9)(A), both the RPS and the biosimilar applicant may sue for declaratory relief.

§ 4:23 The Statute governing NCM

Section (*l*)(8)(A) states:

(A) Notice of commercial marketing

The subsection (k) applicant shall provide notice to the reference product sponsor not later than 180 days before the date of the first commercial marketing of the biological product licensed under subsection (k).

§ 4:24 The Statute governing NCM—Timing of NCM

In the early days of the BPCIA, there was significant litigation regarding when the biosimilar applicant could provide its NCM, particularly whether NCM could be provided before the FDA approved the biosimilar applicant's aBLA, or if, instead, the biosimilar applicant had to wait until it received FDA approval. The Supreme Court, in *Sandoz v. Amgen*, clarified the law: NCM under Section 262(*l*)(8)(A) may be provided at any time prior to 180 days before the date of first commercial marketing, including before FDA approval.[1]

[Section 4:24]

[1]*Sandoz Inc. v. Amgen Inc.*, 137 S. Ct. 1664, 1678, 198 L. Ed. 2d 114, 122 U.S.P.Q.2d 1685 (2017). In that case, Sandoz provided NCM the day

§ 4:25   The Statute governing NCM—Requirements for providing NCM

The BPCIA does not set forth how NCM is to be provided, other than stating that the biosimilar applicant shall provide notice to the RPS. Such notice has typically been provided through correspondence from the biosimilar applicant to the RPS, and there has not yet been any litigation as to the sufficiency of the notice.

One issue that has arisen is whether, regardless of the date of NCM, the actual date of commercial marketing must be tied to the expiration of any patent(s) that the biosimilar applicant identifies to the RPS pursuant to Section $(l)(3)(B)(ii)(II)$, which states that for any patents identified in the RPS's Section $(l)(3)(A)$ list, the biosimilar applicant may provide the RPS "a statement that the [biosimilar] applicant does not intend to begin commercial marketing of the biological product before the date that [a Section (l)(3)(A) listed] patent expires." This leads to several questions. For example, what is the remedy if an applicant provides NCM more than 180 days before the expiration of a patent previously identified pursuant to Section $(l)(3)(B)(ii)(II)$? Is the biosimilar applicant bound by its Section $(l)(3)(B)(ii)(II)$ statement? Can the RPS obtain a declaratory judgment that the biosimilar applicant cannot begin marketing until expiration of the

---

after the FDA accepted the Sandoz aBLA for review. In the district court, Amgen alleged that Sandoz engaged in unlawful activity by, among other things, providing NCM before the FDA approval in violation of Section $(l)(8)(A)$. *Amgen Inc. v. Sandoz Inc.*, 2015 WL 1264756, at *4 (N.D. Cal. 2015), aff'd in part, vacated in part, remanded, 794 F.3d 1347 (Fed. Cir. 2015), and cert. granted, 137 S. Ct. 808, 196 L. Ed. 2d 594 (2017) and rev'd in part, vacated in part, 137 S. Ct. 1664, 198 L. Ed. 2d 114, 122 U.S.P.Q.2d 1685 (2017) and aff'd, 877 F.3d 1315, 125 U.S.P.Q.2d 1001 (Fed. Cir. 2017). The district court found that Sandoz was permitted to provide NCM when it did. *Amgen Inc. v. Sandoz Inc.*, 2015 WL 1264756, at *8 (N.D. Cal. 2015), aff'd in part, vacated in part, remanded, 794 F.3d 1347 (Fed. Cir. 2015), cert. granted, 137 S. Ct. 808, 196 L. Ed. 2d 594 (2017) and rev'd in part, vacated in part, 137 S. Ct. 1664, 198 L. Ed. 2d 114, 122 U.S.P.Q.2d 1685 (2017) and aff'd, 877 F.3d 1315, 125 U.S.P.Q.2d 1001 (Fed. Cir. 2017). The Federal Circuit reversed, holding that an applicant must wait until obtaining FDA approval before providing NCM, and enjoined Sandoz from marketing its product until 180 days after approval. *Amgen Inc. v. Sandoz Inc.*, 794 F.3d 1347, 1358, 1362, (Fed. Cir. 2015), cert. granted, 137 S. Ct. 808, 196 L. Ed. 2d 594 (2017) and rev'd in part, vacated in part, 137 S. Ct. 1664, 198 L. Ed. 2d 114, 122 U.S.P.Q.2d 1685 (2017). The Supreme Court reversed the Federal Circuit, ruling that "the applicant may provide notice either before or after receiving FDA approval." *Sandoz*, 137 S. Ct. at 1678.

patent(s) identified pursuant to Section $(l)(3)(B)(ii)(II)$? While the Courts have not resolved many of these issues, a motion for a declaratory judgment may be denied for lack of sufficient immediacy if the biosimilar applicant's actions do not indicate that it would actually launch its product before expiration of identified patents.[1]

One district court recently addressed the issue of whether Section $(l)(8)(A)$ requires a biosimilar applicant to provide a new NCM after FDA approval of a supplement to its aBLA.[2] In that case, the FDA had approved Amgen's biosimilar, Mvasi® (bevacizumab-awwb), in September 2017; thereafter, Amgen provided its NCM in October 2017, and the FDA approved supplements to Amgen's aBLA in 2018 and 2019. Genentech argued that the approval of those supplements meant that Amgen was seeking to market a different "biological product" than the Mvasi® that was subject to the original approval and Amgen's original NCM. Accordingly, Genentech argued, the supplements voided Amgen's original NCM, and required Amgen to provide a new NCM and wait an additional 180 days before it could market Mvasi® in the United States. The district court, however, found that Amgen's original NCM was still legally effective and denied Genentech's motion, clearing the path for Amgen to launch Mvasi®.

§ 4:26 The statute governing NCM—Enforcement of NCM provisions

Prior to the Supreme Court's decision in *Sandoz v. Amgen*,

[Section 4:25]

[1]*See Genentech, Inc. et al. v. Amgen Inc.*, No. 1:17-cv-01407-CFC, D.I. 84 at 1 (D. Del. April 17, 2018), where Amgen's NCM indicated Amgen would not begin commercial marketing of its bevacizumab biosimilar before April 4, 2018, even though Amgen had previously indicated, in a Section $(l)(3)(B)$ statement, that Amgen did not intend to begin commercial marketing before December 18, 2018 expiration of certain patents. Genentech sought a declaratory judgment that Amgen could not market its biosimilar before December 18, 2018. The Court, about two weeks after the April 4, 2018 NCM date, denied Genentech's motion without prejudice, finding that there was no indication that Amgen would actually launch its product before December 18, 2018, and that accordingly Genentech's "commercial marketing claim is not of 'sufficient immediacy' to warrant the issuance of a novel declaratory judgment." *Genentech*, D.I. 84 at 4 (D. Del. Apr. 17, 2018).

[2]*See Genentech, Inc. v. Immunex Rhode Island Corp.*, No. 19-602, slip op. (D. Del. July 19, 2019).

the Federal Circuit had held that NCM under Section (l)(8)(A) is both mandatory and enforceable by injunction.[1] Section (l)(8)(A) provides that "[t]he subsection (k) applicant *shall* provide notice to the reference product sponsor not later than 180 days before the date of the first commercial marketing of the biological product licensed under subsection (k)."

While *Sandoz v. Amgen* did not expressly address these questions, the Supreme Court's reasoning suggests that NCM—like the other steps of the patent dance—is required[2] but not enforceable by an injunction.[3] Section (l)(9)(B) provides that an RPS may bring an immediate action for a declaration of "infringement, validity or enforceability" of any 3(A)-listed patent if the applicant violates Section (l)(8)(A) by not providing NCM, or providing it later than 180 days before launch.[4] If a biosimilar applicant fails to provide the required NCM, it thus appears that the RPS may bring an immediate declaratory judgment action prior to launch and seek a temporary restraining order and preliminary injunction barring marketing prior to resolution of the RPS's patent infringement claims. Although an RPS might also seek an injunction requiring the biosimilar applicant to provide NCM and wait at least 180 days before marketing its biosimilar product regardless of whether it prevails on the preliminary injunction motion, such injunctive relief would appear to be inconsistent with the Supreme Court's reasoning in *Sandoz v. Amgen* that the declaratory judgment action authorized by Section (l)(9)(C) is the sole statutory remedy for a biosimilar applicant's failure to comply with Section (l)(2)(A). Section (l)(9)(B) sets forth the same sole statutory remedy for a biosimilar applicant's failure to comply with, among other things, the NCM requirement of Section (l)(8)(A). This statutory scheme does not appear to authorize an injunction to enforce compliance with

---

[Section 4:26]

[1]*Amgen Inc. v. Apotex Inc.*, 827 F.3d 1052, 1061, 119 U.S.P.Q.2d 1318 (Fed. Cir. 2016).

[2]*See Sandoz Inc. v. Amgen Inc.*, 137 S. Ct. 1664, 1677, 198 L. Ed. 2d 114, 122 U.S.P.Q.2d 1685 (2017) ("The applicant *must* give 'notice' at least 180 days 'before the date of the first commercial marketing.'" (emphasis added)).

[3]*See Sandoz*, 137 S. Ct. at 1674–75.

[4]42 U.S.C.A. § 262(l)(9)(B).

Section $(l)(8)(A)$ any more than it does to enforce compliance with Section $(l)(2)(A)$.

§4:27 The Statute governing NCM—Some open NCM-related questions

There are still many questions related to NCM that have not been fully litigated or addressed by the courts. For example, what happens if the biosimilar applicant changes its product? Does the biosimilar applicant have to provide a new NCM after making a change? Does the question of whether the biosimilar applicant needs to provide a new NCM depend on the extent of the change? For example, if a change is made in an excipient, is a new NCM required? What if it is a change that requires filing a supplement to the aBLA? As discussed above, so far, one district court has ruled that a new NCM was not required in the case of a supplement concerning certain manufacturing and labeling information. But what if it is a change that requires an entirely new aBLA? Is a new NCM required if an aBLA is resubmitted after being withdrawn for safety reasons? Does it depend on if/how the product has been modified? These questions await resolution by the courts.

§4:28 Second wave litigation

Second wave litigation may be initiated after the applicant gives NCM. Any 3(A)-listed patent not included in the first wave litigation may be included in the second wave. Such patents may not be asserted prior to NCM. In practice, if NCM is given during the patent dance, e.g., at the initiation of the dance, all 3(A)-listed patents become eligible for enforcement at the commencement of the patent infringement litigation.

§4:29 Second wave litigation—Who can bring suit after the applicant provides NCM?

Section $(l)(9)(A)$ states that if the biosimilar applicant provides the application and information required under Section $(l)(2)(A)$, neither the RPS nor the biosimilar applicant may, prior to NCM, bring an action for a declaration of infringement, validity, or enforceability of any patent that is described in clauses (i) and (ii) of Section $(l)(8)(B)$. Thus, after NCM is given, both the biosimilar applicant and the RPS have the right to initiate a patent infringement action. Two district courts, however, have held that if the biosimilar applicant initiates a declaratory judgment action, this so-called "second wave" litigation is limited to the remnant patents— *i.e.*, the patents that could have been litigated in the first wave of BPCIA patent litigation, but were not litigated. One court reasoned that this must be the case because otherwise a biosimilar applicant could circumvent the BPCIA provisions barring the applicant from bringing a declaratory judgment action after, e.g., declining to engage in the patent dance, by simply providing its NCM early.[1] Separately, another district court ruled that providing NCM only "lifts the prohibition imposed by Section (*l*)(9)(A)—and Section (*l*)(9)(A) alone"—which thereby limits declaratory judgment actions in this phase of the BPCIA to patents not litigated in the first wave, and that NCM "only opens the door for an applicant to file a declaratory judgment action if the applicant complies with the rest of the statute."[2]

§ 4:30   Second wave litigation—Factors that could impact bringing suit after providing NCM

With respect to either the biosimilar applicant or RPS bringing suit after NCM is provided, there are many potential issues that have neither arisen nor been addressed

---

[Section 4:29]

[1]*See Amgen, Inc. v. Genentech, Inc.*, 2018 WL 910198 (C.D. Cal. 2018), subsequent determination, 2018 WL 718418 (C.D. Cal. 2018). In *Amgen*, the parties were unable to reach agreement during the Section (*l*)(4) negotiations. Prior to the Section (*l*)(5) patent exchange, Amgen provided NCM and filed a complaint seeking declaratory judgment regarding all patents identified in Genentech's Section (*l*)(3) list. Genentech filed its own complaint and moved to dismiss the Amgen complaint. The Court tentatively granted Genentech's motion reasoning that the BPCIA only allows NCM to trigger the second wave of patent litigation, *i.e.*, litigation on patents that were included in the Section (*l*)(3) lists but not litigated in the first wave. *Amgen, Inc. v. Genentech, Inc.*, 2018 WL 910198, at *4 (C.D. Cal. 2018), subsequent determination, 2018 WL 718418 (C.D. Cal. 2018).

[2]*See Celltrion, Inc. v. Genentech, Inc.*, 2018 WL 2448254, at *7–8 (N.D. Cal. 2018), appeal dismissed, 2018 WL 7046651 (Fed. Cir. 2018). Celltrion had filed applications to market biosimilars of Genentech's Herceptin® (trastuzumab) and Rituxan® (rituximab) products. After undergoing the initial steps of the patent dance (but not all steps of the patent dance), Celltrion provided its NCM as to both biosimilar products and filed declaratory judgment actions in the Northern District of California. The district court found that providing NCM alone, without completing the patent dance steps required for first wave litigation, did not give Celltrion the right to file these second-wave declaratory judgment actions.

by the courts. For example, if a biosimilar applicant has complied with all aspects of the patent dance and is involved in first wave litigation when NCM is provided, can the RPS bring a suit on second wave patents at any time before the biosimilar applicant begins commercial marketing? Can the RPS wait until day 178 to bring suit? In this scenario, can the biosimilar applicant initiate a declaratory judgment action on the remnant patents at any time during the 180 days? Do the answers to these questions depend in any way on whether a first wave litigation is already pending? The courts have not yet had to address any of these issues.

Another outstanding question is whether a biosimilar applicant who has fully participated in the patent dance and provided NCM can initiate a declaratory judgment action on second wave remnant patents in any venue, or if the biosimilar applicant has to bring such an action in the same jurisdiction as any ongoing first wave case. This is a fact specific question that will likely have to be resolved on a case-by-case basis.

§ 4:31 Second wave litigation—What will second wave litigation look like?

There has only been one second wave litigation: *Amgen v. Apotex*, which concerns a single patent that issued and was listed by Amgen pursuant to Section (*l*)(7) only after the parties' first wave litigation had already concluded. This limited example does not shed much light on what a more complex second wave litigation will look like. In theory, second wave litigation could involve any, or all, of the remnant patents. Such litigation might only involve a few remnant patents (or newly issued patents, as in the case of *Amgen v. Apotex*), or potentially a very large number of patents. Moreover, because second wave litigation will likely often begin during the NCM period, it could lead to almost immediate preliminary injunction proceedings in an effort to resolve issues before the biosimilar applicant can begin commercial marketing. Expedited discovery in support of such proceedings might also be necessary.

In practice, however, parties have often settled before second wave litigation is initiated. It is possible that the parties are choosing to litigate the patents of most interest to the RPS and the applicant during the first wave litigation.

V.   COMMENCEMENT OF SUIT

§ 4:32   Venue for biosimilar litigation

The BPCIA does not itself specify where litigation relating to a biologic or biosimilar product may be filed. Accordingly, the general venue statutes codified in Title 28 of the United States Code apply. Those statutes distinguish between actions *for patent infringement*, which are subject to a very narrow venue rule, and actions that are *not* for patent infringement, which are subject to a very generous venue rule that will often give the plaintiff considerable flexibility about where to sue. Many, if not all, actions for a declaratory judgment will fall into the latter category—and many of the actions that are filed pursuant to the BPCIA will be actions for a declaratory judgment.

One significant exception to both rules is that *foreign* defendants have no venue privilege; they therefore can be sued anywhere they are subject to personal jurisdiction.

§ 4:33   Venue for biosimilar litigation—Venue in patent-infringement actions generally

Venue in lawsuits for patent infringement, including lawsuits invoking one of the artificial acts of infringement created by the BPCIA,[1] is governed by 28 U.S.C.A. § 1400(b). That statute provides:

> Any civil action for patent infringement may be brought in the judicial district where the defendant resides, or where the defendant has committed acts of infringement and has a regular and established place of business.

Thus, there are two ways to establish venue in a patent-infringement action: based on the defendant's residence or based on the combination of *both* the defendant's infringement *and* the defendant's regular business. Each of these is discussed below.

Notably, venue must be proper under at least one prong of this test as to *each* defendant as of the time the complaint is filed, not just *a* defendant.[2] In a patent-infringement case, the burden of establishing venue is on the plaintiff, at least

---

[Section 4:33]

[1]*See* 35 U.S.C.A. § 271(e)(2)(C).

[2]*Camp v. Gress*, 250 U.S. 308, 311–16, 39 S. Ct. 478, 63 L. Ed. 997 (1919); *see, e.g., Flexible Technologies, Inc. v. SharkNinja Operating LLC,*

once the defendant challenges venue.[3] If venue is improper as to even one defendant, the entire action may be dismissed,[4] although there is some precedent for dismissing only the defendants that successfully assert improper venue.[5]

Venue is a waivable privilege. If the defendant files a Rule 12 motion to dismiss, it must assert that venue is improper, or else the venue objection will be waived. If the defendant does not file a Rule 12 motion to dismiss, the venue objection must be raised in the answer.[6]

§ 4:34 Venue for biosimilar litigation—Venue in patent-infringement actions generally—Venue based on defendant's residence

For purposes of the venue statute that governs patent-infringement cases, a defendant that is a domestic corporation "resides" in only one state: the state where it is incorporated.[1] For a Delaware corporation, that also establishes the federal judicial district where the corporation resides: the District of Delaware, which has only one judicial district.

If the defendant is incorporated in a state with more than one federal judicial district, the analysis gets somewhat more complicated, but under the Federal Circuit's interpretation, a corporation still always has only one district of residence. If the defendant maintains its *principal place of business*

2018 WL 1175043, *4 (D.S.C. 2018), report and recommendation adopted, 2018 WL 1158425 (D.S.C. 2018) ("[I]n a case with multiple claims and multiple defendants, the Plaintiff bears the burden to establish that venue is proper as to each claim and as to each defendant."), *report and recommendation adopted*, 2018 WL 1158425 (Mar. 5, 2018).

[3]*In re ZTE (USA) Inc.*, 890 F.3d 1008, 1013, 126 U.S.P.Q.2d 1626 (Fed. Cir. 2018) (applying Federal Circuit law to this question, rather than the law of the regional circuit).

[4]*AGIS Software Development, LLC v. ZTE Corporation*, 2018 WL 4854023, *4 (E.D. Tex. 2018).

[5]*See, e.g., Camp*, 250 U.S. at 316; *Stonite Products Co. v. Melvin Lloyd Co.*, 315 U.S. 561, 563 n.2, 62 S. Ct. 780, 86 L. Ed. 1026, 52 U.S.P.Q. 507 (1942) (noting that only the defendant raising the venue objection was dismissed).

[6]*See* Fed. R. Civ. P. 12(g)(2), (h)(1); *In re Micron Technology, Inc.*, 875 F.3d 1091, 1096, 124 U.S.P.Q.2d 1661, 99 Fed. R. Serv. 3d 210 (Fed. Cir. 2017).

[Section 4:34]

[1]*TC Heartland LLC v. Kraft Foods Group Brands LLC*, 137 S. Ct. 1514, 1521, 197 L. Ed. 2d 816, 122 U.S.P.Q.2d 1553 (2017).

(meaning its corporate "nerve center," from which the officers direct and control the corporation) in the state of incorporation, then the corporation resides in the district where the principal place of business is located.[2] If the defendant does not maintain its principal place of business in the state of incorporation, then the location of the corporation's *registered office* in the state of incorporation, "as recorded in its corporate filings," will control.[3]

If the defendant is *not* a corporation, but a limited liability company (LLC) or another unincorporated entity, the analysis is not perfectly clear. Neither the Supreme Court nor the Federal Circuit has yet resolved the venue question for such entities under Section 1400(b).[4] Some courts have held (often without much analysis) that LLCs should be treated like corporations for venue purposes—*i.e.*, that an LLC created under the law of a particular state should reside only in that state.[5] Plaintiffs in many cases have declined to argue that a different rule applies to LLCs, even when venue is contested. But because the Supreme Court has never passed on where an LLC "resides"—to the contrary, it has previously held that an unincorporated association "resides" for venue purposes wherever it is "doing business"[6]—there remains an argument that LLCs, partnerships, and similar unincorporated entities are subject to a broader venue rule.

§ 4:35   Venue for biosimilar litigation—Venue in patent-infringement actions generally—Venue based on infringement and place of business

The alternative venue path requires that the defendant (a) have committed acts of infringement in the district and (b)

---

[2]*In re BigCommerce, Inc.*, 890 F.3d 978, 985, 126 U.S.P.Q.2d 1632 (Fed. Cir. 2018). The concept of "principal place of business" as "nerve center" is borrowed from the diversity-jurisdiction statute, 28 U.S.C.A. § 1332(c)(1), and cases interpreting it, chiefly *Hertz Corp. v. Friend*, 559 U.S. 77, 130 S. Ct. 1181, 175 L. Ed. 2d 1029 (2010). The nerve center need not be the place where the largest number of employees work.

[3]*BigCommerce*, 890 F.3d at 985–86.

[4]*TC Heartland*, 137 S. Ct. at 1517 n.1.

[5]*Maxchief Investments Limited v. Plastic Development Group, LLC*, 2017 WL 3479504, at *2 (E.D. Tenn. 2017).

[6]*See Denver & R. G. W. R. Co. v. Brotherhood of R. R. Trainmen*, 387 U.S. 556, 559, 87 S. Ct. 1746, 18 L. Ed. 2d 954, 65 L.R.R.M. (BNA) 2385, 55 Lab. Cas. (CCH) P 11954, 11 Fed. R. Serv. 2d 361 (1967). The unincorporated association in *Denver & Rio Grande* was a labor union.

maintain a regular and established place of business in the district.

In the biosimilar context, applying the first prong creates an interpretive difficulty: in many biosimilars cases, an action will be filed based on an "artificial" act of infringement, making it necessary to figure out where the defendant "has committed" that act of infringement. Other actions relating to biosimilars will be filed to *prevent* the defendant from committing acts of infringement; the plaintiff may not be able to say that the defendant "has committed acts of infringement yet," but may be alleging that the defendant will infringe in the near future.

Artificial Act of Infringement: District courts are divided on the question whether an artificial act of infringement, for venue purposes, occurs in many districts or just one. This question so far has arisen in small-molecule cases under the Hatch-Waxman Act, but the same analysis may apply to an artificial act of infringement under the BPCIA.

Some district courts have adopted the view that a defendant that files an ANDA containing a Paragraph IV certification "has committed" an artificial act of infringement everywhere the defendant plans to sell the generic ANDA product—which likely means in every judicial district.[1] On this view, the act of infringement necessary for venue therefore can be established through "an applicant's submission of an ANDA, in conjunction with other acts the ANDA applicant non-speculatively intends to take if its ANDA receives final FDA approval, plus steps already taken by the applicant indicating its intent to market the ANDA product in [a] District."[2] Applying this reasoning to an applicant that has filed an aBLA for permission to market in the U.S. generally, the artificial act of infringement has occurred everywhere the applicant intends to sell the biosimilar.

Other district courts, however, have rejected that reasoning and have held that a defendant that submits an ANDA containing a paragraph IV certification "has committed" an

---

[Section 4:35]

[1]*Bristol-Myers Squibb Company v. Mylan Pharmaceuticals Inc.*, 2017 WL 3980155, at *13 (D. Del. 2017); *accord Celgene Corporation v. Hetero Labs Limited*, 2018 WL 1135334, at *3 (D.N.J. 2018) (collecting cases following *Bristol-Myers Squibb*).

[2]*Bristol-Myers Squibb Company v. Mylan Pharmaceuticals Inc.*, 2017 WL 3980155, *13 (D. Del. 2017).

act of infringement only in the single judicial district from which it "prepared and submitted" the ANDA.[3] Applying that reasoning to biosimilars, a defendant that files a qualifying aBLA has committed acts of infringement in the judicial district from which it submitted the aBLA. That is likely to be the defendant's home district, or at least the home district of its generic or biosimilar operation—although conceivably it could be open to manipulation, if the defendant set up a location in a favored venue in which to press the final button dispatching submissions to the FDA.

Future Infringement: The BPCIA allows a reference product sponsor to bring an action for a preliminary injunction once it receives a notice of commercial marketing from the biosimilar applicant.[4] For venue purposes, do the alleged "acts of infringement" also include the *anticipated* infringement that the preliminary injunction seeks to enjoin? Federal Circuit caselaw suggests that the answer may be "no": the Federal Circuit has held that "alleged threatened patent infringement" is not infringement, so an action to restrain future infringement is not an action for infringement.[5] That decision came outside the venue context, however, and district courts have not yet confronted this issue squarely since *TC Heartland*.

Regular and Established Place of Business: This prong of the test, as interpreted by the Federal Circuit, has three requirements: "(1) there must be a physical place in the district; (2) it must be a regular and established place of business; and (3) it must be the place of the defendant."[6] Notably, places of business *of a subsidiary* of the defendant will not do; "[a] subsidiary's presence in the district cannot be imputed to the parent for venue purposes so long as the two entities maintain formal corporate separateness."[7]

---

[3]*See, e.g. Galderma Laboratories, L.P. v. Teva Pharmaceuticals USA, Inc.*, 290 F. Supp. 3d 599, 608-09 (N.D. Tex. 2017).

[4]42 U.S.C.A. § 262(*l*)(8)(B).

[5]*Lang v. Pacific Marine and Supply Co., Ltd.*, 895 F.2d 761, 765, 13 U.S.P.Q.2d 1820 (Fed. Cir. 1990).

[6]*In re Cray Inc.*, 871 F.3d 1355, 1360, 124 U.S.P.Q.2d 1001 (Fed. Cir. 2017).

[7]*E.g., Galderma*, 290 F. Supp. 3d at 611.

§4:36 Venue for biosimilar litigation—Venue in patent-infringement actions generally—Venue based on infringement and place of business—Foreign defendants

Foreign defendants generally have no venue privilege. The general venue statute, for example, specifies that "[a] defendant not resident in the United States may be sued in any judicial district."[1] While the general venue statute does not determine corporate citizenship for purposes of venue in patent-infringement cases,[2] the Supreme Court has held that alien defendants may not raise a venue objection even in patent-infringement cases,[3] and the Federal Circuit has reaffirmed that rule even after *TC Heartland* and the most recent amendments to the venue statute.[4] Indeed, if foreign defendants could be sued only where they reside, and if a corporation resides only where it is incorporated, no foreign corporation could ever be sued based on residence. That is not the law.[5] Instead, if the only defendant is a foreign corporation, venue is proper in any district. If there are multiple defendants, any foreign defendants' citizenship may be disregarded.[6] Note, however, that the plaintiff must still establish personal jurisdiction over each defendant.

§4:37 Venue for biosimilar litigation—Venue in actions for a declaratory judgment

As explained above, a special and restrictive venue rule applies only to a "civil action for patent infringement."[1] An action for a declaratory judgment often will not be "for patent infringement," and in that case a very different rule will

---

[Section 4:36]

[1]28 U.S.C.A. § 1391(c)(3).

[2]*See TC Heartland*, 137 S. Ct. at 1521.

[3]*Brunette Mach. Works, Limited v. Kockum Industries, Inc.*, 406 U.S. 706, 714, 92 S. Ct. 1936, 32 L. Ed. 2d 428, 174 U.S.P.Q. 1 (1972).

[4]*In re HTC Corporation*, 889 F.3d 1349, 1361, 126 U.S.P.Q.2d 1618 (Fed. Cir. 2018), cert. denied, 139 S. Ct. 1271, 203 L. Ed. 2d 279 (2019).

[5]*See HTC Corp.*, 889 F.3d at 1360–61.

[6]*Cf.* 28 U.S.C.A. § 1319(c)(3) ("[T]he joinder of [a foreign] defendant shall be disregarded in determining where the action may be brought with respect to other defendants.").

[Section 4:37]

[1]28 U.S.C.A. § 1400(b).

apply. The general venue statute is much more permissive than the patent venue statute.

§ 4:38   Venue for biosimilar litigation—Venue in patent-infringement actions generally—Is a declaratory-judgment action ever "For Patent Infringement"?

For many years it has been clear that a declaratory-judgment action brought *by the alleged infringer* is not "for patent infringement." Whether the action seeks a declaration of non-infringement, invalidity, or both, it is not "for patent infringement" and is not subject to the patent venue statute.[1] Instead it is subject to the much more permissive general venue statute.

The BPCIA, however, places heavy reliance on declaratory-judgment actions *by the patent owner*. When a biosimilar applicant fails to participate in the patent dance at various steps, the BPCIA authorizes the reference product sponsor to bring not just any action, but an action "for a declaration of infringement, validity, or enforceability of" qualifying patents.[2]

Is an action "for a declaration of [patent] infringement" different from an action "for patent infringement"? Patent owners seeking a broader choice of venue than the patent venue statute allows have sometimes argued that *all* declaratory judgments are subject to the general venue statute, even if brought by the patent owner for a declaration *of infringement*. In the first reported case to discuss that tactic (a Hatch-Waxman case), the Eastern District of Texas rejected it. The court concluded that because the patent owners had an available remedy under the Patent Act, based on the artificial act of infringement created by statute, the case was one "for patent infringement" and the patent venue statute applied. In the court's view, the patent owners "s[ought] to directly enforce their patent rights—nothing more," and

---

[Section 4:38]

[1]*See VE Holding Corp. v. Johnson Gas Appliance Co.*, 917 F.2d 1574, 1583–84, 16 U.S.P.Q.2d 1614 (Fed. Cir. 1990) (abrogated on other grounds by, TC Heartland LLC v. Kraft Foods Group Brands LLC, 137 S. Ct. 1514, 1521, 197 L. Ed. 2d 816, 122 U.S.P.Q.2d 1553 (2017)); *accord Bristol-Myers Squibb Company v. Mylan Pharmaceuticals Inc.*, 2017 WL 3980155, *6 (D. Del. 2017) (collecting cases).

[2]42 U.S.C.A. § 262(*l*)(9)(B), (C) (cross-referencing the Declaratory Judgment Act, 28 U.S.C.A. § 2201); *see also* 35 U.S.C.A. § 271(e)(2)(C).

they could not "avoid the requirements of [the patent venue statute] by wrapping its patent infringement claim inside the blanket of a declaratory judgment action."[3]

Actions seeking only a declaration of "validity" or "enforceability," by contrast, would appear not to be actions "for patent infringement," largely for the same reasons an action for a declaration of *non*-infringement is not. They do not have an infringement claim at their core.

§ 4:39 Venue for biosimilar litigation—Venue in patent-infringement actions generally—Where can a declaratory judgment action be brought?

The general venue statute allows a plaintiff to sue either "where any defendant resides," or "where a substantial part of the events or omissions giving rise to the claim occurred."[1] Residence under the general venue statute is construed much more broadly than under the patent venue statute: a corporation or other business entity is deemed to "reside" anywhere it is subject to personal jurisdiction.[2] And defendants cannot be sued where they are not subject to personal jurisdiction anyway. Therefore, where all defendants are corporations or other business entities *and* the general venue statute applies, venue does not narrow the plaintiff's choices at all. The defendants can be sued anywhere they are subject to personal jurisdiction.

Accordingly, to the extent a BPCIA litigant can bring its claims as a true declaratory-judgment action, therefore, it will generally have a wide choice of venues.

§ 4:40 Subject matter jurisdiction

Subject matter jurisdiction refers to a court's ability to hear cases or controversies, and make legal decisions and judgments, regarding a particular subject matter.

---

[3]*Apicore US LLC v. Beloteca, Inc.*, 2019 WL 1746079, *7 (E.D. Tex. 2019).

[Section 4:39]

[1]28 U.S.C.A. § 1391(b)(1) to (2).

[2]28 U.S.C.A. § 1391(c)(2).

Subject matter jurisdiction over BPCIA litigations is provided by statute to United States district courts.[1] Section 1331 generally provides that district courts have jurisdiction "of all civil actions arising under the . . . laws of the United States." Section 1338(a) more specifically provides that patent cases can be heard by district courts, and not state courts: "The district courts shall have original jurisdiction of any civil action arising under any Act of Congress relating to patents. . ... No State court shall have jurisdiction over any claim for relief arising under any Act of Congress relating to patents. . .." 35 U.S.C.A. § 271(e)(2)(C), under which BPCIA infringement claims arise, is, of course, a law of the United States, and therefore implicates both sections 1331 and 1338(a).

Declaratory judgment actions brought by an RPS or a biosimilar applicant also fall within the subject matter jurisdiction of United States district courts.[2] These sections establish a federal court's ability to hear a case or controversy where a party seeks a declaratory judgment. Moreover, 42 U.S.C. § 262(*l*)(9) limits the circumstances under which an RPS or biosimilar applicant can file a declaratory judgment action for infringement, validity, and enforceability arising under the BPCIA. To date, no biosimilar applicant has successfully maintained a declaratory judgment in a BPCIA case.

§ 4:41   Personal jurisdiction

The exercise of personal jurisdiction over a defendant in any litigation, including infringement actions filed under the BPCIA, is limited by the Due Process Clause of the Fourteenth Amendment.[1] A court may properly assert personal jurisdiction over a defendant under one of two theories: general jurisdiction or specific jurisdiction.[2]

General jurisdiction is applicable when a corporation's "affiliations with the State are so continuous and systematic as

---

[Section 4:40]

[1]*See* 28 U.S.C.A. §§ 1331 and 1338(a).

[2]*See* 28 U.S.C.A. §§ 2201(a) and 2202.

[Section 4:41]

[1]*See Helicopteros Nacionales de Colombia, S.A. v. Hall*, 466 U.S. 408, 413–14, 104 S. Ct. 1868, 80 L. Ed. 2d 404 (1984).

[2]*See Daimler AG v. Bauman*, 571 U.S. 117, 134 S. Ct. 746, 187 L. Ed. 2d 624 (2014).

to render it essentially at home in the forum State."[3] Although the Supreme Court has allowed for the possibility of a broader reach in "exceptional cases," general jurisdiction is typically only available where a corporation either is incorporated or has its principle place of business.[4] Thus, an applicant for a biological product would be subject to general subject matter jurisdiction at least in the state in which such applicant is incorporated and/or has its principle place of business.

Specific jurisdiction is applicable when a corporation "has certain minimum contacts with the forum such that the maintenance of the suit does not offend traditional notions of fair play and substantial justice."[5] This "minimum contacts" threshold is satisfied—and specific jurisdiction proper— where "the defendant purposefully directed activities at the forum, and the litigation results from alleged injuries that arise out of or relate to those activities."[6] In addition to "minimum contacts," specific jurisdiction requires that other factors—e.g., the burden on defendant, the state's interest in adjudicating the dispute, the plaintiff's interest in obtaining convenient and effective relief, and the interstate judicial systems interest in obtaining the most efficient resolution of controversies—do not render the exercise of personal jurisdiction unreasonable under the circumstances.[7]

The basis for an infringement action under the BPCIA is provided by 35 U.S.C.A. § 271(e)(2), which makes it an act of infringement to file an application to market a biological product covered by a patent.[8] Section 271(e)(2) analogously defines the filing of an abbreviated new drug application to market a drug product as an act of infringement. 35 U.S.C.A. § 271(e)(2)(A). In this latter context, the Federal Circuit has explained that filing an application with the FDA to market a generic drug satisfies the "minimum contacts" standard for any state in which the applicant intends to market the drug because (1) such marketing will be "purposefully directed" at

---

[3]*Daimler*, 571 U.S. at 122 (quotations removed).

[4]*Daimler*, 571 U.S. at 122.

[5]*See Acorda Therapeutics Inc. v. Mylan Pharmaceuticals Inc.*, 817 F.3d 755, 759, 118 U.S.P.Q.2d 1304 (Fed. Cir. 2016), cert. denied, 137 S. Ct. 625, 196 L. Ed. 2d 580 (2017) (quotations removed).

[6]*See Accorda*, 817 F.3d at 759.

[7]*See Accorda*, 817 F.3d at 759.

[8]*See Sandoz Inc. v. Amgen Inc.*, 137 S. Ct. 1664, 198 L. Ed. 2d 114, 122 U.S.P.Q.2d 1685 (2017); 35 U.S.C.A. § 271(e)(2)(C).

that state; and (2) the litigation arises from alleged infringement related to the application.[9] Accordingly, courts have specific personal jurisdiction over an applicant for purposes of adjudicating infringement allegations arising under section 271(e)(2) provided that the applicant intends to market the drug in the forum state upon approval, and the unfairness considerations discussed above are consistent with fair play and substantial justice.[10]

§ 4:42   Standing

Article III, section 2, of the Constitution requires that there be a "case or controversy" in order for a court to render judgment. "This requires the [plaintiff] to prove that he has suffered a concrete and particularized injury that is fairly traceable to the challenged conduct, and is likely to be redressed by a favorable judicial decision."[1] "In other words, for a federal court to have authority under the Constitution to settle a dispute, the party before it must seek a remedy for a personal and tangible harm. 'The presence of a disagreement, however sharp and acrimonious it may be, is insufficient by itself to meet Art. III's requirements.' "[2]

Standing to assert patent infringement is provided by 35 U.S.C.A. § 281, which states that "[a] patentee shall have remedy by civil action for infringement of his patent." Accordingly, to have a case or controversy in the context of a patent case, there generally must be an alleged act of infringement. And, infringement typically does not occur unless and until one manufactures, uses, sells, offers for sale, or imports into the United States a claimed invention.[3] The BPCIA, however, "facilitates litigation during the period preceding FDA approval so that the parties do not have to wait until commercial marketing to resolve their patent disputes. It enables the parties to bring infringement actions at certain points in the application process, even if the applicant has

---

[9]*See Accorda*, 817 F.3d at 759–64.

[10]*Accorda*, 817 F.3d at 759–64.

[Section 4:42]

[1]*Hollingsworth v. Perry*, 570 U.S. 693, 133 S. Ct. 2652, 2661, 186 L. Ed. 2d 768, 57 Employee Benefits Cas. (BNA) 1605, 118 Fair Empl. Prac. Cas. (BNA) 1446 (2013).

[2]*Hollingsworth*, 133 S. Ct. at 2661 (quoting *Diamond v. Charles*, 476 U.S. 54, 62, 106 S. Ct. 1697, 90 L. Ed. 2d 48 (1986)).

[3]35 U.S.C.A. § 271(a).

not yet committed an act that would traditionally constitute patent infringement."[4]

In particular, 35 U.S.C.A. § 271(e)(2)(C)—which was amended when the BPCIA was passed—"provides that the mere submission of a biosimilar application constitutes an act of infringement," or more specifically, sometimes referred to as "artificial" infringement.[5] This amendment thereby established the requisite "case or controversy" to permit federal courts to adjudicate patent disputes premised on the filing of a biosimilar application.[6] More specifically, the BPCIA creates artificial infringement under two scenarios, one in which the parties fully dance and a litigation then ensues under 42 U.S.C. § 262(l)(6), and the other in which the applicant opts not to dance and the RPS brings a lawsuit under 42 U.S.C. § 262(l)(9).

The "patentee" identified in section 281 includes "not only the patentee to whom the patent was issued but also the successors in title to the patentee."[7] In certain circumstances, a patent licensee may also have standing to sue for patent infringement.[8] In the event that a patent has multiple owners, all must join as plaintiffs to confer standing.[9]

The burden of proving standing rests with the plaintiff, and must be established by a preponderance of the evidence.[10] If a plaintiff is unable to establish standing, the case must

---

[4]*Sandoz*, 137 S. Ct. at 1670.

[5]*Sandoz*, 137 S. Ct. at 1670.

[6]*See Sandoz*, 773 F.3d at 1281 ("In the Hatch-Waxman Act Congress did provide for certain early adjudications of patent issues that would be presented by future market-entry activity in the FDA setting. It created an 'artificial' act of infringement to allow suit by a patent holder, 35 U.S.C.A. § 271(e)(2)(A); . . . and in the BPCIA, Congress extended the provision to biological products, 35 U.S.C.A. § 271(e)(2)(C)."; *see also Glaxo, Inc. v. Novopharm, Ltd.*, 110 F.3d 1562, 1569, 42 U.S.P.Q.2d 1257 (Fed. Cir. 1997) ("Thus, § 271(e)(2) provided patentees with a defined act of infringement sufficient to create case or controversy jurisdiction to enable a court to promptly resolve any dispute concerning infringement and validity.").

[7]35 U.S.C.A. § 100(d).

[8]*See Rite-Hite Corp. v. Kelley Co., Inc.*, 56 F.3d 1538, 1551–52, 35 U.S.P.Q.2d 1065 (Fed. Cir. 1995).

[9]*See Ethicon, Inc. v. U.S. Surgical Corp.*, 135 F.3d 1456, 1467, 45 U.S.P.Q.2d 1545, 48 Fed. R. Evid. Serv. 1226 (Fed. Cir. 1998).

[10]*See Lujan v. Defenders of Wildlife*, 504 U.S. 555, 561, 112 S. Ct. 2130, 119 L. Ed. 2d 351, 34 Env't. Rep. Cas. (BNA) 1785, 22 Envtl. L. Rep. 20913 (1992).

be dismissed.[11] Dismissal for lack of standing is generally without prejudice, but a district court has discretion to dismiss the case with prejudice, particularly where it appears unlikely the plaintiff will be able to cure the standing problem.[12]

The issue of standing has been addressed in one litigation arising under the BPCIA.[13] Defendants moved to dismiss the Complaint with respect to one of the asserted patents on the grounds that several co-owners of that patent were not joined as plaintiffs, and the patentee therefore lacked standing.[14] The dispute revolved around whether the inventors' conveyance of their ownership interest in the patent to "the COMPANY" transferred title to the patentee alone or to additional entities as well.[15] Concluding that the patentee was, in fact, the sole owner of the patent at issue, the Court held standing was proper and accordingly denied defendants' motion to dismiss.[16]

§ 4:43   The right of an RPS to bring a declaratory judgment action

Under the BPCIA, the right of an RPS to bring an action for declaratory relief is directly tied to whether the applicant has complied with the steps of the patent dance. There are three potential scenarios:

— The applicant fails to disclose the information regarding its biosimilar product required by Section 262(l)(2).

— The applicant provides the information required by Section 262(l)(2), but then fails to complete one of several expressly enumerated steps of the patent dance.

— The applicant completes the statutorily required steps of the patent dance before providing its notice of commercial marketing ("NCM") under section 262(l)(8)(B).

---

[11]See Schreiber Foods, Inc. v. Beatrice Cheese, Inc., 402 F.3d 1198, 1203, 74 U.S.P.Q.2d 1204, 61 Fed. R. Serv. 3d 174 (Fed. Cir. 2005).

[12]See Tyco Healthcare Group LP v. Ethicon Endo-Surgery, Inc., 587 F.3d 1375, 1380, 92 U.S.P.Q.2d 1940 (Fed. Cir. 2009).

[13]Janssen Biotech, Inc. v. Celltrion Healthcare Co., Ltd., 296 F. Supp. 3d 336 (D. Mass. 2017).

[14]Janssen, 296 F. Supp. 3d at 340–41.

[15]Janssen, 296 F. Supp. 3d at 343–53.

[16]Janssen, 296 F. Supp. 3d at 353.

§ 4:44 The right of an RPS to bring a declaratory judgment action—RPS declaratory judgment suits based on section 262(*l*)(9)(C)

If the biosimilar applicant fails to initiate the patent dance by disclosing its application and other information required by Section 262(*l*)(2)(A), then the RPS has a right to bring a declaratory judgment action regarding infringement, validity, or enforceability of any patent that claims the biological product or a use of the biological product.[1] This right to seek declaratory relief is "a remedy" for the applicant's noncompliance with Section 262(*l*)(2)(A), since the BPCIA only authorizes the RPS to bring a declaratory action in this circumstance.[2] When the biosimilar applicant fails to initiate the dance, the statute "thus vests in the sponsor the control that the applicant would otherwise have exercised over the scope and timing of the patent litigation."[3]

When pursuing a declaratory judgment action under this provision, the RPS is authorized to sue based on any patents that " '*could* be identified' under paragraph (*l*)(3)" of the BPCIA."[4] Section 262(*l*)(3), in turn, allows the sponsor to list "patents for which . . . [it] believes a claim of patent infringement could reasonably be asserted [against the applicant]."[5] This means that, when the biosimilar applicant chooses not to dance, the RPS may file a declaratory judgment action on any patent that can be reasonably asserted against the biosimilar applicant.

§ 4:45 The right of an RPS to bring a declaratory judgment action—RPS declaratory judgment suits based on section 262(*l*)(9)(C)—RPS declaratory judgment suits based on section 262(*l*)(9)(B)

The BPCIA also provides the RPS with a remedy if the applicant begins the patent dance by providing the information

---

[Section 4:44]

[1]42 U.S.C.A. § 262(*l*)(9)(C).

[2]*Sandoz*, 137 S. Ct. at 1675 (2017).

[3]*Sandoz*, 137 S. Ct. at 1675 (2017).

[4]*Amgen Inc. v. Hospira, Inc.*, 866 F.3d 1355, 1360–61, 123 U.S.P.Q.2d 1697 (Fed. Cir. 2017) (emphasis in original) (quoting 35 U.S.C.A. § 271(e)(2)(C)(ii)).

[5]42 U.S.C.A. § 262(*l*)(3)(A).

required by Section 262(*l*)(2), but then fails to complete one of several further mandatory steps of the dance. Specifically, the Act designates five mandatory steps of the dance: (1) the statement provided by the applicant identifying (a) the patents included in the RPS's list that either the applicant believes are invalid, unenforceable, or will not be infringed, and (b) the patents that will expire before the applicant intends to begin commercial marketing;[1] (2) the exchange of patent lists required in the absence of an agreement between the parties, which identifies the patents selected for the first wave of litigation;[2] (3) the provision of notice to the Secretary of Health and Human Services after the complaint is filed to initiate the first wave of patent litigation;[3] (4) statements as to any newly issued or licensed patents identified by the RPS;[4] and (5) the provision of NCM to the RPS no later than 180 days before the date of the first commercial marketing of the product.[5] If the applicant does not complete one of these required steps, then the RPS, but not the applicant, may bring an immediate action for declaratory relief as to any patent included in the list provided by the RPS that is described in paragraph (3)(A).[6] The declaratory judgment action may involve not only patents identified during the patent dance, but also any newly issued or licensed patents designated by the RPS pursuant to Section 262(*l*)(7).[7]

§ 4:46 The right of an RPS to bring a declaratory judgment action—RPS declaratory judgment suits based on section 262(*l*)(9)(C)— Restrictions on the timing of an RPS declaratory judgment suit under section 262(*l*)(9)(A)

Section 262(*l*)(9)(A) restricts the RPS from bringing an action for declaratory relief in cases in which the applicant complies with the steps of the patent dance. Specifically, if the applicant provides its biosimilar application and the in-

---

[Section 4:45]

  [1]42 U.S.C.A. § 262(*l*)(3)(B)(ii).

  [2]42 U.S.C.A. § 262(*l*)(5).

  [3]42 U.S.C.A. § 262(*l*)(6)(C)(i).

  [4]42 U.S.C.A. § 262(*l*)(7).

  [5]42 U.S.C.A. § 262(*l*)(8)(A).

  [6]42 U.S.C.A. § 262(*l*)(9)(B).

  [7]42 U.S.C.A. § 262(*l*)(9)(B); *see also* 35 U.S.C.A. § 271(e)(2)(c).

formation required under paragraph (2)(A), neither the RPS nor the applicant may bring an action for declaratory relief as to any patent that is described in clauses (i) and (ii) of Section 262(*l*)(8)(B) until the applicant provides NCM under that Section 262(*l*)(8)(A).[1] Read together, clauses (i) and (ii) of Section 262(*l*)(8)(B) identify the patents that appeared in either the RPS's or the applicant's list under paragraph (3) and were not included in the first phase of patent litigation because they were not included in the lists described in paragraph (4) or paragraph (5)(B).[2]

§ 4:47 The right of an RPS to bring a declaratory judgment action—Limits on the ability of biosimilar applicants to seek declaratory relief

As noted, Section 262(*l*)(9)(A) imposes a restriction on declaratory actions potentially relating to the subsection (k) application that applies "prior to the date" NCM "is received under paragraph (8)(A)."[1] Relying on the text of this provision, some biosimilar applicants have attempted to file declaratory actions immediately after providing NCM, even though the parties had not yet completed the first phase of patent litigation or the related steps of the patent dance. Two district courts, however, have held that NCM does not, by itself, give the biosimilar applicant the right to file a declaratory judgment action.[2] Instead, post-NCM patent litigation may only relate to the remaining patents—*i.e.*, the

---

[Section 4:46]

[1]42 U.S.C.A. § 262(*l*)(9)(A).

[2]42 U.S.C.A. § 262(*l*)(8)(B).

[Section 4:47]

[1]42 U.S.C.A. § 262(*l*)(9)(A).

[2]In *Amgen, Inc. v. Genentech, Inc.*, 2018 WL 910198 (C.D. Cal. 2018), subsequent determination, 2018 WL 718418 (C.D. Cal. 2018), the district court granted Genentech's motion to dismiss Amgen's declaratory judgment action, which concerned patents held by Genentech with respect to its biologic Avastin® (bevacizumab). In the case, Genentech identified the patents that it proposed to litigate pursuant to Section 262(*l*)(5)(A). *Amgen, Inc., 2018 WL 910198 at *2*. But instead of negotiating pursuant to Section 262(*l*)(5)(B), Amgen provided its NCM, and then filed a declaratory judgment action against Genentech for non-infringement, invalidity, and unenforceability of the 27 patents that Genentech had listed. *Amgen, Inc., 2018 WL 910198 at *2*. Genentech promptly filed a competing suit against Amgen in the District of Delaware. *Genentech Inc. v. Amgen Inc.*, No. 1:17-cv-01407-CFC (D. Del. 2017). Amgen moved to transfer the Delaware liti-

patents that could have been litigated in the first phase of BPCIA patent litigation, but were not.[3] These courts reasoned that providing NCM "only opens the door for an applicant to file a declaratory judgment action if the applicant complies with the rest of the statute" and does not allow the biosimilar applicant to skip mandatory steps of the patent dance before filing a declaratory judgment action.[4]

§ 4:48   The right of an RPS to bring a declaratory judgment action—Courts have treated the BPCIA's limits on declaratory judgment actions as non-jurisdictional

In cases applying section 262(*l*)(9)'s restrictions on declara-

---

gation to the Central District of California, and Genentech moved to dismiss the California action for lack of subject matter jurisdiction based on the restrictions on declaratory actions set by Section 262(*l*)(9). In a tentative ruling, the Central District of California held that "pursuant to the discretion provided by the Declaratory Judgment Act" the court would grant the motion and decline jurisdiction over Amgen's declaratory judgment action, but the court stayed its decision pending resolution of the motion to transfer in the District of Delaware. *Amgen, Inc.*, 2018 WL 910198 at *5. After Amgen's motion to transfer was denied, the court issued a final order granting the motion to dismiss, reaffirming its reasoning from the tentative ruling. *Amgen*, D.I. 63, (C.D. Cal. Feb. 2, 2018).

A district court in the Northern District of California reached a similar conclusion in *Celltrion, Inc. v. Genentech, Inc.*, 2018 WL 2448254 (N.D. Cal. 2018), appeal dismissed, 2018 WL 7046651 (Fed. Cir. 2018). In the case, Celltrion had filed applications to market biosimilars of Genentech's Herceptin® (trastuzumab) and Rituxan® (rituximab) products. *Celltrion, 2018 WL 2448254 at *3*. After undergoing the initial steps of the patent dance, Celltrion provided its NCM as to both biosimilar products and filed declaratory judgment actions in the Northern District of California. *Celltrion, 2018 WL 2448254 at *3*. In support of these actions, Celltrion argued that the NCM it had provided for both products enabled Celltrion to file these declaratory judgment actions, regardless of whether Celltrion had completed all of the steps of the patent dance before filing suit. *Celltrion, 2018 WL 2448254 at *7*. The district court disagreed, holding that providing NCM did not remove the bar to Celltrion's declaratory judgment action under section 262(*l*)(9)(B) because Celltrion had not completed all of the mandatory steps of the patent dance. *Celltrion, 2018 WL 2448254 at *7*.

[3]*See Amgen, 2018 WL 910198, at *3* (explaining that "[t]he BPCIA is . . . structured so that after the applicant provides notice of commercial marketing, either party can bring suit with respect to any of the leftover patents that were not selected for litigation through the parties' exchanges and negotiations," but not the patents that were to be litigated in a "first phase" litigation).

[4]*Celltrion, 2018 WL 2448254, at *8; see also Amgen, 2018 WL 910198, at *4*.

tory actions, the parties have debated whether those limits are properly understood as raising an issue of subject-matter jurisdiction rather than a mandatory claims-processing rule. The answer to that question has implications for whether the district court may look outside the pleadings to resolve disputed questions of fact, as well as to whether a party could waive a defense to declaratory relief based on section 262(*l*)(9). To this point, the only court to squarely address the issue held that the BPCIA requirements are not jurisdictional prerequisites, but rather are statutory conditions that function like "claim processing rules.[1] Under that approach, a motion to dismiss premised on non-compliance with the patent dance requirements will be reviewed under Rule 12(b)(6), rather than under Rule 12(b)(1), which limits the district court's ability to reach outside the pleadings or resolve factual disputes.[2]

§4:49 The right of an RPS to bring a declaratory judgment action—Whether the BPCIA's restrictions on declaratory judgment actions apply to counterclaims

The restrictions set by Section 262(*l*)(9) limit the ability of the RPS or biosimilar applicant "to bring an action" for declaratory relief. It remains unsettled whether and to what extent this provision limits the ability of either the RPS or the applicant to file a counterclaim seeking declaratory relief under this provision—and thus potentially to compel litigation on patents that were otherwise excluded from the first phase.

In one early decision on the issue, the district court in the *Amgen v. Sandoz* litigation held that the paragraph (9) bars do *not* apply to counterclaims.[1] This decision was not at is-

---

[Section 4:48]

[1]*Celltrion, 2018 WL 2448254, at *4* (citation omitted). The court in *Amgen v. Genentech* also identified this issue but declined to resolve it, on the ground that it would decline to exercise declaratory judgment jurisdiction in any event. *See 2018 WL 910198, at *4.*

[2]*See Celltrion, 2018 WL 2448254, at *7.*

[Section 4:49]

[1]*Amgen Inc. v. Sandoz Inc.*, 2015 WL 1264756 (N.D. Cal. 2015), aff'd in part, vacated in part, remanded, 794 F.3d 1347 (Fed. Cir. 2015) and cert. granted, 137 S. Ct. 808, 196 L. Ed. 2d 594 (2017) and rev'd in part, vacated in part, 137 S. Ct. 1664, 198 L. Ed. 2d 114, 122 U.S.P.Q.2d 1685

sue in subsequent appeals in that litigation to the Federal Circuit and the Supreme Court in that litigation.

The application of Section 262(*l*)(9) to counterclaims was also raised but not resolved in litigation between Celltrion and Genentech involving Celltrion's biosimilar application for trastuzumab and rituximab. As discussed above, a district judge in the Northern District of California dismissed Celltrion's declaratory judgment action as barred by the BPCIA on the ground that Celltrion had not completed the patent dance.[2] Following dismissal, Genentech went forward with its own action for declaratory relief and patent infringement in the District of Delaware (for trastuzumab)[3] and the District of New Jersey (for rituximab).[4] Celltrion then reasserted claims for declaratory relief as counterclaims in its answer. In subsequent motion to dismiss briefing, Genentech argued that paragraph 9(b) also extended to bar these counterclaims, but Celltrion argued that the paragraph did not apply because asserting a counterclaim in an existing action is not equivalent to "bring[ing] an action." The issue was not resolved, because the parties settled before a ruling on the motion to dismiss.

The same issue also surfaced in litigation between Genentech and Amgen with regard to Bevacizumab.[5] The matter has not yet been ruled on by the district court.

§ 4:50   The right of an RPS to bring a declaratory judgment action—The exercise of declaratory judgment jurisdiction is discretionary

Even if the district court has subject-matter jurisdiction and there is no statutory bar to bringing a declaratory judgment action, the court may still decline declaratory judgment jurisdiction as a matter of discretion.[1] Trial courts "must determine whether hearing the case would serve the

---

(2017) and aff'd, 877 F.3d 1315, 125 U.S.P.Q.2d 1001 (Fed. Cir. 2017).

[2]2018 WL 2448254, at *7.

[3]Nos. 18-cv-95, 18-cv-1025 (D. Del.).

[4]No. 18-cv-574 (D. N.J.).

[5]*See Genentech, Inc. et al. v. Amgen, Inc.*, No. 1:17-cv-01407-CFC, D.I. 129, (D. Del. Nov. 14, 2017).

[Section 4:50]

[1]*See MedImmune, Inc. v. Genentech, Inc.*, 549 U.S. 118, 127 S. Ct. 764, 166 L. Ed. 2d 604, 81 U.S.P.Q.2d 1225, 2007-1 Trade Cas. (CCH) ¶ 75543 (2007) (explaining that the text of the Declaratory Judgment Act

objectives for which the Declaratory Judgment Act was created, namely, allowing a party who is reasonably at legal risk because of an unresolved legal dispute[ ] to obtain judicial resolution of that dispute without having to await the commencement of legal action by the other side."[2] Applying these principles, one district court relied on the discretionary nature of the Declaratory Judgment Act to decline jurisdiction, as the court reasoned that exercising jurisdiction would subvert the BPCIA's purpose and structure by allowing the biosimilar applicant "to bypass the BPCIA's scheme for negotiations and eventual litigation."[3]

§ 4:51 Limitation on claims

As explained elsewhere, the BPCIA provides for waves of patent litigation concerning proposed biosimilars. The course of the litigation proceeds under the terms set out in Section 262(*l*). The Supreme Court has explained that "[t]he applicant has substantial control over the timing and scope of both phases of litigation."[1] Depending on the particular circumstances of the case—for example, whether the parties are able to reach agreement on the proper scope of the litigation—as set out in the various subsections under Section 262(*l*), there are certain consequences as to which claims and patents may be included in either wave.

§ 4:52 Limitation on claims—Applicant who fails to provide notice under § 262(*l*)(2)(A)

A biosimilar applicant initiates the patent dance under Section 262(*l*) by disclosing certain required information to the RPS following the FDA's acceptance of the aBLA for

---

"has long been understood to 'confer on federal courts unique and substantial discretion in deciding whether to declare the rights of litigants.'" (quoting *Wilton v. Seven Falls Co.*, 515 U.S. 277, 286, 115 S. Ct. 2137, 132 L. Ed. 2d 214 (1995)).

[2]*Ford Motor Co. v. U.S.*, 811 F.3d 1371, 1378, 37 Int'l Trade Rep. (BNA) 2313 (Fed. Cir. 2016) (internal quotation marks and citations omitted).

[3]*Amgen, 2018 WL 910198, at *5.*

[Section 4:51]

[1]*Sandoz Inc. v. Amgen Inc.*, 137 S. Ct. 1664, 1666, 198 L. Ed. 2d 114, 122 U.S.P.Q.2d 1685 (2017); *see also Amgen Inc. v. Apotex Inc.*, 827 F.3d 1052, 1056, 119 U.S.P.Q.2d 1318 (Fed. Cir. 2016) ("Th[e] process gives the applicant a scope-limiting ability, based on an exchange of lists of patents to be litigated.").

filing.[1] As a preliminary matter, and as set forth in detail elsewhere, no claim can be brought to enforce compliance with the patent dance.[2] The consequence of a biosimilar applicant choosing not to participate in the dance is that the RPS—but not the applicant—may bring an action for a declaratory judgment of infringement, validity, or enforceability of "any patent that claims the biological product or a use of the biological product."[3] This action is not otherwise limited with respect to the patents or claims that the RPS may assert, nor is amendment to later assert additional patents precluded by the statute in this instance.[4]

§ 4:53   Limitation on claims—Scope-limiting ability of applicant in first wave litigation

The BPCIA allows the applicant to limit the number of patents that can be asserted in the first wave litigation, provided that the applicant first initiates the dance. Not later than 60 days after acceptance of filing of the aBLA, under Section 262(*l*)(3), the RPS must provide the applicant with a list of patents for which the RPS believes a claim of patent infringement could reasonably be asserted.[1] Under Section 262(*l*)(4), the parties are then obligated to engage in negotiations to reach an agreement on the patents that will be included in the first wave litigation.[2] If the RPS and applicant cannot agree on a list within 15 days of beginning negotiations, they must undertake the information exchange process in Section 262(*l*)(5). This requires that the applicant first notify the RPS of the number of patents that the applicant will provide to the RPS.[3] Following this notification, the parties will exchange lists, with the RPS being limited to

---

[Section 4:52]

[1]42 U.S.C.A. § 262(*l*)(2).

[2]*Sandoz*, 137 S. Ct. at 1674; *see also* Section V.B.1., regarding disclosure of information regarding the applicant's biosimilar product.

[3]42 U.S.C.A. § 262(*l*)(9)(C).

[4]42 U.S.C.A. § 262(*l*)(9)(C); *see also* Section V.B.G., concerning the reduction in patents and claims as part of the scheduling and staging of BPCIA cases.

[Section 4:53]

[1]42 U.S.C.A. § 262(*l*)(3)(A); *See* 3(A) Statement for further information.

[2]42 U.S.C.A. § 262(*l*)(4) to (5).

[3]42 U.S.C.A. § 262(*l*)(5)(B)(i)(I).

the number of patents that the applicant identified.[4] This limitation is subject to a sole exception that should the applicant list zero patents, the RPS is permitted to list one.[5] In other words, if the applicant lists no patents on its initial list, then the first wave litigation will be limited to a single patent, no matter how many patents the RPS designated in its Section 262(*l*)(3)(A) list as reasonably assertable against the product.

The BPCIA also places limits on the RPS's damages remedy in certain circumstances. Specifically, if the RPS fails to sue for infringement within 30 days of the exchange of lists under Section 262(*l*)(5), the sole remedy is reasonable royalty and lost profits will not be available.[6]

One issue worth noting that will not necessarily be considered in the first wave litigation is the 35 U.S.C. 271(e)(1) safe harbor defense. Section 271(e)(1) protects pre-marketing manufacturing activity from liability, but may not be an issue appropriate for first wave litigation, which occurs prior to the filing of the notice of commercial marketing.[7]

---

[4]*AbbVie Inc. et al. v. Boehringer Ingelheim Int'l GmbH et al.*, No. 1:17-cv-01065-MSG-RL (D. Del. 2017) provides an example of how this works. As set forth in its complaint, following its receipt of information pursuant to 262(*l*)(2) from Boehringer, AbbVie listed 72 patents that it reasonably believed could be infringed. It then supplemented its list with two newly issued patents. After negotiations, the parties failed to come to an agreement on the patents to be included in the litigation. Boehringer provided that its list would be capped at five patents, and the parties' ultimately ended up with eight patents in the first-wave litigation.

[5]42 U.S.C.A. § 262(*l*)(5)(B)(ii)(II).

[6]42 U.S.C.A. § 262(*l*)(6)(B).

[7]*Abbvie*, No. 1:17-cv-01065-MSG-RL, D.I. 476 (D. Del. Apr. 15, 2019). AbbVie moved to require defendants to more fully respond to its Interrogatories directed to its safe harbor defense.

Abbvie argued that the information it sought was relevant to show inducement for infringement. The Court explained that "[a] theory of inducement does not make sense in the first phase of a case involving 'artificial infringement' . . . [t]he BCPIA was designed to encourage the filing of an aBLA by making the application—or preparatory steps—a potential source of liability for inducement of infringement." The court further explained that "[t]he probative value of the information sought by the interrogatory is remote and unlikely to be material to the resolution of issues in this first phase of the litigation, which is triggered by the 'artificial infringement' created by the filing of a biosimilar application with the FDA." *Abbvie*, D.I. 476 (D. Del. Apr. 15, 2019).

§ 4:54   Limitation on claims—Second wave litigation

After the applicant gives the RPS notice of commercial marketing (at least 180 days before commercially marketing its licensed product), the RPS may seek a preliminary injunction on any patent that appeared on the original Section 262(*l*)(3) list. As described above, the Section 262(*l*)(3) list is provided by the RPS to the applicant no later than 60 days after receipt of the application and information. The RPS lists the patents that the RPS reasonably believes could be asserted. Patents that were the subject of the first phase litigation are excluded from this category.[1]

Unlike the limitation on an applicant filing a declaratory judgment action in the first wave litigation as described above, in the second wave either party is permitted to sue for declaratory relief.[2]

§ 4:55   Right to a jury trial—General overview

Under Federal Law, "[a] litigant has a right to a jury trial if provided by statute, or if required by the Seventh Amendment."[1] The BPCIA statute does not specifically provide for trial by jury.

The Seventh Amendment to the Constitution preserves the right to a jury trial for "[s]uits at common law."[2] The phrase "suits at common law" refers to lawsuits in "which only legal rights and remedies were at issue, as opposed to

---

[Section 4:54]

[1]42 U.S.C.A. § 262(*l*)(8)(B). For example, in the *Abbvie* example described above, the second phase litigation would allow for the assertion of any of the remainder of the 72 patents on the Section 262(*l*)(3)(A) list (minus the five listed that were actually included in the first wave litigation).

[2]42 U.S.C.A. § 262(*l*)(9)(A); *Sandoz*, 137 S.Ct. at 1672; *See* Notice of Commercial Marketing for further information.

[Section 4:55]

[1]*AIA America, Inc. v. Avid Radiopharmaceuticals*, 866 F.3d 1369, 1372, 123 U.S.P.Q.2d 1703 (Fed. Cir. 2017).

[2]U.S. Const. Amend. VII ("In suits at common law, where the value in controversy shall exceed twenty dollars, the right of trial by jury shall be preserved, and no fact tried by a jury, shall be otherwise reexamined in any court of the United States, than according to the rules of the common law."); *see also* Fed. R. Civ. P. 38(a) ("The right of trial by jury as declared by the Seventh Amendment to the Constitution—or as provided by a federal statute—is preserved to the parties inviolate.").

equitable rights and remedies."[3] Therefore, a party has a right to a jury trial when legal rights and remedies are at issue, while an equitable remedy does not implicate the right to a jury trial.[4] A two-step inquiry is used to determine whether a modern statutory cause of action involves only legal rights and remedies.[5] First, one must "compare the statutory action to 18th-century actions brought in the courts of England prior to the merger of the courts of law and equity."[6] Second, one must "examine the remedy sought and determine whether it is legal or equitable in nature."[7] The Supreme Court has stressed that the second step of this test is the more important of the two.[8]

Patent Litigation Generally: In patent litigation, courts generally recognize a Seventh Amendment right to a jury trial in cases where the patentee seeks money damages, which is a legal remedy, and deny it in cases where the patentee seeks only an equitable remedy (for example, an injunction or a declaratory judgment).[9] When a patentee seeks damages, the right to a jury trial is triggered to resolve infringement and validity of the patent.[10]

In patent cases, a patentee often seeks both legal and equitable relief, for example, monetary damages and an injunction. When a patentee joins legal and equitable claims, it is entitled to a jury trial with respect to the legal claims,

---

[3]*AIA Am., Inc.*, 866 F.3d at 1373.

[4]*Curtis v. Loether*, 415 U.S. 189, 196 n.11, 94 S. Ct. 1005, 39 L. Ed. 2d 260, 18 Fed. R. Serv. 2d 189 (1974); *AIA Am., Inc.*, 866 F.3d at 1372.

[5]*Tull v. U.S.*, 481 U.S. 412, 417–18, 107 S. Ct. 1831, 95 L. Ed. 2d 365, 25 Env't. Rep. Cas. (BNA) 1857, 7 Fed. R. Serv. 3d 673, 17 Envtl. L. Rep. 20667 (1987).

[6]*Tull*, 481 U.S. at 417.

[7]*Tull*, 481 U.S. at 417–18.

[8]*Chauffeurs, Teamsters and Helpers, Local No. 391 v. Terry*, 494 U.S. 558, 565, 110 S. Ct. 1339, 108 L. Ed. 2d 519, 133 L.R.R.M. (BNA) 2793, 114 Lab. Cas. (CCH) P 11930 (1990) ("The second inquiry is the more important in our analysis.").

[9]*See, e.g., In re Technology Licensing Corp.*, 423 F.3d 1286, 1291, 76 U.S.P.Q.2d 1450 (Fed. Cir. 2005) ("[I]f the patentee has abandoned any claim for damages, the related invalidity claims are triable to the bench, not to a jury."); *Tegal Corp. v. Tokyo Electron America, Inc.*, 257 F.3d 1331, 1341, 59 U.S.P.Q.2d 1385 (Fed. Cir. 2001) ("[A] defendant, asserting only affirmative defenses and no counterclaims, does not have a right to a jury trial in a patent infringement suit if the only remedy sought by the plaintiff-patentee is an injunction.").

[10]*See supra* Section 3:2.

but not on the equitable claims.[11] For example, there is no right to a jury trial with respect to claims for an injunction,[12] unenforceability (for example, unclean hands, inequitable conduct),[13] or attorneys' fees.[14]

Even if a claim triggers the Seventh Amendment right to a jury trial, there is no right to have a jury decide questions of law. The Seventh Amendment only preserves a jury trial with respect to issues of fact, not issues of law.[15] For example, claim construction is for the court to decide, not the jury.[16]

Declaratory Judgment Claims: As the Federal Circuit has explained, "declaratory judgment actions are, for Seventh Amendment purposes, only as legal or equitable in nature as the controversies on which they are founded."[17]

---

[11]*See, e.g., Beacon Theatres, Inc. v. Westover*, 359 U.S. 500, 510, 79 S. Ct. 948, 3 L. Ed. 2d 988, 2 Fed. R. Serv. 2d 650 (1959) ("In the Federal courts [the right to a jury trial] cannot be dispensed with, except by the assent of the parties entitled to it, nor can it be impaired by any blending with a claim, properly cognizable at law, of a demand for equitable relief in aid of the legal action.") (quoting *Scott v. Neely*, 140 U.S. 106, 109–10, 11 S. Ct. 712, 35 L. Ed. 358 (1891)).

[12]*Tegal Corp.*, 257 F.3d at 1341.

[13]*Agfa Corp. v. Creo Products Inc.*, 451 F.3d 1366, 1373, 79 U.S.P.Q.2d 1385 (Fed. Cir. 2006).

[14]*AIA Am., Inc.*, 866 F.3d at 1373.

[15]*See, e.g., Byrd v. Blue Ridge Rural Elec. Co-op., Inc.*, 356 U.S. 525, 537, 78 S. Ct. 893, 2 L. Ed. 2d 953 (1958) ("[I]n civil common-law actions, [the federal court system] distributes trial functions between judge and jury and, under the influence—if not the command—of the Seventh Amendment, assigns the decisions of disputes questions of fact to the jury."); *Markman v. Westview Instruments, Inc.*, 517 U.S. 370, 376, 116 S. Ct. 1384, 134 L. Ed. 2d 577, 38 U.S.P.Q.2d 1461 (1996) (patent claim construction is a question of law for the court, not the jury).

[16]*Markman*, 517 U.S. at 376.

[17]*In re Lockwood*, 50 F.3d 966, 973, 33 U.S.P.Q.2d 1406 (Fed. Cir. 1995), judgment vacated, 515 U.S. 1182, 116 S. Ct. 29, 132 L. Ed. 2d 911 (1995); *In re Tech. Licensing Corp.*, 423 F.3d at 1288 ("We have made clear that for purposes of the right to a jury trial in patent cases, it is inconsequential whether the parties are aligned in the conventional manner (patent as plaintiff and accused infringer as defendant and invalidity counterclaimant) or in the manner that results when the accused infringer initiates the actions as a declaratory judgment (accused infringer as plaintiff and patentee as defendant and infringement counterclaimant."); *see also Beacon Theatres, Inc.*, 359 U.S. at 504 ("The District Court's finding that the Complaint for Declaratory Relief presented basically equitable issues draws no support from the Declaratory Judgment Act[.] That statute, while allowing prospective defendants to sue to establish their nonliability, specifically preserves the right to jury trial for both parties. It

Thus, in cases where a party sues a patentee for a declaratory judgment of invalidity or non-infringement, the party has no right to a jury trial because only equitable relief is at issue.[18] If the patentee-defendant in a declaratory action case were to assert a counterclaim for patent infringement and seek monetary damages, then the jury trial right is triggered.[19]

§ 4:56   Right to a jury trial—General overview—Right to jury trial in BPCIA cases

The BPCIA statute does not provide the right to a jury trial.

Patent cases brought under the analogous Hatch-Waxman Act are instructive on how courts may view the right to a jury trial for claims brought under the BPCIA statute. Under the Hatch-Waxman Act, a company may seek regulatory approval for a generic version of a patented drug that has already been approved by the FDA by making a "Paragraph IV filing" with respect to the patents covering the branded drug.[1] By statute, the Paragraph IV filing constitutes an act of infringement, and provides a basis for the patentee to bring a suit for declaratory judgment of future infringement.[2] In most Hatch-Waxman disputes initiated by a Paragraph

---

follows that if Beacon would have been entitled to a jury trial in a treble damage suit against Fox it cannot be deprived of that right merely because Fox took advantage of the availability of declaratory relief to sue Beacon first.").

[18]*See, e.g., In re Tech. Licensing Corp.*, 423 F.3d at 1290 ("Thus, if the patentee seeks only equitable relief, the accused infringer has no right to a jury trial, regardless of whether the accused infringer asserts invalidity as a defense (as in the *Tegal* case) or as a separate claim (as in this case).").

[19]*See, e.g., General Motors Corp. v. California Research Corp.*, 9 F.R.D. 565, 83 U.S.P.Q. 282 (D. Del. 1949) (right to jury trial triggered in a declaratory judgment action for invalidity and non-infringement where defendant-patentee raised a counterclaim for infringement and sought damages).

[Section 4:56]

[1]*See* 21 U.S.C.A. § 355(j)(2)(A)(vii)(IV).

[2]35 U.S.C.A. § 271(e)(2) ("It shall be an act of infringement to submit (A) an [ANDA] application . . . for a drug claimed in a patent for the use of which is claimed in a patent . . . if the purpose of such submission is to obtain approval under the Act to engage in the commercial manufacture, use, or sale of a drug, veterinary biological product, or biological product claimed in a patent or the use of which is claimed in a patent before the expiration of such patent.").

IV filing, the alleged infringement is prospective only because the generic applicant has not yet commercially marketed any product. In this situation, the patentee only seeks injunctive relief because no money damages are at issue, and therefore the patentee's claim does not trigger a right to a jury trial.[3] Likewise, unless money damages are at issue, the generic-drug manufacturer does not have a right to a jury trial with respect to any counterclaims raised in response to a patentee's claim brought under § 271(e)(2)(A).[4] If the situation changes such that a patentee in a Hatch-Waxman has a claim for damages, the right to a jury trial is triggered.[5] For example, if a generic company begins commercial marketing of its product (for example, by launching a generic version of the brand drug following FDA approval, but while the litigation remains unresolved,) a patentee has a claim for infringement under § 271(a) and may seek damages, thus triggering the right to a jury trial.

The submission of an aBLA—like the submission of an ANDA—is an artificial act of infringement establishing a

---

[3]*See, e.g., Novartis Pharmaceuticals Corp. v. Roxane Laboratories, Inc.*, 2009 WL 1140440, at *1 (D.N.J. 2009) (in a Hatch-Waxman litigation, granting motion to strike patentee's jury demand because patentee's "claims arise solely from the filing of the ANDA and thus entitle [it] only to injunctive relief. It is well settled that a patentee seeking only injunctive relief does not have a right to a trial by jury."); *Glaxo Group Ltd. v. Apotex, Inc.*, 2001 WL 1246628 (N.D. Ill. 2001) (holding that, in an action brought pursuant to § 271(e)(2), neither party is entitled to a jury).

[4]*In re Apotex, Inc.*, 49 Fed. Appx. 902, 903 (Fed. Cir. 2002) (denying ANDA defendant's petition for mandamus seeking to overturn the district court's order striking its jury demand for its counterclaims for declaratory judgment of patent invalidity and non-infringement where patentee had no right to money damages under 271(e)(2)) ("We agree with the district court that under the unusual circumstances of this case, involving only possible future infringement, and in which there can be no damages because no infringing products have been marketed, the only relief that is before the district court is equitable in nature. Because the nature of the underlying controversy is entirely equitable, there can be no right to a jury trial.").

[5]*See, e.g., Minnesota Mining and Mfg. Co. v. Alphapharm Pty. Ltd.*, 2002 WL 1352426 (D. Minn. 2002) (denying patentee's motion to strike jury demand where generic company started commercial shipments of accused products); *In re Gabapentin Patent Litigation*, 503 F.3d 1254, 84 U.S.P.Q.2d 1651 (Fed. Cir. 2007) (jury trial in a Hatch-Waxman case where defendants launched at risk while litigation was pending); see also *GlaxosmithKline LLC v. Teva Pharm. USA, Inc.*, No. 1:14-cv-00878-LPS-CJB (D. Del. 2014) (jury trial in a Hatch-Waxman case where Teva had launched its generic product seven years before the case was filed).

jurisdictional basis for a patent owner to file suit.[6] Pursuant to 35 U.S.C.A. § 271(e)(2)(C), the biosimilar applicant's filing with the FDA constitutes an act of infringement, and provides a basis for the patentee to bring a suit for declaratory judgment of future infringement.[7] The BPCIA "create[s] an artificial 'act of infringement,' similar to that of 35 U.S.C.A. § 271(e)(2)(A), and [allows] infringement suits to begin based on the filing of a biosimilar application prior to FDA approval and prior to marketing of the biological product."[8] As in the Hatch-Waxman context, the alleged infringement in a BPCIA case may be prospective only where the biosimilar applicant has not yet commercially marketed any product. In this situation, the patentee typically only seeks injunctive relief because no money damages are at issue, and therefore the patentee's claim is not expected to trigger a right to a jury trial.[9]

A reference product sponsor has a claim for infringement under § 271(a) for infringing acts taken by a biosimilar applicant prior to marketing that are not covered under the "safe harbor" defense of § 271(e)(1).[10] Section 271(e)(1) creates a "safe harbor" defense for defendants when their otherwise-infringing activities are "solely for uses reasonably related to obtaining FDA approval."[11] For example, when a biosimilar applicant stockpiles commercial batches for sale

---

[6]35 U.S.C.A. § 271(e)(2)(C) ("It shall be an act of infringement to submit . . .an application seeking approval of a biological product . . . .").

[7]35 U.S.C.A. § 271(e)(2)(C).

[8]*Amgen Inc. v. Sandoz Inc.*, 877 F.3d 1315, 1321, 125 U.S.P.Q.2d 1001 (Fed. Cir. 2017).

[9]*See, e.g., Genentech, Inc. et al. v. Samsung Bioepis Co., Ltd.*, No. 1:18-cv-01363-CFC, D.I. 1 (D. Del. Sept. 4, 2018) (alleging infringement pursuant to 35 U.S.C.A. § 271(e)(1) based on submission of Samsung Bioepis's aBLA for its biosimilar trastuzumab product); *AbbVie Inc. v. Sandoz, Inc.*, C.A. No. 3:18-cv-12668-FLW-LHG D.I. 1 (D. N.J. Aug. 10, 2018) (alleging infringement pursuant to 35 U.S.C.A. § 271(e)(1) based on submission of Sandoz's aBLA for its biosimilar adalimumab product).

[10]*See Amgen Inc. v. Hospira, Inc.*, 336 F. Supp. 3d 333 (D. Del. 2018).

[11]35 U.S.C.A. § 271(e)(1) ("It shall not be an act of infringement to make, use, offer to sell, or sell within the United States or import into the United States a patented invention (other than a new animal drug or veterinary biological product (as those terms are used in the Federal Food, Drug, and Cosmetic Act and the Act of March 4, 1913) which is primarily manufactured using recombinant DNA, recombinant RNA, hybridoma technology, or other processes involving site specific genetic manipulation techniques) solely for uses reasonably related to the development and submission of information under a Federal law which regulates the

after FDA approval, its activities may not fall within the "safe harbor" of § 271(e)(1).[12] In that situation, the RPS may have a claim for a damages for infringing activity and its right to a jury trial may be triggered.[13]

The right to a jury trial in a BPCIA litigation is also triggered when the RPS has a claim for infringement under § 271(a) and may seek damages for ongoing and past infringement. For example, a reference product sponsor has a claim for infringement under § 271(a) if a biosimilar applicant were to begin commercial marketing of its biosimilar product.[14] Thus, if a biosimilar applicant were to obtain FDA approval for its product and launch its product prior to patent resolution, the RPS may allege infringement under § 271(a) and seek damages, triggering a right to a jury trial on infringement and validity of the patents at issue.

§ 4:57   Right to a jury trial—General overview—Right to jury trial in biosimilar v. biosimilar patent cases

A biosimilar company may also assert its patents against another biosimilar company. For these types of case, the submission of an aBLA does not provide an artificial act of infringement establishing a jurisdictional basis for a patent

---

manufacture, use, or sale of drugs or veterinary biological products.").

[12]*See, e.g., Amgen*, 336 F. Supp. 3d at 345 (concluding that substantive evidence supported the jury verdict that some batches manufactured by Amgen were not covered by the safe harbor defense); see also *Genentech, Inc. v. Pfizer, Inc.*, No. 1:19-cv-00638-CFC (D. Del. 2019) (demanding a jury trial in case involving a bevacizumab biosimilar, and alleging that "Pfizer's pre-expiration manufacture and/or use of its aBLA product was not protected by the "safe harbor" provision of 35 U.S.C.A. § 271(e)(1)").

[13]*See, e.g., Amgen Inc. v. Hospira, Inc.*, 336 F. Supp. 3d 333, 345 (D. Del. 2018); *Genentech, Inc. et al. v. Pfizer, Inc.*, No. 1:19-cv-00638-CFC, D.I. 1 at 10 (D. Del. Apr. 5, 2019) (seeking a jury trial, and alleging infringement under 271(a) of Pfizer's bevacizumab biosimilar, and that "Pfizer's pre-expiration manufacture and/or use of its aBLA product was not protected by the 'safe harbor provision of 35 U.S.C.A. § 271(e)(1)"); *Merck KGaA v. Integra Lifesciences I, Ltd.*, 545 U.S. 193, 125 S. Ct. 2372, 162 L. Ed. 2d 160, 74 U.S.P.Q.2d 1801 (2005) (clarifying the legal standard).

[14]*See Minnesota Mining and Mfg. Co. v. Alphapharm Pty. Ltd.*, 2002 WL 1352426 (D. Minn. 2002).

owner to file suit.[1] Rather, a biosimilar company may bring suit against another biosimilar company, alleging infringement under 35 U.S.C.A. § 271(a) to (c), (f), and/or (g). A party's right to a jury trial will depend on whether any legal remedies are sought. For example, Coherus filed a patent infringement complaint against Amgen alleging that the commercial manufacture of Amgen's biosimilar Amgevita in the United States for the European market constitutes an act of infringement under 35 U.S.C.A. § 271(a), which warrants an award of damages.[2] Coherus seeks a jury trial on "all issues so triable."[3]

VI. PRELIMINARY INJUNCTIONS

§ 4:58 Preliminary injunctions

To obtain a preliminary injunction, the plaintiff-patentee must establish that: 1) it is likely to succeed on the merits of its claims; 2) it is likely to suffer irreparable harm in the absence of preliminary injunctive relief; 3) the balance of equities favors the plaintiff; and 4) the preliminary injunction is in the public interest.[1] Because of the "extraordinary nature" preliminary injunctive relief, "the patentee carries the burden of showing likelihood of success on the merits with respect to the [asserted] patent's validity, enforceability, and infringement."[2] That is, although the burden of establishing invalidity or unenforceability normally rests on the patent challenger, it is the patentee's burden in seeking a preliminary injunction to show both that "it will likely prove infringement" and that "any challenges to the validity and

---

[Section 4:57]

[1]35 U.S.C.A. § 271(e)(2)(C) ("It shall be an act of infringement to submit . . . an application seeking approval of a biological product . . . .").

[2]*See Coherus Biosciences, Inc. v. Amgen Inc.*, No. 1:19-cv-00139-RGA D.I. 7 (D. Del. Mar. 5, 2019.

[3]*Coherus Biosciences*, No. 1:19-cv-00139-RGA D.I. 7 (D. Del. Mar. 5, 2019).

[Section 4:58]

[1]*E.g., Winter v. Natural Resources Defense Council, Inc.*, 555 U.S. 7, 20, 129 S. Ct. 365, 172 L. Ed. 2d 249, 67 Env't. Rep. Cas. (BNA) 1225 (2008).

[2]*Nutrition 21 v. U.S.*, 930 F.2d 867, 869, 18 U.S.P.Q.2d 1347 (Fed. Cir. 1991).

enforceability of its patent lack substantial merit."[3] Although no one factor is dispositive, "no injunction will issue, temporary or otherwise, unless the movant 'establishes both . . . likelihood of success on the merits and irreparable harm.'"[4]

Second wave BPCIA litigation can begin once an applicant has provided its notice of commercial marketing under Section 262(*l*)(8)(A). A biosimilar applicant must give notice of commercial marketing at least 180 days prior to the date on which it intends to launch its biosimilar product.[5] In the second wave litigation that follows such notice, the RPS can seek a preliminary injunction to prevent the launch of the biosimilar product during the pendency of the litigation.[6] In this way, the 180-day timeframe under Section 262(*l*)(8)(A) provides a period of time in which preliminary injunction proceedings can be completed before the district court prior to the time that the biosimilar may launch.[7]

---

[3]*Anton / Bauer, Inc. v. PAG, Ltd.*, 329 F.3d 1343, 1348, 66 U.S.P.Q.2d 1675 (Fed. Cir. 2003); *see also Titan Tire Corp. v. Case New Holland, Inc.*, 566 F.3d 1372, 1380, 90 U.S.P.Q.2d 1918 (Fed. Cir. 2009).

[4]*Otsuka Pharmaceutical Co., Ltd. v. Torrent Pharmaceuticals Ltd., Inc.*, 99 F. Supp. 3d 461, 475 (D.N.J. 2015).

[5]*Supra* Section 4:23, discussing timing of NCM.

[6]*AbbVie Inc. v. Boehringer Ingelheim International GmbH*, 2019 WL 917990, *2 (D. Del. 2019) ("A 'sponsor'—the manufacturer of the patented drug, or 'reference drug'—can begin second wave litigation once the applicant has provided 180 days' notice of its intent to commercially launch its biosimilar product. As part of second wave litigation, the sponsor can seek a preliminary injunction to prevent the launch of the biosimilar. Before the 180-day notice is filed, a preliminary injunction is off the table.").

[7]*Amgen Inc. v. Sandoz Inc.*, 877 F.3d 1315, 1321, 125 U.S.P.Q.2d 1001 (Fed. Cir. 2017) ("Subsection 262(*l*) also provides that the applicant give notice of commercial marketing to the RPS at least 180 days prior to commercial marketing of its product licensed under subsection (k). The RPS thus has a period of time to seek a preliminary injunction . . ."); *Amgen Inc. v. Apotex Inc.*, 827 F.3d 1052, 1063, 119 U.S.P.Q.2d 1318 (Fed. Cir. 2016) ("The 180-day period gives the reference product sponsor time to assess its infringement position for the final the FDA-approved product as to yet-to-be-litigated patents. And if there is such litigation, it gives the parties and the district court the time for adjudicating such matters without the reliability-reducing rush that would attend requests for relief against immediate market entry that could cause irreparable injury. This is evident on the face of § 262(*l*). And the Biologics Act's legislative history confirms the aim to avoid the uncertainties and deficiencies associated with a process in which requests for temporary restraining orders and preliminary injunctions are presented and adjudicated on short notice.");

Preliminary injunctions in second wave BPCIA litigations, but not first wave litigation, are governed by Section 262(*l*)(8)(B) of the statute, which provides:

Preliminary injunction

After receiving the notice under subparagraph (A) and before such date of the first commercial marketing of such biological product, the reference product sponsor may seek a preliminary injunction prohibiting the subsection (k) applicant from engaging in the commercial manufacture or sale of such biological product until the court decides the issue of patent validity, enforcement, and infringement with respect to any patent that is-

(i) included in the list provided by the reference product sponsor under paragraph (3)(A) or in the list provided by the subsection (k) applicant under paragraph (3)(B); and

(ii) not included, as applicable, on-

(I) the list of patents described in paragraph (4); or

(II) the lists of patents described in paragraph (5)(B).[8]

Pursuant to Section 262(*l*)(8)(B), an RPS may seek a preliminary injunction with respect to patents that were included on the parties' Section 262(*l*)(3) lists, but that were not included on the Section 262(*l*)(4) and (*l*)(5)(B) lists and therefore were not asserted in the phase one litigation.[9]

Section 262(*l*)(8)(B) does not address patents that are is-

___

Abbvie Inc. v. Boehringer Ingelheim International GmbH, 2019 WL 917990, *2 (D. Del. 2019) ("The 180-day notice requirement . . . is designed to avoid a preliminary injunction proceeding unless one is needed, that is, because a commercial launch is planned in six months. It is also designed to provide a reasonable period of 180 days within which to resolve the preliminary injunction, rather than the usual highly compressed time schedule forced on the parties and court by a commercial launch.").

[8]42 U.S.C.A. § 262(*l*)(8)(B).

[9]*See Sandoz*, 137 S. Ct. at 1672 ("In this second phase of litigation, . . . prior to the date of first commercial marketing, the sponsor may 'seek a preliminary injunction prohibiting the [biosimilar] applicant from engaging in the commercial manufacture or sale of [the biosimilar] until the court decides the issue of patent validity, enforcement, and infringement with respect to any patent that' was included on the § 262(*l*)(3) lists but not litigated in the first phase. § 262(*l*)(8)(B)." (quoting 42 U.S.C.A. § 262(*l*)(8)(B))); *Amgen Inc. v. Apotex Inc.*, 827 F.3d 1052, 1056–57, 119 U.S.P.Q.2d 1318 (Fed. Cir. 2016) ("[T]he Biologics Act . . . provides, in paragraph (8), for a second stage of patent litigation. Paragraph (8) does so by first requiring, in (8)(A), that the applicant give the reference product sponsor notice at least 180 days before commercially marketing its 'licensed' product. . . . (8)(B) then declares that, after receiving the (8)(A) [ ] notice but before the applicant's commercial marketing begins, the ref-

sued to or licensed by the RPS after the patent list exchanges during the patent dance. Instead, newly issued or licensed patents are addressed by Section 262(*l*)(7), which provides:

> Newly issued or licensed patents
>
> In the case of a patent that-
>
> (A) is issued to, or exclusively licensed by, the reference product sponsor after the date that the reference product sponsor provided the list to the subsection (k) applicant under paragraph (3)(A); and
>
> (B) the reference product sponsor reasonably believes that, due to the issuance of such patent, a claim of patent infringement could reasonably be asserted by the reference product sponsor if a person not licensed by the reference product sponsor engaged in the making, using, offering to sell, selling, or importing into the United States of the biological product that is the subject of the subsection (k) application,
>
> not later than 30 days after such issuance or licensing, the reference product sponsor shall provide to the subsection (k) applicant a supplement to the list provided by the reference product sponsor under paragraph (3)(A) that includes such patent, not later than 30 days after such supplement is provided, the subsection (k) applicant shall provide a statement to the reference product sponsor in accordance with paragraph (3)(B), and such patent shall be subject to paragraph (8).[10]

That is, an RPS may seek a preliminary injunction in second wave litigation on newly issued or licensed patents, as well as the patents expressly described by Section 262(*l*)(8)(B).[11]

---

erence product sponsor may seek a preliminary injunction based on any patent within either of two classes. The first class, expressly described in (8)(B), consists of the patents that appeared on any of the original paragraph (3) lists, minus patents that were the subject of paragraph (6) litigation (by agreement under (4) or by the narrowing process under (5)).").

[10]42 U.S.C.A. § 262(*l*)(7).

[11]*Amgen Inc. v. Sandoz Inc.*, 877 F.3d 1315, 1321, 125 U.S.P.Q.2d 1001 (Fed. Cir. 2017) ("The RPS thus has a period of time to seek a preliminary injunction based on patents that the parties initially identified during information exchange, but which were not selected for an immediate infringement action, as well as any newly issued or licensed patents (collectively, 'non-listed patents')."); *Amgen Inc. v. Apotex Inc.*, 827 F.3d 1052, 1056–57, 119 U.S.P.Q.2d 1318 (Fed. Cir. 2016) ("[T]he Biologics Act . . . provides, in paragraph (8), for a second stage of patent litigation. Paragraph (8) does so by first requiring, in (8)(A), that the applicant give the reference product sponsor notice at least 180 days before commercially marketing its 'licensed' product. . . . (8)(B) then declares that, after receiving the (8)(A) [ ] notice but before the applicant's commercial marketing begins, the reference product sponsor may seek a preliminary injunction

If the RPS seeks a preliminary injunction pursuant to Section 262(l)(8)(B), the statute provides that the RPS and the biosimilar applicant "shall reasonably cooperate to expedite such further discovery as is needed in connection with the preliminary injunction motion."[12] This discovery may include documents concerning the sales and profits for the biologic and other financials, the extent to which the biologic has planned and prepared for biosimilar market entry, and public interest factors, as well as depositions of any witnesses, both fact and expert, who provide declarations in support of the parties' briefing in the preliminary injunction proceeding.

As noted above, these statutory provisions are silent as to, and therefore appear not to control, the extent to which a preliminary injunction may be available for patents that were asserted in first wave litigation but for which there has not yet been a resolution on the merits of patent infringement, validity, or enforceability. In other words, if first wave litigation is still pending at the time the biosimilar applicant provides notice of commercial marketing, the RPS may be able to seek a preliminary injunction from the court on first wave patents.

VII. SCHEDULING AND STAGING

§ 4:59 General scheduling & staging

Like other civil litigation in federal district courts, BPCIA litigation is governed by the Federal Rules of Civil Procedure, which dictate to some extent the procedures that district courts must adhere to in scheduling and staging the case. Regardless of the district in which a given case is pending, BPCIA patent cases normally include certain phases: (1) pleadings; (2) claim construction; (3) fact discovery; (4) expert

---

based on any patent within either of two classes. . . . The second class consists of certain patents that were issued to or exclusively licensed by the reference product sponsor after it gave the applicant its (3)(A) list. As to those patents, paragraph (7) prescribes an information exchange and states that they 'shall be subject to paragraph (8)'—which evidently means that patents within (7) are to be treated as falling under (8)(B)." (citations omitted)).

[12]42 U.S.C.A. § 262(l)(8)(C); *see Amgen Inc. v. Apotex Inc.*, 827 F.3d 1052, 1057, 119 U.S.P.Q.2d 1318 (Fed. Cir. 2016) ("For this second-stage litigation, (8)(C) requires that the parties reasonably cooperate to expedite new discovery needed in connection with the preliminary-injunction motion.").

discovery; (5) pre-trial; (6) trial; (7) post-trial; and (8) appeal.[1] The exact schedule adopted in a given case, and the timing and order of deadlines in that schedule can be affected by a number of factors, including the district in which the case is pending, the specific judge assigned to the case, the number of asserted patents, the expiration dates of the asserted patents, whether the aBLA filer has launched its product, and whether a safe harbor defense has been asserted. The length of time from the filing of the complaint to the scheduled trial varies by case, but can be as short as 14 months[2] or as long as 39 months.[3]

BPCIA patent suits are initiated by the filing of a complaint by a plaintiff.[4] Thereafter, the case is assigned to a judge in the district where the lawsuit was filed. The plaintiff must then serve the complaint on the defendant or request that the defendant waive service of the complaint.[5] After the complaint is served, the judge who is assigned the case must issue a scheduling order as soon as practicable, but unless the judge finds good cause for delay, the judge must issue the scheduling order within the earlier of 90 days after any defendant has been served with the complaint or 60 days after any defendant has entered an appearance.[6] While some case deadlines are directly dictated by the Federal Rules of Civil Procedure (e.g., time for the defendant to answer the complaint[7]), the scheduling order issued by the judge must contain certain other deadlines that are not specifically recited in the Federal Rules of Civil Procedure: (i) limit the

---

[Section 4:59]

[1]aBLA cases may also include preliminary injunction proceedings. *See e.g., Genentech, Inc. et al. v. Celltrion, Inc. et al.*, No. 1:18-cv-00574-RMB-KMW, D.I. 78 (D. N.J. Aug. 8, 2018); *Amgen Inc., et al. v. Sandoz Inc., et al.*, No. 3:14-cv-04741-RS, D.I. 55 (N.D. Cal. Feb. 5, 2015).

[2]*Janssen Biotech, Inc. v. Celltrion Healthcare Co., Ltd. et al.*, No. 1:17-cv-11008-MLW, D.I. 176 (D. Mass. Feb. 15, 2018).

[3]*AbbVie Inc. et al v. Amgen Inc. et al.*, No. 1:16-cv-00666-MSG, D.I. 26 (D. Del. Nov. 17, 2016).

[4]Fed. R. Civ. P. 3.

[5]*See* Fed. R. Civ. P. 4(c) to (d).

[6]Fed. R. Civ. P. 16(b)(2).

[7]Fed. R. Civ. P. 12(a)(1)(a) (a defendant must serve an answer to the complaint "(i) within 21 days after being served with the summons and complaint; or (ii) if it has timely waived service under Rule 4(d), within 60 days after the request for a waiver was sent, or within 90 days after it was sent to the defendant outside any judicial district of the United States.")

time to join other parties; (ii) amend the pleadings; (iii) complete discovery; and (iv) file motions.[8] The scheduling order may also contain other provisions such as: (i) modify the timing of initial disclosures under Rules 26(a) and 26(e)(1); (ii) modify the extent of discovery; (iii) provide for disclosure, discovery, or preservation of electronically stored information; (iv) include any agreements the parties reach for asserting claims of privilege or of protection as trial-preparation material after information is produced, including agreements reached under Federal Rule of Evidence 502; (v) direct that before moving for an order relating to discovery, the movant must request a conference with the court; (vi) set dates for pretrial conferences and for trial; and (vii) include other appropriate matters.[9]

As mentioned above, the exact schedule adopted in a given case is dictated by the district court judge who has been assigned the case. For example, each of the four judges in the District of Delaware—a district that has been the venue for a number of biosimilars patent cases[10]—have model scheduling orders for patent cases. Chief Judge Stark's model scheduling order[11] includes deadlines and procedures for the following:

- Initial Disclosures under FRCP 26(a)(1)
- Joinder of Parties and Amendment of Pleadings
- Application to the Court for Protective Order
- Disclosure of Accused Product and Asserted Patents with Initial Infringement Claim Chart
- Initial and Final Invalidity Contentions
- Final Infringement Contentions
- Fact Discovery Limits for Depositions, Requests for Admission, and Interrogatories
- Substantial Completion of Document Production
- Fact Discovery Cut-off
- Expert Report Procedure and Deadlines
- Expert Discovery Cut-off

---

[8]Fed. R. Civ. P. 16(b)(3)(A).

[9]Fed. R. Civ. P. 16(b)(3)(B).

[10]*See, e.g., AbbVie Inc.*, No. 1:16-cv-00666-MSG; *Genentech, Inc. et al v. Pfizer, Inc.*, No. 1:17-cv-01672-CFC; *Amgen Inc. et al. vs. Hospira, Inc. et al.*, No. 1:18-cv-01064-CFC.

[11]Chief Judge Leonard P. Stark Patent Scheduling Order, available at https://www.ded.uscourts.gov/sites/ded/files/LPS-PatentSchedOrder-Non-A NDA.pdf.

- Claim Construction Procedure and Briefing Schedule
- Claim Construction Hearing Date
- Case Dispositive Motion and Daubert Motion Procedure and Briefing Schedule
- Case Dispositive Motion Hearing Date
- Final Pre-trial Order Procedure and Schedule
- Final Pre-trial Hearing
- Jury Instruction, Voir Dire, and Verdict Form Procedure and Schedule
- Trial Date and Length of Trial
- Post-Trial Motions

After the filing of the complaint, but prior to the entry of the scheduling order, the parties must confer as soon as practicable, and in any event at least 21 days before a scheduling conference is to be held or a scheduling order is due under Rule 16(b).[12] During the conference, the parties must consider the nature and basis of their claims and defenses and the possibilities for promptly settling or resolving the case; make or arrange for the disclosures required by Rule 26(a)(1), which is discussed below; discuss any issues about preserving discoverable information; and develop a proposed discovery plan.[13] A party must make Rule 26(a) initial disclosures at or within 14 days after the parties' Rule 26(f) conference unless a different time is set by stipulation or court order, or unless a party objects during the Rule 26(f) conference.[14]

The Rule 26(a) initial disclosures must contain the following information: (i) the name and, if known, the address and telephone number of each individual likely to have discoverable information—along with the subjects of that information—that the disclosing party may use to support its claims or defenses, unless the use would be solely for impeachment; (ii) a copy—or a description by category and location—of all documents, electronically stored information, and tangible things that the disclosing party has in its possession, custody, or control and may use to support its claims or defenses, unless the use would be solely for impeachment; (iii) a computation of each category of damages claimed by the disclosing party—who must also make available for inspec-

---

[12]Fed. R. Civ. P. 26(f)(1).

[13]Fed. R. Civ. P. 26(f)(2).

[14]Fed. R. Civ. P. 26(a)(1)(C).

tion and copying as under Rule 34 the documents or other evidentiary material, unless privileged or protected from disclosure, on which each computation is based, including materials bearing on the nature and extent of injuries suffered; and (iv) for inspection and copying as under Rule 34, any insurance agreement under which an insurance business may be liable to satisfy all or part of a possible judgment in the action or to indemnify or reimburse for payments made to satisfy the judgment.[15]

§ 4:60 BPCIA scheduling issues

In order to manage cases, however, courts have sometimes ordered parties to narrow the number of patents asserted as the case progresses.[1] Some BLA holders have challenged the

---

[15]Fed. R. Civ. P. 26(a)(1)(A).

[Section 4:60]

[1]In *Genentech v. Amgen*, Genentech filed a complaint asserting infringement of 26 patents. Genentech, Inc. and City of Hope v. Amgen, Inc., C.A. No. 17-1407-GMS, Complaint (D.I. 2) (D. Del. Oct. 6, 2017). In a Scheduling Order, Judge Sleet directed the plaintiff Genentech to reduce the number of asserted patents from 26 to no more than eight within six months of the scheduling order—and prior to claim construction proceedings. *See* Initial Scheduling Order, Genentech, Inc. et al. v. Amgen, Inc., C.A. No. 17-1407-GMS (D. Del. Apr. 13, 2018). Genentech further agreed to identify no more than 20 claims for claim construction and trial. Proposed Scheduling Order, Genentech, Inc. et al. v. Amgen, Inc., C.A. No. 17-1407-GMS (D. Del. May 8, 2018). In order to determine which patents to proceed with in the litigation, Genentech suggested an "an initial phase of discovery" whereby Genentech could take discovery on Amgen regarding its manufacturing process, including depositions. Joint Status Report at p. 19-20, Genentech, Inc. et al. v. Amgen, Inc., C.A. No. 17-1407-GMS (D. Del. Feb. 12, 2018).

In *Genentech, Inc. et al v. Pfizer, Inc.*, Genentech filed a complaint asserting infringement of 40 patents. Complaint, Genentech, Inc. et al v. Pfizer, Inc., C.A. No. 17-1672 (D. Del. Nov. 17, 2017). In an initial joint status report, Pfizer asserted that Genentech did not have a reasonable basis to allege infringement for numerous patents in its complaint. Joint Status Report at p. 6, Genentech, Inc. et al v. Pfizer, Inc., C.A. No. 17-1672 (D. Del. Feb. 12, 2018). In the same joint status report, Genentech stated that it believed that it had a reasonable basis for asserting the patents based upon the information that it had available to it at the time, but expected to be able to reduce the number of asserted patents based upon information subsequently provided pursuant to the parties' exchanges under the BPCIA. Joint Status Report at p. 6. In the joint status report, the parties agreed that were engaging in the exchanges of information provided under the BPCIA and that they believe that they will be in a position to reduce the number of asserted patents when the parties complete

constitutionality of being ordered to limit the number of patents asserted in a given case.[2]

The BPCIA does not include any provision whereby an aBLA filer is automatically estopped from launching a biosimilar product while the litigation proceeds. Therefore, in order to stop the launch of a biosimilar product during litigation, a plaintiff may file a preliminary injunction[3] requesting that the court enjoin an aBLA filer from launching its biosimilar product while the litigation proceeds.[4] Preliminary injunction proceedings usually include: (1) an opening brief in support of the motion for preliminary injunction with supporting evidence; (2) a responsive brief in opposition to motion for preliminary injunction with supporting evidence; (3) a reply brief in support of the motion for preliminary injunction with supporting evidence; (4) depositions of witnesses; and (5) preliminary injunction hearing.[5] Preliminary injunction proceedings are often expedited, and can be completed in as little as one month.[6]

In some BPCIA litigations, defendants have asserted that their pre-marketing manufacturing activity is protected by

---

their exchanges under the BPCIA and proposed deadlines in the schedule to facilitate narrowing the number of asserted patents. Joint Status Report at p. 6. Once those exchanges were completed, Genentech dismissed 20 of the asserted patents. Stipulation and Proposed Order of Dismissal with Respect to Certain Asserted Patents, Genentech, Inc. et al v. Pfizer, Inc., C.A. No. 17-1672 (D. Del. Mar. 23, 2018).

[2]*See e.g.,* Letter to Court re: Scheduling Order, Genentech, Inc., et al. v. Amgen Inc., C.A. Nos. 17-1407-GMS, 17-1471-GMS (D. Del. May 2, 2018) (Genentech stated that it "has been given little more than four months (and no assurance of sufficient discovery) to evaluate the infringement of its 26 asserted patents, and on that highly compressed basis dismiss 18 asserted patents from this case concerning the protection of its multi-billion dollar cancer treatment, Avastin," and "[a]bsent Genentech's consent to this case management order, it is plainly unconstitutional, as an order prohibiting assertion of unique patent claims violates the patentee's due process rights.")

[3]*See* Fed. R. Civ. P. 65(a).

[4]*See e.g.,* Preliminary Injunction Schedule, Genentech, Inc. et al. v. Celltrion, Inc. et al., C.A. No. 18-574 (RMB) (KMW) (D.N.J. Aug. 8, 2018); Preliminary Injunction Scheduling Order, Amgen Inc., et al. v. Sandoz Inc., et al., C.A. No. 14-4741-RS (N.D. Cal. Feb. 5, 2015).

[5]*See e.g.,* Preliminary Injunction Schedule, Genentech, Inc. et al. v. Celltrion, Inc. et al., C.A. No. 18-574 (RMB) (KMW) (D.N.J. Aug. 8, 2018); Preliminary Injunction Scheduling Order, Amgen Inc., et al. v. Sandoz Inc., et al., C.A. No. 14-4741-RS (N.D. Cal. Feb. 5, 2015).

[6]*See e.g.,* Preliminary Injunction Scheduling Order, Amgen Inc., et al. v. Sandoz Inc., et al., C.A. No. 14-4741-RS (N.D. Cal. Feb. 5, 2015).

the 35 U.S.C.A. § 271(e)(1) "safe harbor" and therefore the plaintiff is not entitled to any damages for pre-marketing manufacturing activities.[7] In some cases, courts have ordered early discovery and summary judgment briefing to determine whether the safe harbor applies to the pre-marketing manufacturing activities in that case, and whether plaintiffs can seek damages for that manufacturing activity.[8]

VIII.   DISCOVERY ISSUES IN BPCIA LITIGATIONS

§ 4:61   General scope of discovery

Discovery in BPCIA litigations generally follows the same procedures as any other patent litigation, particularly Hatch-Waxman litigations, including production of documents, written discovery, and depositions, that are tailored to the patent(s)-in-dispute. Disputes specific to issues arising in BPCIA cases, however, have arisen over a variety of issues, including the discoverability of information regarding biological manufacturing processes (both of the RPS and applicant), documents exchanged during patent dances preceding other BPCIA litigations where one or more of the same patents are at issue, and the statutorily-required expedited production of documents in the event that that RPS moves for a preliminary injunction. Like Hatch-Waxman litigations, parties in a BPCIA litigation may also dispute the general scope of discovery, the terms of protective order, and

---

[7]If a plaintiff is not entitled to seek damages in the case, then a jury trial is not available.

[8]*See e.g.,* Initial Scheduling Order, Genentech, Inc. et al. v. Amgen, Inc., C.A. No. 17-1407-GMS (D. Del. Apr. 13, 2018) ("The parties shall make all reasonable efforts to cooperate with one another to complete all fact discovery necessary to . . . to enable the court to make an early determination as to whether Genentech will be permitted to seek damages for conduct by Amgen described in Genentech's complaint, which conduct Amgen asserts was protected under the safe harbor provisions of Section 271 of the Patent Act, and whether it is entitled to a jury trial regarding the alleged infringing conduct."); Scheduling Order, Genentech, Inc., et al. v. Amgen Inc., C.A. Nos. 17-1407-GMS, 17-1471-GMS (D. Del. May 18, 2018) (ordering that Defendant may file "a summary judgment motion solely directed to the availability of damages for Plaintiffs' claims for infringement arising from Defendant's manufacturing activities and whether Plaintiffs are entitled to a jury trial" and limiting the summary judgment briefing to "availability of such damages claims (*e.g.,* whether Plaintiffs have satisfied the marking statute and whether Amgen's alleged manufacturing activities are protected under the safe harbor provisions of Section 271 of the Patent Act) and shall not address the quantum of damages.")

the discoverability of settlement agreements from related cases.

Just as would be the case in a Hatch-Waxman litigation, the scope of discovery in a BPCIA litigation is generally reflective of the number of patents-at-issue, as well as the what the asserted claims cover. Although in some cases the RPS has asserted a small number of patents,[1] in others cases the RPS has asserted 40 or more patents.[2] Courts have taken this into account when determining the scope of discovery and may set limits that go beyond what would be appropriate in a case with fewer asserted patents when the scope of discovery is disputed. For example, one court (in a case involving eight patents) allowed "275 hours of depositions for 50 depositions for each party."[3] On the other hand, courts have also been cognizant of the practicalities of trying these cases and have, for example, required parties to reduce the number of topics noticed for a corporate deposition under FRCP 30(b)(6)[4].

[Section 4:61]

[1]*See e.g.,* Janssen Biotech, Inc. v. Samsung Bioepis Co. Ltd., 4:17-cv-3524 (D.N.J.) (filed complaint alleging infringement of three patents); Janssen Biotech, Inc. v. Samsung Bioepis Co. Ltd., 3:17-cv-11008 (D. Mass.) (filed complaint alleging infringement of one patent); Amgen, Inc. v. Hospira, Inc., 15-cv-00839 (D. Del.) (filed complaint alleging infringement of two patents).

[2]*See e.g.,* AbbVie Inc. v. Amgen Inc., 16-cv-00666 (D. Del.) (filed complaint alleging infringement 60 patents); AbbVie, Inc. v. Boehringer Ingelheim Int'l GmbH, 17-cv-01065 (D. Del) (filed complaint alleging infringement of 74 patents); AbbVie, Inc. v. Sandoz, Inc., 5:18-cv-12668 (D. N.J.) (filed complaint alleging infringement of 84 patents); Genentech, Inc. v. Pfizer Inc., 17-cv-1672 (D. Del.) (filed complaint alleging infringement of 40 patents).

[3]AbbVie, Inc. v. Boehringer Ingelheim Int'l GMBH, 17-cv-01065, D.I. 190 (D. Del. September 6, 2018).

[4]In *Genentech, Inc. v. Amgen Inc.*, in an effort to narrow the number of patents asserted, the parties agreed Genentech would issue a 30(b)(6) deposition notice and Amgen would provide one or more witness to address the topics. 17-cv-1407, D.I. 155 at 2 (D. Del. Aug. 2, 2018). Genentech's first deposition notice included 236 topics. 17-cv-1407, D.I. 155 at 2. Shortly after the 30(b)(6) deposition was noticed the parties appeared for the court to address ongoing discovery disputes. 17-cv-1407, D.I. 155 at 2. At that time, Amgen informed the court it was "unworkable" to prepare a witness for that many topics. Genentech was ordered to pare down the list and ultimately the Court found 49 topics were appropriate in scope and breath. D.I. 155 at 2–4.

§ 4:62   Discovery of manufacturing information

In most, if not all, BPCIA cases, the RPS asserts one or more manufacturing-related patents.[1] In contrast to Hatch-Waxman litigations, this is somewhat unique to BPCIA litigations. Starting before litigation formally began, during what is called the "patent dance"[2] and extending into the discovery period, RPSs have sought discovery of manufacturing information to evaluate infringement of the patents-in-suit and also to assess the potential infringement of non-asserted patents. Discovery disputes often arise regarding the scope of relevant manufacturing information.

Although in cases where manufacturing-related patents are asserted, information regarding the applicants' manufacturing process is generally discoverable, courts have recognized the proprietary nature of this information and have limited its discoverability based on the issues in the case. For example, an RPS's assertion of manufacturing patents likely will not open the door to broad discovery of all manufacturing information. Where the asserted patents are limited to a specific manufacturing step, courts will likely tailor discovery to the specific step(s) at issue.[3] Furthermore, courts likely will not compel discovery of manufacturing information solely related to patents that the patentee did not

---

[Section 4:62]

[1]*See e.g.,* Genentech Inc. v. Amgen Inc., 17-cv-0140 (D. Del.); Genentech Inc. v. Amgen Inc., 17-cv-01471 (D. Del.); Genentech Inc. v. Pfizer Inc. , 17-cv-01672 (D. Del.); Genentech Inc. v. Sandoz Inc., 17-cv-13507 (D. N.J); Genentech Inc. v. Celltrion Inc., 18-cv-00095 (D. Del.); Genentech Inc. v. Celltrion Inc., 18-cv-01025 (D. Del.); Genentech Inc. v. Celltrion Inc., 18-cv-00574 (D. N.J.); Genentech Inc. v. Amgen Inc., 18-cv-00924 (D. Del.); Genentech Inc. v. Celltrion Inc., 18-cv-11553 (D. N.J.); AbbVie Inc. v. Amgen Inc., 16-cv-00666 (D. Del.); AbbVie v. Sandoz Inc., 5:18-cv-12668 (D. N.J.); AbbVie v. Boehringer Ingelheim Int'l GmbH, 17-cv-01065 (D. Del.); Janssen Biotech Inc. v. Celltrion Healthcare Co., Ltd., 16-cv-11008 (D. Mass.).

[2]*Supra* Sections 4:3 to 4:20, discussing the patent dance

[3]Amgen Inc. v. Sandoz, 5:14-cv-04741, D.I. 266 (N.D. Cal. Aug. 4, 2017) Amgen sought discovery of information related to Sandoz's, the aBLA applicant, plans to respond to the FDA's Complete Response Letter, including information related to all aspects of Sandoz's manufacturing process. Sandoz argued that only information related to the manufacturing step allegedly covered by the asserted claims should be discoverable. The Court held that Amgen was only entitled to the changes in manufacturing as they related to the asserted claims, noting that "Amgen offere[ed] no reason as to why limited discovery as to changes or modifications to the AEX step does not suffice.").

list in its 3(A) statement[4] and then asserted in the ensuing litigation, even where the RPS alleges that the applicant improperly withheld manufacturing information during the patent dance.[5]

There are also scenarios where an aBLA applicant may be entitled to discovery of manufacturing information from the patentee.[6] Information related to the patentee's manufacturing process, is potentially relevant to comparisons to the prior art, secondary considerations of non-obviousness, and the existence of non-infringing alternatives.[7]

§ 4:63   Discovery of information from litigations concerning the same biological product or one or more overlapping patents-in-suit

In the BPCIA context, there have often been multiple parallel litigations that involved the same biologic product or overlapping asserted patents.[1] These parallel proceedings raise the issue of what information from these related

---

[4]*Supra* Section 4:14, regarding RPS's Section 262(*l*)(3)(A) statement.

[5]*Supra* Section 4:5, regarding applicant's production manufacturing information; *see* Amgen, Inc. v. Hospira Inc., 15-cv-00839, D.I. 47 (D. Del. May 8, 2016) (Amgen sought discovery of manufacturing information unrelated to any patents in its 3(A) statement. Because the manufacturing process was not relevant to the asserted claims, defenses or counterclaims, the district court found Amgen was precluded from seeking any discovery related to the unlisted manufacturing patents); *see also Amgen Inc. v. Hospira, Inc.*, 866 F.3d 1355, 123 U.S.P.Q.2d 1697 (Fed. Cir. 2017) (finding the Court lacked jurisdiction over Amgen's appeal under the collateral order doctrine).

[6]Amgen Inc., , v. Sandoz Inc.,., 5:14-cv-04741, D.I. 165 (N.D. Cal. Mar. 14, 2016) (Court ordering Amgen to produce documents related to purification of Neupogen as well as documents related to the "Chemistry, Manufacturing and Controls ("CMC") sections from its regulatory submissions for each approved or unapproved product for which Amgen has used a process claimed in an asserted patent."); *see also* AbbVie Inc. v. Boehringer Ingelheim Int'l GMBH, 17-cv-01065, D.I. 82, 101, 110 (D. Del. 2018) (where Boehringer Ingelheim moved to compel production of documents related, in part, to the manufacturing of AbbVie's biologic. The court granted Boehringer Ingelheim's request stating it was reasonably related to their on sale defense. D.I. 110.

[7]Amgen Inc. v. Sandoz Inc., 5:14-cv-04741, D.I. 163 at 2 (N.D. Cal. Mar. 14, 2016).

[Section 4:63]

[1]*See e.g.,* Janssen Biotech, Inc. v. Celltrion Healthcare Co., Ltd., 17-cv-11008 (D. Mass) and Janssen Biotech Inc. v. Samsung Bioepis Co. Ltd., 4:17-cv-3524 (D.N.J.) (both involving Janssen's biologic REMICADE®); and AbbVie Inc. v. Amgen Inc., 16-cv-00666 (D. Del); AbbVie Inc. v.

proceedings is discoverable. Thus far, courts have addressed three categories of information that may be discoverable from parallel litigations: manufacturing information of other aBLA filers, 3(B) and 3(C) statements[2] exchanged during the "patent dance," and settlement agreements.

In seeking information from a related litigation, an aBLA applicant may try to compel a non-party to produce documents and even provide a witness for deposition, in order to obtain evidence related to the asserted claims.[3] Non-parties have typically objected to these requests on the grounds that they force competitors to disclose highly sensitive information and are wholly irrelevant. Courts have allowed limited discovery, for example permitting a deposition relating to the licensing and developing of subject matter covered by the asserted claims.[4]

Patent dance exchanges, specifically 3(B) and 3(C) statements, may be discoverable where the same patents are asserted in other litigations. For example, where seven of the eight patents in suit were also asserted in another litigation, the court required production of the patent dance contentions because statements in the 3(C) disclosures were admis-

---

Boehringer Ingelheim Int'l GmbH, 17-cv-01065 (D. Del.); and AbbVie Inc. v. Sandoz Inc., 5:18-cv-12668 (D.N.J.) (these cases all involved AbbVie's HUMIRA® biologic).

[2]*Supra* Sections 4:14 to 4:18, regarding applicants' Section 262(*l*)(3)(A) statement and RPS's Section 262(*l*)(3)(A) statement, respectively.

[3]In *Janssen Biotech, Inc. v. Celltrion Healthcare Co. Ltd*, Celltrion filed a motion to compel non-party Biogen, Inc. to produce documents and information and provide a witness for deposition. 17-cv-11008, D.I. 86 (D. Mass. Dec. 5, 2017). Celltrion's request was specifically related to Biogen's cell culture medium used in the process of making Renflexis®, which Celltrion argued had "clear relevance to damages issues." D.I. 87 at 5.

[4]The Court ultimately denied Celltrion's motion to compel but did allow a limited deposition to go forward of Biogen's Vice President of Technical Development John Ruesch. Janssen Biotech, Inc. v. Celltrion Healthcare Co. Ltd, 17-cv-11008, D.I. 182 at 1–2 (D. Mass. February 20, 2018). The deposition was limited to, *inter alia*, credibility of Mr. Ruesch's previously submitted declaration, including whether the cell culture medium is confidential, whether the cell culture medium was ever licensed or sold to third parties, and the process of developing it. Janssen Biotech, Inc. v. Celltrion Healthcare Co. Ltd, 17-cv-11008, D.I. 182 at 1–2 (D. Mass. February 20, 2018).

sions by the patentee and the 3(B) contentions were required to provide context for the 3(C) disclosures.[5]

Settlement agreements may also be discoverable, but the scope of discovery of these agreements has varied. On the one hand, courts have held that settlement agreements are "routinely produced in patent litigation, with adequate confidentially protections."[6] On the other, however, courts have allowed patentees and third parties to redact particularly sensitive information, such as agreed-upon launch dates.[7]

§ 4:64   Expedited discovery in advance of a preliminary injunction

When the aBLA applicant provides notice to the RPS of commercial marketing, the RPS may seek a preliminary injunction. When the RPS will seek a preliminary injunction, Section 262 (*l*)(8)(C) directs the parties to cooperate on expediting any discovery needed for the motion. Section 262 (*l*)(8)(C) states that the RPS and the aBLA applicant shall "reasonably cooperate" in an effort to "expedite such further discovery as is needed." No court has interpreted the language of Section 262(*l*)(8)(C),[1] however, there have been several disputes related to discovery during a preliminary injunction.

The time frame for discovery in a preliminary injunction is truncated. In cases where a party has moved for a preliminary injunction there have only been a matter of months between the initial motion and the hearing.[2] In that time, parties may be expected to produce documents relevant to the

---

[5]AbbVie v. Boehringer Ingelheim, 17-cv-01065, D.I. 471 (D. Del. April 11, 2019).

[6]AbbVie v. Boehringer, 17-cv-1065, D.I. 471 at 4–6 (D. Del April 11, 2019) (citing *Allergan, Inc. v. Teva Pharmaceuticals USA, Inc.*, 2017 WL 132265, *1 (E.D. Tex. 2017).

[7]Genentech Inc. v. Amgen, 17-cv-1407, D.I. 383 (D. Del. May 23, 2019).

[Section 4:64]

[1]The section reads in full: If the reference product sponsor has sought a preliminary injunction under subparagraph (B), the reference product sponsor and the subsection (k) applicant shall reasonably cooperate to expedite such further discovery as is needed in connection with the preliminary injunction motion.

[2]In *Genentech Inc. v. Celltrion Inc.*, the parties reached out to the court in July regarding a proposed briefing scheduling for the preliminary

preliminary injunction and provide corporate deposition testimony pursuant to Rule 30(b)(6).

During the course of preparing for a preliminary injunction hearing, parties may only be entitled to discovery that is directly related to the motion,[3] and the court may order the parties to produce specific discovery related to the preliminary injunction.[4]

§ 4:65 Protective orders

Due to the sensitive nature of the information being disclosed, parties will negotiate and seek entry of a protective order governing the disclosure of and access to confidential information in the case. Protective orders are often filed as agreed-upon stipulations.

The BPCIA includes default confidentiality provisions, including a use restriction[1] and a general patent prosecution bar,[2] that can apply during the patent dance, and an ensuing litigation.[3] Parties, however, may negotiate, and dispute, the scope of the bars to extend beyond the BPCIA's default provisions. As such, there are several provisions that are commonly raised in BPCIA protective orders, such as more

---

injunction, Genentech filed the motion in August 2018 and the hearing was scheduled for October 2018. 18-cv-574, D.I. 64, 68 (D. N.J. 2018). In *Amgen Inc. v. Apotex Inc.*, the parties filed a motion to set briefing schedule for preliminary injunction (D.I. 37) and less than two months later the preliminary injunction hearing was held. 15-cv-61631, D.I. 70 (S.D. Fla. Dec. 7, 2015). In *Amgen, Inc. v. Sandoz Inc.*, the parties stipulated to extend the date for hearing. However, the hearing was still held less than one month after Amgen filed for preliminary injunction. 5:14-cv-4741, D.I. 64 (N.D. Cal. Feb. 19, 2015).

[3]For example, an aBLA applicant was unable to obtain the RPS manufacturing information. The court found that the information sought, in addition to being 12 years old and not directly related to the product at issue, was most importantly not pertinent specifically to the preliminary injunction motion. Genentech Inc. v. Celltrion Inc., 18-cv-00574, D.I 128 (D. N.J. Sep. 10, 2018).

[4]The court ordered Genentech to produce information related to conception and reduction to practice necessary to the preliminary injunction motion. Genentech Inc. v. Celltrion Inc., 18-cv-00574, D.I. 72 (D.N.J. Aug. 2, 2018).

[Section 4:65]

[1]42 U.S.C.A. § 262(*l*)(1)(D).

[2]42 U.S.C.A. § 262(*l*)(1)(B)(ii).

[3]*See* 42 U.S.C. § 262(*l*)(1); *supra* Section 4:8 to 4:13, regarding confidentiality of applicant's information produced during the patent dance.

robust patent prosecution bars, regulatory bars, and multi-tier access.

§ 4:66   Protective orders—Prosecution bars

Prosecution bars are included in protective orders to prevent lawyers exposed to their adversary's confidential information from directly or indirectly engaging in prosecution of patents directed to related technology, including drafting, amending, or advising patent prosecution before the United States Patent and Trademark Office or foreign patent agency. The default BPCIA patent prosecution bar prohibits recipients of confidential information from engaging "formally or informally, in patent prosecution relevant or related to the reference product."[1] Protective orders entered in BPCIA cases often provide more explanation regarding the scope and contours of this bar. For example, parties negotiate if and when the bar expires.[2]

Parties may also agree to alter the scope of the prosecution bar, carving out certain allowable activities. For example, the parties may agree that the bar does not prevent applicable counsel from representing a party challenging a patent before a domestic or foreign agency. Indeed, courts have upheld the validity of such a caveat, even when only providing an exception to patent challengers.[3]

[Section 4:66]

[1]§ 262(*l*)(1)(B)(ii).

[2]In *AbbVie, Inc. v. Amgen, Inc.*, the parties agreed to the prosecution bar generally and that the bars should expire one year after the last litigation involving an Amgen biosimilar of Humira. 16-cv-666, D.I. 38, 40, 41 (D. Del 2017). However, AbbVie sought an exception, wherein any person could resume barred activity after a year of stopping working on the litigation. *AbbVie, Inc.*, 16-cv-666 at D.I. 40. Amgen argued that a year was not sufficient amount of time for counsel to have forgotten confidential information "to the point they can fairly engage in previously-restricted activities." *AbbVie, Inc.*, 16-cv-666 at D.I. 38, 40. Ultimately, the parties agreed the bars would expire one year after the conclusion of the instant litigation or a related litigation, whichever was later. *AbbVie, Inc.*, 16-cv-666 at D.I. 43 (D. Del. Feb. 6, 2017).

[3]In *Amgen, Inc. v. Sandoz, Inc.*, the parties disputed whether a provision providing an exception to the prosecution bar, allowing counsel under the protective order to participate in challenging a related patent at the patent office, should be reciprocal and allow patent owner's counsel to also participate to defend the patent. 5:14-cv-4741, D.I. 48 at 5 (N.D. Cal. Jan. 29, 2015). The district court ultimately held that the prosecution bar would apply to the representation in defense of a patent in post-grant

§ 4:67 Protective orders—Regulatory bars

Similar to patent prosecution bars, regulatory bars are included in protective orders to prevent individuals with access to confidential information from being involved in communications with the FDA regarding issues related to the product involved in the litigation.[1] BPCIA protective orders include regulatory bars that prevent those with access to confidential information from participating in regulatory work, including for example citizen petitions.[2] Like patent prosecution bars, parties can negotiate a time restriction to the regulatory bar tied to the final disposition of the case. For example, the parties may agree to expiration immediately after the final disposition or one year after the final disposition.[3]

§ 4:68 Protective orders—Confidentiality tiers

The default provisions in the BPCIA provide for access to confidential information for both outside and in-house counsel.[1] Because of the highly sensitive nature of the information exchanged, and the increasing involvement of in-house counsel, parties have placed restrictions on the scope of the information that in-house counsel can access. This restriction is often in the form of multi-tiered confidentiality structure. For example, a two-tiered system is a common approach. In it, the protective order establishes who may access all confidential information and provides for more

---

proceedings, but not the representation challenging a patent. *AbbVie, Inc.,* 16-cv-666at D.I. 54.

[Section 4:67]

[1]In *AbbVie Inc. v. Amgen, Inc.,* Amgen proposed that those exposed to confidential information not be allowed to work on citizens petitions to the FDA involving adalimumab. 16-cv-666, D.I. 38 at 2 (D. Del. Jan. 26, 2017). AbbVie argued Amgen had no support for their proposal of a citizen's petition bar. *AbbVie, Inc.,* 16-cv-666 at 40 (D. Del. Jan 27, 2017). The parties ultimately filed a stipulated protective order with no regulatory bar, which the Court so ordered. *AbbVie, Inc.,* 16-cv-666 at 43 (D. Del. Feb. 6, 2017).

[2]A citizen petition could target a competitor's products or seek to influence the FDA regulations concerning the competitor.

[3]Amgen Inc. v. Sandoz Inc., 5:14-cv-4741, D.I. 60 at ¶ 8.3 (N.D. Cal. Feb. 29, 2015).

[Section 4:68]

[1]42 U.S.C.A. § 262(*l*)(1)(B)(ii).

limited access to a sub-set of specifically designated materials, for example to "outside counsel only."[2]

IX. LIABILITY

§ 4:69   Patent infringement

Patent infringement is governed by 35 U.S.C.A. § 271. In BPCIA cases, the RPS, as the patentee or exclusive patent licensee, has the burden of proving infringement by a preponderance of the evidence, namely that "every limitation of the patent claims asserted to be infringed is found in the accused [product], either literally or by an equivalent."[1] Determination of infringement is a question of fact.[2]

Under the BPCIA, the submission of an aBLA is considered an "artificial" act of infringement of (a) the patents identified by the RFP pursuant to Section 262(*l*)(3)(A), or (b) in the event that the applicant does not dance, any patents that could have been identified.[3] Much like in a Hatch-Waxman context, however, "artificially" infringing a patent does not mean that it would actually be infringed by, for example, the proposed biosimilar product itself.[4]

While traditional infringement principles apply in BPCIA

---

[2]In *Immunex Corp. v. Sandoz Inc.*, Sandoz sought to use the outside counsel only designation for all documents related to the FDA communications on Sandoz's pending aBLA. 4:16-cv-01118, D.I. 79 (D.N.J. July 11, 2016). The court found that such the FDA communications could be "temporarily designated" outside counsel only. D.I. 82. However, the court held that FDA approval of the aBLA would eliminate the outside counsel only tier. D.I. 113 at 2. Ultimately, the parties agreed to allow Sandoz to designate the FDA communications related to the aBLA as outside counsel's eyes only indefinitely. D.I. 115 at ¶¶ 4, 19. Sandoz attempted to set up the same two-tiered confidentiality structure in the District of New Jersey, but the court held that it was premature to make the determination as to what in-house counsel were actual competitive decision makers and should be excluded. Sandoz was permitted to move for the outside counsels only designation at a later date. Amgen Inc. v. Sandoz, Inc., 5:16-cv-2581, D.I. 64, 66 (N.D. Cal. Dec. 23, 2016).

[Section 4:69]

[1]*SmithKline Diagnostics, Inc. v. Helena Laboratories Corp.*, 859 F.2d 878, 889, 8 U.S.P.Q.2d 1468 (Fed. Cir. 1988).

[2]*Bai v. L & L Wings, Inc.*, 160 F.3d 1350, 1353, 48 U.S.P.Q.2d 1674 (Fed. Cir. 1998).

[3]35 U.S.C.A. § 271(e)(2)(C)(i), (ii).

[4]*See, e.g., Sandoz Inc. v. Amgen Inc.*, 137 S. Ct. 1664, 1671–72, 198 L. Ed. 2d 114, 122 U.S.P.Q.2d 1685 (2017); *see generally Ferring B.V. v. Watson Laboratories, Inc.-Florida*, 764 F.3d 1401, 1408, 112 U.S.P.Q.2d

litigation, BPCIA litigation, much like Hatch-Waxman litigation, is unique in that the infringement inquiry typically focuses on a proposed product that has not yet been marketed. Before any launch, the inquiry focuses on the product likely to be sold after FDA approval.[5] Therefore, during the BPCIA litigation, whether the accused product (or the process for making it or its use) infringes any asserted patent claim is determined based on information in the aBLA and—if that is not conclusive—other information concerning the accused product, such as testing, manufacturing guidelines, batch records, product samples, and certifications pledging not to infringe.[6] If the aBLA authorizes activity that would infringe, internal guidelines and certifications that may provide otherwise may not always preclude a finding of infringement.[7] After a biosimilar product has launched,

---

1050 (Fed. Cir. 2014) ("The district court here thus erred to the extent that it read § 271(e) to mean that Watson's act of filing an ANDA, by itself, established infringement sufficient to preclude consideration of the ANDA specification and any amendments before the FDA. The filing only constituted a technical act of infringement for jurisdictional purposes. As we have explained, once jurisdiction is established, the ultimate infringement inquiry provoked by such filing is focused on a comparison of the asserted patent claims against the product that is likely to be sold following ANDA approval and determined by traditional patent law principles."(citation omitted)); *Sunovion Pharmaceuticals, Inc. v. Teva Pharmaceuticals USA, Inc.*, 731 F.3d 1271, 1278, 108 U.S.P.Q.2d 1486 (Fed. Cir. 2013) ("Although no traditional patent infringement has occurred until a patented product is made, used, or sold, under the Hatch-Waxman framework, the filing of an ANDA itself constitutes a technical infringement for jurisdictional purposes. But the ultimate infringement question is determined by traditional patent law principles and, if a product that an ANDA applicant is asking the FDA to approve for sale falls within the scope of an issued patent, a judgment of infringement must necessarily ensue." (citations omitted)).

[5]*Amgen Inc. v. Apotex Inc.*, 712 Fed. Appx. 985, 991–92 (Fed. Cir. 2017) (citing *Sunovion Pharmaceuticals, Inc. v. Teva Pharmaceuticals USA, Inc.*, 731 F.3d 1271, 1278, 108 U.S.P.Q.2d 1486 (Fed. Cir. 2013)); *see also Abbott Laboratories v. TorPharm, Inc.*, 300 F.3d 1367, 1373, 63 U.S.P. Q.2d 1929 (Fed. Cir. 2002).

[6]*Amgen Inc. v. Apotex Inc.*, No. 15-61631, D.I. 267 (S.D. Fl. Sept. 6, 2016) (citing *Sunovion Pharm. Inc.*, 731 F.3d at 1278), aff'd, 712 F. App'x 985 (Fed. Cir. 2017); *see also Amgen Inc. v. Sandoz Inc.*, 923 F.3d 1023 (Fed. Cir. 2019), reh'g granted, opinion modified, 776 Fed. Appx. 707 (Fed. Cir. 2019).

[7]*Amgen*, 712 F. App'x at 991–92 (citing *Sunovion Pharm.*, 731 F.3d at 1278).

courts could consider other information, such as testing of the marketed product and how the product is actually used.[8]

Compared to Hatch-Waxman litigation, however, applicants in BPCIA litigation may find themselves with more opportunities to contest infringement of certain asserted patents. Given that small molecule generic products must in many respects "copy" the branded pharmaceutical product, and that the asserted patents generally relate to compounds, formulations, and methods of use, there are limited opportunities for a generic manufacturer to avoid infringement. Process patents are sometimes litigated in Hatch-Waxman cases, and such patents, like formulation patents, often present design-around opportunities. But process patents are more important in the world of biologics. Whether a proposed biosimilar product is in fact biosimilar to a reference product is highly dependent on the specifications of the manufacturing process.[9] Therefore, RPSs often have procured, and will continue to try to procure, a number of patents covering various steps of manufacturing processes, and then later assert those patents. As a result, process patents will be litigated far more in BPCIA litigation, which presents biosimilar applicants with more design-around opportunities as compared to generic applicants in Hatch-Waxman litigation. Indeed, in the handful of infringement rulings thus far handed down in BPCIA cases, all have related to process patents.[10] In all of these cases but one, the court found that the applicant did not infringe any asserted process claims.[11]

There are multiple infringement theories that may be raised in BPCIA litigation, and the following sections discuss each infringement theory in turn, including how courts have addressed them in BPCIA cases.

---

[8]*See Amgen Inc. v. Sandoz Inc.*, 923 F.3d at 1030–31.

[9]*Supra* Section 3:6.

[10]*See Amgen Inc. v. Apotex Inc.*, 712 Fed. Appx. 985 (Fed. Cir. 2017); *Amgen Inc. v. Sandoz Inc.*, 923 F.3d 1023 (Fed. Cir. 2019), reh'g granted, opinion modified, 776 Fed. Appx. 707 (Fed. Cir. 2019); *Amgen Inc. v. Coherus BioSciences Inc.*, 931 F.3d 1154 (Fed. Cir. 2019); *Amgen Inc. v. Hospira, Inc.*, 336 F. Supp. 3d 333 (D. Del. 2018); *Janssen Biotech, Inc v. Celltrion Healthcare Co., Ltd.*, No. 1:17-11008-MLW, D.I. 393 (D. Mass. July 30, 2018).

[11]In *Amgen*, the court, after a jury trial, ruled that some, but not all, of the asserted claims were infringed. 336 F. Supp. 3d 333 (D. Del. 2018).

§ 4:70 Patent infringement—Claim construction

The determination of whether an accused product or process infringes a claim in a patent involves two steps.[1] The first step is for the court to construe any terms of the asserted claims over which the parties dispute the meaning of the term.[2] Few claim construction disputes have been resolved in BPCIA litigation to date. Courts, however, apply the same claim construction principles in construing the terms of patents asserted in BPCIA litigation as in patent infringement suits generally.[3] An overview of those principles is provided herein.

Claim construction is a question of law, but can involve subsidiary factual findings.[4] Proper claim construction entails an analysis of the intrinsic evidence: the claim language, the written description in the specification, and the prosecution history.[5] If the meaning of a claim term is unambiguous from the intrinsic evidence, then a court usually may not rely on extrinsic evidence for purposes of claim construction.[6] However, extrinsic evidence may be used in claim construction to: (1) resolve any ambiguity in the

---

[Section 4:70]

[1]*See, e.g., Tanabe Seiyaku Co., Ltd. v. U.S. Int'l Trade Com'n*, 109 F.3d 726, 731, 41 U.S.P.Q.2d 1976 (Fed. Cir. 1997) (citing *Markman v. Westview Instruments, Inc.*, 52 F.3d 967, 976, 34 U.S.P.Q.2d 1321 (Fed. Cir. 1995), aff'd, 517 U.S. 370, 116 S. Ct. 1384, 134 L. Ed. 2d 577, 38 U.S.P.Q.2d 1461 (1996)).

[2]*O2 Micro Intern. Ltd. v. Beyond Innovation Technology Co., Ltd.*, 521 F.3d 1351, 1362, 86 U.S.P.Q.2d 1304 (Fed. Cir. 2008) ("When the parties present a fundamental dispute regarding the scope of a claim term, it is the court's duty to resolve it.").

[3]*See, e.g., Amgen Inc. v. Apotex Inc.*, 712 Fed. Appx. 985 (Fed. Cir. 2017); *Amgen Inc. v. Hospira, Inc., 2016 Markman 7013483*, 2016 WL 7013483 (D. Del. 2016); *Amgen Inc. v. Sandoz Inc.*, 923 F.3d 1023 (Fed. Cir. 2019), *reh'g granted, opinion modified*, 776 Fed. Appx. 707 (Fed. Cir. 2019).

[4]*Markman*, 52 F.3d at 979; *Teva Pharmaceuticals USA, Inc. v. Sandoz, Inc.*, 574 U.S. 318, 135 S. Ct. 831, 190 L. Ed. 2d 719, 113 U.S.P.Q.2d 1269 (2015).

[5]*Vitronics Corp. v. Conceptronic, Inc.*, 90 F.3d 1576, 1582–83, 39 U.S.P.Q.2d 1573 (Fed. Cir. 1996); *Phillips v. AWH Corp.*, 415 F.3d 1303, 1312, 75 U.S.P.Q.2d 1321 (Fed. Cir. 2005) (en banc) (reaffirming "the basic principles of claim construction" outlined in, e.g., *Vitronics*, 90 F.3d at 1582).

[6]*Key Pharmaceuticals v. Hercon Laboratories Corp.*, 161 F.3d 709, 716, 48 U.S.P.Q.2d 1911 (Fed. Cir. 1998).

intrinsic record; and (2) "ensure that [the judge's] understanding of the technical aspects of the patent is not entirely at variance with the understanding of one skilled in the art."[7]

With respect to the claim language itself, the words of the claims govern and are generally given their ordinary and customary meaning.[8] The focus of this analysis is "what one of ordinary skill in the art at the time of the invention would have understood the term to mean."[9] However, there are situations in which a claim term may be given a definition other than what one of ordinary skill in the art would give it.[10] An inventor is entitled to be his or her own lexicographer; thus, where it is apparent from the patent and prosecution history that the inventor intended a meaning different from that understood by one ordinarily skilled in the art, the inventor's meaning governs.[11]

The patent specification is always relevant to claim construction, because, pursuant to 35 U.S.C.A. § 112, it is the specification that must provide a written description of the invention in such full, clear, and exact terms as to allow a person of ordinary skill in the art to make and use the invention. Thus, "a claim must be read in view of the specification of which it is part."[12] Usually, the patent specification is the single best guide to the meaning of a disputed term.[13]

The prosecution history of a patent is also important for claim construction, because "it may contain contemporaneous exchanges between the patent applicant and the PTO about what the claims mean."[14] "Arguments and amendments made during the prosecution of a patent application . . . as well as the specification and other claims must be

---

[7]*Pitney Bowes, Inc. v. Hewlett-Packard Co.*, 182 F.3d 1298, 1309, 51 U.S.P.Q.2d 1161 (Fed. Cir. 1999).

[8]*Vitronics*, 90 F.3d at 1582. See also *Renishaw PLC v. Marposs Societa' per Azioni*, 158 F.3d 1243, 1249, 48 U.S.P.Q.2d 1117 (Fed. Cir. 1998); *Phillips*, 415 F.3d at 1315.

[9]*Markman*, 52 F.3d at 986.

[10]*Renishaw*, 158 F.3d at 1248.

[11]*Markman*, 52 F.3d at 979–80.

[12]*Renishaw*, 158 F.3d at 1248.

[13]*Vitronics*, 90 F.3d at 1582.

[14]*Digital Biometrics, Inc. v. Identix, Inc.*, 149 F.3d 1335, 1344, 47 U.S.P.Q.2d 1418 (Fed. Cir. 1998).

examined to determine the meaning of terms in the claims."[15] Moreover, statements made in the prosecution history may modify the ordinary meaning of a claim term.[16] A court may also consider the prior art cited in the prosecution history, which may contain clues as to what the claims do not cover.[17]

If the claim language remains genuinely ambiguous after consideration of the intrinsic evidence, reliance upon extrinsic evidence to construe the claims is appropriate, but only to the extent that such reliance does not "contradict the claim construction unambiguously apparent from the intrinsic evidence."[18] Extrinsic sources that may be used include dictionaries, treatises and encyclopedias.[19] However, the use of such extrinsic sources to interpret claims must be done with caution, because "[t]he resulting definitions . . . do not necessarily reflect the inventor's goal of distinctly setting forth his invention as a person of ordinary skill in that particular art would understand it."[20] In addition, opinion testimony, "whether by an attorney or artisan in the field of technology to which the patent is directed . . . should be treated with utmost caution, for it is no better than opinion testimony on the meaning of statutory terms."[21]

Typically, claim construction proceedings are held early in a case to determine the scope of the asserted patents prior to proceedings on the merits of infringement. However, the timing of when a court conducts its claim construction analysis is within its discretion.[22] A court may also have discretion to revise its construction at any time.[23]

---

[15]*Southwall Technologies, Inc. v. Cardinal IG Co.*, 54 F.3d 1570, 1576, 34 U.S.P.Q.2d 1673 (Fed. Cir. 1995).

[16]See, e.g., *Hockerson-Halberstadt, Inc. v. Avia Group Intern., Inc.*, 222 F.3d 951, 956, 55 U.S.P.Q.2d 1487 (Fed. Cir. 2000).

[17]*Vitronics*, 90 F.3d at 1583.

[18]*Pitney Bowes, Inc. v. Hewlett-Packard Co.*, 182 F.3d 1298, 1308–09, 51 U.S.P.Q.2d 1161 (Fed. Cir. 1999) (quoting *Bell & Howell Document Management Products Co. v. Altek Systems*, 132 F.3d 701, 706, 45 U.S.P. Q.2d 1033 (Fed. Cir. 1997)).

[19]See *Phillips v. AWH Corp.*, 415 F.3d 1303, 1318, 75 U.S.P.Q.2d 1321 (Fed. Cir. 2005).

[20]*Phillips*, 415 F.3d at 1322.

[21]*Vitronics*, 90 F.3d at 1585.

[22]*E.g., CollegeNet, Inc. v. ApplyYourself, Inc.*, 418 F.3d 1225, 1234, 75 U.S.P.Q.2d 1733 (Fed. Cir. 2005).

[23]*Jack Guttman, Inc. v. Kopykake Enterprises, Inc.*, 302 F.3d 1352,

§ 4:71   Patent infringement—Literal direct infringement

Infringement under Section 271(a) is typically referred to as "direct infringement." Section 271(a) provides that "whoever without authority makes, uses, offers to sell, or sells any patented invention, within the United States, or imports into the United States any patented invention during the term of the patent therefore, infringes the patent."[1] There are two kinds of direct infringement: literal infringement and infringement under the doctrine of equivalents.

Literal infringement of a patent claim requires that the accused infringing instrumentality contain each and every limitation recited in the claim.[2] Each of the limitations of the claim must be exactly met by the accused device or process. If there is any deviation or if any limitation is missing, there can be no literal infringement as a matter of law.[3] Literal infringement of a process patent claim, as is often asserted in BPCIA litigation, therefore requires each step of the claimed process to be performed, in the order (if any) claimed.[4]

As noted above, the infringement inquiry in BPCIA litigation, before a biosimilar launch, focuses on the product likely to be sold after FDA approval and the process for making that product. Courts will therefore look to information about the accused biosimilar product and processes found in the aBLA, and if that is inconclusive, supplemental information, such as batch records, manufacturing information, test results, etc.[5] Moreover, contentions provided by the aBLA applicant during the patent dance are entitled to *some proba-*

1361, 64 U.S.P.Q.2d 1302 (Fed. Cir. 2002).

[Section 4:71]

[1]35 U.S.C.A. § 271(a).

[2]*See Carroll Touch, Inc. v. Electro Mechanical Systems, Inc.*, 15 F.3d 1573, 1579, 27 U.S.P.Q.2d 1836 (Fed. Cir. 1993).

[3]*Lantech, Inc. v. Keip Mach. Co.*, 32 F.3d 542, 547, 31 U.S.P.Q.2d 1666 (Fed. Cir. 1994).

[4]*Canton Bio Medical, Inc. v. Integrated Liner Technologies, Inc.*, 216 F.3d 1367, 1370, 55 U.S.P.Q.2d 1378 (Fed. Cir. 2000).

[5]*Supra* Section 4:62. For example, in *Amgen Inc. v. Apotex Inc.*, the RPS and applicant disputed whether the aBLA file "constrain[ed] the [manufacturing] process to non-infringing levels." 712 F. App'x 985, 992 (Fed. Cir. 2017). The Federal Circuit ruled that it did, because, inter alia, the application referenced "key process parameters" that were non-infringing, and although such parameters were not "absolute limits," "the applications indicate that close adherence to [them] is critical to the func-

tive weight—as party admissions—in assessing infringement.[6] Such evidence, however, is *not binding* and may be contradicted by additional evidence presented at trial, such as information in the aBLA itself and trial testimony.[7]

After a biosimilar launch, courts apply more "conventional principles of patent infringement."[8] When a biosimilar is actually marketed, "it is unnecessary to determine 'what is likely to be sold,' as is required for a technical act of infringement."[9] Therefore, to determine whether a biosimilar manufacturer literally infringes a process claim by making its marketed biosimilar, courts will evaluate the current process used to make that product.[10]

§4:72 Patent infringement—direct infringement under the doctrine of equivalents

If an RPS is unable to prove literal infringement, the RPS may be able to prove infringement under doctrine of equivalents by showing that the accused product or process is equivalent to the subject matter claimed. Thus far, no RPS has, however, demonstrated that an applicant infringes under the doctrine of equivalents, or that as a factual matter, an applicant's product or process is equivalent to the subject matter claimed. In at least two BPCIA cases, courts have found that the RPS was legally barred from arguing in-

---

tion of the process." *Amgen*, 712 F. Appx at 992. And even if the aBLA did not "affirmatively constrain[] the processes" to non-infringing levels, batch records of the applicant's actual process demonstrated further indicated that the process did not literally fall within the claimed parameters.

[6]*Amgen*, 712 F. App'x at 989 ("[W]e agree that a district court cannot ignore letters sent during the BPCIA's information exchange if properly offered into evidence. Indeed, the prelitigation information exchange is part of the BPCIA's 'carefully calibrated scheme for preparing to adjudicate, and then adjudicating, claims of infringement.' ") (quoting *Sandoz Inc. v. Amgen Inc.*, 137 S. Ct. 1664, 1670, 198 L. Ed. 2d 114, 122 U.S.P.Q.2d 1685 (2017)).

[7]*Amgen*, 712 F. App'x at 989 ("[T]he district court did not ignore the prelitigation letters. Rather, it first concluded that the letters were not binding on Apotex, a conclusion that Amgen does not dispute, and it then found that the letters lacked probative value in light of the other evidence presented at trial. Thus, the court gave the letters their evidentiary due.").

[8]*Amgen Inc. v. Sandoz Inc.*, 923 F.3d 1023, 1030 (Fed. Cir. 2019), reh'g granted, opinion modified, 776 Fed. Appx. 707 (Fed. Cir. 2019).

[9]*Amgen*, 923 F.3d at 1030.

[10]*Amgen*, 923 F.3d at 1030.

fringement under the doctrine of equivalents.[1] Bars to assertion of the doctrine are discussed in Sections 4:73 and 4:74.

Infringement under the doctrine of equivalents is an issue of fact[2] and requires the patentee to prove that the accused product or process includes only insubstantial differences when compared to the patent claims. A patentee may prove that an insubstantial difference exists by showing that the substituted element in the accused product or process performs substantially the same function, in substantially the same way, to obtain substantially the same result as the claimed element.[3] Stated another way, an element of an accused process is equivalent if the differences between the element and the relevant claim limitation are "insubstantial" to one of ordinary skill in the art.[4]

In addition to the function-way-result test, a court may also consider whether one skilled in the art would know of the interchangeability of the claim limitation with the accused product's alleged substituted element.[5]

However, "[t]he doctrine of equivalents applies only in exceptional cases and is not 'simply the second prong of every infringement charge, regularly available to extend protection beyond the scope of the claims.' "[6] Furthermore, several principles limit the use of the doctrine of equivalents to find

---

[Section 4:72]

[1]*Janssen v. Celltrion*, No. 17-11008-MLW (D. Mass July 30, 2018); *Amgen Inc. et al. v. Mylan Inc. et al.*, No. 17-1235 (W.D. Pa. Sept. 13, 2019).

[2]*Tanabe Seiyaku Co., Ltd. v. U.S. Intern. Trade Com'n*, 109 F.3d 726, 731, 41 U.S.P.Q.2d 1976 (Fed. Cir. 1997).

[3]*Eastman Kodak Co. v. Goodyear Tire & Rubber Co.*, 114 F.3d 1547, 1560, 42 U.S.P.Q.2d 1737, 1997-1 Trade Cas. (CCH) ¶ 71824 (Fed. Cir. 1997) (*abrogated on other grounds by, Cybor Corp. v. FAS Technologies, Inc.*, 138 F.3d 1448, 46 U.S.P.Q.2d 1169 (Fed. Cir. 1998)) (citing *Warner-Jenkinson Co., Inc. v. Hilton Davis Chemical Co.*, 520 U.S. 17, 39–40, 117 S. Ct. 1040, 137 L. Ed. 2d 146, 41 U.S.P.Q.2d 1865 (1997); *Graver Tank & Mfg. Co. v. Linde Air Products Co.*, 339 U.S. 605, 608, 70 S. Ct. 854, 94 L. Ed. 1097, 85 U.S.P.Q. 328 (1950)).

[4]*See, e.g., Eagle Comtronics, Inc. v. Arrow Communication Laboratories, Inc.*, 305 F.3d 1303, 1315, 64 U.S.P.Q.2d 1481 (Fed. Cir. 2002), as amended on denial of reh'g and reh'g en banc, (Nov. 1, 2002).

[5]*Multiform Desiccants, Inc. v. Medzam, Ltd.*, 133 F.3d 1473, 1480–81, 45 U.S.P.Q.2d 1429 (Fed. Cir. 1998).

[6]*Amgen Inc. v. Sandoz Inc.*, 923 F.3d 1023 (Fed. Cir. 2019), reh'g granted, opinion modified, 776 Fed. Appx. 707 (Fed. Cir. 2019) (citing *London v. Carson Pirie Scott & Co.*, 946 F.2d 1534, 1538, 20 U.S.P.Q.2d

infringement. For example, application of the doctrine of equivalents does not allow "such broad play as to effectively eliminate [a claim] element in its entirety."[7]

§ 4:73 Patent infringement—direct infringement under the doctrine of equivalents— prosecution history estoppel

An aBLA filer may avoid a finding of infringement under the doctrine of equivalents by relying on the doctrine of prosecution history estoppel. "Prosecution history estoppel . . . preclud[es] a patentee from regaining, through litigation, coverage of subject matter relinquished during prosecution of the application for the patent."[1] The entire record of proceedings in the PTO, including representations made to the Examiner that the invention is patentable, are included in a patent's prosecution history.[2] "Prosecution history estoppel can occur . . . in one of two ways, either (1) by making a narrowing amendment to the claim ('amendment-based estoppel') or (2) by surrendering claim scope through argument to the patent examiner ('argument-based estoppel')."[3] Thus, "a narrowing amendment made to satisfy any requirement of the Patent Act may give rise to an estoppel."[4] Accordingly, prosecution history estoppel is not limited to amendments intended to narrow the patented invention's subject matter, e.g., to avoid prior art, but may apply to a narrowing amendment made to satisfy any requirement of patent law, including the utility, novelty and non-obviousness requirements of 35 U.S.C.A. §§ 101 to 103, respectively, and the written description, enablement and best mode requirements of 35 U.S.C.A. § 112.[5]

However, prosecution history estoppel is not a *per se*

1456 (Fed. Cir. 1991)).

[7]*Warner-Jenkinson*, 520 U.S. at 29.

[Section 4:73]

[1]*Festo Corp. v. Shoketsu Kinzoku Kogyo Kabushiki Co., Ltd.*, 535 U.S. 722, 734, 122 S. Ct. 1831, 152 L. Ed. 2d 944, 62 U.S.P.Q 2d 1705 (2002) (quoting *Wang Laboratories, Inc. v. Mitsubishi Electronics America, Inc.*, 103 F.3d 1571, 1577–78, 41 U.S.P.Q.2d 1263 (Fed. Cir. 1997)).

[2]*Jonsson v. Stanley Works*, 903 F.2d 812, 817, 14 U.S.P.Q 2d 1863 (Fed. Cir. 1990).

[3]*Conoco, Inc. v. Energy & Environmental Intern., L.C.*, 460 F.3d 1349, 1363, 79 U.S.P.Q.2d 1801 (Fed. Cir. 2006).

[4]*Festo*, 535 U.S. at 736.

[5]*Festo*, 535 U.S. at 736–38.

complete bar to the assertion of infringement against all equivalents of the amended claim element. Instead, the reasons for the narrowing amendment must be examined to determine if the particular equivalent in question has been surrendered.[6] The patentee bears the burden of proving that an amendment did not surrender the particular equivalent in question.[7] Thus, a patentee's decision to narrow the claims by amendment is presumed to be a general disclaimer of the territory between the original claim and the amended claim.[8] If the patentee is unable to rebut this presumption by explaining the reason for amendment, prosecution history estoppel applies and bars the application of the doctrine of equivalents as to that claim element.[9]

The presumption that prosecution history estoppel bars application of the doctrine of equivalents may be overcome if one or more of the following three criteria are met: (1) the patentee demonstrates that the alleged equivalent would have been unforeseeable at the time the narrowing amendment was made;[10] (2) the patentee demonstrates that the rationale underlying the amendment bears no more than a tangential relation to the equivalent in question; or (3) another reason exists that the patentee could not reasonably have been expected to have described the insubstantial substitute in question.[11]

To invoke argument-based estoppel, the "prosecution history must evince a clear and unmistakable surrender of subject matter."[12] Argument-based estoppel can apply, however, whether or not the arguments in question were

---

[6]*Festo*, 535 U.S. at 738.

[7]*Festo*, 535 U.S. at 740.

[8]*Festo*, 535 U.S. at 740–41.

[9]*Festo*, 535 U.S. at 741.

[10]The Supreme Court's decision in *Festo* states that the relevant time for this inquiry is "at the time of the [patent] *application*." *Festo*, 535 U.S. at 740 (emphasis added). However, after remand, the Federal Circuit has stated that the relevant time period is "at the time of the narrowing amendment . . . ." *Festo Corp. v. Shoketsu Kinzoku Kogyo Kabushiki Co., Ltd.*, 344 F.3d 1359, 1365 n.2, 68 U.S.P.Q.2d 1321 (Fed. Cir. 2003) (emphasis added).

[11]*Festo*, 535 U.S. at 740–41.

[12]*Conoco, Inc. v. Energy & Environmental Intern., L.C.*, 460 F.3d 1349, 1364, 79 U.S.P.Q.2d 1801 (Fed. Cir. 2006) (quoting *Deering Precision Instruments, L.L.C. v. Vector Distribution Systems, Inc.*, 347 F.3d 1314, 1326, 68 U.S.P.Q.2d 1716 (Fed. Cir. 2003).

actually required to secure allowance of the patented claim.[13] Therefore, "[t]here is no requirement that argument-based estoppel apply only to arguments made in the most recent submission before allowance."[14] In at least one BPCIA litigation, an RPS was legally barred, *at the pleading stage*, from presenting its equivalents argument because of argument-based estoppel.[15]

Statements that merely provide clarification do not give rise to estoppel.[16] However, estoppel arises when "a competitor would reasonably believe that the applicant has surrendered the relevant subject matter."[17] A reasonable belief can be found based on, for example, statements made to distinguish the claims from the prior art and statements

---

[13]*Southwall Technologies, Inc. v. Cardinal IG Co.*, 54 F.3d 1570, 1583, 34 U.S.P.Q.2d 1673 (Fed. Cir. 1995). See also *Canton Bio Medical, Inc. v. Integrated Liner Technologies, Inc.*, 216 F.3d 1367, 1371, 55 U.S.P.Q.2d 1378 (Fed. Cir. 2000) (holding that arguments made during prosecution in response to a prior art rejection to distinguish claimed subject matter from the prior art give rise to prosecution history estoppel).

[14]*Amgen Inc. v. Coherus BioSciences Inc.*, 931 F.3d 1154, 1161 (Fed. Cir. 2019)

[15]*Amgen*, 931 F.3d 1154. Amgen sued Coherus for infringing Amgen's process patent based on Coherus's aBLA. In particular, the claims at issue required a salt combination chosen from one of three pairs, as part of a protein purification process. Amgen, 931 F.3d at 1157. "Amgen alleged infringement under the doctrine of equivalents because the salt combination used in Coherus's process did not match any of the three expressly claimed salt combinations." Amgen, 931 F.3d at 1158. Coherus moved to dismiss under Federal Rule of Civil Procedure 12(b)(6), arguing that the doctrine of argument-based prosecution history estoppel applied. The district court agreed with Coherus, and so did the Federal Circuit, holding "that that argument-based prosecution history estoppel applies here because Amgen clearly and unmistakably surrendered unclaimed salt combinations during prosecution." *Amgen*, 931 F.3d at 1160. During prosecution, the patentee distinguished the prior art on the basis that, among other things, the prior art did not teach the particular claimed combinations of salt. *Amgen*, 931 F.3d at 1160. Estoppel applied with respect to unclaimed combinations, even though the patentee asserted other bases for distinguishing the prior art during prosecution, and even though other arguments may have ultimately convinced the patent office to grant the claims. *Amgen*, 931 F.3d at 1160–61.

[16]*Deering Precision Instruments, L.L.C. v. Vector Distribution Systems, Inc.*, 347 F.3d 1314, 1326, 68 U.S.P.Q.2d 1716 (Fed. Cir. 2003).

[17]*Cybor Corp. v. FAS Technologies, Inc.*, 138 F.3d 1448, 1457, 46 U.S.P.Q.2d 1169 (Fed. Cir. 1998).

made in a declaration by a named inventor narrowly defining the claimed invention.[18]

§ 4:74   Patent infringement—direct infringement under the doctrine of equivalents—Ensnarement

An aBLA filer may also use prior art itself to avoid being liable for infringement under the doctrine of equivalents. "Ensnarement" precludes "a patentee from asserting a scope of equivalency that would encompass, or 'ensnare,' the prior art."[1] Ensnarement is determined using the "hypothetical claim analysis" first articulated in *Wilson Sporting Goods Co. v. David Geoffrey & Associates*, 904 F.2d 677, 684, 14 U.S.P.Q.2d 1942 (Fed. Cir. 1990) (disapproved of by, Cardinal Chemical Co. v. Morton Intern., Inc., 508 U.S. 83, 113 S. Ct. 1967, 124 L. Ed. 2d 1, 26 U.S.P.Q.2d 1721 (1993)) (emphasis in original):

> Whether prior art restricts the range of equivalents of what is literally claimed can be a difficult question to answer. To simplify analysis and bring the issue onto familiar turf, it may be helpful to conceptualize the limitation on the scope of equivalents by visualizing a *hypothetical* patent claim, sufficient in scope to *literally* cover the accused product. The pertinent question then becomes whether that hypothetical claim could have been allowed by the PTO over the prior art. If not, then it would be improper to permit the patentee to obtain that coverage in an infringement suit under the doctrine of equivalents. If the hypothetical claim could have been allowed, then *prior art* is not a bar to infringement under the doctrine of equivalents.

However, "[t]he *Wilson* hypothetical claim analysis does not envision application of a full-blown patentability analy-

---

[18]In *Amgen Inc. v. Coherus Biosciences Inc.*, No. 17-546-LPS-CJB, D.I. 50 (D. Del. December 7, 2017) (redacted version at D.I. 59), patentee was found to have surrendered processes using all combinations of salts other than those recited in the claim. During prosecution, patentee argued that the claimed purification process requires use of particular combinations of salts that are not disclosed in the prior art. In fact, the process disclosed in the prior art did not disclose use of any combinations of salts. Patentee also submitted a declaration of a named inventor stating that the inventors has discovered a benefit of the particular combination of salts claimed.

[Section 4:74]

[1]*DePuy Spine, Inc. v. Medtronic Sofamor Danek, Inc.*, 567 F.3d 1314, 1322, 90 U.S.P.Q.2d 1865 (Fed. Cir. 2009).

sis to a hypothetical claim. *Wilson* simply acknowledges that prior art limits the coverage available under the doctrine of equivalents."[2]

Ensnarement analysis does not require that the hypothetical claim be anticipated by the prior art; it may suffice that the hypothetical claims are obvious.[3] Traditional anticipation and obviousness principles are applied to the hypothetical claim.[4] The hypothetical claims are compared to the closest prior art, which may include more than one reference.[5] Furthermore, the analysis is not limited to a single hypothetical claim; more than one hypothetical claim that would cover the alleged infringing product or process can be analyzed for ensnarement.[6] Patentee bears the burden of proving that the hypothetical claim is patentable over the prior art.[7]

In at least one BPCIA litigation, an RPS was legally barred at the summary judgment stage from presenting its equivalents argument, because the asserted scope of equivalents ensnared the prior art.[8]

---

[2]*Key Mfg. Group, Inc. v. Microdot, Inc.*, 925 F.2d 1444, 1449, 17 U.S.P.Q.2d 1806 (Fed. Cir. 1991).

[3]See *Janssen v. Celltrion*, No. 17-11008-MLW, D.I. 393 (D. Mass July 30, 2018).

[4]See *Wilson*, 904 F.2d at 684.

[5]See *Wilson*, 904 F.2d at 684.

[6]See *Wilson*, 904 F.2d at 684.

[7]*DePuy*, 567 F.3d at 1325.

[8]See *Janssen*, No. 17-11008-MLW, D.I. 393. The patent at issue in *Janssen v. Celltrion* concerned a composition for producing a cell culture media. The asserted claim listed 61 ingredients for the media and a concentration range for each. Moreover, only 52 of those ingredients were required, because the concentration range for nine had a low end of zero. While the accused media had all 52 of these ingredients, several were present in amounts that fell outside the claimed concentration ranges. Janssen argued that those amounts, however, were not substantially different from the amounts claimed, and that defendants infringed under the doctrine of equivalents. Defendants moved for summary judgment of noninfringement on the grounds that the scope of equivalents argument ensnared the prior art. In particular, defendants argued that the hypothetical invention was obvious over the prior art. The district court agreed, concluding:

> Undisputed and strong evidence compels the conclusion that a [POSA] would have had the ability and motivation to combine familiar ingredients from prior art cell culture media compositions in predictable concentrations to create what Janssen claims as its hypothetical invention. Moreover, the POSA would have

§ 4:75   Patent infringement—Indirect infringement

Indirect infringement refers to induced infringement or contributory infringement under Sections 271(b) and (c). Absent direct infringement of the patent claims, either literally or under the doctrine of equivalents, there can be no inducement of infringement and no contributory infringement.[1]

§ 4:76   Patent infringement—Indirect infringement— Induced infringement

Induced infringement is governed by Section 271(b), which provides that "[w]hoever actively induces infringement of a patent shall be liable as an infringer."[1] A person induces infringement under Section 271(b) by actively and knowingly aiding and abetting another's direct infringement.[2] Thus, to succeed on a claim of inducement, "the patentee must show, first that there has been direct infringement" and "second, that the alleged infringer knowingly induced infringement and possessed specific intent to encourage another's infringement."[3] "Evidence of active steps taken to encourage direct infringement, such as advertising an infringing use or instructing how to engage in an infringing use, show an affirmative intent that the product be used to infringe."[4] The patentee "has the burden of showing that the alleged

---

predicted the combination's successful results. Therefore, ensnarement bars Janssen from prevailing under the doctrine of equivalents.

Janssen, No. 17-11008-MLW, D.I. 383 at 6.

[Section 4:75]

[1]*Joy Technologies, Inc. v. Flakt, Inc.*, 6 F.3d 770, 774, 28 U.S.P.Q.2d 1378 (Fed. Cir. 1993) ("Liability for either active inducement of infringement or for contributory infringement is dependent upon the existence of direct infringement.").

[Section 4:76]

[1]35 U.S.C.A. § 271(b).

[2]*C.R. Bard, Inc. v. Advanced Cardiovascular Systems, Inc.*, 911 F.2d 670, 675, 15 U.S.P.Q.2d 1540 (Fed. Cir. 1990).

[3]*MEMC Electronic Materials, Inc. v. Mitsubishi Materials Silicon Corp.*, 420 F.3d 1369, 1378, 76 U.S.P.Q.2d 1276 (Fed. Cir. 2005) (citation omitted); see also *Limelight Networks, Inc. v. Akamai Technologies, Inc.*, 572 U.S. 915, 921, 134 S. Ct. 2111, 189 L. Ed. 2d 52, 110 U.S.P.Q.2d 1681 (2014) "([L]iability for inducement must be predicated on direct infringement.").

[4]MEMC, 420 F.3d at 1379 (quoting *Metro-Goldwyn-Mayer Studios Inc. v. Grokster, Ltd.*, 545 U.S. 913, 125 S. Ct. 2764, 2768, 162 L. Ed. 2d

infringer's actions induced infringing acts and that he knew or should have known his actions would induce actual infringement."[5] In other words, "the intent requirement for inducement requires more than just intent to cause the acts that produce direct infringement."[6] "Beyond that threshold knowledge, the inducer must have an affirmative intent to cause direct infringement."[7] Direct evidence of actual intent is not required; rather, proof of willful blindness, i.e., evidence that the alleged infringer subjectively believes that there is a high probability of infringement by a third party and (2) the alleged infringer took deliberate actions to avoid learning of that infringement, may suffice.[8]

As in Hatch-Waxman litigation, induced infringement claims in BPCIA litigation will most likely arise in the context of method of use claims, i.e., claims directed to a method of using a drug product or drug substance to treat a certain medical condition. Such claims may include, for example, limitations covering the dosage amount, dosage frequency, and intended results of the method, among other things. Because biosimilar manufacturers themselves do not administer or prescribe the biosimilars they plan to sell, an RPS will generally have no *direct* infringement claims against a biosimilar manufacturer for these types of claims. Instead, the RPS will allege that the biosimilar manufacturer will induce infringement, on the theory that the biosimilar manufacturer will encourage physicians and/or patients to use the biosimilar product in an infringing way, either with the product label, in advertising, or by some other means. To date, no court in a BPCIA litigation has addressed whether a biosimilar applicant will induce or has induced infringement of a method claim.

Prior to the biosimilar launch, these claims will likely hinge on the content of the proposed product label, as has been seen in the Hatch-Waxman context. Where an RPS bases its induced infringement claim on the biosimilar prod-

---

781, 33 Media L. Rep. (BNA) 1865, 75 U.S.P.Q.2d 1001 (2005)).

[5]*DSU Medical Corp. v. JMS Co., Ltd.*, 471 F.3d 1293, 1304, 81 U.S.P. Q.2d 1238 (Fed. Cir. 2006) (en banc) (quoting *Manville Sales Corp. v. Paramount Systems, Inc.*, 917 F.2d 544, 554, 16 U.S.P.Q.2d 1587 (Fed. Cir. 1990)).

[6]*DSU*, 471 F.3d at 1306.

[7]*DSU*, 471 F.3d at 1306.

[8]*Global-Tech Appliances, Inc. v. SEB S.A.*, 563 U.S. 754, 131 S. Ct. 2060, 179 L. Ed. 2d 1167, 98 U.S.P.Q.2d 1665 (2011).

uct label, for there to be an induced infringement finding of a method of use claim,

> [t]he label must encourage, recommend, or promote infringement. The mere existence of direct infringement by physicians, while necessary to find liability for induced infringement, is not sufficient for inducement. . . . .. It is well-established that mere knowledge of possible infringement by others does not amount to inducement; specific intent and action to induce must be proven.[9]

Moreover, "[t]he question is not just whether instructions [in a label] describ[e] the infringing mode, . . . but whether the instructions teach an infringing use *such that* we are willing to infer from those instructions an affirmative intent to infringe the patent."[10] "[V]ague label language cannot be combined with speculation about how physicians may act to find inducement."[11]

In these circumstances, where the infringement claim is based on the biosimilar label, a biosimilar applicant may be able to avoid infringement liability by carving out[12] the indication that is claimed. That, of course, assumes that the reference drug label has one or more other indications that remain in the biosimilar product label. The mere fact that a physician or patient still uses the biosimilar in an infringing manner, notwithstanding the carve-out, will not alone establish inducement because, as indicated above, specific intent and action to induce must be proven.[13]

To use a carve-out to avoid infringement, the applicant may need to excise additional information in the label beyond the indication itself. That may not always be possible, however, such as where the FDA does not permit the applicant to excise the information that induces infringement.[14] There may, however, be nuances to whether a biosimilar can

---

[9]*Takeda Pharmaceuticals U.S.A., Inc. v. West-Ward Pharmaceutical Corp.*, 785 F.3d 625, 630–31, 114 U.S.P.Q.2d 1679 (Fed. Cir. 2015) (citations, footnote, and internal quotation marks omitted)

[10]*Takeda*, 785 F.3d at 631 (citations and internal quotation marks omitted; emphasis in original).

[11]*Takeda*, 785 F.3d at 632.

[12]*See supra* Section 3:11, regarding carve-outs of indications from biosimilar applicant's labeling.

[13]*See Takeda*, 785 F.3d at 632, 634.

[14]*See AstraZeneca LP v. Apotex, Inc.*, 633 F.3d 1042, 1060, 97 U.S.P. Q.2d 1029 (Fed. Cir. 2010). In this case, Apotex attempted to excise the claimed method of use. The FDA, however, would not let Apotex carve out

successfully carve out a patented method of use. For instance, it remains an open question whether a biosimilar applicant can be found liable for induced infringement where its original aBLA contains a patented indication that is later carved out before the product is brought to market.[15]

Moreover, in litigation involving biosimilar products, additional theories of induced infringement may arise that have not previously been seen in the Hatch-Waxman context. Because non-interchangeable biosimilar products are not automatically substitutable for prescriptions written for the RLP, biosimilar manufacturers will need to actively market their biosimilar products.[16] Small molecule generics, on the other hand, are automatically substitutable for the reference product and therefore traditionally are not marketed. As a result, an RPS may sue a biosimilar manufacturer for induced infringement not only based on the label for the biosimilar product, but also based on marketing claims the biosimilar manufacturer may make in the course of promoting the product. These marketing claims may provide an additional basis for the RPS to allege induced infringement of method claims, and should be considered by the biosimilar manufacturer when preparing its marketing materials.

§ 4:77 Patent infringement—Indirect infringement—Contributory infringement

Contributory infringement is governed by Section 271(c), which provides that "[w]hoever offers to sell or sells within the United States or imports into the United States a component of a patented machine, manufacture, combination or composition, or a material or apparatus for use in practicing a patented process, constituting a material part of the invention, knowing the same to be especially made or especially adapted for use in an infringement of such patent, and not a staple article or commodity of commerce suitable

---

certain safety information, and, notwithstanding the language that Apotex did remove, the court concluded that the remaining safety information provided evidence that Apotex induced infringement.

[15]*See Immunex Corp. v. Sandoz Inc.*, No. 16-cv-01118 (D.N.J. Sept. 14, 2017), ECF No. 226 (redacted public version at ECF No. 311, Dec. 18, 2017). According to Amgen, an applicant's submission of an aBLA seeking approval of a patented use constitutes infringement under 35 U.S.C.A. § 271(e)(2)(C), and that a later label amendment cannot retroactively undo this. This issue, however, was never addressed by the court.

[16]*See supra* Section 3:13, regarding interchangeability requirements.

for substantial non-infringing use, shall be liable as a contributory infringer."[1] To date, no issues of contributory infringement have been fully litigated in a BPCIA litigation.

Contributory infringement allegations, much like inducement allegations, are more likely to arise when the RPS asserts method-of-use patents. For example, a biosimilar applicant may be accused of contributing to a physician's infringement of a method claim by selling a biosimilar product with instructions that induce the physician to use the product in an infringing manner.

As noted above, to establish liability for contributory infringement, an RPS must show, among other things, that there are no substantial noninfringing uses for the biosimilar product. Substantial non-infringing uses are "not unusual, far-fetched, illusory, impractical, occasional, aberrant, or experimental."[2] That said, off-label, non-infringing use of a biosimilar may not qualify as a substantial non-infringing use, where the product labeling itself instructs the infringing use.[3]

§ 4:78   Patent infringement—Products manufactured abroad using a domestically patented process

Manufacturing process patents have been a key feature of BPCIA litigation. Biosimilar manufacturers may work with other companies, including companies located outside the United States, to complete all or part of the manufacturing process for a biosimilar product. Accordingly, biosimilar applicants should be mindful of potential infringement liability for infringement under 35 U.S.CA. § 271(g). To date, however, no court in a BPCIA case has resolved the question of infringement under Section 271(g).

Section 271(g) provides for infringement liability where a product is made abroad by a process patented in the United

---

[Section 4:77]

[1]35 U.S.C.A. § 271(c).

[2]*Toshiba Corp. v. Imation Corp.*, 681 F.3d 1358, 1362, 103 U.S.P.Q.2d 1097 (Fed. Cir. 2012) (quoting *Vita-Mix Corp. v. Basic Holding, Inc.*, 581 F.3d 1317, 1327, 92 U.S.P.Q.2d 1340 (Fed. Cir. 2009))

[3]See *Eli Lilly and Co. v. Actavis Elizabeth LLC*, 435 Fed. Appx. 917, 927 (Fed. Cir. 2011). The Federal Circuit held in this non-precedential decision that "unauthorized [i.e., off-label] activity does not avoid infringement by a product that is authorized to be sold solely for the infringing use."

States, and is imported into or sold, offered for sale, or used in the United States. Section 271(g) provides specifically: "Whoever without authority imports into the United States or offers to sell, sells, or uses within the United States a product which is made by a process patented in the United States shall be liable as an infringer, if the importation, offer to sell, sale, or use of the product occurs during the term of such process patent." Infringement under Section 271(g) requires that the process by which the product is made falls within the scope of a United States patent.[1] Accordingly, Section 271(g) applies the same standards of infringement as though the process were practiced in the United States.[2]

"The ordinary meaning of 'made' as used in § 271(g) means 'manufacture,' and extends to the creation or transformation of a product, such as by synthesizing, combining components, or giving raw materials new properties."[3] It does not, however, "extend to testing to determine whether an already synthesized drug substance possesses existing qualities or properties"[4] or "whether the intended product of a separate and perhaps separately-patented process has in fact already been manufactured."[5]

Moreover, "[w]hen the process used abroad is the same as the process covered by a United States patent, liability for infringement arises only upon importation, sale or offers, or use in the United States as set forth in § 271(g)."[6] Conversely, "without authority" in Section 271(g) does not simply mean whether the patented process was authorized for practice abroad; rather, it means whether the *importation* of the prod-

---

[Section 4:78]

[1]*Novo Nordisk of North America, Inc. v. Genentech, Inc.*, 77 F.3d 1364, 1367–68, 37 U.S.P.Q.2d 1773 (Fed. Cir. 1996) ("Section 271(g) requires that a patentee establish, inter alia, that an accused infringer imported, offered to sell, sold, or used a product made by a process falling within the scope of one or more claims of the patentee's United States patent.").

[2]*Novo Nordisk*, 77 F.3d at 1367–68.

[3]*Momenta Pharmaceuticals, Inc. v. Teva Pharmaceuticals USA Inc.*, 809 F.3d 610, 616, 116 U.S.P.Q.2d 1961 (Fed. Cir. 2015).

[4]*Momenta*, 809 F.3d at 616.

[5]*Momenta*, 809 F.3d at 617.

[6]*Ajinomoto Co., Inc. v. Archer-Daniels-Midland Co.*, 228 F.3d 1338, 1348, 56 U.S.P.Q.2d 1332 (Fed. Cir. 2000).

uct made by that process was authorized.[7] Therefore, a license to practice a patented method abroad will not, without more, necessarily absolve an accused infringer of liability under Section 271(g).

Section 271(g) also provides two exceptions to liability. A product made by a patented process will not infringe under Section 271(g) if the product is either: (1) materially changed by subsequent processes; or (2) becomes a trivial and nonessential component of another product.[8] Whether something is materially changed is "context dependent,"[9] and "requires, at a minimum, that there be a real difference between the product imported, offered for sale, sold, or used in the United States and the products produced by the patented process."[10] Moreover, in the case of biologic process patents:

> a significant change in a protein's structure and/or properties would constitute a material change. A good source for determining whether a change in a product of a process is material under § 271(g) is the patent. Where the specification or asserted claims recite a structure or function for the product of the processes, then significant variations from the recited structure and function are material. What makes a variation significant enough to be a "material change," however, is a question of degree.[11]

Whether the product of a patented process is a "trivial and nonessential component" is also a "question of degree."[12] These exceptions have not been addressed in the BPCIA context, but undoubtedly will in the future.

§ 4:79 Patent infringement—Safe harbor under section 271(e)

The development of a biosimilar product prior to FDA approval inevitably involves actions that may be considered infringing and subject an applicant to liability but for the safe harbor provided under 35 U.S.C.A. § 271(e)(1):

---

[7]*Ajinomoto*, 228 F.3d at 1347–48.

[8]See 35 U.S.C.A. § 271(g)(1), (2).

[9]*Amgen Inc. v. F. Hoffman-La Roche Ltd*, 580 F.3d 1340, 1379, 92 U.S.P.Q.2d 1289 (Fed. Cir. 2009).

[10]*Bio-Technology General Corp. v. Genentech, Inc.*, 80 F.3d 1553, 1560, 38 U.S.P.Q.2d 1321 (Fed. Cir. 1996).

[11]*Amgen*, 580 F.3d at 1379 (citation omitted).

[12]*Eli Lilly and Co. v. American Cyanamid Co.*, 82 F.3d 1568, 1572, 38 U.S.P.Q.2d 1705 (Fed. Cir. 1996).

It shall not be an act of infringement to make, use, offer to sell, or sell within the United States or import into the United States a patented invention (other than a new animal drug or veterinary biological product (as those terms are used in the Federal Food, Drug, and Cosmetic Act and the Act of March 4, 1913) which is primarily manufactured using recombinant DNA, recombinant RNA, hybridoma technology, or other processes involving site specific genetic manipulation techniques) solely for uses reasonably related to the development and submission of information under a Federal law which regulates the manufacture, use, or sale of drugs or veterinary biological products.

Section 271(e)(1) "exempt[s] from infringement *all* uses of patented compounds 'reasonably related' to the process of developing information for submission under *any* federal law regulating the manufacture, use, or distribution of drugs."[1] It is also "not restricted to preapproval activities."[2] And even if the testing of patented materials is not ultimately included in an FDA submission, the applicant is not automatically deemed liable for infringement.[3] Because there is uncertainty regarding the type and amount of information required by the FDA to gain approval for a drug, the safe harbor provision only requires that "there is a reasonable basis for believing that the experiments will produce 'the types of information that are relevant to an IND or NDA.' "[4] Section 271 is "sufficiently broad" enough so as to "leave[] adequate space for experimentation and failure on the road to regulatory approval."[5]

Section 271(e)(1) also "does not look to the underlying purposes or attendant consequences of the activity . . . as long as the use is reasonably related to FDA approval."[6] Therefore, the safe harbor may still apply even if data is

---

[Section 4:79]

[1]*Merck KGaA v. Integra Lifesciences I, Ltd.*, 545 U.S. 193, 206, 125 S. Ct. 2372, 162 L. Ed. 2d 160, 74 U.S.P.Q.2d 1801 (2005) (emphasis in original).

[2]*Momenta Pharmaceuticals, Inc. v. Amphastar Pharmaceuticals, Inc.*, 686 F.3d 1348, 1358–59, 103 U.S.P.Q.2d 1800 (Fed. Cir. 2012).

[3]*Merck*, 545 U.S. at 206.

[4]*Merck*, 545 U.S. at 208.

[5]*Merck*, 545 U.S. at 206–07.

[6]*Abtox, Inc. v. Exitron Corp.*, 122 F.3d 1019, 1030, 43 U.S.P.Q.2d 1545 (Fed. Cir. 1997), opinion amended on reh'g, 131 F.3d 1009 (Fed. Cir. 1997).

used for additional purposes other than FDA approval.[7] For example, the exemption could extend to activities that are promotional rather than regulatory in nature, at least where such activities are "consistent with the collection of data necessary for" seeking FDA approval.[8] Certain activities, however, that are not, or may not, be reasonably related to FDA approval include "information that may be routinely reported to the FDA, long after marketing approval has been obtained,"[9] including "routine quality control testing . . . as part of the post-approval, commercial production process,"[10] and "research tools or devices that are not themselves subject to FDA approval."[11]

To date, only one court—the district court in *Amgen Inc. v. Hospira, Inc.*—has addressed whether the safe harbor provision protects otherwise infringing activity in the BPCIA context.[12] There, the court did not disturb a jury's finding that some, but not all, of Hospira's batches were reasonably related to FDA approval and protected by the safe harbor. Although that case is on appeal, and the question as to whether Hospira's batches were entitled to safe harbor protection was very factual in nature, certain cautionary notes may be gleaned from it. For example, it suggests that at least some courts may be inclined to decide on a batch-by-batch basis whether the use of a patented manufacturing process is reasonably related to FDA approval, and that although biosimilarity testing is required for the FDA approval, not *all* biosimilarity testing may fall within the safe harbor. The FDA guidances setting forth testing requirements may be instructive in determining whether certain

---

[7]*Abtox*, 122 F.3d at 1030.

[8]*Momenta Pharmaceuticals, Inc. v. Teva Pharmaceuticals USA Inc.*, 809 F.3d 610, 613, 116 U.S.P.Q.2d 1961 (Fed. Cir. 2015).

[9]*Momenta*, 809 F.3d at 619.

[10]*Momenta*, 809 F.3d at 620.

[11]*Momenta*, 809 F.3d at 619.

[12]See *Amgen Inc. v. Hospira, Inc.*, 336 F. Supp. 3d 333, 342 (D. Del. 2018). There, Amgen asserted that Hospira's pre-approval production of its epogen batches infringed Amgen's process patents. A jury found that Hospira infringed one of those patents, and that only seven of the 21 lots of epogen were entitled to safe harbor protection. Hospira challenged the jury's findings, but the court overruled them. According to the court, a reasonable juror could have concluded that not all of the 21 batches were protected based on "Amgen's presentation of FDA guidance documents, admissions in Hospira's internal documents, and post-litigation changes to Hospira's representations to the FDA." The case is currently on appeal.

biosimilarity testing is reasonably related to the FDA approval.[13] Simply submitting testing to the FDA may not be enough to show that such testing is needed for approval. Moreover, intent may be a relevant factor in determining whether certain activities are reasonably related to obtaining FDA approval.[14] That said, "once it is determined that 'the activity is reasonably related to obtaining FDA approval, [] intent or alternative uses are irrelevant to its qualification to invoke the section 271(e) shield.' "[15]

§ 4:80 Patent validity

Although a limited number of invalidity challenges have actually been resolved by courts in BPCIA litigations, this chapter discusses some invalidity challenges—*i.e.*, unpatentable subject matter under 35 U.S.C.A. § 101, anticipation under 35 U.S.C.A. § 102, obviousness under 35 U.S.C.A. § 103, lack of written description, lack of enablement and indefiniteness under 35 U.S.C.A. § 112, and obviousness-type double patenting—that have arisen, or may arise in future cases.

§ 4:81 Patent validity—Ineligible subject matter (Section 101)

35 U.S.C.A. § 101[1] excludes as patent ineligible "laws of nature, natural phenomena, and abstract ideas."[2] "Whether a claim recites patent eligible subject matter is a question of law which may contain disputes over underlying facts."[3]

To determine whether a patent is invalid under Section

---

[13]*See Amgen*, 336 F. Supp. 3d at 342.

[14]*See Amgen*, 336 F. Supp. 3d at 354.

[15]*See Amgen*, 336 F. Supp. 3d at 354 (quoting *Abtox, Inc. v. Exitron Corp.*, 122 F.3d 1019, 1030, 43 U.S.P.Q.2d 1545 (Fed. Cir. 1997), opinion amended on reh'g, 131 F.3d 1009 (Fed. Cir. 1997)).

[Section 4:81]

[1]35 U.S.C.A. § 101: "Whoever invents or discovers any new and useful process, machine, manufacture, or composition of matter, or any new and useful improvement thereof, may obtain a patent therefor, subject to the conditions and requirements of this title."

[2]*Association for Molecular Pathology v. Myriad Genetics, Inc.*, 569 U.S. 576, 589, 133 S. Ct. 2107, 186 L. Ed. 2d 124, 106 U.S.P.Q.2d 1972 (2013) (quoting *Mayo Collaborative Services v. Prometheus Laboratories, Inc.*, 566 U.S. 66, 70, 132 S. Ct. 1289, 182 L. Ed. 2d 321, 101 U.S.P.Q.2d 1961, 90 A.L.R. Fed. 2d 685 (2012)).

[3]*Berkheimer v. HP Inc.*, 881 F.3d 1360, 1368, 125 U.S.P.Q.2d 1649

101, courts must apply a two-step test, which requires (1) determining if the patented technology touches upon ineligible subject matter and if so, (2) whether there are sufficient inventive elements such that the invention is "significantly more" than a patent on an ineligible concept.[4] "[T]o transform an unpatentable law of nature into a patent-eligible *application* of such a law, one must do more than simply state the law of nature while adding the words 'apply it.' "[5] Moreover, "adding 'conventional steps, specified at a high level of generality,' to a law of nature does not make a claim to the law of nature patentable."[6] Put another way, " 'conventional or obvious' '[pre]-solution activity' is normally not sufficient to transform an unpatentable law of nature into a patent-eligible application of such a law."[7] Still, "[t]he inventive concept inquiry requires more than recognizing that each claim element, by itself, was known in the art."[8] A claim's limitations, taken individually, may all be conventional, but when taken together, in the order as claimed, they may nevertheless make the claim patent-eligible under step two.[9] Furthermore, the Supreme Court has cautioned "that too broad an interpretation of this exclusionary principle could eviscerate patent law. For all inventions at some level embody, use, reflect, rest upon, or apply laws of nature, natural phenomena, or abstract ideas."[10]

No court in a BPCIA litigation has ruled on a dispute concerning a Section 101 challenge. Such disputes are likely to arise in the future, when RPSs assert claims directed to,

---

(Fed. Cir. 2018), petition for certiorari filed (U.S. Sept. 28, 2018).

[4]*See DDR Holdings, LLC v. Hotels.com, L.P.*, 773 F.3d 1245, 1255, 113 U.S.P.Q.2d 1097 (Fed. Cir. 2014) (quoting *Alice Corp. Pty. Ltd. v. CLS Bank Intern.*, 573 U.S. 208, 215, 134 S. Ct. 2347, 189 L. Ed. 2d 296, 110 U.S.P.Q.2d 1976 (2014)); *see also Alice*, 573 U.S. at 217 ("[A]n invention is not rendered ineligible for patent simply because it involves an abstract concept."); *Athena Diagnostics, Inc. v. Mayo Collaborative Services, LLC*, 927 F.3d 1333 (Fed. Cir. 2019).

[5]*Mayo Collaborative Servs.*, 566 U.S. at 72.

[6]*Athena Diagnostics, Inc. v. Mayo Collaborative Services, LLC*, 915 F.3d 743, 749 (Fed. Cir. 2019) (quoting *Mayo Collaborative Servs.*, 566 U.S. at 82).

[7]*Mayo Collaborative Servs.*, 566 U.S. at 79 (alteration in original) (quoting *Flook*, 437 U.S. at 590, 98 S.Ct. 2522).

[8]*Bascom Global Internet Services, Inc. v. AT&T Mobility LLC*, 827 F.3d 1341, 119 U.S.P.Q.2d 1236 (Fed. Cir. 2016).

[9]*Bascom*, 827 F.3d at 1349.

[10]*Mayo Collaborative Servs.*, 566 U.S. at 71–72.

or covering, isolated products of nature, like DNA or proteins, or to diagnostic methods—such as the use of a companion diagnostic with a biological product. Courts, including the Federal Circuit and the Supreme Court, have frequently ruled on Section 101 challenges to such claims.

Diagnostic claims, in particular, have been a repeated target of Section 101 challenges, and are frequently invalidated. Diagnostic claims are often directed to the application of a natural correlation, such as between (a) some marker in the body, like a metabolite, gene, mutation, antibody, etc., and (b) a particular disease, or outcome from using a particular treatment. Such natural correlations themselves are laws of nature that cannot be patented.[11] And when patent claims are directed to such correlations, and merely recite methods for detecting or applying them that are well understood or conventional (whether that method is as simple as making a visual observation or requires something like making a special tagged antibody to find the marker), then the result is that they are unpatentable under Section 101.[12] A claim can be invalid even where it involves a step of administering a drug, where the administration is part of the diagnostic test itself. Other diagnostic claims are directed to the comparison of a patient's genetic information to wild-type information from the general population to determine when the patient has a genetic mutation. Such a comparison may be considered abstract, and not patentable, if the claims merely recite conventional methods for observing that comparison. For example, the following types of claims have been found invalid as directed to unpatentable subject matter:

- Method for optimizing therapeutic efficacy by administering a known drug, determining serum level of drug in patient, and adjusting amount of drug administered when levels of drug in patient's blood exceed or fall below certain amounts.[13]
- Methods for screening for BRCA1 mutation by comparing gene/RNA from tissue sample to wild-type, by (a)(i) hybridizing a BRCA gene probe and (ii) detecting the presence of a hybridization product; or (b)(i) amplifica-

---

[11]See, e.g., Mayo Collaborative Servs., 566 U.S. at 71–72.

[12]Mayo Collaborative Servs., 566 U.S. at 71–72.

[13]Mayo Collaborative Servs., 566 U.S. at 73–74.

tion of the BRCA1 gene and (ii) sequencing of the amplified nucleic acids.[14]

- Diagnostic methods for detecting a paternally inherited nucleic acid of fetal origin performed on a maternal serum or plasma sample from a pregnant female.[15]

- Detecting genetic variations by amplifying and analyzing "non-coding regions."[16]

- Diagnostic methods by subjecting DNA to PCR using primers and detecting the presence of an amplification product as indicative of M. tuberculosis.[17]

- Diagnosing neurotransmission or developmental disorders related to muscle specific tyrosine kinase (MuSK) by contacting a bodily fluid sample with MuSK and detecting antibody-antigen complex formation using an anti-IgG antibody tagged with a reporter molecule[18]

Some courts, however, have ruled the other way. One set of claims was held patent eligible where they applied a relationship between the core body temperature and the temporal artery temperature "into an unconventional method of temperature measurement."[19] In other cases, the following claims were not invalidated early in the case on a motion to dismiss:

- Quantifying metabolites in a urine sample to determine compliance with a drug regimen (where *urine* screening in particular—as opposed to using any bodily fluid—presented an improvement).[20]

---

[14]*In re BRCA1– and BRCA2-Based Hereditary Cancer Test Patent Litigation*, 774 F.3d 755, 113 U.S.P.Q.2d 1241 (Fed. Cir. 2014).

[15]*Ariosa Diagnostics, Inc. v. Sequenom, Inc.*, 788 F.3d 1371, 115 U.S.P.Q.2d 1152 (Fed. Cir. 2015).

[16]*Genetic Technologies Ltd. v. Merial L.L.C.*, 818 F.3d 1369, 118 U.S.P.Q.2d 1541 (Fed. Cir. 2016).

[17]*Roche Molecular Systems, Inc. v. CEPHEID*, 905 F.3d 1363, 128 U.S.P.Q.2d 1221 (Fed. Cir. 2018).

[18]*Cleveland Clinic Foundation v. True Health Diagnostics LLC*, 760 Fed. Appx. 1013 (Fed. Cir. 2019).

[19]*Exergen Corporation v. Kaz USA, Inc.*, 725 Fed. Appx. 959, 966 (Fed. Cir. 2018) (non-precedential).

[20]*Ameritox, Ltd. v. Millennium Health, LLC*, 88 F. Supp. 3d 885 (W.D. Wis. 2015).

- Detecting whether a human has been exposed to the bacteria that causes tuberculosis.[21]

Method of treatment claims that incorporate diagnostic elements have also withstood Section 101 challenges, in particular where the diagnostic step is used to figure out an appropriate dose for the patient.[22] Such claims are not directed to laws of nature, but rather they "recite a method for treating a patient," "specific treatment steps," and "a specific method of treatment for specific patients using a specific compound at specific doses to achieve a specific outcome."[23]

Courts have also heard Section 101 challenges to claims directed to isolated DNA sequence. When such a sequence is indistinguishable chemically and structurally from a sequence that naturally exists in a living thing, it is considered a product of nature and not patent eligible.[24] The mere fact that the claimed molecule is isolated or synthesized does not make it patent eligible.[25] On the other hand, complementary DNA (cDNA) is patent eligible because it is not naturally-occurring.[26] cDNA is "synthetically created DNA" that "contains the same protein-coding information found in a segment of natural DNA but omits portions within the DNA segment that do not code for proteins."[27]

---

[21]*Rutgers v. Qiagen N.V.*, 2016 WL 828101 (D.N.J. 2016). Tests for TB infection were also held not invalid under Section 101 at the motion to dismiss phase in *Oxford Immunotec Ltd. v. Qiagen, Inc.*, No. 15-13124-NMG, D.I. 87 (D. Mass. Sept. 30, 2016).

[22]*See Vanda Pharmaceuticals Inc. v. West-Ward Pharmaceuticals International Limited*, 887 F.3d 1117, 126 U.S.P.Q.2d 1266 (Fed. Cir. 2018), petition for certiorari filed (U.S. Dec. 27, 2018); *Endo Pharmaceuticals Inc. v. Teva Pharmaceuticals USA, Inc.*, 919 F.3d 1347 (Fed. Cir. 2019). In *Vanda*, the asserted claims were directed to a method of using iloperidone to treat schizophrenia that included a step of analyzing a patient's genetic information for predicting toxicity. The claims instructed how the patient's dose varied depending on the outcome of that test. In *Endo*, the asserted claims covered methods for treating pain in a renally impaired patient by tailoring the patient's oxymorphone dose after measuring the drug's bioavailability in the patient.

[23]*Endo*, 919 F.3d at 1354; *Vanda*, 887 F.3d at 1136.

[24]*Roche Molecular Systems, Inc. v. CEPHEID*, 905 F.3d 1363, 1370, 128 U.S.P.Q.2d 1221 (Fed. Cir. 2018); *Association for Molecular Pathology v. Myriad Genetics, Inc.*, 569 U.S. 576, 594, 133 S. Ct. 2107, 186 L. Ed. 2d 124, 106 U.S.P.Q.2d 1972 (2013).

[25]*Myriad*, 569 U.S. at 594.

[26]*Myriad*, 569 U.S. at 594.

[27]*Myriad*, 569 U.S. at 594.

The mere fact that a claim *references* a naturally-existing substance, such as an isolated genetic sequence, does not end the inquiry, however. An invention referencing a naturally-existing substance can be patentable under Section 101 where it involves the use of such a substance, present "in unnatural quantities to alter a patient's natural state, to treat a patient with specific dosages outlined" or where the naturally-existing substance is incorporated into "specific treatment formulations" that has "different characteristics and can be used in a manner that [the natural substance] as it appears in nature cannot."[28]

§ 4:82   Patent validity—Anticipation (Section 102)

To anticipate a claim, a single prior art reference must expressly or inherently disclose each claim limitation.[1] 35 U.S.C.A. § 102 describes the categories of prior art that could anticipate a patent claim.[2] Anticipation requires "the presence in a single prior art disclosure of all elements of a

---

[28]*Natural Alternatives International, Inc. v. Creative Compounds, LLC*, 918 F.3d 1338, 1346–48 (Fed. Cir. 2019).

[Section 4:82]

[1]*Celeritas Technologies, Ltd. v. Rockwell Intern. Corp.*, 150 F.3d 1354, 1361, 47 U.S.P.Q.2d 1516 (Fed. Cir. 1998).

[2]For any patents with effective filing dates on or before March 16, 2013, the pre-AIA version of Section 102 applies, setting forth the following categories of prior art:

A person shall be entitled to a patent unless—

(a) the invention was known or used by others in this country, or patented or described in a printed publication in this or a foreign country, before the invention thereof by the applicant for patent, or

(b) the invention was patented or described in a printed publication in this or a foreign country or in public use or on sale in this country, more than one year prior to the date of the application for patent in the United States, or

(c) he has abandoned the invention, or

(d) the invention was first patented or caused to be patented, or was the subject of an inventor's certificate, by the applicant or his legal representatives or assigns in a foreign country prior to the date of the application for patent in this country on an application for patent or inventor's certificate filed more than 12 months before the filing of the application in the United States, or

(e) the invention was described in—(1) an application for patent, published under section 122(b), by another filed in the United States before the invention by the applicant for patent or (2) a patent granted on an application for patent by another filed in the United States before the invention by the applicant for patent, except that an international application filed under the treaty defined in section 351(a) shall have the effects for the purposes of this subsection of an application filed in the United States only if the international application designated the United States and was published under Article 21(2) of such treaty in the English language; or

claimed invention arranged as in the claim."[3] A prior art ref-

_____

(f) he did not himself invent the subject matter sought to be patented, or

(g) (1) during the course of an interference conducted under section 135 or section 291, another inventor involved therein establishes, to the extent permitted in section 104, that before such person's invention thereof the invention was made by such other inventor and not abandoned, suppressed, or concealed, or (2) before such person's invention thereof, the invention was made in this country by another inventor who had not abandoned, suppressed, or concealed it. In determining priority of invention under this subsection, there shall be considered not only the respective dates of conception and reduction to practice of the invention, but also the reasonable diligence of one who was first to conceive and last to reduce to practice, from a time prior to conception by the other.

Patents with effective filing dates after March 16, 2013, are subject to the first-inventor-to file provisions of the amended version of Section 102. Specifically, Section 102 describes the following kinds of prior art, with certain exceptions:

(a) Novelty; prior art—A person shall be entitled to a patent unless—

(1) the claimed invention was patented, described in a printed publication, or in public use, on sale, or otherwise available to the public before the effective filing date of the claimed invention; or

(2) the claimed invention was described in a patent issued under section 151, or in an application for patent published or deemed published under section 122(b), in which the patent or application, as the case may be, names another inventor and was effectively filed before the effective filing date of the claimed invention.

(b) Exceptions—

(1) Disclosures made 1 year or less before the effective filing date of the claimed invention—A disclosure made 1 year or less before the effective filing date of a claimed invention shall not be prior art to the claimed invention under subsection (a)(1) if—

(A) the disclosure was made by the inventor or joint inventor or by another who obtained the subject matter disclosed directly or indirectly from the inventor or a joint inventor; or

(B) the subject matter disclosed had, before such disclosure, been publicly disclosed by the inventor or a joint inventor or another who obtained the subject matter disclosed directly or indirectly from the inventor or a joint inventor.

(2) A disclosure shall not be prior art to a claimed invention under subsection (a)(2) if—

(A) the subject matter disclosed was obtained directly or indirectly from the inventor or a joint inventor;

(B) the subject matter disclosed had, before such subject matter was effectively filed under subsection (a)(2), been publicly disclosed by the inventor or a joint inventor or another who obtained the subject matter disclosed directly or indirectly from the inventor or a joint inventor;

or (C) the subject matter disclosed and the claimed invention, not later than the effective filing date of the claimed invention, were owned by the same person or subject to an obligation of assignment to the same person.

[3]*Connell v. Sears, Roebuck & Co.*, 722 F.2d 1542, 1548, 220 U.S.P.Q. 193 (Fed. Cir. 1983) (citing *Soundscriber Corp. v. U. S.*, 175 Ct. Cl. 644, 360 F.2d 954, 960, 149 U.S.P.Q. 640 (1966)). Moreover, in order to anticipate a claim, a prior art reference must also "enable one of skill in the

erence can also anticipate without disclosing a feature or aspect if that missing characteristic is "necessarily present, or inherent" in the reference.[4] Inherent anticipation does not require that the inherent characteristic be recognized in the prior art[5] or be "appreciated at the time" of the disclosure.[6] Instead, where the "natural result flowing from the operation as taught" in the prior art would be the invention claimed in the patent-in-suit, that invention is inherently anticipated.[7]

In BPCIA cases, anticipation arguments can arise in a number of contexts, but interesting ones may be raised concerning process claims—e.g., claims directed to cell culture or purification processes to manufacture an antibody.[8]

For example, an RPS may use one or more of the same process steps for manufacturing multiple biologics. Under pre-AIA case law, "a party's placing of the product of a method invention on sale more than a year before that party's application filing date . . . act[s] as a forfeiture of any right to the grant of a valid patent on the method."[9] Similarly, under post-AIA § 102, a patent claim to a manu-

---

field of the invention to make and use the claimed invention." *Merck & Co., Inc. v. Teva Pharmaceuticals USA, Inc.*, 347 F.3d 1367, 1372, 68 U.S.P. Q.2d 1857 (Fed. Cir. 2003). Prior art patents are presumed enabled, *Amgen Inc. v. Hoechst Marion Roussel, Inc.*, 314 F.3d 1313, 1355, 65 U.S.P.Q.2d 1385 (Fed. Cir. 2003), and at least one district court ruled that in the context of a patent litigation (as opposed to in a proceeding before the PTO) all prior art publications are presumed enabled as well, *Cubist Pharmaceuticals, Inc. v. Hospira, Inc.*, 75 F. Supp. 3d 641, 661 n.10 (D. Del. 2014), aff'd, 805 F.3d 1112, 117 U.S.P.Q.2d 1054 (Fed. Cir. 2015).

[4]*Schering Corp. v. Geneva Pharmaceuticals*, 339 F.3d 1373, 1377, 67 U.S.P.Q.2d 1664 (Fed. Cir. 2003).

[5]*E.g.*, *Schering*, 339 F.3d at 1377 (citing *In re Cruciferous Sprout Litigation*, 301 F.3d 1343, 1351, 64 U.S.P.Q.2d 1202 (Fed. Cir. 2002)).

[6]*Abbott Laboratories v. Baxter Pharmaceutical Products, Inc.*, 471 F.3d 1363, 1367, 80 U.S.P.Q.2d 1860 (Fed. Cir. 2006).

[7]*See Finnigan Corp. v. International Trade Com'n*, 180 F.3d 1354, 1365, 51 U.S.P.Q.2d 1001 (Fed. Cir. 1999) (*quoting, Continental Can Co. USA, Inc. v. Monsanto Co.*, 948 F.2d 1264, 1268–69, 20 U.S.P.Q.2d 1746 (Fed. Cir. 1991)); *Eli Lilly and Co. v. Barr Laboratories, Inc.*, 251 F.3d 955, 970, 58 U.S.P.Q.2d 1869 (Fed. Cir. 2001)).

[8]*See, e.g., Genentech, Inc. v. Samsung Bioepis, Inc.*, No. 1:18-01363, D.I. 1 (D. Del. Sept. 14, 2018) (complaint asserting patents directed to techniques developed by Genentech relating to various aspects of cell culture, purification, and antibody purification); *AbbVie, Inc. v. Sandoz, Inc.*, No. 3:18-12668, D.I. 1 (D.N.J. Aug. 10, 2018) (complaint asserting patents directed to various purification methods).

[9]*D.L. Auld Co. v. Chroma Graphics Corp.*, 714 F.2d 1144, 1148, 219

facturing process is invalid if the "claimed invention was . . . in public use, on sale, or otherwise available to the public before the effective filing date of the claimed invention."[10] Therefore, if an RPS sold a biologic made by the claimed process more than a year before the patent was filed, the process claims may be anticipated by the prior sales.

Furthermore, where a process in a prior art reference is expressly missing one or more claim elements, the biosimilar applicant may try to recreate the process to show that those elements are actually inherently disclosed. That was attempted in at least one BPCIA case, but was ultimately not successful. Ultimately, the applicant failed to show that the prior art processes "necessarily and inevitably" met each of the claimed limitations.[11]

Other anticipation challenges could arise in the context of method of treatment claims directed to patient subpopulations. Because of the targeted nature of biologics, RPSs are likely to procure and assert patents directed to methods for treating a disease in a particular patient subpopulation, e.g., a subpopulation of patients having a common symptoms, genetic mutations or predisposition, or having a tumor with a particular genotype. In such a case, the prior art may include a reference disclosing the use of the claimed drug for treating the claimed disease, but in a broader patient population. Biosimilar applicants may look

---

U.S.P.Q. 13 (Fed. Cir. 1983) (citing *Metallizing Engineering Co. v. Kenyon Bearing & Auto Parts Co.*, 153 F.2d 516, 519, 68 U.S.P.Q. 54 (C.C.A. 2d Cir. 1946)); *W.L. Gore & Associates, Inc. v. Garlock, Inc.*, 721 F.2d 1540, 1550, 220 U.S.P.Q. 303 (Fed. Cir. 1983); *Scaltech, Inc. v. Retec/Tetra, LLC*, 269 F.3d 1321, 1328, 60 U.S.P.Q.2d 1687, 45 U.C.C. Rep. Serv. 2d 1036 (Fed. Cir. 2001).

[10]35 U.S.C.A. § 102(a)(1).

[11]*See Amgen Inc. v. Hospira, Inc.*, 336 F. Supp. 3d 333, 347–48 (D. Del. 2018). For example, one claim at issue, claim 24, was directed to "a method of preparing erythropoietin molecules having a predetermined number of sialic acids per molecule said number selected from the group consisting of 1-14, comprising applying material containing erythropoietin to an ion exchange column and selectively eluting said molecules from the column." Relying on expert testimony and testing, Hospira argued that the prior art Lai reference inherently met the "selectively eluting" and "predetermined number of sialic acids" limitations of claim 24. But the jury disagreed. The Court then ruled that the evidence adequately supported the jury's finding because, *inter alia*, Hospira's expert admitted that the prior art process could not have eluted isoforms with a predetermined number of sialic acids, and no other expert witness testified that the anticipating reference necessarily and inevitably met the claimed limitations.

for ways to argue that that the claimed subpopulation would have necessarily been a part of the population described in the prior art.

§ 4:83   Patent validity—Obviousness (Section 103)

A determination of obviousness under Section 103[1] considers (1) the "level of ordinary skill in the pertinent art," (2) the "scope and content of the prior art," (3) the "differences between the prior art and the claims at issue," and (4) "secondary considerations" of non-obviousness such as "commercial success, long-felt but unsolved needs, failure of others, etc."[2] For a claim to be obvious, it must be demonstrated that "a skilled artisan would have had reason to combine the teachings of the prior art references to achieve the claimed invention, and that the skilled artisan would have had a reasonable expectation of success from doing so."[3]

No court in a BPCIA litigation has found a claim obvious. In one BPCIA case, the Court did not disturb a jury's verdict that the biosimilar applicant did not meet its burden.[4] In another case, the Court held after a bench trial that the

---

[Section 4:83]

[1]Patents with filing dates on or before March 16, 2013 are subject to the pre-AIA version of 35 U.S.C.A. § 103(a), which states that "[a] patent may not be obtained, notwithstanding that the claimed invention is not identically disclosed or described as set forth in section 102, if the differences between the subject matter sought to be patented and the prior art are such that the subject matter as a whole would have been obvious at the time the invention was made to a person having ordinary skill in the art to which said subject matter pertains." For patents with filing dates after March 16, 2013, the post-AIA 35 U.S.C.A. § 103 applies, which states that "[a] patent for a claimed invention may not be obtained, notwithstanding that the claimed invention is not identically disclosed as set forth in section 102, if the differences between the claimed invention and the prior art are such that the claimed invention as a whole would have been obvious before the effective filing date of the claimed invention to a person having ordinary skill in the art to which the claimed invention pertains." The temporal focus for the obviousness inquiry for post-AIA patents is before the effective filing date of the claimed invention, rather than at the time of the invention as set forth in the pre-AIA statute.

[2]KSR Intern. Co. v. Teleflex Inc., 550 U.S. 398, 406, 127 S. Ct. 1727, 167 L. Ed. 2d 705, 82 U.S.P.Q.2d 1385 (2007).

[3]In re Cyclobenzaprine Hydrochloride Extended-Release Capsule Patent Litigation, 676 F.3d 1063, 1068–69, 102 U.S.P.Q.2d 1760 (Fed. Cir. 2012) (quoting Procter & Gamble Co. v. Teva Pharmaceuticals USA, Inc., 566 F.3d 989, 994, 90 U.S.P.Q.2d 1947 (Fed. Cir. 2009)).

[4]See Amgen, 336 F. Supp. 3d at 348-349. The claims there were

biosimilar applicant had not established the asserted claims were obvious.[5]

In general, as in any other patent case, whether a claim— e.g., one directed to a manufacturing process or method of treatment—asserted in a BPCIA litigation is obvious will turn on the closeness of the prior art to the claimed invention, whether there was reason to combine the prior art in a way to practice the invention, and whether there would have been a reasonable expectation of success.

In Hatch-Waxman cases, however, courts often analyze pharmaceutical-related claims differently from other patent claims. For example, to prove that the chemical structure of a synthetic small molecule is obvious, a patent challenger typically has to provide grounds that would have led a chemist to modify a "lead compound"—one that would be a "natural choice for further development efforts."[6] From there, the challenger has to demonstrate why a person of skill in the art would have modified the "lead compound" to arrive at the claimed invention.[7] The law does not require patent challengers in any other context to prove, as part of an obviousness defense, why a particular prior art reference would have been selected as a starting point. Moreover, courts repeatedly find that various pharmaceutical arts are more unpredictable than non-pharmaceuticals arts, in some cases raising the bar for the patent challenger to make its case for

---

directed to methods "of preparing erythropoietin molecules having a predetermined number of sialic acids per molecule" by "applying material containing erythropoietin to an ion exchange column and selectively eluting said molecules from the column." Hospira argued that (1) it was known that more sialylated forms of erythropoietin were more biologically active, (2) it was known that sialic acid negatively charged erythropoietin, (3) ion exchange chromatography was known method for separating protein molecules by charge, and (4) an additional reference taught that reference taught that glycoproteins could be separated by charge using ion exchange chromatography. Hospira further argued this gave a person of ordinary skill in the art motivation to separate isoforms of erythropoietin with a predetermined number of sialic acids. The Court concluded, however, the prior art references did not teach erythropoietin isoforms, or predetermined mixtures, or in vivo specific activities of erythropoietin isoforms, and that Hospira's motivation arguments lacked any explanation.

[5]See Immunex Corp. v. Sandoz Inc., 2019 WL 3761915 (D.N.J. 2019).

[6]Bristol-Myers Squibb Co. v. Teva Pharmaceuticals USA, Inc., 752 F.3d 967, 973, 111 U.S.P.Q.2d 1293 (Fed. Cir. 2014).

[7]Bristol-Myers Squibb, 752 F.3d at 973.

obviousness.[8] Because biologics are designed differently than small molecules, and often have vastly more complicated structure, it is unclear whether courts will ultimately develop new tests for evaluating whether the structure of a novel biologic would have been obvious.[9]

BPCIA cases may, in particular, involve patent claims directed to modified structures of known biologics—for example, claims directed to antibodies with certain post-translational modifications (e.g., glycosylation, sialylation, methylation), or an antibody with a modified acidic or base variant profile. For such claims, the question of obviousness may turn "on the structural similarities and differences between the claimed compound and the prior art compound[ ]" and whether a person of skill in the art would have been motivated to modify the known biologic to have the claimed profile.[10]

BPCIA cases may also concern patents directed to methods of using a biologic agent for therapy. Like a method of use patent in a Hatch-Waxman case, whether those claims are obvious may turn on what was known about the biologic agent and other drugs in the same class, including the extent of any animal or human testing, and the efficacy of prior art treatments for the claimed disease.

§ 4:84   Patent validity—Lack of written description, lack of enablement, and indefiniteness (section 112)

35 U.S.C.A. § 112 includes written description and enablement requirements for a patent specification, and definite-

---

[8]*See, e.g., Otsuka Pharmaceutical Co., Ltd. v. Sandoz, Inc.*, 678 F.3d 1280, 1298, 102 U.S.P.Q.2d 1729 (Fed. Cir. 2012) (crediting the district court's finding of "evidence demonstrating the high degree of unpredictability in antipsychotic drug discovery as of the priority date" and noting that "[a]s *KSR* makes clear, predictability is a vital consideration in the obviousness analysis."); *see also Procter & Gamble Co. v. Teva Pharmaceuticals USA, Inc.*, 566 F.3d 989, 996, 90 U.S.P.Q.2d 1947 (Fed. Cir. 2009) ("[T]o the extent an art is unpredictable, as the chemical arts often are, *KSR's* focus on [] 'identified, predictable solutions' may present a difficult hurdle because potential solutions are less likely to be genuinely predictable.").

[9]*See Immunex Corp. v. Sandoz Inc.*, 2019 WL 3761915 (D.N.J. 2019) (evaluating obviousness of patent claiming etanercept without explicit reference to "lead compound" analysis).

[10]*Eisai Co. Ltd. v. Dr. Reddy's Laboratories, Ltd.*, 533 F.3d 1353, 1356–57, 87 U.S.P.Q.2d 1452 (Fed. Cir. 2008).

ness requirement for patent claims.[1] If any of these requirements are not met, an invalidity ruling will follow.

The test for enablement is that the specification must provide "sufficient teaching such that one skilled in the art could make and use the full scope of the invention without undue experimentation."[2] If some experimentation is required to practice the full scope of the claims, the patent will not necessarily lack enablement, but if the amount of experimentation is "undue," then it is invalid.[3] The factors that may be utilized in determining whether a disclosure would require undue experimentation include: (1) the quantity of experimentation necessary; (2) the amount of direction or guidance disclosed in the patent; (3) the presence or absence of working examples in the patent; (4) the nature of the invention; (5) the state of the prior art; (6) the relative skill of those in the art; (7) the predictability of the art; and (8) the breadth of the claims.[4]

The written description requirement contained in 35 U.S.C.A. § 112 requires that "disclosure of the application relied upon reasonably conveys to those skilled in the art that the inventor had possession of the claimed subject mat-

---

[Section 4:84]

[1]Pre-AIA, the relevant portion of Section 112 read as follows:

The specification shall contain a written description of the invention, and of the manner and process of making and using it, in such full, clear, concise, and exact terms as to enable any person skilled in the art to which it pertains, or with which it is most nearly connected, to make and use the same, and shall set forth the best mode contemplated by the inventor of carrying out his invention.

The specification shall conclude with one or more claims particularly pointing out and distinctly claiming the subject matter which the inventor or a joint inventor regards as the invention.

Post-AIA Section 112(a) has the same written description, enablement and indefiniteness requirements as pre-AIA Section 112. Section 112 also identified best mode as a requirement, and pre-AIA, lack of best mode was a defense to patent infringement. The AIA, however, amended 35 U.S.C.A. § 282 such that failure to disclose best mode is no longer a grounds for invalidity for proceedings commenced on or after September 16, 2011.

[2]*Warner-Lambert Co. v. Teva Pharmaceuticals USA, Inc.*, 418 F.3d 1326, 1337, 75 U.S.P.Q.2d 1865 (Fed. Cir. 2005).

[3]*Cephalon, Inc. v. Watson Pharmaceuticals, Inc.*, 707 F.3d 1330, 1338, 105 U.S.P.Q.2d 1817 (Fed. Cir. 2013).

[4]*In re Wands*, 858 F.2d 731, 737, 8 U.S.P.Q.2d 1400 (Fed. Cir. 1988). These factors are sometimes referred to as the "Wands factors."

ter as of the filing date."[5] For a specification to provide written description for a claimed invention, "the specification must describe an invention understandable to that skilled artisan and show that the inventor actually invented the invention claimed."[6] For claims directed to a genus of biological products, the patentee must include a disclosure of "either a representative number of species falling within the scope of the genus or structural features common to the members of the genus so that one of skill in the art can 'visualize or recognize' the members of the genus."[7] The written description must further include "a precise definition, such as by structure, formula, chemical name, physical properties, or other properties, of species falling within the genus sufficient to distinguish the genus from other materials," although functional language may suffice "when the art has established a correlation between structure and function."[8]

A patent is invalid for indefiniteness "if its claims, read in light of the specification delineating the patent, and the prosecution history, fail to inform, with reasonable certainty, those skilled in the art about the scope of the invention."[9] A patent is not indefinite merely because there is some uncertainty in the claim language as "[s]ome modicum of uncertainty . . . is the 'price of ensuring the appropriate incentives for innovation.' "[10] However, if a claim term requires measurement, "the patent and prosecution history must disclose a single known approach or establish that, where multiple known approaches exist, a person having ordinary skill in the art would know which approach to select."[11] The definiteness requirement is intended to provide notice to the public "what is still open to them" and what

---

[5]*Ariad Pharmaceuticals, Inc. v. Eli Lilly and Co.*, 598 F.3d 1336, 1351, 94 U.S.P.Q.2d 1161 (Fed. Cir. 2010).

[6]*Ariad*, 598 F.3d at 1351.

[7]*Ariad*, 598 F.3d at 1350.

[8]*Ariad*, 598 F.3d at 1350.

[9]*Nautilus, Inc. v. Biosig Instruments, Inc.*, 572 U.S. 898, 901, 134 S. Ct. 2120, 189 L. Ed. 2d 37, 110 U.S.P.Q.2d 1688 (2014).

[10]*Nautilus*, 572 U.S. at 901 (quoting *Festo Corp. v. Shoketsu Kinzoku Kogyo Kabushiki Co., Ltd.*, 535 U.S. 722, 732, 122 S. Ct. 1831, 152 L. Ed. 2d 944, 62 U.S.P.Q.2d 1705 (2002)).

[11]*Dow Chemical Co. v. Nova Chemicals Corp. (Canada)*, 803 F.3d 620, 630, 115 U.S.P.Q.2d 2024 (Fed. Cir. 2015).

they would infringe.[12] Unlike enablement, written description, or best mode, indefiniteness is often raised at the claim construction stage of a case.

In BPCIA cases, written description, enablement, and indefiniteness arguments are likely to arise with respect to claims directed to antibodies or other proteins that are drafted according to their characteristics or interactions with targets in the body, as opposed to their structural characteristics.[13] While no BPCIA cases have addressed the issue of written description in the context of an antibody claim, other patent litigations have.[14] The Federal Circuit has indicated that the description of a "newly characterized antigen" is not sufficient as a matter of law to provide adequate written description for antibody genus claims.[15]

---

[12]*Markman v. Westview Instruments, Inc.*, 517 U.S. 370, 373, 116 S. Ct. 1384, 134 L. Ed. 2d 577, 38 U.S.P.Q.2d 1461 (1996) (quoting *McClain v. Ortmayer*, 141 U.S. 419, 424, 12 S. Ct. 76, 35 L. Ed. 800 (1891)).

[13]*See, e.g., Immunex Corporation v. Sanofi*, 2018 WL 6252460, at *3, *11 (C.D. Cal. 2018) (denying motion for summary judgment that claims to "[a]n isolated human antibody that *competes* with a reference antibody for binding to [a specific] receptor" were indefinite) (emphasis added); *Amgen, Inc. v. Chugai Pharmaceutical Co., Ltd.*, 927 F.2d 1200, 18 U.S.P. Q.2d 1016 (Fed. Cir. 1991) (finding that claims to "generic DNA sequence" encoding a protein and claims to "homogenous erythropoietin" with specific molecular weights and activity levels did not satisfy enablement requirement and that claim limitations requiring protein to have activity of "at least about 160,000" was indefinite).

[14]*See Amgen Inc. v. Sanofi*, 872 F.3d 1367, 124 U.S.P.Q.2d 1354 (Fed. Cir. 2017), cert. denied, 139 S. Ct. 787, 202 L. Ed. 2d 568 (2019) (affirming denial of motion for judgment as a matter of law that claims covering "the entire genus of antibodies that bind to specific amino acid residues" lack written description); *MorphoSys AG v. Janssen Biotech, Inc.*, 358 F. Supp. 3d 354 (D. Del. 2019) (*MorphoSys AG v. Janssen Biotech, Inc.*, 358 F. Supp. 3d 354, 366–367 (D. Del. 2019) (granting summary judgment that claim directed to antibodies lacked written description where the specification identified functional characteristics the antibodies had to meet but failed to disclose the structural characteristics of antibody sequence that would achieve those functions, and granting summary judgment that claims to "any and all CD38 antibodies that satisfy broad functional tests" lack enablement); *Centocor Ortho Biotech, Inc. v. Abbott Laboratories*, 636 F.3d 1341, 1350–1351, 97 U.S.P.Q.2d 1870 (Fed. Cir. 2011) (reversing the denial of the accused infringer's JMOL motion of invalidity because the specification "at best describes a plan for making fully-human antibodies" but "the specification does not describe a single antibody that satisfies the claim limitations" or otherwise indicate that the inventors had constructive possession of the claimed invention).

[15]*Amgen*, 872 F.3d at 1378-79 ("[T]he 'newly characterized antigen' test flouts basic legal principles of the written description requirement.

Likewise, the description of large number of structurally similar antibodies is not sufficient to support claims that cover a structurally diverse genus of antibodies.[16] In BPCIA cases concerning antibody patents, therefore, biosimilar applicants are likely to compare the scope of the asserted antibody claims to that disclosed in the patent specification. Because the adequacy of disclosure is evaluated in view of knowledge is the field, "the maturity of the science or technology, [and] the predictability of the aspect at issue" will factor into whether a disclosure satisfies § 112.[17] Whether the specification discloses a "representative number of species" required to claim the genus and thereby satisfy the written description requirement will depend on how much was known about the claimed genus.[18]

Challenges under 35 U.S.C.A. § 112 to process and method of use claims in the BPCIA context will be similar to those raised in Hatch-Waxman litigation, or other litigation concerning biologics. Similar to composition claims, a court will consider what was known in the art about a claimed process or method, and whether the specification provides adequate disclosures to comply with the various requirements of 35 U.S.C.A. § 112.[19]

Section 112 requires a 'written description of the invention.' But this test allows patentees to claim antibodies by describing something that is not the invention, *i.e.*, the antigen.").

[16]*See AbbVie Deutschland GmbH & Co., KG v. Janssen Biotech, Inc.*, 759 F.3d 1285, 111 U.S.P.Q.2d 1780 (Fed. Cir. 2014).

[17]*Ariad Pharmaceuticals, Inc. v. Eli Lilly and Co.*, 598 F.3d 1336, 1351, 94 U.S.P.Q.2d 1161 (Fed. Cir. 2010).

[18]*MorphoSys AG*, 358 F. Supp. 3d at 364 (considering whether the binding sites using peptide mapping experiments disclosed in the specification would convey to a person of skill in the art that peptide mapping experiments "reliably identify binding sites"); *Amgen Inc. v. Sanofi*, 872 F.3d 1367, 1378–79, 124 U.S.P.Q.2d 1354 (Fed. Cir. 2017), cert. denied, 139 S. Ct. 787, 202 L. Ed. 2d 568 (2019) (holding that same written description standard applies to patents claiming antibodies and noting that the court has "generally eschewed judicial exceptions to the written description requirement based on the subject matter of the claims").

[19]*Butamax Advanced Biofuels LLC v. Gevo, Inc.*, 117 F. Supp. 3d 632, 641 (D. Del. 2015) (finding claim to method for engineering yeast strains indefinite when "the specification identifies a non-inclusive list of five methods to calculate [the claimed] '% identity' " and "such methods of measurement can yield different results").

Method of use claims have been challenged under Section 112 where the claims at issue recite "effective amounts" of a given biologic product. *Ariad*, 598 F.3d at 1357–58 (Fed. Cir. 2010) (en banc) (reversing jury's

§ 4:85 Patent validity—Obviousness-Type double patenting

The doctrine of obviousness-type double patenting serves to bar a patentee from obtaining a later-expiring patent for the same invention.[1] This issue often arises where patent applicants seek to file separate applications for overlapping subject matter and claim different priority dates, thereby obtaining differing expiration dates.[2] In the obviousness-type double patenting analysis, after construing the claims in the two patents the court evaluates whether the differences render the claims patentably distinct.[3] If available, obviousness-type double patenting challenges may prove particularly useful to biosimilar applicants, because the relatively large families of biologic patents may create more opportunities to find invalidating references.[4]

---

verdict that claims directed to a method of "reducing" a certain type of cell activity were not invalid for lack of a written description where specification failed to describe how the claimed reduction would be done, and only provided theoretical ideas of how to achieve the reduced activity); *Immuno-medics, Inc. v. Roger Williams Medical Center, 2017 Markman 788122*, 2017 WL 788122, at *2, *5 (D.N.J. 2017) (holding the term "effective amount" is not indefinite in patents claiming methods of treatment using monoclonal antibodies "in an effective amount for treatment"). They have also been challenged when they were directed to treatment of a specific disease with a broad class of biological products. *Phigenix, Inc. v. Genentech Inc.*, 238 F. Supp. 3d 1177 (N.D. Cal. 2017) (denying summary judgment that claims to a method of treating breast cancer by administering compositions to inhibit expression of a specific protein or to increase expression of another protein lacked an adequate written description because there were issues of fact as to whether the claims were supported based on the structural information contained in the specification).

[Section 4:85]

[1]*Abbvie Inc. v. Mathilda and Terence Kennedy Institute of Rheumatology Trust*, 764 F.3d 1366, 1373, 112 U.S.P.Q.2d 1001 (Fed. Cir. 2014).

[2]*AbbVie*, 764 F.3d at 1373.

[3]*AbbVie*, 764 F.3d at 1374.

[4]For instance, Janssen's antibody claims, which had been asserted in a BPCIA litigation against Celltrion, were invalidated on obviousness-type double patenting grounds by the PTAB in an *ex parte* reexamination over another patent with substantially similar claims. The question as to whether the claims were invalid boiled down to a couple of legal technicalities, *i.e.*, whether the safe harbor exception to double patenting protected Janssen's claims, and whether the "so-called" two-way double patenting test needed to be applied. Ultimately, on both issues, the PTAB, and the Federal Circuit on appeal, sided against Janssen. *In re Janssen Biotech, Inc.*, 880 F.3d 1315, 125 U.S.P.Q.2d 1525 (Fed. Cir. 2018). During the cor-

§ 4:86   Patent enforceability

Under 35 U.S.C.A. § 282, "unenforceability" of a patent is a defense to patent infringement.The judicially recognized defenses that, if proven, result in unenforceability of a patent include (1) unclean hands and (2) inequitable conduct committed during the prosecution of the patent before the PTO.[1]

§ 4:87   Patent enforceability—Unclean hands

A determination of unclean hands may be reached when the misconduct of party seeking relief "has immediate and necessary relation to the equity that he seeks in respect of the matter in litigation."[1] The broad doctrine of unclean hands "closes the doors of a court of equity to one tainted with inequitableness or bad faith relative to the matter in which he seeks relief."[2] Unclean hands is a flexible doctrine based on equity, and courts "are not bound by formula or restrained by any limitation that tends to trammel the free and just exercise of discretion."[3] As one example, unclean hands occurred where an employee of the patentee learned of the accused infringer's drug structure by participating in a conference call, "violating a clear 'firewall' understanding . . . that call participants not be involved in related patent

---

responding BPCIA litigation relating to Celltrion's infliximab biosimilar, on summary judgment, the district court invalidated the same claims for obviousness-type patenting on two separate grounds. *Janssen Biotech, Inc. v. Celltrion Healthcare Co. Inc.*, 210 F. Supp. 3d 244, 245, 120 U.S.P.Q.2d 1786 (D. Mass. 2016). Although Janssen appealed those rulings as well, following the Federal Circuit's affirmance of the PTAB's reexamination decision, the Federal Circuit dismissed the appeal of the summary judgment decisions as moot. *In re Janssen Biotech, Inc.*, 880 F.3d 1315, 125 U.S.P. Q.2d 1525 (Fed. Cir. 2018).

[Section 4:86]

[1]*See, e.g., Gilead Sciences, Inc. v. Merck & Co., Inc.*, 888 F.3d 1231, 1241-46, 126 U.S.P.Q.2d 1481 (Fed. Cir. 2018), cert. denied, 139 S. Ct. 797, 202 L. Ed. 2d 572 (2019) (unclean hands); *Therasense, Inc. v. Becton, Dickinson and Co.*, 649 F.3d 1276, 1287–89, 99 U.S.P.Q.2d 1065 (Fed. Cir. 2011) (inequitable conduct).

[Section 4:87]

[1]*Keystone Driller Co. v. General Excavator Co.*, 290 U.S. 240, 245, 54 S. Ct. 146, 78 L. Ed. 293, 19 U.S.P.Q. 228 (1933).

[2]*Precision Instrument Mfg. Co. v. Automotive Maintenance Machinery Co.*, 324 U.S. 806, 814–15, 65 S. Ct. 993, 89 L. Ed. 1381, 65 U.S.P.Q. 133 (1945).

[3]*Keystone Driller Co.*, 290 U.S. at 245–46.

prosecutions," and then continued to involve the employee in the patent prosecution after the call, leading to narrowed claims that were directed to the accused infringer's product.[4]

In the BPCIA context, a reference product sponsor may face an unclean hands counterclaim based on their development of a "patent thicket" as a means to delay competition.[5] For example, engaging "in a pattern of pursuing numerous overlapping and non-inventive patents for the purpose of developing a 'patent thicket,' using the patenting process itself as a means to seek to delay competition" has served as the basis for an unclean hands allegation.[6] Specifically, unclean hands may be based on allegations that the reference product sponsor's patents "share common specifications and have overlapping and nearly identical claims,"[7] and "do not represent innovation, but rather are attempts to claim methods of treatment, methods of production, and formulations derived from the prior art for the purpose of creating a patent thicket or estate that competitors must . . . 'contend with' to sell" their biosimilar product.[8]

§ 4:88 Patent enforceability—Inequitable conduct

Inequitable conduct arises from misrepresentations or omissions by the patent owner during prosecution before the PTO.[1] The defense of inequitable conduct requires proof that the patent applicant "misrepresented or omitted material information with the specific intent to deceive the PTO."[2] As a general matter, "the materiality required to establish inequitable conduct is but-for materiality," and thus, "in assessing the materiality of a withheld reference, the court must determine whether the PTO would have allowed the claim if

---

[4]See Gilead Sciences, Inc., 888 F.3d at 1241 (finding that the employee's knowledge "acquired improperly, influenced Merck's filing of narrowed claims, a filing that held the potential for expediting patent issuance and for lowering certain invalidity risks," amounting to "serious misconduct, violating clear standards of probity in the circumstances").

[5]See, e.g., AbbVie Inc. et al. v. Boehringer Ingelheim Int'l GmbH et al., No. 17-01065, D.I. 20 (D. Del. Sept. 11, 2017) at 42-44.

[6]AbbVie Inc., No. 17-01065, D.I. 20 at 44.

[7]AbbVie Inc., No. 17-01065, D.I. 20 at 44.

[8]AbbVie Inc., No. 17-01065, D.I. 20 at 45.

[Section 4:88]

[1]Therasense, Inc. v. Becton, Dickinson and Co., 649 F.3d 1276, 1287, 99 U.S.P.Q.2d 1065 (Fed. Cir. 2011).

[2]Therasense Inc., 649 F.3d at 1287.

it had been aware of the undisclosed reference."[3] "Although but-for materiality generally must be proved to satisfy the materiality prong of inequitable conduct," the Federal Circuit also "recognizes an exception in cases of affirmative egregious misconduct," such as "the filing of an unmistakably false affidavit," which is deemed material even if the "but-for test" is not satisfied.[4]

§ 4:89   Patent enforceability—Unenforceability allegations in the BPCIA patent dance

A biosimilar applicant that opts to participate in the patent dance pursuant to the BPCIA may include an allegation of unenforceability in its detailed statement.[1] If a biosimilar applicant includes an allegation of unenforceability in its detailed statement, the reference product sponsor is obligated to respond "not later than 60 days after receipt of the list and statement under subparagraph (B)," including "a response to the statement concerning . . . unenforceability provided under subparagraph (B)(ii)(1)."[2]

X.   POTENTIAL REMEDIES FOR INFRINGEMENT

§ 4:90   Infringement remedies generally

In the event that a court finds that a biosimilar applicant has infringed a patent that is valid and enforceable, the RPS may be entitled to relief, such as injunctive relief or damages. When Congress passed the BPCIA, it made conforming amendments to 35 U.S.C.A. § 271(e)(4) to account for the newly enacted biosimilars regime. As amended, the statute addresses what remedies would or may be available for the RPS in the event that the applicant is found to infringe one

---

[3]*Therasense Inc.*, 649 F.3d at 1291.

[4]*Therasense Inc.*, 649 F.3d at 1292.

[Section 4:89]

[1]42 U.S.C.A. § 262(*l*)(3)(B)(ii)(I) (West) (stating that the biosimilar applicant "shall provide to the reference product sponsor . . . (I) a detailed statement that describes, on a claim by claim basis, the factual and legal basis of the opinion of the subsection (k) applicant that such patent is invalid, **unenforceable**, or will not be infringed by the commercial marketing of the biological product that is the subject of the subjection (k) application[.]" (emphasis added).

[2]42 U.S.C.A. § 262(*l*)(3)(C).

or more patents.[1] The amendments also limit the remedies that are available to an RPS. "The remedies prescribed by [35 U.S.C.A. § 271(e)(4)] are the only remedies which may be granted by a court for an act of infringement described in paragraph (2), except that a court may award attorney fees under section 285."[2] Once an applicant has launched its biosimilar product, 35 U.S.C.A. § 283 theoretically defines the categories of monetary recovery to which the RPS may be entitled.

§ 4:91 The BPCIA's conforming amendments to 35 U.S.C.A. § 271(e)(4)

Section 271(e)(4) of the U.S. Code provides the remedies available for the acts of infringement defined in Section 271(e)(2). For acts of infringement relating to applications seeking approval for drug or veterinary biological products under the Federal Food, Drug, and Cosmetic Act or the Act of March 4, 1913, Section 271(e)(4) had provided for (A) court orders delaying the effective date of approval for the product until the expiry of the infringed patent, and the possibility of (B) injunctive relief and (C) monetary damages, if the drug product had been commercialized.

As part of the BPCIA, Congress amended Section 271(e)(4) to add references to "biological products." In view of Section 271(e)(2), these references mean biosimilar products. These new provisions for biosimilars were added to subparagraphs (B) and (C), regarding injunctive relief and damages for approved products, and subparagraph (D), addressing not-yet-approved biological products.

(4) For an act of infringement described in paragraph (2)—

(A) the court shall order the effective date of any approval of the drug or veterinary biological product involved in the infringement to be a date which is not earlier than the date of the expiration of the patent which has been infringed,

(B) injunctive relief may be granted against an infringer to prevent the commercial manufacture, use, offer to sell, or sale within the United States or importation into the United States of an approved drug, veterinary biological product, *or biological product,*

[Section 4:90]

[1]*See* Biologics Price Competition and Innovation Act of 2009 ("BPCIA"); 35 U.S.C.A. § 271(e)(4).

[2]35 U.S.C.A. § 271(e)(4)(D).

(C) damages or other monetary relief may be awarded against an infringer only if there has been commercial manufacture, use, offer to sell, or sale within the United States or importation into the United States of an approved drug, veterinary biological product, *or biological product,* and

(D) the court shall order a permanent injunction prohibiting any infringement of the patent by the biological product involved in the infringement until a date which is not earlier than the date of the expiration of the patent that has been infringed under paragraph (2)(C), provided the patent is the subject of a final court decision, as defined in section 351(k)(6) of the Public Health Service Act, in an action for infringement of the patent under section 351(l)(6) of such Act, and the biological product has not yet been approved because of section 351(k)(7) of such Act.[1]

§ 4:92   Delaying the effective date of FDA approval

In the event that one or more patents are found valid and infringed in a BPCIA litigation, it is unsettled whether an RPS may be able to use Section 271(e)(4)(A) to have the court effectively stay FDA approval of the aBLA until a date no earlier than patent expiration.[1] No court has yet addressed this provision in a BPCIA litigation. In Hatch-Waxman litigations, where the generic challenger is found to infringe one or more valid patents:

> [T]he court is required [under this provision] to order the effective date of the ANDA approval to be a date "not earlier than" the expiration date of the patent. If the FDA has not approved the ANDA at the time of the district court's decision, the FDA may not approve the ANDA (and the generic may not sell its drug) until after the patent expires. If the FDA has already approved the ANDA, the district court's order alters the effective date of that approval.[2]

At least one court has ruled, however, that once the generic applicant launches its product, this provision is "inapplicable . . . because the infringing acts fall under 35 U.S.C.A.

[Section 4:91]

[1]35 U.S.C.A. § 271(e)(4) (emphases added).

[Section 4:92]

[1]35 U.S.C.A. § 271(e)(4)(A).

[2]*AstraZeneca AB v. Apotex Corp.*, 782 F.3d 1324, 1341, 114 U.S.P. Q.2d 1416 (Fed. Cir. 2015) (citations omitted). In the latter scenario, the final approval would be converted into a tentative approval. *See Ortho-McNeil Pharmaceutical, Inc. v. Mylan Laboratories, Inc.*, 520 F.3d 1358, 1366, 86 U.S.P.Q.2d 1196 (Fed. Cir. 2008).

§ 271(a) (direct infringement), § 271(b) (inducement), and § 271(c) (contributory infringement), not under § 271(e)(4)(A) (infringement based on the act of filing the ANDA)."[3] In that case, 35 U.S.C.A. § 284 provides the potential remedies to which the patentee could be entitled, including a reasonable royalty.

It is unclear whether Section 271(e)(4)(A)—which refers to "drugs," but not "biological products"—applies to the approval of aBLAs in the event that a court finds that one or more patents are infringed in a BPCIA litigation. One the one hand, Congress specifically added references to "biological products" to sub-paragraphs (B) and (C), which respectively addresses injunctive relief and damages. No such change was made to paragraph (A). On the other hand, Section 271(e)(1), which carves out an exception to patent infringement known as the "safe harbor,"[4] refers to "drugs" and "veterinary biological products." It does not specifically refer to "biological products" like Section 271(e)(4) does.

To date, no court in a BPCIA litigation has ruled that a biosimilar applicant has infringed a valid, enforceable, and *unexpired* patent. Therefore, no court has had an opportunity to weigh in on whether Section 271(e)(4)(A) applies to aBLAs.

§ 4:93 Awarding monetary relief

In the event that a biosimilar applicant is found to infringe one or more valid and enforceable patents, the RPS may be entitled to monetary relief in one or more of the three scenarios:

- The safe harbor defense did not protect the biosimilar applicant's pre-market activities;[1]
- The applicant launched its biosimilar product; and
- A court finds that the case was exceptional, and that the RPS is entitled to attorney fees.

For the first two scenarios described above, although Sec-

---

[3]*See Sanofi-Aventis Deutschland GmbH v. Glenmark Pharmaceuticals Inc.*, 821 F. Supp. 2d 681, 697 (D.N.J. 2011), aff'd and remanded, 748 F.3d 1354, 110 U.S.P.Q.2d 1571 (Fed. Cir. 2014).

[4]*Supra* Section 4:69, addressing infringement and the safe harbor provision.

[Section 4:93]

[1]*See supra* Section 4:79 regarding the safe harbor defense to infringement. *See also* 35 U.S.C.A. § 271(e)(1).

tion 271(e)(4) states that "[t]he remedies prescribed by [it] are the only remedies which may be granted by a court for an act of infringement described in paragraph (2), except that a court may award attorney fees under section 285,"[2] Section 284 theoretically defines the categories of monetary recovery to which the RPS may be entitled. In particular, it states that a damages award shall not be less than a reasonable royalty. A reasonable royalty represents the minimum the patent owner is entitled to for the infringement of its patents. A reasonable royalty is determined by imagining a "hypothetical negotiation" between the two parties before the time of the alleged infringement.[3] There are a variety of factors that are considered when determining the reasonable royalty[4] which in essence attempts to represent the royalty the parties would arrive at during a friendly business negotiation.

Often times, a patent owner will attempt to recover more damages than what a reasonable royalty would grant them and seek what is referred to as "lost profits." Lost profits damages compensates the patent owner for the money they lost due to the infringing activities.[5] To be awarded lost profits, the patentee must show a show a reasonable probability that "but for" the infringement, plaintiff would have made the defendant's infringing sales.[6] In general, to demonstrate it is entitled to lost profits, the patentee must show the so-called *Panduit* factors: "(1) demand for the patented product; (2) absence of acceptable non-infringing substitutes; (3) manufacturing and marketing capability to exploit the demand; and (4) the amount of the profit [the patent owner] would have made."[7]

In some cases, enhanced damages may be awarded if the patent owner can prove there was "egregious infringement

---

[2]35 U.S.C.A. § 271(e)(4).

[3]*Wang Laboratories, Inc. v. Toshiba Corp.*, 993 F.2d 858, 870, 26 U.S.P.Q.2d 1767 (Fed. Cir. 1993).

[4]*Georgia-Pacific Corp. v. U.S. Plywood Corp.*, 318 F. Supp. 1116, 1120, 166 U.S.P.Q. 235 (S.D. N.Y. 1970), judgment aff'd modified, 446 F.2d 295, 170 U.S.P.Q. 369 (2d Cir. 1971).

[5]*Grain Processing Corp. v. American Maize-Products Co.*, 185 F.3d 1341, 1349, 51 U.S.P.Q.2d 1556 (Fed. Cir. 1999).

[6]*Grain Processing*, 185 F.3d at 1350.

[7]*Rite-Hite Corp. v. Kelley Co., Inc.*, 56 F.3d 1538, 1545, 35 U.S.P.Q.2d 1065 (Fed. Cir. 1995).

behavior" or where the infringer acted "deliberately or willfully."[8]

35 U.S.C.A. § 285 controls whether attorneys' fees may be awarded in a given case. It states that "[t]he court in exceptional cases may award reasonable attorney fees to the prevailing party." An " 'exceptional' case is simply one that stands out from others with respect to the substantive strength of a party's litigating position . . . or the unreasonable manner in which the case was litigated," to be determined at the district court's discretion under the totality of the circumstances based on a preponderance of the evidence.[9]

To date, such monetary relief has only been awarded in one BPCIA litigation, in which a jury, and then the court following post-trial motions, found that an applicant's safe harbor defense did not apply, and awarded an RPS a reasonable royalty. In Hatch-Waxman cases, monetary damages are rarely granted in Hatch-Waxman cases, because most judgments are entered before a generic applicant launches its product. Whether that pattern continues with BPCIA cases remains to be same.

§ 4:94 Patent enforceability—Monetary damages where safe harbor provision does not protect pre-market activity

The "safe harbor" provision of Section 271(e)(1) provides that it shall not be an act of infringement to perform otherwise infringing activities if those activities are "reasonably related to the development and submission of information" for regulatory purposes.[1] If an activity is deemed not be protected by the safe-harbor provision, a party could be liable for damages to the RPS for the unauthorized, pre-market use of the patented invention. Without any actual infringing sales, such pre-market activity would probably only entitle the RPS to a reasonable royalty. Still, in the one BPCIA litigation where the safe harbor provision did not protect the biosimilar applicant's premarket activity, the

---

[8]*Halo Electronics, Inc. v. Pulse Electronics, Inc.*, 136 S. Ct. 1923, 195 L. Ed. 2d 278, 118 U.S.P.Q.2d 1761 (2016).

[9]*Octane Fitness, LLC v. ICON Health & Fitness, Inc.*, 572 U.S. 545, 134 S. Ct. 1749, 1756, 1758, 188 L. Ed. 2d 816, 110 U.S.P.Q.2d 1337 (2014).

[Section 4:94]

[1]*See supra* Section 4:79 regarding the safe harbor defense to infringement.

district court did not disturb a jury's verdict that the RPS was owed a reasonable royalty amounting to $70 million.[2]

§ 4:95   Patent enforceability—Monetary damages for an at-risk launch

There has been no lost profits or reasonable royalty award in a BPCIA case as a result of an at-risk, biosimilar launch. Such awards are infrequent in Hatch-Waxman cases, as generic applicants infrequently launch their products before a final judgment is entered—whether by their own choice or as a result of a preliminary injunction. It is not clear whether the trend will be the same for BPCIA litigations. Thus far, at least one biosimilar applicant launched its product at risk before final judgment, but it ultimately prevailed on non-infringement at the summary judgment-stage, and there was never any jury trial on its potential liability to the RPS.[1]

Still, damages inquiries may raise interesting issues in the context of litigating manufacturing process patents in BPCIA cases. To avoid having to pay lost profits on the infringing use of a process patent, biosimilar applicants will likely look for acceptable non-infringing alternatives to the claimed process—evidence of that alone could defeat, or substantially diminish, an RPS's lost profits claim.[2] In this context, the biosimilar applicant that has been sued on a process patent may want to take discovery of other companies that are developing a biosimilar of the same molecule, but that were not sued for infringement. Non-infringing alternatives include products not accused of infringement.[3] Therefore, an RPS's decision not to sue a competitor making a

---

[2]Amgen Inc., et al. v. Hospira, Inc., Case No. 15-cv-839-RGA (Order, August 27, 2018). The case is currently on appeal to the Federal Circuit.

[Section 4:95]

[1]*See* "Pfizer Announces the U.S. Availability of Biosimilar Inflectra® (Inflimixmab-dyyb)," Oct. 17, 2016 (*available at* https://www.pfizer.com/ne ws/press-release/press-release-detail/pfizer_announces_the_u_s_availabilit y_of_biosimilar_inflectra_infliximab_dyyb). *See also* Janssen Biotech, Inc. v. Celltrion Healthcare Co., Case 3:17-cv-11008-MLW, D.I. 393 (D.Mass. July 30, 2018) (finding that Pfizer's process was noninfringing).

[2]*Grain Processing Corp. v. American Maize-Products Co.*, 185 F.3d 1341, 1352-53, 51 U.S.P.Q.2d 1556 (Fed. Cir. 1999) ("Market sales of an acceptable noninfringing substitute often suffice alone to defeat a case for lost profits."); *Panduit*, 575 F.2d at 1156.

[3]*SRI Intern. Inc. v. Internet Sec. Systems, Inc.*, 2011 WL 5166436, *1 (D. Del. 2011).

biosimilar of the same molecule cannot be ignored when analyzing lost profits.[4]

§ 4:96 Patent enforceability—Attorneys' fees

A Court may award attorneys' fees, in its discretion, when it determines that a case is exceptional, considering the totality of the circumstances.[1] In Hatch-Waxman litigation, courts have awarded attorney fees where patent challengers engaged in a pattern of litigation misconduct, including serving paragraph IV certifications that contained only "baseless" defenses.[2] Moreover, when a party fails to present any evidence to support an allegation it made attorneys' fees may also be warranted.[3] Not only is the accused infringer potentially on the hook for attorneys' fees, the patent owner may also be forced to pay fees when they fail to put forth any evidence of infringement.[4]

§ 4:97 Awarding permanent injunctive relief

If a court in a BPCIA litigation finds that an asserted patent is infringed, valid, and enforceable, the court may enjoin the manufacture, use, offer to sell, or sale within the United States or importation into the United States of a biosimilar product. To date, no court has, in a BPCIA litigation, entered a permanent injunction.

The standard for granting a permanent injunction in any kind of patent litigation is provided in 35 U.S.C.A. § 283, as further elaborated by the Supreme Court. In particular, courts "may grant injunctions in accordance with the principles of equity to prevent the violation of any right

---

[4]*In re Gabapentin Patent Litigation*, 2011 WL 1807448, *6 (D.N.J. 2011); *Pall Corp. v. Micron Separations, Inc.*, 66 F.3d 1211, 1223, 36 U.S.P. Q.2d 1225, 43 Fed. R. Evid. Serv. 97 (Fed. Cir. 1995) (explaining that the presence of a product that the patentee allowed into the marketplace cannot be ignored in analyzing lost profits).

[Section 4:96]

[1]*Octane Fitness, LLC v. ICON Health & Fitness, Inc.*, 572 U.S. 545, 553–54, 134 S. Ct. 1749, 188 L. Ed. 2d 816, 110 U.S.P.Q.2d 1337 (2014).

[2]*Yamanouchi Pharmaceutical Co. v. Danbury Pharmacal, Inc.*, 21 F. Supp. 2d 366, 48 U.S.P.Q.2d 1741 (S.D. N.Y. 1998), aff'd, 231 F.3d 1339, 56 U.S.P.Q.2d 1641, 180 A.L.R. Fed. 743 (Fed. Cir. 2000).

[3]*Takeda Chemical Industries, Ltd. v. Mylan Laboratories, Inc.*, 549 F.3d 1381, 89 U.S.P.Q.2d 1218 (Fed. Cir. 2008).

[4]*Astrazeneca AB v. Dr. Reddy's Laboratories, Ltd.*, 2010 WL 1375176, *4 (S.D. N.Y. 2010).

secured by patent, on such terms as the court deems reasonable."[1] To obtain a permanent injunction, a patentee must demonstrate that analysis of the following factors—known as the *eBay* factors—warrant such relief:

(i)   the patent holder has suffered or will suffer irreparable injury or harm,

(ii)   legal remedies are inadequate to compensate that injury,

(iii)   balance of hardships, and

(iv)   the public interest.[2]

Generally speaking, a finding of patent infringement does not necessarily mean that the patentee is entitled to a permanent injunction.

Section 271(e)(4)(B) and (D) speak to permanent injunctions in the biosimilar context. Both provisions above could apply to where a permanent injunction is sought before launch. Section 271(e)(4)(B) arguably could also apply where an injunction is sought after launch, although it is duplicative of the relief otherwise available to a patentee under Section 283.

Section 271(e)(4)(B), specifically, does not entitle patentees to an automatic permanent injunction.[3] Rather, under that provision, a patentee must demonstrate that a permanent injunction is warranted by analysis of the *eBay* factors.[4] In some, Hatch-Waxman cases, courts have refused to grant relief under Section 271(e)(4)(B) because the date of final FDA approval of the ANDA is already delayed under Section 271(e)(4)(A).[5] In such cases, for example, the relief already available to the patentee—a stay of FDA approval—supports a finding that adequate legal remedies for the patentee do

---

[Section 4:97]

[1]35 U.S.C.A. § 283.

[2]*See eBay Inc. v. MercExchange, L.L.C.*, 547 U.S. 388, 391, 126 S. Ct. 1837, 164 L. Ed. 2d 641, 78 U.S.P.Q.2d 1577, 27 A.L.R. Fed. 2d 685 (2006); *Bayer Pharma AG v. Watson Laboratories, Inc.*, 2016 WL 7468172 (D. Del. 2016).

[3]*See, e.g., Alcon, Inc. v. Teva Pharmaceuticals USA, Inc.*, 2010 WL 3081327, *2 (D. Del. 2010).

[4]*Bayer Pharma AG v. Watson Laboratories, Inc.*, 2016 WL 7468172, at *2 (D. Del. 2016).

[5]*See, e.g., Bayer Pharma*, 2016 WL 7468172, at *4; *Alcon*, 2010 WL 3081327, at *2.

exist.[6] In other cases, however, courts have granted permanent injunctions on top of the relief provided under Section 271(e)(4)(A).[7]

Under Section 271(e)(4)(D), a permanent injunction on infringing acts is *mandatory* if certain requirements are met. In other words, the *eBay* test is inapplicable. Sub-paragraph (D) includes many textual limitations worth noting. First, the provision applies only to proposed biosimilar products that have not yet been approved *due to the reference product's statutory period of exclusivity* under section 351(k)(7) of the BPCIA (42 U.S.C. § 262(k)(7))—in other words, due to the RPS's 12-year market exclusivity.[8] In theory, this provision should not apply if the market exclusivity has expired, but FDA approval has been delayed for another reason. It is also questionable whether such a permanent injunction would stay in effect after expiration of the market exclusivity.

Second, the provision applies only if the infringed patent "is the subject of a final court decision, as defined in section 351(k)(6) of the Public Health Service Act."[9] Section 351(k)(6) of the Public Health Service Act defines a "final court decision" as "a final decision of a court from which no appeal (other than a petition to the United States Supreme Court for a writ of certiorari) has been or can be taken."[10] This suggests that, unlike the remedies provided in Section 271(e)(4)(A)-(C), the remedy in sub-paragraph (D) is applicable only after appeal or expiration of the time for appeal.

Third, sub-paragraph (D) applies only "in an action for infringement of the patent under section 351(*l*)(6) of such Act."[11] Section 351(*l*)(6) of the Act—otherwise known as 42 U.S.C. 262(*l*)(6)—relates to the "immediate" patent infringement that the RPS files after the parties have completed the patent dance.[12] Not all BPCIA cases are filed under this provision; for instance, declaratory judgment actions of infringe-

---

[6]*See, e.g., Bayer Pharma*, 2016 WL 7468172, at *4; *Alcon*, 2010 WL 3081327, at *2.

[7]*See Mytee Products, Inc. v. Harris Research, Inc.*, 439 Fed. Appx. 882, 884, 888 (Fed. Cir. 2011); *Ortho-McNeil Pharmaceutical, Inc. v. Mylan Laboratories Inc.*, 2007 WL 869545, *1 (D.N.J. 2007), aff'd in part, 520 F.3d 1358, 86 U.S.P.Q.2d 1196 (Fed. Cir. 2008).

[8]*See* 35 U.S.C.A. § 271(e)(4)(D).

[9]35 U.S.C.A. § 271(e)(4)(D).

[10]42 U.S.C.A. § 262(k)(6).

[11]35 U.S.C.A. § 271(e)(4)(D).

[12]*See supra* Section 4:20 relating to patent infringement lawsuit filed

ment may be filed by the RPS where the RPS does not dance at all under a different provision of the BPCIA. Thus, 35 U.S.C. 271(e)(4)(D) may only apply where the parties fully engaged in the patent dance prior to the RPS filing the instant litigation.

§ 4:98   Limitations on remedies Under 35 U.S.C.A. § 271(e)(6)

There are limitations to remedies that RPSs are otherwise available under Section 271(e)(4)(A). In particular, Section 271(e)(6)(A) and (B) dictate two conditions under which the RPS will only be entitled to a reasonable royalty as a remedy to patent infringement.[1] In particular, the RPS will be penalized, and only be entitled to a reasonable royalty where: (a) the parties dance, but the RPS does not file suit within the 30 day period proscribed by 42 U.S.C. § 262(k)(6); and/or (b) the RPS did not prosecute its claims to judgment in good faith, or had its claims dismissed without prejudice. According to one court, however, an RPS's failure to file suit within the 30-day period mentioned above did not limit the RPS to a reasonable royalty, where the applicant allegedly failed to engage in good faith negotiations during the patent dance.[2]

---

pursuant to 42 U.S.C. 262(*l*)(6) following completion of the patent dance.

[Section 4:98]

[1]35 U.S.C.A. § 271(e)(6): **(6)(A)** Subparagraph (B) applies, in lieu of paragraph (4), in the case of a patent—

(i) that is identified, as applicable, in the list of patents described in section 351(l)(4) of the Public Health Service Act or the lists of patents described in section 351(*l*)(5)(B) of such Act with respect to a biological product; and

(ii) for which an action for infringement of the patent with respect to the biological product—

(I) was brought after the expiration of the 30-day period described in subparagraph (A) or (B), as applicable, of section 351(*l*)(6) of such Act; or

(II) was brought before the expiration of the 30-day period described in subclause (I), but which was dismissed without prejudice or was not prosecuted to judgment in good faith.

(B) In an action for infringement of a patent described in subparagraph (A), the sole and exclusive remedy that may be granted by a court, upon a finding that the making, using, offering to sell, selling, or importation into the United States of the biological product that is the subject of the action infringed the patent, shall be a reasonable royalty.

[2]*Janssen Biotech, Inc. v. Celltrion Healthcare Co. Inc.*, 239 F. Supp. 3d 328 (D. Mass. 2017).

Chapter 5

Post-Grant Proceedings and BPCIA Litigations

§ 5:1   Introduction
§ 5:2   Background on Post-Grant Proceedings
§ 5:3   Parallel post-grant proceedings and BPCIA litigations
§ 5:4   Stays
§ 5:5   —The stage of the litigation
§ 5:6   —Simplification of issues
§ 5:7   —Undue prejudice
§ 5:8   — —Timing of review request
§ 5:9   — —Timing of stay request
§ 5:10   — —Status of review proceedings
§ 5:11   — —Relationship of the parties
§ 5:12   Motions to stay in BPCIA litigation
§ 5:13   Estoppel generally
§ 5:14   Real parties in interest & privity
§ 5:15   Scope of estoppel
§ 5:16   Patent owner estoppel
§ 5:17   Settlement
§ 5:18   Joinder
§ 5:19   Serial petitions
§ 5:20   Appeals

KeyCite®: Cases and other legal materials listed in KeyCite Scope can be researched through the KeyCite service on Westlaw®. Use KeyCite to check citations for form, parallel references, prior and later history, and comprehensive citator information, including citations to other decisions and secondary materials.

---

§ 5:1 Introduction

Post-grant proceedings may be attractive to an aBLA filer who does not want to wait until BPCIA litigation ensues to challenge RPS patents. In particular, if an RPS's patent portfolio contains a large number of patents, an aBLA filer may wish to begin challenging the patents as early as possible.[1]

§ 5:2   Background on Post-Grant Proceedings

Under the America Invents Act, new post-grant review proceedings, including *Inter Partes* Review ("IPR") and Post-Grant Review ("PGR"), became available on September 16, 2012. IPR and PGR proceedings provide an alternative to district court litigation by allowing third parties to challenge the patentability of issued patent claims before the Patent Trial & Appeals Board ("PTAB," or "the Board"). The patent challenger's burden of proof in post-grant proceedings is lower than that in district court litigations: in IPRs and PGRs, the burden of proof is a preponderance of the evidence, and in district court, the burden is clear and convincing evidence.[1]

For patents issued post-enactment of the America Invents Act (AIA), IPR petitions can be filed nine (9) months after issuance of the challenged patent, or later.[2] IPR petitions can be filed at any time against patents issues pre-AIA. IPR challenges are limited to anticipation grounds (under 35 U.S.C.A. § 102) and/or obviousness grounds (under 35 U.S.C.A. § 103) and only on the basis of "prior art consisting of patents or printed publications."[3] Institution of an IPR requires a "reasonable likelihood" that petitioner will prevail on at least one claim.[4] In IPRs, discovery is "limited to the deposition of witnesses submitting declarations or affidavits and what is otherwise necessary in the interest of justice."[5]

PGR petitions may be filed challenging patents with an effective filing date on or after March 16, 2013, and must be

---

[Section 5:1]

[1]For example, Amgen filed two IPR petitions challenging two of AbbVie's Humira patents on June 26, 2015 but did not file their aBLA until November 25, 2015.

[Section 5:2]

[1]*See* 35 U.S.C.A. § 316(e); *see also* 35 U.S.C.A. § 326(e); *see also Cuozzo Speed Technologies, LLC v. Lee*, 136 S. Ct. 2131, 2143–2144, 195 L. Ed. 2d 423, 119 U.S.P.Q.2d 1065 (2016).

[2]35 U.S.C.A. § 311(c)(1).

[3]35 U.S.C.A. § 311(b).

[4]35 U.S.C.A. § 314(a).

[5]35 U.S.C.A. § 316(a)(5).

filed within nine (9) months of issuance.[6] PGR challenges can be based on any grounds of invalidity. The threshold for institution of a PGR is that it is "more likely than not" that at least one claim is unpatentable.[7] Discovery is broader in PGRs than in IPRs and may include any evidence directly related to factual assertions by either party.[8]

When an IPR or PGR petition is filed, the patent owner has three months to file a preliminary response.[9] The Board then has three months to issue a decision on institution.[10] Once a trial is instituted, the Board has one year to issue a final written decision,[11] although there are exceptions to this, such as in the case of joinder.[12] After the Board issues a final written decision, the losing party can (a) request a rehearing of the Board's decision;[13] and/or (b) appeal to the Federal Circuit.[14] The IPR/PGR process, from filing a petition, to the Federal Circuit issuing a decision takes approximately 2.5 years.[15] This timeline is significantly shorter than for district court litigation, which can take over 4 years[16] to run its course, from the filing of a complaint until the Federal Circuit issues a decision on appeal.

§ 5:3 Parallel post-grant proceedings and BPCIA litigations

The implementation of IPRs and PGRs was intended by Congress to serve as an alternative to district court litigation but Congress did not foreclose the possibility that patents may be challenged in both forums. If an aBLA filer files an IPR or PGR petition, there is likely to be an overlap

---

[6]35 U.S.C.A. § 321(c).

[7]35 U.S.C.A. § 324(a).

[8]35 U.S.C.A. § 326(a)(5).

[9]37 C.F.R. § 42.120(b).

[10]35 U.S.C.A. § 314(b).

[11]37 C.F.R. § 42.100(c).

[12]37 C.F.R. § 42.100(c).

[13]37 C.F.R. § 42.71(d)(2).

[14]35 U.S.C. § 141(c).

[15]See http://www.cafc.uscourts.gov/sites/default/files/the-court/statistics/06_Med_Disp_Time_MERITS_table_-_Final.pdf.

[16]The average time to a bench trial in U.S. district court is 35 months. The average time for an appeal is 14 months. See http://www.cafc.uscourts.gov/sites/default/files/the-court/statistics/06_Med_Disp_Time_MERITS_table_-_Final.pdf.

of the IPR/PGR proceeding(s) and BPCIA litigation. Once district court litigation ensues, there are limitations on a patent challenger's ability to file IPR and PGR petitions. For instance, an IPR or PGR may not be instituted if the petitioner or real party in interest files a civil action first challenging the validity of the same patent.[1] The bar is triggered by filing a suit for declaratory judgment regardless of a subsequent voluntary dismissal of the complaint.[2] Once a petitioner, real party in interest, or privy of the petitioner is served with a complaint alleging infringement of a patent, the petitioner has one year to file an IPR petition challenging the validity of claims of that patent.[3] Service of a complaint triggers the one year time bar, regardless of a subsequent voluntary dismissal of the complaint.[4]

§ 5:4   Stays

If an IPR or PGR petition is timely filed and not otherwise barred, the district court has discretion to stay litigation pending resolution of IPR or PGR. Determining whether to stay the litigation until resolution of a PTAB proceeding is within "district courts' broad discretion to manage their dockets."[1] A court's grant or denial of a stay is reviewed for abuse of discretion.[2] When determining whether to grant a stay pending a PTAB decision, courts will consider the following factors: "(1) whether discovery is complete and whether a trial date has been set; (2) whether a stay will simplify the issues in question and trial of the case; and (3) whether a stay would unduly prejudice or present a clear tactical disadvantage to the non-moving party."[3]

[Section 5:3]

[1]35 U.S.C.A. § 315(a)(1); 325(a)(1).

[2]*Cisco Sys., Inc. v. ChriMar Sys., Inc.*, IPR2018-01511 (P.T.A.B. Jan. 31, 2019) (Paper 11).

[3]35 U.S.C.A. § 315(b).

[4]*Click-To-Call Technologies, LP v. Ingenio, Inc., YellowPages.com, LLC*, 899 F.3d 1321, 127 U.S.P.Q.2d 1747 (Fed. Cir. 2018), certiorari granted in part, 139 S. Ct. 2742 (2019).

[Section 5:4]

[1]*See Procter & Gamble Co. v. Kraft Foods Global, Inc.*, 549 F.3d 842, 848–49, 89 U.S.P.Q.2d 1085 (Fed. Cir. 2008).

[2]*Procter & Gamble*, 549 F.3d at 845.

[3]*Evolutionary Intelligence, LLC v. Apple, Inc.*, 2014 WL 93954, *3

§ 5:5 Stays—The stage of the litigation

When determining whether to grant a stay, the court will first consider how far the litigation has progressed. The court will consider: (1) whether the parties have engaged in costly expert discovery and dispositive motion practice; (2) whether the court has issued its claim construction order; and (3) whether the court has set a trial date.[1]

In general, if the litigation is at an early stage, this may weigh in favor of granting a stay.[2] In particular, when the court has yet to set deadlines for the close of fact and expert discovery, dispositive motions, or trial, this factor weighs in favor of granting a stay.[3] Even when contentions have been exchanged and the case in the midst of discovery, if significant deadlines in the case remain, a stay may still be appropriate.[4] However, at an early stage of litigation the risk of evidentiary staleness may weigh in favor of denying a stay.[5]

If the litigation is in a later stage, this factor may weigh against a stay.[6] A stay may be denied where there has been significant discovery, Markman briefing is underway, and a

---

(N.D. Cal. 2014).

[Section 5:5]

[1]*Finjan, Inc. v. Symantec Corp.*, 139 F. Supp. 3d 1032 (N.D. Cal. 2015).

[2]*See Cannarella v. Volvo Car USA LLC*, 2016 WL 9450451, *14–15 (C.D. Cal. 2016) (". . .this is the quintessential patent case in the infancy of its proceedings, and courts have concluded this factor weighs in favor of a stay even when the parties are significantly more immersed in litigation.").

[3]*Wi-Lab, Inc. v. LG Elecs., Inc.*, No. 5:17-cv-00358-BEN-MDD (S.D. Cal. May 2, 2018).

[4]*TAS Energy, Inc. v. San Diego Gas & Elec. Co.*, 2014 WL 794215, *6 (S.D. Cal. 2014).

[5]*General Electric Company v. Vibrant Media, Inc.*, 2013 WL 6328063, *1 (D. Del. 2013) ("[T]he Court will permit fact discovery to be completed—reducing any risk of evidentiary staleness that might otherwise be present during the pendency of the stay—but will allow the parties to avoid the expense of expert discovery until after the results of the IPR are known."). *But see Evolutionary Intelligence, LLC v. Apple, Inc.*, 2014 WL 93954, *3 (N.D. Cal. 2014). ("Without specific evidence based on sworn testimony that spoliation has in fact occurred, a vague generalized 'loss of evidence' argument is unpersuasive.").

[6]*See Intellectual Ventures II LLC v. FedEx Corporation*, 2017 WL 4812434, *2 (E.D. Tex. 2017) (Substantial efforts and resources expended by the parties during discovery and in preparing claim construction brief-

Markman hearing is approaching.[7] A stay also may not be appropriate if the litigation is at a critical point, for example, a pending summary judgment motion has been filed and fully briefed.[8] However, even if a litigation at a later stage and trial is approaching, this factor may not outweigh other benefits of a stay because the upcoming trial would imposes burdensome expenses on the parties.[9]

§ 5:6   Stays—Simplification of issues

Courts will consider whether the PTAB has issued an institution decision when determining the likelihood that resolution of a PTAB proceeding will simplify the issues in litigation. Institution of an IPR or PGR increases the likelihood that at least some of the challenged claims will be canceled,[1] and a stay may be favored where the outcome of the IPR or PGR is likely to render infringement issue moot.[2] If the claims are found to be unpatentable, the Board's decision can be used as evidence that the court must consider.[3] Even if the claims are found not to be unpatentable, the case may be simplified because defendant would be estopped from relying on the grounds that were asserted or reasonably could have been asserted in the IPR or PGR.[4]

Courts are generally reluctant to grant a stay if the PTAB has yet to issue an institution decision.[5] Prior to institution, there is more uncertainty that the issues will be simplified,

---

ing weighed against a stay.)

[7]*Realtime Data LLC v. Actian Corp.*, No. 8:15-CV-463-RWS-JDL (E.D. Tex. Jun. 14, 2016).

[8]*Immunex Corp. v. Sanofi*, 2018 WL 2717852, at *8–9 (C.D. Cal. 2018).

[9]*CyWee Grp. Ltd. v. Samsung Elecs. Co., Ltd.*, No. 4:17-CV-00140-WCB-RSP, D.I. 331 (E.D. Tex. Feb. 14, 2019).

[Section 5:6]

[1]*Evolutionary Intelligence, LLC v. Sprint Nextel Corporation*, 2014 WL 819277, at *2 (N.D. Cal. 2014).

[2]*Evolutionary Intelligence, LLC v. Apple, Inc.*, 2014 WL 93954 (N.D. Cal. 2014).

[3]*TAS Energy, Inc. v. San Diego Gas & Elec. Co.*, 2014 WL 794215, at *4 (S.D. Cal. 2014).

[4]*TAS Energy, Inc. v. San Diego Gas & Elec. Co.*, 2014 WL 794215, at *4 (S.D. Cal. 2014).

[5]*TAS Energy, Inc. v. San Diego Gas & Elec. Co.*, 2014 WL 794215, at *4 (S.D. Cal. 2014).

which may weigh in favor of denying a stay.[6] Such uncertainty has prompted district courts to be creative in their stay determinations. A court may deny the stay pending the PTAB's institution decision.[7] A court may choose to stay the litigation only until the Board has made an institution decision, in which case, if institution is denied, the litigation will have only been delayed a few months.[8] Alternatively, a court may deny the stay but then renew the motion to stay if the Board institutes the IPR.[9] Once an IPR or PGR has been instituted, "the parallel litigation ordinarily should be stayed."[10]

If not all patents asserted in litigation are challenged by IPR or PGR and issues such as noninfringement and validity under 35 U.S.C.A. § 112 are raised in litigation, it is less likely that granting the stay will simplify the issues in the litigation.[11]

§ 5:7 Stays—Undue prejudice

A stay will obviously delay the litigation but this alone is not enough to establish undue prejudice.[1] Courts looks to the following four sub-factors to determine whether the non-moving party would be unacceptably prejudiced if a stay is granted: (1) the timing of the review request; (2) the timing of the request for stay; (3) the status of the review proceedings; and (4) the relationship of the parties.[2]

---

[6]*See Endotach LLC v. Cook Med. Inc.*, No. 3:13-cv-01135-LJM-DKL (S.D. Ind. Jan. 28, 2014), D.I. 124.

[7]*See Trover Group, Inc. v. Dedicated Micros USA*, 2015 WL 1069179, *5–6 (E.D. Tex. 2015).

[8]*See Fisher-Price, Inc. v. Dynacraft BSC, Inc.*, 2017 WL 5153588, *1 (N.D. Cal. 2017).

[9]*Infogation Corp. v. ZTE Corporation*, 2017 WL 2123625, *2 (S.D. Cal. 2017).

[10]*NFC Technology LLC v. HTC America, Inc.*, 2015 WL 106911, *7 (E.D. Tex. 2015).

[11]*See Davol, Inc. v Atrium Medical Corp.*, No. 12-958-GMS (D. Del. June 17, 2013); *see also Endotach LLC v. Cook Med. Inc.*, No. 3:13-cv-01135-LJM-DKL (S.D. Ind Jan. 28, 2014).

[Section 5:7]

[1]*Immunex Corp. v. Sanofi*, 2018 WL 2717852, at *7 (C.D. Cal. 2018).

[2]*ImageVision.Net, Inc. v. Internet Payment Exchange, Inc.*, 2013 WL 663535, at *5 (D. Del. 2013), report and recommendation adopted, 2013 WL 1743854 (D. Del. 2013); *Boston Scientific Corp. v. Cordis Corp.*, 777 F.

§ 5:8   Stays—Undue prejudice—Timing of review request

A petitioner can file an IPR petition up to one year after being served with a complaint alleging infringement of the patent.[1] Filing an IPR petition immediately before the statutory deadline may weigh against a stay if the petitioner is viewed as trying to gain an unfair tactical advantage.[2] Filing close to the statutory deadline may also be viewed as a lack of diligence, weighing against a stay.[3] A four month delay in filing an IPR petition after being served plaintiff's infringement contentions has been deemed reasonable.[4]

However, a court may find that filing close to the deadline is merely a "timely exercise of statutory rights."[5] Other courts have found it reasonable for a defendant to wait to file an IPR petition until after having received infringement contentions.[6]

§ 5:9   Stays—Undue prejudice—Timing of stay request

The longer a defendant waits to file a motion to stay pending a PTAB decision, the more it looks like the delay may be

---

Supp. 2d 783, 789 (D. Del. 2011); *Ever Win Intern. Corp. v. Radioshack Corp.*, 902 F. Supp. 2d 503, 508–509 (D. Del. 2012).

[Section 5:8]

[1]35 U.S.C.A. § 315(b).

[2]*See, e.g., TruePosition, Inc., v. Polaris Wireless, Inc.*, 2013 WL 5701529, at *6 (D. Del. 2013), report and recommendation adopted, 2013 WL 6020798 (D. Del. 2013) ("Filings for IPR made well after the initiation of litigation, however, may suggest an unfair tactical advantage or dilatory motive").

[3]*See, e.g., Realtime Data LLC v. Actian Corp.*, 2016 WL 3277259, *3 (E.D. Tex. 2016) ("All Defendants waited between seven and 11 months to file their IPR petitions and between one month and seven months after the petitions to file the current motion, which demonstrates a lack of diligence on the part of the Defendants, and they have not attempted to provide an explanation for this unjustifiable delay.")

[4]*NFC Technology LLC v. HTC America, Inc.*, 2015 WL 1069111, at *6 (E.D. Tex. 2015).

[5]*See, e.g., Finjan, Inc. v. Symantec Corp.*, 139 F. Supp. 3d 1032, 1036 (N.D. Cal. 2015) ("[T]he Court declines to condition a stay on Symantec seeking IPR earlier than the end of its statutory deadline, or to read a dilatory motive into the timely exercise of its statutory rights.").

[6]*See, e.g., ACQIS, LLC v. EMC Corp.*, 109 F. Supp. 3d 352, 359 (D. Mass. 2015); *see also NFC Tech., 2015 WL 1069111 at *4.*

impermissibly tactical.[1] A delay in filing a motion to stay, coupled with waiting until a few days before the statutory deadline to file a PTAB petition, may show a pattern of delay that weighs against granting the stay.[2] Courts will generally not fault a petitioner for waiting until institution to file a motion to stay since it is likely.[3]

§ 5:10   Stays—Undue prejudice—Status of review proceedings

When the PTAB proceeding has not yet been instituted, a stay could potentially delay resolution of the case for almost two years. Therefore, at an early stage, the patentee risks impairment of patent rights and this factor may weigh against a stay.[1]

§ 5:11   Stays—Undue prejudice—Relationship of the parties

The relationship between the parties, and in particular, whether they are direct competitors, is an important factor in determining if a stay will prejudice the plaintiff.[1] If the parties are direct competitors, delay in the district court

---

[Section 5:9]

[1]*ImageVision.Net, Inc. v. Internet Payment Exchange, Inc.*, 2013 WL 663535, at *5 (D. Del. 2013), report and recommendation adopted, 2013 WL 1743854 (D. Del. 2013).

[2]*Trover Group, Inc. v. Dedicated Micros USA*, 2015 WL 1069179, *5–6 (E.D. Tex. 2015) (". . .[B]y delaying in filing their petition and then further delaying in filing their motion to stay, the defendants have allowed the case to progress to a point at which the proceedings have become more active, and thus more expensive, for the parties.")

[3]*See CyWee Group Ltd. v. Samsung Electronics Co.*, No. 4:17-CV-00140-WCB-RSP (E.D. Tex. February 14, 2019).

[Section 5:10]

[1]*Davol, Inc. v. Atrium Medical Corp.*, 2013 WL 3013343, at *2 (D. Del. 2013).

[Section 5:11]

[1]*See ImageVision.Net, Inc. v. Internet Payment Exchange, Inc.*, 2013 WL 663535, at *6 (D. Del. 2013), report and recommendation adopted, 2013 WL 1743854 (D. Del. 2013); *Mission Abstract Data L.L.C. v. Becsley Broadcast Group, Inc.*, 2011 WL 5523315, at *4 (D. Del. 2011); *Boston Scientific Corp. v. Cordis Corp.*, 777 F. Supp. 2d 783, 788 (D. Del. 2011); *Cooper Notification, Inc. v. Twitter, Inc.*, 2010 WL 5149351, at *5 (D. Del. 2010); *Textron Innovations Inc. v. Toro Co.*, 2007 WL 7772169, at *3 (D. Del. 2007).

case may result in loss of market share or erosion of goodwill for plaintiff.[2] However, the risk of such harms is lower if there are other competitors in the market.[3] Non-practicing entities are not considered competitors even though they license their technology.[4]

§ 5:12   Motions to stay in BPCIA litigation

In the biosimilar context, many IPR petitions are filed well before the biosimilar applicant submits their aBLA and litigation ensues. Therefore, there have only been limited circumstances in BPCIA litigations that warrant the filing of a motion to stay pending resolution of a PTAB proceeding.

The BPCIA, however, brings an additional factor to the analysis not seen in traditional patent infringement cases. The BPCIA incentivizes plaintiffs to timely bring infringement claims and the intent of the BPCIA is to expeditiously resolve patent disputes. A delay in the litigation would contradict these principles and may weigh against the grant of stay.[1]

§ 5:13   Estoppel generally

An aBLA filer who challenges RPS patents via an IPR or PGR runs the risk of limiting the invalidity arguments that can be presented later in a BPCIA litigation. When the Board issues a final written decision in an IPR, estoppel arises under 35 U.S.C.A. § 315(e)(2):

> The petitioner in an inter partes review of a claim in a patent under this chapter that results in a final written decision under section 318(a), or the real party in interest or privy of the petitioner, may not assert either in a civil action arising in whole or in part under section 1338 of title 28 or in a proceeding before the International Trade Commission under section

---

[2]*Neste Oil Oyj v. Dynamic Fuels, LLC*, 2013 WL 424754, at *2 (D. Del. 2013) (quoting *SenoRx, Inc. v. Hologic, Inc.*, 2013 WL 144255, *5 (D. Del. 2013)).

[3]*Neste Oil Oyj v. Dynamic Fuels, LLC*, 2013 WL 424754, at *3 (D. Del. 2013); *Air Vent, Inc. v. Owens Corning Corp.*, 2012 WL 1607145, *3 (W.D. Pa. 2012).

[4]*CyWee Grp. Ltd. v. Samsung Elecs. Co.*, No. 4:17-CV-00140-WCB-RSP, D.I. 331 (E.D. Tex. Feb. 14, 2019).

[Section 5:12]

[1]*See Janssen Biotech Inc. v. Celltrion Healthcare Co.*, No. 3:15-cv-10698, D.I. 164 (D. Mass. Mar. 14, 2016).

337 of the Tariff Act of 1930 that the claim is invalid on any ground that the petitioner raised or reasonably could have raised during that inter partes review.

35 U.S.C.A. § 325(e)(2) recites the same estoppel rule for PGRs. The proponent of estoppel bears the burden of showing that estoppel is appropriate.[1] Estoppel will apply both during a district court action and post-trial where the court has not entered a final judgment on the relevant ground.[2] At least one district court has ruled that estoppel can apply when a final written decision is issued after the district court trial but before the district court issues its opinion.[3]

§ 5:14 Real parties in interest & privity

The estoppel provisions recited above apply to any "real party in interest or privy of petitioner." All real parties in interest ("RPIs") must be identified in the IPR petition.[1]

Real parties in interest include third parties who the petitioner is acting at the behest of or on behalf of.[2] A party having a "specially structured, preexisting, and well established business relationship with one another, including indemnification and exclusivity arrangements" will be considered a real party in interest and in privity with the petitioner.[3] In a litigation with multiple defendants where one defendant has filed an IPR petition, the other co-defendants will be found to be privies of the petitioner if the petitioner has sufficient control over the district court litigation.[4]

If a real party in interest is inadvertently omitted from

[Section 5:13]

[1]*See Clearlamp, LLC v. LKQ Corporation*, 2016 WL 4734389, at *9 (N.D. Ill. 2016), judgment entered, 2016 WL 7013478 (N.D. Ill. 2016).

[2]*Novartis Pharm. Corp. v. Par Pharm. Inc.*, No. 14-1289-RGA, D.I. 198 (D. Del. Apr. 11, 2019).

[3]*Senju Pharm. Co., Ltd. v. Lupin Ltd.*, No. 14-667 (D.N.J.) (case settled before the issue was decided).

[Section 5:14]

[1]35 U.S.C.A. § 322(a)(2).

[2]*Wi-Fi One, LLC v. Broadcom Corporation*, 887 F.3d 1329, 1340, 126 U.S.P.Q.2d 1370 (Fed. Cir. 2018), cert. denied, 139 S. Ct. 826, 202 L. Ed. 2d 579 (2019).

[3]*Ventex Co., Ltd. v. Columbia Sportswear N. Am., Inc.*, IPR2017-00651 (P.T.A.B. Jan. 24, 2019) (Paper 152).

[4]*Wi-Fi One*, 887 F.3d at 1340–41.

the petition, the petitioner can file a Motion to Amend Mandatory Notices to add the real party in interest without altering filing date of the petition, even if the addition occurs after the petitioner would otherwise be barred from filing the petition. In determining whether a party may add an RPI without disrupting the filing date of the petition, the Board will consider: (1) whether Petitioners/RPI's attempts to circumvent the time bar or estoppel rules; (2) prejudice to the Patent Owner caused by the delay; (3) bad faith by the Petitioner; or (4) gamesmanship by the petitioner regarding the timing or manner of identifying the RPI.[5]

§ 5:15   Scope of estoppel

Estoppel applies to any grounds that petitioner "raised or reasonably could have raised" during the post grant review or *inter partes* review.[1]

By statute, a petitioned, but non-instituted, ground cannot be addressed in an IPR or PGR. Therefore, such grounds cannot reasonably be raised in an instituted IPR or PGR, through no fault of the petitioner.[2] However, since partial institution is no longer permitted and the PTAB must institute a proceeding on all petitioned grounds or deny the petition,[3] the question of estoppel regarding non-instituted grounds no longer arises.

The Federal Circuit has not addressed whether estoppel applies to non-petitioned grounds. However, a number of district courts have interpreted the statute's "reasonably could have been raised" language broadly.[4] "[A]n inter partes review petitioner is estopped from relying on any ground that could have been raised based on prior art that could

---

[5]*Proppant Express Invs., LLC v. Oren Techs., LLC*, IPR2017-01917 (P.T.A.B. Feb. 13, 2019) (Paper 86).

[Section 5:15]

[1]35 U.S.C.A. § 315(e); § 325(e).

[2]*Shaw Industries Group, Inc. v. Automated Creel Systems, Inc.*, 817 F.3d 1293, 1299–1300, 118 U.S.P.Q.2d 1316 (Fed. Cir. 2016).

[3]*SAS Institute, Inc. v. Iancu*, 138 S. Ct. 1348, 200 L. Ed. 2d 695, 126 U.S.P.Q.2d 1307 (2018).

[4]*See Clearlamp, LLC v. LKQ Corporation*, 2016 WL 4734389 (N.D. Ill. 2016), judgment entered, 2016 WL 7013478 (N.D. Ill. 2016); *see also Am. Tech. Ceramics Corp. v. Presidio Components, Inc.*, No. 14-CV-6544 (E.D.N.Y. Jan. 30, 2019).

have been found by a skilled searcher's diligent search."[5] Estoppel may apply to alternative combinations of prior art or subsets of prior art that reasonably could have been included in the petition.[6]

Since the basis for grounds of invalidity in IPRs is limited to printed publications certain types of prior art cannot be included in an IPR petition by statute.[7] These types of prior art, "exempt prior art," include, for example, products and videos. Estoppel will not apply to exempt prior art unless it is described in sufficient detail in a printed publication such that it could have been relied on in an IPR.[8] Even if the exempt prior art is described in a printed publication, it will not be subject to estoppel if the petitioner did not have reasonable access to the printed publication.[9] Furthermore, estoppel may not apply to printed publications if the ground for invalidity requires a combination of the printed publication with exempt prior art.[10]

§ 5:16 Patent owner estoppel

An adverse judgment against one patent may preclude a patent owner from obtaining subsequent patents. Patent owners are specifically precluded from obtaining claims that are not patentably distinct from a finally refused or canceled claim according to an adverse judgment.[1] Disclaimer of a patent can be construed as a request for adverse judgment despite a patent owner's express statement that an adverse judgment was not being requested upon disclaimer of the patent.[2] Therefore, attempts to disclaim a patent in a PTAB proceeding is not effective to prevent the Board from issuing an adverse judgment, and the patent owner will be subject to estoppel.

---

[5]*Clearlamp*, 2016 WL 4734389, at *8.

[6]*Milwaukee Electric Tool Corporation v. Snap-On Incorporated*, 271 F. Supp. 3d 990 (E.D. Wis. 2017).

[7]35 U.S.C.A. § 311(b).

[8]*Oil-Dri Corporation of America v. Nestle Purina Petcare Company*, 2019 WL 861394, at *10 (N.D. Ill. 2019).

[9]*Oil-Dri*, 2019 WL 861394, at *10; *Milwaukee Elec.*, 271 F. Supp. 3d 990.

[10]*Oil-Dri*, 2019 WL 861394.

[Section 5:16]

[1]37 C.F.R. § 42.73(d)(3).

[2]*Arthrex, Inc. v. Smith & Nephew, Inc.*, 880 F.3d 1345, 1347, 125 U.S.P.Q.2d 1532 (Fed. Cir. 2018).

§ 5:17   Settlement

Estoppel does not arise until the Board issues a final written decision. Issuance of a final written decision may be avoided if the parties settle their dispute and file a joint motion to terminate the PTAB proceeding. However, the Board may deny the motion to terminate and proceed with a final written decision if it finds that the "public's interest in the status of the challenged claims of each patent is at its peak."[1] Moreover, if the PTAB issues a decision finding the patentee's claims unpatentable, and the parties settle (either before or after the decision issues), the PTO has standing to intervene in an appeal filed by the patentee to defend its position.[2]

§ 5:18   Joinder

Since there are likely to be multiple aBLA filers for a single RP, it follows that multiple parties may seek to challenge the same RPS patents. In such cases, the petitioner or patent owner can seek joinder.[1] Once a PTAB proceeding is instituted, the Board has discretion to join any party who files a petition that the Board has also decided to institute.[2] The party requesting joinder must file a motion within one month of institution of the PTAB proceeding it wishes to join.[3] An IPR petition accompanied by a motion for joinder will be not be barred if filed more than a year after petitioner is served with a complaint alleging infringement of the same patent.[4] There is no comparable statutory exemption for PGR petitions filed with a joinder motion after nine months after patent issuance.[5]

A motion for joinder should (1) set forth reasons why joinder is appropriate; (2) identify any new grounds of

---

[Section 5:17]

[1]*Rubicon Commc'ns, LP v. Lego A/S*, IPR2016-01187, (P.T.A.B. Dec. 15, 2017) (Paper 100 at p.2).

[2]*Knowles Electronics LLC v. Iancu*, 886 F.3d 1369, 1372 n. 2, 126 U.S.P.Q.2d 1137 (Fed. Cir. 2018).

[Section 5:18]

[1]37 C.F.R. § 42.122(b).

[2]35 U.S.C.A. § 315(c).

[3]35 U.S.C.A. § 315(c).

[4]35 U.S.C.A. § 315(c).

[5]35 U.S.C.A. § 325(e).

unpatentability asserted in the petition; (3) explain what impact (if any) joinder would have on the trial schedule for the existing review; and (4) address specifically how briefing and discovery may be simplified through joinder.[6] The petitioner bears the burden of proving that it should be allowed to join the preceding PTAB proceeding.[7] The non-moving party can oppose the motion for joinder.

As a result of joinder, the one-year deadline for issuance of a final written decision after institution of an IPR can be extended.[8]

When a petitioner and patent owner settle their dispute and file a motion to terminate while another PTAB petition and motion for joinder is pending, the Board has discretion to terminate the proceeding only as to the petitioner moving to terminate and otherwise continue the proceeding.[9] The Board may choose not to terminate the entire proceeding even when the party seeking to join the proceeding challenges fewer claims than the original petitioner.[10]

§ 5:19 Serial petitions

Under 35 U.S.C.A. § 314(a), the Board has discretion to deny institution of follow-on petitions filed against previously-challenged patents.[1] The Board considers the following "baseline" factors:[2]

1. Whether the same petitioner previously filed a petition directed to the same claims of the same patent;

2. Whether at the time of filing of the first petition the petitioner knew of the prior art asserted in the second petition or should have known of it;

3. Whether at the time of filing of the second petition the

---

[6]*See Ever Win Intern. Corp. v. Radioshack Corp.*, 902 F. Supp. 2d 503 (D. Del. 2012) (Paper 15).

[7]37 C.F.R. § 42.20(c).

[8]37 C.F.R. § 42.100(c).

[9]*Facebook, Inc. v. Windy City Innovations, LLC*, IPR2016-01067 (P.T.A.B. Aug. 14, 2017) (Paper 54).

[10]*Facebook, Inc. v. Windy City Innovations, LLC*, IPR2016-01067 (P.T.A.B. Aug. 14, 2017) (Paper 54).

[Section 5:19]

[1]*See, e.g., NVIDIA Corp. v. Samsung Elec. Co.*, IPR2016-00124 (P.T.A.B. May 4, 2016) (Paper 9).

[2]*General Plastic Indus. Co. v. Canon Kabushiki Kaisha*, IPR2016-01357 (P.T.A.B. Sep. 6, 2017) (Paper 19) (precedential).

petitioner already received the patent owner's preliminary response to the first petition or received the Board's decision on whether to institute review in the first petition;

4. The length of time that elapsed between the petitioner learning of the prior art asserted in the second petition and the filing of the second petition;

5. Whether the petitioner provides adequate explanation for the time elapsed between the filing of multiple petitions directed to the same claims of the same patent;

6. The finite resources of the Board; and

7. The requirement under 35 U.S.C.A. § 316(a)(11) to issue a final determination not later than 1 year after the date on which the Director notices institution of review.

The Board will deny institution when the petitioner fails to distinguish its arguments from those made by a prior petitioner.[3] However, the Board may institute a follow-on petition if it is sufficiently distinct from prior petitions.[4] Moreover, the Board may institute similar petitions that are filed around the same time.[5]

§ 5:20   Appeals

An aBLA filer who challenges RPS patents well before filing their aBLA runs the risk of lacking standing to appeal an adverse final written decision. A party to an IPR has the right to appeal a final written decision to the Federal Circuit if the party has standing under Article III.[1] Standing requires that a party (1) "has suffered an injury in fact that is both concrete and particularized, and actual or imminent"; (2) "the injury is fairly traceable to the challenged action";

---

[3]*Apple, Inc. v. California Instit. of Tech.*, IPR2017-00703, (P.T.A.B. Sep. 12, 2017) (Paper 11 at 9).

[4]*Panduit Corp. v. CCS Tech., Inc.*, IPR2017-01323, (P.T.A.B. Nov. 8, 2017) (Paper 8).

[5]*See, e.g,* IPR2017-1373 and IPR2017-01374.

[Section 5:20]

[1]35 U.S.C. §§ 319 and 329; *Consumer Watchdog v. Wisconsin Alumni Research Foundation*, 753 F.3d 1258, 1260, 111 U.S.P.Q.2d 1241 (Fed. Cir. 2014).

and (3) "that it is likely, rather than merely speculative, that a favorable judicial decision will redress the injury."[2]

Neither an adverse decision by the Board on its own, nor the resulting estoppel provided under 35 U.S.C.A. § 315 constitute an injury in fact.[3] A "general grievance" concerning the patent at issue is not enough to show an injury in fact.[4] If the petitioner does not engage in activity that could constitute a basis for a claim of infringement and does not allege an intent to engage in such conduct, that it is an actual or prospective licensee, or that is has any connection to the patent-in-suit, the petitioner does not have standing under Article III to appeal an adverse final written decision.[5] Economic injury caused by increased competition and loss of licensing revenue is insufficient to show an injury in fact.[6] Petitioners who are joined as parties to an IPR are considered within the zone of interests of 35 U.S.C.A. § 319, even if, absent joinder, their petition would have been time-barred.[7]

A petitioner may have standing to appeal a final written decision even if petitioner cannot obtain the FDA approval for its product before expiration of the patent.[8] The petitioner may have an injury in fact if a decision from the Federal Circuit invalidating the patent would enable the petitioner "to launch its competing product substantially earlier than it otherwise could."[9] However, in the biosimilar context, a petitioner who abandons plans to market a biosimilar product at the time of appeal and therefore will not engage in potentially infringing activity, does not have standing to appeal.[10]

---

[2]*Consumer Watchdog*, 753 F.3d at 1260–61.

[3]*Consumer Watchdog*, 753 F.3d at 1262.

[4]*Consumer Watchdog*, 753 F.3d at 1261.

[5]*Consumer Watchdog*, 753 F.3d at 1261.

[6]*Phigenix, Inc. v. Immunogen, Inc.*, 845 F.3d 1168, 1173, 121 U.S.P. Q.2d 1242 (Fed. Cir. 2017).

[7]*Mylan Pharmaceuticals Inc. v. Research Corporation Technologies, Inc.*, 914 F.3d 1366, 1372 (Fed. Cir. 2019).

[8]*Amerigen Pharmaceuticals Limited v. UCB Pharma GmBH*, 913 F.3d 1076, 1084 (Fed. Cir. 2019).

[9]*Amerigen*, 913 F.3d at 1084.

[10]*Momenta Pharmaceuticals, Inc. v. Bristol-Myers Squibb Company*, 915 F.3d 764, 768 (Fed. Cir. 2019).

Chapter 6

ITC Section 337 Actions

§ 6:1   ITC Section 337 actions generally
§ 6:2   Elements of a section 337 violation
§ 6:3   ITC remedies
§ 6:4   Comparison between section 337 investigations
         and district court litigations

> **KeyCite®:** Cases and other legal materials listed in KeyCite Scope can be researched through the KeyCite service on Westlaw®. Use KeyCite to check citations for form, parallel references, prior and later history, and comprehensive citator information, including citations to other decisions and secondary materials.

§ 6:1   ITC Section 337 actions generally

The U.S. International Trade Commission (ITC) is a venue for technology disputes involving products, or components, that are or will be imported into the United States. Section 337 matters are considered "investigations" by the ITC, culminating, if successful, in the issuance of exclusion orders by the ITC. A Section 337 investigation offers a patent holder an alternative venue to federal district courts to prevent importation of a biosimilar manufactured outside the United States. Although the ITC has not yet brought any investigations for biosimilar products, the ITC has previously resolved Section 337 actions for other biologic products, including recombinant erythropoietin (rEPO),[1] recombinant factor VIII products,[2] recombinant factor IX products,[3] botulinum neurotoxin products,[4] and snake antivenom.[5]

[Section 6:1]

[1]*In re Certain Prods. and Pharm. Compositions Containing Recombinant Human Erythropoieten*, Inv. No. 337-TA-568.

[2]*In re Recombinant Factor VIII Prods.*, Inv. No. 337-TA-956.

[3]*Certain Recombinant Factor IX Prods.*, Inv. No. 337-TA-1066.

[4]*Certain Botulinum Toxin Products, Process for Manufacturing or Relating to Same and Certain Products Containing Same*, Inv. No. 337-

§ 6:2   Elements of a section 337 violation

In a Section 337 action, a complainant must prove the following major elements: (1) an unfair act; (2) importation; (3) domestic industry; and (4) injury to the complainant.

Unfair Act: Section 337 authorizes the ITC to declare unlawful "unfair methods of competition and unfair acts in the importation of articles" and the importation into the United States articles that "infringe a valid and enforceable U.S. Patent."[1] For example, a reference product sponsor or a competing biosimilar company could seek an exclusion order from the ITC preventing importation of a biosimilar product that infringes a valid and enforceable patent directed to a biosimilar formulation or composition.

The ITC is also authorized to issue exclusion orders for products made outside the United States using a patented process.[2] This type of infringement arises under 35 U.S.C.A. § 271(g).[3] However, there is a significant and important difference between actions brought under Section 271(g) in a Federal District Court, and Section 337 investigations alleging infringement under Section 271(g)—certain defenses that are available to accused infringers in District Court are not available to respondents in a Section 337 investigation. Under Section 271(g) in the district court, there is no liability for infringement if the product made by the patented

---

TA-1145.

[5]*Certain Antivenom Prods. & Components Thereof*, Inv. No. 337-TA-903.

[Section 6:2]

[1]19 U.S.C.A. § 1337(a).

[2]*See Certain Sweeteners Containing Sucralose, and Related Intermediate Compounds Thereof*, Inv. No. 337-TA-604, (I.T.C. Apr. 28, 2009) (Comm'n Op.).

[3]35 U.S.C.A. § 271(g) ("Whoever without authority imports into the United States or offers to sell, sells, or uses within the United States a product which is made by a process patented in the United States shall be liable as an infringer, if the importation, offer to sell, sale, or use of the product occurs during the term of such process patent. In an action for infringement of a process patent, no remedy may be granted for infringement on account of the noncommercial use or retail sale of a product unless there is no adequate remedy under this title for infringement on account of the importation or other use, offer to sell, or sale of that product. A product which is made by a patented process will, for purposes of this title, not be considered to be so made after—(1) it is materially changed by subsequent processes; or (2) it becomes a trivial and nonessential component of another product.").

process is materially changed by subsequent processes or if the product made by the patented process becomes a "trivial and nonessential component of another product."[4] These defenses are not recognized in Section 337 actions; rather, the ITC looks to the interdependence between the patented process and the production of the imported product.[5] For example, the ITC found a "close interdependence" where imported sucralose was alleged to be "made, produced, or processed" by means of the claimed process, even though the patented process occurred several steps prior to the final steps to make the imported product.[6]

In addition to allegations of patent or trademark infringement, which are the most common, "unfair methods of competition and unfair" acts under Section 337 also include trade secret theft, copyright infringement, common law trademark infringement, trade dress infringement, and price fixing.[7] The ITC has authority to consider whether conduct of a foreign company outside the United States violates U.S. laws, including trade secret laws.[8] For example, the ITC is currently investigating whether a former employee of one Korean company stole trade secrets relating to the manufacture of Botox® and provided them to another Korean company who used them to develop and manufacture DWP-450, a purified botulinum toxin type A complex, that would directly compete with Botox®.[9]

Importation Requirement: Section 337 prohibits "unfair

---

[4]35 U.S.C.A. § 271(g).

[5]*See Certain Sucralose*, Inv. No. 337-TA-604, (I.T.C. Apr. 28, 2009) (Comm'n Op.).

[6]*See Certain Sucralose*, Inv. No. 337-TA-604, (I.T.C. Apr. 28, 2009) (Comm'n Op.).

[7]*See* 19 U.S.C.A. § 1337(a); *Certain Light-Emitting Diode Prods. & Components Thereof*, ITC Inv. No. 337-TA-947 (I.T.C. Feb. 12, 2015) (false advertising); *Certain Footwear Prods.*, Inv. No. 337-TA-936, (I.T.C. Nov. 12, 2014) (false designation of origin, common law trademark infringement, and trademark dilution); *Certain Elec. Fireplaces, Components, Manuals, Certain Processes for Mfg.*, Inv. No. 337-TA-791/826, (I.T.C. May 1, 2013) (USITC Pub. 4552) (breach of contract and tortious interference with contract relations); *Certain Food Water Disposers*, Inv. No. 337-TA-838, (I.T.C. Apr. 16, 2012) (common law trademark infringement, passing off, and trade dress infringement).

[8]*TianRui Group Co. Ltd. v. International Trade Com'n*, 661 F.3d 1322, 33 Int'l Trade Rep. (BNA) 1385, 100 U.S.P.Q.2d 1401 (Fed. Cir. 2011).

[9]*In re Certain Botulinum Toxin Products*, Inv. No. 337-TA-1145 (U.S. Int'l Trade Comm'n May 24, 2019).

methods of competition and unfair acts in the importation of articles" and "the importation into the United States, the sale for importation, or the sale within the United States after importation . . . of articles that" infringe a U.S. patent, registered trademark or copyright."[10] The importation requirement includes the importation of even a small quantity of an accused article, for example an importation of products for a U.S. trade show.[11]

The goal of the ITC is the protection of domestic industries from unfair acts occurring abroad which result in competition against the domestic industry in the United States.[12] As long as the accused company is importing goods established to violate Section 337, the remedial measures of the statute are available. For example, the importation requirement would be satisfied if an FDA-approved biosimilar has been imported, or in situations where a biosimilar subject to a pending aBLA has been imported for uses not protected by the safe harbor of § 271(e)(1).

Although in most cases the accused article has already been imported, Section 337 also extends to the imminent importation of a product, such as a contract for a future sale for importation.[13] The importation requirement may be a hurdle for biosimilar cases in which the biosimilar applicant's product is not yet approved by the FDA. The Federal Circuit previously approved ITC jurisdiction based on likely future infringement where the FDA approval was projected to occur, but the Federal Circuit later withdrew its opinion.[14] If a biosimilar applicant provides notice of commercial marketing before its product is approved by the

---

[10]19 U.S.C.A. § 1337(a).

[11]*See, e.g., Certain Acesulfame Potassium and Blends*, Inv. No. 337-TA-403 (U.S. Int'l Trade Comm'n Jan. 15, 1999) (Comm'n Op.).

[12]*See* 19 U.S.C.A. § 1337(a)(1)(A) (limiting ITC jurisdiction to only "unfair methods of competition and unfair acts in the importation of articles" that "the threat or effect of which is (i) to destroy or substantially injure an industry in the United States; (ii) to prevent the establishment of such an industry; or (iii) to restrain or monopolize trade and commerce in the United States.").

[13]*See, e.g., Certain Variable Speed Wind Turbines and Components Thereof*, Inv. No. 337- TA-376 (U.S. Int'l Trade Comm'n Oct. 19, 1995) (Comm'n Op.).

[14]*Amgen, Inc. v. Roche Holding Ltd.*, 519 F.3d 1343, 1352, 30 Int'l Trade Rep. (BNA) 1467, 86 U.S.P.Q.2d 1188 (Fed. Cir. 2008), reh'g en banc granted, opinion withdrawn by, , Returned to Panel by564 F.3d 1358, 31 Int'l Trade Rep. (BNA) 1984, 90 U.S.P.Q.2d 1843 (Fed. Cir. 2009) and

FDA,[15] then importation may not be sufficiently imminent to confer ITC jurisdiction. In that scenario, the complainant may need to show additional facts indicating that importation is imminent, for example, by citing to statements by the biosimilar applicant indicating an expectation that the FDA approval is imminent.

Domestic Industry Requirement: The domestic industry requirement is another element necessary to establish a violation of Section 337. In understanding the domestic industry requirement, it is important to remember that Section 337 is a trade statute that was enacted to protect American industries from unfairly traded imports. A complainant thus must establish that an "industry" exists or an "industry is in the process of being established" in the United States for the intellectual property sought to be protected under the investigation.[16] The domestic industry requirement has two prongs: a technical prong and an economic prong.[17]

Under the "technical prong" of the domestic industry requirement, a complainant must identify "articles" that

---

opinion revised and superseded, 565 F.3d 846, 31 Int'l Trade Rep. (BNA) 1984, 90 U.S.P.Q.2d 1842 (Fed. Cir. 2009), and opinion revised and superseded sub nom. *Amgen Inc. v. International Trade Com'n*, 565 F.3d 846, 31 Int'l Trade Rep. (BNA) 1984, 90 U.S.P.Q.2d 1842 (Fed. Cir. 2009) ("Statute, precedent, and the policies they reflect, negate the Commission's rejection of its own authority to consider the issues of unfair competition based on infringement by product imported for purposes of obtaining federal approval, whether or not sale has already occurred. Although § 271(e)(1) negates infringement by the imported EPO, the projected the FDA approval established the Commission's jurisdiction to review and provide remedy to take effect as appropriate after the approval is granted and § 271(e)(1) no longer shelters liability.").

[15]A biosimilar applicant may provide notice of commercial marketing "either before or after receiving the FDA approval." *Sandoz Inc. v. Amgen Inc.*, 137 S. Ct. 1664, 1667, 198 L. Ed. 2d 114, 122 U.S.P.Q.2d 1685 (2017) ("The applicant must give 'notice' at least 180 days 'before the date of the first commercial marketing.' '[C]ommercial marketing,' in turn, must be 'of the biological product licensed under subsection (k).' § 262(*l*) (8)(A). Because this latter phrase modifies 'commercial marketing' rather than 'notice,' 'commercial marketing' is the point in time by which the biosimilar must be 'licensed.' The statute's use of the word 'licensed' merely reflects the fact that, on the 'date of the first commercial marketing,' the product must be 'licensed.' *See* § 262(a)(1)(A). Accordingly, the applicant may provide notice either before or after receiving the FDA approval.").

[16]19 U.S.C.A. § 1337(a)(2).

[17]19 U.S.C.A. § 1337(a)(2).

practice the intellectual property right at issue.[18] For patents, this is typically akin to an infringement analysis under Section 271, and requires that a complainant establish that it, or one of its licensees, practices at least one valid claim of each asserted patent.[19] Importantly, the valid claim alleged to be practiced does not have to be one of the claims allegedly infringed.[20]

Generally, the "economic prong" of the domestic industry requirement is met when the complainant can show a nexus between substantial or significant economic activity in the United States and the asserted intellectual property right.[21] The standard for proving the economic prong of domestic industry depends in part on the type of unfair act being alleged, e.g., patent or trademark infringement or unfair competition. In general, a complainant can satisfy the economic prong by proving: (A) significant investment in plant and equipment; (B) significant employment of labor or capital; or (C) substantial investment in its exploitation, including engineering, research and development, or

---

[18]19 U.S.C.A. § 1337(a)(2).

[19]*See Microsoft Corp. v. International Trade Com'n*, 731 F.3d 1354, 1361–62, 35 Int'l Trade Rep. (BNA) 2081, 108 U.S.P.Q.2d 1443 (Fed. Cir. 2013) ("To establish a violation of section 337, Microsoft had to show not just infringement by Motorola's products but the existence of a domestic industry relating to the articles protected by the patent. The ALJ determined that Microsoft failed to make that domestic-industry showing because it did not offer sufficient proof of articles that were actually protected by the patent. . . . There is no question about the substantiality of Microsoft's investment in its operating system or about the importance of that operating system to mobile phones on which it runs. But that is not enough under the statute. Section 337, though not requiring that an article protected by the patent be produced in the United States, unmistakably requires that the domestic company's substantial investments relate to actual 'articles protected by the patent.' 19 U.S.C.A. § 1337(a)(2), (3).") (internal citations and quotations omitted).

[20]*See Certain Batteries and Electrochemical Devices Containing Composite Separators, Components Thereof, and Prods. Containing the Same*, Inv. No. 337-TA-1087, (I.T.C. Aug. 8, 2018) (Order No. 32 at 8) ("The Commission has long held that in order to satisfy the technical prong of the domestic industry requirement, it is sufficient to show that a domestic industry practices *any* claim of the asserted patent.") (emphasis in original).

[21]*See, e.g., In re Certain Multimedia Display and Navigation Devices and Systems, Components Thereof, and Products Containing Same*, Inv. No. 337-TA-694 (I.T.C. Aug. 11, 2001) (Op.).

licensing.[22] Subsections (A) and (B) apply to all types of unfair acts. Subsection (C) applies to unfair acts based on patent, registered trademark, copyright or mask work infringements.[23]

Injury to the Complainant: Where the "unfair act" is one of patent, trademark, or copyright infringement, there is no requirement to prove any additional injury beyond proof of the infringement itself.[24] When the unfair act is not infringement of a patent, trademark, copyright, the complainant must also prove economic injury based on the unfairly traded imports.[25] In the latter case, the following factors are often considered: (1) lost sales due to the unfairly traded imports; (2) respondent's volume of imports; (3) underselling by the respondent; (4) evidence of complainant's declining production, profitability and sales; and (5) harm to goodwill and reputation.[26]

§ 6:3 ITC remedies

Upon finding a violation of Section 337, the ITC can issue an exclusion order and/or a cease and desist order, barring the importation and sale of the accused articles in the United States. There are two types of exclusion orders: general exclusion orders ("GEOs"), which exclude all articles found to infringe regardless of the identity of the importer or manufacturer, and limited exclusion orders ("LEOs"), which exclude infringing articles by parties named as respondents in the investigation. To obtain a GEO, the complainant must establish one of two criteria under Section 337(d)(2): (a) a GEO is "necessary to prevent circumvention of an [LEO]"; or

---

[22]19 U.S.C.A. § 1337(a)(3).

[23]19 U.S.C.A. § 1337(a)(3).

[24]Prior to 1988, proof of economic injury was required in all Section 337 actions. The Omnibus Trade & Competitiveness Act of 1988, 19 U.S.C.A. § 2191 (2012), eliminated the injury requirement for unfair acts based on infringement of a patent, registered trademark, copyright or mask work.

[25]See, e.g., Certain Digital Multimeters, Inv. No. 337-TA-588 (I.T.C. Jan. 14, 2008).

[26]Certain Digital Multimeters, Inv. No. 337-TA-588 (I.T.C. Jan. 14, 2008).

(b) "there is a pattern of violation of this section and it is difficult to identify the source of infringing products."[1]

The ITC may also issue cease and desist orders to prevent all sales in the U.S. of the infringing articles, including those that are already in U.S. inventory.[2] Cease and desist orders are directed to specific parties—respondents in the investigation—and prevent the U.S. sale, distribution, or other use of the infringing articles. To issue a cease and desist order, the ITC must find that a domestic entity maintains a "commercially significant" inventory of the infringing articles in the U.S.[3]

Before issuing any remedial order, the ITC must consider the effect of such orders on four public interest factors.[4] The public interest factors are: 1) public health and welfare; 2) competitive conditions in the U.S. economy; 3) production of like or competitive articles in the U.S.; and 4) U.S. consumers.[5] The ITC must also consult with administrative agencies such as the Federal Trade Commission, the Department of Health and Human Services, the Department of Justice, and other agencies it deems appropriate in order to evaluate the effect of a potential remedy on the public interest.[6] The ITC also invites public comment from interested parties and members of the public on the public interest factors.[7] The ITC considers only the four public interest factors listed above and need not consider the *eBay* factors

---

[Section 6:3]

[1]19 U.S.C.A. § 1337(d); *Certain Airless Spray Pumps and Components Thereof*, Inv. No. 337-TA-90 (I.T.C. Nov. 24, 1981).

[2]*See* 19 U.S.C.A. § 1337(f)(1) ("[T]he Commission may issue and cause to be served on any person violating this section, or believed to be violating this section, as the case may be, an order directing such person to cease and desist from engaging in the unfair methods or acts involved, unless after considering the effect of such order upon the public health and welfare, competitive conditions in the United States economy, the production of like or directly competitive articles in the United States, and United States consumers, it finds that such order should not be issued.").

[3]*See Certain Voltage Regulators*, Inv. No. 337-TA-654 (I.T.C. Aug. 3, 2010) (Comm'n Op.) (finding that respondent's domestic inventory of 5,800 samples of infringing articles and 75,000 engineering parts was not a "significant inventory" given the "millions of parts maintained and sold abroad" by the respondent).

[4]19 U.S.C.A. § 1337(e).

[5]19 U.S.C.A. § 1337(e).

[6]19 U.S.C.A. § 1337(b)(2).

[7]19 U.S.C.A. § 1337(b)(1).

applied by federal district courts in determining whether to issue injunctive relief to remedy patent infringement.[8]

After the ITC issues a remedial order, the President of the United States has 60 days to review the order and has the power to veto the order for policy reasons.[9] During this 60 day period, products covered by the propose order may enter the United States if a bond is posted.[10]

§ 6:4 Comparison between section 337 investigations and district court litigations

Interplay with the BPCIA: The BPCIA does not set any limits on the scope or timing of a Section 337 action, unlike actions brought in district court. Thus, a reference product sponsor does not need to engage in the patent dance with a biosimilar applicant prior to filing a complaint with the ITC. A patent owner may assert any number of patents in an ITC investigation without identifying patents in the patent dance as required by the BPCIA.

Timing: Within 45 days of institution, the presiding Administrative Law Judge establishes a target date for a final determination. Typically, an investigation lasts between 12 and 18 months, which is, in general, much faster than patent litigation in the district courts. The general timeline for Section 337 investigations includes a bench trial before the ALJ, an Initial Determination by the ALJ, and the Commission's Final Determination. To enable the Commission to issue a final determination within 12 to 18 months, litigants can expect hearings to occur as early as six months from the filing of the complaint.

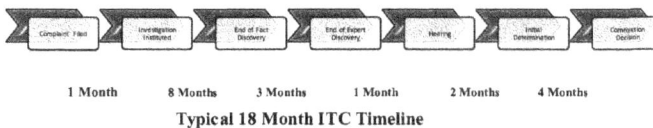

Complaint Filed	Investigation Instituted	End of Fact Discovery	End of Expert Discovery	Hearing	Initial Determination	Commission Decision
1 Month	8 Months	3 Months	1 Month	2 Months	4 Months	

Typical 18 Month ITC Timeline

---

[8]*See Spansion, Inc. v. International Trade Com'n*, 629 F.3d 1331, 1358, 97 U.S.P.Q.2d 1417 (Fed. Cir. 2010) ("The ITC responds that the Commission properly considered the public interest factors prior to issuing the exclusion order and that *eBay* does not apply to Commission remedy determinations."). The Commission will also consider the public interest issue in deciding whether to institute an Investigation in the first instance. *See* 19 U.S.C.A. § 1337(d)(1).

[9]19 U.S.C.A. § 1337(j).

[10]19 U.S.C.A. § 1337(j).

Stay of Section 337 Investigations: Unlike district court actions, stays of Section 337 actions are seldom granted, even if a petition for *inter partes* review is instituted by the U.S. Patent and Trademark Office. For example, in one investigation, even though IPRs were instituted and set to conclude prior to the ITC investigation target date, Judge Shaw denied a request for a stay.[1]

Substantive Proceedings: Similar to district court judges, each of the Administrative Law Judges (ALJ) has their own set of substantive rules and procedures. ITC investigations are conducted before a sole fact finder, and there is no jury available. Many ALJs will conduct claim construction proceedings if requested by the parties, and this will often involve and incorporate an extensive technology tutorial. In appropriate cases, summary determination, akin to summary judgment, may be available. With many of the ALJs, at trial, direct testimony is provided by written witness statements, and cross-examination and re-direct testimony are live.

Injunctive relief: Injunctive relief is the primary remedy available at the ITC. The ITC has the power to issue broad injunctive relief in the form of exclusion orders that prevent the importation of the unfairly imported goods, or issue cease and desist order that prohibit the sale of infringing products from inventory already in the United States.[2] By prevailing on the merits, a patent holder is generally entitled to obtain an injunction in an ITC action, whereas district courts must follow the Supreme Court's *eBay* standard in analyzing whether to grant an injunction.

Damages: Unlike district courts, the ITC is not authorized to award money damages as a remedy for patent infringement or other unfair acts.[3]

Personal Jurisdiction: In the ITC, jurisdiction turns on whether an accused *product* is imported into the United

---

[Section 6:4]

[1]*Certain Laser-Driven Light Sources*, Inv. No. 337-TA-983 (U.S. Int'l Trade Comm'n Mar. 4, 2016) (Order No. 8).

[2]19 U.S.C.A. § 1337(d), (e), and (f).

[3]*Bio-Technology General Corp. v. Genentech, Inc.*, 80 F.3d 1553, 1564, 38 U.S.P.Q.2d 1321 (Fed. Cir. 1996) ("[T]he ITC does not have the power to award damages for patent infringement. This form of relief may only be provided by the United States District Courts, which have original and exclusive jurisdiction over patent infringement cases.").

States.[4] This is called *in rem* jurisdiction, and jurisdiction can be established regardless of whether there is personal jurisdiction over the company importing the product. As a result, single complaints can name multiple manufacturers and all parties in the chain of distribution, including, for example, a foreign biosimilar manufacture and any other entities involved in the manufacture, sale, marketing or distribution of the product, regardless of their location. Relatedly, because jurisdiction is over the products crossing the borders, foreign entities are subject to the Commission's jurisdiction as long as their products are being imported into the U.S. Thus, there are no special service of process requirements for binding foreign companies to the Commission's decisions.

---

[4]19 U.S.C.A. § 1337(a).

Chapter 7

Discovery in the United States for Use in Foreign Litigation

§ 7:1   The use of U.S. discovery in foreign litigation generally
§ 7:2   Procedures for a Section 1782 Action
§ 7:3   —The Ex Parte application
§ 7:4   —discretion under section 1782

KeyCite®: Cases and other legal materials listed in KeyCite Scope can be researched through the KeyCite service on Westlaw®. Use KeyCite to check citations for form, parallel references, prior and later history, and comprehensive citator information, including citations to other decisions and secondary materials.

---

§ 7:1   The use of U.S. discovery in foreign litigation generally

Litigants in foreign proceedings can seek discovery from individuals and entities located in the United States by filing an action in Federal District Court under 28 U.S.C.A. § 1782. This statute is available for use by both innovator biological product manufacturers and biosimilar manufacturers to seek discovery from United States-based parties for use in foreign patent litigation, including proceedings before foreign patent offices such as the European Patent Office. Such discovery may include written responses, documents, things, and testimony. This discovery procedure has been used in biologics and biosimilar cases.[1]

Section 1782 states that a district court "may" order a

"person," which can be a corporation, who "resides or is found" in the district to give their "testimony or statement or to produce a document or other thing for use in a proceeding in a foreign or international tribunal."[2] The district court's order "may be made pursuant to a letter rogatory issued, or request made, by a foreign or international tribunal" or based upon "the application of any interested person."[3] By default, discovery ordered under § 1782 will be conducted according to the Federal Rules of Civil Procedure, but the district court can order alternative procedures, "which may be in whole or part the practice and procedure of the foreign country or the international tribunal."

§ 7:2   Procedures for a Section 1782 Action

Section 1782 actions typically begin with an *ex parte* application by the applicant seeking discovery.[1] If the application is granted, the court authorizes the applicant to serve subpoenas and/or discovery requests on the party from whom discovery is sought. Once the target of the discovery receives the requests, it may respond to the request, negotiate a narrower scope of discovery, or move to quash the discovery entirely.[2] A motion to quash is the target's opportunity to respond to and oppose the discovery sought.

Practice tip: although § 1782 applications are usually considered *ex parte*, some district courts have required that notice of the application be provided to the target of the

---

U.S. importation, manufacturing and sales for use in infringement action in Japan); *In re Application of Teva Pharma B.V. for an Order Permitting Issuance of Subpoenas to Take Discovery for Use in a Foreign Proceeding*, No. 14-MC-697-PJWx, D.I. 1 (C.D. Cal. Sep. 11, 2014) (seeking discovery of information regarding inventorship and assignment of rights to patent application for use in proceedings in various European jurisdictions).

[2]28 U.S.C.A. § 1782(a).

[3]28 U.S.C.A. § 1782(a).

[Section 7:2]

[1]*See, e.g., In re O'Keeffe*, 650 Fed. Appx. 83, 85 (2d Cir. 2016); *In re Letters Rogatory from Tokyo Dist., Tokyo, Japan*, 539 F.2d 1216, 1217, 46 A.L.R. Fed. 950 (9th Cir. 1976); *In re Application of Masters for an Order Pursuant to 28 U.S.C. § 1782 to Conduct Discovery for Use in a Foreign Proceeding*, 315 F. Supp. 3d 269, 272 (D.D.C. 2018).

[2]*See, e.g., In re Letters Rogatory from Tokyo Dist., Tokyo, Japan*, 539 F.2d 1216, 1217, 46 A.L.R. Fed. 950 (9th Cir. 1976); *IPCom GMBH & Co. KG v. Apple Inc.*, 61 F. Supp. 3d 919, 922 (N.D. Cal. 2014).

discovery request before the court will consider the application.[3]

§ 7:3 Procedures for a Section 1782 Action—The Ex Parte application

In an application for an order to obtain discovery under § 1782, the applicant must demonstrate that four statutory requirements are met:

> (1) the request must be made "by a foreign or international tribunal," or by "any interested person"; (2) the request must seek evidence, whether it be the "testimony or statement" of a person or the production of "a document or other thing"; (3) the evidence must be "for use in a proceeding in a foreign or international tribunal"; and (4) the person from whom discovery is sought must reside or be found in the district of the district court ruling on the application for assistance.[1]

"Interested persons" includes not only litigants in the foreign proceedings, but also "any other person whether he be designated by foreign law or international convention or merely possess a reasonable interest in obtaining [judicial] assistance."[2] Some courts have interpreted the requirement that the evidence sought must be "for use" in the foreign proceedings includes a relevance element and therefore excludes evidence that is "plainly irrelevant" to the foreign proceeding.[3] An application under § 1782 typically also includes a detailed description of the discovery sought, including, for example, a copy of the proposed subpoena, a list of documents or categories of documents, or a list of deposition topics.

Practice tip: the European Patent Office has been found to

---

[3]*E.g.*, *In re Penner*, 2017 WL 5632658, *1 (D. Mass. 2017); *In re Harbour Victoria Inv. Holdings Ltd. Section 1782 Petitions*, 2015 WL 4040420, *3 (S.D. N.Y. 2015); *In re Anglin*, 2009 WL 4739481, *2 (D. Neb. 2009); *In re Merck & Co., Inc.*, 197 F.R.D. 267, 271 (M.D. N.C. 2000).

[Section 7:3]

[1]*In re Clerici*, 481 F.3d 1324, 1331–32 (11th Cir. 2007) (quoting 28 U.S.C.A. § 1782(a))

[2]*Intel Corp. v. Advanced Micro Devices, Inc.*, 542 U.S. 241, 256–57, 124 S. Ct. 2466, 159 L. Ed. 2d 355, 71 U.S.P.Q.2d 1001, 2004-1 Trade Cas. (CCH) ¶ 74453, 64 Fed. R. Evid. Serv. 742, 58 Fed. R. Serv. 3d 696 (2004). *See also, Akebia Therapeutics, Inc. v. FibroGen, Inc.*, 793 F.3d 1108, 1111, 115 U.S.P.Q.2d 1864 (9th Cir. 2015) (a party seeking to invalidate patents in a foreign patent office is an "interested party" for purposes of § 1782).

[3]*See, e.g.*, *In re Schlich*, 893 F.3d 40, 52 (1st Cir. 2018).

be a foreign tribunal for purposes of § 1782, and discovery has been ordered under § 1782 for use in opposition proceedings before the European Patent Office.[4]

§ 7:4   Procedures for a Section 1782 Action— discretion under section 1782

If the statutory requirements are met, then § 1782 "authorizes, but does not require, a federal district court to provide assistance."[1]

Courts consider several discretionary factors when deciding whether to grant an application under § 1782.[2] First, whether "the person from whom discovery is sought is a participant in the foreign proceeding," because "the need for § 1782(a) aid generally is not as apparent as it ordinarily is when evidence is sought from a nonparticipant" who "may be outside the foreign tribunal's jurisdictional reach."[3] Second, "the nature of the foreign tribunal, the character of the proceedings underway abroad, and the receptivity of the foreign government or the court or agency abroad to U.S. federal-court judicial assistance."[4] Third, "whether the § 1782(a) request conceals an attempt to circumvent foreign proof-gathering restrictions or other policies of a foreign country or the United States."[5] However, there is no requirement that the requested discovery be available under the rules of the foreign tribunal or that "United States law would allow discovery in domestic litigation analogous to the foreign proceeding."[6] Rather, the second and third discretionary factors concern whether "the foreign tribunal would readily accept relevant information discovered in the United States," and whether the foreign country has an affirmative policy precluding the discovery such that the "foreign govern-

---

[4]*E.g., Akebia Therapeutics, Inc. v. FibroGen, Inc.*, 793 F.3d 1108, 1111, 115 U.S.P.Q.2d 1864 (9th Cir. 2015); *Oncology Foundation v. Avanza Development Services, LLC*, 2017 WL 2376769, *1 (D. Md. 2017).

[Section 7:4]

[1]*Intel Corp. v. Advanced Micro Devices, Inc.*, 542 U.S. 241, 255, 124 S. Ct. 2466, 159 L. Ed. 2d 355, 71 U.S.P.Q.2d 1001, 2004-1 Trade Cas. (CCH) ¶ 74453, 64 Fed. R. Evid. Serv. 742, 58 Fed. R. Serv. 3d 696 (2004).

[2]*Intel*, 542 U.S. at 264–65.

[3]*Intel*, 542 U.S. at 264.

[4]*Intel*, 542 U.S. at 264.

[5]*Intel*, 542 U.S. at 264–65.

[6]*Intel*, 542 U.S. at 262–63.

ment[ ] would in fact be offended" by a grant of discovery in the United States.[7] Fourth and finally, courts take into consideration whether or not the request is otherwise "unduly intrusive or burdensome."[8] If a request is unduly intrusive or burdensome, it may be rejected outright or "trimmed" and limited in scope.[9]

If the district court decides that the statutory requirements are satisfied and that the discretionary factors favor granting the requested discovery, the court may issue subpoenas. At that point the applicant typically serves the subpoenas on the target of the discovery. Once the target receives the subpoenas, it may choose to respond to the discovery request, attempt to negotiate a narrower scope of discovery with the applicant, or move to quash the subpoenas.

Practice tip: foreign attorneys representing a party in a foreign tribunal can submit declarations explaining the foreign proceeding and procedural rules of the tribunal. These declarations provide an opportunity to explain to the U.S. court the context of the discovery request and provide factual support for the *Intel* discretionary factors that weigh in favor of granting the requested discovery.

---

[7]*Intel*, 542 U.S. at 261–62.

[8]*Intel*, 542 U.S. at 265.

[9]*Intel*, 542 U.S. at 265.

Chapter 8

Antitrust Actions

§ 8:1   Antitrust actions generally
§ 8:2   Challenges to patent settlement agreements
§ 8:3   Filing agreements with the government
§ 8:4   Intellectual property acquisition and
         enforcement—Sham litigation and walker process
         fraud
§ 8:5   —Patent thickets
§ 8:6   Exclusionary contracting and rebating strategies

> **KeyCite®:** Cases and other legal materials listed in KeyCite Scope can be researched through the KeyCite service on Westlaw®. Use KeyCite to check citations for form, parallel references, prior and later history, and comprehensive citator information, including citations to other decisions and secondary materials.

§ 8:1   Antitrust actions generally

The pharmaceutical industry has been subject to intense antitrust scrutiny for decades. Antitrust law is intended to preserve competition with the goals of promoting innovation, fostering price competition, and enhancing consumer welfare. Public and private concern about the rising costs of healthcare, and the prices of prescription medicines, has prompted scrutiny of the industry from many angles. Antitrust investigations have been pursued and lawsuits have been filed against pharmaceutical companies by the U.S. Department of Justice, the Federal Trade Commission, state attorneys general, drug wholesalers, retail pharmacy chains, insurance companies, union welfare plans, consumers, and competing drug manufacturers, among others.

In addition, the scrutiny has been turned on a wide variety of conduct. Some recent antitrust actions involve conduct that is not unique to the pharmaceutical industry. One example includes allegations of price-fixing among generic drug competitors.[1] Other actions, by contrast, focus on unique features of the industry and likely would not arise in any other context. One example involves so-called "product hopping" by brand companies in the Hatch-Waxman space, in which brand companies allegedly undertake to switch the market to new, patented variants of old drugs in order to thwart the operation of AB-rated generic substitution under state drug selection laws.[2] In addition to actions challenging conduct by drug manufacturers, the antitrust agencies scrutinize pharmaceutical mergers and routinely require divestitures of products or other remedies to maintain competition.

There is every reason to believe that this same intensity of antitrust scrutiny will be brought to bear on biologic and biosimilar products—indeed, the process has already started. The sections below provide a brief overview of antitrust issues that have arisen in relation to biosimilars.

§ 8:2   Challenges to patent settlement agreements

One of the most active areas of antitrust enforcement for the past two decades has involved challenges to settlements of patent litigation between brand and generic drug companies, under the so-called "reverse payment" or "pay for delay" doctrine. The theory of these cases is that the brand company pays the generic company to accept a later entry date in exchange for granting the generic company some other economic benefit, such as a payment or commercial deal on more favorable terms than would otherwise be granted. The payment is allegedly funded by the increased monopoly profits the brand would earn by postponing generic entry, benefiting the settling parties but harming the public, which is denied earlier access to lower-cost generic alternatives. The theory arose in relation to brand/generic settlements, and the degree to which it will be implicated by biologic/biosimilar settlements remains unclear.

Prior to 2013, these types of antitrust challenges routinely failed. The majority of courts applied what came to be known

---

[Section 8:1]

[1]*See Heritage Pharmaceuticals Pays Over $7 Million to Resolve Civil False Claims Act Allegations*, U.S. Attorney's Office E.D. Pa. (May 31, 2019), https://www.justice.gov/usao-edpa/pr/heritage-pharmaceuticals-pay s-over-7-million-resolve-civil-false-claims-act-allegations.

[2]*E.g.*, *New York ex rel. Schneiderman v. Actavis PLC*, 787 F.3d 638, 2015-1 Trade Cas. (CCH) ¶ 79178 (2d Cir. 2015).

as the scope-of-the-patent test.[1] Under that test, a settlement agreement that permitted generic entry prior to expiration of the patent(s) at issue could not be anticompetitive as a matter of law, regardless of whether the agreement included a reverse payment, because the agreement did not prevent competition beyond the potential exclusionary scope of the patent. As a result, any exclusion was deemed to result from the patent, not the agreement.

In 2013, the Supreme Court addressed the proper antitrust standard to apply to reverse-payment challenges, in *FTC v. Actavis, Inc.*[2] The FTC had filed a lawsuit challenging several settlement agreements involving generic versions of Androgel as containing improper reverse payments. On the basis of the scope-of-the-patent test, the district court dismissed the case, and the Eleventh Circuit affirmed. In the Supreme Court, the FTC argued that any agreement containing a reverse payment should be presumptively unlawful, regardless of whether it allowed generic entry prior to patent expiry. The industry defendants argued the Court should affirm the scope-of-the-patent test. The Supreme Court rejected both positions and adopted a middle ground. In the Court's view, reverse payments are "unusual," and it stated that "there is reason for concern that settlements taking this form tend to have significant adverse effects on competition."[3] The Court also recognized that there may be justifications for reverse payments, including traditional settlement considerations.[4] While justifications may mean that the agreement did not produce anticompetitive results,

---

[Section 8:2]

[1]*E.g., In re Tamoxifen Citrate Antitrust Litigation*, 466 F.3d 187, 2006-2 Trade Cas. (CCH) ¶ 75382 (2d Cir. 2006) (rejected by, In re K-Dur Antitrust Litigation, 686 F.3d 197, 103 U.S.P.Q.2d 1497, 2012-2 Trade Cas. (CCH) ¶ 77971 (3d Cir. 2012)) and (abrogated by, F.T.C. v. Actavis, Inc., 570 U.S. 136, 133 S. Ct. 2223, 186 L. Ed. 2d 343, 106 U.S.P.Q.2d 1953, 2013-1 Trade Cas. (CCH) ¶ 78419 (2013)); *In re Ciprofloxacin Hydrochloride Antitrust Litigation*, 544 F.3d 1323, 88 U.S.P.Q.2d 1801, 2008-2 Trade Cas. (CCH) ¶ 76336 (Fed. Cir. 2008) (rejected by, In re K-Dur Antitrust Litigation, 686 F.3d 197, 103 U.S.P.Q.2d 1497, 2012-2 Trade Cas. (CCH) ¶ 77971 (3d Cir. 2012)) and (abrogated by, F.T.C. v. Actavis, Inc., 570 U.S. 136, 133 S. Ct. 2223, 186 L. Ed. 2d 343, 106 U.S.P. Q.2d 1953, 2013-1 Trade Cas. (CCH) ¶ 78419 (2013)).

[2]*F.T.C. v. Actavis, Inc.*, 570 U.S. 136, 133 S. Ct. 2223, 186 L. Ed. 2d 343, 106 U.S.P.Q.2d 1953, 2013-1 Trade Cas. (CCH) ¶ 78419 (2013).

[3]*FTC v. Actavis*, 570 U.S. at 147–48.

[4]*FTC v. Actavis*, 570 U.S. at 156.

the Court held that possibility did not justify dismissing an antitrust complaint because "these anticompetitive consequences will at least sometimes prove unjustified."[5] As a result, the Court reversed the grant of a motion to dismiss and allowed the case to continue. The Court also declined to apply any presumption of unlawfulness or anticompetitive effect, holding that in a reverse payment case, "the FTC [or a private plaintiff] must prove its case as in other rule-of-reason cases."[6]

Following *Actavis*, courts have allowed reverse-payment challenges to patent settlements to go forward based on allegations of various types of purported reverse payments including: (1) agreements under which the generic company is paid to provide goods or services to the brand (including on products other than the one at issue in the settlement), such as co-promotion agreements or back-up supply agreements;[7] (2) agreements by the brand company not to market an authorized generic version of its product during the generic first-filer's 180-day exclusivity period;[8] and (3) situations in which the parties settle cases involving two drugs at the same time, one of which resolves a damages claim by the brand against the generic involving one product allegedly for less than it is worth, as a form of compensation for delayed entry on the second product.[9] Several cases also have addressed "accelerator" or "contingent launch" provisions, which allow the generic company to launch its products earlier than a default entry date if certain events occur, such as the launch by competing generics or an authorized generic, or the occurrence of a final court decision that could lead a first-filer to forfeit its 180-day exclusivity if it does not begin marketing its product within 75 days. Most courts

---

[5]*FTC v. Actavis*, 570 U.S. at 156.

[6]*FTC v. Actavis*, 570 U.S. at 159.

[7]*E.g.*, *In re Niaspan Antitrust Litigation*, 42 F. Supp. 3d 735 (E.D. Pa. 2014); *In re Aggrenox Antitrust Litigation*, 94 F. Supp. 3d 224, 236, 2015-1 Trade Cas. (CCH) ¶ 79115 (D. Conn. 2015).

[8]*E.g.*, *King Drug Co. of Florence, Inc. v. Smithkline Beecham Corp.*, 791 F.3d 388, 404, 2015-2 Trade Cas. (CCH) ¶ 79223 (3d Cir. 2015); *In re Loestrin 24 Fe Antitrust Litigation*, 261 F. Supp. 3d 307, 332–33, 2017-2 Trade Cas. (CCH) ¶ 80200 (D.R.I. 2017).

[9]*E.g.*, *In re Nexium (Esomeprazole) Antitrust Litigation*, 842 F.3d 34, 44–45, 2016-2 Trade Cas. (CCH) ¶ 79835 (1st Cir. 2016); *In re Lipitor Antitrust Litigation*, 868 F.3d 231, 253, 2017-2 Trade Cas. (CCH) ¶ 80101 (3d Cir. 2017), cert. denied, 138 S. Ct. 983, 200 L. Ed. 2d 300 (2018) and cert. denied, 138 S. Ct. 984, 200 L. Ed. 2d 300 (2018).

have held that such provisions are not actionable reverse payments, though one court denied a motion to dismiss a complaint where there were fact issues as to whether alleged reverse payments were larger than necessary to compensate the generic company for its litigation expenses, among other issues.[10]

It remains unclear whether, and to what degree, the reverse-payment doctrine will apply in the biologic/biosimilar space. The question is not a legal one: if a biosimilar applicant and the RPS entered into a settlement containing a large and unexplained reverse payment, there is no reason why the principles of *Actavis* might not apply. Instead, the question is more practical: reverse payments arguably arose as a result of the unique regulatory and economic features of competition under Hatch-Waxman and state drug substitution laws, including automatic AB-rated substitution of generic products for prescriptions written for the brand and the presence of the 180-day exclusivity period, which arguably allows a brand company to pay off the first-filer to "park" its exclusivity and thereby delay not just its own entry, but the entry of all other later ANDA filers. To the extent that those or comparable features do not exist in the biosimilar space, the incentives for parties to enter into reverse-payment agreements may be reduced, and such agreements simply may not occur.

To date, only one set of cases challenging biosimilar settlements under the reverse-payment doctrine has been filed.[11] Those cases involve biosimilars of Humira. The complaints allege that several biosimilar applicants settled with Ab-bVie, the RPS, in agreements that allowed biosimilar entry in the European Union years earlier than in the United States. According to the complaints, the earnings that the biosimilar applicants would receive from the EU entry amounts to a reverse payment that delayed US entry. The court has not yet issued any rulings on the viability of that theory.

---

[10]*E.g.*, *In re Actos End Payor Antitrust Litigation*, 2015-2 Trade Cas. (CCH) ¶ 79309, 2015 WL 5610752, *15–16 (S.D. N.Y. 2015), aff'd in part, vacated in part, 848 F.3d 89, 2017-1 Trade Cas. (CCH) ¶ 79893 (2d Cir. 2017); *Sergeants Benevolent Association Health & Welfare Fund v. Acta Vis, PLC*, 2016 WL 4992690, *14–15 (S.D. N.Y. 2016).

[11]*UFCW Local 1500 Welfare Fund v. AbbVie Inc.*, C.A. No. 1:19-cv-01873 (N.D. Ill).

§ 8:3   Filing agreements with the government

Since 2003, a federal law referred to as the Medicare Modernization Act ("MMA") has required that certain agreements between brand and generic drug companies, or between two or more generic drug companies, must be filed with FTC and the Justice Department. The coverage of MMA originally was limited to agreements pertaining to ANDAs with Paragraph IV certifications under Hatch-Waxman. In 2018, Congress amended MMA to extend its coverage to biosimilars.

Under MMA, certain agreements between biosimilar applicants and the RPS must be filed.[1] An agreement must be filed if it pertains to (a) the manufacturing, marketing, or sale of the reference product; (b) the manufacturing, marketing, or sale of the biosimilar; or (c) any of the time periods referred to in Section 351(k)(6) that apply to the biosimilar.[2] Certain agreements between two or more biosimilar applicants for the same RP also must be filed.[3] The filing requirement is triggered in those circumstances if the agreement concerns any of the time periods referred to in Section 351(k)(6) that apply to the biosimilar product or the manufacturing, marketing, or sale of the biosimilar product.[4]

The filing requirements extend beyond the specific agreement(s) that fall into one of the categories described above. Parties must also file certain "other agreements." This category, too, expanded in 2018. "Other agreements" that need to be filed fall into two categories. The first one is based on content: other agreements between the parties that are contingent on, or related to, the agreement that is subject to the statute must be filed, even if the other agreement itself would not otherwise meet the filing requirement. The second category of "other agreements" is based on timing: other agreements between the parties that are entered into within 30 days of the agreement that is subject to the statute must be filed, whether related or not.[5] To the extent such agreements have not been reduced to writing, the parties must

---

[Section 8:3]

[1]21 U.S.C.A. § 355 note (Section 1112(a)(1)).

[2]21 U.S.C.A. § 355 note (Section 1112(a)(2)).

[3]21 U.S.C.A. § 355 note (Section 1112(b)(1)).

[4]21 U.S.C.A. § 355 note (Section 1112(b)(2)).

[5]21 U.S.C.A. § 355 note (Section 1112(c)(2)).

prepare and filed a written description sufficient to disclose its terms.[6]

Filings required by the MMA must be filed no later than 10 business days after the agreements are executed.[7] Failure to file may result in civil penalties.[8] Materials submitted under the MMA are exempt from disclosure.[9] Filing does not trigger any waiting period. The filing is for notice purposes only, and the filing parties may hear nothing from the agencies in response. That said, the FTC has initiated certain enforcement actions on the basis of information it received under the MMA. The FTC also periodically publishes reports describing information it receives under MMA (with company- and product-identifying information removed).[10]

§ 8:4 Intellectual property acquisition and enforcement—Sham litigation and walker process fraud

The sham litigation doctrine addresses the alleged misuse of the litigation process to harm competition. The premise of a sham litigation claim is that the party that initiated or continued to press the challenged lawsuit is using the pendency of the lawsuit itself, rather than the outcome, as an anticompetitive weapon. In the Hatch-Waxman context, such claims often allege that a brand company has filed or is maintaining a patent infringement lawsuit it knows to be meritless, simply to benefit from the automatic 30-month stay of an ANDA's approval in order to postpone generic entry.[1] That said, sham litigation claims often are pursued outside the Hatch-Waxman context. The absence in the BPCIA of an analog to the 30-month stay does not itself preclude biosimilar applicants or others from being able to assert sham litigation claims.

---

[6]21 U.S.C.A. § 355 note (Section 1112(c)(3)).

[7]21 U.S.C.A. § 355 note (Section 1113).

[8]21 U.S.C.A. § 355 note (Section 1115).

[9]21 U.S.C.A. § 355 note (Section 1114).

[10]*See Medicare Modernization Act (MMA)*, FEDERAL TRADE COMMISSION, https://www.ftc.gov/taxonomy/term/388/type/report.

[Section 8:4]

[1]*E.g., In re Wellbutrin XL Antitrust Litigation Indirect Purchaser Class*, 868 F.3d 132, 147 (3d Cir. 2017), judgment entered, 2017-2 Trade Cas. (CCH) ¶ 80099, 2017 WL 3529114 (3d Cir. 2017); *Rochester Drug Co-op., Inc. v. Braintree Laboratories*, 712 F. Supp. 2d 308, 311, 2010-2 Trade Cas. (CCH) ¶ 77140 (D. Del. 2010).

Antitrust plaintiffs pursuing claims of sham litigation face high burdens. As an initial matter, a patentee's act of filing a lawsuit to enforce its patent rights is a form of petitioning. Under the First Amendment and the *Noerr-Pennington* doctrine, that act of petitioning is immune from antitrust challenge, unless an exception applies.[2] Proof that the lawsuit is sham is an established exception and lifts *Noerr-Pennington* immunity.[3] To prove the sham exception, the antitrust plaintiff must establish that both (a) the lawsuit against it was "objectively baseless," in the sense that no reasonable litigant could have expected to prevail on the merits, and (2) the lawsuit was "subjectively intended to interfere directly with a competitor's business" through the litigation process itself.[4] If the antitrust plaintiff clears those hurdles, it also must prove all the remaining elements of a traditional antitrust claim, including market power and harm to competition.

Sham litigation claims in the pharmaceutical industry have been brought as counterclaims in patent litigation, as part of freestanding antitrust claims filed by consumers, and in government enforcement actions.[5] The FTC recently won in a sham litigation case against a brand drug company based on the argument that patent lawsuits against two generic competitors were objectively baseless because prosecution history estoppel prevented the brand company from asserting the theory of infringement on which its cases relied. One court recently applied the doctrine to reject claims that a patent litigation brought by the reference drug company against a biosimilar application was a sham.

---

[2]*Eastern R. R. Presidents Conference v. Noerr Motor Freight, Inc.*, 365 U.S. 127, 81 S. Ct. 523, 5 L. Ed. 2d 464 (1961); *United Mine Workers of America v. Pennington*, 381 U.S. 657, 85 S. Ct. 1585, 14 L. Ed. 2d 626 (1965).

[3]*Professional Real Estate Investors, Inc. v. Columbia Pictures Industries, Inc.*, 508 U.S. 49, 113 S. Ct. 1920, 123 L. Ed. 2d 611, 26 U.S.P. Q.2d 1641, 1993-1 Trade Cas. (CCH) ¶ 70207 (1993).

[4]*Professional Real Estate Investors*, 508 U.S. at 60–61; *Federal Trade Commission v. AbbVie Inc.*, 329 F. Supp. 3d 98, 117, 2018-1 Trade Cas. (CCH) ¶ 80431 (E.D. Pa. 2018).

[5]*See, e.g., Otsuka Pharmaceutical Co., Ltd. v. Torrent Pharmaceuticals Ltd., Inc.*, 118 F. Supp. 3d 646, 2015-1 Trade Cas. (CCH) ¶ 79218 (D.N.J. 2015); *In re Wellbutrin XL Antitrust Litigation Indirect Purchaser Class*, 868 F.3d 132 (3d Cir. 2017), judgment entered, 2017-2 Trade Cas. (CCH) ¶ 80099, 2017 WL 3529114 (3d Cir. 2017); *Federal Trade Commission v. AbbVie Inc.*, 329 F. Supp. 3d 98, 2018-1 Trade Cas. (CCH) ¶ 80431 (E.D. Pa. 2018).

Closely related to sham litigation is the *Walker Process* doctrine, which addresses situations in which a patentee seeks to enforce a patent that was procured by fraud.[6] To make out a *Walker Process* claim, an antitrust plaintiff must show that the patent at issue would not have issued but-for intentional fraud, and that the party asserting the patents knows of the fraud.[7] If proven, *Walker Process* fraud strips the patentee of *Noerr-Pennington* immunity for its actions, meaning that the antitrust plaintiff can assert that the filing and prosecution of the case was an antitrust violation.[8] As with sham litigation, an antitrust plaintiff that proves the elements of *Walker Process* still must satisfy the remaining elements of an antitrust claim to prevail.[9]

One recent case asserted both sham litigation and *Walker Process* claims in an antitrust action brought by consumers challenging the legality of patent infringement claims pursued by a RPS against a biosimilar applicant. The court rejected both claims on a motion to dismiss, but it raised no question about whether the doctrines would apply in the biosimilars context in appropriate circumstances.[10]

§8:5 Intellectual property acquisition and enforcement—Patent thickets

In addition to the well-established doctrines of sham litigation and *Walker Process* fraud, the newer concept of a so-called "patent thicket" has attracted considerable attention recently, particularly in the biosimilar space. The notion of a patent thicket is not well defined but rests on the premise that a company has obtained multiple, overlapping, unnecessary patents for the purpose of deterring or delaying competitive entry, and that at some point such conduct becomes improper. Much of the conversation has arisen in relation to

---

[6]*Walker Process Equipment, Inc. v. Food Machinery & Chemical Corp.*, 382 U.S. 172, 86 S. Ct. 347, 15 L. Ed. 2d 247, 147 U.S.P.Q. 404 (1965); *In re Lipitor Antitrust Litigation*, 868 F.3d 231, 266, 2017-2 Trade Cas. (CCH) ¶ 80101 (3d Cir. 2017), cert. denied, 138 S. Ct. 983, 200 L. Ed. 2d 300 (2018) and cert. denied, 138 S. Ct. 984, 200 L. Ed. 2d 300 (2018).

[7]*Abbott Laboratories v. Teva Pharmaceuticals USA, Inc.*, 432 F. Supp. 2d 408, 432, 2006-1 Trade Cas. (CCH) ¶ 75270 (D. Del. 2006).

[8]*Nobelpharma AB v. Implant Innovations, Inc.*, 141 F.3d 1059, 1068, 46 U.S.P.Q.2d 1097, 1998-1 Trade Cas. (CCH) ¶ 72100 (Fed. Cir. 1998).

[9]*Lipitor*, 868 F.3d at 266.

[10]*In re Remicade Antitrust Litigation*, 345 F. Supp. 3d 566, 581–82, 2018-2 Trade Cas. (CCH) ¶ 80612 (E.D. Pa. 2018).

Humira, a biologic product with over 100 patents in the United States. One company seeking to sell a biosimilar of Humira premised an unclean hands defense on allegations that the RLD company had acted improperly in erecting a patent thicket to protect its product.[1] Various consumer groups have filed follow-on antitrust litigation making similar allegations and asserting that the patent thicket has improperly delayed the entry of biosimilar products in the United States.[2]

To date, no court has ruled on the viability of patent defenses or antitrust claims premised on an alleged patent thicket, nor even articulated a standard to assess how one would evaluate such a claim. In the Humira patent litigation, while the court allowed certain discovery on the patent-thicket allegations to proceed as part of an unclean-hands defense, it also noted that "[w]hether the creation of a 'patent thicket' can amount to a cognizable defense to a claim of patent infringement, such as unclean hands, and where the boundary line between licit and illicit conduct might be, is not clear. The simple act of applying for, and receiving a patent, standing alone, can hardly be the basis for patent invalidation."[3] Decisions in the recently filed consumer antitrust cases about Humira may begin to shed light on how the courts will assess such claims. Legislation about patent thickets also has been proposed in Congress.[4]

§ 8:6   Exclusionary contracting and rebating strategies

Another area of emerging antitrust scrutiny involving biosimilar products concerns the use of potentially exclusionary contracting strategies. Antitrust law has long recognized that, in certain circumstances, exclusive contracts and

---

[Section 8:5]

[1]*AbbVie Inc. v. Boehringer Ingelheim International GmbH*, 2019 WL 1571666, at *3 (D. Del. 2019) (noting that "the unclean hands defense alleges that AbbVie created a 'patent thicket' of 'overlapping and noninventive patents for the purpose of . . . delaying competition' ").

[2]*UFCW Local 1500 Welfare Fund v. AbbVie Inc.*, C.A. No. 1:19-cv-01873 (N.D. Ill.).

[3]*AbbVie Inc. v. Boehringer Ingelheim Int'l GmbH*, No. 17-cv-01065-MSG-RL (D. Del. June 4, 2018), ECF No. 112.

[4]*E.g.*, Biologic Patent Transparency Act, S. 659 (116th Congress).

bundled rebate agreements are potentially anticompetitive, including in the sale of pharmaceuticals.[1]

In one case, a biosimilar applicant filed an antitrust lawsuit against the RPS challenging its contracting policies. The biosimilar applicant alleged that the reason its product achieved minimal sales after approval, despite its lower price, is that the reference product owner had entered into exclusive dealing contracts and bundled rebate agreements with payors and providers. The biosimilar applicant further alleged that the effect of those contracts was to block access to its biosimilar product, even though it allegedly was a less-expensive alternative. The court denied a motion to dismiss and allowed the case to proceed to discovery.[2] Given the nature of competition between biologics and biosimilars, which often will not involve automatic substitution and instead will require the companies to compete for coverage and prescriptions, these types of issues may become increasingly prevalent in this space.

[Section 8:6]

[1]*E.g.*, *SmithKline Corp. v. Eli Lilly & Co.*, 575 F.2d 1056, 1978-1 Trade Cas. (CCH) ¶ 62007 (3d Cir. 1978) (affirming antitrust liability for bundled rebate strategy in pharmaceuticals).

[2]*Pfizer Inc. v. Johnson & Johnson*, 333 F. Supp. 3d 494, 2018-2 Trade Cas. (CCH) ¶ 80464 (E.D. Pa. 2018); *see also In re Remicade Antitrust Litigation*, 345 F. Supp. 3d 566, 2018-2 Trade Cas. (CCH) ¶ 80612 (E.D. Pa. 2018). *But see Shire US, Inc. v. Allergan, Inc.*, 375 F. Supp. 3d 538, 2019-1 Trade Cas. (CCH) ¶ 80716 (D.N.J. 2019) (dismissing complaint alleging use of exclusive contracts and anticompetitive bundling to exclude competing product from Medicare Part D prescription plans).

Chapter 9

Product Liability Claims Against Biosimilars

§ 9:1 Failure to warn claims
§ 9:2 FDA biosimilar labeling
§ 9:3 Manufacturing defect claims
§ 9:4 Product design defect claims
§ 9:5 Field preemption and primary jurisdiction

> **KeyCite®:** Cases and other legal materials listed in KeyCite Scope can be researched through the KeyCite service on Westlaw®. Use KeyCite to check citations for form, parallel references, prior and later history, and comprehensive citator information, including citations to other decisions and secondary materials.

---

§ 9:1 Failure to warn claims

Product liability failure to warn claims arise from the principle that a manufacturer or seller must provide adequate warnings regarding the dangers associated with the use, or foreseeable misuse, of its products.[1] A plaintiff must usually show that the manufacturer had a duty to warn of a known or foreseeable risk, that the manufacturer breached that duty, and that the manufacturer's breach caused injury to the plaintiff.

For generic drug products approved pursuant to the Hatch-

[Section 9:1]

[1]Failure to warn claims are widely recognized. *See, e.g., Gurley By and Through Gurley v. American Honda Motor Co., Inc.*, 505 So. 2d 358, Prod. Liab. Rep. (CCH) ¶ 11385 (Ala. 1987); *Aguayo v. Crompton & Knowles Corp.*, 183 Cal. App. 3d 1032, 228 Cal. Rptr. 768, Prod. Liab. Rep. (CCH) ¶ 11111 (2d Dist. 1986); *Evridge v. American Honda Motor Co.*, 685 S.W.2d 632 (Tenn. 1985); *Billiar v. Minnesota Min. and Mfg. Co.*, 623 F.2d 240 (2d Cir. 1980); *Nolan v. Dillon*, 261 Md. 516, 276 A.2d 36 (1971); *Campos v. Firestone Tire & Rubber Co.*, 98 N.J. 198, 485 A.2d 305 (1984); *Bloxom v. Bloxom*, 512 So. 2d 839, Prod. Liab. Rep. (CCH) ¶ 11572, 72 A.L.R.4th 43 (La. 1987); *Kozlowski v. John E. Smith's Sons Co.*, 87 Wis. 2d 882, 275 N.W.2d 915 (1979); *Libbey-Owens Ford Glass Co. v. L & M Paper Co.*, 189 Neb. 792, 205 N.W.2d 523 (1973).

Waxman Act, federal law preempts failure to warn claims brought against generic drug manufacturers. This is because federal law requires that the generic product label be "the same as the labeling approved for the [brand-name] drug[.]"[2] As a consequence, this federal law preempts any failure to warn claims arising under state law, since it would be impossible for the generic drug manufacturer to comply with both the federal requirement of sameness and the state tort law standards requiring additional or different warnings.[3]

Unlike small-molecule generic drugs, the label of a biosimilar may differ to a certain extent from the reference product label and still comply with federal law. This raises the possibility that a state-law tort claimant may attempt to argue that the biosimilar applicant can include more or different warning information in its labeling, thereby enabling the biosimilar manufacturer to both comply with federal law and state tort law standards. If the FDA permits biosimilar manufacturers to change their labels unilaterally in response to post-marketing reports, without involving the FDA, federal law may not preempt state tort law claims with respect to the adequacy of warnings.[4] Moreover, if a biosimilar's label merely recites information about the reference biologic

---

[2]*See* 21 U.S.C.A. § 355(j)(2)(A)(v); *PLIVA, Inc. v. Mensing,* 564 U.S. 604, 131 S. Ct. 2567, 180 L. Ed. 2d 580, Prod. Liab. Rep. (CCH) P 18642 (2011).

[3]*Guarino v. Wyeth LLC,* 823 F. Supp. 2d 1289 (M.D. Fla. 2011), aff'd, 719 F.3d 1245, Prod. Liab. Rep. (CCH) P 19156 (11th Cir. 2013) (granting generic defendant's motion to dismiss based on *Mensing* because "Plaintiff's claims are, on their face, premised on allegedly inadequate warnings"); *Morris v. Wyeth, Inc.,* 2011 WL 4973839 (W.D. La. 2011), aff'd, 713 F.3d 774 (5th Cir. 2013); *Strayhorn v. Wyeth Pharmaceuticals, Inc.,* 887 F. Supp. 2d 799 (W.D. Tenn. 2012), judgment aff'd, 737 F.3d 378, Prod. Liab. Rep. (CCH) P 19284 (6th Cir. 2013); *Chatman v. Pfizer, Inc.,* 960 F. Supp. 2d 641, Prod. Liab. Rep. (CCH) P 19092 (S.D. Miss. 2013), modified, 2014 WL 4546042 (S.D. Miss. 2014); *Lashley v. Pfizer, Inc.,* 750 F.3d 470, Prod. Liab. Rep. (CCH) P 19333 (5th Cir. 2014); *Bowman v. Wyeth, LLC,* 2012 WL 684116 (D. Minn. 2012).

[4]*Compare Mensing,* 564 U.S. at 604 with *Wyeth v. Levine,* 555 U.S. 555, 569–71, 129 S. Ct. 1187, 173 L. Ed. 2d 51, Prod. Liab. Rep. (CCH) P 18176 (2009) (holding that preemption did not bar claims when there is no evidence that the FDA would prohibit a label change, and it was thus not impossible for the drug manufacturer to satisfy both federal regulatory and state tort duties); *see also Felix v. Hoffmann-LaRoche, Inc.,* 540 So. 2d 102, 105, Prod. Liab. Rep. (CCH) P 12063 (Fla. 1989) (examining text of package insert and explaining that the adequacy of a prescription drug warning "become[s] a question of law where the warning is accurate, clear, and unambiguous").

product and does not include specific information pertaining to additional risks that a manufacturer may be aware of that are specific to the biosimilar product, a court may find the biosimilar's label fails to provide a warning that is adequate. Conversely, plaintiffs might even claim that the biosimilar label mirrored the biologic reference product label *too* much, since a biosimilar does not have the exact same chemical make-up as the biologic reference product. In other words, the approach that the FDA takes to biosimilar labeling, whether as a whole or with respect to a particular product, may have an impact on the extent to which failure to warn claims are preempted.

§ 9:2 FDA biosimilar labeling

FDA labeling guidelines for biosimilars may provide insight into how courts will handle label preemption claims. In July 2018, the FDA released a Final Guidance titled "Labeling for Biosimilar Products." This Guidance explains that "[t]he goal of a biosimilar product development program is to demonstrate biosimilarity between the proposed product and the reference product—*not to independently establish safety and effectiveness* of the proposed product."[1]

In the Guidance, the FDA recommends that biosimilar product labeling incorporate relevant data and information from the reference product labeling, but notes that some differences between the two may be appropriate.[2] For example, "biosimilar product labeling may include information specific to the biosimilar product that is necessary to inform safe and effective use of the [biosimilar] product, including

---

[Section 9:2]

[1]U.S. DEPARTMENT OF HEALTH AND HUMAN SERVICES FOOD AND DRUG ADMINISTRATION, LABELING FOR BIOSIMILAR PRODUCTS: GUIDANCE FOR INDUSTRY 3 (July 2018) (emphasis added), https://www.fda.gov/regulatory-information/search-fda-guidance-documents/labeling-biosimilar-products-guidance-industry.

[2]U.S. DEPARTMENT OF HEALTH AND HUMAN SERVICES FOOD AND DRUG ADMINISTRATION, LABELING FOR BIOSIMILAR PRODUCTS: GUIDANCE FOR INDUSTRY 5 ("Certain differences between the biosimilar and reference product labeling may be appropriate. . . . [B]iosimilar product labeling may include information specific to the biosimilar product that is necessary to inform safe and effective use of the product, including administration, preparation, storage, or safety information.")

administration, preparation, storage, or safety information."[3] The Guidance further advises that the "relevant data and information from the reference product labeling that should be incorporated into the biosimilar product labeling will depend on whether the applicant is seeking licensure for all conditions of use (e.g., indication(s), dosing regimen(s)) or fewer than all conditions of use of the reference product for the biosimilar product."[4] In sections of the biosimilar product labeling that are based on the reference product labeling, the text should be similar to the corresponding text in the reference product labeling, but "need not be identical to the reference product labeling."[5] The biosimilar product labeling "should reflect currently available information necessary for the safe and effective use of the biosimilar product."[6]

For warnings and precautions on biosimilar labels, when the risk warned of applies to both the biosimilar product and the reference product, the biosimilar label should use the core name[7] of the reference product to indicate that the risk or other safety information applies to both the biosimilar and the reference product. When the risk or safety information applies only to the biosimilar, the label should indicate this by using the proper name of the biosimilar (the core name, followed by the approved suffix). For example, when warning of a risk that applies to all adalimumab products (both reference product and biosimilar product), the biosimilar label should warn that certain adverse events were associated with "adalimumab products." When warning of a risk that applies only to the biosimilar, the label should

---

[3]U.S. DEPARTMENT OF HEALTH AND HUMAN SERVICES FOOD AND DRUG ADMINISTRATION, LABELING FOR BIOSIMILAR PRODUCTS: GUIDANCE FOR INDUSTRY 5.

[4]U.S. DEPARTMENT OF HEALTH AND HUMAN SERVICES FOOD AND DRUG ADMINISTRATION, LABELING FOR BIOSIMILAR PRODUCTS: GUIDANCE FOR INDUSTRY 5.

[5]U.S. DEPARTMENT OF HEALTH AND HUMAN SERVICES FOOD AND DRUG ADMINISTRATION, LABELING FOR BIOSIMILAR PRODUCTS: GUIDANCE FOR INDUSTRY 5.

[6]U.S. DEPARTMENT OF HEALTH AND HUMAN SERVICES FOOD AND DRUG ADMINISTRATION, LABELING FOR BIOSIMILAR PRODUCTS: GUIDANCE FOR INDUSTRY 5 ("Text based on the reference product labeling need not be identical to the reference product labeling and should reflect currently available information necessary for the safe and effective use of the biosimilar product.")

[7]Biosimilars follow a specified naming guidance, described further in Section 3:21. "Core names" are shared among the reference biologic product and any related biosimilar products, and indicate relatedness between products. "Proper names" include a distinguishing suffix of four lowercase letters attached to the core name. For example, "adalimumab" is a core name, and "adalimumab-adaz" is a proper name.

warn that certain adverse events were associated with "adalimumab-[xxxx]."

When new information becomes available that causes information in labeling to be inaccurate, false, or misleading, the biosimilar applicant must take steps to change the content of its product labeling. Under 21 C.F.R. 601.12, a biosimilar manufacturer must submit to the FDA a supplement for any change in the package insert, package label, or container label to reflect newly acquired information intended to add or strengthen an instruction about dosage and administration that is intended to increase the safety of the use of the product. Under 21 C.F.R. 601.12, a manufacturer can even distribute the drug with the updated labeling before FDA approval of the updated labeling, so long as the changes are made in order to:

- Add or strengthen a contraindication, warning, precaution, or adverse reaction for which the evidence of a causal association satisfies the standard for inclusion in the labeling;
- Add or strengthen a statement about abuse, dependence, psychological effect, or overdosage;
- Add or strengthen an instruction about dosage and administration that is intended to increase the safety of the use of the product; or
- Delete false, misleading, or unsupported indications for use or claims for effectiveness.

If the proposed changes are to any of the other labeling requirements set forth in 21 C.F.R. 201.57(a) (which details the information that must appear in all prescription drug labeling), the biosimilar manufacturer must wait for FDA approval before distributing the updated labeling. In situations where the biosimilar manufacturer must wait for FDA approval after submitting a supplement regarding labeling changes, it is possible that impossibility preemption may apply.[8]

---

[8]*See PLIVA, Inc. v. Mensing*, 564 U.S. 604, 131 S. Ct. 2567, 180 L. Ed. 2d 580, Prod. Liab. Rep. (CCH) P 18642 (2011) (holding that federal drug regulations that prevented manufacturers from independently changing generic drugs' safety labels preempted state-law failure to warn claims); *see also Mutual Pharmaceutical Co., Inc. v. Bartlett*, 570 U.S. 472, 492, 133 S. Ct. 2466, 186 L. Ed. 2d 607, Prod. Liab. Rep. (CCH) P 19155 (2013) (holding that state-law design defect claims that place a duty on manufacturers to render a drug safer by either altering its composition or

§ 9:3   Manufacturing defect claims

Manufacturing defect claims arise from an alleged deviation from the intended design of a product. For example, a departure from the manufacturer's own design specification for that product is said to be a deviation from its "intended design."[1] In a product liability drug context, this could include contamination of a product.

One potential issue in the biosimilar field is the complexity of biosimilar and biologic products. Variability in their manufacture could potentially lead to a greater risk of vari-

---

altering its labeling are in conflict with federal laws that prohibit manufacturers from unilaterally altering drug composition or labeling).

[Section 9:3]

[1]*See, e.g., Caterpillar Tractor Co. v. Beck*, 593 P.2d 871, 881 (Alaska 1979) (deviation from the manufacturer's norm); *Barker v. Lull Engineering Co.*, 20 Cal. 3d 413, 143 Cal. Rptr. 225, 573 P.2d 443, 454, 96 A.L.R.3d 1 (1978) (rejected by, Vineyard v. Empire Machinery Co., Inc., 119 Ariz. 502, 581 P.2d 1152 (Ct. App. Div. 1 1978)) ("a defective product differs from the manufacturer's intended result or from other ostensibly identical units of the same product line"); *Banks v. ICI Americas, Inc.*, 264 Ga. 732, 450 S.E.2d 671, 673, Prod. Liab. Rep. (CCH) P 14107 (1994) (In a manufacturing defect case ". . . it is assumed that the design of the product is safe and had the product been manufactured in accordance with the design it would have been safe for consumer use."); La. Rev. Stat. Ann. § 9:2800.55 (West 1988) ("product deviated in a material way from the manufacturer's or designer's specifications or performance standards for the product or from otherwise identical products manufactured by the same manufacturer."); *Singleton v. International Harvester Co.*, 685 F.2d 112, 115 (4th Cir. 1981) (applying Maryland law) ("In manufacturing defect cases, the plaintiff proves that the product is defective by simply showing that it does not conform to the manufacturer's specifications."); *Back v. Wickes Corp.*, 375 Mass. 633, 378 N.E.2d 964, 970, 24 U.C.C. Rep. Serv. 1164 (1978) (deviation from the manufacturer's design standard); *Prentis v. Yale Mfg. Co.*, 421 Mich. 670, 365 N.W.2d 176, 182 (1984) ("In the case of a 'manufacturing defect,' the product may be evaluated against the manufacturer's own production standards, as manifested by that manufacturer's other like products."); Miss. Code Ann. § 11-1-63 (1993) (product "deviated in a material way from the manufacturer's or designer's specifications or from otherwise identical units manufactured to the same manufacturing specifications"); *Rix v. General Motors Corp.*, 222 Mont. 318, 723 P.2d 195, 200, Prod. Liab. Rep. (CCH) P 11181 (1986) (product is "flawed or defective because it was not constructed correctly by the manufacturer"; product does not conform to its intended design); *Thibault v. Sears, Roebuck & Co.*, 118 N.H. 802, 395 A.2d 843, 846 (1978) (rejected by, Armstrong v. Cione, 69 Haw. 176, 738 P.2d 79, Prod. Liab. Rep. (CCH) P 11543 (1987)) ("defect is an accidental variation caused by a mistake in the manufacturing process; . . . product does not 'conform to the great majority of products manufactured in accordance with that design' ").

ability within the product. The regulations applicable to vaccines and biosimilars require that an application for a license "spells out the manufacturing method that must be followed and the directions and warnings that must accompany the product."[2] In the vaccine context, the Supreme Court has commented that deviation from the manufacturing method spelled out in the license is "objective evidence" of a manufacturing defect.[3] But because biosimilars, unlike conventional pharmaceuticals, are composed of large molecule natural resources rather than pure chemical substances with known structures, there is an intrinsic risk of variations within the product. How will courts interpret "intended design" in this field? Courts may conclude that small variations among batches of a biosimilar product are insufficient to constitute "defects" within the spirit of the law governing manufacturing-defect claims.[4] Instead, a plaintiff may be required to demonstrate that a variation falls outside the scope of normal biosimilar variability, and that the deviation was responsible for the alleged injury.

§ 9:4   Product design defect claims

Design defects are alleged flaws in the products design, rendering a product unreasonably dangerous. Unlike a manufacturing defect, it applies not just to single products (or batches) deviating from the norm, but to every product manufactured according to the allegedly defective design.[1] A plaintiff must typically show that a "reasonable alternative

---

[2]*Bruesewitz v. Wyeth LLC*, 562 U.S. 223, 237, 131 S. Ct. 1068, 179 L. Ed. 2d 1, Prod. Liab. Rep. (CCH) P 18580 (2011).

[3]In *Wyeth*, the Supreme Court held that plaintiff's design defect claims were expressly preempted by federal statute; the Court also discussed manufacturing defects, noting that *"[d]eviations from the license thus provide objective evidence of manufacturing defects or inadequate warnings.* Further objective evidence comes from the FDA's regulations . . . that pervasively regulate the manufacturing process, down to the requirements for plumbing and ventilation systems at each manufacturing facility. Material noncompliance with any one of them, or with any other the FDA regulation, could cost the manufacturer its regulatory-compliance defense." 562 U.S. at 237 (emphasis added).

[4]*See In re Genentech, Inc.*, 367 F. Supp. 3d 1274 (N.D. Okla. 2019) regarding "reasonable variations" in biologic packaging.

[Section 9:4]

[1]*See* Restatement (Third) of Torts: Prod. Liab. § 2 (1998) ("Whereas a manufacturing defect consists of a product unit's failure to meet the manufacturer's design specifications, a product asserted to have a defec-

design" existed for the product.[2] No court has yet ruled on a design defect claim regarding a biosimilar product.

42 U.S.C.A. § 262(i)(2) regulates similarity between biosimilars and biologics. A biosimilar is "highly similar" to the biologic product "notwithstanding minor differences in inactive components" and it must have "no clinically meaningful differences" in terms of safety, purity and potency.[3] Biosimilarity is established by: (1) analytical "fingerprint" studies proving "high similarity"; (2) animal studies (including toxicity studies); or (3) at least one clinical study sufficient to demonstrate safety, purity and potency for at least one condition of use for which the reference product is approved.[4]

Under biosimilar regulations, a biosimilar cannot have any "clinically meaningful differences" from its reference product.[5] It is unclear how this will be applied to product design defect claims. It is possible that courts may consider the reference biologic product to be evidence of a "reasonable alternative design" for the purposes of a negligent design defect claim. Conversely, courts may decide that since biosimilars have "no clinically meaningful differences" to biologics,[6] there is no difference for purposes of a "reasonable alternative design." Plaintiffs might be required to demonstrate that the biosimilar varied from the biologic in a "meaningful" way; however, this may implicate the FDA preemption.

Courts have not yet interpreted "clinically meaningful difference," but it is possible that if this statutory term is treated the same as "bioequivalence" for generic drugs, impossibility preemption may apply to biosimilar product design defect claims in the same way that it applies to generic small molecule design defect claims. For generic drugs,

---

tive design meets the manufacturer's design specifications but raises the question whether the specifications themselves create unreasonable risks.")

[2]Restatement (Third) of Torts: Prod. Liab. § 2 (1998) ("[T]he test is whether a reasonable alternative design would, at reasonable cost, have reduced the foreseeable risks of harm posed by the product and, if so, whether the omission of the alternative design by the seller or a predecessor in the distributive chain rendered the product not reasonably safe.")

[3]42 U.S.C.A. § 262(i)(2).

[4]42 U.S.C.A. § 262(k)(2).

[5]42 U.S.C.A. § 262(i)(2)(B).

[6]*See* 42 U.S.C.A. § 262(i)(2)(B).

the FDA requires a new drug applicant to file an abbreviated new drug application ("ANDA") containing data showing that it is bioequivalent to the branded drug.[7] A generic drug is considered bioequivalent if there is no "significant difference" in the time it takes for the generic drug's active ingredient to become available when administered at the same dose under similar conditions, compared with the time it takes for the branded drug.[8] For this reason, state law claims that seek to hold a manufacturer of a generic drug liable for failing to alter the composition of the generic drug are subject to impossibility preemption.[9]

Like the biologic reference product, and like generic small molecule drugs, biosimilar products are required to receive FDA approval for any manufacturing changes. State-law design defect claims allege that a drug manufacture should change its manufacturing process in order to comply with tort standards. Because a drug manufacturer cannot change its manufacturing process without FDA approval, courts have found that manufacturing defect claims as to small molecule products are preempted by federal law.[10] The same preemption theory may apply to claims involving alleged design defects in a biologic reference product,[11] but it is still

---

[7]See 21 C.F.R. 314.94(a)(7).

[8]See 21 C.F.R. 314.3.

[9]See *Mutual Pharmaceutical Co., Inc. v. Bartlett*, 570 U.S. 472, 492, 133 S. Ct. 2466, 186 L. Ed. 2d 607, Prod. Liab. Rep. (CCH) P 19155 (2013) (holding that state-law design-defect claims that place a duty on manufacturers to render a generic drug safer by either altering its composition or altering its labeling are in conflict with federal laws that prohibit generic drug manufacturers from unilaterally altering drug composition or labeling).

[10]See *Bartlett*, 570 U.S. at 492.

[11]For example, in *In re Genentech, Inc.*, 367 F. Supp. 3d 1274 (N.D. Okla. 2019), the court held that the plaintiffs' labeling claims conflicted with federal law, which allowed a range of "reasonable variations" for solid drugs sold in vials. The court also held that plaintiffs' claims that defendant could comply with plaintiffs' state law-based demands by changing either the manufacturing process of the biologic or the labeling of the biologic failed as a matter of law under the doctrine of impossibility preemption, because these changes required FDA approval. Citing *Jones v. Rath Packing Co.*, 430 U.S. 519, 97 S. Ct. 1305, 51 L. Ed. 2d 604 (1977), and distinguishing *Wyeth v. Levine*, 555 U.S. 555, 129 S. Ct. 1187, 173 L. Ed. 2d 51, Prod. Liab. Rep. (CCH) P 18176 (2009), the court held that "Plaintiffs' labeling claims conflict with federal law, which permits reasonable variations for solid drugs sold in vials. . . . [T]he regulatory scheme expressly allows a range of 'reasonable variations' for solid drugs sold in

unclear whether courts will also apply this theory to biosimilars.

§ 9:5 Field preemption and primary jurisdiction

In addition to impossibility preemption (discussed, *supra*, in Sections 9:2 to 9:4), other theories may also be applied to block state-law product liability claims relating to biosimilars.

For example, courts might infer that Congress did not intend for the states to interfere with the federal regulatory scheme pertaining to biosimilars.[1] In this instance, field preemption could apply to bar state-law product liability claims against biosimilars.

Alternatively, courts could apply the primary jurisdiction doctrine. The primary jurisdiction doctrine "is concerned with 'promoting proper relationships between the courts and administrative agencies charged with particular regulatory duties.' "[2] Courts can stay proceedings, deferring issues to a federal agency, where state-law claims involve issues specifically within that agency's ambit and expertise. Relevant factors for invoking the primary jurisdiction doctrine are: (1) whether the question at issue is within the conventional experience of judges or whether it involves technical or policy considerations within the agency's particular field of expertise; (2) whether the question at issue is particularly within the agency's discretion; (3) whether there exists a substantial danger of inconsistent rulings; and (4) whether a

---

vials, and Plaintiffs' state-law claims conflict with these regulations." In granting the motion for summary judgment, the court also held that plaintiffs' claims that defendant could comply with plaintiffs' state-law-based demands by changing either the manufacturing process or the labeling of Herceptin failed as a matter of law under the doctrine of impossibility preemption, because these changes required FDA approval. *In re Genentech, Inc.*, 367 F. Supp. 3d 1274, 1288–89 (N.D. Okla. 2019).

[Section 9:5]

[1]*Com. of Pa. v. Nelson*, 350 U.S. 497, 502–04, 76 S. Ct. 477, 100 L. Ed. 640 (1956) (holding that if "the scheme of federal regulation [is] so pervasive as to make reasonable the inference that Congress left no room for the States to supplement it," state law is preempted "regardless of whether it purports to supplement the federal law").

[2]*Ellis v. Tribune Television Co.*, 443 F.3d 71, 81 (2d Cir. 2006) (quoting *U.S. v. Western Pac. R. Co.*, 352 U.S. 59, 63, 77 S. Ct. 161, 1 L. Ed. 2d 126, 16 Pub. Util. Rep. 3d (PUR) 265 (1956)).

prior application to the agency has been made.[3]

---

[3]*Ellis*, 443 F.3d at 82–83.

APPENDICES

Appendix A.   Compilation of Relevant Statutes (42 USC 262 and 35 USC 271)

Appendix B.   Compilation of Relevant Regulations (21 CFR 10.115, 21 CFR Part 600, 37 CFR 42)

Appendix C1.   Scientific Considerations in Demonstrating Biosimilarity to a Reference Product

Appendix C2.   Clinical Pharmacology Data to Support a Demonstration of Biosimilarity to a Reference Product

Appendix C3.   Assessing User Fees Under the Biosimilar User Fee Amendments of 2017

Appendix C4.   Labeling for Biosimilar Products Guidance

Appendix C5.   Interpretation of the "Deemed to be a License" Provision of the Biologics Price Competition and Innovation Act of 2009

Appendix C6.   Questions and Answers on Biosimilar Development and the BPCI Act

Appendix C7.   Considerations in Demonstrating Interchangeability With a Reference Product

Appendix D1.   Guidance for Industry Reference Product Exclusivity for Biological Products Filed Under Section 351(a) of the PHS Act

Appendix D2.   Citizen Petitions and Petitions for Stay of Action Subject to Section 505(q) of the Federal Food, Drug, and Cosmetic Act

Appendix D3.   Formal Meetings Between the FDA and Sponsors or Applicants of BsUFA Products

Appendix D4.   New and Revised Draft Q&As on Biosimilar Development and the BPCI Act (Revision 2)

Appendix D5.   Development of Therapeutic Protein Biosimilars: Comparative Analytical Assessment and Other Quality-Related Considerations

Appendix E.   FDA Approvals and U.S. Launches of
               Biosimilars
Appendix F.   BPCIA Litigations

APPENDIX A

Compilation of Relevant Statutes (42 USC 262 and 35 USC 271)

42 USC 262.	Regulation of biological products
35 USC 271.	Infringement of patent

42 USC 262. Regulation of biological products

(a) Biologics license

(1) No person shall introduce or deliver for introduction into interstate commerce any biological product unless—

(A) a biologics license under this subsection or subsection (k) is in effect for the biological product; and

(B) each package of the biological product is plainly marked with—

(i) the proper name of the biological product contained in the package;

(ii) the name, address, and applicable license number of the manufacturer of the biological product; and

(iii) the expiration date of the biological product.

(2) (A) The Secretary shall establish, by regulation, requirements for the approval, suspension, and revocation of biologics licenses.

(B) **Pediatric studies** A person that submits an application for a license under this paragraph shall submit to the Secretary as part of the application any assessments required under section 505B of the Federal Food, Drug, and Cosmetic Act.

(C) The Secretary shall approve a biologics license application—

(i) on the basis of a demonstration that—

(I) the biological product that is the subject of the application is safe, pure, and potent; and

249

(II) the facility in which the biological product is manufactured, processed, packed, or held meets standards designed to assure that the biological product continues to be safe, pure, and potent; and

(ii) if the applicant (or other appropriate person) consents to the inspection of the facility that is the subject of the application, in accordance with subsection (c).

(D) Postmarket studies and clinical trials; labeling; risk evaluation and mitigation strategy A person that submits an application for a license under this paragraph is subject to sections 505(o), 505(p), and 505-1 of the Federal Food, Drug, and Cosmetic Act.

(E) (i) The Secretary may rely upon qualified data summaries to support the approval of a supplemental application, with respect to a qualified indication for a drug, submitted under this subsection, if such supplemental application complies with the requirements of subparagraph (B) of section 505(c)(5) of the Federal Food, Drug, and Cosmetic Act.

(ii) In this subparagraph, the terms "qualified indication" and "qualified data summary" have the meanings given such terms in section 505(c)(5) of the Federal Food, Drug, and Cosmetic Act.

(3) The Secretary shall prescribe requirements under which a biological product undergoing investigation shall be exempt from the requirements of paragraph (1).

(b) Falsely labeling or marking package or container; altering label or mark No person shall falsely label or mark any package or container of any biological product or alter any label or mark on the package or container of the biological product so as to falsify the label or mark.

(c) Inspection of establishment for propagation and preparation Any officer, agent, or employee of the Department of Health and Human Services, authorized by the Secretary for the purpose, may during all reasonable hours enter and inspect any establishment for the propagation or manufacture and preparation of any biological product.

(d) Recall of product presenting imminent hazard; violations

(1) Upon a determination that a batch, lot, or other

quantity of a product licensed under this section presents an imminent or substantial hazard to the public health, the Secretary shall issue an order immediately ordering the recall of such batch, lot, or other quantity of such product. An order under this paragraph shall be issued in accordance with section 554 of Title 5.

(2) Any violation of paragraph (1) shall subject the violator to a civil penalty of up to $100,000 per day of violation. The amount of a civil penalty under this paragraph shall, effective December 1 of each year beginning 1 year after the effective date of this paragraph, be increased by the percent change in the Consumer Price Index for the base quarter of such year over the Consumer Price Index for the base quarter of the preceding year, adjusted to the nearest 110 of 1 percent. For purposes of this paragraph, the term "base quarter", as used with respect to a year, means the calendar quarter ending on September 30 of such year and the price index for a base quarter is the arithmetical mean of such index for the 3 months comprising such quarter.

(e) **Interference with officers** No person shall interfere with any officer, agent, or employee of the Service in the performance of any duty imposed upon him by this section or by regulations made by authority thereof.

(f) **Penalties for offenses** Any person who shall violate, or aid or abet in violating, any of the provisions of this section shall be punished upon conviction by a fine not exceeding $500 or by imprisonment not exceeding one year, or by both such fine and imprisonment, in the discretion of the court.

(g) **Construction with other laws** Nothing contained in this chapter shall be construed as in any way affecting, modifying, repealing, or superseding the provisions of the Federal Food, Drug, and Cosmetic Act.

(h) **Exportation of partially processed biological products** A partially processed biological product which—

(1) is not in a form applicable to the prevention, treatment, or cure of diseases or injuries of man;

(2) is not intended for sale in the United States; and

(3) is intended for further manufacture into final dosage form outside the United States,

shall be subject to no restriction on the export of the product under this chapter or the Federal Food, Drug, and

Cosmetic Act if the product is manufactured, processed, packaged, and held in conformity with current good manufacturing practice requirements or meets international manufacturing standards as certified by an international standards organization recognized by the Secretary and meets the requirements of section 801(e)(1) of the Federal Food, Drug, and Cosmetic Act (21 U.S.C. 381(e)).

(i) "Biological product" defined In this section:

(1) The term "biological product" means a virus, therapeutic serum, toxin, antitoxin, vaccine, blood, blood component or derivative, allergenic product, protein (except any chemically synthesized polypeptide), or analogous product, or arsphenamine or derivative of arsphenamine (or any other trivalent organic arsenic compound), applicable to the prevention, treatment, or cure of a disease or condition of human beings.

(2) The term "biosimilar" or "biosimilarity", in reference to a biological product that is the subject of an application under subsection (k), means—

(A) that the biological product is highly similar to the reference product notwithstanding minor differences in clinically inactive components; and

(B) there are no clinically meaningful differences between the biological product and the reference product in terms of the safety, purity, and potency of the product.

(3) The term "interchangeable" or "interchangeability", in reference to a biological product that is shown to meet the standards described in subsection (k)(4), means that the biological product may be substituted for the reference product without the intervention of the health care provider who prescribed the reference product.

(4) The term "reference product" means the single biological product licensed under subsection (a) against which a biological product is evaluated in an application submitted under subsection (k).

(j) Application of Federal Food, Drug, and Cosmetic Act The Federal Food, Drug, and Cosmetic Act, including the requirements under sections 505(o), 505(p), and 505-1 of such Act, applies to a biological product subject to regulation under this section, except that a product for which a license has been approved under subsection (a) shall not be required to have an approved application under section 505 of such Act.

(k) Licensure of biological products as biosimilar or interchangeable

(1) In general Any person may submit an application for licensure of a biological product under this subsection.

(2) Content

(A) In general

(i) Required information An application submitted under this subsection shall include information demonstrating that—

(I) the biological product is biosimilar to a reference product based upon data derived from—

(aa) analytical studies that demonstrate that the biological product is highly similar to the reference product notwithstanding minor differences in clinically inactive components;

(bb) animal studies (including the assessment of toxicity); and

(cc) a clinical study or studies (including the assessment of immunogenicity and pharmacokinetics or pharmacodynamics) that are sufficient to demonstrate safety, purity, and potency in 1 or more appropriate conditions of use for which the reference product is licensed and intended to be used and for which licensure is sought for the biological product;

(II) the biological product and reference product utilize the same mechanism or mechanisms of action for the condition or conditions of use prescribed, recommended, or suggested in the proposed labeling, but only to the extent the mechanism or mechanisms of action are known for the reference product;

(III) the condition or conditions of use prescribed, recommended, or suggested in the labeling proposed for the biological product have been previously approved for the reference product;

(IV) the route of administration, the dosage form, and the strength of the biological product are the same as those of the reference product; and

(V) the facility in which the biological product is manufactured, processed, packed, or held meets standards designed to assure that the biological product continues to be safe, pure, and potent.

(ii) Determination by Secretary The Secretary may determine, in the Secretary's discretion, that an element described in clause (i)(I) is unnecessary in an application submitted under this subsection.

(iii) Additional information An application submitted under this subsection—

(I) shall include publicly-available information regarding the Secretary's previous determination that the reference product is safe, pure, and potent; and

(II) may include any additional information in support of the application, including publicly-available information with respect to the reference product or another biological product.

(B) Interchangeability An application (or a supplement to an application) submitted under this subsection may include information demonstrating that the biological product meets the standards described in paragraph (4).

(3) Evaluation by Secretary Upon review of an application (or a supplement to an application) submitted under this subsection, the Secretary shall license the biological product under this subsection if—

(A) the Secretary determines that the information submitted in the application (or the supplement) is sufficient to show that the biological product—

(i) is biosimilar to the reference product; or

(ii) meets the standards described in paragraph (4), and therefore is interchangeable with the reference product; and

(B) the applicant (or other appropriate person) consents to the inspection of the facility that is the subject of the application, in accordance with subsection (c).

(4) Safety standards for determining interchangeability Upon review of an application submitted under this subsection or any supplement to such application, the Secretary shall determine the biological product to be interchangeable with the reference product if the Secretary determines that the information submitted in the application (or a supplement to such application) is sufficient to show that—

(A) the biological product—

(i) is biosimilar to the reference product; and

(ii) can be expected to produce the same clinical result as the reference product in any given patient; and

(B) for a biological product that is administered more than once to an individual, the risk in terms of safety or diminished efficacy of alternating or switching between use of the biological product and the reference product is not greater than the risk of using the reference product without such alternation or switch.

(5) General rules

(A) One reference product per application A biological product, in an application submitted under this subsection, may not be evaluated against more than 1 reference product.

(B) Review An application submitted under this subsection shall be reviewed by the division within the Food and Drug Administration that is responsible for the review and approval of the application under which the reference product is licensed.

(C) Risk evaluation and mitigation strategies The authority of the Secretary with respect to risk evaluation and mitigation strategies under the Federal Food, Drug, and Cosmetic Act shall apply to biological products licensed under this subsection in the same manner as such authority applies to biological products licensed under subsection (a).

(6) Exclusivity for first interchangeable biological product Upon review of an application submitted under this subsection relying on the same reference product for which a prior biological product has received a determination of interchangeability for any condition of use, the Secretary shall not make a determination under paragraph (4) that the second or subsequent biological product is interchangeable for any condition of use until the earlier of—

(A) 1 year after the first commercial marketing of the first interchangeable biosimilar biological product to be approved as interchangeable for that reference product;

(B) 18 months after—

(i) a final court decision on all patents in suit in an action instituted under subsection (l)(6) against the applicant that submitted the application for the first approved interchangeable biosimilar biological product; or

(ii) the dismissal with or without prejudice of an action instituted under subsection (l)(6) against the applicant that submitted the application for the first approved interchangeable biosimilar biological product; or

(C) (i) 42 months after approval of the first interchangeable biosimilar biological product if the applicant that submitted such application has been sued under subsection (l)(6) and such litigation is still ongoing within such 42-month period; or

(ii) 18 months after approval of the first interchangeable biosimilar biological product if the applicant that submitted such application has not been sued under subsection (l)(6).

For purposes of this paragraph, the term "final court decision" means a final decision of a court from which no appeal (other than a petition to the United States Supreme Court for a writ of certiorari) has been or can be taken.

(7) Exclusivity for reference product

(A) Effective date of biosimilar application approval Approval of an application under this subsection may not be made effective by the Secretary until the date that is 12 years after the date on which the reference product was first licensed under subsection (a).

(B) Filing period An application under this subsection may not be submitted to the Secretary until the date that is 4 years after the date on which the reference product was first licensed under subsection (a).

(C) First licensure Subparagraphs (A) and (B) shall not apply to a license for or approval of—

(i) a supplement for the biological product that is the reference product; or

(ii) a subsequent application filed by the same sponsor or manufacturer of the biological product that is the reference product (or a licensor, predecessor in interest, or other related entity) for—

(I) a change (not including a modification to the structure of the biological product) that results in a new indication, route of administration, dosing schedule, dosage form, delivery system, delivery device, or strength; or

(II) a modification to the structure cf the biological product that does not result in a change in safety, purity, or potency.

(8) Guidance documents

(A) In general The Secretary may, after opportunity for public comment, issue guidance in accordance, except as provided in subparagraph (B)(i), with section 701(h) of the Federal Food, Drug, and Cosmetic Act with respect to the licensure of a biological product under this subsection. Any such guidance may be general or specific.

(B) Public comment

(i) In general The Secretary shall provide the public an opportunity to comment on any proposed guidance issued under subparagraph (A) before issuing final guidance.

(ii) Input regarding most valuable guidance The Secretary shall establish a process through which the public may provide the Secretary with input regarding priorities for issuing guidance.

(C) No requirement for application consideration The issuance (or non-issuance) of guidance under subparagraph (A) shall not preclude the review of, or action on, an application submitted under this subsection.

(D) Requirement for product class-specific guidance If the Secretary issues product class-specific guidance under subparagraph (A), such guidance shall include a description of—

(i) the criteria that the Secretary will use to determine whether a biological product is highly similar to a reference product in such product class; and

(ii) the criteria, if available, that the Secretary will use to determine whether a biological product meets the standards described in paragraph (4).

(E) Certain product classes

(i) Guidance The Secretary may indicate in a guidance document that the science and experience, as of the date of such guidance, with respect to a product or product class (not including any recombinant protein) does not allow approval of an application for a license as provided under this subsection for such product or product class.

(ii) Modification or reversal The Secretary may issue a subsequent guidance document under subparagraph (A) to modify or reverse a guidance document under clause (i).

(iii) No effect on ability to deny license Clause (i) shall not be construed to require the Secretary to approve a product with respect to which the Secretary has not indicated in a guidance document that the science and experience, as described in clause (i), does not allow approval of such an application.

(l) Patents

(1) Confidential access to subsection (k) application

(A) Application of paragraph Unless otherwise agreed to by a person that submits an application under subsection (k) (referred to in this subsection as the "subsection (k) applicant") and the sponsor of the application for the reference product (referred to in this subsection as the "reference product sponsor"), the provisions of this paragraph shall apply to the exchange of information described in this subsection.

(B) In general

(i) Provision of confidential information When a subsection (k) applicant submits an application under subsection (k), such applicant shall provide to the persons described in clause (ii), subject to the terms of this paragraph, confidential access to the information required to be produced pursuant to paragraph (2) and any other information that the subsection (k) applicant determines, in its sole discretion, to be appropriate (referred to in this subsection as the "confidential information").

(ii) Recipients of information The persons described in this clause are the following:

(I) Outside counsel One or more attorneys designated by the reference product sponsor who are employees of an entity other than the reference product sponsor (referred to in this paragraph as the "outside counsel"), provided that such attorneys do not engage, formally or informally, in patent prosecution relevant or related to the reference product.

(II) In-house counsel One attorney that represents the reference product sponsor who is an employee of the reference product sponsor, provided that such attorney does not engage, formally or informally, in patent prosecution relevant or related to the reference product.

(iii) Patent owner access A representative of the owner of a patent exclusively licensed to a reference product sponsor with respect to the reference product and who has retained a right to assert the patent or participate in litigation concerning the patent may be provided the confidential information, provided that the representative informs the reference product sponsor and the subsection (k) applicant of his or her agreement to be subject to the confidentiality provisions set forth in this paragraph, including those under clause (ii).

(C) Limitation on disclosure No person that receives confidential information pursuant to subparagraph (B) shall disclose any confidential information to any other person or entity, including the reference product sponsor employees, outside scientific consultants, or other outside counsel retained by the reference product sponsor, without the prior written consent of the subsection (k) applicant, which shall not be unreasonably withheld.

(D) Use of confidential information Confidential information shall be used for the sole and exclusive purpose of determining, with respect to each patent assigned to or exclusively licensed by the reference product sponsor, whether a claim of patent infringement could reasonably be asserted if the subsection (k) applicant engaged in the manufacture, use, offering for sale, sale, or importation into the United States of the biological product that is the subject of the application under subsection (k).

(E) Ownership of confidential information The confidential information disclosed under this paragraph is, and shall remain, the property of the subsection (k) applicant. By providing the confidential information pursuant to this paragraph, the subsection (k) applicant does not provide the reference product sponsor or the outside counsel any interest in or license to use the confidential information, for purposes other than those specified in subparagraph (D).

(F) Effect of infringement action　In the event that the reference product sponsor files a patent infringement suit, the use of confidential information shall continue to be governed by the terms of this paragraph until such time as a court enters a protective order regarding the information. Upon entry of such order, the subsection (k) applicant may redesignate confidential information in accordance with the terms of that order. No confidential information shall be included in any publicly-available complaint or other pleading. In the event that the reference product sponsor does not file an infringement action by the date specified in paragraph (6), the reference product sponsor shall return or destroy all confidential information received under this paragraph, provided that if the reference product sponsor opts to destroy such information, it will confirm destruction in writing to the subsection (k) applicant.

(G) Rule of construction　Nothing in this paragraph shall be construed—

(i)　as an admission by the subsection (k) applicant regarding the validity, enforceability, or infringement of any patent; or

(ii)　as an agreement or admission by the subsection (k) applicant with respect to the competency, relevance, or materiality of any confidential information.

(H) Effect of violation　The disclosure of any confidential information in violation of this paragraph shall be deemed to cause the subsection (k) applicant to suffer irreparable harm for which there is no adequate legal remedy and the court shall consider immediate injunctive relief to be an appropriate and necessary remedy for any violation or threatened violation of this paragraph.

(2) Subsection (k) application information　Not later than 20 days after the Secretary notifies the subsection (k) applicant that the application has been accepted for review, the subsection (k) applicant—

(A)　shall provide to the reference product sponsor a copy of the application submitted to the Secretary under subsection (k), and such other information that describes the process or processes used to manufacture the biological product that is the subject of such application; and

(B) may provide to the reference product sponsor additional information requested by or on behalf of the reference product sponsor.

(3) List and description of patents

(A) List by reference product sponsor Not later than 60 days after the receipt of the application and information under paragraph (2), the reference product sponsor shall provide to the subsection (k) applicant—

(i) a list of patents for which the reference product sponsor believes a claim of patent infringement could reasonably be asserted by the reference product sponsor, or by a patent owner that has granted an exclusive license to the reference product sponsor with respect to the reference product, if a person not licensed by the reference product sponsor engaged in the making, using, offering to sell, selling, or importing into the United States of the biological product that is the subject of the subsection (k) application; and

(ii) an identification of the patents on such list that the reference product sponsor would be prepared to license to the subsection (k) applicant.

(B) List and description by subsection (k) applicant Not later than 60 days after receipt of the list under subparagraph (A), the subsection (k) applicant—

(i) may provide to the reference product sponsor a list of patents to which the subsection (k) applicant believes a claim of patent infringement could reasonably be asserted by the reference product sponsor if a person not licensed by the reference product sponsor engaged in the making, using, offering to sell, selling, or importing into the United States of the biological product that is the subject of the subsection (k) application;

(ii) shall provide to the reference product sponsor, with respect to each patent listed by the reference product sponsor under subparagraph (A) or listed by the subsection (k) applicant under clause (i)—

(I) a detailed statement that describes, on a

claim by claim basis, the factual and legal basis of the opinion of the subsection (k) applicant that such patent is invalid, unenforceable, or will not be infringed by the commercial marketing of the biological product that is the subject of the subsection (k) application; or

(II)   a statement that the subsection (k) applicant does not intend to begin commercial marketing of the biological product before the date that such patent expires; and

(iii)   shall provide to the reference product sponsor a response regarding each patent identified by the reference product sponsor under subparagraph (A)(ii).

(C) Description by reference product sponsor
Not later than 60 days after receipt of the list and statement under subparagraph (B), the reference product sponsor shall provide to the subsection (k) applicant a detailed statement that describes, with respect to each patent described in subparagraph (B)(ii)(I), on a claim by claim basis, the factual and legal basis of the opinion of the reference product sponsor that such patent will be infringed by the commercial marketing of the biological product that is the subject of the subsection (k) application and a response to the statement concerning validity and enforceability provided under subparagraph (B)(ii)(I).

(4) Patent resolution negotiations

(A) In general   After receipt by the subsection (k) applicant of the statement under paragraph (3)(C), the reference product sponsor and the subsection (k) applicant shall engage in good faith negotiations to agree on which, if any, patents listed under paragraph (3) by the subsection (k) applicant or the reference product sponsor shall be the subject of an action for patent infringement under paragraph (6).

(B) Failure to reach agreement   If, within 15 days of beginning negotiations under subparagraph (A), the subsection (k) applicant and the reference product sponsor fail to agree on a final and complete list of which, if any, patents listed under paragraph (3) by the subsection (k) applicant or the reference product sponsor shall be the subject of an action for patent infringement under paragraph (6), the provisions of paragraph (5) shall apply to the parties.

(5) Patent resolution if no agreement

(A) Number of patents The subsection (k) applicant shall notify the reference product sponsor of the number of patents that such applicant will provide to the reference product sponsor under subparagraph (B)(i)(I).

(B) Exchange of patent lists

(i) In general On a date agreed to by the subsection (k) applicant and the reference product sponsor, but in no case later than 5 days after the subsection (k) applicant notifies the reference product sponsor under subparagraph (A), the subsection (k) applicant and the reference product sponsor shall simultaneously exchange—

(I) the list of patents that the subsection (k) applicant believes should be the subject of an action for patent infringement under paragraph (6); and

(II) the list of patents, in accordance with clause (ii), that the reference product sponsor believes should be the subject of an action for patent infringement under paragraph (6).

(ii) Number of patents listed by reference product sponsor

(I) In general Subject to subclause (II), the number of patents listed by the reference product sponsor under clause (i)(II) may not exceed the number of patents listed by the subsection (k) applicant under clause (i)(I).

(II) Exception If a subsection (k) applicant does not list any patent under clause (i)(I), the reference product sponsor may list 1 patent under clause (i)(II).

(6) Immediate patent infringement action

(A) Action if agreement on patent list If the subsection (k) applicant and the reference product sponsor agree on patents as described in paragraph (4), not later than 30 days after such agreement, the reference product sponsor shall bring an action for patent infringement with respect to each such patent.

(B) Action if no agreement on patent list If the provisions of paragraph (5) apply to the parties as described in paragraph (4)(B), not later than 30 days after the exchange of lists under paragraph (5)(B), the reference product sponsor shall bring an action for patent infringement with respect to each patent that is included on such lists.

(C) Notification and publication of complaint

(i) **Notification to Secretary** Not later than 30 days after a complaint is served to a subsection (k) applicant in an action for patent infringement described under this paragraph, the subsection (k) applicant shall provide the Secretary with notice and a copy of such complaint.

(ii) **Publication by Secretary** The Secretary shall publish in the Federal Register notice of a complaint received under clause (i).

(7) Newly issued or licensed patents In the case of a patent that—

(A) is issued to, or exclusively licensed by, the reference product sponsor after the date that the reference product sponsor provided the list to the subsection (k) applicant under paragraph (3)(A); and

(B) the reference product sponsor reasonably believes that, due to the issuance of such patent, a claim of patent infringement could reasonably be asserted by the reference product sponsor if a person not licensed by the reference product sponsor engaged in the making, using, offering to sell, selling, or importing into the United States of the biological product that is the subject of the subsection (k) application, not later than 30 days after such issuance or licensing, the reference product sponsor shall provide to the subsection (k) applicant a supplement to the list provided by the reference product sponsor under paragraph (3)(A) that includes such patent, not later than 30 days after such supplement is provided, the subsection (k) applicant shall provide a statement to the reference product sponsor in accordance with paragraph (3)(B), and such patent shall be subject to paragraph (8).

(8) Notice of commercial marketing and preliminary injunction

(A) **Notice of commercial marketing** The subsection (k) applicant shall provide notice to the reference product sponsor not later than 180 days before the date of the first commercial marketing of the biological product licensed under subsection (k).

(B) **Preliminary injunction** After receiving the

notice under subparagraph (A) and before such date of the first commercial marketing of such biological product, the reference product sponsor may seek a preliminary injunction prohibiting the subsection (k) applicant from engaging in the commercial manufacture or sale of such biological product until the court decides the issue of patent validity, enforcement, and infringement with respect to any patent that is—

(i) included in the list provided by the reference product sponsor under paragraph (3)(A) or in the list provided by the subsection (k) applicant under paragraph (3)(B); and

(ii) not included, as applicable, on—

(I) the list of patents described in paragraph (4); or

(II) the lists of patents described in paragraph (5)(B).

(C) **Reasonable cooperation** If the reference product sponsor has sought a preliminary injunction under subparagraph (B), the reference product sponsor and the subsection (k) applicant shall reasonably cooperate to expedite such further discovery as is needed in connection with the preliminary injunction motion.

(9) Limitation on declaratory judgment action

(A) **Subsection (k) application provided** If a subsection (k) applicant provides the application and information required under paragraph (2)(A), neither the reference product sponsor nor the subsection (k) applicant may, prior to the date notice is received under paragraph (8)(A), bring any action under section 2201 of Title 28 for a declaration of infringement, validity, or enforceability of any patent that is described in clauses (i) and (ii) of paragraph (8)(B).

(B) **Subsequent failure to act by subsection (k) applicant** If a subsection (k) applicant fails to complete an action required of the subsection (k) applicant under paragraph (3)(B)(ii), paragraph (5), paragraph (6)(C)(i), paragraph (7), or paragraph (8)(A), the reference product sponsor, but not the subsection (k) applicant, may bring an action under section 2201 of Title 28 for a declaration of infringement, validity, or enforceability of any patent included in the list described in paragraph (3)(A), including as provided under paragraph (7).

(C) Subsection (k) application not provided If a subsection (k) applicant fails to provide the application and information required under paragraph (2)(A), the reference product sponsor, but not the subsection (k) applicant, may bring an action under section 2201 of Title 28 for a declaration of infringement, validity, or enforceability of any patent that claims the biological product or a use of the biological product.

(m) Pediatric studies

(1) Application of certain provisions The provisions of subsections (a), (d), (e), (f), (h), (i), (j), (k), (l), (n), and (p) of section 505A of the Federal Food, Drug, and Cosmetic Act shall apply with respect to the extension of a period under paragraphs (2) and (3) to the same extent and in the same manner as such provisions apply with respect to the extension of a period under subsection (b) or (c) of section 505A of the Federal Food, Drug, and Cosmetic Act.

(2) Market exclusivity for new biological products If, prior to approval of an application that is submitted under subsection (a), the Secretary determines that information relating to the use of a new biological product in the pediatric population may produce health benefits in that population, the Secretary makes a written request for pediatric studies (which shall include a timeframe for completing such studies), the applicant agrees to the request, such studies are completed using appropriate formulations for each age group for which the study is requested within any such timeframe, and the reports thereof are submitted and accepted in accordance with section 505A(d)(4) of the Federal Food, Drug, and Cosmetic Act—

(A) the periods for such biological product referred to in subsection (k)(7) are deemed to be 4 years and 6 months rather than 4 years and 12 years and 6 months rather than 12 years; and

(B) if the biological product is designated under section 526 for a rare disease or condition, the period for such biological product referred to in section 526(a) is deemed to be 7 years and 6 months rather than 7 years.

(3) Market exclusivity for already-marketed biological products If the Secretary determines that information relating to the use of a licensed biological product in the pediatric population may produce health benefits in that population and makes a written request to the holder of an approved application under subsection (a) for pediatric studies (which shall include a timeframe for completing such studies), the holder agrees to the request, such studies are completed using appropriate formulations for each age group for which the study is requested within any such timeframe, and the reports thereof are submitted and accepted in accordance with section 505A(d)(4) of the Federal Food, Drug, and Cosmetic Act—

(**A**) the periods for such biological product referred to in subsection (k)(7) are deemed to be 4 years and 6 months rather than 4 years and 12 years and 6 months rather than 12 years; and

(**B**) if the biological product is designated under section 526 for a rare disease or condition, the period for such biological product referred to in section 527(a) is deemed to be 7 years and 6 months rather than 7 years.

(**4**) **Exception** The Secretary shall not extend a period referred to in paragraph (2)(A), (2)(B), (3)(A), or (3)(B) if the determination under section 505A(d)(4) is made later than 9 months prior to the expiration of such period.

(**n**) **Date of approval in the case of recommended controls under the CSA**

(**1**) **In general** In the case of an application under subsection (a) with respect to a biological product for which the Secretary provides notice to the sponsor that the Secretary intends to issue a scientific and medical evaluation and recommend controls under the Controlled Substances Act,[1] approval of such application shall not take effect until the interim final rule controlling the biological product is issued in accordance with section 201(j) of the Controlled Substances Act.[2]

(**2**) **Date of approval** For purposes of this section, with respect to an application described in paragraph (1), references to the date of approval of such application, or licensure of the product subject to such application, shall mean the later of—

---

[1]21 U.S.C.A. §§ 801 et seq.
[2]21 U.S.C.A. §§ 811(j).

(A) the date an application is approved under subsection (a); or

(B) the date of issuance of the interim final rule controlling the biological product.

(July 1, 1944, c. 373, Title III, §§ 351, 58 Stat. 702; 1953 Reorg. Plan No. 1, §§ 5, 8, eff. Apr. 11, 1953, 18 F.R. 2053, 67 Stat. 631; Pub.L. 85-881, §§ 2, Sept. 2, 1958, 72 Stat. 1704; Pub.L. 91-515, Title II, §§ 291, Oct. 30, 1970, 84 Stat. 1308; Pub.L. 96-88, Title V, §§ 509(b), Oct. 17, 1979, 93 Stat. 695; Pub.L. 99-660, Title I, §§ 105(a), Title III, §§ 315, Nov. 14, 1986, 100 Stat. 3751, 3783; Pub.L. 102-300, §§ 6(b)(1), June 16, 1992, 106 Stat. 240; Pub.L. 104-134, Title II, §§ 2102(d)(2), 2104, Apr. 26, 1996, 110 Stat. 1321-319, 1321-320; Pub.L. 105-115, Title I, §§ 123(a) to (d), (g), Nov. 21, 1997, 111 Stat. 2323, 2324; Pub.L. 108-155, §§ 2(b)(3), Dec. 3, 2003, 117 Stat. 1941; Pub.L. 110-85, Title IX, §§ 901(c), Sept. 27, 2007, 121 Stat. 939; Pub.L. 111-148, Title VII, §§ 7002(a), (b), (g)(1), Mar. 23, 2010, 124 Stat. 804, 814, 819; Pub.L. 112-144, Title V, §§ 502(a)(2), July 9, 2012, 126 Stat. 1040; Pub.L. 114-89, §§ 2(a)(2), Nov. 25, 2015, 129 Stat. 698; Pub.L. 114-255, Div. A, Title III, §§ 3031(b), Dec. 13, 2016, 130 Stat. 1100; Pub.L. 115-52, Title V, §§ 505(b)(2)(B), Aug. 18, 2017, 131 Stat. 1046.)

35 USC 271. Infringement of patent

(a) Except as otherwise provided in this title, whoever without authority makes, uses, offers to sell, or sells any patented invention, within the United States or imports into the United States any patented invention during the term of the patent therefor, infringes the patent.

(b) Whoever actively induces infringement of a patent shall be liable as an infringer.

(c) Whoever offers to sell or sells within the United States or imports into the United States a component of a patented machine, manufacture, combination or composition, or a material or apparatus for use in practicing a patented process, constituting a material part of the invention, knowing the same to be especially made or especially adapted for use in an infringement of such patent, and not a staple article or commodity of commerce suitable for substantial noninfringing use, shall be liable as a contributory infringer.

(d) No patent owner otherwise entitled to relief for infringement or contributory infringement of a patent shall be denied relief or deemed guilty of misuse or illegal extension of the patent right by reason of his having done one or more of the following: (1) derived revenue from acts which if performed by another without his consent would constitute contributory infringement of the patent; (2) licensed or authorized another to perform acts which if performed without his consent would constitute contributory infringement of the patent; (3) sought to enforce his patent rights against infringement or contributory infringement; (4) refused to license or use any rights to the patent; or (5) conditioned the license of any rights to the patent or the sale of the patented product on the acquisition of a license to rights in another patent or purchase of a separate product, unless, in view of the circumstances, the patent owner has market power in the relevant market for the patent or patented product on which the license or sale is conditioned.

(e) (1) It shall not be an act of infringement to make, use, offer to sell, or sell within the United States or import into the United States a patented invention (other than a new animal drug or veterinary biological product (as those terms are used in the Federal Food, Drug, and Cosmetic Act and the Act of March 4, 1913) which is primarily manufactured using recombinant DNA, recombinant RNA, hybridoma technology, or other processes involving site specific genetic manipulation techniques) solely for uses reasonably related to the development and submission of information under a Federal law which regulates the manufacture, use, or sale of drugs or veterinary biological products.

(2) It shall be an act of infringement to submit—

(A) an application under section 505(j) of the Federal Food, Drug, and Cosmetic Act or described in section 505(b)(2) of such Act for a drug claimed in a patent or the use of which is claimed in a patent,

(B) an application under section 512 of such Act or under the Act of March 4, 1913 (21 U.S.C. 151 to 158) for a drug or veterinary biological product which is not primarily manufactured using recombinant DNA, recombinant RNA, hybridoma technology, or other processes involving site specific genetic manipulation techniques and which is claimed in a patent or the use of which is claimed in a patent, or

(C) (i) with respect to a patent that is identified in the list of patents described in section 351(l)(3) of the Public Health Service Act (including as provided under section 351(l)(7) of such Act), an application seeking approval of a biological product, or

(ii) if the applicant for the application fails to provide the application and information required under section 351(l)(2)(A) of such Act, an application seeking approval of a biological product for a patent that could be identified pursuant to section 351(l)(3)(A)(i) of such Act,

if the purpose of such submission is to obtain approval under such Act to engage in the commercial manufacture, use, or sale of a drug, veterinary biological product, or biological product claimed in a patent or the use of which is claimed in a patent before the expiration of such patent.

(3) In any action for patent infringement brought under this section, no injunctive or other relief may be granted which would prohibit the making, using, offering to sell, or selling within the United States or importing into the United States of a patented invention under paragraph (1).

(4) For an act of infringement described in paragraph (2)—

(A) the court shall order the effective date of any approval of the drug or veterinary biological product involved in the infringement to be a date which is not earlier than the date of the expiration of the patent which has been infringed,

(B) injunctive relief may be granted against an infringer to prevent the commercial manufacture, use, offer to sell, or sale within the United States or importation into the United States of an approved drug, veterinary biological product, or biological product,

(C) damages or other monetary relief may be awarded against an infringer only if there has been commercial manufacture, use, offer to sell, or sale within the United States or importation into the United States of an approved drug, veterinary biological product, or biological product, and

(D) the court shall order a permanent injunction prohibiting any infringement of the patent by the biological product involved in the infringement until a date which is not earlier than the date of the expiration of the patent that has been infringed under paragraph (2)(C), provided the patent is the subject of a final court decision, as defined in section 351(k)(6) of the Public Health Service Act, in an action for infringement of the patent under section 351(l)(6) of such Act, and the biological product has not yet been approved because of section 351(k)(7) of such Act.

The remedies prescribed by subparagraphs (A), (B), (C),

and (D) are the only remedies which may be granted by a court for an act of infringement described in paragraph (2), except that a court may award attorney fees under section 285.

(5) Where a person has filed an application described in paragraph (2) that includes a certification under subsection (b)(2)(A)(iv) or (j)(2)(A)(vii)(IV) of section 505 of the Federal Food, Drug, and Cosmetic Act (21 U.S.C. 355), and neither the owner of the patent that is the subject of the certification nor the holder of the approved application under subsection (b) of such section for the drug that is claimed by the patent or a use of which is claimed by the patent brought an action for infringement of such patent before the expiration of 45 days after the date on which the notice given under subsection (b)(3) or (j)(2)(B) of such section was received, the courts of the United States shall, to the extent consistent with the Constitution, have subject matter jurisdiction in any action brought by such person under section 2201 of title 28 for a declaratory judgment that such patent is invalid or not infringed.

(6) (A) Subparagraph (B) applies, in lieu of paragraph (4), in the case of a patent—

(i) that is identified, as applicable, in the list of patents described in section 351(l)(4) of the Public Health Service Act or the lists of patents described in section 351(l)(5)(B) of such Act with respect to a biological product; and

(ii) for which an action for infringement of the patent with respect to the biological product—

(I) was brought after the expiration of the 30-day period described in subparagraph (A) or (B), as applicable, of section 351(l)(6) of such Act; or

(II) was brought before the expiration of the 30-day period described in subclause (I), but which was dismissed without prejudice or was not prosecuted to judgment in good faith.

(B) In an action for infringement of a patent described in subparagraph (A), the sole and exclusive remedy that may be granted by a court, upon a finding that the making, using, offering to sell, selling, or importation into the United States of the biological product that is the subject of the action infringed the patent, shall be a reasonable royalty.

(C) The owner of a patent that should have been included in the list described in section 351(l)(3)(A) of the Public Health Service Act, including as provided under section 351(l)(7) of such Act for a biological product, but was not timely included in such list, may not bring an action under this section for infringement of the patent with respect to the biological product.

(f) (1) Whoever without authority supplies or causes to be supplied in or from the United States all or a substantial portion of the components of a patented invention, where such components are uncombined in whole or in part, in such manner as to actively induce the combination of such components outside of the United States in a manner that would infringe the patent if such combination occurred within the United States, shall be liable as an infringer.

(2) Whoever without authority supplies or causes to be supplied in or from the United States any component of a patented invention that is especially made or especially adapted for use in the invention and not a staple article or commodity of commerce suitable for substantial noninfringing use, where such component is uncombined in whole or in part, knowing that such component is so made or adapted and intending that such component will be combined outside of the United States in a manner that would infringe the patent if such combination occurred within the United States, shall be liable as an infringer.

(g) Whoever without authority imports into the United States or offers to sell, sells, or uses within the United States a product which is made by a process patented in the United States shall be liable as an infringer, if the importation, offer to sell, sale, or use of the product occurs during the term of such process patent. In an action for infringement of a process patent, no remedy may be granted for infringement on account of the noncommercial use or retail sale of a product unless there is no adequate remedy under this title for infringement on account of the importation or other use, offer to sell, or sale of that product. A product which is made by a patented process will, for purposes of this title, not be considered to be so made after—

(1) it is materially changed by subsequent processes; or

(2) it becomes a trivial and nonessential component of another product.

(h) As used in this section, the term "whoever" includes any State, any instrumentality of a State, and any officer or employee of a State or instrumentality of a State acting in his official capacity. Any State, and any such instrumentality, officer, or employee, shall be subject to the provisions of this title in the same manner and to the same extent as any nongovernmental entity.

(i) As used in this section, an "offer for sale" or an "offer to sell" by a person other than the patentee, or any designee of the patentee, is that in which the sale will occur before the expiration of the term of the patent.

(July 19, 1952, c. 950, 66 Stat. 811; Pub.L. 98-417, Title II, §§ 202, Sept. 24, 1984, 98 Stat. 1603; Pub.L. 98-622, Title I, §§ 101(a), Nov. 8, 1984, 98 Stat. 3383; Pub.L. 100-418, Title IX, §§ 9003, Aug. 23, 1988, 102 Stat. 1564; Pub.L. 100-670, Title II, §§ 201(i), Nov. 16, 1988, 102 Stat. 3988; Pub.L. 100-703, Title II, §§ 201, Nov. 19, 1988, 102 Stat. 4676; Pub.L. 102-560, §§ 2(a)(1), Oct. 28, 1992, 106 Stat. 4230; Pub.L. 103-465, Title V, §§ 533(a), Dec. 8, 1994, 108 Stat. 4988; Pub.L. 108-173, Title XI, §§ 1101(d), Dec. 8, 2003, 117 Stat. 2457; Pub.L. 111-148, Title VII, §§ 7002(c)(1), Mar. 23, 2010, 124 Stat. 815.)

APPENDIX B

Compilation of Relevant Regulations (21 CFR 10.115, 21 CFR Part 600, 37 CFR 42)

21 CFR 10.115   Good guidance practices.
      PART 600—BIOLOGICAL PRODUCTS: GENERAL
          SUBPART A—GENERAL PROVISIONS
21 CFR 600.2   Mailing addresses.
21 CFR 600.3   Definitions.
      SUBPART B—ESTABLISHMENT STANDARDS
21 CFR 600.10   Personnel.
21 CFR 600.11   Physical establishment, equipment, animals, and care.
21 CFR 600.12   Records.
21 CFR 600.13   Retention samples.
21 CFR 600.14   Reporting of biological product deviations by licensed manufacturers.
21 CFR 600.15   Temperatures during shipment.
      SUBPART C—ESTABLISHMENT INSPECTION
21 CFR 600.20   Inspectors.
21 CFR 600.21   Time of inspection.
21 CFR 600.22   [Reserved by 84 FR 12508]
      Subpart D—Reporting of Adverse Experiences
21 CFR 600.80   Postmarketing reporting of adverse experiences.
21 CFR 600.81   Distribution reports.
21 CFR 600.82   Notification of a permanent discontinuance cr an interruption in manufacturing.
21 CFR 600.90   Waivers.
  PART 42—TRIAL PRACTICE BEFORE THE PATENT TRIAL AND APPEAL BOARD
  SUBPART A—TRIAL PRACTICE AND PROCEDURE
          GENERAL
37 CFR 42.1   Policy.
37 CFR 42.2   Definitions.

37 CFR 42.3   Jurisdiction.
37 CFR 42.4   Notice of trial.
37 CFR 42.5   Conduct of the proceeding.
37 CFR 42.6   Filing of documents, including exhibits; service.
37 CFR 42.7   Management of the record.
37 CFR 42.8   Mandatory notices.
37 CFR 42.9   Action by patent owner.
37 CFR 42.10   Counsel.
37 CFR 42.11   Duty of candor; signing papers; representations to the Board; sanctions.
37 CFR 42.12   Sanctions.
37 CFR 42.13   Citation of authority.
37 CFR 42.14   Public availability.

FEES

37 CFR 42.15   Fees.

PETITION AND MOTION PRACTICE

37 CFR 42.20   Generally.
37 CFR 42.21   Notice of basis for relief.
37 CFR 42.22   Content of petitions and motions.
37 CFR 42.23   Oppositions and replies.
37 CFR 42.24   Type-volume or page-limits for petitions, motions, oppositions, and replies.
37 CFR 42.25   Default filing times.

TESTIMONY AND PRODUCTION

37 CFR 42.51   Discovery.
37 CFR 42.52   Compelling testimony and production.
37 CFR 42.53   Taking testimony.
37 CFR 42.54   Protective order.
37 CFR 42.55   Confidential information in a petition.
37 CFR 42.56   Expungement of confidential information.
37 CFR 42.57   Privilege for patent practitioners.
37 CFR 42.61   Admissibility.
37 CFR 42.62   Applicability of the Federal rules of evidence.
37 CFR 42.63   Form of evidence.
37 CFR 42.64   Objection; motion to exclude.
37 CFR 42.65   Expert testimony; tests and data.

ORAL ARGUMENT, DECISION, AND SETTLEMENT

37 CFR 42.70   Oral argument.
37 CFR 42.71   Decision on petitions or motions.
37 CFR 42.72   Termination of trial.
37 CFR 42.73   Judgment.

37 CFR 42.74   Settlement.

CERTIFICATE

37 CFR 42.80   Certificate.

SUBPART B—INTER PARTES REVIEW

GENERAL

37 CFR 42.100   Procedure; pendency.

37 CFR 42.101   Who may petition for inter partes review.

37 CFR 42.102   Time for filing.

37 CFR 42.103   Inter partes review fee.

37 CFR 42.104   Content of petition.

37 CFR 42.105   Service of petition.

37 CFR 42.106   Filing date.

37 CFR 42.107   Preliminary response to petition.

INSTITUTING INTER PARTES REVIEW

37 CFR 42.108   Institution of inter partes review.

AFTER INSTITUTION OF INTER PARTES REVIEW

37 CFR 42.120   Patent owner response.

37 CFR 42.121   Amendment of the patent.

37 CFR 42.122   Multiple proceedings and Joinder.

37 CFR 42.123   Filing of supplemental information.

SUBPART C—POST-GRANT REVIEW

GENERAL

37 CFR 42.200   Procedure; pendency.

37 CFR 42.201   Who may petition for a post-grant review.

37 CFR 42.202   Time for filing.

37 CFR 42.203   Post-grant review fee.

37 CFR 42.204   Content of petition.

37 CFR 42.205   Service of petition.

37 CFR 42.206   Filing date.

37 CFR 42.207   Preliminary response to petition.

INSTITUTING POST–GRANT REVIEW

37 CFR 42.208   Institution of post-grant review.

AFTER INSTITUTION OF POST–GRANT REVIEW

37 CFR 42.220   Patent owner response.

37 CFR 42.221   Amendment of the patent.

37 CFR 42.222   Multiple proceedings and Joinder.

37 CFR 42.223   Filing of supplemental information.

37 CFR 42.224   Discovery.

SUBPART D—TRANSITIONAL PROGRAM FOR COVERED
BUSINESS METHOD PATENTS

37 CFR 42.300   Procedure; pendency.

37 CFR 42.301   Definitions.
37 CFR 42.302   Who may petition for a covered business
                 method patent review.
37 CFR 42.303   Time for filing.
37 CFR 42.304   Content of petition.
                 SUBPART E—DERIVATION
                 GENERAL
37 CFR 42.400   Procedure; pendency.
37 CFR 42.401   Definitions.
37 CFR 42.402   Who may file a petition for a derivation
                 proceeding.
37 CFR 42.403   Time for filing.
37 CFR 42.404   Derivation fee.
37 CFR 42.405   Content of petition.
37 CFR 42.406   Service of petition.
37 CFR 42.407   Filing date.
          INSTITUTING DERIVATION PROCEEDING
37 CFR 42.408   Institution of derivation proceeding.
      AFTER INSTITUTION OF DERIVATION PROCEEDING
37 CFR 42.409   Settlement agreements.
37 CFR 42.410   Arbitration.
37 CFR 42.411   Common interests in the invention.
37 CFR 42.412   Public availability of Board records.

21 CFR 10.115. Good guidance practices.

(a) What are good guidance practices? Good guidance practices (GGP's) are FDA's policies and procedures for developing, issuing, and using guidance documents.

(b) What is a guidance document?

(1) Guidance documents are documents prepared for FDA staff, applicants/sponsors, and the public that describe the agency's interpretation of or policy on a regulatory issue.

(2) Guidance documents include, but are not limited to, documents that relate to: The design, production, labeling, promotion, manufacturing, and testing of regulated products; the processing, content, and evaluation or approval of submissions; and inspection and enforcement policies.

(3) Guidance documents do not include: Documents relating to internal FDA procedures, agency reports, general information documents provided to consumers

or health professionals, speeches, journal articles and editorials, media interviews, press materials, warning letters, memoranda of understanding, or other communications directed to individual persons or firms.

(c) What other terms have a special meaning?

(1) "Level 1 guidance documents" include guidance documents that:

(i) Set forth initial interpretations of statutory or regulatory requirements;

(ii) Set forth changes in interpretation or policy that are of more than a minor nature;

(iii) Include complex scientific issues; or

(iv) Cover highly controversial issues.

(2) "Level 2 guidance documents" are guidance documents that set forth existing practices or minor changes in interpretation or policy. Level 2 guidance documents include all guidance documents that are not classified as Level 1.

(3) "You" refers to all affected parties outside of FDA.

(d) Are you or FDA required to follow a guidance document?

(1) No. Guidance documents do not establish legally enforceable rights or responsibilities. They do not legally bind the public or FDA.

(2) You may choose to use an approach other than the one set forth in a guidance document. However, your alternative approach must comply with the relevant statutes and regulations. FDA is willing to discuss an alternative approach with you to ensure that it complies with the relevant statutes and regulations.

(3) Although guidance documents do not legally bind FDA, they represent the agency's current thinking. Therefore, FDA employees may depart from guidance documents only with appropriate justification and supervisory concurrence.

(e) Can FDA use means other than a guidance document to communicate new agency policy or a new regulatory approach to a broad public audience? The agency may not use documents or other means of communication that are excluded from the definition of guidance document to informally communicate new or different regulatory expectations to a broad public audience for the first time.

These GGP's must be followed whenever regulatory expectations that are not readily apparent from the statute or regulations are first communicated to a broad public audience.

(f) How can you participate in the development and issuance of guidance documents?

(1) You can provide input on guidance documents that FDA is developing under the procedures described in paragraph (g) of this section.

(2) You can suggest areas for guidance document development. Your suggestions should address why a guidance document is necessary.

(3) You can submit drafts of proposed guidance documents for FDA to consider. When you do so, you should mark the document "Guidance Document Submission" and submit it to Division of Dockets Management (HFA-305), 5630 Fishers Lane, rm. 1061, Rockville, MD 20852. If you wish to submit the draft of a proposed guidance document electronically, submit it through https://www.regulations.gov at Docket No. FDA-2013-S-0610. It is only necessary to submit one copy.

(4) You can, at any time, suggest that FDA revise or withdraw an already existing guidance document. Your suggestion should address why the guidance document should be revised or withdrawn and, if applicable, how it should be revised.

(5) Once a year, FDA will publish, both in the Federal Register and on the Internet, a list of possible topics for future guidance document development or revision during the next year. You can comment on this list (e.g., by suggesting alternatives or making recommendations on the topics that FDA is considering).

(6) To participate in the development and issuance of guidance documents through one of the mechanisms described in paragraphs (f)(1), (f)(2), or (f)(4) of this section, you should contact the center or office that is responsible for the regulatory activity covered by the guidance document.

(7) If FDA agrees to draft or revise a guidance document, under a suggestion made under paragraphs (f)(1), (f)(2), (f)(3) or (f)(4) of this section, you can participate in the development of that guidance document under the procedures described in paragraph (g) of this section.

(g) What are FDA's procedures for developing and issuing guidance documents?

(1) FDA's procedures for the development and issuance of Level 1 guidance documents are as follows:

(i) Before FDA prepares a draft of a Level 1 guidance document, FDA can seek or accept early input from individuals or groups outside the agency. For example, FDA can do this by participating in or holding public meetings and workshops.

(ii) After FDA prepares a draft of a Level 1 guidance document, FDA will:

(A) Publish a notice in the Federal Register announcing that the draft guidance document is available;

(B) Post the draft guidance document on the Internet and make it available in hard copy; and

(C) Invite your comment on the draft guidance document. Paragraph (h) of this section tells you how to submit your comments.

(iii) After FDA prepares a draft of a Level 1 guidance document, FDA also can:

(A) Hold public meetings or workshops; or

(B) Present the draft guidance document to an advisory committee for review.

(iv) After providing an opportunity for public comment on a Level 1 guidance document, FDA will:

(A) Review any comments received and prepare the final version of the guidance document that incorporates suggested changes, when appropriate;

(B) Publish a notice in the Federal Register announcing that the guidance document is available;

(C) Post the guidance document on the Internet and make it available in hard copy; and

(D) Implement the guidance document.

(v) After providing an opportunity for comment, FDA may decide that it should issue another draft of the guidance document. In this case, FDA will follow the steps in paragraphs (g)(1)(ii), (g)(1)(iii), and (g)(1)(iv) of this section.

(2) FDA will not seek your comment before it implements a Level 1 guidance document if the agency determines that prior public participation is not feasible or appropriate.

(3) FDA will use the following procedures for developing and issuing Level 1 guidance documents under the circumstances described in paragraph (g)(2) of this section:

(i)   After FDA prepares a guidance document, FDA will:

(A)   Publish a notice in the Federal Register announcing that the guidance document is available;

(B)   Post the guidance document on the Internet and make it available in hard copy;

(C)   Immediately implement the guidance document; and

(D)   Invite your comment when it issues or publishes the guidance document. Paragraph (h) of this section tells you how to submit your comments.

(ii)   If FDA receives comments on the guidance document, FDA will review those comments and revise the guidance document when appropriate.

(4) FDA will use the following procedures for developing and issuing Level 2 guidance documents:

(i)   After it prepares a guidance document, FDA will:

(A)   Post the guidance document on the Internet and make it available in hard copy;

(B)   Immediately implement the guidance document, unless FDA indicates otherwise when the document is made available; and

(C)   Invite your comment on the Level 2 guidance document. Paragraph (h) of this section tells you how to submit your comments.

(ii)   If FDA receives comments on the guidance document, FDA will review those comments and revise the document when appropriate. If a version is revised, the new version will be placed on the Internet.

(5) You can comment on any guidance document at any time. Paragraph (h) of this section tells you how to submit your comments. FDA will revise guidance documents in response to your comments when appropriate.

(h) How should you submit comments on a guidance document?

(1) If you choose to submit comments on any guidance document under paragraph (g) of this section, you must

send them to the Division of Dockets Management (HFA-305), 5630 Fishers Lane, rm. 1061, Rockville, MD 20852.

(2) Comments should identify the docket number on the guidance document, if such a docket number exists. For documents without a docket number, the title of the guidance document should be included.

(3) Comments will be available to the public in accordance with FDA's regulations on submission of documents to the Division of Dockets Management specified in §§ 10.20(j).

(i) What standard elements must FDA include in a guidance document?

(1) A guidance document must:

(i) Include the term "guidance,"

(ii) Identify the center(s) or office(s) issuing the document,

(iii) Identify the activity to which and the people to whom the document applies,

(iv) Prominently display a statement of the document's nonbinding effect,

(v) Include the date of issuance,

(vi) Note if it is a revision to a previously issued guidance and identify the document that it replaces, and

(vii) Contain the word "draft" if the document is a draft guidance.

(2) Guidance documents must not include mandatory language such as "shall," "must," "required," or "requirement," unless FDA is using these words to describe a statutory or regulatory requirement.

(3) When issuing draft guidance documents that are the product of international negotiations (e.g., guidances resulting from the International Conference on Harmonisation), FDA need not apply paragraphs (i)(1) and (i)(2) of this section. However, any final guidance document issued according to this provision must contain the elements in paragraphs (i)(1) and (i)(2) of this section.

(j) Who, within FDA, can approve issuance of guidance documents? Each center and office must have written procedures for the approval of guidance documents. Those procedures must ensure that issuance of all documents is approved by appropriate senior FDA officials.

(k) How will FDA review and revise existing guidance documents?

(1) The agency will periodically review existing guidance documents to determine whether they need to be changed or withdrawn.

(2) When significant changes are made to the statute or regulations, the agency will review and, if appropriate, revise guidance documents relating to that changed statute or regulation.

(3) As discussed in paragraph (f)(3) of this section, you may at any time suggest that FDA revise a guidance document.

(l) How will FDA ensure that FDA staff are following GGP's?

(1) All current and new FDA employees involved in the development, issuance, or application of guidance documents will be trained regarding the agency's GGP's.

(2) FDA centers and offices will monitor the development and issuance of guidance documents to ensure that GGP's are being followed.

(m) How can you get copies of FDA's guidance documents? FDA will make copies available in hard copy and, as feasible, through the Internet.

(n) How will FDA keep you informed of the guidance documents that are available?

(1) FDA will maintain on the Internet a current list of all guidance documents. New documents will be added to this list within 30 days of issuance.

(2) Once a year, FDA will publish in the Federal Register its comprehensive list of guidance documents. The comprehensive list will identify documents that have been added to the list or withdrawn from the list since the previous comprehensive list.

(3) FDA's guidance document lists will include the name of the guidance document, issuance and revision dates, and information on how to obtain copies of the document.

(o) What can you do if you believe that someone at FDA is not following these GGP's? If you believe that someone at FDA did not follow the procedures in this section or that someone at FDA treated a guidance document as a binding requirement, you should contact that person's supervisor in the center or office that issued the guidance document. If the issue cannot be resolved, you should contact the next highest supervisor. You can also contact the center or office ombudsman for assistance in resolving the issue. If you are unable to resolve the issue at the center or office level or if you feel that you are not making progress by going through the chain of command, you may ask the Office of the Chief Mediator and Ombudsman to become involved.

[65 FR 56477, Sept. 19, 2000; 83 FR 13416, March 29, 2018]

PART 600 —BIOLOGICAL PRODUCTS: GENERAL

SUBPART A —GENERAL PROVISIONS

21 CFR 600.2. Mailing addresses.

(a) Licensed biological products regulated by the Center for Biologics Evaluation and Research (CBER). Unless otherwise stated in paragraph (c) of this section, or as otherwise prescribed by FDA regulation, all submissions to CBER referenced in parts 600 through 680 of this chapter, as applicable, must be sent to: Food and Drug Administration, Center for Biologics Evaluation and Research, Document Control Center, 10903 New Hampshire Ave., Bldg. 71, Rm. G112, Silver Spring, MD 20993-0002. Examples of such submissions include: Biologics license applications (BLAs) and their amendments and supplements, biological product deviation reports, fatality reports, and other correspondence. Biological products samples must not be sent to this address but must be sent to the address in paragraph (c) of this section.

(b) Licensed biological products regulated by the Center for Drug Evaluation and Research (CDER). Unless otherwise stated in paragraphs (b)(1), (b)(2), or (c) of this section, or as otherwise prescribed by FDA regulation, all submissions to CDER referenced in parts 600, 601, and 610 of this chapter, as applicable, must be sent to: CDER Central Document Room, Center for Drug Evaluation and Research, Food and Drug Administration, 5901B Ammendale Rd., Beltsville, MD 20705. Examples of such submissions include: BLAs and their amendments and supplements, and other correspondence.

(1) Biological Product Deviation Reporting (CDER). All biological product deviation reports required under §§ 600.14 must be sent to: Division of Compliance Risk Management and Surveillance, Office of Compliance,

Center for Drug Evaluation and Research, Food and Drug Administration, 10903 New Hampshire Ave., Silver Spring, MD 20993-0002.

(2) Advertising and Promotional Labeling (CDER). All advertising and promotional labeling supplements required under §§ 601.12(f) of this chapter must be sent to: Division of Drug Marketing, Advertising and Communication, Center for Drug Evaluation and Research, Food and Drug Administration, 5901-B Ammendale Rd., Beltsville, MD 20705-1266.

(c) Samples and Protocols for licensed biological products regulated by CBER or CDER.

(1) Biological product samples and/or protocols, other than radioactive biological product samples and protocols, required under §§ 600.13, 600.22, 601.15, 610.2, 660.6, 660.36, or 660.46 of this chapter must be sent by courier service to: Food and Drug Administration, Center for Biologics Evaluation and Research, ATTN: Sample Custodian, 10903 New Hampshire Ave., Bldg. 75, Rm. G707, Silver Spring, MD 20993-0002. The protocol(s) may be placed in the box used to ship the samples to CBER. A cover letter should not be included when submitting the protocol with the sample unless it contains pertinent information affecting the release of the lot.

(2) Radioactive biological products required under §§ 610.2 of this chapter must be sent by courier service to: Food and Drug Administration, Center for Biologics Evaluation and Research, ATTN: Sample Custodian, c/o White Oak Radiation Safety Program, 10903 New Hampshire Ave., Bldg. 52-72, Rm. G406A, Silver Spring, MD 20993-0002.

(d) Address information for submissions to CBER and CDER other than those listed in parts 600 through 680 of this chapter are included directly in the applicable regulations.

(e) Obtain updated mailing address information for biological products regulated by CBER at http://www.fda.g ov/BiologicsBloodVaccines/default.htm, or for biological products regulated by CDER at http://www.fda.gov/Drugs/ default.htm.

[70 FR 14981, March 24, 2005; 74 FR 13114, March 26, 2009; 78 FR 19585, April 2, 2013; 79 FR 33090, June 10, 2014; 80 FR 18091, April 3, 2015; 80 FR 30152, May 27, 2015]

21 CFR 600.3. Definitions.

For statute(s) affecting validity, see: 21 USCA §§ 321, 351, 352, 353, 355, 360, 360i, 371, 374; 42 USCA §§ 216, 262, 263, 263a, 264, 300aa-25.

As used in this subchapter:

(a) Act means the Public Health Service Act (58 Stat. 682), approved July 1, 1944.

(b) Secretary means the Secretary of Health and Human Services and any other officer or employee of the Department of Health and Human Services to whom the authority involved has been delegated.

(c) Commissioner of Food and Drugs means the Commissioner of the Food and Drug Administration.

(d) Center for Biologics Evaluation and Research means Center for Biologics Evaluation and Research of the Food and Drug Administration.

(e) State means a State or the District of Columbia, Puerto Rico, or the Virgin Islands.

(f) Possession includes among other possessions, Puerto Rico and the Virgin Islands.

(g) Products includes biological products and trivalent organic arsenicals.

(h) Biological product means any virus, therapeutic serum, toxin, antitoxin, or analogous product applicable to the prevention, treatment or cure of diseases or injuries of man:

(1) A virus is interpreted to be a product containing the minute living cause of an infectious disease and includes but is not limited to filterable viruses, bacteria, rickettsia, fungi, and protozoa.

(2) A therapeutic serum is a product obtained from blood by removing the clot or clot components and the blood cells.

(3) A toxin is a product containing a soluble substance poisonous to laboratory animals or to man in doses of 1 milliliter or less (or equivalent in weight) of the product, and having the property, following the injection of nonfatal doses into an animal, of causing to be produced therein another soluble substance which specifically neutralizes the poisonous substance and which is demonstrable in the serum of the animal thus immunized.

(4) An antitoxin is a product containing the soluble

substance in serum or other body fluid of an immunized animal which specifically neutralizes the toxin against which the animal is immune.

(5) A product is analogous:

(i) To a virus if prepared from or with a virus or agent actually or potentially infectious, without regard to the degree of virulence or toxicogenicity of the specific strain used.

(ii) To a therapeutic serum, if composed of whole blood or plasma or containing some organic constituent or product other than a hormone or an amino acid, derived from whole blood, plasma, or serum.

(iii) To a toxin or antitoxin, if intended, irrespective of its source of origin, to be applicable to the prevention, treatment, or cure of disease or injuries of man through a specific immune process.

(i) Trivalent organic arsenicals means arsphenamine and its derivatives (or any other trivalent organic arsenic compound) applicable to the prevention, treatment, or cure of diseases or injuries of man.

(j) A product is deemed applicable to the prevention, treatment, or cure of diseases or injuries of man irrespective of the mode of administration or application recommended, including use when intended through administration or application to a person as an aid in diagnosis, or in evaluating the degree of susceptibility or immunity possessed by a person, and including also any other use for purposes of diagnosis if the diagnostic substance so used is prepared from or with the aid of a biological product.

(k) Proper name, as applied to a product, means the name designated in the license for use upon each package of the product.

(l) Dating period means the period beyond which the product cannot be expected beyond reasonable doubt to yield its specific results.

(m) Expiration date means the calendar month and year, and where applicable, the day and hour, that the dating period ends.

(n) The word standards means specifications and procedures applicable to an establishment or to the manufacture or release of products, which are prescribed in this subchapter or established in the biologics license application designed to insure the continued safety, purity, and potency of such products.

(o) The word continued as applied to the safety, purity and potency of products is interpreted to apply to the dating period.

(p) The word safety means the relative freedom from harmful effect to persons affected, directly or indirectly, by a product when prudently administered, taking into consideration the character of the product in relation to the condition of the recipient at the time.

(q) The word sterility is interpreted to mean freedom from viable contaminating microorganisms, as determined by the tests conducted under §§ 610.12 of this chapter.

(r) Purity means relative freedom from extraneous matter in the finished product, whether or not harmful to the recipient or deleterious to the product. Purity includes but is not limited to relative freedom from residual moisture or other volatile substances and pyrogenic substances.

(s) The word potency is interpreted to mean the specific ability or capacity of the product, as indicated by appropriate laboratory tests or by adequately controlled clinical data obtained through the administration of the product in the manner intended, to effect a given result.

(t) Manufacturer means any legal person or entity engaged in the manufacture of a product subject to license under the act; "Manufacturer" also includes any legal person or entity who is an applicant for a license where the applicant assumes responsibility for compliance with the applicable product and establishment standards.

(u) Manufacture means all steps in propagation or manufacture and preparation of products and includes but is not limited to filling, testing, labeling, packaging, and storage by the manufacturer.

(v) Location includes all buildings, appurtenances, equipment and animals used, and personnel engaged by a manufacturer within a particular area designated by an address adequate for identification.

(w) Establishment has the same meaning as "facility" in section 351 of the Public Health Service Act and includes all locations.

(x) Lot means that quantity of uniform material identified by the manufacturer as having been thoroughly mixed in a single vessel.

(y) A filling refers to a group of final containers identical in all respects, which have been filled with the same product from the same bulk lot without any change that will affect the integrity of the filling assembly.

(z) Process refers to a manufacturing step that is performed on the product itself which may affect its safety, purity or potency, in contrast to such manufacturing steps which do not affect intrinsically the safety, purity or potency of the product.

(aa) Selling agent or distributor means any person engaged in the unrestricted distribution, other than by sale at retail, of products subject to license.

(bb) Container (referred to also as "final container") is the immediate unit, bottle, vial, ampule, tube, or other receptacle containing the product as distributed for sale, barter, or exchange.

(cc) Package means the immediate carton, receptacle, or wrapper, including all labeling matter therein and thereon, and the contents of the one or more enclosed containers. If no package, as defined in the preceding sentence, is used, the container shall be deemed to be the package.

(dd) Label means any written, printed, or graphic matter on the container or package or any such matter clearly visible through the immediate carton, receptacle, or wrapper.

(ee) Radioactive biological product means a biological product which is labeled with a radionuclide or intended solely to be labeled with a radionuclide.

(ff) Amendment is the submission of information to a pending license application or supplement, to revise or modify the application as originally submitted.

(gg) Supplement is a request to approve a change in an approved license application.

(hh) Distributed means the biological product has left the control of the licensed manufacturer.

(ii) Control means having responsibility for maintaining the continued safety, purity, and potency of the product and for compliance with applicable product and establishment standards, and for compliance with current good manufacturing practices.

(jj) Assess the effects of the change, as used in §§ 601.12 of this chapter, means to evaluate the effects of a manufacturing change on the identity, strength, quality, purity, and potency of a product as these factors may relate to the safety or effectiveness of the product.

(kk) Specification, as used in §§ 601.12 of this chapter, means the quality standard (i.e., tests, analytical procedures, and acceptance criteria) provided in an approved application to confirm the quality of products, intermediates, raw materials, reagents, components, in-process materials, container closure systems, and other materials used in the production of a product. For the purpose of this definition, acceptance criteria means numerical limits, ranges, or other criteria for the tests described.

(ll) Complete response letter means a written communication to an applicant from FDA usually describing all of the deficiencies that the agency has identified in a biologics license application or supplement that must be satisfactorily addressed before it can be approved.

(mm) Resubmission means a submission by the biologics license applicant or supplement applicant of all materials needed to fully address all deficiencies identified in the complete response letter. A biologics license application or supplement for which FDA issued a complete response letter, but which was withdrawn before approval and later submitted again, is not a resubmission.

[38 FR 32048, Nov. 20, 1973, as amended at 40 FR 31313, July 25, 1975; 49 FR 23833, June 8, 1984; 55 FR 11014, March 26, 1990; 61 FR 24232, May 14, 1996; 62 FR 39901, July 24, 1997; 64 FR 56449, Oct. 20, 1999; 65 FR 66634, Nov. 7, 2000; 65 FR 67477, Nov. 9, 2000; 69 FR 18766, April 8, 2004; 70 FR 14982, March 24, 2005; 73 FR 39610, July 10, 2008; 77 FR 26174, May 3, 2012]

SUBPART B —ESTABLISHMENT STANDARDS

21 CFR 600.10.   Personnel.

(a) [Reserved]

(b) Personnel. Personnel shall have capabilities commensurate with their assigned functions, a thorough understanding of the manufacturing operations which they perform, the necessary training and experience relating to individual products, and adequate information concerning the application of the pertinent provisions of this subchapter to their respective functions. Personnel shall include such professionally trained persons as are necessary to insure the competent performance of all manufacturing processes.

(c) Restrictions on personnel—

(1) Specific duties. Persons whose presence can affect adversely the safety and purity of a product shall be excluded from the room where the manufacture of a product is in progress.

(2) Sterile operations. Personnel performing sterile operations shall wear clean or sterilized protective clothing and devices to the extent necessary to protect the product from contamination.

(3) Pathogenic viruses and spore-forming organisms. Persons working with viruses pathogenic for man or with spore-forming microorganisms, and persons engaged in the care of animals or animal quarters, shall be excluded from areas where other products are manufactured, or such persons shall change outer clothing, including shoes, or wear protective covering prior to entering such areas.

(4) Live vaccine work areas. Persons may not enter a live vaccine processing area after having worked with other infectious agents in any other laboratory during the same working day. Only persons actually concerned with propagation of the culture, production of the vaccine, and unit maintenance, shall be allowed in live vaccine processing areas when active work is in progress. Casual visitors shall be excluded from such units at all times and all others having business in such areas shall be admitted only under supervision. Street clothing, including shoes, shall be replaced or covered by suitable laboratory clothing before entering a live vaccine processing unit. Persons caring for animals used in the manufacture of live vaccines shall be excluded from other animal quarters and from contact with other animals during the same working day.

[49 FR 23833, June 8, 1984; 55 FR 11014, March 26, 1990; 62 FR 53538, Oct. 15, 1997; 68 FR 75119, Dec. 30, 2003; 69 FR 26768, May 14, 2004]

21 CFR 600.11. Physical establishment, equipment, animals, and care.

(a) Work areas. All rooms and work areas where products are manufactured or stored shall be kept orderly, clean, and free of dirt, dust, vermin and objects not required for manufacturing. Precautions shall be taken to avoid clogging and back-siphonage of drainage systems. Precautions shall be taken to exclude extraneous infectious agents from manufacturing areas. Work rooms shall be well lighted and ventilated. The ventilation system shall be arranged so as to prevent the dissemination of microorganisms from one manufacturing area to another and to avoid other conditions unfavorable to the safety of the product. Filling rooms, and other rooms where open, sterile operations are conducted, shall be adequate to meet manufacturing needs and such rooms shall be constructed and equipped to permit thorough cleaning and to keep airborne contaminants at a minimum. If such rooms are used for other purposes, they shall be cleaned and prepared prior to use for sterile operations. Refrigerators, incubators and warm rooms shall be maintained at temperatures within applicable ranges and shall be free of extraneous material which might affect the safety of the product.

(b) Equipment. Apparatus for sterilizing equipment and the method of operation shall be such as to insure the destruction of contaminating microorganisms. The effectiveness of the sterilization procedure shall be no less than that achieved by an attained temperature of 121.5 degrees C maintained for 20 minutes by saturated steam or by an attained temperature of 170 degrees C maintained for 2 hours with dry heat. Processing and storage containers, filters, filling apparatus, and other pieces of apparatus and accessory equipment, including pipes and tubing, shall be designed and constructed to permit thorough cleaning and, where possible, inspection for cleanliness. All surfaces that come in contact with products shall be clean and free of surface solids, leachable contaminants, and other materials that will hasten the deterioration of the product or otherwise render it less suitable for the intended use. For products for which sterility is a factor, equipment shall be sterile, unless sterility of the product is assured by subsequent procedures.

(c) Laboratory and bleeding rooms. Rooms used for the processing of products, including bleeding rooms, shall be effectively fly-proofed and kept free of flies and vermin. Such rooms shall be so constructed as to insure freedom from dust, smoke and other deleterious substances and to permit thorough cleaning and disinfection. Rooms for animal injection and bleeding, and rooms for smallpox vaccine animals, shall be disinfected and be provided with the necessary water, electrical and other services.

(d) Animal quarters and stables. Animal quarters, stables and food storage areas shall be of appropriate construction, fly-proofed, adequately lighted and ventilated, and maintained in a clean, vermin-free and sanitary condition. No manure or refuse shall be stored as to permit the breeding of flies on the premises, nor shall the establishment be located in close proximity to off-property manure or refuse storage capable of engendering fly breeding.

(e) Restrictions on building and equipment use—

(1) Work of a diagnostic nature. Laboratory procedures of a clinical diagnostic nature involving materials that may be contaminated, shall not be performed in space used for the manufacture of products except that

manufacturing space which is used only occasionally may be used for diagnostic work provided spore-forming pathogenic microorganisms are not involved and provided the space is thoroughly cleaned and disinfected before the manufacture of products is resumed.

(2) Spore-forming organisms for supplemental sterilization procedure control test. Spore-forming organisms used as an additional control in sterilization procedures may be introduced into areas used for the manufacture of products, only for the purposes of the test and only immediately before use for such purposes: *Provided*, That (i) the organism is not pathogenic for man or animals and does not produce pyrogens or toxins, (ii) the culture is demonstrated to be pure, (iii) transfer of test cultures to culture media shall be limited to the sterility test area or areas designated for work with spore-forming organisms, (iv) each culture be labeled with the name of the microorganism and the statement "Caution: microbial spores. See directions for storage, use and disposition.", and (v) the container of each culture is designed to withstand handling without breaking.

(3) Work with spore-forming microorganisms.

(i) Manufacturing processes using spore-forming microorganisms conducted in a multiproduct manufacturing site must be performed under appropriate controls to prevent contamination of other products and areas within the site. Prevention of spore contamination can be achieved by using a separate dedicated building or by using process containment if manufacturing is conducted in a multiproduct manufacturing building. All product and personnel movement between the area where the spore-forming microorganisms are manufactured and other manufacturing areas must be conducted under conditions that will prevent the introduction of spores into other areas of the facility.

(ii) If process containment is employed in a multiproduct manufacturing area, procedures must be in place to demonstrate adequate removal of the spore-forming microorganism(s) from the manufacturing area for subsequent manufacture of other products. These procedures must provide for adequate removal or decontamination of the spore-forming microorganisms on and within manufacturing equipment, facilities, and ancillary room items as well as the removal of disposable or product dedicated items from the manufacturing area. Environmental monitoring specific for the spore-forming microorganism(s) must be conducted in adjacent areas during manufacturing operations and in the manufacturing area after completion of cleaning and decontamination.

(4) Live vaccine processing. Live vaccine processing must be performed under appropriate controls to prevent cross contamination of other products and other manufacturing areas within the building. Appropriate controls must include, at a minimum:

(i) (A) Using a dedicated manufacturing area that is either in a separate building, in a separate wing of a building, or in quarters at the blind end of a corridor and includes adequate space and equipment for all processing steps up to, but not including, filling into final containers; and

(B) Not conducting test procedures that potentially involve the presence of microorganisms other than the vaccine strains or the use of tissue culture cell lines other than primary cultures in space used for processing live vaccine; or

(ii) If manufacturing is conducted in a multiproduct manufacturing building or area, using procedural controls, and where necessary, process containment. Process containment is deemed to be necessary unless procedural controls are sufficient to prevent cross contamination of other products and other manufacturing areas within the building. Process containment is a system designed to mechanically isolate equipment or an area that involves manufacturing using live vaccine organisms. All product, equipment, and personnel movement between distinct live vaccine processing areas and between live vaccine processing areas and other manufacturing areas, up to, but not including, filling in final containers, must be conducted under conditions that will prevent cross contamination of other products and manufacturing areas within the building, including the introduction of live vaccine organisms into other areas. In addition, written procedures and effective processes must be in place to adequately remove or decontaminate live vaccine organisms from the manufacturing area and equipment for subsequent manufacture of other products. Written procedures must be in place for verification that processes to remove or decontaminate live vaccine organisms have been followed.

(5) Equipment and supplies—contamination. Equipment and supplies used in work on or otherwise exposed to any pathogenic or potentially pathogenic agent shall be kept separated from equipment and supplies used in the manufacture of products to the extent necessary to prevent cross-contamination.

(f) Animals used in manufacture—

(1) Care of animals used in manufacturing. Caretakers and attendants for animals used for the manufacture of products shall be sufficient in number and have adequate experience to insure adequate care. Animal quarters and cages shall be kept in sanitary condition. Animals on production shall be inspected daily to observe response to production procedures. Animals that become ill for reasons not related to production shall be isolated from other animals and shall not be used for production until recovery is complete. Competent veterinary care shall be provided as needed.

(2) Quarantine of animals—

(i) General. No animal shall be used in processing unless kept under competent daily inspection and preliminary quarantine for a period of at least 7 days before use, or as otherwise provided in this subchapter. Only healthy animals free from detectable communicable diseases shall be used. Animals must remain in overt good health throughout the quarantine periods and particular care shall be taken during the quarantine periods to reject animals of the equine genus which may be infected with glanders and animals which may be infected with tuberculosis.

(ii) Quarantine of monkeys. In addition to observing the pertinent general quarantine requirements, monkeys used as a source of tissue in the manufacture of vaccine shall be maintained in quarantine for at least 6 weeks prior to use, except when otherwise provided in this part. Only monkeys that have reacted negatively to tuberculin at the start of the quarantine period and again within 2 weeks prior to use shall be used in the manufacture of vaccine. Due precaution shall be taken to prevent cross-infection from any infected or potentially infected monkeys on the premises. Monkeys to be used in the manufacture of a live vaccine shall be maintained throughout the quarantine period in cages closed on all sides with solid materials except the front which shall be screened, with no more than two monkeys housed in one cage. Cage mates shall not be interchanged.

(3) Immunization against tetanus. Horses and other animals susceptible to tetanus, that are used in the processing steps of the manufacture of biological products, shall be treated adequately to maintain immunity to tetanus.

(4) Immunization and bleeding of animals used as a source of products. Toxins or other nonviable antigens administered in the immunization of animals used in the manufacture of products shall be sterile. Viable antigens, when so used, shall be free of contaminants, as determined by appropriate tests prior to use. Injections shall not be made into horses within 6 inches of bleeding site. Horses shall not be bled for manufacturing purposes while showing persistent general reaction or local reaction near the site of bleeding. Blood shall not be used if it was drawn within 5 days of injecting the animals with viable microorganisms. Animals shall not be bled for manufacturing purposes when they have an intercurrent disease. Blood intended for use as a source of a biological product shall be collected in clean, sterile vessels. When the product is intended for use by injection, such vessels shall also be pyrogen-free.

(5) [Reserved]

(6) Reporting of certain diseases. In cases of actual or suspected infection with foot and mouth disease, glanders, tetanus, anthrax, gas gangrene, equine infectious anemia; equine encephalomyelitis, or any of the pock diseases among animals intended for use or used in the manufacture of products, the manufacturer shall immediately notify the Director, Center for Biologics Evaluation and Research or the Director, Center for Drug Evaluation and Research (see mailing addresses in §§ 600.2(a) or (b)).

(7) Monkeys used previously for experimental or test purposes. Monkeys that have been used previously for experimental or test purposes with live microbiological agents shall not be used as a source of kidney tissue for the manufacture of vaccine. Except as provided otherwise in this subchapter, monkeys that have been used previously for other experimental or test purposes may be used as a source of kidney tissue upon their return to a normal condition, provided all quarantine requirements have been met.

(8) Necropsy examination of monkeys. Each monkey used in the manufacture of vaccine shall be examined at necropsy under the direction of a qualified pathologist, physician, or veterinarian having experience with diseases of monkeys, for evidence of ill health, particularly for (i) evidence of tuberculosis, (ii) presence of herpes-like lesions, including eruptions or plaques on or around the lips, in the buccal cavity or on the gums, and (iii) signs of conjunctivitis. If there are any such signs or other significant gross pathological lesions, the tissue shall not be used in the manufacture of vaccine.

(g) Filling procedures. Filling procedures shall be such as will not affect adversely the safety, purity or potency of the product.

(h) Containers and closures. All final containers and closures shall be made of material that will not hasten the deterioration of the product or otherwise render it less suitable for the intended use. All final containers and closures shall be clean and free of surface solids, leachable contaminants and other materials that will hasten the deterioration of the product or otherwise render it less suitable for the intended use. After filling, sealing shall be performed in a manner that will maintain the integrity of the product during the dating period. In addition, final containers and closures for products intended for use by injection shall be sterile and free from pyrogens. Except as otherwise provided in the regulations of this subchapter, final containers for products intended for use by injection shall be colorless and sufficiently transparent to permit visual examination of the contents under normal light. As soon as possible after filling final containers shall be labeled as prescribed in §§ 610.60 et seq. of this chapter, except that final containers may be stored without such prescribed labeling provided they are stored in a sealed receptacle labeled both inside and outside with at least the name of the product, the lot number, and the filling identification.

[38 FR 32048, Nov. 20, 1973, as amended at 41 FR 10428, March 11, 1976; 49 FR 23833, June 8, 1984; 55 FR 11013, March 26, 1990; 68 FR 75119, Dec. 30, 2003; 69 FR 26768, May 14, 2004; 70 FR 14982, March 24, 2005; 72 FR 59003, Oct. 18, 2007; 73 FR 12262, March 7, 2008; 80 FR 18092, April 3, 2015]

21 CFR 600.12. Records.

(a) Maintenance of records. Records shall be made, concurrently with the performance, of each step in the manufacture and distribution of products, in such a manner that at any time successive steps in the manufacture and distribution of any lot may be traced by an inspector. Such records shall be legible and indelible, shall identify the person immediately responsible, shall include dates of the various steps, and be as detailed as necessary for clear understanding of each step by one experienced in the manufacture of products.

(b) Records retention—

(1) General. Records shall be retained for such interval beyond the expiration date as is necessary for the individual product, to permit the return of any clinical report of unfavorable reactions. The retention period shall be no less than five years after the records of manufacture have been completed or six months after the latest expiration date for the individual product, whichever represents a later date.

(2) Records of recall. Complete records shall be maintained pertaining to the recall from distribution of any product upon notification by the Director, Center for Biologics Evaluation and Research or the Director, Center for Drug Evaluation and Research, to recall for failure to conform with the standards prescribed in the regulations of this subchapter, because of deterioration of the product or for any other factor by reason of which the distribution of the product would constitute a danger to health.

(3) Suspension of requirement for retention. The Director, Center for Biologics Evaluation and Research or the Director, Center for Drug Evaluation and Research, may authorize the suspension of the requirement to retain records of a specific manufacturing step upon a showing that such records no longer have significance for the purposes for which they were made: *Provided*, That a summary of such records shall be retained.

(c) Records of sterilization of equipment and supplies. Records relating to the mode of sterilization, date, duration, temperature and other conditions relating to each sterilization of equipment and supplies used in the processing of products shall be made by means of automatic recording devices or by means of a system of recording which gives equivalent assurance of the accuracy and reliability of the record. Such records shall be maintained in a manner that permits an identification of the product with the particular manufacturing process to which the sterilization relates.

(d) *Animal necropsy records.* A necropsy record shall be kept on each animal from which a biological product has been obtained and which dies or is sacrificed while being so used.

(e) *Records in case of divided manufacturing responsibility.* If two or more establishments participate in the manufacture of a product, the records of each such establishment must show plainly the degree of its responsibility. In addition, each participating manufacturer shall furnish to the manufacturer who prepares the product in final form for sale, barter or exchange, a copy of all records relating to the manufacturing operations performed by such participating manufacturer insofar as they concern the safety, purity and potency of the lots of the product involved, and the manufacturer who prepares the product in final form shall retain a complete record of all the manufacturing operations relating to the product.

[49 FR 23833, June 8, 1984; 55 FR 11013, March 26, 1990; 70 FR 14982, March 24, 2005]

21 CFR 600.13.   Retention samples.

Manufacturers shall retain for a period of at least 6 months after the expiration date, unless a different time period is specified in additional standards, a quantity of representative material of each lot of each product, sufficient for examination and testing for safety and potency, except Whole Blood, Cryoprecipitated AHF, Platelets, Red Blood Cells, Plasma, and Source Plasma and Allergenic Products prepared to a physician's prescription. Samples so retained shall be selected at random from either final container material, or from bulk and final containers, provided they include at least one final container as a final package, or package-equivalent of such filling of each lot of the product as intended for distribution. Such sample material shall be stored at temperatures and under conditions which will maintain the identity and integrity of the product. Samples retained as required in this section shall be in addition to samples of specific products required to be submitted to the Center for Biologics Evaluation and Research or the Center for Drug Evaluation and Research (see mailing addresses in §§ 600.2). Exceptions may be authorized by the Director, Center for Biologics Evaluation and Research or the Director, Center for Drug Evaluation and Research, when the lot yields relatively few final containers and when such lots are prepared by the same method in large number and in close succession.

[41 FR 10428, March 11, 1976; 49 FR 23833, June 8, 1984; 50 FR 4133,

Jan. 29, 1985; 55 FR 11013, March 26, 1990; 70 FR 14982, March 24, 2005]

21 CFR 600.14. Reporting of biological product deviations by licensed manufacturers.

(a) Who must report under this section?

(1) You, the manufacturer who holds the biological product license and who had control over the product when the deviation occurred, must report under this section. If you arrange for another person to perform a manufacturing, holding, or distribution step, while the product is in your control, that step is performed under your control. You must establish, maintain, and follow a procedure for receiving information from that person on all deviations, complaints, and adverse events concerning the affected product.

(2) Exceptions:

(i) Persons who manufacture only in vitro diagnostic products that are not subject to licensing under section 351 of the Public Health Service Act do not report biological product deviations for those products under this section but must report in accordance with part 803 of this chapter;

(ii) Persons who manufacture blood and blood components, including licensed manufacturers, unlicensed registered blood establishments, and transfusion services, do not report biological product deviations for those products under this section but must report under §§ 606.171 of this chapter;

(iii) Persons who manufacture Source Plasma or any other blood component and use that Source Plasma or any other blood component in the further manufacture of another licensed biological product must report:

(A) Under §§ 606.171 of this chapter, if a biological product deviation occurs during the manufacture of that Source Plasma or any other blood component; or

(B) Under this section, if a biological product deviation occurs after the manufacture of that Source Plasma or any other blood component, and during manufacture of the licensed biological product.

(b) What do I report under this section? You must report

any event, and information relevant to the event, associated with the manufacturing, to include testing, processing, packing, labeling, or storage, or with the holding or distribution, of a licensed biological product, if that event meets all the following criteria:

(1) Either:

(i) Represents a deviation from current good manufacturing practice, applicable regulations, applicable standards, or established specifications that may affect the safety, purity, or potency of that product; or

(ii) Represents an unexpected or unforeseeable event that may affect the safety, purity, or potency of that product; and

(2) Occurs in your facility or another facility under contract with you; and

(3) Involves a distributed biological product.

(c) When do I report under this section? You should report a biological product deviation as soon as possible but you must report at a date not to exceed 45-calendar days from the date you, your agent, or another person who performs a manufacturing, holding, or distribution step under your control, acquire information reasonably suggesting that a reportable event has occurred.

(d) How do I report under this section You must report on Form FDA-3486.

(e) Where do I report under this section?

(1) For biological products regulated by the Center for Biologics Evaluation and Research (CBER), send the completed Form FDA 3486 to the CBER Document Control Center (see mailing address in §§ 600.2(a)), or submit electronically using CBER's electronic Web-based application.

(2) For biological products regulated by the Center for Drug Evaluation and Research (CDER), send the completed Form FDA-3486 to the Division of Compliance Risk Management and Surveillance (HFD-330) (see mailing addresses in §§ 600.2). CDER does not currently accept electronic filings.

(3) If you make a paper filing, you should identify on the envelope that a biological product deviation report (BPDR) is enclosed.

(f) How does this regulation affect other FDA regulations? This part supplements and does not supersede other provisions of the regulations in this chapter. All biological product deviations, whether or not they are required to be reported under this section, should be investigated in accordance with the applicable provisions of parts 211 and 820 of this chapter.

[49 FR 23833, June 8, 1984; 49 FR 36348, Sept. 14, 1984; 49 FR 36644, Sept. 19, 1984; 55 FR 11014, March 26, 1990; 65 FR 66634, Nov. 7, 2000; 65 FR 67477, Nov. 9, 2000; 70 FR 14982, March 24, 2005; 80 FR 18092, April 3, 2015]

21 CFR 600.15.   Temperatures during shipment.

The following products shall be maintained during shipment at the specified temperatures:

(a) Products.

Product	Temperature
Cryoprecipitated AHF	-18 °C or colder.
Measles and Rubella Virus Vaccine Live	10 °C or colder.
Measles Live and Smallpox Vaccine	Do.
Measles, Mumps, and Rubella Virus Vaccine Live	Do.
Measles and Mumps Virus Vaccine Live	Do.
Measles Virus Vaccine Live	Do.
Mumps Virus Vaccine Live	Do.
Fresh Frozen Plasma	-18 °C or colder.
Liquid Plasma	1° to 10°C.
Plasma	-18 °C or colder.
Platelet Rich Plasma	Between 1 and 10 °C if the label indicates storage between 1 and 6 °C, or all reasonable methods to maintain the temperature as close as possible to a range between 20 and 24 °C, if the label indicates storage between 20 and 24 °C.

Product	Temperature
Platelets	Between 1 and 10 °C if the label indicates storage between 1 and 6 °C, or all reasonable methods to maintain the temperature as close as possible to a range between 20 to 24 °C, if the label indicates storage between 20 and 24 °C.
Poliovirus Vaccine Live Oral Trivalent	0 °C or colder.
Poliovirus Vaccine Live Oral Type I	Do.
Poliovirus Vaccine Live Oral Type II	Do.
Poliovirus Vaccine Live Oral Type III	Do.
Red Blood Cells (liquid product)	Between 1 and 10 °C.
Red Blood Cells Frozen	-65 °C or colder.
Rubella and Mumps Virus Vaccine Live	10 °C or colder.
Rubella Virus Vaccine Live	Do.
Smallpox Vaccine (Liquid Product)	0 °C or colder.
Source Plasma	-5 °C or colder.
Source Plasma Liquid	10 °C or colder.
Whole Blood	Blood that is transported from the collecting facility to the processing facility shall be transported in an environment capable of continuously cooling the blood toward a temperature range of 1 ° to 10 °C, or at a temperature as close as possible to 20 ° to 24 °C for a period not to exceed 6 hours. Blood transported from the storage facility shall be placed in an appropriate environment to maintain a temperature range between 1 to 10 °C during shipment.

Product	Temperature
Yellow Fever Vaccine	0 °C or colder.

(b) Exemptions. Exemptions or modifications shall be made only upon written approval, in the form of a supplement to the biologics license application, approved by the Director, Center for Biologics Evaluation and Research.

[39 FR 39872, Nov. 12, 1974, as amended at 40 FR 4304, Jan. 29, 1975; 42 FR 10983, Feb. 25, 1977; 42 FR 59877, Nov. 22, 1977; 47 FR 49020, Oct. 29, 1982; 49 FR 23833, June 8, 1984; 50 FR 4133, Jan. 29, 1985; 50 FR 9000, March 6, 1985; 55 FR 11013, March 26, 1990; 59 FR 49351, Sept. 28, 1994; 64 FR 56449, Oct. 20, 1999]

SUBPART C —ESTABLISHMENT INSPECTION
21 CFR 600.20. Inspectors.

Inspections shall be made by an officer of the Food and Drug Administration having special knowledge of the methods used in the manufacture and control of products and designated for such purposes by the Commissioner of Food and Drugs, or by any officer, agent, or employee of the Department of Health and Human Services specifically designated for such purpose by the Secretary.

21 CFR 600.21. Time of inspection.

The inspection of an establishment for which a biologics license application is pending need not be made until the establishment is in operation and is manufacturing the complete product for which a biologics license is desired.

[38 FR 32048, Nov. 20, 1973, as amended at 48 FR 26314, June 7, 1983; 64 FR 56449, Oct. 20, 1999; 83 FR 3589, Jan. 26, 2018; 83 FR 19936, May 7, 2018; 84 FR 12508, April 2, 2019]

21 CFR 600.22. [Reserved by 84 FR 12508]
[Reserved]

[84 FR 12508, April 2, 2019]

Subpart D —Reporting of Adverse Experiences
21 CFR 600.80. Postmarketing reporting of adverse experiences.

(a) Definitions. The following definitions of terms apply to this section:

Adverse experience. Any adverse event associated with the use of a biological product in humans, whether or not considered product related, including the following: An adverse event occurring in the course of the use of a biological product in professional practice; an adverse event occurring from overdose of the product whether accidental or intentional; an adverse event occurring from abuse of the product; an adverse event occurring from withdrawal of the product; and any failure of expected pharmacological action.

Blood Component. As defined in §§ 606.3(c) of this chapter.

Disability. A substantial disruption of a person's ability to conduct normal life functions.

Individual case safety report (ICSR). A description of an adverse experience related to an individual patient or subject.

ICSR attachments. Documents related to the adverse experience described in an ICSR, such as medical records, hospital discharge summaries, or other documentation.

Life-threatening adverse experience. Any adverse experience that places the patient, in the view of the initial reporter, at immediate risk of death from the adverse experience as it occurred, i.e., it does not include an adverse experience that, had it occurred in a more severe form, might have caused death.

Serious adverse experience. Any adverse experience occurring at any dose that results in any of the following outcomes: Death, a life-threatening adverse experience, inpatient hospitalization or prolongation of existing hospitalization, a persistent or significant disability/incapacity, or a congenital anomaly/birth defect. Important medical events that may not result in death, be life-threatening, or require hospitalization may be considered a serious adverse experience when, based upon appropriate medical judgment, they may jeopardize the patient or subject and may require medical or surgical intervention to prevent one of the outcomes listed in this definition. Examples of such medical events include allergic bronchospasm requiring intensive treatment in an emergency room or at home, blood dyscrasias or convulsions that do not result in inpatient hospitalization, or the development of drug dependency or drug abuse.

Unexpected adverse experience: Any adverse experience that is not listed in the current labeling for the biological product. This includes events that may be symptomatically and pathophysiologically related to an event listed in the labeling, but differ from the event because of greater severity or specificity. For example, under this definition, hepatic necrosis would be unexpected (by virtue of greater severity) if the labeling only referred to elevated hepatic enzymes or hepatitis. Similarly, cerebral thromboembolism and cerebral vasculitis would be unexpected (by virtue of greater specificity) if the labeling only listed cerebral vascular accidents. "Unexpected," as used in this definition, refers to an adverse experience that has not been previously observed (i.e., included in the labeling) rather than from the perspective of such experience not being anticipated from the pharmacological properties of the pharmaceutical product.

(b) Review of adverse experiences. Any person having a biologics license under §§ 601.20 of this chapter must promptly review all adverse experience information pertaining to its product obtained or otherwise received by the applicant from any source, foreign or domestic, including information derived from commercial marketing experience, postmarketing clinical investigations, postmarketing epidemiological/surveillance studies, reports in the scientific literature, and unpublished scientific papers. Applicants are not required to resubmit to FDA adverse product experience reports forwarded to the applicant by FDA; applicants, however, must submit all followup information on such reports to FDA. Any person subject to the reporting requirements under paragraph (c) of this section must also develop written procedures for the surveillance, receipt, evaluation, and reporting of postmarketing adverse experiences to FDA.

(c) Reporting requirements. The applicant must submit to FDA postmarketing 15-day Alert reports and periodic safety reports pertaining to its biological product as described in this section. These reports must be submitted to the Agency in electronic format as described in paragraph (h)(1) of this section, except as provided in paragraph (h)(2) of this section.

(1) (i) Postmarketing 15-day "Alert reports". The applicant must report each adverse experience that is both serious and unexpected, whether foreign or domestic, as soon as possible but no later than 15 calendar days from initial receipt of the information by the applicant.

(ii) Postmarketing 15-day "Alert reports"— followup. The applicant must promptly investigate all adverse experiences that are the subject of these postmarketing 15-day Alert reports and must submit followup reports within 15 calendar days of receipt of new information or as requested by FDA. If additional information is not obtainable, records should be maintained of the unsuccessful steps taken to seek additional information.

(iii) Submission of reports. The requirements of paragraphs (c)(1)(i) and (c)(1)(ii) of this section, concerning the submission of postmarketing 15-day Alert reports, also apply to any person whose name appears on the label of a licensed biological product as a manufacturer, packer, distributor, shared manufacturer, joint manufacturer, or any other participant involved in divided manufacturing. To avoid unnecessary duplication in the submission to FDA of reports required by paragraphs (c)(1)(i) and (c)(1)(ii) of this section, obligations of persons other than the applicant of the final biological product may be met by submission of all reports of serious adverse experiences to the applicant of the final product. If a person elects to submit adverse experience reports to the applicant rather than to FDA, the person must submit, by any appropriate means, each report to the applicant within 5 calendar days of initial receipt of the information by the person, and the applicant must then comply with the requirements of this section. Under this circumstance, a person who elects to submit reports to the applicant of the final product shall maintain a record of this action which must include:

(A) A copy of all adverse biological product experience reports submitted to the applicant of the final product;

(B) The date the report was received by the person;

(C) The date the report was submitted to the applicant of the final product; and—

(D) The name and address of the applicant of the final product.

(2) Periodic adverse experience reports.

(i) The applicant must report each adverse experience not reported under paragraph (c)(1)(i) of this section at quarterly intervals, for 3 years from the date of issuance of the biologics license, and then at annual intervals. The applicant must submit each quarterly report within 30 days of the close of the quarter (the first quarter beginning on the date of issuance of the biologics license) and each annual report within 60 days of the anniversary date of the issuance of the biologics license. Upon written notice, FDA may extend or reestablish the requirement that an applicant submit quarterly reports, or require that the applicant submit reports under this section at different times than those stated. Followup information to adverse experiences submitted in a periodic report may be submitted in the next periodic report.

(ii) Each periodic report is required to contain:

(A) Descriptive information.

(1) A narrative summary and analysis of the information in the report;

(2) An analysis of the 15-day Alert reports submitted during the reporting interval (all 15-day Alert reports being appropriately referenced by the applicant's patient identification code for nonvaccine biological product reports or by the unique case identification number for vaccine reports, adverse reaction term(s), and date of submission to FDA);

(3) A history of actions taken since the last report because of adverse experiences (for example, labeling changes or studies initiated);

(4) An index consisting of a line listing of the applicant's patient identification code for nonvaccine biological product reports or by the unique case identification number for vaccine reports and adverse reaction term(s) for ICSRs submitted under paragraph (c)(2)(ii)(B) of this section; and

(B) ICSRs for serious, expected and, nonserious adverse experiences. An ICSR for each adverse experience not reported under paragraph (c)(1)(i) of this section (all serious, expected and nonserious adverse experiences). All such ICSRs must be submitted to FDA (either individually or in one or more batches) within the timeframe specified in paragraph (c)(2)(i) of this section. ICSRs must only be submitted to FDA once.

(iii) Periodic reporting, except for information regarding 15-day Alert reports, does not apply to adverse experience information obtained from postmarketing studies (whether or not conducted under an investigational new drug application), from reports in the scientific literature, and from foreign marketing experience.

(d) Scientific literature. A 15-day Alert report based on information in the scientific literature must be accompanied by a copy of the published article. The 15-day Alert reporting requirements in paragraph (c)(1)(i) of this section (i.e., serious, unexpected adverse experiences) apply only to reports found in scientific and medical journals either as case reports or as the result of a formal clinical trial.

(e) Postmarketing studies. Applicants are not required to submit a 15-day Alert report under paragraph (c) of this section for an adverse experience obtained from a postmarketing clinical study (whether or not conducted under a biological investigational new drug application) unless the applicant concludes that there is a reasonable possibility that the product caused the adverse experience.

(f) Information reported on ICSRs for nonvaccine biological products. ICSRs for nonvaccine biological products include the following information:

(1) Patient information.

(i)   Patient identification code;

(ii)   Patient age at the time of adverse experience, or date of birth;

(iii)   Patient gender; and

(iv)   Patient weight.

(2) Adverse experience.

(i)   Outcome attributed to adverse experience;

(ii)   Date of adverse experience;

(iii)   Date of report;

(iv)   Description of adverse experience (including a concise medical narrative);

(v)   Adverse experience term(s);

(vi)   Description of relevant tests, including dates and laboratory data; and

(vii)   Other relevant patient history, including preexisting medical conditions.

(3) Suspect medical product(s).

(i)   Name;

(ii)   Dose, frequency, and route of administration used;

(iii)   Therapy dates;

(iv)   Diagnosis for use (indication);

(v)   Whether the product is a combination product as defined in §§ 3.2(e) of this chapter;

(vi) Whether the product is a prescription or nonprescription product;

(vii) Whether adverse experience abated after product use stopped or dose reduced;

(viii) Whether adverse experience reappeared after reintroduction of the product;

(ix) Lot number;

(x) Expiration date;

(xi) National Drug Code (NDC) number, or other unique identifier; and

(xii) Concomitant medical products and therapy dates.

(4) Initial reporter information.

(i) Name, address, and telephone number;

(ii) Whether the initial reporter is a health care professional; and

(iii) Occupation, if a health care professional.

(5) Applicant information.

(i) Applicant name and contact office address;

(ii) Telephone number;

(iii) Report source, such as spontaneous, literature, or study;

(iv) Date the report was received by applicant;

(v) Application number and type;

(vi) Whether the ICSR is a 15-day "Alert report";

(vii) Whether the ICSR is an initial report or followup report; and

(viii) Unique case identification number, which must be the same in the initial report and any subsequent followup report(s).

(g) Information reported on ICSRs for vaccine products. ICSRs for vaccine products include the following information:

(1) Patient information.

(i) Patient name, address, telephone number;

(ii) Patient age at the time of vaccination, or date of birth;

(iii) Patient gender; and

(iv) Patient birth weight for children under age 5.

(2) Adverse experience.

(i)   Outcome attributed to adverse experience;

(ii)   Date and time of adverse experience;

(iii)   Date of report;

(iv)   Description of adverse experience (including a concise medical narrative);

(v)   Adverse experience term(s);

(vi)   Illness at the time of vaccination;

(vii)   Description of relevant tests, including dates and laboratory data; and

(viii)   Other relevant patient history, including preexisting medical conditions.

(3) Suspect medical product(s), including vaccines administered on the same date.

(i)   Name;

(ii)   Dose, frequency, and route or site of administration used;

(iii)   Number of previous vaccine doses;

(iv)   Vaccination date(s) and time(s);

(v)   Diagnosis for use (indication);

(vi)   Whether the product is a combination product (as defined in §§ 3.2(e) of this chapter);

(vii)   Whether the adverse experience abated after product use stopped or dose reduced;

(viii)   Whether the adverse experience reappeared after reintroduction of the product;

(ix)   Lot number;

(x)   Expiration date;

(xi)   National Drug Code (NDC) number, or other unique identifier; and

(xii)   Concomitant medical products and therapy dates.

(4) Vaccine(s) administered in the 4 weeks prior to the vaccination date.

(i)   Name of vaccine;

(ii)   Manufacturer;

(iii)   Lot number;

(iv)   Route or site of administration;

(v)   Date given; and

(vi)   Number of previous doses.

(5) Initial reporter information.

(i) Name, address, and telephone number;

(ii) Whether the initial reporter is a health care professional; and

(iii) Occupation, if a health care professional.

(6) Facility and personnel where vaccine was administered.

(i) Name of person who administered vaccine;

(ii) Name of responsible physician at facility where vaccine was administered; and

(iii) Name, address (including city, county, and state), and telephone number of facility where vaccine was administered.

(7) Applicant information.

(i) Applicant name and contact office address;

(ii) Telephone number;

(iii) Report source, such as spontaneous, literature, or study;

(iv) Date received by applicant;

(v) Application number and type;

(vi) Whether the ICSR is a 15-day "Alert report";

(vii) Whether the ICSR is an initial report or followup report; and

(viii) Unique case identification number, which must be the same in the initial report and any subsequent followup report(s).

(h) Electronic format for submissions.

(1) Safety report submissions, including ICSRs, ICSR attachments, and the descriptive information in periodic reports, must be in an electronic format that FDA can process, review, and archive. FDA will issue guidance on how to provide the electronic submission (e.g., method of transmission, media, file formats, preparation and organization of files).

(2) Persons subject to the requirements of paragraph (c) of this section may request, in writing, a temporary waiver of the requirements in paragraph (h)(1) of this section. These waivers will be granted on a limited basis for good cause shown. FDA will issue guidance on requesting a waiver of the requirements in paragraph (h)(1) of this section. Requests for waivers must be submitted in accordance with §§ 600.90.

(i) Multiple reports. An applicant should not include in reports under this section any adverse experience that occurred in clinical trials if they were previously submitted as part of the biologics license application. If a report refers to more than one biological product marketed by an applicant, the applicant should submit the report to the biologics license application for the product listed first in the report.

(j) Patient privacy. For nonvaccine biological products, an applicant should not include in reports under this section the names and addresses of individual patients; instead, the applicant should assign a unique code for identification of the patient. The applicant should include the name of the reporter from whom the information was received as part of the initial reporter information, even when the reporter is the patient. The names of patients, health care professionals, hospitals, and geographical identifiers in adverse experience reports are not releasable to the public under FDA's public information regulations in part 20 of this chapter. For vaccine adverse experience reports, these data will become part of the CDC Privacy Act System 09-20-0136, "Epidemiologic Studies and Surveillance of Disease Problems." Information identifying the person who received the vaccine or that person's legal representative will not be made available to the public, but may be available to the vaccinee or legal representative.

(k) Recordkeeping. The applicant must maintain for a period of 10 years records of all adverse experiences known to the applicant, including raw data and any correspondence relating to the adverse experiences.

(l) Revocation of biologics license. If an applicant fails to establish and maintain records and make reports required under this section with respect to a licensed biological product, FDA may revoke the biologics license for such a product in accordance with the procedures of §§ 601.5 of this chapter.

(m) Exemptions. Manufacturers of the following listed products are not required to submit adverse experience reports under this section:

(1) Whole blood or components of whole blood.

(2) In vitro diagnostic products, including assay systems for the detection of antibodies or antigens to retroviruses. These products are subject to the reporting requirements for devices.

(n) Disclaimer. A report or information submitted by an

applicant under this section (and any release by FDA of that report or information) does not necessarily reflect a conclusion by the applicant or FDA that the report or information constitutes an admission that the biological product caused or contributed to an adverse effect. An applicant need not admit, and may deny, that the report or information submitted under this section constitutes an admission that the biological product caused or contributed to an adverse effect. For purposes of this provision, this paragraph also includes any person reporting under paragraph (c)(1)(iii) of this section.

[62 FR 34168, June 25, 1997; 62 FR 52252, Oct. 7, 1997; 63 FR 14612, March 26, 1998; 64 FR 56449, Oct. 20, 1999; 70 FR 14982, March 24, 2005; 79 FR 33090, June 10, 2014; 80 FR 30152, May 27, 2015]

21 CFR 600.81. Distribution reports.

(a) Reporting requirements. The applicant must submit to the Center for Biologics Evaluation and Research or the Center for Drug Evaluation and Research, information about the quantity of the product distributed under the biologics license, including the quantity distributed to distributors. The interval between distribution reports must be 6 months. Upon written notice, FDA may require that the applicant submit distribution reports under this section at times other than every 6 months. The distribution report must consist of the bulk lot number (from which the final container was filled), the fill lot numbers for the total number of dosage units of each strength or potency distributed (e.g., fifty thousand per 10-milliliter vials), the label lot number (if different from fill lot number), labeled date of expiration, number of doses in fill lot/label lot, date of release of fill lot/label lot for distribution at that time. If any significant amount of a fill lot/label lot is returned, include this information. Disclosure of financial or pricing data is not required. As needed, FDA may require submission of more detailed product distribution information. Upon written notice, FDA may require that the applicant submit reports under this section at times other than those stated. Requests by an applicant to submit reports at times other than those stated should be made as a request for a waiver under §§ 600.90.

(b) (1) Electronic format. Except as provided for in paragraph (b)(2) of this section, the distribution reports required under paragraph (a) of this section must be submitted to the Agency in an electronic format that FDA can process, review, and archive. FDA will issue guidance on how to provide the electronic submission (e.g., method of transmission, media, file formats, preparation and organization of files).

(2) Waivers. An applicant may request, in writing, a temporary waiver of the requirements in paragraph (b)(1) of this section. These waivers will be granted on a limited basis for good cause shown. FDA will issue guidance on requesting a waiver of the requirements in paragraph (b)(1) of this section. Requests for waivers must be submitted in accordance with §§ 600.90.

[64 FR 56449, Oct. 20, 1999; 70 FR 14983, March 24, 2005; 79 FR 33091, June 10, 2014; 80 FR 30152, May 27, 2015]

21 CFR 600.82. Notification of a permanent discontinuance or an interruption in manufacturing.

(a) Notification of a permanent discontinuance or an interruption in manufacturing.

(1) An applicant of a biological product, other than blood or blood components for transfusion, which is licensed under section 351 of the Public Health Service Act, and which may be dispensed only under prescription under section 503(b)(1) of the Federal Food, Drug, and Cosmetic Act (21 U.S.C. 353(b)(1)), must notify FDA in writing of a permanent discontinuance of manufacture of the biological product or an interruption in manufacturing of the biological product that is likely to lead to a meaningful disruption in supply of that biological product in the United States if:

(i) The biological product is life supporting, life sustaining, or intended for use in the prevention or treatment of a debilitating disease or condition, including any such biological product used in emergency medical care or during surgery; and

(ii) The biological product is not a radiopharmaceutical biological product.

(2) An applicant of blood or blood components for transfusion, which is licensed under section 351 of the Public Health Service Act, and which may be dispensed only under prescription under section 503(b) of the Federal Food, Drug, and Cosmetic Act, must notify FDA in writing of a permanent discontinuance of manufacture of any product listed in its license or an interruption in manufacturing of any such product that is likely to lead to a significant disruption in supply of that product in the United States if:

(i) The product is life supporting, life sustaining, or intended for use in the prevention or treatment of a debilitating disease or condition, including any such product used in emergency medical care or during surgery; and

(ii) The applicant is a manufacturer of a significant percentage of the U.S. blood supply.

(b) Submission and timing of notification. Notifications required by paragraph (a) of this section must be submitted to FDA electronically in a format that FDA can process, review, and archive:

(1) At least 6 months prior to the date of the permanent discontinuance or interruption in manufacturing; or

(2) If 6 months' advance notice is not possible because the permanent discontinuance or interruption in manufacturing was not reasonably anticipated 6 months in advance, as soon as practicable thereafter, but in no case later than 5 business days after such a permanent discontinuance or interruption in manufacturing occurs.

(c) Information included in notification. Notifications required by paragraph (a) of this section must include the following information:

(1) The name of the biological product subject to the notification, including the National Drug Code for such biological product, or an alternative standard for identification and labeling that has been recognized as acceptable by the Center Director;

(2) The name of the applicant of the biological product;

(3) Whether the notification relates to a permanent discontinuance of the biological product or an interruption in manufacturing of the biological product;

(4) A description of the reason for the permanent discontinuance or interruption in manufacturing; and

(5) The estimated duration of the interruption in manufacturing.

(d)

(1) Public list of biological product shortages. FDA will maintain a publicly available list of biological products that are determined by FDA to be in shortage. This biological product shortages list will include the following information:

(i) The names and National Drug Codes for such

biological products, or the alternative standards for identification and labeling that have been recognized as acceptable by the Center Director;

(ii)   The name of each applicant for such biological products;

(iii)   The reason for the shortage, as determined by FDA, selecting from the following categories: Requirements related to complying with good manufacturing practices; regulatory delay; shortage of an active ingredient; shortage of an inactive ingredient component; discontinuation of the manufacture of the biological product; delay in shipping of the biological product; demand increase for the biological product; or other reason; and

(iv)   The estimated duration of the shortage.

(2) Confidentiality. FDA may choose not to make information collected to implement this paragraph available on the biological product shortages list or available under section 506C(c) of the Federal Food, Drug, and Cosmetic Act (21 U.S.C. 356c(c)) if FDA determines that disclosure of such information would adversely affect the public health (such as by increasing the possibility of hoarding or other disruption of the availability of the biological product to patients). FDA will also not provide information on the public shortages list or under section 506C(c) of the Federal Food, Drug, and Cosmetic Act that is protected by 18 U.S.C. 1905 or 5 U.S.C. 552(b)(4), including trade secrets and commercial or financial information that is considered confidential or privileged under §§ 20.61 of this chapter.

(e) Noncompliance letters. If an applicant fails to submit a notification as required under paragraph (a) of this section and in accordance with paragraph (b) of this section, FDA will issue a letter to the applicant informing it of such failure.

(1) Not later than 30 calendar days after the issuance of such a letter, the applicant must submit to FDA a written response setting forth the basis for noncompliance and providing the required notification under paragraph (a) of this section and including the information required under paragraph (c) of this section; and

(2) Not later than 45 calendar days after the issuance of a letter under this paragraph, FDA will make the letter and the applicant's response to the letter public, un-

less, after review of the applicant's response, FDA determines that the applicant had a reasonable basis for not notifying FDA as required under paragraph (a) of this section.

(f) Definitions. The following definitions of terms apply to this section:

Biological product shortage or shortage means a period of time when the demand or projected demand for the biological product within the United States exceeds the supply of the biological product.

Intended for use in the prevention or treatment of a debilitating disease or condition means a biological product intended for use in the prevention or treatment of a disease or condition associated with mortality or morbidity that has a substantial impact on day-to-day functioning.

Life supporting or life sustaining means a biological product that is essential to, or that yields information that is essential to, the restoration or continuation of a bodily function important to the continuation of human life.

Meaningful disruption means a change in production that is reasonably likely to lead to a reduction in the supply of a biological product by a manufacturer that is more than negligible and affects the ability of the manufacturer to fill orders or meet expected demand for its product, and does not include interruptions in manufacturing due to matters such as routine maintenance or insignificant changes in manufacturing so long as the manufacturer expects to resume operations in a short period of time.

Significant disruption means a change in production that is reasonably likely to lead to a reduction in the supply of blood or blood components by a manufacturer that substantially affects the ability of the manufacturer to fill orders or meet expected demand for its product, and does not include interruptions in manufacturing due to matters such as routine maintenance or insignificant changes in manufacturing so long as the manufacturer expects to resume operations in a short period of time.

[80 FR 38939, July 8, 2015]

21 CFR 600.90. Waivers.

(a) An applicant may ask the Food and Drug Administration to waive under this section any requirement that applies to the applicant under §§ 600.80 and 600.81. A waiver request under this section is required to be submitted with supporting documentation. The waiver request is required to contain one of the following:

(1) An explanation why the applicant's compliance with the requirement is unnecessary or cannot be achieved,

(2) A description of an alternative submission that satisfies the purpose of the requirement, or

(3) Other information justifying a waiver.

(b) FDA may grant a waiver if it finds one of the following:

(1) The applicant's compliance with the requirement is unnecessary or cannot be achieved,

(2) The applicant's alternative submission satisfies the requirement, or

(3) The applicant's submission otherwise justifies a waiver.

[79 FR 33092, June 10, 2014; 80 FR 30152, May 27, 2015]

PART 42— TRIAL PRACTICE BEFORE THE PATENT TRIAL AND APPEAL BOARD

SUBPART A— TRIAL PRACTICE AND PROCEDURE

GENERAL

§ 42.1.   Policy.

(a) Scope. Part 42 governs proceedings before the Patent Trial and Appeal Board. Sections 1.4, 1.7, 1.14, 1.16, 1.22, 1.23, 1.25, 1.26, 1.32, 1.34, and 1.36 of this chapter also apply to proceedings before the Board, as do other sections of part 1 of this chapter that are incorporated by reference into this part.

(b) Construction. This part shall be construed to secure the just, speedy, and inexpensive resolution of every proceeding.

(c) Decorum. Every party must act with courtesy and decorum in all proceedings before the Board, including in interactions with other parties.

(d) Evidentiary standard. The default evidentiary standard is a preponderance of the evidence.

§ 42.2.   Definitions.

The following definitions apply to this part:

Affidavit means affidavit or declaration under § 1.68 of this chapter. A transcript of an ex parte deposition or a declaration under 28 U.S.C. 1746 may be used as an affidavit.

Board means the Patent Trial and Appeal Board. Board means a panel of the Board, or a member or employee acting with the authority of the Board, including:

(1) For petition decisions and interlocutory decisions, a Board member or employee acting with the authority of the Board.

(2) For final written decisions under 35 U.S.C. 135(d), 318(a), and 328(a), a panel of the Board.

Business day means a day other than a Saturday, Sunday, or Federal holiday within the District of Columbia.

Confidential information means trade secret or other confidential research, development, or commercial information.

Final means final for the purpose of judicial review to the extent available. A decision is final only if it disposes of all necessary issues with regard to the party seeking judicial review, and does not indicate that further action is required.

Hearing means consideration of the trial.

Involved means an application, patent, or claim that is the subject of the proceeding.

Judgment means a final written decision by the Board, or a termination of a proceeding.

Motion means a request for relief other than by petition.

Office means the United States Patent and Trademark Office.

Panel means at least three members of the Board.

Party means at least the petitioner and the patent owner and, in a derivation proceeding, any applicant or assignee of the involved application.

Petition is a request that a trial be instituted.

Petitioner means the party filing a petition requesting that a trial be instituted.

Preliminary Proceeding begins with the filing of a petition for instituting a trial and ends with a written decision as to whether a trial will be instituted.

Proceeding means a trial or preliminary proceeding.

Rehearing means reconsideration.

Trial means a contested case instituted by the Board based upon a petition. A trial begins with a written decision notifying the petitioner and patent owner of the institution of the trial. The term trial specifically includes a derivation proceeding under 35 U.S.C. 135; an inter partes review under Chapter 31 of title 35, United States Code; a post-grant review under Chapter 32 of title 35, United States Code; and a transitional business-method review under section 18 of the Leahy–Smith America Invents Act. Patent interferences are administered under part 41 and not under part 42 of this title, and therefore are not trials.

§ 42.3.   Jurisdiction.

(a) The Board may exercise exclusive jurisdiction within the Office over every involved application and patent during the proceeding, as the Board may order.

(b) A petition to institute a trial must be filed with the Board consistent with any time period required by statute.

§ 42.4.   Notice of trial.

(a) Institution of trial. The Board institutes the trial on behalf of the Director.

(b) Notice of a trial will be sent to every party to the proceeding. The entry of the notice institutes the trial.

(c) The Board may authorize additional modes of notice, including:

(1) Sending notice to another address associated with the party, or

(2) Publishing the notice in the Official Gazette of the United States Patent and Trademark Office or the Federal Register.

§ 42.5.   Conduct of the proceeding.

(a) The Board may determine a proper course of conduct in a proceeding for any situation not specifically covered by this part and may enter non-final orders to administer the proceeding.

(b) The Board may waive or suspend a requirement of parts 1, 41, and 42 and may place conditions on the waiver or suspension.

(c) Times.

(1) Setting times. The Board may set times by order. Times set by rule are default and may be modified by order. Any modification of times will take any applicable statutory pendency goal into account.

(2) Extension of time. A request for an extension of time must be supported by a showing of good cause.

(3) Late action. A late action will be excused on a showing of good cause or upon a Board decision that consideration on the merits would be in the interests of justice.

(d) Ex parte communications. Communication regarding a specific proceeding with a Board member defined in 35 U.S.C. 6(a) is not permitted unless both parties have an opportunity to be involved in the communication.

§ 42.6. Filing of documents, including exhibits; service.

(a) General format requirements.

(1) Page size must be 8½ inch x 11 inch except in the case of exhibits that require a larger size in order to preserve details of the original.

(2) In documents, including affidavits, created for the proceeding:

(i) Markings must be in black or must otherwise provide an equivalent dark, high-contrast image;

(ii) 14–point, Times New Roman proportional font, with normal spacing, must be used;

(iii) Double spacing must be used except in claim charts, headings, tables of contents, tables of authorities, indices, signature blocks, and certificates of service. Block quotations may be 1.5 spaced, but must be indented from both the left and the right margins; and

(iv) Margins must be at least 2.5 centimeters (1 inch) on all sides.

(3) Incorporation by reference; combined documents. Arguments must not be incorporated by reference from one document into another document. Combined motions, oppositions, replies, or other combined documents are not permitted.

(4) Signature; identification. Documents must be signed in accordance with §§ 1.33 and 11.18(a) of this title, and should be identified by the trial number (where known).

(b) Modes of filing.

(1) Electronic filing. Unless otherwise authorized, submissions are to be made to the Board electronically via the Internet according to the parameters established by the Board and published on the Web site of the Office.

(2) (i) Filing by means other than electronic filing. A document filed by means other than electronic filing must:

(A) Be accompanied by a motion requesting acceptance of the submission; and

(B) Identify a date of transmission where a party seeks a filing date other than the date of receipt at the Board.

(ii) Mailed correspondence shall be sent to: Mail Stop PATENT BOARD, Patent Trial and Appeal Board, United States Patent and Trademark Office, PO Box 1450, Alexandria, Virginia 22313–1450.

(c) Exhibits. Each exhibit must be filed with the first document in which it is cited except as the Board may otherwise order.

(d) Previously filed paper. A document already in the record of the proceeding must not be filed again, not even as an exhibit or an appendix, without express Board authorization.

(e) Service.

(1) Electronic or other mode. Service may be made electronically upon agreement of the parties. Otherwise, service may be by Priority Mail Express® or by means at least as fast and reliable as Priority Mail Express®.

(2) Simultaneous with filing. Each document filed with the Board, if not previously served, must be served simultaneously on each opposing party.

(3) Counsel of record. If a party is represented by counsel of record in the proceeding, service must be on counsel.

(4) Certificate of service.

(i) Each document, other than an exhibit, must include a certificate of service at the end of that document. Any exhibit filed with the document may be included in the certification for the document.

(ii) For an exhibit filed separately, a transmittal letter incorporating the certificate of service must be filed. If more than one exhibit is filed at one time, a single letter should be used for all of the exhibits filed together. The letter must state the name and exhibit number for every exhibit filed with the letter.

(iii) The certificate of service must state:

(A) The date and manner of service; and

(B) The name and address of every person served.

[79 FR 63043, Oct. 22, 2014; 80 FR 28565, May 19, 2015]

§ 42.7. Management of the record.

(a) The Board may expunge any paper directed to a proceeding or filed while an application or patent is under the jurisdiction of the Board that is not authorized under this part or in a Board order or that is filed contrary to a Board order.

(b) The Board may vacate or hold in abeyance any non–Board action directed to a proceeding while an application or patent is under the jurisdiction of the Board unless the action was authorized by the Board.

§ 42.8. Mandatory notices.

(a) Each notice listed in paragraph (b) of this section must be filed with the Board:

(1) By the petitioner, as part of the petition;

(2) By the patent owner, or applicant in the case of derivation, within 21 days of service of the petition; or

(3) By either party, within 21 days of a change of the information listed in paragraph (b) of this section stated in an earlier paper.

(b) Each of the following notices must be filed:

(1) Real party-in-interest. Identify each real party-in-interest for the party.

(2) Related matters. Identify any other judicial or administrative matter that would affect, or be affected by, a decision in the proceeding.

(3) Lead and back-up counsel. If the party is represented by counsel, then counsel must be identified.

(4) Service information. Identify (if applicable):

(i) An electronic mail address;

(ii) A postal mailing address;

(iii) A hand-delivery address, if different than the postal mailing address;

(iv) A telephone number; and

(v) A facsimile number.

§ 42.9. Action by patent owner.

(a) Entire interest. An owner of the entire interest in an involved application or patent may act to the exclusion of the inventor (see § 3.71 of this title).

(b) Part interest. An owner of a part interest in the

subject patent may move to act to the exclusion of an inventor or a co-owner. The motion must show the inability or refusal of an inventor or co-owner to prosecute the proceeding or other cause why it is in the interests of justice to permit the owner of a part interest to act in the trial. In granting the motion, the Board may set conditions on the actions of the parties.

§ 42.10. Counsel.

(a) If a party is represented by counsel, the party must designate a lead counsel and at least one back-up counsel who can conduct business on behalf of the lead counsel.

(b) A power of attorney must be filed with the designation of counsel, except the patent owner should not file an additional power of attorney if the designated counsel is already counsel of record in the subject patent or application.

(c) The Board may recognize counsel pro hac vice during a proceeding upon a showing of good cause, subject to the condition that lead counsel be a registered practitioner and to any other conditions as the Board may impose. For example, where the lead counsel is a registered practitioner, a motion to appear pro hac vice by counsel who is not a registered practitioner may be granted upon showing that counsel is an experienced litigating attorney and has an established familiarity with the subject matter at issue in the proceeding.

(d) A panel of the Board may disqualify counsel for cause after notice and opportunity for hearing. A decision to disqualify is not final for the purposes of judicial review until certified by the Chief Administrative Patent Judge.

(e) Counsel may not withdraw from a proceeding before the Board unless the Board authorizes such withdrawal.

[80 FR 28565, May 19, 2015]

§ 42.11. Duty of candor; signing papers; representations to the Board; sanctions.

(a) Duty of candor. Parties and individuals involved in the proceeding have a duty of candor and good faith to the Office during the course of a proceeding.

(b) Signature. Every petition, response, written motion, and other paper filed in a proceeding must comply with the signature requirements set forth in § 11.18(a) of this chapter. The Board may expunge any unsigned submission unless the omission is promptly corrected after being called to the counsel's or party's attention.

(c) Representations to the Board. By presenting to the

Board a petition, response, written motion, or other paper—whether by signing, filing, submitting, or later advocating it—an attorney, registered practitioner, or unrepresented party attests to compliance with the certification requirements under § 11.18(b)(2) of this chapter.

(d) Sanctions—

(1) In general. If, after notice and a reasonable opportunity to respond, the Board determines that paragraph (c) of this section has been violated, the Board may impose an appropriate sanction on any attorney, registered practitioner, or party that violated the rule or is responsible for the violation.

(2) Motion for sanctions. A motion for sanctions must be made separately from any other motion and must describe the specific conduct that allegedly violates paragraph (c) of this section. The motion must be authorized by the Board under § 42.20 prior to filing the motion. At least 21 days prior to seeking authorization to file a motion for sanctions, the moving party must serve the other party with the proposed motion. A motion for sanctions must not be filed or be presented to the Board if the challenged paper, claim, defense, contention, or denial is withdrawn or appropriately corrected within 21 days after service of such motion or within another time the Board sets. If warranted, the Board may award to the prevailing party the reasonable expenses, including attorney's fees, incurred for the motion.

(3) On the Board's initiative. On its own, the Board may order an attorney, registered practitioner, or party to show cause why conduct specifically described in the order has not violated paragraph (c) of this section and why a specific sanction authorized by the Board should not be imposed.

(4) Nature of a sanction. A sanction imposed under this rule must be limited to what suffices to deter repetition of the conduct or comparable conduct by others similarly situated and should be consistent with § 42.12.

(5) Requirements for an order. An order imposing a sanction must describe the sanctioned conduct and explain the basis for the sanction.

[81 FR 18765, April 1, 2016]

§ 42.12. Sanctions.

(a) The Board may impose a sanction against a party for misconduct, including:

(1) Failure to comply with an applicable rule or order in the proceeding;

(2) Advancing a misleading or frivolous argument or request for relief;

(3) Misrepresentation of a fact;

(4) Engaging in dilatory tactics;

(5) Abuse of discovery;

(6) Abuse of process; or

(7) Any other improper use of the proceeding, including actions that harass or cause unnecessary delay or an unnecessary increase in the cost of the proceeding.

(b) Sanctions include entry of one or more of the following:

(1) An order holding facts to have been established in the proceeding;

(2) An order expunging or precluding a party from filing a paper;

(3) An order precluding a party from presenting or contesting a particular issue;

(4) An order precluding a party from requesting, obtaining, or opposing discovery;

(5) An order excluding evidence;

(6) An order providing for compensatory expenses, including attorney fees;

(7) An order requiring terminal disclaimer of patent term; or

(8) Judgment in the trial or dismissal of the petition.

§ 42.13. Citation of authority.

(a) For any United States Supreme Court decision, citation to the United States Reports is preferred.

(b) For any decision other than a United States Supreme Court decision, citation to the West Reporter System is preferred.

(c) Citations to authority must include pinpoint citations whenever a specific holding or portion of an authority is invoked.

(d) Non-binding authority should be used sparingly. If the authority is not an authority of the Office and is not reproduced in the United States Reports or the West Reporter System, a copy of the authority should be provided.

§ 42.14. Public availability.

The record of a proceeding, including documents and things, shall be made available to the public, except as otherwise ordered. A party intending a document or thing to be sealed shall file a motion to seal concurrent with the filing of the document or thing to be sealed. The document or thing shall be provisionally sealed on receipt of the motion and remain so pending the outcome of the decision on the motion.

FEES

§ 42.15. Fees.

(a) On filing a petition for inter partes review of a patent, payment of the following fees are due:

(1) Inter Partes Review request fee: $15,500.00.

(2) Inter Partes Review Post–Institution fee: $15,000.00.

(3) In addition to the Inter Partes Review request fee, for requesting review of each claim in excess of 20: $300.00.

(4) In addition to the Inter Partes Post–Institution request fee, for requesting review of each claim in excess of 15: $600.00.

(b) On filing a petition for post-grant review or covered business method patent review of a patent, payment of the following fees are due:

(1) Post–Grant or Covered Business Method Patent Review request fee: $16,000.00.

(2) Post–Grant or Covered Business Method Patent Review Post–Institution fee: $22,000.00.

(3) In addition to the Post–Grant or Covered Business Method Patent Review request fee, for requesting review of each claim in excess of 20: $375.00

(4) In addition to the Post–Grant or Covered Business Method Patent Review Post–Institution fee, for requesting review of each claim in excess of 15: $825.00.

(c) On the filing of a petition for a derivation proceeding, payment of the following fees is due:

(1) Derivation petition fee: $400.00.

(d) Any request requiring payment of a fee under this part, including a written request to make a settlement agreement available: $400.00.

[78 FR 4291, Jan. 18, 2013; 80 FR 28565, May 19, 2015; 82 FR 52817, Nov. 14, 2017]

PETITION AND MOTION PRACTICE

§ 42.20.   Generally.

(a) Relief. Relief, other than a petition requesting the institution of a trial, must be requested in the form of a motion.

(b) Prior authorization. A motion will not be entered without Board authorization. Authorization may be provided in an order of general applicability or during the proceeding.

(c) Burden of proof. The moving party has the burden of proof to establish that it is entitled to the requested relief.

(d) Briefing. The Board may order briefing on any issue involved in the trial.

§ 42.21.   Notice of basis for relief.

(a) Notice of request for relief. The Board may require a party to file a notice stating the relief it requests and the basis for its entitlement to relief. A notice must include sufficient detail to place the Board and each opponent on notice of the precise relief requested. A notice is not evidence except as an admission by a party-opponent.

(b) Filing and service. The Board may set the times and conditions for filing and serving notices required under this section. The Board may provide for the notice filed with the Board to be maintained in confidence for a limited time.

(c) Effect. If a notice under paragraph (a) of this section is required:

(1) A failure to state a sufficient basis for relief may result in a denial of the relief requested;

(2) A party will be limited to filing motions consistent with the notice; and

(3) Ambiguities in the notice will be construed against the party.

(d) Correction. A party may move to correct its notice. The motion should be filed promptly after the party becomes aware of the basis for the correction. A correction filed after the time set for filing notices will only be entered if entry would serve the interests of justice.

§ 42.22.   Content of petitions and motions.

(a) Each petition or motion must be filed as a separate paper and must include:

(1) A statement of the precise relief requested; and

(2) A full statement of the reasons for the relief requested, including a detailed explanation of the significance of the evidence including material facts, and the governing law, rules, and precedent.

(b) *Relief requested.* Where a rule in part 1 of this title ordinarily governs the relief sought, the petition or motion must make any showings required under that rule in addition to any showings required in this part.

(c) *Statement of material facts.* Each petition or motion may include a statement of material fact. Each material fact preferably shall be set forth as a separately numbered sentence with specific citations to the portions of the record that support the fact.

(d) The Board may order additional showings or explanations as a condition for authorizing a motion (see § 42.20(b)).

§ 42.23. Oppositions and replies.

(a) Oppositions and replies must comply with the content requirements for motions and, if the paper to which the opposition or reply is responding contains a statement of material fact, must include a listing of facts that are admitted, denied, or cannot be admitted or denied. Any material fact not specifically denied may be considered admitted.

(b) All arguments for the relief requested in a motion must be made in the motion. A reply may only respond to arguments raised in the corresponding opposition, patent owner preliminary response, or patent owner response.

[80 FR 28565, May 19, 2015; 81 FR 18765, April 1, 2016]

§ 42.24. Type-volume or page-limits for petitions, motions, oppositions, and replies.

(a) *Petitions and motions.*

(1) The following word counts or page limits for petitions and motions apply and include any statement of material facts to be admitted or denied in support of the petition or motion. The word count or page limit does not include a table of contents, a table of authorities, mandatory notices under § 42.8, a certificate of service or word count, or appendix of exhibits or claim listing.

(i) Petition requesting inter partes review: 14,000 words.

(ii) Petition requesting post-grant review: 18,700 words.

(iii)   Petition requesting covered business method patent review: 18,700 words.

(iv)   Petition requesting derivation proceeding: 14,000 words.

(v)   Motions (excluding motions to amend): 15 pages.

(vi)   Motions to Amend: 25 pages.

(2) Petitions to institute a trial must comply with the stated word counts but may be accompanied by a motion to waive the word counts. The petitioner must show in the motion how a waiver of the word counts is in the interests of justice and must append a copy of proposed petition exceeding the word count to the motion. If the motion is not granted, the proposed petition exceeding the word count may be expunged or returned. Any other motion to waive word counts or page limits must be granted in advance of filing a motion, opposition, or reply for which the waiver is necessary.

(b) Patent owner responses and oppositions. The word counts or page limits set forth in this paragraph (b) do not include a listing of facts which are admitted, denied, or cannot be admitted or denied.

(1) The word counts for a patent owner preliminary response to petition are the same as the word counts for the petition.

(2) The word counts for a patent owner response to petition are the same as the word counts for the petition.

(3) The page limits for oppositions are the same as those for corresponding motions.

(c) Replies. The following word counts or page limits for replies apply and include any statement of facts in support of the reply. The word counts or page limits do not include a table of contents, a table of authorities, a listing of facts which are admitted, denied, or cannot be admitted or denied, a certificate of service or word count, or appendix of exhibits.

(1) Replies to patent owner responses to petitions: 5,600 words.

(2) Replies to oppositions (excluding replies to oppositions to motions to amend): 5 pages.

(3) Replies to oppositions to motions to amend: 12 pages.

(d) Certification. Any paper whose length is specified by

type-volume limits must include a certification stating the number of words in the paper. A party may rely on the word count of the word-processing system used to prepare the paper.

[80 FR 28565, May 19, 2015; 81 FR 18765, April 1, 2016; 81 FR 24703, April 27, 2016]

§ 42.25. Default filing times.

(a) A motion may only be filed according to a schedule set by the Board. The default times for acting are:

(1) An opposition is due one month after service of the motion; and

(2) A reply is due one month after service of the opposition.

(b) A party should seek relief promptly after the need for relief is identified. Delay in seeking relief may justify a denial of relief sought.

TESTIMONY AND PRODUCTION

§ 42.51. Discovery.

(a) Mandatory initial disclosures.

(1) With agreement. Parties may agree to mandatory discovery requiring the initial disclosures set forth in the Office Patent Trial Practice Guide.

(i) The parties must submit any agreement reached on initial disclosures by no later than the filing of the patent owner preliminary response or the expiration of the time period for filing such a response. The initial disclosures of the parties shall be filed as exhibits.

(ii) Upon the institution of a trial, parties may automatically take discovery of the information identified in the initial disclosures.

(2) Without agreement. Where the parties fail to agree to the mandatory discovery set forth in paragraph (a)(1), a party may seek such discovery by motion.

(b) Limited discovery. A party is not entitled to discovery except as provided in paragraph (a) of this section, or as otherwise authorized in this subpart.

(1) Routine discovery. Except as the Board may otherwise order:

(i) Unless previously served or otherwise by agreement of the parties, any exhibit cited in a paper or in testimony must be served with the citing paper or testimony.

(ii) Cross examination of affidavit testimony prepared for the proceeding is authorized within such time period as the Board may set.

(iii) Unless previously served, a party must serve relevant information that is inconsistent with a position advanced by the party during the proceeding concurrent with the filing of the documents or things that contains the inconsistency. This requirement does not make discoverable anything otherwise protected by legally recognized privileges such as attorney-client or attorney work product. This requirement extends to inventors, corporate officers, and persons involved in the preparation or filing of the documents or things.

(2) Additional discovery.

(i) The parties may agree to additional discovery between themselves. Where the parties fail to agree, a party may move for additional discovery. The moving party must show that such additional discovery is in the interests of justice, except in post-grant reviews where additional discovery is limited to evidence directly related to factual assertions advanced by either party in the proceeding (see § 42.224). The Board may specify conditions for such additional discovery.

(ii) When appropriate, a party may obtain production of documents and things during cross examination of an opponent's witness or during authorized compelled testimony under § 42.52.

(c) Production of documents. Except as otherwise ordered by the Board, a party producing documents and things shall either provide copies to the opposing party or make the documents and things available for inspection and copying at a reasonable time and location in the United States.

[80 FR 28565, May 19, 2015]

§ 42.52.   Compelling testimony and production.

(a) Authorization required. A party seeking to compel testimony or production of documents or things must file a motion for authorization. The motion must describe the general relevance of the testimony, document, or thing, and must:

(1) In the case of testimony, identify the witness by name or title; and

(2) In the case of a document or thing, the general nature of the document or thing.

(b) Outside the United States. For testimony or production sought outside the United States, the motion must also:

(1) In the case of testimony.

(i) Identify the foreign country and explain why the party believes the witness can be compelled to testify in the foreign country, including a description of the procedures that will be used to compel the testimony in the foreign country and an estimate of the time it is expected to take to obtain the testimony; and

(ii) Demonstrate that the party has made reasonable efforts to secure the agreement of the witness to testify in the United States but has been unsuccessful in obtaining the agreement, even though the party has offered to pay the travel expenses of the witness to testify in the United States.

(2) In the case of production of a document or thing.

(i) Identify the foreign country and explain why the party believes production of the document or thing can be compelled in the foreign country, including a description of the procedures that will be used to compel production of the document or thing in the foreign country and an estimate of the time it is expected to take to obtain production of the document or thing; and

(ii) Demonstrate that the party has made reasonable efforts to obtain the agreement of the individual or entity having possession, custody, or control of the document or thing to produce the document or thing in the United States but has been unsuccessful in obtaining that agreement, even though the party has offered to pay the expenses of producing the document or thing in the United States.

§ 42.53.   Taking testimony.

(a) Form. Uncompelled direct testimony must be submitted in the form of an affidavit. All other testimony, including testimony compelled under 35 U.S.C. 24, must be in the form of a deposition transcript. Parties may agree to video-recorded testimony, but may not submit such testimony without prior authorization of the Board. In addition, the Board may authorize or require live or video-recorded testimony.

(b) Time and location.

(1) Uncompelled direct testimony may be taken at any time to support a petition, motion, opposition, or reply; otherwise, testimony may only be taken during a testimony period set by the Board.

(2) Except as the Board otherwise orders, during the testimony period, deposition testimony may be taken at any reasonable time and location within the United States before any disinterested official authorized to administer oaths at that location.

(3) Uncompelled deposition testimony outside the United States may only be taken upon agreement of the parties or as the Board specifically directs.

(c) Duration.

(1) Unless stipulated by the parties or ordered by the Board, direct examination, cross-examination, and redirect examination for compelled deposition testimony shall be subject to the following time limits: Seven hours for direct examination, four hours for cross-examination, and two hours for redirect examination.

(2) Unless stipulated by the parties or ordered by the Board, cross-examination, redirect examination, and re-cross examination for uncompelled direct testimony shall be subject to the follow time limits: Seven hours for cross-examination, four hours for redirect examination, and two hours for re-cross examination.

(d) Notice of deposition.

(1) Prior to the taking of deposition testimony, all parties to the proceeding must agree on the time and place for taking testimony. If the parties cannot agree, the party seeking the testimony must initiate a conference with the Board to set a time and place.

(2) Cross-examination should ordinarily take place after any supplemental evidence relating to the direct testimony has been filed and more than a week before the filing date for any paper in which the cross-examination testimony is expected to be used. A party requesting cross-examination testimony of more than one witness may choose the order in which the witnesses are to be cross-examined.

(3) In the case of direct deposition testimony, at least three business days prior to the conference in paragraph (d)(1) of this section, or if there is no conference, at least ten days prior to the deposition, the party seeking the direct testimony must serve:

(i)   A list and copy of each document under the party's control and on which the party intends to rely; and

(ii)   A list of, and proffer of reasonable access to, anything other than a document under the party's control and on which the party intends to rely.

(4) The party seeking the deposition must file a notice of the deposition at least ten business days before a deposition.

(5) Scope and content—

(i)   For direct deposition testimony, the notice limits the scope of the testimony and must list:

(A)   The time and place of the deposition;

(B)   The name and address of the witness;

(C)   A list of the exhibits to be relied upon during the deposition; and

(D)   A general description of the scope and nature of the testimony to be elicited.

(ii)   For cross-examination testimony, the scope of the examination is limited to the scope of the direct testimony.

(iii)   The notice must list the time and place of the deposition.

(iv)   Where an additional party seeks to take direct testimony of a third party witness at the time and place noticed in paragraph (d)(5) of this section, the additional party must provide a counter notice that lists the exhibits to be relied upon in the deposition and a general description of the scope and nature of the testimony to be elicited.

(6) Motion to quash—Objection to a defect in the notice is waived unless the objecting party promptly seeks authorization to file a motion to quash.

(e) Deposition in a foreign language. If an interpreter will be used during the deposition, the party calling the witness must initiate a conference with the Board at least five business days before the deposition.

(f) Manner of taking deposition testimony.

(1) Before giving deposition testimony, each witness shall be duly sworn according to law by the officer before whom the deposition is to be taken. The officer must be authorized to take testimony under 35 U.S.C. 23.

(2) The testimony shall be taken with any questions and answers recorded in their regular order by the officer, or by some other disinterested person in the presence of the officer, unless the presence of the officer is waived on the record by agreement of all parties.

(3) Any exhibits used during the deposition must be numbered as required by § 42.63(c), and must, if not previously served, be served at the deposition. Exhibits objected to shall be accepted pending a decision on the objection.

(4) All objections made at the time of the deposition to the qualifications of the officer taking the deposition, the manner of taking it, the evidence presented, the conduct of any party, and any other objection to the deposition shall be noted on the record by the officer.

(5) When the testimony has been transcribed, the witness shall read and sign (in the form of an affidavit) a transcript of the deposition unless:

(i)   The parties otherwise agree in writing;

(ii)   The parties waive reading and signature by the witness on the record at the deposition; or

(iii)   The witness refuses to read or sign the transcript of the deposition.

(6) The officer shall prepare a certified transcript by attaching a certificate in the form of an affidavit signed and sealed by the officer to the transcript of the deposition. Unless the parties waive any of the following requirements, in which case the certificate shall so state, the certificate must state:

(i)   The witness was duly sworn by the officer before commencement of testimony by the witness;

(ii)   The transcript is a true record of the testimony given by the witness;

(iii)   The name of the person who recorded the testimony, and if the officer did not record it, whether the testimony was recorded in the presence of the officer;

(iv)   The presence or absence of any opponent;

(v)   The place where the deposition was taken and the day and hour when the deposition began and ended;

(vi)   The officer has no disqualifying interest, personal or financial, in a party; and

(vii) If a witness refuses to read or sign the transcript, the circumstances under which the witness refused.

(7) Except where the parties agree otherwise, the proponent of the testimony must arrange for providing a copy of the transcript to all other parties. The testimony must be filed as an exhibit.

(8) Any objection to the content, form, or manner of taking the deposition, including the qualifications of the officer, is waived unless made on the record during the deposition and preserved in a timely filed motion to exclude.

(g) Costs. Except as the Board may order or the parties may agree in writing, the proponent of the direct testimony shall bear all costs associated with the testimony, including the reasonable costs associated with making the witness available for the cross-examination.

[80 FR 28565, May 19, 2015]

§ 42.54. Protective order.

(a) A party may file a motion to seal where the motion to seal contains a proposed protective order, such as the default protective order set forth in the Office Patent Trial Practice Guide. The motion must include a certification that the moving party has in good faith conferred or attempted to confer with other affected parties in an effort to resolve the dispute. The Board may, for good cause, issue an order to protect a party or person from disclosing confidential information, including, but not limited to, one or more of the following:

(1) Forbidding the disclosure or discovery;

(2) Specifying terms, including time and place, for the disclosure or discovery;

(3) Prescribing a discovery method other than the one selected by the party seeking discovery;

(4) Forbidding inquiry into certain matters, or limiting the scope of disclosure or discovery to certain matters;

(5) Designating the persons who may be present while the discovery is conducted;

(6) Requiring that a deposition be sealed and opened only by order of the Board;

(7) Requiring that a trade secret or other confidential research, development, or commercial information not be revealed or be revealed only in a specified way; and

(8) Requiring that the parties simultaneously file specified documents or information in sealed envelopes, to be opened as the Board directs.

(b) [Reserved]

§ 42.55.   Confidential information in a petition.

A petitioner filing confidential information with a petition may, concurrent with the filing of the petition, file a motion to seal with a proposed protective order as to the confidential information. The institution of the requested trial will constitute a grant of the motion to seal unless otherwise ordered by the Board.

(a) Default protective order. Where a motion to seal requests entry of the default protective order set forth in the Office Patent Trial Practice Guide, the petitioner must file, but need not serve, the confidential information under seal. The patent owner may only access the filed sealed information prior to the institution of the trial by agreeing to the terms of the default protective order or obtaining relief from the Board.

(b) Protective orders other than default protective order. Where a motion to seal requests entry of a protective order other than the default protective order, the petitioner must file, but need not serve, the confidential information under seal. The patent owner may only access the sealed confidential information prior to the institution of the trial by:

(1) agreeing to the terms of the protective order requested by the petitioner;

(2) agreeing to the terms of a protective order that the parties file jointly; or

(3) obtaining entry of a protective order (e.g., the default protective order).

§ 42.56.   Expungement of confidential information.

After denial of a petition to institute a trial or after final judgment in a trial, a party may file a motion to expunge confidential information from the record.

§ 42.57.   Privilege for patent practitioners.

(a) Privileged communications. A communication between a client and a USPTO patent practitioner or a foreign jurisdiction patent practitioner that is reasonably necessary and incident to the scope of the practitioner's authority shall receive the same protections of privilege under Federal law as if that communication were between a client and an attorney authorized to practice in the United States, including all limitations and exceptions.

(b) Definitions. The term "USPTO patent practitioner" means a person who has fulfilled the requirements to practice patent matters before the United States Patent and Trademark Office under § 11.7 of this chapter. "Foreign jurisdiction patent practitioner" means a person who is authorized to provide legal advice on patent matters in a foreign jurisdiction, provided that the jurisdiction establishes professional qualifications and the practitioner satisfies them. For foreign jurisdiction practitioners, this rule applies regardless of whether that jurisdiction provides privilege or an equivalent under its laws.

(c) Scope of coverage. USPTO patent practitioners and foreign jurisdiction patent practitioners shall receive the same treatment as attorneys on all issues affecting privilege or waiver, such as communications with employees or assistants of the practitioner and communications between multiple practitioners.

[82 FR 51575, Nov. 7, 2017]

§ 42.61. Admissibility.

(a) Evidence that is not taken, sought, or filed in accordance with this subpart is not admissible.

(b) Records of the Office. Certification is not necessary as a condition to admissibility when the evidence to be submitted is a record of the Office to which all parties have access.

(c) Specification and drawings. A specification or drawing of a United States patent application or patent is admissible as evidence only to prove what the specification or drawing describes. If there is data in the specification or a drawing upon which a party intends to rely to prove the truth of the data, an affidavit by an individual having first-hand knowledge of how the data was generated must be filed.

§ 42.62. Applicability of the Federal rules of evidence.

(a) Generally. Except as otherwise provided in this subpart, the Federal Rules of Evidence shall apply to a proceeding.

(b) Exclusions. Those portions of the Federal Rules of Evidence relating to criminal proceedings, juries, and other matters not relevant to proceedings under this subpart shall not apply.

(c) Modifications in terminology. Unless otherwise clear

from context, the following terms of the Federal Rules of Evidence shall be construed as indicated:

Appellate court means United States Court of Appeals for the Federal Circuit.

Civil action, civil proceeding, and action mean a proceeding before the Board under part 42.

Courts of the United States, U.S. Magistrate, court, trial court, trier of fact, and judge mean Board.

Hearing means, as defined in Federal Rule of Evidence 804(a)(5), the time for taking testimony.

Judicial notice means official notice.

Trial or hearing in Federal Rule of Evidence 807 means the time for taking testimony.

(d) In determining foreign law, the Board may consider any relevant material or source, including testimony, whether or not submitted by a party or admissible under the Federal Rules of Evidence.

§ 42.63. Form of evidence.

(a) Exhibits required. Evidence consists of affidavits, transcripts of depositions, documents, and things. All evidence must be filed in the form of an exhibit.

(b) Translation required. When a party relies on a document or is required to produce a document in a language other than English, a translation of the document into English and an affidavit attesting to the accuracy of the translation must be filed with the document.

(c) Exhibit numbering. Each party's exhibits must be uniquely numbered sequentially in a range the Board specifies. For the petitioner, the range is 1001–1999, and for the patent owner, the range is 2001–2999.

(d) Exhibit format. An exhibit must conform with the requirements for papers in § 42.6 and the requirements of this paragraph.

(1) Each exhibit must have an exhibit label.

(i) An exhibit filed with the petition must include the petitioner's name followed by a unique exhibit number.

(ii) For exhibits not filed with the petition, the exhibit label must include the party's name followed by a unique exhibit number, the names of the parties, and the trial number.

(2) When the exhibit is a paper:

(i) Each page must be uniquely numbered in sequence; and

(ii) The exhibit label must be affixed to the lower right corner of the first page of the exhibit without obscuring information on the first page or, if obscuring is unavoidable, affixed to a duplicate first page.

(e) Exhibit list. Each party must maintain an exhibit list with the exhibit number and a brief description of each exhibit. If the exhibit is not filed, the exhibit list should note that fact. A current exhibit list must be served whenever evidence is served and the current exhibit list must be filed when filing exhibits.

§ 42.64. Objection; motion to exclude.

(a) Deposition evidence. An objection to the admissibility of deposition evidence must be made during the deposition. Evidence to cure the objection must be provided during the deposition, unless the parties to the deposition stipulate otherwise on the deposition record.

(b) Other evidence. For evidence other than deposition evidence:

(1) Objection. Any objection to evidence submitted during a preliminary proceeding must be filed within ten business days of the institution of the trial. Once a trial has been instituted, any objection must be filed within five business days of service of evidence to which the objection is directed. The objection must identify the grounds for the objection with sufficient particularity to allow correction in the form of supplemental evidence.

(2) Supplemental evidence. The party relying on evidence to which an objection is timely served may respond to the objection by serving supplemental evidence within ten business days of service of the objection.

(c) Motion to exclude. A motion to exclude evidence must be filed to preserve any objection. The motion must identify the objections in the record in order and must explain the objections. The motion may be filed without prior authorization from the Board.

[80 FR 28565, May 19, 2015]

§ 42.65. Expert testimony; tests and data.

(a) Expert testimony that does not disclose the underlying facts or data on which the opinion is based is entitled to little or no weight. Testimony on United States patent law or patent examination practice will not be admitted.

(b) If a party relies on a technical test or data from such a test, the party must provide an affidavit explaining:

(1) Why the test or data is being used;

(2) How the test was performed and the data was generated;

(3) How the data is used to determine a value;

(4) How the test is regarded in the relevant art; and

(5) Any other information necessary for the Board to evaluate the test and data.

ORAL ARGUMENT, DECISION, AND SETTLEMENT

§ 42.70. Oral argument.

(a) Request for oral argument. A party may request oral argument on an issue raised in a paper at a time set by the Board. The request must be filed as a separate paper and must specify the issues to be argued.

(b) Demonstrative exhibits must be served at least seven business days before the oral argument and filed no later than the time of the oral argument.

[81 FR 18765, April 1, 2016]

§ 42.71. Decision on petitions or motions.

(a) Order of consideration. The Board may take up petitions or motions for decisions in any order, may grant, deny, or dismiss any petition or motion, and may enter any appropriate order.

(b) Interlocutory decisions. A decision on a motion without a judgment is not final for the purposes of judicial review. If a decision is not a panel decision, the party may request that a panel rehear the decision. When rehearing a non-panel decision, a panel will review the decision for an abuse of discretion. A panel decision on an issue will govern the trial.

(c) Petition decisions. A decision by the Board on whether to institute a trial is final and nonappealable. A party may request rehearing on a decision by the Board on whether to institute a trial pursuant to paragraph (d) of this section. When rehearing a decision on petition, a panel will review the decision for an abuse of discretion.

(d) Rehearing. A party dissatisfied with a decision may file a single request for rehearing without prior authorization from the Board. The burden of showing a decision should be modified lies with the party challenging the decision. The request must specifically identify all matters the party believes the Board misapprehended or overlooked, and the place where each matter was previously addressed in a motion, an opposition, or a reply. A request for rehearing does not toll times for taking action. Any request must be filed:

(1) Within 14 days of the entry of a non-final decision or a decision to institute a trial as to at least one ground of unpatentability asserted in the petition; or

(2) Within 30 days of the entry of a final decision or a decision not to institute a trial.

[80 FR 28565, May 19, 2015]

§ 42.72. Termination of trial.

The Board may terminate a trial without rendering a final written decision, where appropriate, including where the trial is consolidated with another proceeding or pursuant to a joint request under 35 U.S.C. 317(a) or 327(a).

§ 42.73. Judgment.

(a) A judgment, except in the case of a termination, disposes of all issues that were, or by motion reasonably could have been, raised and decided.

(b) Request for adverse judgment. A party may request judgment against itself at any time during a proceeding. Actions construed to be a request for adverse judgment include:

(1) Disclaimer of the involved application or patent;

(2) Cancellation or disclaimer of a claim such that the party has no remaining claim in the trial;

(3) Concession of unpatentability or derivation of the contested subject matter; and

(4) Abandonment of the contest.

(c) Recommendation. The judgment may include a recommendation for further action by an examiner or by the Director.

(d) Estoppel.

(1) Petitioner other than in derivation proceeding. A petitioner, or the real party in interest or privy of the petitioner, is estopped in the Office from requesting or maintaining a proceeding with respect to a claim for which it has obtained a final written decision on patentability in an inter partes review, post-grant review, or a covered business method patent review, on any ground that the petitioner raised or reasonably could have raised during the trial, except that estoppel shall not apply to a petitioner, or to the real party in interest or privy of the petitioner who has settled under 35 U.S.C. 317 or 327.

(2) In a derivation, the losing party who could have properly moved for relief on an issue, but did not so move, may not take action in the Office after the judgment that is inconsistent with that party's failure to move, except that a losing party shall not be estopped with respect to any contested subject matter for which that party was awarded a favorable judgment.

(3) Patent applicant or owner. A patent applicant or owner is precluded from taking action inconsistent with the adverse judgment, including obtaining in any patent:

(i) A claim that is not patentably distinct from a finally refused or canceled claim; or

(ii) An amendment of a specification or of a drawing that was denied during the trial proceeding, but this provision does not apply to an application or patent that has a different written description.

§ 42.74. Settlement.

(a) Board role. The parties may agree to settle any issue in a proceeding, but the Board is not a party to the settlement and may independently determine any question of jurisdiction, patentability, or Office practice.

(b) Agreements in writing. Any agreement or understanding between the parties made in connection with, or in contemplation of, the termination of a proceeding shall be in writing and a true copy shall be filed with the Board before the termination of the trial.

(c) Request to keep separate. A party to a settlement may request that the settlement be treated as business confidential information and be kept separate from the files of an involved patent or application. The request must be filed with the settlement. If a timely request is filed, the settlement shall only be available:

(1) To a Government agency on written request to the Board; or

(2) To any other person upon written request to the Board to make the settlement agreement available, along with the fee specified in § 42.15(d) and on a showing of good cause.

CERTIFICATE

§ 42.80. Certificate.

After the Board issues a final written decision in an inter partes review, post-grant review, or covered business method patent review and the time for appeal has expired or any appeal has terminated, the Office will issue and publish a certificate canceling any claim of the patent finally determined to be unpatentable, confirming any claim of the patent determined to be patentable, and incorporating in the patent any new or amended claim determined to be patentable by operation of the certificate.

SUBPART B— INTER PARTES REVIEW

GENERAL

§ 42.100. Procedure; pendency.

(a) An inter partes review is a trial subject to the procedures set forth in subpart A of this part.

(b) In an inter partes review proceeding, a claim of a patent, or a claim proposed in a motion to amend under § 42.121, shall be construed using the same claim construction standard that would be used to construe the claim in a civil action under 35 U.S.C. 282(b), including construing the claim in accordance with the ordinary and customary meaning of such claim as understood by one of ordinary skill in the art and the prosecution history pertaining to the patent. Any prior claim construction determination concerning a term of the claim in a civil action, or a proceeding before the International Trade Commission, that is timely made of record in the inter partes review proceeding will be considered.

(c) An inter partes review proceeding shall be administered such that pendency before the Board after institution is normally no more than one year. The time can be extended by up to six months for good cause by the Chief Administrative Patent Judge, or adjusted by the Board in the case of joinder.

[81 FR 18766, April 1, 2016; 83 FR 51358, Oct. 11, 2018]

§ 42.101. Who may petition for inter partes review.

A person who is not the owner of a patent may file with the Office a petition to institute an inter partes review of the patent unless:

(a) Before the date on which the petition for review is filed, the petitioner or real party-in-interest filed a civil action challenging the validity of a claim of the patent;

(b) The petition requesting the proceeding is filed more than one year after the date on which the petitioner, the petitioner's real party-in-interest, or a privy of the petitioner is served with a complaint alleging infringement of the patent; or

(c) The petitioner, the petitioner's real party-in-interest, or a privy of the petitioner is estopped from challenging the claims on the grounds identified in the petition.

§ 42.102.   Time for filing.

(a) A petition for inter partes review of a patent must be filed after the later of the following dates, where applicable:

(1) If the patent is a patent described in section 3(n)(1) of the Leahy–Smith America Invents Act, the date that is nine months after the date of the grant of the patent;

(2) If the patent is a patent that is not described in section 3(n)(1) of the Leahy–Smith American Invents Act, the date of the grant of the patent; or

(3) If a post-grant review is instituted as set forth in subpart C of this part, the date of the termination of such post-grant review.

Subsection (b) reserved effective Oct. 31, 2019; see 84 FR 51982.

(b) The Director may impose a limit on the number of inter partes reviews that may be instituted during each of the first four one-year periods in which the amendment made to chapter 31 of title 35, United States Code, is in effect by providing notice in the Office's Official Gazette or Federal Register. Petitions filed after an established limit has been reached will be deemed untimely.

[78 FR 17874, March 25, 2013; 84 FR 51982, Oct. 1, 2019]

§ 42.103.   Inter partes review fee.

(a) An inter partes review fee set forth in § 42.15(a) must accompany the petition.

(b) No filing date will be accorded to the petition until full payment is received.

§ 42.104.   Content of petition.

In addition to the requirements of §§ 42.6, 42.8, 42.22, and 42.24, the petition must set forth:

(a) Grounds for standing. The petitioner must certify that the patent for which review is sought is available for inter partes review and that the petitioner is not barred or estopped from requesting an inter partes review challenging the patent claims on the grounds identified in the petition.

(b) Identification of challenge. Provide a statement of

the precise relief requested for each claim challenged. The statement must identify the following:

(1) The claim;

(2) The specific statutory grounds under 35 U.S.C. 102 or 103 on which the challenge to the claim is based and the patents or printed publications relied upon for each ground;

(3) How the challenged claim is to be construed. Where the claim to be construed contains a means-plus-function or step-plus-function limitation as permitted under 35 U.S.C. 112(f), the construction of the claim must identify the specific portions of the specification that describe the structure, material, or acts corresponding to each claimed function;

(4) How the construed claim is unpatentable under the statutory grounds identified in paragraph (b)(2) of this section. The petition must specify where each element of the claim is found in the prior art patents or printed publications relied upon; and

(5) The exhibit number of the supporting evidence relied upon to support the challenge and the relevance of the evidence to the challenge raised, including identifying specific portions of the evidence that support the challenge. The Board may exclude or give no weight to the evidence where a party has failed to state its relevance or to identify specific portions of the evidence that support the challenge.

(c) A motion may be filed that seeks to correct a clerical or typographical mistake in the petition. The grant of such a motion does not change the filing date of the petition.

§ 42.105.   Service of petition.

In addition to the requirements of § 42.6, the petitioner must serve the petition and exhibits relied upon in the petition as follows:

(a) The petition and supporting evidence must be served on the patent owner at the correspondence address of record for the subject patent. The petitioner may additionally serve the petition and supporting evidence on the patent owner at any other address known to the petitioner as likely to effect service.

(b) Upon agreement of the parties, service may be made electronically. Service may be by Priority Mail Express® or by means at least as fast and reliable as Priority Mail Express®. Personal service is not required.

[79 FR 63043, Oct. 22, 2014]

§ 42.106. Filing date.

(a) Complete petition. A petition to institute inter partes review will not be accorded a filing date until the petition satisfies all of the following requirements:

(1) Complies with § 42.104;

(2) Effects service of the petition on the correspondence address of record as provided in § 42.105(a); and

(3) Is accompanied by the fee to institute required in § 42.15(a).

(b) Incomplete petition. Where a party files an incomplete petition, no filing date will be accorded, and the Office will dismiss the petition if the deficiency in the petition is not corrected within one month from the notice of an incomplete petition.

§ 42.107. Preliminary response to petition.

(a) The patent owner may file a preliminary response to the petition. The response is limited to setting forth the reasons why no inter partes review should be instituted under 35 U.S.C. 314 and can include supporting evidence. The preliminary response is subject to the word count under § 42.24.

(b) Due date. The preliminary response must be filed no later than three months after the date of a notice indicating that the request to institute an inter partes review has been granted a filing date. A patent owner may expedite the proceeding by filing an election to waive the patent owner preliminary response.

(c) [Reserved by 81 FR 18766]

(d) No amendment. The preliminary response shall not include any amendment.

(e) Disclaim Patent Claims. The patent owner may file a statutory disclaimer under 35 U.S.C. 253(a) in compliance with § 1.321(a) of this chapter, disclaiming one or more claims in the patent. No inter partes review will be instituted based on disclaimed claims.

[81 FR 18766, April 1, 2016]

INSTITUTING INTER PARTES REVIEW

§ 42.108. Institution of inter partes review.

For statute(s) affecting validity of § 42.108(a), see: 35 USCA § 318(a).

(a) When instituting inter partes review, the Board may

authorize the review to proceed on all or some of the challenged claims and on all or some of the grounds of unpatentability asserted for each claim.

(b) At any time prior to institution of inter partes review, the Board may deny some or all grounds for unpatentability for some or all of the challenged claims. Denial of a ground is a Board decision not to institute inter partes review on that ground.

(c) Sufficient grounds. Inter partes review shall not be instituted for a ground of unpatentability unless the Board decides that the petition supporting the ground would demonstrate that there is a reasonable likelihood that at least one of the claims challenged in the petition is unpatentable. The Board's decision will take into account a patent owner preliminary response where such a response is filed, including any testimonial evidence, but a genuine issue of material fact created by such testimonial evidence will be viewed in the light most favorable to the petitioner solely for purposes of deciding whether to institute an inter partes review. A petitioner may seek leave to file a reply to the preliminary response in accordance with §§ 42.23 and 42.24(c). Any such request must make a showing of good cause.

[81 FR 18766, April 1, 2016]

AFTER INSTITUTION OF INTER PARTES REVIEW

§ 42.120. Patent owner response.

(a) Scope. A patent owner may file a response to the petition addressing any ground for unpatentability not already denied. A patent owner response is filed as an opposition and is subject to the page limits provided in § 42.24.

(b) Due date for response. If no time for filing a patent owner response to a petition is provided in a Board order, the default date for filing a patent owner response is three months from the date the inter partes review was instituted.

§ 42.121. Amendment of the patent.

(a) Motion to amend. A patent owner may file one motion to amend a patent, but only after conferring with the Board.

(1) Due date. Unless a due date is provided in a Board order, a motion to amend must be filed no later than the filing of a patent owner response.

(2) Scope. A motion to amend may be denied where:

(i) The amendment does not respond to a ground of unpatentability involved in the trial; or

(ii) The amendment seeks to enlarge the scope of the claims of the patent or introduce new subject matter.

(3) A reasonable number of substitute claims. A motion to amend may cancel a challenged claim or propose a reasonable number of substitute claims. The presumption is that only one substitute claim would be needed to replace each challenged claim, and it may be rebutted by a demonstration of need.

(b) Content. A motion to amend claims must include a claim listing, which claim listing may be contained in an appendix to the motion, show the changes clearly, and set forth:

(1) The support in the original disclosure of the patent for each claim that is added or amended; and

(2) The support in an earlier-filed disclosure for each claim for which benefit of the filing date of the earlier filed disclosure is sought.

(c) Additional motion to amend. In addition to the requirements set forth in paragraphs (a) and (b) of this section, any additional motion to amend may not be filed without Board authorization. An additional motion to amend may be authorized when there is a good cause showing or a joint request of the petitioner and the patent owner to materially advance a settlement. In determining whether to authorize such an additional motion to amend, the Board will consider whether a petitioner has submitted supplemental information after the time period set for filing a motion to amend in paragraph (a)(1) of this section.
[80 FR 28566, May 19, 2015]

§ 42.122. Multiple proceedings and Joinder.

(a) Multiple proceedings. Where another matter involving the patent is before the Office, the Board may during the pendency of the inter partes review enter any appropriate order regarding the additional matter including providing for the stay, transfer, consolidation, or termination of any such matter.

(b) Request for joinder. Joinder may be requested by a patent owner or petitioner. Any request for joinder must be filed, as a motion under § 42.22, no later than one month after the institution date of any inter partes review for which joinder is requested. The time period set forth in § 42.101(b) shall not apply when the petition is accompanied by a request for joinder.

§ 42.123. Filing of supplemental information.

(a) Motion to submit supplemental information. Once a trial has been instituted, a party may file a motion to submit supplemental information in accordance with the following requirements:

(1) A request for the authorization to file a motion to submit supplemental information is made within one month of the date the trial is instituted.

(2) The supplemental information must be relevant to a claim for which the trial has been instituted.

(b) Late submission of supplemental information. A party seeking to submit supplemental information more than one month after the date the trial is instituted, must request authorization to file a motion to submit the information. The motion to submit supplemental information must show why the supplemental information reasonably could not have been obtained earlier, and that consideration of the supplemental information would be in the interests-of-justice.

(c) Other supplemental information. A party seeking to submit supplemental information not relevant to a claim for which the trial has been instituted must request authorization to file a motion to submit the information. The motion must show why the supplemental information reasonably could not have been obtained earlier, and that consideration of the supplemental information would be in the interests-of-justice.

SUBPART C— POST-GRANT REVIEW

GENERAL

§ 42.200. Procedure; pendency.

(a) A post-grant review is a trial subject to the procedures set forth in subpart A of this part.

(b) In a post-grant review proceeding, a claim of a patent, or a claim proposed in a motion to amend under § 42.221, shall be construed using the same claim construction standard that would be used to construe the claim in a civil action under 35 U.S.C. 282(b), including construing the claim in accordance with the ordinary and customary meaning of such claim as understood by one of ordinary skill in the art and the prosecution history pertaining to the patent. Any prior claim construction determination concerning a term of the claim in a civil action, or a proceeding before the International Trade Commission, that is timely made of record in the post-grant review proceeding will be considered.

(c) A post-grant review proceeding shall be administered such that pendency before the Board after institution is normally no more than one year. The time can be extended by up to six months for good cause by the Chief Administrative Patent Judge, or adjusted by the Board in the case of joinder.

(d) Interferences commenced before September 16, 2012, shall proceed under part 41 of this chapter except as the Chief Administrative Patent Judge, acting on behalf of the Director, may otherwise order in the interests-of-justice.

[81 FR 18766, April 1, 2016; 83 FR 51358, Oct. 11, 2018]

§ 42.201. Who may petition for a post-grant review.

A person who is not the owner of a patent may file with the Office a petition to institute a post-grant review of the patent unless:

(a) Before the date on which the petition for review is filed, the petitioner or real party-in-interest filed a civil action challenging the validity of a claim of the patent; or

(b) The petitioner, the petitioner's real party-in-interest, or a privy of the petitioner is estopped from challenging the claims on the grounds identified in the petition.

§ 42.202. Time for filing.

(a) A petition for a post-grant review of a patent must be filed no later than the date that is nine months after the date of the grant of a patent or of the issuance of a reissue patent. A petition, however, may not request a post-grant review for a claim in a reissue patent that is identical to or narrower than a claim in the original patent from which the reissue patent was issued unless the petition is filed not later than the date that is nine months after the date of the grant of the original patent.

Subsection (b) reserved effective Oct. 31, 2019; see 84 FR 51982.

(b) The Director may impose a limit on the number of post-grant reviews that may be instituted during each of the first four one-year periods in which 35 U.S.C. 321 is in effect by providing notice in the Office's Official Gazette or Federal Register. Petitions filed after an established limit has been reached will be deemed untimely.

[84 FR 51982, Oct. 1, 2019]

§ 42.203. Post-grant review fee.

(a) A post-grant review fee set forth in § 42.15(b) must accompany the petition.

(b) No filing date will be accorded to the petition until full payment is received.

§ 42.204. Content of petition.

In addition to the requirements of §§ 42.6, 42.8, 42.22, and 42.24, the petition must set forth:

(a) Grounds for standing. The petitioner must certify that the patent for which review is sought is available for post-grant review and that the petitioner is not barred or estopped from requesting a post-grant review challenging the patent claims on the grounds identified in the petition.

(b) Identification of challenge. Provide a statement of the precise relief requested for each claim challenged. The statement must identify the following:

(1) The claim;

(2) The specific statutory grounds permitted under 35 U.S.C. 282(b)(2) or (3) on which the challenge to the claim is based;

(3) How the challenged claim is to be construed. Where the claim to be construed contains a means-plus-function or step-plus-function limitation as permitted under 35 U.S.C. 112(f), the construction of the claim must identify the specific portions of the specification that describe the structure, material, or acts corresponding to each claimed function;

(4) How the construed claim is unpatentable under the statutory grounds identified in paragraph (b)(2) of this section. Where the grounds for unpatentability are based on prior art, the petition must specify where each element of the claim is found in the prior art. For all other grounds of unpatentability, the petition must identify the specific part of the claim that fails to comply with the statutory grounds raised and state how the identified subject matter fails to comply with the statute; and

(5) The exhibit number of the supporting evidence relied upon to support the challenge and the relevance of the evidence to the challenge raised, including identifying specific portions of the evidence that support the challenge. The Board may exclude or give no weight

to the evidence where a party has failed to state its relevance or to identify specific portions of the evidence that support the challenge.

(c) A motion may be filed that seeks to correct a clerical or typographical mistake in the petition. The grant of such a motion does not change the filing date of the petition.

§ 42.205.   Service of petition.

In addition to the requirements of § 42.6, the petitioner must serve the petition and exhibits relied upon in the petition as follows:

(a) The petition and supporting evidence must be served on the patent owner at the correspondence address of record for the subject patent. The petitioner may additionally serve the petition and supporting evidence on the patent owner at any other address known to the petitioner as likely to effect service.

(b) Upon agreement of the parties, service may be made electronically. Service may be by Priority Mail Express® or by means at least as fast and reliable as Priority Mail Express®. Personal service is not required.

[79 FR 63043, Oct. 22, 2014]

§ 42.206.   Filing date.

(a) Complete petition. A petition to institute a post-grant review will not be accorded a filing date until the petition satisfies all of the following requirements:

(1) Complies with § 42.204 or § 42.304, as the case may be,

(2) Effects service of the petition on the correspondence address of record as provided in § 42.205(a); and

(3) Is accompanied by the filing fee in § 42.15(b).

(b) Incomplete petition. Where a party files an incomplete petition, no filing date will be accorded and the Office will dismiss the request if the deficiency in the petition is not corrected within the earlier of either one month from the notice of an incomplete petition, or the expiration of the statutory deadline in which to file a petition for post-grant review.

§ 42.207.   Preliminary response to petition.

(a) The patent owner may file a preliminary response to the petition. The response is limited to setting forth the reasons why no post-grant review should be instituted under 35 U.S.C. 324 and can include supporting evidence. The preliminary response is subject to the word count under § 42.24.

(b) Due date. The preliminary response must be filed no later than three months after the date of a notice indicating that the request to institute a post-grant review has been granted a filing date. A patent owner may expedite the proceeding by filing an election to waive the patent owner preliminary response.

(c) [Reserved by 81 FR 18766]

(d) No amendment. The preliminary response shall not include any amendment.

(e) Disclaim Patent Claims. The patent owner may file a statutory disclaimer under 35 U.S.C. 253(a) in compliance with § 1.321(a), disclaiming one or more claims in the patent. No post-grant review will be instituted based on disclaimed claims.

[81 FR 18766, April 1, 2016]

INSTITUTING POST–GRANT REVIEW

§ 42.208.   Institution of post-grant review.

(a) When instituting post-grant review, the Board may authorize the review to proceed on all or some of the challenged claims and on all or some of the grounds of unpatentability asserted for each claim.

(b) At any time prior to institution of post-grant review, the Board may deny some or all grounds for unpatentability for some or all of the challenged claims. Denial of a ground is a Board decision not to institute post-grant review on that ground.

(c) Sufficient grounds. Post-grant review shall not be instituted for a ground of unpatentability unless the Board decides that the petition supporting the ground would, if unrebutted, demonstrate that it is more likely than not that at least one of the claims challenged in the petition is unpatentable. The Board's decision will take into account a patent owner preliminary response where such a response is filed, including any testimonial evidence, but a genuine issue of material fact created by such testimonial evidence will be viewed in the light most favorable to the petitioner solely for purposes of deciding whether to institute a post-grant review. A petitioner may seek leave to file a reply to the preliminary response in accordance with §§ 42.23 and 42.24(c). Any such request must make a showing of good cause.

(d) Additional grounds. Sufficient grounds under § 42.208(c) may be a showing that the petition raises a novel or unsettled legal question that is important to other patents or patent applications.

[81 FR 18766, April 1, 2016]

AFTER INSTITUTION OF POST–GRANT REVIEW

§ 42.220.   Patent owner response.

(a) Scope. A patent owner may file a response to the petition addressing any ground for unpatentability not already denied. A patent owner response is filed as an opposition and is subject to the page limits provided in § 42.24.

(b) Due date for response. If no date for filing a patent owner response to a petition is provided in a Board order, the default date for filing a patent owner response is three months from the date the post-grant review is instituted.

§ 42.221.   Amendment of the patent.

(a) Motion to amend. A patent owner may file one motion to amend a patent, but only after conferring with the Board.

(1) Due date. Unless a due date is provided in a Board order, a motion to amend must be filed no later than the filing of a patent owner response.

(2) Scope. A motion to amend may be denied where:

(i)   The amendment does not respond to a ground of unpatentability involved in the trial; or

(ii)   The amendment seeks to enlarge the scope of the claims of the patent or introduce new subject matter.

(3) A reasonable number of substitute claims. A motion to amend may cancel a challenged claim or propose a reasonable number of substitute claims. The presumption is that only one substitute claim would be needed to replace each challenged claim, and it may be rebutted by a demonstration of need.

(b) Content. A motion to amend claims must include a claim listing, which claim listing may be contained in an appendix to the motion, show the changes clearly, and set forth:

(1) The support in the original disclosure of the patent for each claim that is added or amended; and

(2) The support in an earlier-filed disclosure for each claim for which benefit of the filing date of the earlier filed disclosure is sought.

(c) Additional motion to amend. In addition to the

requirements set forth in paragraphs (a) and (b) of this section, any additional motion to amend may not be filed without Board authorization. An additional motion to amend may be authorized when there is a good cause showing or a joint request of the petitioner and the patent owner to materially advance a settlement. In determining whether to authorize such an additional motion to amend, the Board will consider whether a petitioner has submitted supplemental information after the time period set for filing a motion to amend in paragraph (a)(1) of this section.

[80 FR 28566, May 19, 2015]

§ 42.222. Multiple proceedings and Joinder.

(a) Multiple proceedings. Where another matter involving the patent is before the Office, the Board may during the pendency of the post-grant review enter any appropriate order regarding the additional matter including providing for the stay, transfer, consolidation, or termination of any such matter.

(b) Request for joinder. Joinder may be requested by a patent owner or petitioner. Any request for joinder must be filed, as a motion under § 42.22, no later than one month after the institution date of any post-grant review for which joinder is requested.

§ 42.223. Filing of supplemental information.

(a) Motion to submit supplemental information. Once a trial has been instituted, a party may file a motion to submit supplemental information in accordance with the following requirements:

(1) A request for the authorization to file a motion to submit supplemental information is made within one month of the date the trial is instituted.

(2) The supplemental information must be relevant to a claim for which the trial has been instituted.

(b) Late submission of supplemental information. A party seeking to submit supplemental information more than one month after the date the trial is instituted, must request authorization to file a motion to submit the information. The motion to submit supplemental information must show why the supplemental information reasonably could not have been obtained earlier, and that consideration of the supplemental information would be in the interests-of-justice.

(c) Other supplemental information. A party seeking to submit supplemental information not relevant to a claim for which the trial has been instituted must request authorization to file a motion to submit the information. The motion must show why the supplemental information reasonably could not have been obtained earlier, and that consideration of the supplemental information would be in the interests-of-justice.

§ 42.224. Discovery.

Notwithstanding the discovery provisions of subpart A:

(a) Requests for additional discovery may be granted upon a showing of good cause as to why the discovery is needed; and

(b) Discovery is limited to evidence directly related to factual assertions advanced by either party in the proceeding.

SUBPART D— TRANSITIONAL PROGRAM FOR COVERED BUSINESS METHOD PATENTS

§ 42.300. Procedure; pendency.

(a) A covered business method patent review is a trial subject to the procedures set forth in subpart A of this part and is also subject to the post-grant review procedures set forth in subpart C except for §§ 42.200, 42.201, 42.202, and 42.204.

(b) In a covered business method patent review proceeding, a claim of a patent, or a claim proposed in a motion to amend under § 42.221, shall be construed using the same claim construction standard that would be used to construe the claim in a civil action under 35 U.S.C. 282(b), including construing the claim in accordance with the ordinary and customary meaning of such claim as understood by one of ordinary skill in the art and the prosecution history pertaining to the patent. Any prior claim construction determination concerning a term of the claim in a civil action, or a proceeding before the International Trade Commission, that is timely made of record in the covered business method patent review proceeding will be considered.

(c) A covered business method patent review proceeding shall be administered such that pendency before the Board after institution is normally no more than one year. The time can be extended by up to six months for good cause by the Chief Administrative Patent Judge, or adjusted by the Board in the case of joinder.

(d) The rules in this subpart are applicable until

September 15, 2020, except that the rules shall continue to apply to any petition for a covered business method patent review filed before the date of repeal.

[80 FR 28566, May 19, 2015; 81 FR 18766, April 1, 2016; 83 FR 51359, Oct. 11, 2018]

§ 42.301. Definitions.

In addition to the definitions in § 42.2, the following definitions apply to proceedings under this subpart D:

(a) Covered business method patent means a patent that claims a method or corresponding apparatus for performing data processing or other operations used in the practice, administration, or management of a financial product or service, except that the term does not include patents for technological inventions.

(b) Technological invention. In determining whether a patent is for a technological invention solely for purposes of the Transitional Program for Covered Business Methods (section 42.301(a)), the following will be considered on a case-by-case basis: whether the claimed subject matter as a whole recites a technological feature that is novel and unobvious over the prior art; and solves a technical problem using a technical solution.

[77 FR 48753, Aug. 14, 2012]

§ 42.302. Who may petition for a covered business method patent review.

(a) A petitioner may not file with the Office a petition to institute a covered business method patent review of the patent unless the petitioner, the petitioner's real party-in-interest, or a privy of the petitioner has been sued for infringement of the patent or has been charged with infringement under that patent. Charged with infringement means a real and substantial controversy regarding infringement of a covered business method patent exists such that the petitioner would have standing to bring a declaratory judgment action in Federal court.

(b) A petitioner may not file a petition to institute a covered business method patent review of the patent where the petitioner, the petitioner's real party-in-interest, or a privy of the petitioner is estopped from challenging the claims on the grounds identified in the petition.

(c) A petitioner may not file a petition to institute a covered business method patent review of the patent where, before the date on which the petition is filed, the petitioner or real party-in-interest filed a civil action challenging the validity of a claim of the patent.

[80 FR 28566, May 19, 2015]

§ 42.303. Time for filing.

A petition requesting a covered business method patent review may be filed any time except during the period in which a petition for a post-grant review of the patent would satisfy the requirements of 35 U.S.C. 321(c).

§ 42.304. Content of petition.

In addition to any other notices required by subparts A and C of this part, a petition must request judgment against one or more claims of a patent identified by patent number. In addition to the requirements of §§ 42.6, 42.8, 42.22, and 42.24 the petition must set forth:

(a) Grounds for standing. The petitioner must demonstrate that the patent for which review is sought is a covered business method patent, and that the petitioner meets the eligibility requirements of § 42.302.

(b) Identification of challenge. Provide a statement of the precise relief requested for each claim challenged. The statement must identify the following:

(1) The claim;

(2) The specific statutory grounds permitted under paragraph (2) or (3) of 35 U.S.C. 282(b), except as modified by section 18(a)(1)(C) of the Leahy-Smith America Invents Act (Pub. L. 112-29, 125 Stat. 284 (2011)), on which the challenge to the claim is based;

(3) How the challenged claim is to be construed. Where the claim to be construed contains a means-plus-function or step-plus-function limitation as permitted under 35 U.S.C. 112(f), the construction of the claim must identify the specific portions of the specification that describe the structure, material, or acts corresponding to each claimed function;

(4) How the construed claim is unpatentable under the statutory grounds identified in paragraph (b)(2) of this section. Where the grounds for unpatentability are based on prior art, the petition must specify where each element of the claim is found in the prior art. For all other grounds of unpatentability, the petition must identify the specific part of the claim that fails to comply with the statutory grounds raised and state how the identified subject matter fails to comply with the statute; and

(5) The exhibit number of supporting evidence relied

upon to support the challenge and the relevance of the evidence to the challenge raised, including identifying specific portions of the evidence that support the challenge. The Board may exclude or give no weight to the evidence where a party has failed to state its relevance or to identify specific portions of the evidence that support the challenge.

(c) A motion may be filed that seeks to correct a clerical or typographical mistake in the petition. The grant of such a motion does not change the filing date of the petition.

SUBPART E— DERIVATION

GENERAL

§ 42.400. Procedure; pendency.

(a) A derivation proceeding is a trial subject to the procedures set forth in subpart A of this part.

(b) The Board may for good cause authorize or direct the parties to address patentability issues that arise in the course of the derivation proceeding.

§ 42.401. Definitions.

In addition to the definitions in § 42.2, the following definitions apply to proceedings under this subpart:

Agreement or understanding under 35 U.S.C. 135(e) means settlement for the purposes of § 42.74.

Applicant includes a reissue applicant.

Application includes both an application for an original patent and an application for a reissued patent.

First publication means either a patent or an application publication under 35 U.S.C. 122(b), including a publication of an international application designating the United States as provided by 35 U.S.C. 374.

Petitioner means a patent applicant who petitions for a determination that another party named in an earlier-filed patent application allegedly derived a claimed invention from an inventor named in the petitioner's application and filed the earlier application without authorization.

Respondent means a party other than the petitioner.

Same or substantially the same means patentably indistinct.

§ 42.402. Who may file a petition for a derivation proceeding.

An applicant for patent may file a petition to institute a derivation proceeding in the Office.

§ 42.403.   Time for filing.

A petition for a derivation proceeding must be filed within the one-year period beginning on the date of the first publication of a claim to an invention that is the same or substantially the same as the earlier application's claim to the allegedly derived invention.

§ 42.404.   Derivation fee.

(a) A derivation fee set forth in § 42.15(c) must accompany the petition.

(b) No filing date will be accorded to the petition until payment is complete.

§ 42.405.   Content of petition.

(a) Grounds for standing. The petition must:

(1) Demonstrate compliance with §§ 42.402 and 42.403; and

(2) Show that the petitioner has at least one claim that is:

(i) The same or substantially the same as the respondent's claimed invention; and

(ii) The same or substantially the same as the invention disclosed to the respondent.

(b) In addition to the requirements of §§ 42.8 and 42.22, the petition must:

(1) Provide sufficient information to identify the application or patent for which the petitioner seeks a derivation proceeding;

(2) Demonstrate that a claimed invention was derived from an inventor named in the petitioner's application, and that the inventor from whom the invention was derived did not authorize the filing of the earliest application claiming such invention; and

(3) For each of the respondent's claims to the derived invention,

(i) Show why the claimed invention is the same or substantially the same as the invention disclosed to the respondent, and

(ii) Identify how the claim is to be construed. Where the claim to be construed contains a means-plus-function or step-plus-function limitation as permitted under 35 U.S.C. 112(f), the construction of the claim must identify the specific portions of the specification that describe the structure, material, or acts corresponding to each claimed function.

(c) *Sufficiency of showing.* A derivation showing is not sufficient unless it is supported by substantial evidence, including at least one affidavit addressing communication of the derived invention and lack of authorization that, if unrebutted, would support a determination of derivation. The showing of communication must be corroborated.

§ 42.406. Service of petition.

In addition to the requirements of § 42.6, the petitioner must serve the petition and exhibits relied upon in the petition as follows:

(a) The petition and supporting evidence must be served on the respondent at the correspondence address of record for the earlier application or subject patent. The petitioner may additionally serve the petition and supporting evidence on the respondent at any other address known to the petitioner as likely to effect service.

(b) Upon agreement of the parties, service may be made electronically. Service may be by Priority Mail Express® or by means at least as fast and reliable as Priority Mail Express®. Personal service is not required.

[79 FR 63043, Oct. 22, 2014]

§ 42.407. Filing date.

(a) *Complete petition.* A petition to institute a derivation proceeding will not be accorded a filing date until the petition satisfies all of the following requirements:

(1) Complies with §§ 42.404 and 42.405, and

(2) Service of the petition on the correspondence address of record as provided in § 42.406.

(b) *Incomplete petition.* Where the petitioner files an incomplete petition, no filing date will be accorded, and the Office will dismiss the petition if the deficiency in the petition is not corrected within the earlier of either one month from notice of the incomplete petition, or the expiration of the statutory deadline in which to file a petition for derivation.

INSTITUTING DERIVATION PROCEEDING

§ 42.408. Institution of derivation proceeding.

(a) An administrative patent judge institutes, and may as necessary reinstitute, the derivation proceeding on behalf of the Director.

(b) *Additional derivation proceeding.* The petitioner may suggest the addition of a patent or application to the derivation proceeding. The suggestion should make the showings required under § 42.405 and explain why the suggestion could not have been made in the original petition.

AFTER INSTITUTION OF DERIVATION PROCEEDING

§ 42.409. Settlement agreements.

An agreement or understanding under 35 U.S.C. 135(e) is a settlement for the purposes of § 42.74.

§ 42.410. Arbitration.

(a) Parties may resort to binding arbitration to determine any issue. The Office is not a party to the arbitration. The Board is not bound by, and may independently determine, any question of patentability.

(b) The Board will not set a time for, or otherwise modify the proceeding for, an arbitration unless:

(1) It is to be conducted according to Title 9 of the United States Code;

(2) The parties notify the Board in writing of their intention to arbitrate;

(3) The agreement to arbitrate:

(i) Is in writing;

(ii) Specifies the issues to be arbitrated;

(iii) Names the arbitrator, or provides a date not more than 30 days after the execution of the agreement for the selection of the arbitrator;

(iv) Provides that the arbitrator's award shall be binding on the parties and that judgment thereon can be entered by the Board;

(v) Provides that a copy of the agreement is filed within 20 days after its execution; and

(vi) Provides that the arbitration is completed within the time the Board sets.

(c) The parties are solely responsible for the selection of the arbitrator and the conduct of the arbitration.

(d) The Board may determine issues the arbitration does not resolve.

(e) The Board will not consider the arbitration award unless it:

(1) Is binding on the parties;

(2) Is in writing;

(3) States in a clear and definite manner each issue arbitrated and the disposition of each issue; and

(4) Is filed within 20 days of the date of the award.

(f) Once the award is filed, the parties to the award may not take actions inconsistent with the award. If the award is dispositive of the contested subject matter for a party, the Board may enter judgment as to that party.

§ 42.411. Common interests in the invention.

The Board may decline to institute, or if already instituted the Board may issue judgment in, a derivation proceeding between an application and a patent or another application that are commonly owned.

§ 42.412. Public availability of Board records.

(a) Publication.

(1) Generally. Any Board decision is available for public inspection without a party's permission if rendered in a file open to the public pursuant to § 1.11 of this chapter or in an application that has been published in accordance with §§ 1.211 to 1.221 of this chapter. The Office may independently publish any Board decision that is available for public inspection.

(2) Determination of special circumstances. Any Board decision not publishable under paragraph (a)(1) of this section may be published or made available for public inspection if the Director believes that special circumstances warrant publication and a party does not petition within two months after being notified of the intention to make the decision public, objecting in writing on the ground that the decision discloses the objecting party's trade secret or other confidential information and stating with specificity that such information is not otherwise publicly available.

(b) Record of proceeding.

(1) The record of a Board proceeding is available to the public, unless a patent application not otherwise available to the public is involved.

(2) Notwithstanding paragraph (b)(1) of this section, after a final Board decision in or judgment in a Board proceeding, the record of the Board proceeding will be made available to the public if any involved file is or becomes open to the public under § 1.11 of this chapter or an involved application is or becomes published under §§ 1.211 to 1.221 of this chapter.

APPENDIX C1

Scientific Considerations in Demonstrating Biosimilarity to a Reference Product

---

Scientific Considerations in Demonstrating Biosimilarity to a Reference Product

Guidance for Industry

U.S. Department of Health and Human Services
Food and Drug Administration
Center for Drug Evaluation and Research (CDER)
Center for Biologics Evaluation and Research (CBER)

April 2015
Biosimilarity

Scientific Considerations in Demonstrating Biosimilarity to a Reference Product

Guidance for Industry

Additional copies are available from:

Office of Communications, Division of Drug Information
Center for Drug Evaluation and Research
Food and Drug Administration
10001 New Hampshire Ave., Hillandale Bldg., 4th Floor
Silver Spring, MD 20993-0002
Phone: 855-543-3784 or 301-796-3400; Fax: 301-431-6353
Email: druginfo@fda.hhs.gov
http://www.fda.gov/Drugs/GuidanceComplianceRegulatoryInformation/Guidances/default.htm

and/or

Office of Communication, Outreach and Development
Center for Biologics Evaluation and Research
Food and Drug Administration
10903 New Hampshire Ave., Bldg. 71, Room 3128
Silver Spring, MD 20993-0002
Phone: 800-835-4709 or 240-402-7800
Email: ocod@fda.hhs.gov
http://www.fda.gov/BiologicsBloodVaccines/GuidanceComplianceRegulatoryInformation/Guidances/default.htm

U.S. Department of Health and Human Services
Food and Drug Administration
Center for Drug Evaluation and Research (CDER)
Center for Biologics Evaluation and Research (CBER)

April 2015
Biosimilarity

Contains Nonbinding Recommendations

TABLE OF CONTENTS

I.   INTRODUCTION... 1

II.   SCOPE 2

III.   BACKGROUND 3

IV.   COMPLEXITIES OF PROTEIN PRODUCTS... 4

    A.   Nature of Protein Products and Related Scientific Considerations 5

    B.   Manufacturing Process Considerations 5

V.   U.S.-LICENSED REFERENCE PRODUCT AND OTHER COMPARATORS 6

VI.   APPROACHES TO DEVELOPING AND ASSESSING EVIDENCE TO
DEMONSTRATE BIOSIMILARITY 7

    A.   Using a Stepwise Approach to Demonstrate Biosimilarity 7

    B.   Using a *Totality-of-the-Evidence* Approach to Assess a Demonstration of Biosimilarity 8

VII.   DEMONSTRATING BIOSIMILARITY 9

    A.   Structural Analyses... 9

    B.   Functional Assays 10

    C.   Animal Data.. 11

        1. Animal Toxicity Studies.. 11

        2. Inclusion of Animal PK and PD Measures 13

        3. Interpreting Animal Immunogenicity Results 13

    D.   Clinical Studies – General Considerations 13

        1. Human Pharmacology Data 14

        2. Clinical Immunogenicity Assessment.. 16

        3. Comparative Clinical Studies 18

        4. Extrapolation of Clinical Data Across Indications... 21

VIII.   POSTMARKETING SAFETY MONITORING CONSIDERATIONS..................... 22

IX.   CONSULTATION WITH FDA... 22

GLOSSARY.. 24

i

Scientific Considerations in Demonstrating Biosimilarity to a Reference Product
Guidance for Industry[1]

I.   INTRODUCTION

This guidance is intended to assist sponsors in demonstrating that a proposed therapeutic protein product (hereinafter *proposed product*[2]) is biosimilar to a reference product for purposes of the submission of a marketing application under section 351(k) of the Public Health Service Act (PHS Act).[3] The Biologics Price Competition and Innovation Act of 2009 (BPCI Act) amends the PHS Act and other statutes to create an abbreviated licensure pathway in section 351(k) of the PHS Act for biological products shown to be biosimilar to or interchangeable with an FDA-licensed biological reference product (see sections 7001 through 7003 of the Patient Protection and Affordable Care Act (Affordable Care Act) (Public Law 111-148). Although the 351(k) pathway applies generally to biological products, this guidance focuses on therapeutic protein products and gives an overview of important scientific considerations for demonstrating biosimilarity. The scientific principles described in this guidance may also apply to other types of proposed biosimilar biological products.

This guidance is one in a series of guidances that FDA is developing to implement the BPCI Act. These guidances address a broad range of issues, including:

- Quality Considerations in Demonstrating Biosimilarity of a Therapeutic Protein Product to a Reference Product

---

[1] This guidance has been prepared by the Office of Medical Policy in the Center for Drug Evaluation and Research (CDER) in cooperation with the Center for Biologics Evaluation and Research (CBER) at the Food and Drug Administration.

[2] In Section II (Scope) of this document, the term *proposed product* is also used to describe a product that is the subject of a new drug application (NDA) submitted through the pathway described by section 505(b)(2) of the Federal Food, Drug, and Cosmetic Act (FD&C Act).

[3] The statutory definition of *biosimilar* and definitions of selected other terms used in this guidance are provided in the glossary at the end of the document.

1

- Scientific Considerations in Demonstrating Biosimilarity to a Reference Product

- Biosimilars: Questions and Answers Regarding Implementation of the Biologics Price Competition and Innovation Act of 2009

- Formal Meetings Between the FDA and Biosimilar Biological Product Sponsors or Applicants

- Clinical Pharmacology Data to Support a Demonstration of Biosimilarity to a Reference Product

When applicable, references to information in these guidances are included in this guidance.

In general, FDA's guidance documents do not establish legally enforceable responsibilities. Instead, guidances describe the Agency's current thinking on a topic and should be viewed only as recommendations, unless specific regulatory or statutory requirements are cited. The use of the word *should* in Agency guidances means that something is suggested or recommended, but not required.

II.   SCOPE

This guidance gives an overview of FDA's approach to determining biosimilarity and discusses important scientific considerations in demonstrating biosimilarity, including:

- A stepwise approach to demonstrating biosimilarity, which can include a comparison of the proposed product and the reference product with respect to structure, function, animal toxicity, human pharmacokinetics (PK) and pharmacodynamics (PD), clinical immunogenicity, and clinical safety and effectiveness

- The *totality-of-the-evidence* approach that FDA will use to review applications for biosimilar products, consistent with a longstanding Agency approach to evaluation of scientific evidence[4]

- General scientific principles in conducting comparative structural analyses, functional assays, animal testing, human PK and PD studies, clinical immunogenicity assessments, and comparative clinical studies (including clinical study design issues)

---

[4] The guidance for industry *Providing Clinical Evidence of Effectiveness for Human Drug and Biological Products* provides insight into the concept of the *totality-of-the-evidence* approach in a different context (i.e., considerations of both the quantity and quality of the evidence to support effectiveness for drugs and biological products). Some of the principles discussed in that guidance may also be relevant in the design of a development program to support a demonstration of biosimilarity.

We update guidances periodically. For the most recent version of a guidance, check the FDA guidance Web page at http://www.fda.gov/RegulatoryInformation/Guidances/default.htm.

2

Additional topics discussed include the following:

- Considerations of the complexities of therapeutic protein products when designing a biosimilar development program, including manufacturing process considerations

- Use of data derived from studies comparing a proposed product with a non-U.S.-licensed comparator product

- Postmarketing safety monitoring considerations

This guidance applies to applications submitted under section 351(k) of the PHS Act. However, some scientific principles described in this guidance may be informative for the development of certain biological products under section 505(b)(2) of the FD&C Act.[5] Section 505(b)(2) of the FD&C Act and section 351(k) of the PHS Act are two separate statutory schemes. This guidance is not intended to describe any relationship between the standards for approval under these schemes.

III. BACKGROUND

The BPCI Act was enacted as part of the Affordable Care Act on March 23, 2010. The BPCI Act creates an abbreviated licensure pathway for biological products demonstrated to be biosimilar to or interchangeable with a reference product. Section 351(k) of the PHS Act (42 U.S.C. 262(k)), added by the BPCI Act, sets forth the requirements for an application for a proposed biosimilar product and an application or a supplement for a proposed interchangeable product.[6] Section 351(i) of the PHS Act defines *biosimilarity* to mean "that the biological product is highly similar to the reference product notwithstanding minor differences in clinically inactive components" and that "there are no clinically meaningful differences between the biological product and the reference product in terms of the safety, purity, and potency of the product."[7] The BPCI Act also amended the definition of biological product to include "protein (except any chemically synthesized polypeptide)."[8]

Under section 351(k) of the PHS Act, a proposed biological product that is demonstrated to be biosimilar to a reference product can rely on certain existing scientific knowledge about the

---

[5] A 505(b)(2) application is an NDA that contains full reports of investigations of safety and effectiveness, where at least some of the information required for approval comes from studies not conducted by or for the applicant and for which the applicant has not obtained a right of reference or use (e.g., the Agency's finding of safety and/or effectiveness for a listed drug or published literature). A 505(b)(2) application that seeks to rely on a listed drug (i.e., the reference product) must contain adequate data and information to demonstrate that the proposed product is sufficiently similar to the listed drug to justify reliance, in part, on FDA's finding of safety and/or effectiveness for the listed drug. Any aspects of the proposed product that differ from the listed drug must be supported by adequate data and information to support the safety and effectiveness of the proposed product.

[6] General scientific issues relating to the demonstration of interchangeability will be addressed separately.

[7] Section 7002(b)(3) of the Affordable Care Act, adding section 351(i)(2) of the PHS Act.

[8] Section 7002(b)(2) of the Affordable Care Act, amending section 351(i) of the PHS Act.

3

safety, purity, and potency[9] of the reference product to support licensure. FDA will license a proposed biological product submitted under section 351(k) of the PHS Act if FDA "determines that the information submitted in the application . . . is sufficient to show that the biological product is biosimilar to the reference product . . ." and the 351(k) applicant (or other appropriate person) consents to an inspection of the facility that is the subject of the application (i.e., a facility in which the proposed biological product is manufactured, processed, packed, or held).[10]

An application submitted under section 351(k) of the PHS Act must contain, among other things, information demonstrating that "the biological product is biosimilar to a reference product" based upon data derived from:[11]

- Analytical studies that demonstrate that the biological product is highly similar to the reference product notwithstanding minor differences in clinically inactive components;

- Animal studies (including the assessment of toxicity); and

- A clinical study or studies (including the assessment of immunogenicity and pharmacokinetics or pharmacodynamics) that are sufficient to demonstrate safety, purity, and potency in one or more appropriate conditions of use for which the reference product is licensed and intended to be used and for which licensure is sought for the biological product.

The Agency has the discretion to determine that an element described above is unnecessary in a 351(k) application.[12] FDA advises sponsors intending to develop biosimilar products to meet with FDA to present their product development plans and establish a schedule of milestones that will serve as landmarks for future discussions with the Agency. FDA anticipates that early discussions with FDA about product development plans and about approaches to providing adequate scientific justifications will facilitate biosimilar development.[13]

IV. COMPLEXITIES OF PROTEIN PRODUCTS

A sponsor should consider the complexities of protein products and related scientific issues when designing a development program to support a demonstration of biosimilarity.

---

[9] The standard for licensure of a biological product as *potent* under section 351(a) of the PHS Act has long been interpreted to include effectiveness (see 21 CFR 600.3(s) and the guidance for industry on *Providing Clinical Evidence of Effectiveness for Human Drug and Biological Products*). In this guidance, we use the terms *safety and effectiveness* and *safety, purity, and potency* interchangeably in the discussions pertaining to biosimilar products.

[10] Section 7002(a)(2) of the Affordable Care Act, adding section 351(k)(3) of the PHS Act.

[11] Section 7002(a)(2) of the Affordable Care Act, adding section 351(k)(2)(A)(i)(I) of the PHS Act.

[12] Section 7002(a)(2) of the Affordable Care Act, adding section 351(k)(2)(A)(ii) of the PHS Act.

[13] See the draft guidance for industry *Formal Meetings Between the FDA and Biosimilar Biological Product Sponsors or Applicants* for a detailed discussion. When final, this guidance will represent FDA's current thinking on this topic.

4

A. Nature of Protein Products and Related Scientific Considerations

Unlike small molecule drugs, whose structure can usually be completely defined and entirely reproduced, proteins are typically more complex and are unlikely to be shown to be structurally identical to a reference product. Many potential differences in protein structure can arise. Because even minor structural differences (including certain changes in glycosylation patterns) can significantly affect a protein's safety and/or effectiveness, it is important to evaluate these differences.

In general, proteins can differ in at least three ways: (1) primary amino acid sequence; (2) modification to amino acids, such as sugar moieties (glycosylation) or other side chains; and (3) higher order structure (protein folding and protein-protein interactions). Modifications to amino acids may lead to heterogeneity and can be difficult to control. Protein modifications and higher order structure can be affected by formulation and environmental conditions, including light, temperature, moisture, packaging materials, container closure systems, and delivery device materials. Additionally, process- as well as product-related impurities may increase the likelihood and/or the severity of an immune response to a protein product, and certain excipients may limit the ability to characterize the protein product.

Advances in analytical sciences enable some protein products to be extensively characterized with respect to their physicochemical and biological properties, such as higher order structures and functional characteristics. These analytical methodologies have increasingly improved the ability to identify and characterize not only the drug substance of a protein product but also excipients and product- and process-related impurities.

Despite such significant improvements in analytical techniques, however, current analytical methodology may not be able to detect all relevant structural and functional differences between two protein products. In addition, there may be incomplete understanding of the relationship between a product's structural attributes and its clinical performance. Thus, as set forth in the PHS Act, data derived from analytical studies, animal studies, and a clinical study or studies are required to demonstrate biosimilarity unless FDA determines an element unnecessary.[14]

B. Manufacturing Process Considerations

Different manufacturing processes may alter a protein product in a way that could affect the safety or effectiveness of the product. For example, differences in biological systems used to manufacture a protein product may cause different posttranslational modifications, which in turn may affect the safety and/or effectiveness of the product. Thus, when the manufacturing process for a marketed protein product is changed, the application holder must assess the effects of the change and demonstrate—through appropriate analytical testing, functional assays, and/or in some cases animal and/or clinical studies—that the change does not have an adverse effect on the identity, strength, quality, purity, or potency of the product as they relate to the safety or

---

[14] Section 7002(a)(2) of the Affordable Care Act, adding section 351(k)(2)(A)(i)(I) of the PHS Act.

5

effectiveness of the product.[15] The International Conference on Harmonisation (ICH) guidance for industry *Q5E Comparability of Biotechnological/Biological Products Subject to Changes in Their Manufacturing Process* (ICH Q5E) describes scientific principles in the comparability assessment for manufacturing changes.

Demonstrating that a proposed product is biosimilar to a reference product typically will be more complex than assessing the comparability of a product before and after manufacturing changes made by the same manufacturer. This is because a manufacturer that modifies its own manufacturing process has extensive knowledge and information about the product and the existing process, including established controls and acceptance parameters. By contrast, the manufacturer of a proposed product is likely to have a different manufacturing process (e.g., different cell line, raw materials, equipment, processes, process controls, and acceptance criteria) from that of the reference product and no direct knowledge of the manufacturing process for the reference product. Therefore, even though some of the scientific principles described in ICH Q5E may also apply in the demonstration of biosimilarity, in general, FDA anticipates that more data and information will be needed to establish biosimilarity than would be needed to establish that a manufacturer's post-manufacturing change product is comparable to the pre-manufacturing change product.

V. U.S.-LICENSED REFERENCE PRODUCT AND OTHER COMPARATORS

To obtain licensure of a proposed product under section 351(k) of the PHS Act, a sponsor must demonstrate that the proposed product is biosimilar to a single reference product that previously has been licensed by FDA.[16] In general, a sponsor needs to provide information to demonstrate biosimilarity based on data directly comparing the proposed product with the reference product. As a scientific matter, analytical studies and at least one clinical PK study and, if appropriate, at least one PD study, intended to support a demonstration of biosimilarity for purposes of section 351(k) of the PHS Act must include an adequate comparison of the proposed biosimilar product directly with the U.S.-licensed reference product unless it can be scientifically justified that such a study is not needed. However, a sponsor may seek to use data derived from animal or clinical studies comparing a proposed product with a non-U.S.-licensed comparator product to address, in part, the requirements under section 351(k)(2)(A) of the PHS Act. In such a case, the sponsor should provide adequate data or information to scientifically justify the relevance of these comparative data to an assessment of biosimilarity and establish an acceptable bridge to the U.S.-licensed reference product.[17] Sponsors are encouraged to discuss with FDA during the development program their plans to provide an adequate scientific justification and bridge to the U.S.-licensed reference product. A final decision about the adequacy of such justification and bridge will be made by FDA during review of the 351(k) application.

---

[15] See 21 CFR 601.12 and 21 CFR 314.70 for regulatory requirements for changes (including manufacturing changes) made to a licensed biologics license application (BLA) and an approved NDA, respectively.

[16] Sections 7002(a)(2) and (b)(3) of the Affordable Care Act, adding sections 351(k), 351(i)(2), and 351(i)(4) of the PHS Act.

[17] For examples of issues that a sponsor may need to address, see the guidance for industry *Biosimilars: Questions and Answers Regarding Implementation of the Biologics Price Competition and Innovation Act of 2009.*

VI. APPROACHES TO DEVELOPING AND ASSESSING EVIDENCE TO DEMONSTRATE BIOSIMILARITY

FDA recommends that sponsors use a stepwise approach to develop the evidence needed to demonstrate biosimilarity. FDA intends to consider the *totality of the evidence* provided by a sponsor when the Agency evaluates the sponsor's demonstration of biosimilarity, consistent with a longstanding Agency approach to evaluating scientific evidence.[18]

A. Using a Stepwise Approach to Demonstrate Biosimilarity

The purpose of a biosimilar development program is to support a demonstration of biosimilarity between a proposed product and a reference product, including an assessment of the effects of any observed differences between the products, but not to independently establish the safety and effectiveness of the proposed product. FDA recommends that sponsors use a stepwise approach to developing the data and information needed to support a demonstration of biosimilarity. At each step, the sponsor should evaluate the extent to which there is residual uncertainty about the biosimilarity of the proposed product and identify next steps to try to address that uncertainty. Where possible, studies conducted should be designed to maximize their contribution to demonstrating biosimilarity. For example, a clinical immunogenicity study may also provide other useful information about the safety profile of the proposed product.

The stepwise approach should start with extensive structural and functional characterization of both the proposed product and the reference product, which serves as the foundation of a biosimilar development program (sections VII.A and VII.B). The more comprehensive and robust the comparative structural and functional characterization—the extent to which these studies are able to identify (qualitatively or quantitatively) differences in relevant product attributes between the proposed product and the reference product (including the drug substance, excipients, and impurities)—the more useful such characterization will be in determining what additional studies may be needed. For example, rigorous structural and functional comparisons that show minimal or no difference between the proposed product and the reference product will strengthen the scientific justification for a selective and targeted approach to animal and/or clinical testing to support a demonstration of biosimilarity. It may be useful to further quantify the similarity or differences between the two products using a meaningful *fingerprint*-like analyses algorithm that covers a large number of additional product attributes and their combinations with high sensitivity using orthogonal methods. Such a strategy may further reduce the possibility of undetected structural differences between the products and lead to a more selective and targeted approach to animal and/or clinical testing. A sufficient understanding of the mechanism of action (MOA) of the drug substance and clinical relevance of any observed structural differences, clinical knowledge of the reference product and its class that indicates low overall safety risks, and the availability of a relevant PD measure(s) may provide further scientific justification for a selective and targeted approach to animal and/or clinical studies.

---

[18] See footnote 4.

7

Contains Nonbinding Recommendations

The sponsor should then consider the role of animal data in assessing toxicity and, in some cases, in providing additional support for demonstrating biosimilarity and in contributing to the immunogenicity assessment (section VII.C). The sponsor should then conduct comparative human PK and PD studies (if there is a relevant PD measure(s)) (section VII.D.1) and compare the clinical immunogenicity of the two products in an appropriate study population (section VII.D.2). If there is residual uncertainty about biosimilarity after conducting structural analyses, functional assays, animal testing, human PK and PD studies, and the clinical immunogenicity assessment, the sponsor should then consider what additional clinical data may be needed to adequately address that uncertainty (section VII.D.3). FDA encourages sponsors to consult extensively with the Agency after completion of comparative structural and functional analyses (before finalizing the clinical program) and throughout development as needed.

FDA recognizes that some of the aforementioned investigations could be performed in parallel; however, the Agency recommends that sponsors use a stepwise approach to better address residual uncertainty about biosimilarity that might remain at each step and incorporate FDA's advice provided after FDA review of data and information collected at certain milestones.

B. Using a *Totality-of-the-Evidence* Approach to Assess a Demonstration of Biosimilarity

In evaluating a sponsor's demonstration of biosimilarity, FDA will consider the totality of the data and information submitted in the application, including structural and functional characterization, nonclinical evaluation, human PK and PD data, clinical immunogenicity data, and comparative clinical study(ies) data. FDA intends to use a risk-based approach to evaluate all available data and information submitted in support of the biosimilarity of the proposed product.

Thus, a sponsor may be able to demonstrate biosimilarity even though there are formulation or minor structural differences, provided that the sponsor provides sufficient data and information demonstrating that the differences are not clinically meaningful and the proposed product otherwise meets the statutory criteria for biosimilarity. For example, differences in certain posttranslational modifications or differences in certain excipients (e.g., human serum albumin) might not preclude a finding of biosimilarity if data and information provided by the sponsor show that the proposed product is highly similar to the reference product notwithstanding minor differences in clinically inactive components and that there are no clinically meaningful differences between the products in terms of safety, purity, and potency.[19] Clinically meaningful differences could include a difference in the expected range of safety, purity, or potency of the proposed product and the reference product. By contrast, slight differences in rates of occurrence of certain adverse events between the two products ordinarily would not be considered clinically meaningful differences.

---

[19] In this example, because some excipients may affect the ability to characterize products, a sponsor should provide evidence that the excipients used in the reference product will not affect the ability to characterize and compare the products.

VII. DEMONSTRATING BIOSIMILARITY

This section discusses scientific considerations in the stepwise approach to developing data and information needed to support a demonstration of biosimilarity. To demonstrate biosimilarity, a sponsor must provide sufficient data and information to show that the proposed product and the reference product are highly similar notwithstanding minor differences in clinically inactive components and that there are no clinically meaningful differences between the two products in terms of safety, purity, and potency.[20] The type and amount of analyses and testing that will be sufficient to demonstrate biosimilarity will be determined on a product-specific basis.

A. Structural Analyses

The PHS Act requires that a 351(k) application include information demonstrating biosimilarity based on data derived from, among other things, analytical studies that demonstrate that the biological product is highly similar to the reference product notwithstanding minor differences in clinically inactive components, unless FDA determines that an element is unnecessary in a 351(k) application.[21] FDA expects that first, a sponsor will extensively characterize the proposed product and the reference product with state-of-the-art technology, because extensive characterization of both products serves as the foundation for a demonstration of biosimilarity. It is expected that the expression construct for a proposed product will encode the same primary amino acid sequence as its reference product. However, minor modifications such as N- or C-terminal truncations that are not expected to change the product performance may be justified and should be explained by the sponsor. Additionally, sponsors should consider all relevant characteristics of the protein product (e.g., the primary, secondary, tertiary, and quaternary structure; posttranslational modifications; and biological activities) to demonstrate that the proposed product is highly similar to the reference product notwithstanding minor differences in clinically inactive components. The more comprehensive and robust the comparative structural and functional characterization is, the stronger the scientific justification for a selective and targeted approach to animal and/or clinical testing.

Sponsors should use appropriate analytical methodologies with adequate sensitivity and specificity for structural characterization of the proteins. Generally, such tests include the following comparisons of the proposed product and the reference product:

- Primary structures, such as amino acid sequence

- Higher order structures, including secondary, tertiary, and quaternary structure (including aggregation)

- Enzymatic posttranslational modifications, such as glycosylation and phosphorylation

---

[20] Section 7002(b)(3) of the Affordable Care Act, adding section 351(i)(2) of the PHS Act.

[21] Section 7002(a)(2) of the Affordable Care Act, adding sections 351(k)(2)(A)(i)(I)(aa) and 351(k)(2)(A)(ii) of the PHS Act.

9

- Other potential variations, such as protein deamidation and oxidation

- Intentional chemical modifications, such as PEGylation sites and characteristics

Sponsors should conduct extensive structural characterization of both the proposed product and the reference product in multiple representative lots to understand the lot-to-lot variability of both products in the manufacturing processes. Lots used for the analyses should support the biosimilarity of both the clinical material used in the clinical study(ies) intended to support a demonstration of biosimilarity, and the to-be-marketed proposed product, to the reference product. Characterization of lots manufactured during process development for the proposed product may also be useful. Sponsors should justify the selection of the representative lots, including the number of lots.

In addition, FDA recommends that sponsors analyze the finished dosage form of multiple lots of the proposed product and the reference product, assessing excipients and any formulation effect on purity, product- and process-related impurities, and stability.[22] Differences in formulation between the proposed product and the reference product are among the factors that may affect the extent and nature of subsequent animal or clinical testing.[23] A sponsor considering manufacturing changes after completing the initial analytical similarity assessment or after completing clinical testing intended to support a 351(k) application should perform an additional analytical similarity assessment with lots manufactured by the new process and the reference product and establish comparability of the proposed product manufactured by the old and new manufacturing processes. The nature and extent of the changes may determine the extent of the analytical similarity and comparability studies and any necessary additional studies.

If the reference product or the proposed product cannot be adequately characterized with state-of-the-art technology, the application for the proposed product may not be appropriate for submission under section 351(k) of the PHS Act; and the sponsor should consult FDA for guidance on the appropriate submission pathway.

B.   **Functional Assays**

The pharmacologic activity of protein products should be evaluated by in vitro and/or in vivo functional assays. In vitro assays may include, but are not limited to, biological assays, binding assays, and enzyme kinetics. In vivo assays may include the use of animal models of disease (e.g., models that exhibit a disease state or symptom) to evaluate functional effects on pharmacodynamic markers or efficacy measures. A functional evaluation comparing a proposed product to the reference product using these types of assays is also an important part of the foundation that supports a demonstration of biosimilarity and may be used to scientifically justify a selective and targeted approach to animal and/or clinical testing.

---

[22] See also the guidance for industry *Quality Considerations in Demonstrating Biosimilarity of a Therapeutic Protein Product to a Reference Product.*

[23] See also the guidance for industry *Quality Considerations in Demonstrating Biosimilarity of a Therapeutic Protein Product to a Reference Product.*

10

Contains Nonbinding Recommendations

Sponsors can use functional assays to provide additional evidence that the biologic activity and potency of the proposed product are highly similar to those of the reference product and/or to support a conclusion that there are no clinically meaningful differences between the proposed product and the reference product. Such assays also may be used to provide additional evidence that the MOA of the two products is the same to the extent the MOA of the reference product is known. Functional assays can be used to provide additional data to support results from structural analyses, investigate the consequences of observed structural differences, and explore structure-activity relationships.[24] These assays are expected to be comparative so they can provide evidence of similarity or reveal differences in the performance of the proposed product compared to the reference product, especially differences resulting from variations in structure that cannot be detected using current analytical methods. FDA also recommends that sponsors discuss limitations of the assays they used when interpreting results in their submissions to FDA. Such discussions would be useful for the evaluation of analytical data and may guide whether additional analytical testing would be necessary to support a demonstration of biosimilarity.

Functional assays can also provide information that complements the animal and clinical data in assessing the potential clinical effects of minor differences in structure between the proposed product and the reference product. For example, cell-based bioactivity assays may be used to detect the potential for inducing cytokine release syndrome in vivo. The available information about these assays, including sensitivity, specificity, and extent of validation, can affect the amount and type of additional animal or clinical data that may be needed to establish biosimilarity. As is the case for the structural evaluation, sponsors should justify the selection of the representative lots, including the number of lots.

C.   Animal Data

The PHS Act also requires that a 351(k) application include information demonstrating biosimilarity based on data derived from animal studies (including the assessment of toxicity), unless FDA determines that such studies are not necessary in a 351(k) application.[25] Results from animal studies may be used to support the safety evaluation of the proposed product and more generally to support the demonstration of biosimilarity between the proposed product and the reference product.

1.   Animal Toxicity Studies

As a scientific matter, animal toxicity data are considered useful when, based on the results of extensive structural and functional characterization, uncertainties remain about the safety of the proposed product that need to be addressed before initiation of clinical studies in humans (assuming results from animal studies can meaningfully address the remaining uncertainties).

---

[24] See also the guidance for industry *Quality Considerations in Demonstrating Biosimilarity of a Therapeutic Protein Product to a Reference Product.*

[25] Section 7002(a)(2) of the Affordable Care Act, adding sections 351(k)(2)(A)(i)(I)(bb) and 351(k)(2)(A)(ii) of the PHS Act.

11

Contains Nonbinding Recommendations

The scope and extent of any animal toxicity studies will depend on information about the reference product, information about the proposed product, and the extent of known similarities or differences between the two. As described further in section IX, FDA encourages sponsors to initiate early discussions with the Agency with regard to their biosimilar development plans, including identifying appropriate scientific justifications for not conducting an animal toxicity study or for the scope and extent of such a study.

If comparative structural and functional data using the proposed product provide strong support for analytical similarity to a reference product, then limited animal toxicity data may be sufficient to support initial clinical use of the proposed product. Such a study may be non-sacrificial and include endpoints that measure in-life parameters, PD, and PK (with an assessment of immunogenicity).

If the structural and functional data are limited in scope or there are concerns about the proposed product quality, a general toxicology study may be needed that includes full animal pathology, histopathology, PD, PK, and immunogenicity assessments. When animal toxicology studies are conducted, it will be useful to perform a comparative study with the proposed product and the reference product (i.e., comparative bridging toxicology studies). The selection of dose, regimen, duration, and test species for these studies should provide a meaningful toxicological comparison between the two products. It is important to understand the limitations of such animal studies (e.g., small sample size, intra-species variations) when interpreting results comparing the proposed product and the reference product. For a detailed discussion on the design of animal toxicology studies relevant to biological products, see the ICH guidance for industry *S6(R1) Preclinical Safety Evaluation of Biotechnology-Derived Pharmaceuticals* (ICH S6(R1)).

Safety data derived from animal toxicity studies generally are not expected if clinical data (e.g., from studies or marketing experience outside the United States) using the proposed product are available (with the same proposed route of administration and formulation) that provide sufficient evidence for its safe use, unless animal toxicity studies are otherwise needed to address a specific product quality concern.

Animal toxicity studies are generally not useful if there is no animal species that can provide pharmacologically relevant data for the product (i.e., no species in which the biologic activity of the product mimics the human response). For a detailed discussion about demonstrating species relevance, see the criteria described in ICH S6(R1). However, there may be some instances when animal data from a pharmacologically nonresponsive species (including rodents) may be useful to support clinical studies with a proposed product that has not been previously tested in human subjects, for example, comparative PK and systemic tolerability studies. If animal toxicity studies are not warranted based on an acceptable scientific justification, additional comparative in vitro testing (using human cells or tissues when appropriate) is encouraged. Data derived using human cells can provide important comparative information between the proposed product and the reference product regarding potential clinical effects (section VII.B), particularly in situations where there are no animal species available for safety testing.

12

Contains Nonbinding Recommendations

In general, nonclinical safety pharmacology, reproductive and developmental toxicity, and carcinogenicity studies are not warranted when the proposed product and the reference product have been demonstrated to be highly similar through extensive structural and functional characterization and animal toxicity studies (if such studies were conducted).

2. Inclusion of Animal PK and PD Measures

Under certain circumstances, a single-dose study in animals comparing the proposed product and the reference product using PK and PD measures may contribute to the totality of evidence that supports a demonstration of biosimilarity. Specifically, sponsors can use results from animal studies to support the degree of similarity based on the PK and PD profiles of the proposed product and the reference product. PK and PD measures also can be incorporated into a single animal toxicity study, where appropriate. Animal PK and PD assessment will not negate the need for human PK and PD studies.

3. Interpreting Animal Immunogenicity Results

Animal immunogenicity assessments are conducted to assist in the interpretation of the animal study results and generally do not predict potential immune responses to protein products in humans. However, when differences in manufacturing (e.g., impurities or excipients) between the proposed product and the reference product may result in differences in immunogenicity, measurement of anti-therapeutic protein antibody responses in animals may provide useful information. Additionally, differences observed in animal immunogenicity assessments may reflect potential structural or functional differences between the two products not captured by other analytical methods.

D. Clinical Studies – General Considerations

The sponsor of a proposed product must include in its submission to FDA information demonstrating that "there are no clinically meaningful differences between the biological product and the reference product in terms of the safety, purity, and potency of the product."[26]

The nature and scope of the clinical study or studies will depend on the nature and extent of residual uncertainty about biosimilarity after conducting structural and functional characterization and, where relevant, animal studies. The frequency and severity of safety risks

---

[26] Section 7002(b)(3) of the Affordable Care Act, adding section 351(i)(2)(B) of the PHS Act. To support a demonstration of biosimilarity, the statute also requires a clinical study or studies (including the assessment of immunogenicity and PK or PD) sufficient to demonstrate safety, purity, and potency in one or more appropriate conditions of use for which the reference product is licensed and intended to be used and for which licensure is sought for the biological product, unless FDA determines an element unnecessary (section 7002(a)(2) of the Affordable Care Act, adding section 351(k)(2)(A)(i)(I)(cc) of the PHS Act). As a general matter, FDA anticipates that the recommendations described in this guidance designed to demonstrate that the proposed product is highly similar to its reference product notwithstanding minor differences in clinically inactive components and to demonstrate that no clinically meaningful differences exist between the two products will provide data sufficient to demonstrate the safety, purity, and potency of the proposed product. FDA recommends that sponsors identify which study or studies will provide data regarding no clinically meaningful differences prior to starting clinical studies.

13

and other safety and effectiveness considerations (e.g., poor relationship between pharmacologic effects and effectiveness) for the reference product may also affect the design of the clinical program. The scope of the clinical program and the type of clinical studies (i.e., comparative human PK, PD, clinical immunogenicity, or clinical safety and effectiveness) should be scientifically justified by the sponsor.

As a scientific matter, FDA expects a sponsor to conduct comparative human PK and PD studies (if there is a relevant PD measure(s))[27] and a clinical immunogenicity assessment. In certain cases, the results of these studies may provide adequate clinical data to support a conclusion that there are no clinically meaningful differences between the proposed biosimilar product and the reference product. However, if residual uncertainty about biosimilarity remains after conducting these studies, an additional comparative clinical study or studies would be needed to further evaluate whether there are clinically meaningful differences between the two products.

1. Human Pharmacology Data[28]

Human PK and PD profiles of a protein product often cannot be adequately predicted from functional assays and/or animal studies alone. Therefore, human PK and PD studies comparing a proposed product to the reference product generally are fundamental components in supporting a demonstration of biosimilarity. Both PK and PD studies (where there is a relevant PD measure(s)) generally will be expected to establish biosimilarity, unless a sponsor can scientifically justify that such a study is not needed.[29] Even if relevant PD measures are not available, sensitive PD endpoints may be assessed if such assessment may help reduce residual uncertainty about biosimilarity.

Sponsors should provide a scientific justification for the selection of the human PK and PD study population (e.g., patients versus healthy subjects) and parameters, taking into consideration the relevance and sensitivity of such population and parameters, the population and parameters studied for the licensure for the reference product, as well as the current knowledge of the intra-subject and inter-subject variability of human PK and PD for the reference product. For example, comparative human PK and PD studies should use a population, dose(s), and route of administration that are adequately sensitive to allow for the detection of differences in PK and PD profiles. FDA recommends that, to the extent possible, the sponsor select PD measures that (1) are relevant to clinical

---

[27] A PD study may also incorporate PK measures (i.e., a combined PK/PD study).

[28] See the draft guidance for industry *Clinical Pharmacology Data to Support a Demonstration of Biosimilarity to a Reference Product* for a more detailed discussion on the design and use of clinical pharmacology studies to support a demonstration of biosimilarity. When final, this guidance will represent FDA's current thinking on this topic.

[29] PK and PD studies provide quite different types of information. In simple terms, a PK study measures how the body acts on a drug (how the drug is absorbed, distributed, metabolized, and eliminated), and a PD study measures how the drug acts on the body (typically assessing a measure(s) related to the drug's biochemical and physiologic effects on the body). Therefore, one type of study does not duplicate or substitute for the information provided by the other. Both PK studies and PD studies provide important information for assessing biosimilarity; and therefore, as a scientific matter, comparative human PK studies and PD studies (where there is a relevant PD measure(s)) generally will be expected.

14

385

outcomes (e.g., on mechanistic path of MOA or disease process related to effectiveness or safety); (2) are measurable for a sufficient period of time after dosing to ascertain the full PD response and with appropriate precision; and (3) have the sensitivity to detect clinically meaningful differences between the proposed product and the reference product. Use of multiple PD measures that assess different domains of activities may also be of value.

When there are established dose-response or systemic exposure-response relationships (response may be PD measures or clinical endpoints), it is important to select, whenever possible, a dose(s) for study on the steep part of the dose-response curve for the proposed product. Studying doses that are on the plateau of the dose-response curve is unlikely to detect clinically meaningful differences between the two products. Sponsors should predefine and justify the criteria for PK and PD parameters for studies included in the application to demonstrate biosimilarity.

A human PK study that demonstrates similar exposure (e.g., serum concentration over time) for the proposed product and the reference product may provide support for a demonstration of biosimilarity. A human PK study may be particularly useful when the exposure correlates with clinical safety and effectiveness. A human PD study that demonstrates a similar effect on a relevant PD measure(s) related to effectiveness or specific safety concerns (except for immunogenicity, which is evaluated separately) represents even stronger support for a biosimilarity determination.

In certain cases, establishing a similar clinical PK, PD, and immunogenicity profile may provide sufficient clinical data to support a conclusion that there are no clinically meaningful differences between the two products. PK and PD parameters are generally more sensitive than clinical efficacy endpoints in assessing the similarity of two products. For example, an effect on thyroid stimulating hormone (TSH) levels would provide a more sensitive comparison of two thyroxine products than an effect on clinical symptoms of euthyroidism.

In cases where there is a meaningful correlation between PK and PD results and clinical effectiveness, convincing PK and PD results may make a comparative efficacy study unnecessary. For example, similar dose-response curves of the proposed product and the reference product on a relevant PD measure, combined with a similar human PK profile and clinical immunogenicity profile, could provide sufficient evidence to support a conclusion of no clinically meaningful differences. Even if there is still residual uncertainty about biosimilarity based on PK and PD results, establishing a similar human PK and PD profile may provide a scientific basis for a selective and targeted approach to subsequent clinical testing.

For PD studies using products with a short half-life (e.g., shorter than 5 days), a rapid PD response, and a low incidence of immunogenicity, a crossover design is appropriate, when feasible. For products with a longer half-life (e.g., more than 5 days), a parallel design will usually be needed. Sponsors should provide a scientific justification for the selection of study dose (e.g., one dose or multiple doses) and route of administration.

15

FDA recommends that sponsors consider the duration of time it takes for a PD measure to change and the possibility of nonlinear PK. FDA also encourages consideration of the role of modeling and simulation in designing comparative human PK and PD studies.

2.   Clinical Immunogenicity Assessment

The goal of the clinical immunogenicity assessment is to evaluate potential differences between the proposed product and the reference product in the incidence and severity of human immune responses. Immune responses may affect both the safety and effectiveness of the product by, for example, altering PK, inducing anaphylaxis, or promoting development of neutralizing antibodies that neutralize the product as well as its endogenous protein counterpart. Thus, establishing that there are no clinically meaningful differences in immune response between a proposed product and the reference product is a key element in the demonstration of biosimilarity. Structural, functional, and animal data[30] are generally not adequate to predict immunogenicity in humans. Therefore, at least one clinical study that includes a comparison of the immunogenicity of the proposed product to that of the reference product will be expected. FDA encourages that, where feasible, sponsors collect immunogenicity data in any clinical study, including human PK or PD studies.

The extent and timing of the clinical immunogenicity assessment will vary depending on a range of factors, including the extent of analytical similarity between the proposed product and the reference product, and the incidence and clinical consequences of immune responses for the reference product. For example, if the clinical consequence is severe (e.g., when the reference product is a therapeutic counterpart of an endogenous protein with a critical, nonredundant biological function or is known to provoke anaphylaxis), a more extensive immunogenicity assessment will likely be needed to support a demonstration of biosimilarity. If the immune response to the reference product is rare, a premarketing evaluation to assess apparent differences in immune responses between the two products may be adequate to support biosimilarity. In addition, in some cases certain safety risks may need to be evaluated through postmarketing surveillance or studies.

The overall immunogenicity assessment should consider the nature of the immune response (e.g., anaphylaxis, neutralizing antibody), the clinical relevance and severity of consequences (e.g., loss of efficacy of life-saving therapeutic and other adverse effects), the incidence of immune responses, and the population being studied. FDA recommends use of a comparative parallel design (i.e., a head-to-head study) in treatment-naïve patients as the most sensitive design for a premarketing study to assess potential differences in the risk of immunogenicity. However, depending on the clinical experience of the reference and proposed products (taking into consideration the conditions of use and patient population), a sponsor may need to evaluate a subset of patients to provide a substantive descriptive assessment of whether a single cross-over

---

[30] Section VII.C.3 of this guidance contains a discussion concerning the interpretation of animal immunogenicity results.

16

from the reference product to the proposed biosimilar would result in a major risk in terms of hypersensitivity, immunogenicity, or other reactions. The design of any study to assess immunogenicity and acceptable differences in the incidence and other parameters of immune response should be discussed with FDA before initiating the study. Differences in immune responses between a proposed product and the reference product in the absence of observed clinical sequelae may be of concern and may warrant further evaluation (e.g., extended period of follow-up evaluation).

The study population used to compare immunogenicity should be justified by the sponsor and agreed to by the Agency. If a sponsor is seeking to extrapolate immunogenicity findings for one condition of use to other conditions of use, the sponsor should consider using a study population and treatment regimen that are adequately sensitive for predicting a difference in immune responses between the proposed product and the reference product across the conditions of use. Usually, this will be the population and regimen for the reference product for which development of immune responses with adverse outcomes is most likely to occur (e.g., patients on background immunosuppressants would be less likely to develop immune responses than patients who are not immunosuppressed).

The selection of clinical immunogenicity endpoints or PD measures associated with immune responses to therapeutic protein products (e.g., antibody formation and cytokine levels) should take into consideration the immunogenicity issues that have emerged during the use of the reference product. Sponsors should prospectively define the clinical immune response criteria (e.g., definitions of significant clinical events such as anaphylaxis), using established criteria where available, for each type of potential immune response and should obtain agreement from FDA on these criteria before initiating the study.

The duration of follow-up evaluation should be determined based on (1) the time course for the generation of immune responses (such as the development of neutralizing antibodies, cell-mediated immune responses) and expected clinical sequelae (informed by experience with the reference product), (2) the time course of disappearance of the immune responses and clinical sequelae following cessation of therapy, and (3) the length of administration of the product. For example, for chronically administered agents, the follow-up period is recommended to be 1 year unless a shorter duration can be scientifically justified based on the *totality of the evidence* to support biosimilarity.

As a scientific matter, a sponsor should evaluate the following antibody parameters in the clinical immunogenicity assessment:

- Titer, specificity, relevant isotype distribution, time course of development, persistence, disappearance, impact on PK, and association with clinical sequelae

- Neutralization of product activity: neutralizing capacity to all relevant functions (e.g., uptake and catalytic activity, neutralization for replacement enzyme therapeutics)

17

Contains Nonbinding Recommendations

The sponsor should develop assays capable of sensitively detecting immune responses, even in the presence of the circulating drug product (proposed product and reference product).[31] The proposed product and the reference product should be assessed in the same assay with the same patient sera whenever possible. FDA recommends that immunogenicity assays be developed and validated early in development, and the validation should consider both the proposed product and the reference product. Sponsors should consult with FDA on the sufficiency of assays before initiating any clinical immunogenicity assessment.

3.   *Comparative Clinical Studies*

As a scientific matter, a comparative clinical study will be necessary to support a demonstration of biosimilarity if there is residual uncertainty about whether there are clinically meaningful differences between the proposed product and the reference product based on structural and functional characterization, animal testing, human PK and PD data, and clinical immunogenicity assessment. A sponsor should provide a scientific justification if it believes that a comparative clinical study is not necessary.

The following are examples of factors that may influence the type and extent of the comparative clinical study data needed:

a.   The nature and complexity of the reference product, the extensiveness of structural and functional characterization, and the findings and limitations of comparative structural, functional, and nonclinical testing, including the extent of observed differences

b.   The extent to which differences in structure, function, and nonclinical pharmacology and toxicology predict differences in clinical outcomes, in conjunction with the degree of understanding of the MOA of the reference product and disease pathology

c.   The extent to which human PK or PD is known to predict clinical outcomes (e.g., PD measures known to be relevant to effectiveness or safety)

d.   The extent of clinical experience with the reference product and its therapeutic class, including the safety and risk-benefit profile (e.g., whether there is a low potential for off-target adverse events), and appropriate endpoints and biomarkers for safety and effectiveness (e.g., availability of established, sensitive clinical endpoints)

e.   The extent of any other clinical experience with the proposed product (e.g., if the proposed product has been marketed outside the United States)

---

[31] See the draft guidance for industry *Assay Development for Immunogenicity Testing of Therapeutic Proteins* for a detailed discussion. When final, this guidance will represent FDA's current thinking on this topic.

18

A sponsor should provide a scientific justification for how it intends to use these factors to determine what type(s) of clinical study(ies) are needed and the design of any necessary study(ies). For example, if a comparative clinical study is needed, a sponsor should explain how these factors were considered in determining the design of such a study, including the endpoint(s), population, similarity margin, and statistical analyses.

Additionally, specific safety or effectiveness concerns regarding the reference product and its class (including history of manufacturing- or source-related adverse events) may warrant more comparative clinical data. Alternatively, if there is information regarding other biological products that could support a biosimilarity determination (with marketing histories that demonstrate no apparent differences in clinical safety and effectiveness profiles), such information may be an additional factor supporting a selective and targeted approach to the clinical program.

Endpoints

A sponsor should use endpoints that can assess clinically meaningful differences between the proposed product and the reference product in a comparative clinical study. The endpoints may be different from those used as primary endpoints in the reference product's clinical studies if they are scientifically supported. As discussed in section VII.D.1, certain endpoints (such as PD measures) are more sensitive than clinical endpoints and, therefore, may enable more precise comparisons of relevant therapeutic effects. There may be situations when the assessment of multiple PD measures in a comparative clinical study will enhance the sensitivity of the study. The adequacy of the endpoints depends on the extent to which PD measures correlate with clinical outcome, the extent of structural and functional data support for biosimilarity, the understanding of MOA, and the nature or seriousness of outcome affected.

Study Population

The choice of study population should allow for an assessment of clinically meaningful differences between the proposed product and the reference product. Often the study population will have characteristics consistent with those of the population studied for the licensure of the reference product for the same indication. However, there are cases where a study population could be different from that in the clinical studies that supported the licensure of the reference product. For example, if a genetic predictor of response was developed following licensure of the reference product, it may be possible to use patients with the response marker as the study population.

Sample Size and Duration of Study

The sample size for and duration of the comparative clinical study should be adequate to allow for the detection of clinically meaningful differences between the two products. As discussed in section VII.D.1, certain endpoints, such as PD measures, may be more sensitive than clinical endpoints and facilitate the conduct of a smaller study of limited duration. In such cases where the size and duration of the comparative clinical study may

19

not be adequate for the detection of relevant safety signals, a separate assessment of safety and immunogenicity may be needed.

Study Design and Analyses

A comparative clinical study for a biosimilar development program should be designed to investigate whether there are clinically meaningful differences between the proposed product and the reference product. The design should take into consideration the nature and extent of residual uncertainty that remains about biosimilarity based on data generated from comparative structural and functional characterization, animal testing, human PK and PD studies, and clinical immunogenicity assessment.

Generally, FDA expects a clinical study or studies designed to establish statistical evidence that the proposed product is neither inferior to the reference product by more than a specified margin nor superior to the reference product by more than a (possibly different) specified margin. Typically, an equivalence design with symmetric inferiority and superiority margins would be used. Symmetric margins would be reasonable when, for example, there are dose-related toxicities.

In some cases, it would be appropriate to use an asymmetric interval with a larger upper bound to rule out superiority than lower bound to rule out inferiority. An asymmetric interval could be reasonable, for example, if the dose used in the clinical study is near the plateau of the dose-response curve and there is little likelihood of dose-related effects (e.g., toxicity). In most cases, use of an asymmetric interval would generally allow for a smaller sample size than would be needed with symmetric margins. However, if there is a demonstration of clear superiority, then further consideration should be given as to whether the proposed product can be considered biosimilar to the reference product.

In some cases, depending on the study population and endpoint(s), ruling out only inferiority may be adequate to establish that there are no clinically meaningful differences between the proposed product and the reference product. For example, if it is well established that doses of a reference product pharmacodynamically saturate the target at the clinical dose level and it would be unethical to use lower than clinically approved doses, a non-inferiority (NI) design may be sufficient.[32]

A sponsor should provide adequate scientific justification for the choice of study design, study population, study endpoint(s), estimated effect size for the reference product, and margin(s) (how much difference to rule out). Sponsors should discuss their study proposal(s) and overall clinical development plan with FDA before initiating the comparative clinical study(ies).

---

[32] If an NI design is considered appropriate, sponsors are encouraged to refer to the draft guidance for industry *Non-inferiority Clinical Trials*. When final, this guidance will represent FDA's current thinking on this topic.

4.   *Extrapolation of Clinical Data Across Indications*

If the proposed product meets the statutory requirements for licensure as a biosimilar product under section 351(k) of the PHS Act based on, among other things, data derived from a clinical study or studies sufficient to demonstrate safety, purity, and potency in an appropriate condition of use, the applicant may seek licensure of the proposed product for one or more additional conditions of use for which the reference product is licensed. However, the applicant would need to provide sufficient scientific justification for extrapolating clinical data to support a determination of biosimilarity for each condition of use for which licensure is sought.

Such scientific justification for extrapolation should address, for example, the following issues for the tested and extrapolated conditions of use:

- The MOA(s) in each condition of use for which licensure is sought; this may include:

    - The target/receptor(s) for each relevant activity/function of the product

    - The binding, dose/concentration response, and pattern of molecular signaling upon engagement of target/receptor(s)

    - The relationships between product structure and target/receptor interactions

    - The location and expression of the target/receptor(s)

- The PK and bio-distribution of the product in different patient populations (Relevant PD measures may also provide important information on the MOA.)

- The immunogenicity of the product in different patient populations

- Differences in expected toxicities in each condition of use and patient population (including whether expected toxicities are related to the pharmacological activity of the product or to off-target activities)

- Any other factor that may affect the safety or efficacy of the product in each condition of use and patient population for which licensure is sought

Differences between conditions of use with respect to the factors described above do not necessarily preclude extrapolation. A scientific justification should address these differences in the context of the *totality of the evidence* supporting a demonstration of biosimilarity.

In choosing which condition of use to study that would permit subsequent extrapolation of clinical data to other conditions of use, FDA recommends that a sponsor consider choosing a condition of use that would be adequately sensitive to detect clinically meaningful differences between the two products.

21

Contains Nonbinding Recommendations

The sponsor of a proposed product may obtain licensure only for a condition of use that has been previously licensed for the reference product. If a reference product has a condition of use that was licensed under section 506(c) of the FD&C Act and 21 CFR part 601, subpart E (accelerated approval), and the reference product's clinical benefit in this condition of use has not yet been verified in postmarketing studies, the proposed product sponsor should consider studying another condition of use for which the reference product is licensed to avoid potential complications in the event that postmarketing studies fail to verify the clinical benefit of the reference product for the condition of use.

VIII. POSTMARKETING SAFETY MONITORING CONSIDERATIONS

Robust postmarketing safety monitoring is an important component in ensuring the safety and effectiveness of biological products, including biosimilar therapeutic protein products.

Postmarketing safety monitoring should first take into consideration any particular safety or effectiveness concerns associated with the use of the reference product and its class, the proposed product in its development and clinical use (if marketed outside the United States), the specific condition of use and patient population, and patient exposure in the biosimilar development program. Postmarketing safety monitoring for a proposed product should also have adequate mechanisms in place to differentiate between the adverse events associated with the proposed product and those associated with the reference product, including the identification of adverse events associated with the proposed product that have not been previously associated with the reference product. Rare, but potentially serious, safety risks (e.g., immunogenicity) may not be detected during preapproval clinical testing because the size of the population exposed likely will not be large enough to assess rare events. In particular cases, such risks may need to be evaluated through postmarketing surveillance or studies. In addition, as with any other biological product, FDA may take any appropriate action to ensure the safety and effectiveness of a proposed product, including, for example, requiring a postmarketing study or clinical trial to evaluate certain safety risks.[33]

Because some aspects of postmarketing safety monitoring are product-specific, FDA encourages sponsors to consult with appropriate FDA divisions to discuss the sponsor's proposed approach to postmarketing safety monitoring.

IX. CONSULTATION WITH FDA

Many product-specific factors can influence the components of a product development program intended to establish that a proposed product is biosimilar to a reference product. Therefore, FDA will ordinarily provide feedback on a case-by-case basis on the components of a development program for a proposed product. In addition, it may not be possible to identify in advance all the necessary components of a development program; and the assessment of one element (e.g., structural analyses) at one step can influence decisions about the type and amount

---

[33] See, for example, sections 505(o)(3) and 505(p)(1)(A)(ii) of the FD&C Act.

22

Contains Nonbinding Recommendations

of subsequent data for the next step. For these reasons, FDA recommends that sponsors use a stepwise approach to establish the *totality of the evidence* that supports a demonstration of biosimilarity.

FDA also advises sponsors intending to develop biosimilar products to meet with FDA to present their product development plans and establish a schedule of milestones that will serve as landmarks for future discussions with the Agency. FDA anticipates that early discussions with FDA about product development plans and about the approaches to providing adequate scientific justifications will facilitate biosimilar development.

23

Contains Nonbinding Recommendations

GLOSSARY

As used in this guidance, the following terms are defined below:

- *Biological product* means "a virus, therapeutic serum, toxin, antitoxin, vaccine, blood, blood component or derivative, allergenic product, protein (except any chemically synthesized polypeptide), or analogous product, or arsphenamine or derivative of arsphenamine (or any other trivalent organic arsenic compound), applicable to the prevention, treatment, or cure of a disease or condition of human beings."[34]

- *Biosimilar* or *biosimilarity* means that "the biological product is highly similar to the reference product notwithstanding minor differences in clinically inactive components," and that "there are no clinically meaningful differences between the biological product and the reference product in terms of the safety, purity, and potency of the product."[35]

- *Chemically synthesized polypeptide* means any alpha amino acid polymer that (a) is made entirely by chemical synthesis and (b) is less than 100 amino acids in size.

- *Product*, when used without modifiers in this guidance, is intended to refer to the intermediates, drug substance, and/or drug product, as appropriate. The use of the term *product* is consistent with the use of the term in ICH Q5E.

- *Protein* means any alpha amino acid polymer with a specific defined sequence that is greater than 40 amino acids in size.

- *Reference product* means the single biological product licensed under section 351(ε) of the PHS Act against which a biological product is evaluated in a 351(k) application.[36]

---

[34] Section 7002(b)(2) of the Affordable Care Act, amending section 351(i)(1) of the PHS Act.

[35] Section 7002(b)(3) of the Affordable Care Act, adding section 351(i)(2) of the PHS Act.

[36] Section 7002(b)(3) of the Affordable Care Act, adding section 351(i)(4) of the PHS Act.

24

APPENDIX C2

Clinical Pharmacology Data to Support a Demonstration of Biosimilarity to a Reference Product

Clinical Pharmacology Data to Support a Demonstration of Biosimilarity to a Reference Product

Guidance for Industry

U.S. Department of Health and Human Services
Food and Drug Administration
Center for Drug Evaluation and Research (CDER)
Center for Biologics Evaluation and Research (CBER)

December 2016
Biosimilars

C:\Users\CAROLANM\AppData\Local\Microsoft\Windows\Temporary Internet Files\Content.Outlook\NRXMQ6DI\FRDTS 2015-739_FINAL clin pharm biosimilar guidance _111616_for RPMS.docx

397

Clinical Pharmacology Data to Support a Demonstration of Biosimilarity to a Reference Product

Guidance for Industry

Additional copies are available from:

Office of Communications, Division of Drug Information
Center for Drug Evaluation and Research
Food and Drug Administration
10001 New Hampshire Ave., Hillandale Bldg., 4th Floor
Silver Spring, MD 20993-0002
Phone: 855-543-3784 or 301-796-3400; Fax: 301-431-6353; Email: druginfo@fda.hhs.gov
http://www.fda.gov/Drugs/GuidanceComplianceRegulatoryInformation/Guidances/default.htm

and/or
Office of Communication, Outreach, and Development
Center for Biologics Evaluation and Research
Food and Drug Administration
10903 New Hampshire Ave., Bldg. 71, rm. 3128
Silver Spring, MD 20993-0002
Phone: 800-835-4709 or 240-402-8010; Email: ocod@fda.hhs.gov
http://www.fda.gov/BiologicsBloodVaccines/GuidanceComplianceRegulatoryInformation/Guidances/default.htm

U.S. Department of Health and Human Services
Food and Drug Administration
Center for Drug Evaluation and Research (CDER)
Center for Biologics Evaluation and Research (CBER)

December 2016
Biosimilars

TABLE OF CONTENTS

I.   INTRODUCTION 1

II.   THE ROLE OF CLINICAL PHARMACOLOGY STUDIES IN THE DEMONSTRATION OF BIOSIMILARITY 2

III.   CRITICAL CONSIDERATIONS IN THE USE OF CLINICAL PHARMACOLOGY STUDIES TO SUPPORT BIOSIMILARITY 3

     A.   Exposure and Response Assessment to Support a Demonstration of Biosimilarity 3

     B.   Evaluation of Residual Uncertainty 4

     C.   Analytical Quality and Similarity 4

     D.   Integrity of the Bioanalytical Methods Used in PK and PD Studies 6

     E.   Safety and Immunogenicity 8

IV.   DEVELOPING CLINICAL PHARMACOLOGY DATA FOR SUPPORTING A DEMONSTRATION OF BIOSIMILARITY 9

     A.   Study Design 9

     B.   Reference Product 10

     C.   Study Population 10

     D.   Dose Selection 11

     E.   Route of Administration 11

     F.   Pharmacokinetic Measures 12

     G.   Pharmacodynamic Measures 12

     H.   Defining the Appropriate Pharmacodynamic Time Profile 13

     I.   Statistical Comparison of PK and PD Results 13

V.   UTILITY OF SIMULATION TOOLS IN STUDY DESIGN AND DATA ANALYSIS 14

VI.   CONCLUSION 14

DEFINITIONS 15

Clinical Pharmacology Data to Support a Demonstration of Biosimilarity to a Reference Product

Guidance for Industry[1]

This guidance represents the current thinking of the Food and Drug Administration (FDA or Agency) on this topic. It does not establish any rights for any person and is not binding on FDA or the public. You can use an alternative approach if it satisfies the requirements of the applicable statutes and regulations. To discuss an alternative approach, contact the FDA office responsible for this guidance as listed on the title page.

I.   INTRODUCTION

This guidance is intended to assist sponsors with the design and use of clinical pharmacology studies to support a decision that a proposed therapeutic biological product is **biosimilar**[2] to its **reference product**. This guidance pertains to those products—such as therapeutic biological products—for which pharmacokinetic (PK) and pharmacodynamic (PD) data are needed to support a demonstration of biosimilarity. Specifically, the guidance discusses some of the overarching concepts related to clinical pharmacology testing for biosimilar products, approaches for developing the appropriate clinical pharmacology database, and the utility of modeling and simulation for designing clinical trials.

This guidance is one in a series that FDA is developing to implement the Biologics Price Competition and Innovation Act of 2009 (BPCI Act).[3] This guidance is intended to assist sponsors in designing clinical pharmacology studies that can support an application submitted under section 351(k) of the Public Health Service Act (PHS Act) (42 U.S.C. 262(k)) (a 351(k) application) as part of a stepwise approach to support a demonstration of biosimilarity.[4]

In general, FDA's guidance documents do not establish legally enforceable responsibilities. Instead, guidances describe the Agency's current thinking on a topic and should be viewed only as recommendations, unless specific regulatory or statutory requirements are cited. The use of

---

[1] This guidance has been prepared by the Center for Drug Evaluation and Research (CDER) and the Center for Biologics Evaluation and Research (CBER) at the Food and Drug Administration.

[2] Terms that appear in bold type are defined in the "Definitions" section at the end of this guidance.

[3] Sections 7001 through 7003 of the Patient Protection and Affordable Care Act (Affordable Care Act), Public Law 111-148.

[4] See FDA's guidance for industry *Scientific Considerations in Demonstrating Biosimilarity to a Reference Product.* We update guidances periodically. To make sure you have the most recent version of a guidance, check the FDA Drugs guidance Web page at http://www.fda.gov/Drugs/GuidanceComplianceRegulatoryInformation/Guidances/default.htm.

1

the word *should* in Agency guidances means that something is suggested or recommended, but not required.

II. THE ROLE OF CLINICAL PHARMACOLOGY STUDIES IN THE DEMONSTRATION OF BIOSIMILARITY

The BPCI Act, which was enacted as part of the Affordable Care Act, established an abbreviated pathway for FDA licensure of biological products that are demonstrated to be biosimilar to or interchangeable with an FDA-licensed reference product. This pathway is described in section 351(k) of the PHS Act.

Under section 351(k)(2) of the PHS Act, a 351(k) application must contain, among other things, information demonstrating that the biological product is biosimilar to a reference product based on data derived from analytical studies, animal studies, and a clinical study or clinical studies, including an assessment of immunogenicity, PK, and PD,[5] unless FDA determines, in its discretion, that certain studies are unnecessary in a 351(k) application.[6]

Biosimilarity is defined at section 351(i)(2) of the PHS Act to mean that the biological product is highly similar to the reference product notwithstanding minor differences in clinically inactive components and that there are no clinically meaningful differences between the biological product and the reference product in terms of the safety, purity, and potency of the product.

Comparative analytical data provide the foundation for a development program for a proposed biosimilar product intended for submission under section 351(k) of the PHS Act. Clinical pharmacology studies build on the comparative analytical studies in the stepwise approach to support a demonstration of biosimilarity, and are normally a critical part of demonstrating biosimilarity by supporting a demonstration that there are no clinically meaningful differences between the proposed biosimilar product and the reference product. These studies provide the data that describe the degree of PK similarity between the proposed biosimilar product and the reference product. In addition, clinical pharmacology studies often include PD endpoints (both therapeutic and toxic) and pharmacometric analysis to assess whether there are clinically meaningful differences between the proposed biosimilar product and the reference product. These clinical pharmacology studies may address residual uncertainties that remain after the analytical evaluation, can add to the totality of the evidence supporting a demonstration of biosimilarity, and can guide both the need for and design of subsequent clinical testing to support a demonstration of no clinically meaningful differences in the overall demonstration of biosimilarity. Clinical pharmacology data can be an important component of the scientific justification supporting extrapolation of data to one or more additional conditions of use.[7]

---

[5] Section 351(k)(2)(A)(i)(I) of the PHS Act.
[6] Section 351(k)(2)(A)(iii) of the PHS Act.
[7] See FDA's guidance for industry *Biosimilars: Questions and Answers Regarding Implementation of the Biologics Price Competition and Innovation Act of 2009* for more information on this topic.

2

Contains Nonbinding Recommendations

The types of clinical pharmacology studies to be conducted will depend on the residual uncertainties about biosimilarity that these studies can address to add to the totality of evidence for biosimilar product development.

III.   CRITICAL CONSIDERATIONS IN THE USE OF CLINICAL PHARMACOLOGY STUDIES TO SUPPORT BIOSIMILARITY

Three key concepts—namely a PK and PD response assessment, an evaluation of residual uncertainty, and assumptions about analytical quality and similarity—are especially relevant to the stepwise development of proposed biosimilar products and are discussed in more detail in this section. Bioanalytical methodology and the use of clinical pharmacology studies to gain safety and immunogenicity information are also examined.

A.   Exposure and Response Assessment to Support a Demonstration of Biosimilarity

The objective of a well-designed clinical PK and PD study in a biosimilar development program is to evaluate the similarities and differences in the PK and PD profiles between the proposed biosimilar product and the reference product. A well-designed clinical PK and PD study should include information about the **exposure** and, when possible, the **exposure-response** to the biological products, which are important for assessing whether there are any potential clinically meaningful differences between two products. Determining the exposure-response to a biological product can be particularly challenging because of the complex nature and heterogeneity of biological products. An evaluation of clinical pharmacology similarity should include assessments of PK similarity, and if applicable, PD similarity.

The PD biomarker(s) used to measure PD response should be a single biomarker or a composite of biomarkers that effectively demonstrate the characteristics of the product's target effects. Use of a single scientifically appropriate PD biomarker or a composite of more than one relevant PD biomarker can reduce residual uncertainty regarding the existence of any clinically meaningful differences between products and can significantly add to the overall demonstration of biosimilarity. Using broader panels of PD biomarkers (e.g., by conducting a protein or mRNA microarray analysis) that capture multiple pharmacological effects of the product can be of additional value. When determining which biomarkers should be used to measure response, it is important to consider the following five characteristics:

- The time of onset of change in the PD biomarker relative to dosing and its return to baseline with discontinuation of dosing

- The dynamic range of the PD biomarker over the exposure range to the biological product

- The sensitivity of the PD biomarker to differences between the proposed biosimilar product and the reference product

3

- The relevance of the PD biomarker to the mechanism of action of the drug (to the extent that the mechanism of action is known for the reference product)

- The analytical validity of the PD biomarker assay

If these characteristics are addressed, through the submission of PK and PD results, the extent of the clinical development program can be refined in both the design and extent of additional clinical trials necessary to assess whether there are clinically meaningful differences between the proposed biosimilar product and the reference product. In some instances, PD biomarkers with the relevant characteristics listed above are not identified, but the sponsor is still encouraged to incorporate PD biomarkers that achieve a large dynamic range over the concentration range in the PK evaluation because these PD biomarkers represent potential orthogonal tests that can support similarity. When PD biomarkers are not sensitive or specific enough to detect clinically meaningful differences, the derived PK parameters should be used as the primary basis for evaluating similarity from a clinical pharmacology perspective, and the PD biomarkers can be used to augment the PK data. A combination of PK and PD similarity can be an important assessment in demonstrating that there are no clinically meaningful differences between the proposed biosimilar product and the reference product.

B.   Evaluation of Residual Uncertainty

In evaluating a sponsor's data to support a demonstration of biosimilarity, FDA will consider the totality of the data and information submitted using a risk-based approach, including data from the structural and functional characterizations, nonclinical evaluations, clinical PK and PD studies, clinical immunogenicity testing and an investigation of clinical safety, and, when appropriate, clinical effectiveness. These data should be collected in a stepwise manner. Especially pertinent to FDA's clinical pharmacology evaluation are the clinical PK and PD data and immunogenicity and other safety data obtained in conjunction with the clinical pharmacology studies. The need for additional studies at each step in this progressive approach will be determined by the degree of residual uncertainty that remains at each step regarding the similarity of the products and whether the study can address these uncertainties.

C.   Analytical Quality and Similarity

In a stepwise assessment of biosimilarity, extensive and robust comparative structural and functional studies (e.g., bioassays, binding assays, and studies of enzyme kinetics) should be performed to evaluate whether the proposed biosimilar product and the reference product are highly similar. A meaningful assessment of biosimilarity depends on, among other things, the capabilities of available state-of-the-art analytical assays to evaluate, for example, the molecular weight, the higher-order structure and post-translational modifications, heterogeneity, functional properties, impurity profiles, and degradation profiles denoting stability of the protein. The sponsor should describe the capabilities and limitations of the methods used in the analytical assessment.

An extensive analytical characterization can reveal differences between the proposed biosimilar product and the reference product. The type, nature, and extent of any differences between the

4

two products should be clearly identified, and the potential effect of these differences should be addressed and supported by appropriate data. In some cases, additional studies can demonstrate that the identified difference is within an appropriate range to consider the proposed biosimilar product to be highly similar to the reference product.[8] However, certain differences in the results of the analytical characterization can preclude a determination by FDA that the proposed biosimilar product is highly similar to the reference product and, therefore, the further development of the proposed biosimilar product through the 351(k) regulatory pathway is not recommended.

It may be useful to compare the quality attributes of the proposed biosimilar product with those of the reference product using a meaningful **fingerprint-like** analysis algorithm that covers a large number of product attributes and their combinations with high sensitivity using orthogonal methods. Comparison of quality attributes in this manner can further quantify the overall similarity between two products and might provide a basis for a more selective and targeted approach to subsequent animal and/or clinical studies.

The result of the comparative analytical characterization during product development can lead to one of the following four assessments within a *development-phase* continuum, with the understanding that FDA does not make the ultimate determination that the proposed biosimilar product is highly similar to the U.S.-licensed reference product until the time of licensure.

- Insufficient analytical similarity: Certain differences in the results of the analytical characterization are sufficiently significant such that further development through the 351(k) regulatory pathway is not recommended unless, for example, modifications are made to the manufacturing process for the proposed biosimilar product that are likely to lead to the minimization or elimination of such differences.

- Analytical similarity with residual uncertainty: Further information, additional analytical data, or other studies are needed to determine if observed analytical differences are likely to fall within an appropriate range when the 351(k) application for the proposed biosimilar product is submitted. As an example, glycosylation plays an important role in the PK of certain protein products. Manufacturing process conditions can affect glycosylation and in some cases PK. Comparative PK and PD studies of the proposed biosimilar product and the reference product, in addition to supporting a demonstration of no clinically meaningful differences, may address residual uncertainties regarding certain glycosylation differences and the impact on PK. Thus PK and PD studies could support that some differences in glycosylation identified in the analytical studies might fall within an appropriate range.

- Tentative analytical similarity: At this stage of development, the results of the comparative analytical characterization permit high confidence in the analytical similarity of the proposed biosimilar product and the reference product, and it can be

---

[8] See FDA's guidance for industry *Quality Considerations in Demonstrating Biosimilarity of a Therapeutic Protein Product to a Reference Product.*

5

appropriate for the sponsor to conduct targeted and selective animal and/or clinical studies to resolve residual uncertainty and support a demonstration of biosimilarity.

- Fingerprint-like analytical similarity: The results of integrated, multi-parameter approaches that are extremely sensitive in identifying analytical differences (i.e., fingerprint-like analyses) permit a very high level of confidence in the analytical similarity of the proposed biosimilar product and the reference product, and it would be appropriate for the sponsor to use a more targeted and selective approach to conducting animal and/or clinical studies to resolve residual uncertainty and to support a demonstration of biosimilarity.

The outcome of the comparative analytical characterization should inform the next steps in the demonstration of biosimilarity.

D. Integrity of the Bioanalytical Methods Used in PK and PD Studies

When performing an evaluation of clinical pharmacology similarity, it is critical to use the appropriate bioanalytical methods to evaluate the PK and PD properties of a proposed biosimilar product and the reference product. Because of the generally complex molecular structure of biological products, conventional analytical methods might not be suitable for biological products. The bioanalytical methods used for PK and PD evaluations should be accurate, precise, specific, sensitive, and reproducible. The scientific requirements of bioanalytical methods are described in a separate FDA guidance document.[9]

1. General PK Assay Considerations

A sponsor should design or choose an assay based on a thorough understanding of the mechanism of action (to the extent that the mechanism of action is known for the reference product) and/or structural elements of the proposed biosimilar product and reference product that are critical for activity. An assay producing concentration data that correlate to the pharmacological/PD activity is preferred. The same assay should be used for measuring concentrations of the proposed biosimilar product and the reference product and validated for use with both products. Analytical assays should have design and performance parameters that are consistent with current industry best practices.

2. General PD Assay Considerations

Sponsors should make every effort to employ the most suitable assays and methodologies to obtain data that are meaningful and reflective of PK, the biological activity, and/or the PD effect of the proposed biosimilar product and the reference product. Furthermore, in submissions to the FDA, the sponsor should provide a rationale for the choice of assay and the relevance of the assay to drug activity.

---

[9] See FDA's revised draft guidance for industry, *Bioanalytical Method Validation*, for more information on this topic. When final, this guidance will represent FDA's current thinking on this issue.

6

3.   *Specific Assays*

Three types of assays are of particular importance for biosimilar product development: ligand binding assays, concentration and activity assays, and PD assays.

- Ligand binding assays

  Currently, the concentration of most biological products in circulation is measured using ligand binding assays. These assays are analytical methods for quantifying high affinity and selective macromolecular interactions between assay reagents (e.g. antibodies, receptors or ligands) and the biological product. The ligand binding assay reagents chosen for detecting the biological product should be carefully evaluated with the goal of producing product concentration data that are meaningful to, and reflective of, the pharmacological activity and/or PD effect of the biological product of interest. Assays that rely upon antibody reagents and epitopes involved in pharmacological/biochemical interactions with targets are most likely to produce concentration data that are meaningful for target binding activity.

  Some biological products exert pharmacological effects only after multiple molecular interactions. For example, in some cases, the in vivo mechanism of action of monoclonal antibodies, bispecific antibodies, or fusion proteins involves binding mediated by different regions of the protein product (e.g. binding to both a ligand or receptor through a target antigen binding epitope of the protein and to Fc gamma receptors with the fragment crystallizable (Fc) region of the protein. A sponsor should choose the most appropriate interactions to measure. Generally, assays for monoclonal antibody product concentrations rely on molecular interactions involving the antigen binding (Fab) region, in particular epitopes in the complementarity determining regions (CDRs).

- Concentration and activity assays

  Bioanalytical methods that are not based on ligand binding can be used for quantification of the proposed biosimilar product and the reference product concentrations. For some biological products, such as those that are used to achieve enzyme replacement, the drug availability measurements may rely on activity and should be captured through an appropriate activity assay. Depending on the complexity of the structural features, some biological products should have more than one assay to characterize the systemic exposure of the proposed biosimilar product and the reference product. If more than one assay is used, mass spectrometry and other assays can be useful for distinguishing the structures of product variants, if relevant.

- PD assays

7

406

Relevant PD biomarkers might not always be available to support a proposed biosimilar product's development through clinical pharmacology studies. However, when PD assessment is a component of the biosimilarity evaluation, sponsors should submit (1) a rationale for the selection of the PD endpoints and/or biomarkers and (2) data to demonstrate the quality of the assay. PD assays should be sensitive for a product or product class and designed to quantitatively evaluate the pharmacological effects of the biologic product. The use of multiple complementary PD assays that reflect different aspects of pharmacologic activity of the product might be particularly useful to reduce residual uncertainty regarding clinically meaningful differences between the products. Because the PD assay is highly dependent on the pharmacological activity of the product, the approach for assay validation and the characteristics of the assay performance might differ depending on the specific PD assay. However, the general guiding principles for choosing PK assays (i.e., demonstration of specificity, reliability, and robustness) also apply to PD assays.

E. Safety and Immunogenicity

When **immunogenicity** results in, for example, either loss of PD effect or efficacy (e.g., neutralizing antibodies) or immune-mediated toxicity, the incidence and severity of the response should be assessed.[10] Safety and immunogenicity data from the clinical pharmacology studies should be collected and evaluated. FDA recognizes that safety and immunogenicity data derived from these studies may need to be supplemented by additional evaluations. The overall immunogenicity assessment should include relevant patient populations that are not immunocompromised and thus are able to mount an immune response. However, as part of their role in the overall assessment of biosimilarity, clinical pharmacology studies can sometimes suggest that there are clinically meaningful differences between the products that can inform the design and the details of additional investigations and/or clinical studies conducted to investigate these potential differences. The extent of such potential differences will determine whether or not further development of the proposed biosimilar product should continue, and if so, what studies should be conducted.

Publicly available information on the safety and immunogenicity profile of the reference product should be considered when incorporating safety and immunogenicity measurements in the clinical pharmacology studies.[11] For example, when the reference product is known to have the potential for immune-mediated toxicity, assays capable of detecting binding antibodies (and their neutralizing potential) should be developed in advance to analyze samples obtained from PK and PD studies, so that immunogenicity can be evaluated in real time. Generally, samples can be stored for future analysis if such assays are not yet developed.[12] In all cases, sponsors should carefully consider assay confounders such as the systemic presence of the proposed biosimilar

---

[10] See FDA's guidance for industry *Immunogenicity Assessment for Therapeutic Protein Products.*
[11] See footnote 4 for more information on this topic.
[12] FDA has issued the draft guidance for industry *Assay Development and Validation for Immunogenicity Testing of Therapeutic Protein Products.*

8

Contains Nonbinding Recommendations

product or the reference product. Recommendations for immunogenicity assay development are described in a separate FDA guidance document.[13]

When evaluating data (e.g., safety or immunogenicity) collected during the PK and PD studies, sponsors should have an understanding of the time course of the appearance and resolution of safety signals or immune responses. The PK profile of the proposed biosimilar product and/or the publicly available PK data for the reference product can be used to inform the duration of follow-up for safety signals or immunogenicity.

IV.   DEVELOPING CLINICAL PHARMACOLOGY DATA FOR SUPPORTING A DEMONSTRATION OF BIOSIMILARITY

Sponsors are encouraged to discuss their clinical pharmacology development plan with FDA in the early stages of the biosimilar product development program. Critical topics that should be discussed with FDA are set forth below.

A.   Study Design

To evaluate clinical PK and PD similarity for the development of proposed biosimilar products, two study designs are of particular relevance: crossover designs and parallel study designs. All clinical pharmacology studies of the proposed biosimilar product should be performed using materials from the final manufacturing process expected to be used for the marketed product if approval is granted. The relevance of data submitted from studies using materials from different manufacturing processes may need to be adequately justified, for example, by establishing an analytical and PK bridge to the to-be-marketed product.

- Crossover design

  For PK similarity assessments, a single-dose, randomized, crossover study is generally preferred. A crossover study is recommended for a product with a short half-life (e.g., shorter than 5 days), a rapid PD response (e.g., the time of onset, maximal effect, and disappearance in conjunction with drug exposure), and a low anticipated incidence of immunogenicity. This design is considered the most sensitive to assess PK similarity, and can provide reliable estimates of differences in exposure with a minimum number of subjects. For PD similarity assessments, a multiple-dose design may be appropriate when the PD effect is delayed or otherwise not parallel to the single-dose drug PK profile. The time course of appearance and disappearance of immunogenicity and its relation to the washout period should be considered for studies using a crossover design.

- Parallel design

---

[13] See footnote 10.

9

Contains Nonbinding Recommendations

Many biological products have a long half-life and elicit immunogenic responses. A parallel group design is appropriate for products that have a long half-life or for products where repeated exposures can lead to an increased immune response that can affect the PK and/or PD similarity assessments. This design is also appropriate for diseases that exhibit time-related changes associated with exposure to the drug.

B.   Reference Product

Analytical studies, clinical PK and, if appropriate, PD studies that are intended to support a demonstration of biosimilarity should include an adequate comparison of the proposed biosimilar product directly with the U.S.-licensed reference product. However, a sponsor could use a non-U.S.-licensed comparator product in certain studies to support a demonstration that the proposed biological product is biosimilar to the U.S.-licensed reference product. If a sponsor seeks to use data from a clinical study comparing its proposed biosimilar product to a non-U.S.-licensed comparator product to address, in part, the requirements under section 351(k)(2)(A) of the PHS Act, the sponsor should provide adequate data or information to scientifically justify the scientific relevance of these comparative data to an assessment of biosimilarity and establish an acceptable bridge to the U.S.-licensed reference product. [14]

C.   Study Population

Healthy Subject vs. Patient: The study population selected should be the most informative for detecting and evaluating differences in PK and PD profiles between the proposed biosimilar product and the reference product. Clinical PK and PD studies should be conducted in healthy subjects if the product can be safely administered to them. A study in healthy subjects is considered to be more sensitive in evaluating the product similarity because it is likely to produce less PK and/or PD variability compared with a study in patients with potential confounding factors such as underlying and/or concomitant disease and concomitant medications. If safety or ethical considerations preclude the participation of healthy subjects in human PK and PD studies for certain products (e.g., immunogenicity or known toxicity from the reference product), or if PD biomarkers can only be relevant in patients with the relevant condition or disease, the clinical pharmacology studies should be conducted in such patients. A population that is representative of the patient population to which the drug is targeted will be appropriate unless a study in a different population would be more sensitive to detect potential differences between the proposed biosimilar product and the reference product.

Demographic Group: Clinical pharmacology studies should be conducted in the subject or patient demographic group most likely to provide a sensitive measure of differences between the proposed biosimilar product and the reference product. The sponsor should justify why the subject or patient group chosen for clinical pharmacology studies will provide an adequately sensitive measure of difference between the proposed biosimilar product and the reference product. The total number of subjects studied should provide adequate statistical power for PK, and, when relevant, PD similarity assessment. Analysis of the data should be conducted

---

[14] See footnote 4 and footnote 7 for more information on the bridging data needed and examples of issues that a sponsor may need to address.

according to the pre-specified analysis plan, and any post hoc statistical analysis is exploratory only.

D.   Dose Selection

As in the selection of study population, the most sensitive dose should be selected to detect and to evaluate differences in the PK and PD profiles between the proposed biosimilar product and the reference product. The dose selected should be one most likely to provide clinically meaningful and interpretable data. If a study is conducted in a patient population, the approved dose for the reference product can be the appropriate choice, because this approved dose can best demonstrate the pharmacological effects in a clinical setting. However, a lower dose on the steep part of the exposure-response curve is generally appropriate when PD is being measured or when healthy subjects are selected for evaluation (See section V, "Utility of Simulation Tools in Study Design and Data Analysis").

In certain cases, a dose selected from a range of doses can be useful for a clinical PK and PD similarity assessment. For example, if the concentration-effect relationship of the reference product is known to be highly variable or nonlinear, a range of doses can be used to assess dose-response (See Section V, "Utility of Simulation Tools in Study Design and Data Analysis").

If the product can only be administered to patients, an alternative dosing regimen such as a single dose for a chronic indication or a lower dose than the approved dose may be preferable to increase the sensitivity for detecting differences if the approved dose either results in nonlinear PK or exceeds the dose required for maximal PD effect. The appropriateness of an alternative dosing regimen will depend on certain factors, e.g., whether the lower dose is known to have the same effect as the approved dose and whether it is ethically appropriate to give lower doses notwithstanding differences in effect. An adequate justification for the selection of an alternative dosing regimen should be provided.

When appropriate, PD biomarkers should be used to assess PK/PD similarity between the proposed biosimilar product and the reference product. Development of an exposure-response profile that includes the steep part of the exposure-response curve is a sensitive test for PK/PD similarity between products; if clinical pharmacology similarity between products is demonstrated, in some instances, the exposure-response profile might support an adequate assessment of whether there are clinically meaningful differences between the products, and in others, the exposure-response profile might support a more targeted clinical development program to address residual uncertainty regarding whether there are any such clinically meaningful differences.

E.   Route of Administration

Clinical PK and PD studies should be conducted using the same route of administration for the proposed biological product and the reference product. If more than one route of administration (e.g., both intravenous and subcutaneous) is approved for the reference product, the route selected for the assessment of PK and PD similarity should be the one most sensitive for detecting clinically meaningful differences. In most cases, the most sensitive route is likely to be

11

Contains Nonbinding Recommendations

the subcutaneous or other extravascular routes of administration, because extravascular routes can provide insight into potential PK differences during the absorption phase in addition to the distribution and elimination phases. In addition, extravascular routes of administration may provide a more sensitive assessment for differences in immunogenicity.

F.   Pharmacokinetic Measures

All PK measures should be obtained for both the proposed biosimilar product and the reference product. The sponsor should obtain measures of peak concentration (C_{max}) and total area under the curve (AUC) in a relevant biological fluid. For single-dose studies, AUC should be calculated as the area under the biological product concentration-time curve from time zero to time infinity ($AUC_{0-\infty}$), where $AUC_{0-\infty} = AUC_{0-t} + C_t/k_{el}$ (or C_t (concentration at the last measurable timepoint) divided by k_{el} (elimination rate constant)) is calculated based on an appropriate method. C_{max} should be determined from the data without interpolation. For intravenous studies, $AUC_{0-\infty}$ will be considered the primary endpoint. For subcutaneous studies, C_{max} and AUC will be considered coprimary study endpoints. For multiple dose studies, the measurement of total exposure should be the area under the concentration-time profile from time zero to the end of the dosing interval at steady-state (AUC_{0-tau}), and is considered the primary endpoint. Both the concentration prior to the next dose during multiple dosing ($C_{trough\ ss}$) and C_{max} are considered secondary endpoints. Population PK data will not provide an adequate assessment for PK similarity.

G.   Pharmacodynamic Measures

In certain circumstances, clinical PK and PD data that demonstrate similar exposure and response between a proposed biosimilar product and the reference product can be sufficient to completely assess whether there are clinically meaningful differences between products, notwithstanding the need for an adequate assessment of immunogenicity. The biosimilarity assessment should be based on similarity in PD using a biomarker that reflects the mechanism of drug action when the PD measure has a wide dynamic range over the range of drug concentrations achieved during the PK study. In such instances, a full evaluation of safety and immunogenicity should still be conducted. When human PD data in a PK/PD study are insufficient to fully assess whether there are clinically meaningful differences between the proposed biosimilar and the reference product, human PD data can nonetheless be helpful to support a more targeted approach for the collection of subsequent clinical safety and effectiveness data. Selection of appropriate time points and durations for the measure of PD biomarkers will depend on the characteristics of the PD biomarkers (e.g., the timing of the PD response after administration of the product based on the half-life of the product and the anticipated duration of the product's effect). When a PD response lags after initiation of product administration, a study of multiple-dose and steady state conditions can be important, especially if the proposed therapy is intended for long-term use. The PD biomarker(s) evaluated for the proposed biosimilar product and the reference product should be compared by determining the area under the effect curve (AUEC). If only one PD measurement is available because of the characteristics of the PD biomarker, the measurement should be linked to a simultaneous drug concentration measurement. The relationship of drug concentration and the PD biomarker should then be used as a basis for comparison between products.

12

411

Use of a single, scientifically appropriate PD biomarker as described above, or a composite of more than one relevant PD biomarkers, can reduce any residual uncertainty about whether there are clinically meaningful differences between products and add significantly to the overall demonstration of biosimilarity. Using broader panels of biomarkers (e.g., by conducting a protein or mRNA microarray analysis) that capture multiple pharmacological effects of the product can also add value.

When available and appropriate, clinical endpoints in clinical pharmacology studies can also provide useful information about the presence of clinically meaningful differences between two products.

H. Defining the Appropriate Pharmacodynamic Time Profile

The optimal sampling strategy for determining PD measures can differ from the strategy used for PK measures. For PK sampling, frequent sampling at early time points following product administration with decreased frequency later is generally most effective to characterize the concentration-time profile. However, the PD-time profile might not mirror the PK-time profile. In such cases, the PD sampling should be well justified. When both PK and PD data are to be obtained during a clinical pharmacology study, the sampling strategy should be optimized for both PK and PD measures.

I. Statistical Comparison of PK and PD Results

The assessment of the clinical pharmacology similarity of a proposed biosimilar product and the reference product in PK and PD studies is based on statistical evaluation. The recommended clinical pharmacology similarity assessment relies on: (1) a criterion to allow the comparison, (2) a confidence interval for the criterion, and (3) an acceptable limit for the biosimilarity assessment. FDA recommends that log-transformation of the exposure measures be performed before the statistical analysis. Sponsors should use an **average equivalence** statistical approach[15] to compare PK and PD parameters for both replicate and nonreplicate design studies. This average equivalence approach involves a calculation of a 90% confidence interval for the ratio between the geometric means of the parameters of the proposed biosimilar product and the reference product. To establish PK and/or PD similarity, the calculated confidence interval should fall within an acceptable limit. Selection of the confidence interval and the acceptable limits can vary among products. An appropriate starting point for an acceptable limit for the confidence interval of the ratio is 80–125%; if other limits are proposed, the sponsor should justify the limits selected for the proposed biosimilar product. There can be situations in which the results of the PK and/or PD study fall outside the pre-defined limits. Because such results can suggest existence of underlying differences between the proposed biosimilar product and the reference product that can preclude development under the 351(k) pathway, FDA encourages sponsors to analyze and explain such findings and discuss them with the FDA before proceeding to the next step in the development program.

---

[15] See FDA's guidance for industry *Statistical Approaches to Establishing Bioequivalence.*

13

V. UTILITY OF SIMULATION TOOLS IN STUDY DESIGN AND DATA ANALYSIS

Modeling and simulation tools can be useful when designing a PK and/or PD study. For instance, these tools can contribute to the selection of an optimally informative dose or doses for evaluating PD similarity. When a biomarker-based comparison is used, it is preferable that the selected dose be on the steep portion of the dose-response curve of the reference product. Sponsors should provide data to support the claim that the selected dose is on the steep part of the dose-response curve and not on the plateau of the dose-response curve where it is not likely to detect differences between the two products. Publicly available data for the dose (or exposure)-response relationship of the reference product can be analyzed using model-based simulations to justify the dose selected for the PK and/or PD study or studies.

If the exposure-response data for the reference product are not available, the sponsor can decide to generate this information using a small study to determine an optimally informative dose (e.g., a dose representing the effective dose to achieve the 50% maximal response [ED_{50}] of the reference product). This small study can involve evaluating the PK/PD relationship at multiple dose levels (e.g., the low, intermediate, and highest approved dose) to obtain dose-response and/or exposure-response data.[16] Alternatively, when possible, sponsors can conduct a PK/PD similarity study between the reference product and the proposed biosimilar product with low, intermediate, and the highest approved doses where a clear dose-response is observed. If multiple doses are studied, PK/PD parameters such as EC_{50}, the maximum PD response (E_{max}), and the slope of the concentration-effect relationship should be evaluated for similarity. Such studies should be useful for the demonstration of PK, PK/PD, and PD similarity when the clinical pharmacology evaluation is likely to be the major source of information to assess clinically meaningful differences. Publicly available information on biomarker-clinical endpoint relationships accompanied with modeling and simulation can also be used to define the appropriate limits for PD similarity.

VI. CONCLUSION

Clinical pharmacology studies play a critical role in the development of biosimilar products. These studies are part of a stepwise process for demonstrating biosimilarity between a proposed biosimilar product and the reference product. These studies may support a demonstration that there are no clinically meaningful differences between the products. These studies may address residual uncertainties that remain after the analytical evaluation, may add to the totality of the evidence supporting a demonstration of biosimilarity, and may also support a selective and targeted approach to the design of any recommended subsequent clinical studies to support a demonstration of biosimilarity.

---

[16] For more information, see FDA's guidance for industry *Topical Dermatologic Corticosteroids: In Vivo Bioequivalence.*

14

DEFINITIONS

Biological product: "[A] virus, therapeutic serum, toxin, antitoxin, vaccine, blood, blood component or derivative, allergenic product, protein (except any chemically synthesized polypeptide), or analogous product, or arsphenamine or derivative of arsphenamine (or any other trivalent organic arsenic compound), applicable to the prevention, treatment, or cure of a disease or condition of human beings."[17]

Biosimilar or biosimilarity: In reference to a biological product that is the subject of an application under subsection 351(k) of the PHS Act, the term 'biosimilar' or 'biosimilarity' means "that the biological product is highly similar to the reference product notwithstanding minor differences in clinically inactive components; and that there are no clinically meaningful differences between the biological product and the reference product in terms of the safety, purity, and potency of the product."[18]

Exposure: In this guidance, we use the broad term *exposure* to refer to PK variables, including input of all active components of the biological product as measured by dose (drug input to the body) and various measures of single or integrated drug concentrations in plasma and other biological fluid, e.g., peak concentration (C_{max}), concentration prior to the next dose during multiple dosing ($C_{trough\ ss}$), and area under the plasma/blood concentration-time curve (AUC).

Fingerprint-like: Integrated, multi-parameter approaches that are extremely sensitive in identifying analytical differences.

Immunogenicity: In this guidance immunogenicity refers to an immune response that a biological product elicits through formation of antibodies to the administered biological product.

Reference product: The single biological product licensed under section 351(a) of the PHS Act against which a biological product is evaluated in a 351(k) application.[19]

Exposure-Response: Pharmacodynamic response, referred to here as PD (a direct measure of the pharmacological or toxicological effect of a drug) in relationship to drug exposure (PK) variables.

Average equivalence: An approach to statistical analysis for pharmacokinetic measures, such as area under the curve (AUC) and peak concentration (C_{max}). It is based on the *two one-sided tests procedure* to determine whether the average values for the pharmacokinetic measures determined after administration of the Test (T) and Reference (R) products are comparable. This approach involves the calculation of a 90% confidence interval for the ratio of the log-transformed averages of the measures for the T and R products.

---

[17] Section 351(i)(1) of the PHS Act.
[18] Section 351(i)(2) of the PHS Act.
[19] Section 351(i)(4) of the PHS Act.

15

414

APPENDIX C3

Assessing User Fees Under the Biosimilar User Fee Amendments of 2017

Assessing User Fees Under the Biosimilar User Fee Amendments of 2017
Guidance for Industry

U.S. Department of Health and Human Services
Food and Drug Administration
Center for Drug Evaluation and Research (CDER)
Center for Biologics Evaluation and Research (CBER)

June 2018
User Fees

Assessing User Fees Under the Biosimilar User Fee Amendments of 2017

Guidance for Industry

Additional copies are available from:

Office of Communications, Division of Drug Information
Center for Drug Evaluation and Research
Food and Drug Administration
10001 New Hampshire Ave., Hillandale Bldg., 4th Floor
Silver Spring, MD 20993-0002
Phone: 855-543-3784 or 301-796-3400; Fax: 301-431-6353; Email: druginfo@fda.hhs.gov
http://www.fda.gov/Drugs/GuidanceComplianceRegulatoryInformation/Guidances/default.htm
and/or
Office of Communication, Outreach, and Development
Center for Biologics Evaluation and Research
Food and Drug Administration
10903 New Hampshire Ave., Bldg. 71, rm. 3128
Silver Spring, MD 20993-0002
Phone: 800-835-4709 or 240-402-8010; Email: ocod@fda.hhs.gov
http://www.fda.gov/BiologicsBloodVaccines/GuidanceComplianceRegulatoryInformation/Guidances/default.htm

U.S. Department of Health and Human Services
Food and Drug Administration
Center for Drug Evaluation and Research (CDER)
Center for Biologics Evaluation and Research (CBER)

June 2018
User Fees

TABLE OF CONTENTS

I. INTRODUCTION 1

II. BACKGROUND 2

III. DEFINITIONS 2

IV. CHANGES TO THE STRUCTURE OF THE BSUFA USER FEE PROGRAM 3

V. BIOSIMILAR BIOLOGICAL PRODUCT DEVELOPMENT FEES 4

    A. Initial BPD Fee 4

    B. Annual BPD Fee 4

    C. Request for Refund of Annual BPD Fee 5

    D. Discontinuation of Annual BPD Fee Obligation 5

    E. Reactivation Fee 6

VI. BIOSIMILAR BIOLOGICAL PRODUCT APPLICATION FEES 7

    A. Exception to the Application Fee 7

    B. Refund of the Application Fee 8

    C. Waiver of Application Fees 8

VII. BIOSIMILAR BIOLOGICAL PRODUCT PROGRAM FEES 10

VIII. FAILURE TO PAY FEES 11

IX. PAYMENT INFORMATION AND PROCEDURES 12

    A. Initial BPD Fees, Reactivation Fees, and Application Fees 12

    B. Annual Billing Cycle 12

    C. Waiver or Refund Requests 14

X. APPEALS PROCESS 14

    A. Reconsideration Request 14

    B. Appeal Request 15

XI. OTHER RESOURCES 16

Contains Nonbinding Recommendations

Assessing User Fees Under the Biosimilar User Fee Amendments of 2017
Guidance for Industry[1]

This guidance represents the current thinking of the Food and Drug Administration (FDA or Agency) on this topic. It does not establish any rights for any person and is not binding on FDA or the public. You can use an alternative approach if it satisfies the requirements of the applicable statutes and regulations. To discuss an alternative approach, contact the FDA staff responsible for this guidance as listed on the title page.

I.   INTRODUCTION

This guidance provides stakeholders information regarding FDA's implementation of the Biosimilar User Fee Amendments of 2017 (BsUFA II) under Title IV of the FDA Reauthorization Act of 2017. Because BsUFA II created changes to the user fee program, this guidance serves to provide an explanation about the new fee structure and types of fees for which entities are responsible.

This guidance describes the types of user fees authorized by BsUFA II, the process for submitting payments to FDA, the consequences for failing to pay BsUFA fees, and the process for requesting a reconsideration of a user fee assessment. This guidance also describes how FDA determines which products are subject to a fee and discusses certain changes to FDA's policies under the new law. This guidance does not address how FDA determines and adjusts fees each fiscal year; nor does it address FDA's implementation of other user fee programs (e.g., Prescription Drug User Fee Amendments, Generic Drug User Fee Amendments).[2] Throughout this guidance, references to *user fees* or the *user-fee program* are to the user fee program for biosimilar biological products under section 744H of the Federal Food, Drug, and Cosmetic Act (FD&C Act).

---

[1] This guidance has been prepared by the Division of User Fee Management and Budget Formulation, Office of Management, in the Center for Drug Evaluation and Research in cooperation with the Center for Biologics Evaluation and Research at the Food and Drug Administration.

[2] FDA will publish in the *Federal Register* the fee revenue and fees resulting from adjustment not later than 60 days before the start of each fiscal year. Section 744H(c)(5) of the FD&C Act, as amended by the FDA Reauthorization Act of 2017.

1

In general, FDA's guidance documents do not establish legally enforceable responsibilities. Instead, guidances describe the Agency's current thinking on a topic and should be viewed only as recommendations unless specific regulatory or statutory requirements are cited. The use of the word *should* in Agency guidances means that something is suggested or recommended, but not required.

Changes to statutory provisions that are described in this guidance are effective with respect to fees assessed beginning on the first day of fiscal year[3] (FY) 2018.

II. BACKGROUND

The Biosimilar User Fee Act of 2012 (BsUFA I) added sections 744G and 744H to the FD&C Act, authorizing FDA to collect user fees for a 5-year period from persons that develop biosimilar biological products. Fees authorized by this legislation help fund the process for the review of biosimilar biological product applications, and have played an important role in expediting the review and approval process. BsUFA was reauthorized for a 5-year period in 2017 under Title IV of the FDA Reauthorization Act of 2017 (BsUFA II), enacted on August 18, 2017.

BsUFA II extends FDA's authority to collect user fees from FY 2018 through FY 2022 and revises the fees that the Agency collects and how it collects some fees. Discussions about the reauthorization of BsUFA are expected to begin before FY 2022, the final fiscal year of BsUFA II.

III. DEFINITIONS

For purposes of this guidance:

- The term ***affiliate*** means a business entity that has a relationship with a second business entity if, directly or indirectly, (A) one business entity controls, or has the power to control, the other business entity, or (B) a third party controls, or has the power to control, both of the business entities.[4]

- The term ***biosimilar biological product*** means a specific strength of a biological product in final dosage form for which a biosimilar biological product application has been approved.[5]

---

[3] FDA's fiscal year begins on October 1 and ends on September 30.
[4] Section 744G(2) of the FD&C Act.
[5] Section 744G(3) of the FD&C Act.

2

Contains Nonbinding Recommendations

- Except as provided by section 744G(4)(B), the term *biosimilar biological product application* means an application for licensure of a biological product under section 351(k) of the Public Health Service Act (PHS Act).[6]

- The term *final dosage form* means, with respect to a biosimilar biological product, a finished dosage form which is approved for administration to a patient without substantial further manufacturing (such as lyophilized products before reconstitution).[7]

- The term *financial hold* means an order issued by the Secretary to prohibit the sponsor of a clinical investigation from continuing the investigation if the Secretary determines that the investigation is intended to support a biosimilar biological product application and the sponsor has failed to pay any of the biosimilar biological product development program fees for the product.[8]

- The term *person* includes an affiliate of such person.[9] The term *person* includes an individual, partnership, corporation, or association.[10] This document will also use the term *person* when referring to a sponsor or applicant.

- The term *supplement* means a request to the Secretary to approve a change in a biosimilar biological product application which has been approved, including a supplement requesting that the Secretary determine that the biosimilar biological product meets the standards for interchangeability described in section 351(k)(4) of the PHS Act.[11]

IV. CHANGES TO THE STRUCTURE OF THE BSUFA USER FEE PROGRAM

BsUFA II authorizes the collection of three types of fees: (1) biosimilar biological product development program fees (BPD fees), (2) biosimilar biological product application fees (application fees), and (3) biosimilar biological product program fees (program fees).

Previously, section 744H of the FD&C Act authorized FDA to collect (1) biosimilar development program fees, (2) biosimilar biological product application and supplement fees, (3) biosimilar biological product establishment fees, and (4) biosimilar biological product fees. BsUFA II eliminates fees for supplements as well as for establishments. Applicants will be assessed annual biosimilar biological product program fees, rather than the biosimilar biological product fees assessed under BsUFA I.

---

[6] Section 744G(4)(A) of the FD&C Act.
[7] Section 744G(10) of the FD&C Act.
[8] Section 744G(11) of the FD&C Act.
[9] Section 744G(12) of the FD&C Act.
[10] Section 201(e) of the FD&C Act.
[11] Section 744G(14) of the FD&C Act.

3

Additionally, BsUFA II eliminates the reduction of an application fee by the cumulative amount of fees paid by the applicant under the BPD program.

The Agency will establish BPD fees, biosimilar biological product application fees, and the biosimilar biological product program fees for each fiscal year as set forth in the statute, and will publish the fees and fee revenue amounts for a fiscal year in the Federal Register not later than 60 days before the start of that year.[12]

V.   BIOSIMILAR BIOLOGICAL PRODUCT DEVELOPMENT FEES

BsUFA II BPD fees are assessed for products in FDA's BPD program. BPD fees include the initial BPD fee, the annual BPD fee, and the reactivation fee.

A. Initial BPD Fee

Under section 744H(a)(1)(A) of the FD&C Act, an *initial BPD fee* is a one-time fee that is assessed to a sponsor to enter the BPD program. A sponsor can enter the BPD program through one of two ways:

- The sponsor submits to FDA a meeting request for a BPD meeting for a product; or

- The sponsor submits a clinical protocol for an investigational new drug application (IND) describing an investigation that FDA determines is intended to support a biosimilar biological product application.

There is no fee for a biosimilar initial advisory meeting.

The initial BPD fee is due within 5 calendar days after FDA grants the first BPD meeting for the product or upon submission of an IND for the product that FDA determines is intended to support a biosimilar biological product application, whichever occurs first.[13] Refer to section VIII of this guidance for consequences of failing to pay the required fees.

B. Annual BPD Fee

Beginning in the next fiscal year after a sponsor has paid the initial BPD fee, the sponsor must pay an *annual BPD fee*[14] for the product in each fiscal year. The annual BPD fee for a product is due on the first business day on or after October 1 of each fiscal year[15] or the first business day after the enactment of an appropriations Act providing for the collection and obligation of such

---

[12] Section 744H(c)(5) of the FD&C Act.
[13] Section 744H(a)(1)(A)(iv) of the FD&C Act.
[14] Section 744H(a)(1)(B) of the FD&C Act.
[15] Section 744H(a)(1)(B)(ii) of the FD&C Act.

4

fees for the year, whichever is later, unless the sponsor has discontinued participation in the BPD program for the product or has submitted a marketing application for the product that was accepted for filing.[16]

C. Request for Refund of Annual BPD Fee

If a person submits a biosimilar biological product application before October 1 of the fiscal year and the application is accepted for filing on or after October 1 of that fiscal year, the applicant may request a refund of the annual BPD fee paid by the applicant for such fiscal year.[17] FDA must receive a written request for a refund not later than 180 calendar days after the application is accepted for filing.[18]

For example, if an applicant submits a biosimilar biological product application for a product in the BPD program on September 15, 2017, the annual BPD fee for the product for FY 2018 is due on the first business day on or after October 1, 2017 (unless one of the exceptions applies; *see* section V.B of this guidance). If the application is accepted for filing by FDA on or after October 1, 2017, the applicant may submit Form FDA 3913 (User Fee Payment Refund Request)[19] to CDERCollections@fda.hhs.gov to request a refund of the annual BPD fee paid for the product for fiscal year 2018 within 180 calendar days from the date the application was accepted for filing.

D. Discontinuation of Annual BPD Fee Obligation

A sponsor may discontinue participation in the BPD program for a product, effective October 1 of a fiscal year, by notifying FDA *on or before August 1 of the preceding fiscal year* as follows:[20]

- If the sponsor has not yet submitted an IND – By submitting a written declaration to FDA that the sponsor has no present intention of further developing the product as a biosimilar biological product.[21] The sponsor should send a courtesy copy to CDERCollections@fda.hhs.gov and include the following information in the letter:

   o Sponsor's contact information including name, address, email, and telephone number
   o Identification of the request at the top of the cover letter as "Request to Discontinue Participation in the BPD Program"
   o Name of product

---

[16] Section 744H(a)(1)(B)(iii) of the FD&C Act.
[17] Section 744H(a)(1)(B)(iv) of the FD&C Act.
[18] Section 744H(a)(1)(B)(iv) of the FD&C Act.
[19] https://www.fda.gov/downloads/AboutFDA/ReportsManualsForms/Forms/UCM492188.pdf
[20] Section 744H(a)(1)(C) of the FD&C Act.
[21] Section 744H(a)(1)(C)(i) of the FD&C Act.

5

- o Pre-IND number
- If the sponsor has already submitted an IND and wishes to discontinue participation in the BPD program – By withdrawing the IND for the product in accordance with Part 312 of Title 21 of the Code of Federal Regulations (available at https://www.ecfr.gov/cgi-bin/text-idx?SID=63f7c466f2cfc85163fc45a67be57ddb&mc=true&node=pt21.5.312&rgn=div5)[22]

In addition to withdrawing the IND, a sponsor who has already submitted an IND and wishes to discontinue participation should also submit to FDA a written request to discontinue participation in the BPD program, as described above, with a courtesy copy to CDERCollections@fda.hhs.gov.

Requests to discontinue participation in the BPD program can be submitted to the FDA Electronic Submissions Gateway or mailed to:

> Food and Drug Administration
> Center for Drug Evaluation and Research
> Central Document Room
> 5901-B Ammendale Road
> Beltsville, MD 20705-1266

FDA must receive the request by August 1 of the preceding fiscal year to avoid assessment of the annual BPD fee. If FDA receives a request to discontinue participation in the BPD program after August 1 of the fiscal year, the sponsor will receive an annual BPD fee invoice for the upcoming fiscal year and must pay the invoice amount by the due date. Under section 744H(a)(1)(F)(i), FDA shall not refund any BPD fee (initial, annual, or reactivation), except as provided in section 744H(a)(1)(B)(iv) (see section V.C of this guidance).

E. Reactivation Fee

A sponsor that has discontinued participation in the BPD program for a product and wants to resume participation in the BPD program for the product must pay a *reactivation fee*.[23] A sponsor may resume participation in the BPD program for a product in one of two ways:

- The sponsor requests a BPD meeting for the product; or

- The sponsor submits a clinical protocol for an IND describing an investigation that FDA determines is intended to support a biosimilar biological product application for the product.

---

[22] Section 744H(a)(1)(C)(ii) of the FD&C Act.
[23] Section 744H(a)(1)(D) of the FD&C Act.

6

Contains Nonbinding Recommendations

The *reactivation fee* is due within 5 calendar days after FDA grants a BPD meeting for the product or upon submission of an IND describing an investigation that FDA determines is intended to support a biosimilar biological product application for the product, whichever occurs first. The reactivation fee for a fiscal year will be equal to twice the amount of the annual BPD fee established for that fiscal year.[24] Refer to section VIII of this guidance for consequences of failing to pay the required fees.

Beginning in the next fiscal year after a sponsor has paid the reactivation fee, the sponsor must pay an annual BPD fee.

VI.   BIOSIMILAR BIOLOGICAL PRODUCT APPLICATION FEES

FDA assesses a user fee for each biosimilar biological product application. Under BsUFA II, application fees are not assessed for supplements to approved biosimilar biological product applications.

Beginning in FY 2018, each person that submits an application is assessed an application fee as follows:

- A biosimilar biological product application for which clinical data (other than comparative bioavailability studies) with respect to safety or effectiveness are required for approval is assessed a full application fee.[25]

- A biosimilar biological product application for which clinical data (other than comparative bioavailability studies) with respect to safety or effectiveness are not required for approval is assessed one-half of a full application fee.[26]

Under BsUFA II, application fees are not reduced by the cumulative amount of BPD fees paid for the product that is the subject of the application.[27] Application fees are due when the application is submitted.[28]

A. Exception to the Application Fee

If a biosimilar biological product application:

- was submitted by a person that paid the fee for the application,

---

[24] Section 744H(b)(3)(D) of the FD&C Act.
[25] Section 744H(a)(2)(A)(i) of the FD&C Act.
[26] Section 744H(a)(2)(A)(ii) of the FD&C Act.
[27] See section 744H(a)(2)(B) of the FD&C Act. For application fees assessed under BsUFA I, the application fee was reduced by the cumulative amount of BPD fees paid for a product that was the subject of the application.
[28] Section 744H(a)(2)(C) of the FD&C Act.

7

- was accepted for filing, and
- was not approved or was withdrawn (without a waiver),

the submission of a biosimilar biological product application for the same product by the same person (or the person's licensee, assignee, or successor) does not require an application fee.[29]

B. Refund of the Application Fee

If an application is refused for filing or is withdrawn without a waiver before filing, FDA will refund seventy-five percent of the application fee paid.[30] A written refund request is not required. An application that was withdrawn before filing or refused for filing will be subject to the full application fee when resubmitted, unless a waiver applies.[31]

C. Waiver of Application Fees[32]

Under section 744H(d)(1) of the FD&C Act, an applicant is eligible for a waiver of the *application fee* if the applicant is a small business submitting its first biosimilar biological product application to the Agency for review and does not have another product that has been approved under a human drug application or a biosimilar biological product application and introduced or delivered for introduction into interstate commerce.

To qualify for a small business waiver of the application fee, an applicant must meet all of the following criteria:

- The applicant employs fewer than 500 employees, including employees of affiliates;

- The applicant does not have a drug product that has been approved under a human drug application or a biosimilar biological product application and introduced or delivered for introduction into interstate commerce; and

- The applicant, including its affiliates, is submitting its first biosimilar biological product application.

1. Small Business Waiver and Refund Request

To qualify for a small business waiver of the biosimilar biological product application fee,[33] an applicant should submit to FDA Form FDA 3971, attached as Appendix I, at least four months

---

[29] Section 744H(a)(2)(D) of the FD&C Act.
[30] Section 744H(a)(2)(E) of the FD&C Act.
[31] Section 744H(a)(2)(F) of the FD&C Act.
[32] This shaded portion of the guidance reflects the provisions for which FDA is seeking an information collection approval from the Office of Management and Budget. When OMB approval is obtained, FDA will provide notice.
[33] Section 744H(d)(1) of the FD&C Act.

8

Contains Nonbinding Recommendations

prior to the submission of the application. If an applicant submitted an application with payment and would like to request a small business waiver and refund, the applicant should complete and submit Form FDA 3971 to request the refund. Such a request must be made within 180 calendar days of when the application fee was due.[34] The completed form should be submitted via email to CDERCollections@fda.hhs.gov.

Upon receipt of Form FDA 3971, FDA may contact the applicant to request additional information and to clarify information provided in Form FDA 3971. Examples of requested information include, but are not limited to, the following:

- An application for size determination;

- A copy of the applicant's Articles of Incorporation and Bylaws;

- The applicant's most recent annual financial statement to shareholders; or

- A breakdown of the number of persons employed full time, part time, temporarily, or otherwise by the applicant and affiliates during each of the pay periods for the 12 months preceding the applicant's certification.

Occasionally, FDA finds entities affiliated with the applicant that the applicant did not identify as one of its affiliates. In such cases, FDA recommends that the applicant submit any agreements between an applicant and the other entities that demonstrate the nature of the relationship the applicant has with the entity.

If the requested information is not submitted, FDA may deny the small business waiver request because there is insufficient evidence that the applicant meets the criteria described in section 744H(d)(1) of the FD&C Act.

2. *Expiration Date of the Small Business Waiver*

If a small business waiver is granted, the applicant should submit its biosimilar biological product application within 1 year after the date of the small business determination since circumstances supporting a small business waiver may change rapidly. For example, an applicant could merge with a larger company and therefore no longer be considered a small business. Similarly, an applicant could purchase a new drug application (NDA) or biologics license application (BLA) from an unaffiliated company and, therefore, would have a drug product that has been approved under a human drug application or a biosimilar biological product application and introduced into or delivered for introduction into interstate commerce.

If an applicant is granted a small business waiver and is unable to submit the application within 1 year of the determination, the applicant should request a new small business waiver. The

---

[34] Section 744H(h) of the FD&C Act.

Agency will examine its records to confirm that the applicant still meets the criteria for a small business waiver. If the criteria are no longer met, the small business waiver request will be denied. If the criteria are still met, the Agency will renew the small business waiver for another year.

3. Small Business Waivers of Application Fees for Future Biosimilar Biological Product Applications

After an applicant or its affiliate is granted a small business waiver and submits its first biosimilar biological product application, the applicant cannot receive another small business waiver.[35] That means the applicant or its affiliate is not eligible to receive a small business waiver for any subsequent biosimilar biological product application. In addition, the applicant or affiliate is ineligible for another small business waiver even if the application is withdrawn or refused for filing. If an applicant does not submit the application for which it was granted a small business waiver, the applicant may qualify again for a small business waiver.

VII. BIOSIMILAR BIOLOGICAL PRODUCT PROGRAM FEES

The biosimilar biological product program fee is assessed annually for each eligible biosimilar biological product. Program fees are assessed for a fiscal year to each person[36] who is named as the applicant in a biosimilar biological product application for each biosimilar biological product identified in a biosimilar biological product application approved as of October 1 of such fiscal year,[37] where the product does not appear on a list of discontinued biosimilar biological products (as of October 1 of such fiscal year).[38] For example, if approval of a biosimilar biological product application occurs on or before October 1, 2017, and the products identified in the approved application are not on the discontinued list as of October 1, 2017, then program fees will be assessed for the products for FY 2018. However, if approval of a biosimilar biological product application occurs after October 1, 2017, then program fees are not assessed for the products identified in the application for FY 2018.

The program fees are due on the first business day on or after October 1 of each fiscal year or the first business day after the enactment of an appropriations Act providing for the collection and obligation of such fees for the year, whichever is later.[39]

---

[35] See section 744H(d)(1) of the FD&C Act.
[36] "The term 'person' includes an affiliate of such person." Section 744G(12) of the FD&C Act. See section III of this document for more information on the meaning of the term "person" for purposes of this guidance.
[37] Section 744H(a)(3)(A)(i) of the FD&C Act.
[38] Section 744H(a)(3)(A)(ii) of the FD&C Act.
[39] Section 744H(a)(3)(B) of the FD&C Act.

10

Applicants may not be assessed more than five program fees for biosimilar biological products identified in each approved application for each fiscal year.[40] For example, if seven biosimilar biological products are approved under the same BLA, the applicant would be assessed five program fees for the fiscal year.

Program fees for liquid parenteral biosimilar biological products. BsUFA II clarifies the definition of a "biosimilar biological product" to mean "a specific strength of a biological product in final dosage form for which a biosimilar biological product application has been approved."[41] For the purposes of assessing program fees for liquid parenteral biosimilar biological products, FDA intends to take into consideration both the total quantity of drug substance in mass or units of activity in a product and the concentration of the drug substance in mass or units of activity per unit volume of product. For example, two biosimilar biological products in final dosage form with the same concentration but with different fill volumes would be considered two separate biosimilar biological products for the purpose of assessing program fees. The applicant would be assessed two program fees for these products. If the applicant has more than five concentrations or fill volumes approved in the BLA, it will not be assessed more than five program fees for each fiscal year for products identified in such application.

An auto-injector that has the same strength or potency in final dosage form as a prefilled syringe or vial will generally be assessed a separate program fee. This is intended to align the Agency's assessment of fees for biological products approved under section 351(k) of the PHS Act with its assessment of fees for products approved under section 351(a) of the PHS Act or section 505 of the FD&C Act.[42, 43]

VIII. FAILURE TO PAY FEES

Under section 744H(a)(1)(E) of the FD&C Act, if a person has failed to pay any BPD fee (initial, annual, or reactivation) for a product as required:

- FDA shall not provide a BPD meeting relating to the product for which fees are owed.[44]

- Except in extraordinary circumstances, FDA shall not consider an IND submitted for the product to have been received under section 505(i)(2) of the FD&C Act if FDA determines that the investigation is intended to support a biosimilar biological product application.[45]

---

[40] Section 744H(a)(3)(D) of the FD&C Act.
[41] Section 744G(3) of the FD&C Act.
[42] See guidance for industry *Assessing User Fees Under the Prescription Drug User Fee Amendments of 2017* (https://www.fda.gov/downloads/Drugs/GuidanceComplianceRegulatoryInformation/Guidances/UCM580099.pdf).
[43] The distinction in this guidance between (1) auto-injectors and (2) prefilled syringes or vials is for the purposes of assessing the biosimilar biological product program fee only and not for any other purpose.
[44] Section 744H(a)(1)(E)(i) of the FD&C Act.
[45] Section 744H(a)(1)(E)(ii) of the FD&C Act.

11

428

- Except in extraordinary circumstances, FDA shall prohibit the sponsor of a clinical investigation from continuing the investigation (this is referred to as a "financial hold") if FDA determines that the investigation is intended to support a biosimilar biological product application.[46]

Under sections 744H(a)(1)(E)(iv) and 744H(e) and of the FD&C Act, a biosimilar biological product application or supplement submitted by a person subject to BsUFA fees shall be considered incomplete and shall not be accepted for filing until all BsUFA fees owed by such person have been paid.

IX.   PAYMENT INFORMATION AND PROCEDURES

This section briefly describes the procedures for assessing and issuing annual invoices for the annual BPD fee and the biosimilar biological product program fees under BsUFA II. More detailed instructions will be provided in FDA's direct notice to affected persons by issuing a "Notification of Annual BsUFA Fees" correspondence.

A. Initial BPD Fees, Reactivation Fees, and Application Fees

Applicants should complete a Biosimilar User Fee Cover Sheet (Form FDA 3792) online and pay by electronic check, wire transfer, money order, or bank draft. Instruction on accessing and completing the Biosimilar User Fee Cover Sheet is located on the BsUFA website (https://www.fda.gov/bsufa).

B. Annual Billing Cycle

1. BPD Sponsor Survey

FDA intends to send sponsors an annual survey to gather pertinent information to assist with fee setting for the next fiscal year. FDA anticipates sending the survey in the third quarter of each fiscal year.

2. Notification of Annual BsUFA Fees Correspondence

FDA will issue a "Notification of Annual BsUFA Fees" correspondence to affected sponsors by July of each fiscal year regarding their active BPD programs and approved biosimilar biological products. Sponsors should review the correspondence and notify FDA of any changes in contact information, changes in the status of Pre-IND/INDs in the BPD program, changes in biosimilar biological product marketing status, and any other information pertinent for the Agency to issue an accurate invoice to the proper person.

3. Annual Invoicing

---

[46] Section 744H(a)(1)(E)(iii) of the FD&C Act.

12

Contains Nonbinding Recommendations

FDA expects to issue annual invoices by September. Because sponsors are invoiced for annual BPD fees and program fees in advance of the upcoming fiscal year, the invoices may not reflect the actual data available as of October 1. FDA will issue additional invoices later, as needed, to capture any new BPD sponsors and program fee-eligible biosimilar biological products that should have been invoiced. For example, if a sponsor pays a FY 2017 initial BPD fee on September 15, 2017, the sponsor can expect to receive a FY 2018 annual BPD fee invoice in December 2017.

Payment instructions are included on the invoice.

4. Moving a Product to the Discontinued Section of the Biosimilar List

FDA maintains a list of approved biosimilar biological products that are user fee-eligible and products that are not marketed (discontinued). This list will be available on the BsUFA website (https://www.fda.gov/bsufa). A biosimilar biological product is not assessed a program fee if it is in the discontinued section of the biosimilar list on the date that fees are assessed as of October 1 of the fiscal year. Applicants who have decided to stop marketing a product, or have decided to delay launch of a product after its approval date, should request to have the product moved to the discontinued section. If a biosimilar biological product remains on the biosimilar list, and has not been moved to the discontinued section, on the date that fees are assessed for a fiscal year, the applicant will be assessed a program fee for the product even if it is not being marketed.[47]

Requests to move an approved biosimilar biological product to the discontinued section of the biosimilar list should be submitted to CDERCollections@fda.hhs.gov no later than September 30 of the preceding fiscal year. The request should clearly identify the product to be moved and the date that its not-marketed status begins and, if applicable, would end. If the applicant submits a request as set forth in this paragraph, FDA intends to consider the product to have been moved to the discontinued section on the date that the request was received or on the date the product is no longer marketed, whichever is later.

Please note that applicants seeking to move a biosimilar biological product to the discontinued section should clearly indicate the date on which their product is no longer marketed. Applicants should not rely on communications with a review division. Communication with the wrong division of FDA, or in a manner that does not make clear when a product is no longer marketed, may mean that the biosimilar biological product is not moved to the discontinued section of the biosimilar list before the date program fees are assessed, and may result in the applicant being required to pay a program fee for the product.

---

[47] Section 744H(a)(3)(A) of the FD&C Act.

13

Contains Nonbinding Recommendations

C. Waiver or Refund Requests

An applicant may request a waiver of the application fee, and may request a refund of fees it has paid, if it meets the applicable statutory criteria.[48] The written waiver or refund request must be submitted not later than 180 calendar days after such fee is due.[49] To request a small business waiver of the application fee, see section VI.C of this guidance. To request a refund of fees paid, the applicant should complete Form FDA 3913 (User Fee Payment Refund Request) and submit to CDERCollections@fda.hhs.gov. This form can be accessed from the User Fees website (https://www.fda.gov/ForIndustry/UserFees/). Any questions can be directed to CDERCollections@fda.hhs.gov.

X.   APPEALS PROCESS

A. Reconsideration Request

If FDA fully or partially denies a request for a waiver or refund of user fees, the applicant may request reconsideration of that decision. A request for reconsideration should be made within 30 calendar days of the issuance of FDA's decision to fully or partially deny a request for a waiver or refund of user fees.

FDA recommends that requests for reconsideration state the applicant's reasons for believing that FDA's decision is in error and include any additional information, including updated financial information that is relevant to the applicant's position. The Agency will issue a response upon reconsideration, setting forth the basis for the decision.

All requests for reconsideration (regardless of whether the product is regulated by CDER or CBER) should be submitted via email to CDERCollections@fda.hhs.gov and should be addressed to the following:

> Division of User Fee Management and Budget Formulation
> Attention: Division Director
> Center for Drug Evaluation and Research

Alternatively, an applicant can mail the request to FDA via the carrier of its choice. For the most updated mailing address, visit the following FDA website: https://www.fda.gov/bsufa.

---

[48] Sections 744H(a)(1)(F) and 744H(d)(1) of the FD&C Act. The FD&C Act does not provide for deferral of user fees, and FDA does not grant deferral of user fees based on pending requests for a refund. FDA therefore expects that all BsUFA fees assessed will be paid when due without regard to a pending request for a refund.
[49] Section 744H(h) of the FD&C Act.

B. Appeal Request

If a request is denied upon reconsideration, the applicant may choose to appeal the denial. A request for an appeal should be made within 30 calendar days of the issuance of FDA's decision to affirm its denial of a request for a waiver or refund of user fees. The following information should be included in the appeal:

- The original request;
- The denial of the original request;
- The reconsideration request;
- The denial of the reconsideration request; and
- A statement of the applicant's reasons for believing that the prior conclusions were in error.

No new information or new analyses should be presented in the appeal request. If new information or analyses are presented in the appeal request the appeal will not be accepted and the matter will be referred back to the original deciding authority to consider the new information or analyses.

All requests for appeals for either CDER or CBER products should be submitted to the Director of CDER's Office of Management via CDERCollections@fda.hhs.gov and a copy should be submitted to the CDER Formal Dispute Resolution Project Manager. The contact information can be found on the CDER Formal Dispute Resolution Web page.[50] Alternatively, an applicant can mail the request to FDA via carrier of its choice. For the most updated mailing address, visit the following FDA website: https://www.fda.gov/bsufa.

After FDA reviews the information submitted in the appeal request, for CDER regulated products the Director of CDER's Office of Management will issue a written decision on the applicant's request; for CBER regulated products the Director of CBER will issue a written decision on the applicant's request.

CDER Products
If the applicant's appeal is denied at one management level, the applicant can appeal the same matter to the next higher management level in the Center chain of command. A new request should be submitted for each appeal to the next management level and should follow the process provided in this guidance. If the applicant has exhausted the Center's management levels and remains unsatisfied with the decision, the applicant may request review of the matter by the Commissioner of Food and Drugs (Commissioner) under 21 C.F.R. §10.75(c). Requests for review by the Commissioner should be submitted to FDA's Ombudsman, with a copy provided to the Center. Review of such matters by the Commissioner is discretionary.[51]

---

[50] See
https://www.fda.gov/AboutFDA/CentersOffices/OfficeofMedicalProductsandTobacco/CDER/ContactCDER/ucm44 4092.htm.
[51] See 40 FR 40682, 40693 (September 3, 1975).

15

CBER Products

If the applicant's appeal is denied by the Director of CBER, the applicant may request review of the matter by the Commissioner under 21 C.F.R. § 10.75(c). Requests for review by the Commissioner should be submitted to the FDA's Ombudsman, with copies provided to the center that denied the appeal. Review of such matters by the Commissioner is discretionary.

XI.   OTHER RESOURCES

The following guidance documents may be helpful:
- Guidance for Industry - Submitting Separate Marketing Applications and Clinical Data for Purposes of Assessing User Fees[52]

The following manuals of policies and procedures (MAPP) may be helpful:
- MAPP 6050.1 Refusal to Accept Applications for Filing From Applicants in Arrears[53]

Additional information is also available on the FDA User Fees web page. For any questions, please email the Biosimilar User Fee staff at CDERCollections@fda.hhs.gov or call 301-796-7900.

XII.   PAPERWORK REDUCTION ACT OF 1995

This guidance contains information collection provisions that are subject to review by the Office of Management and Budget (OMB) under the Paperwork Reduction Act of 1995 (44 U.S.C. 3501-3520).

The guidance refers to collections of information for filling out and submitting Form FDA 3792 (Biosimilar User Fee Cover Sheet) previously approved under OMB control number 0910-0718; collections of information for filling out and submitting Forms FDA 3913 and 3914 (User Fee Payment Refund and Transfer Requests) approved under OMB control number 0910-0805; collections of information associated with review of investigational new drug applications, approved under OMB control number 0910-0014; and collections of information associated with review of new drug applications under the FD&C Act, or biologics license applications submitted under section 351(a) or 351(k) of the PHS Act, approved under OMB control numbers 0910-0001, 0910-0338, and 0910-0719, respectively.

Requests from sponsors to discontinue their participation in the BPD program where an IND may or may not have been submitted consists of a simple written declaration to the IND or the

---

[52] See
https://www.fda.gov/downloads/Drugs/GuidanceComplianceRegulatoryInformation/Guidances/UCM07932C.pdf.
[53] See
https://www.fda.gov/downloads/AboutFDA/CentersOffices/OfficeofMedicalProductsandTobacco/CDER/Manualof
PoliciesProcedures/UCM082029.pdf.

16

Contains Nonbinding Recommendations

FDA. The burden of these requests is estimated to average 2 hours annually per sponsor. FDA also anticipates 5 requests annually from sponsors to move BsUFA products to the discontinued section of the BsUFA list with an associated burden of ½ hour per request.

The guidance also references BsUFA small business waiver requests using the Small Business Waiver and Refund Request Form (Form FDA 3971) approved under OMB control number 0910-0693. Completion of the form and collection of BsUFA waiver supporting documents are estimated to require an average of 16 hours for a BsUFA small business waiver request, 24 hours per response for a reconsideration of a denied waiver request, and 12 hours for an appeal of a waiver, reduction, or refund decision.

Collection of information in response to correspondence notifying sponsors of Annual BsUFA Fees allows FDA to collect and update information necessary for accurate invoicing of sponsors participating in the BsUFA program. The burden of this request is estimated to average 2 hours annually per participating sponsor. In addition, a BPD sponsor survey, to assist FDA in determining appropriate BsUFA fees for the upcoming fiscal year, is estimated to average 1 hour burden annually for each participating sponsor and is approved under OMB Control No. 0718. These estimates include the time to review instructions, gather the data needed, and respond to FDA's information requests.

Send any comments regarding the burden estimate or suggestions for reducing this burden to the following:

> Department of Health and Human Services
> Food and Drug Administration
> Office of Operations
> Paperwork Reduction Act (PRA) Staff
> PRAStaff@fda.hhs.gov

17

Contains Nonbinding Recommendations

APPENDIX I: FORM FDA 3971

DEPARTMENT OF HEALTH AND HUMAN SERVICES Food and Drug Administration *Prescription Drug and Biosimilar User Fee Acts* **Small Business Waiver and Refund Request**	Form Approved: OMB No. 0910-0693 Expiration Date: October 31, 2020 *See PRA Statement on last page.*

Section I: Applicant Information

1. Applicant Name

Former Names *(if applicable)*

2. Telephone Number *(Including area and country codes)*	3. Fax Number *(Including area and country codes)*

4. Address *(No P.O. boxes allowed)*	5. Federal Tax ID Number *(Required for all U.S. applicants)*
Address 1 *(Street address)*	
Address 2 *(Apartment, suite, unit, building, floor, etc.)*	6. DUNS Number
City / State/Province/Region	7. Number of Employees
Country / ZIP or Postal Code	

8. User Fee Program for which the action is requested *(Select one)*   ☐ PDUFA   ☐ BsUFA

9. Human Drug/Biosimilar Biological Product Applications (Applicant)

Product Name

Application Number	Submission Date	Application Status *(Select from drop-down list)*

Is this the first application the Applicant has submitted to the FDA for review?   ☐ Yes   ☐ No

10. Human Drug/Biosimilar Biological Products (Applicant)

Does the Applicant have drug products approved under a human drug or biosimilar biological product application by the FDA that have been introduced or delivered for introduction into interstate commerce?   ☐ Yes   ☐ No

11. Small Business Waiver (Applicant)

Has the Applicant previously received a Small Business Waiver for a human drug or biosimilar biological product? *(See instructions for details.)*   ☐ Yes   ☐ No

Section II: Affiliate Information *(Enter information for each entity affiliated with the Applicant)*

Provide information for each of the Applicant's domestic and foreign affiliates. For multiple affiliates, click the "Add Affiliate" button for each additional entry. Refer to Instructions, Section II for additional information.

The Applicant does NOT have any Affiliates *(Check if applicable):*   ☐

12. Affiliate Name

FORM FDA 3971 (12/16)   PSC Publishing Services (301) 44—4740   EF

13. Affiliate Address *(No P.O. boxes allowed)*		14. DUNS Number
Address 1 *(Street address)*		
Address 2 *(Apartment, suite, unit, building, floor, etc.)*		15. Number of Employees
City	State/Province/Region	
Country	ZIP or Postal Code	

16. Name of Affiliate's Point of Contact	17. E-mail Address	18. Telephone Number

19. Small Business Waiver (Affiliate)

Has the Affiliate previously received a Small Business Waiver for a human drug or biosimilar biological product application? *(See instructions for details.)* ☐ Yes ☐ No

20. Human Drug/Biosimilar Biological Product Applications (Affiliate)

Has the Affiliate ever submitted a human drug or biosimilar biological product application? ☐ Yes ☐ No

Click for an additional set of Section II affiliate entries (includes items 12 through 20). May be repeated.

Section III: Refund

21. Did the Applicant pay a fee for this application for_____prior to requesting this Small Business Waiver? Yes ☐ ☐ No   *Product Name*

NDA or BLA Number	Payment Amount	PIN/Invoice Number	Payment Reference Number	Refund Amount Requested

Section IV: Certification

Review, sign, and date the following certification statement:

I certify that _____
Applicant Name (must be identical to item 1)

BsUFA:

i Has fewer than 500 employees, including employees of Affiliates;

ii. Does not have a drug product that has been approved under a human drug application or biosimilar biological product application by the FDA and introduced or delivered for introduction into interstate commerce;

iii. Requests a Small Business Waiver for the first biosimilar biological product application that the Applicant or its Affiliate has submitted.

PDUFA:

i Has fewer than 500 employees, including employees of Affiliates;

ii. Does not have a drug product that has been approved under a human drug application by the FDA and introduced or delivered for introduction into interstate commerce;

iii. Requests a Small Business Waiver for the first human drug application that the Applicant or its Affiliate has submitted.

I further certify that, to the best of my knowledge, the information I have provided in this form is complete, accurate and has been verified. I understand that submission of a false certification may subject me to criminal penalties under 18 U.S.C. § 1001 and other applicable federal statutes.

FORM FDA 3971 (12/16)

22. Name of Applicant's Responsible Official	23. Title
24. Telephone Number	25. Email Address

26. Responsible Official's Address	
Address 1 *(Street address)*	
Address 2 *(Apartment, suite, unit, building, floor, etc.)*	
City	State/Province/Region
Country	ZIP or Postal Code

27. Signature	28. Date *(mm/dd/yyyy)*
To enable the signature field, please fill out all prior required fields. For a list of required fields which have not yet been filled out, please click here.	

Send Completed Form FDA 3971 to FDA via

Email (preferred): *CDERCollections@FDA.HHS.GOV*   **or**   **Physical Mail:** Division of User Fee Management and Budget Formulation
Food and Drug Administration 10001 New Hampshire Ave. Silver Spring, MD 20993-0002

FDA Use Only

Date Received: _____   ☐ Approved   ☐ Denied

Privacy Act Notice: This notice is provided pursuant to the Privacy Act of 1974, 5 U.S.C. § 552a. The collection of this information is authorized by 21 U.S.C. § 379h and 21 U.S.C. § 379j-52. FDA will use the information to assess, collect and process user fee payments, and, facilitate debt collection under the Debt Collection Improvement Act. FDA may disclose information to courts and the Department of Justice in the context of litigation and requests for legal advice; to other Federal agencies in response to subpoenas issued by such agencies; to HHS and FDA employees and contractors to perform user fee services; to the National Archives and Records Administration and General Services Administration for records management inspections; to the Department of Homeland Security and other Federal agencies and contractors
in order to respond to system breaches; to banks in order to process payment made by credit card; to Dun and Bradstreet to validate submitter contact information, and to other entities as permitted under the Debt Collection Improvement Act. Furnishing the requested information is mandatory unless otherwise indicated. Failure to supply the information could prevent FDA from processing user fee payments and waivers. Additional detail regarding FDA's use of information is available online: Privacy Act and Website Policies.

FORM FDA 3971 (12/16)

This section applies only to requirements of the Paperwork Reduction Act of 1995.
DO NOT SEND YOUR COMPLETED FORM TO THE PRA STAFF EMAIL ADDRESS BELOW.

The burden time for this collection of information is estimated to average 40 minutes per response, including the time to review instructions, search existing data sources, gather and maintain the data needed and complete and review the collection of information. Send comments regarding this burden estimate or any other aspect of this information collection, including suggestions for reducing this burden, to:

Department of Health and Human Services Food and Drug Administration
Office of Operations
Paperwork Reduction Act (PRA) Staff
PRAStaff@fda.hhs.gov

"An agency may not conduct or sponsor, and a person is not required to respond to, a collection of information unless it displays a currently valid OMB number."

FORM FDA 3971 (12/16)

APPENDIX C4

Labeling for Biosimilar Products Guidance

Labeling for Biosimilar Products

Guidance for Industry

U.S. Department of Health and Human Services
Food and Drug Administration
Center for Drug Evaluation and Research (CDER)
Center for Biologics Evaluation and Research (CBER)

July 2018
Labeling

Labeling for Biosimilar Products

Guidance for Industry

Additional copies are available from:

Office of Communications
Division of Drug Information, Division of Drug Information
Center for Drug Evaluation and Research
Food and Drug Administration
10001 New Hampshire Ave., Hillandale Bldg., 4th Floor
Silver Spring, MD 20993-0002
Phone: 855-543-3784 or 301-796-3400; Fax: 301-431-6353
Email: druginfo@fda.hhs.gov
https://www.fda.gov/Drugs/GuidanceComplianceRegulatoryInformation/Guidances/default.htm

and/or

Office of Communication, Outreach and Development
Center for Biologics Evaluation and Research
Food and Drug Administration
10903 New Hampshire Ave., Bldg. 71, Room 3128
Silver Spring, MD 20993-0002
Phone: 800-835-4709 or 240-402-8010
Email: ocod@fda.hhs.gov
https://www.fda.gov/BiologicsBloodVaccines/GuidanceComplianceRegulatoryInformation/Guidances/default.htm

U.S. Department of Health and Human Services
Food and Drug Administration
Center for Drug Evaluation and Research (CDER)
Center for Biologics Evaluation and Research (CBER)

July 2018
Labeling

Contains Nonbinding Recommendations

TABLE OF CONTENTS

I.   INTRODUCTION.. 1

II.   BACKGROUND 1

III.   GENERAL PRINCIPLES FOR DRAFT LABELING OF PROPOSED
BIOSIMILAR PRODUCTS (BIOSIMILAR PRODUCT LABELING) 3

IV.   SPECIFIC RECOMMENDATIONS ON CONTENT OF BIOSIMILAR PRODUCT
LABELING 5

    A.   Approaches to Product Identification 5

    B.   Approaches to Content Presentation 7

    C.   Approaches to Specific Sections of Biosimilar Product Labeling 8

V.   FDA-APPROVED PATIENT LABELING 10

VI.   REVISING BIOSIMILAR PRODUCT LABELING 10

    A.   Updating Safety Information 10

    B.   Additional Conditions of Use 11

VII.   HOW TO SUBMIT INITIAL AND REVISED LABELING 11

VIII.   INTERCHANGEABLE PRODUCTS 12

Labeling for Biosimilar Products
Guidance for Industry[1]

This guidance represents the current thinking of the Food and Drug Administration (FDA or Agency) on this topic. It does not establish any rights for any person and is not binding on FDA or the public. You can use an alternative approach if it satisfies the requirements of the applicable statutes and regulations. To discuss an alternative approach, contact the FDA office responsible for this guidance as listed on the title page.

I. INTRODUCTION

This guidance is intended to help applicants develop draft labeling for proposed biosimilar products for submission in an application under section 351(k) of the Public Health Service Act (PHS Act) (42 U.S.C. 262(k)). The recommendations for prescription drug labeling in this guidance pertain only to the prescribing information (commonly referred to as the package insert), except for certain recommendations in section V pertaining to FDA-approved patient labeling (e.g., Patient Information, Medication Guide, and Instructions for Use).[2] This guidance does not provide specific labeling recommendations for interchangeable products (see section VIII of this guidance).

In general, FDA's guidance documents do not establish legally enforceable responsibilities. Instead, guidances describe the Agency's current thinking on a topic and should be viewed only as recommendations, unless specific regulatory or statutory requirements are cited. The use of the word *should* in Agency guidances means that something is suggested or recommended, but not required.

II. BACKGROUND

The Biologics Price Competition and Innovation Act of 2009 (BPCI Act) was enacted as part of the Patient Protection and Affordable Care Act (Affordable Care Act) (Public Law 111-148) on March 23, 2010. The BPCI Act amends the PHS Act and other statutes to create an abbreviated licensure pathway for biological products shown to be biosimilar to or interchangeable with an

---

[1] This guidance has been prepared by the Office of New Drugs, Therapeutic Biologics and Biosimilars Staff, in the Center for Drug Evaluation and Research (CDER) in cooperation with the Center for Biologics Evaluation and Research (CBER) at the Food and Drug Administration.

[2] Unless otherwise specified, the terms *biosimilar product labeling* and *labeling* as used in this guidance address only the prescribing information as described in 21 CFR 201.56 and 201.57.

1

FDA-licensed reference product[3] (see sections 7001 through 7003 of the Affordable Care Act). Section 351(k) of the PHS Act, added by the BPCI Act, sets forth the requirements for an application for a proposed biosimilar product and an application or a supplement for a proposed interchangeable product.

Section 351(i) of the PHS Act defines *biosimilarity* to mean "that the biological product is highly similar to the reference product notwithstanding minor differences in clinically inactive components" and that "there are no clinically meaningful differences between the biological product and the reference product in terms of the safety, purity, and potency of the product."

To meet the standard for *interchangeability*, an applicant must provide sufficient information to demonstrate biosimilarity and also to demonstrate that the biological product can be expected to produce the same clinical result as the reference product in any given patient and, if the biological product is administered more than once to an individual, the risk in terms of safety or diminished efficacy of alternating or switching between the use of the biological product and the reference product is not greater than the risk of using the reference product without such alternation or switch (see section 351(k)(4) of the PHS Act). Interchangeable products may be substituted for the reference product without the intervention of the prescribing health care provider (see section 351(i)(3) of the PHS Act).

An application submitted under section 351(k) of the PHS Act must contain, among other things, information demonstrating that the biological product is biosimilar to a reference product based upon data derived from:

- Analytical studies that demonstrate that the biological product is highly similar to the reference product notwithstanding minor differences in clinically inactive components;

- Animal studies (including the assessment of toxicity); and

- A clinical study or studies (including the assessment of immunogenicity and pharmacokinetics or pharmacodynamics) that are sufficient to demonstrate safety, purity, and potency in one or more appropriate conditions of use for which the reference product is licensed and intended to be used and for which licensure is sought for the biological product.

Under the PHS Act, FDA has the discretion to determine that an element described above is unnecessary in a 351(k) application.

Under FDA regulations, prescription drug labeling must provide adequate information to enable health care providers to "use the drug safely and for the purposes for which it is intended"; and to this end, the approved prescribing information summarizes the essential scientific information

---

[3] *Reference product* means the single biological product licensed under section 351(a) of the PHS Act against which a biological product is evaluated in a 351(k) application (section 351(i)(4) of the PHS Act).

needed by health care providers for the safe and effective use of a drug.[4] Prescription drug labeling reflects FDA's finding of safety and effectiveness[5,6] for the drug under the labeled conditions of use and facilitates prescribing decisions, thereby enabling the safe and effective use of drugs, including biological products, and reducing the likelihood of medication errors.

III.   GENERAL PRINCIPLES FOR DRAFT LABELING OF PROPOSED BIOSIMILAR PRODUCTS (BIOSIMILAR PRODUCT LABELING)

The goal of a biosimilar product development program is to demonstrate biosimilarity between the proposed product and the reference product — not to independently establish safety and effectiveness of the proposed product. A demonstration of biosimilarity means, among other things, that FDA has determined that there are no clinically meaningful differences between the proposed product and the reference product in terms of safety, purity, and potency.[7] Thus, FDA's finding of safety and effectiveness for the reference product, as reflected in its FDA-approved prescribing information, may be relied upon to provide health care providers with the essential scientific information needed to facilitate prescribing decisions for the proposed biosimilar product's labeled conditions of use (e.g., indication(s), dosing regimen(s)). Accordingly, FDA recommends that biosimilar product labeling incorporate relevant data and information from the reference product labeling, with appropriate modifications, such as those described in sections V and VI of this guidance.[8]

Information and data from a clinical study of a proposed biosimilar product should be described in its labeling only when necessary to inform safe and effective use by a health care provider. As a general matter, it is FDA's view that biosimilar product labeling should not include a description of or data from clinical studies conducted to support a demonstration of biosimilarity.[9] Generally, clinical studies conducted to support a demonstration of biosimilarity

---

[4] See 21 CFR 201.100 and 201.56(a)(1).

[5] The standard for licensure of a biological product as potent under section 351(a) of the PHS Act has long been interpreted to include effectiveness (see 21 CFR 600.3(s) and the guidance for industry *Providing Clinical Evidence of Effectiveness for Human Drug and Biological Products*). We update guidances periodically. For the most recent version of a guidance, check the FDA guidance web page at https://www.fda.gov/RegulatoryInformation/Guidances/default.htm.

[6] In this guidance, we use the terms *safety and effectiveness* and *safety, purity, and potency* interchangeably in the discussions pertaining to biosimilar products.

[7] Section 351(i)(2) of the PHS Act.

[8] Sections V and VI of this guidance describe examples of areas in which the reference product labeling and biosimilar product labeling might differ.

[9] FDA posts on its website certain documents generated by FDA related to its review of a 351(k) application, as appropriate. For products regulated by CDER, see Drugs@FDA (https://www.accessdata.fda.gov/scripts/cder/daf/index.cfm). For products regulated by CBER, see the CBER Freedom of Information Office Electronic Reading Room

3

Contains Nonbinding Recommendations

are not designed to support an independent demonstration of safety or effectiveness of the proposed biosimilar product and thus would generally not be expected to facilitate an understanding of product safety and effectiveness. For example, the endpoints used in a clinical study conducted to support a demonstration of no clinically meaningful differences may not be the same endpoints evaluated to support licensure of the reference product and thus may not inform prescribing decisions regarding safety and effectiveness. Similarly, the patient population may differ from the patient population studied in the clinical trials that supported the determination of safety and effectiveness of the reference product. For example, subjects in a study conducted to support a demonstration of no clinically meaningful differences between the biosimilar product and the reference product may be healthy volunteers, or the condition of use studied may be one for which the reference product is not licensed or for which the applicant of the biosimilar product is not seeking licensure but for which sufficient data indicate that the population or condition of use is adequately sensitive to detect clinically meaningful differences between the products, should they exist.

Because clinical studies conducted to support a demonstration of biosimilarity generally are not designed to support an independent demonstration of safety or effectiveness, such studies may be misinterpreted in the context of drug labeling, resulting in an inaccurate understanding of the risk-benefit profile of the biosimilar product. Therefore, studies conducted to support biosimilarity generally should not be included in biosimilar product labeling. Biosimilar product labeling should incorporate relevant data and information from the reference product labeling, including clinical data that supported FDA's finding of safety and effectiveness of the reference product.

As required under 21 CFR 201.56(c)(1), biosimilar product labeling must meet the content and format requirements of the physician labeling rule (PLR) as described in 21 CFR 201.56(d) and 201.57, regardless of the format of the reference product labeling.[10] In addition, biosimilar product labeling must meet the content and format requirements of the pregnancy and lactation labeling final rule (PLLR) as described in 21 CFR 201.57(c)(9)(i) through (iii), regardless of whether the reference product must meet these requirements.[11]

(https://www.fda.gov/AboutFDA/CentersOffices/OfficeofMedicalProductsandTobacco/CBER/ucm129132.htm). Health care providers and others can refer to those documents if interested in FDA's review of data and information submitted in a 351(k) application to support biosimilarity.

[10] See the final rule "Requirements on Content and Format of Labeling for Human Prescription Drug and Biological Products" (71 FR 3922, January 24, 2006). This rule is commonly referred to as the *physician labeling rule* because it addresses prescription drug labeling that is used by prescribing physicians and other health care providers. Also see additional labeling guidances at
https://www.fda.gov/Drugs/GuidanceComplianceRegulatoryInformation/LawsActsandRules/ucm084159.htm

[11] See the final rule "Content and Format of Labeling for Human Prescription Drug and Biological Products; Requirements for Pregnancy and Lactation Labeling" (79 FR 72064, December 4, 2014). The final rule describes the implementation schedule for applications submitted on or after the effective date of the rule, applications pending at the time the rule became effective, and applications approved before the rule became effective (79 FR 72064 at 72095–96).

4

IV.   SPECIFIC RECOMMENDATIONS ON CONTENT OF BIOSIMILAR PRODUCT LABELING

FDA recommends that biosimilar product labeling incorporate relevant data and information from the reference product labeling, with appropriate modifications, as explained in sections V and VI of this guidance. The relevant data and information from the reference product labeling that should be incorporated into the biosimilar product labeling will depend on whether the applicant is seeking licensure for all conditions of use (e.g., indication(s), dosing regimen(s)) or fewer than all conditions of use of the reference product for the biosimilar product.[12]

In sections of the biosimilar product labeling that are based on the reference product labeling, it is anticipated that the text will be similar to the corresponding text in the reference product labeling. Text based on the reference product labeling need not be identical to the reference product labeling and should reflect currently available information necessary for the safe and effective use of the biosimilar product. Certain differences between the biosimilar and reference product labeling may be appropriate. For example, biosimilar product labeling conforming to PLR and/or PLLR may differ from reference product labeling because the reference product labeling may not be required to conform to those requirements at the time of licensure of the biosimilar product. In addition, biosimilar product labeling may include information specific to the biosimilar product that is necessary to inform safe and effective use of the product, including administration, preparation, storage, or safety information. This information may differ from that of the reference product labeling when it reflects differences between the biosimilar product and the reference product that do not preclude licensure of the biosimilar product.

A.   Approaches to Product Identification

In biosimilar product labeling, the approach to product identification depends on the context of the information being presented. FDA acknowledges that there will be variations on the general concepts outlined in this section because the approach to product identification will depend on the specific statements. The illustrative examples in this section use a fictional reference product JUNEXANT *(replicamab-hjxf)* and a fictional biosimilar product NEXSYMEO *(replicamab-cznm)*.

---

[12] A biosimilar product applicant generally may seek licensure for fewer than all conditions of use for which the reference product is licensed. The 351(k) application must include information demonstrating that the condition or conditions of use prescribed, recommended, or suggested in the proposed labeling submitted for the proposed biosimilar product have been previously licensed for the reference product (see section 351(k)(2)(A)(i)(III) of the PHS Act).

5

1. When use of the biosimilar product name is recommended:

The biosimilar product name should be used in labeling text that is specific to the biosimilar product or that refers solely to the biosimilar product. If a biosimilar product has a proprietary name, the proprietary name (e.g., NEXSYMEO) should be used in the appropriate sections. However, if a proprietary name is not available, or if referring to the drug substance (as discussed below), the biosimilar product's proper name (e.g., *replicamab-cznm*) should be used.[13]

The biosimilar product's proprietary name (or, if a proprietary name is not available, the biosimilar product's proper name) should be used in circumstances such as the following:

- In sections where the information described is specific to the biosimilar product — This includes, but is not limited to, the following sections: INDICATIONS AND USAGE, DOSAGE AND ADMINISTRATION, DESCRIPTION, and HOW SUPPLIED/STORAGE AND HANDLING.

- For directive statements and recommendations for preventing, monitoring, managing, or mitigating risks (e.g., "Discontinue NEXSYMEO in patients with [adverse reaction]") — Such statements are typically included in, but are not limited to, the BOXED WARNING, CONTRAINDICATIONS, WARNINGS AND PRECAUTIONS, and DRUG INTERACTIONS sections.

The biosimilar product's proper name should be used when referring to the drug substance. An example would be to use the biosimilar product's proper name in the DESCRIPTION section.

2. When use of the reference product name is recommended:

When clinical studies or data derived from studies with the reference product are described in biosimilar product labeling, the reference product's proper name (e.g., *replicamab-hjxf*) should be used. This information would typically be included in sections such as, but not limited to, ADVERSE REACTIONS (*Clinical Trials Experience* subsection) and CLINICAL STUDIES.

3. When use of the core name is recommended:[14]

The overall risk-benefit profile of the reference product is relevant to the biosimilar product, even if a particular serious adverse reaction or other risk included in the reference product labeling may not have been reported with the biosimilar product at the time of licensure. In labeling sections where the risk applies to both the biosimilar product and the reference product

---

[13] The *proper name* is the nonproprietary name designated by FDA in the license for a biological product licensed under the PHS Act (see section 351(a)(1)(B)(i) of the PHS Act and 21 CFR 600.3(k)).

[14] Two examples of a *core name* are filgrastim and epoetin alfa. The *proper name* for biological products will include a distinguishing suffix composed of four lowercase letters attached to the *core name* with a hyphen.

6

Contains Nonbinding Recommendations

(e.g., BOXED WARNING, CONTRAINDICATIONS, WARNINGS AND PRECAUTIONS, ADVERSE REACTIONS (*Postmarketing Experience* subsection)), it would be appropriate to use the core name of the reference product followed by the word "*products*" (e.g., *replicamab products*) to convey, for instance, that a risk or other information necessary for the safe use of the product applies to both the biosimilar product and the reference product (see section IV.B of this guidance).

For example, in WARNINGS AND PRECAUTIONS:

Reference Product Labeling	Biosimilar Product Labeling
Treatment with JUNEXANT increases the risk of serious infections involving various organ systems and sites that may lead to hospitalization or death.	Treatment with replicamab products increases the risk of serious infections involving various organ systems and sites that may lead to hospitalization or death.

    4. When use of more than one product name is recommended:

There may be text appropriately based on the reference product labeling where more than one of these product identification approaches should be used to convey information accurately. Therefore, all text in biosimilar product labeling, even sections that have been based on reference product labeling, should be carefully evaluated for the most appropriate product identification approach. In some cases, such as the following example, more than two of the approaches may be used:

> Replicamab products can cause hepatoxicity and acute hepatic failure. In clinical trials of replicamab-hjxf, 10% of patients developed elevated ALT or AST greater than three times the upper limit of normal and 5% progressed to acute hepatic failure. Evaluate serum transaminases (ALT and AST) and bilirubin at baseline and monthly during treatment with NEXSYMEO . . .

B.   **Approaches to Content Presentation**

The labeling for the biosimilar product should be specific to the conditions of use (e.g., indication(s), dosing regimen(s)) sought for the biosimilar product and should be consistent with language previously approved for the reference product for those conditions of use.

When a biosimilar product applicant obtains licensure for fewer than all conditions of use (e.g., indication(s), dosing regimen(s)) for which the reference product is licensed, certain text in the reference product labeling related to condition(s) of use for the reference product that are not licensed for the biosimilar product would generally not be included in the biosimilar product labeling.[15] However, in certain circumstances it may be necessary to include information in the biosimilar product labeling relating to an indication(s) for which the biosimilar product is not

---

[15] See Q.I.7 in the guidance for industry *Biosimilars: Questions and Answers Regarding Implementation of the Biologics Price Competition and Innovation Act of 2009.*

licensed, in order to help ensure safe use (e.g., when safety information in the reference product labeling is related to use of the product and is not specific to a particular licensed indication(s) or when information specific to only the biosimilar product's indication(s) cannot be easily extracted).[16] Such text should be written in a manner that does not imply that the biosimilar product is licensed for a reference product indication(s) or use(s) that has not been licensed for the biosimilar product. In these circumstances, specific sections of labeling that could be affected include BOXED WARNING, CONTRAINDICATIONS, WARNINGS AND PRECAUTIONS, ADVERSE REACTIONS, DRUG INTERACTIONS, and USE IN SPECIFIC POPULATIONS.

For example, for sections such as WARNINGS AND PRECAUTIONS and ADVERSE REACTIONS, the reference product labeling may pool and categorize events from all the reference product clinical trials for all the indications for which the reference product is licensed. In cases where the biosimilar product applicant is not seeking licensure for all the indications for which the reference product is licensed, the pooled data described in the reference product labeling should be included in the biosimilar product labeling in a manner that is not indication-specific. However, any text that refers to an indication for which the biosimilar product applicant is not currently seeking licensure and is included to ensure safe use of the biosimilar product should be revised to avoid an implication that the biosimilar has been licensed for that indication(s).

C.   Approaches to Specific Sections of Biosimilar Product Labeling

1.   HIGHLIGHTS OF PRESCRIBING INFORMATION (Highlights)

    a.   Initial U.S. approval

The initial U.S. approval in the Highlights section is the year that the biosimilar product is licensed.

    b.   Biosimilarity statement

FDA recommends including a statement, placed on the line immediately beneath the initial U.S. approval in the Highlights section, that the product is biosimilar to the reference product. It should read as follows:

[BIOSIMILAR PRODUCT'S PROPRIETARY NAME (biosimilar product's proper name)] is biosimilar* to [REFERENCE PRODUCT'S PROPRIETARY NAME (reference product's proper name)].

The asterisk should appear as a footnote symbol inserted after the word "biosimilar."

---

[16] See also 21 CFR 201.57(c)(6)(i).

8

For example, for the fictitious product NEXSYMEO, the statement should read as follows:

NEXSYMEO (replicamab-cznm) is biosimilar* to JUNEXANT (replicamab-hjxf).

The footnote should appear at the end of the Highlights section (but above the Revision Date) and state the following:

*Biosimilar means that the biological product is approved based on data demonstrating that it is highly similar to an FDA-approved biological product, known as a reference product, and that there are no clinically meaningful differences between the biosimilar product and the reference product. Biosimilarity of [BIOSIMILAR PRODUCT'S PROPRIETARY NAME] has been demonstrated for the condition(s) of use (e.g., indication(s), dosing regimen(s)), strength(s), dosage form(s), and route(s) of administration described in its Full Prescribing Information.

2.   INDICATIONS AND USAGE

Information in the INDICATIONS AND USAGE section should be specific to the licensed indications for the biosimilar product and should be consistent with information previously approved for the reference product. The biosimilar product labeling should include text from the reference product labeling regarding any Limitations of Use relevant to the biosimilar product's indication(s) (see section IV.B of this guidance for recommendations regarding text that refers to an indication for which licensure has not been sought by the biosimilar product applicant).

3.   ADVERSE REACTIONS, Immunogenicity

Immunogenicity information for therapeutic protein products is usually placed in a subsection in the ADVERSE REACTIONS section entitled *Immunogenicity*. To help health care providers interpret the significance of the information, the following or a similar statement should be included as the first paragraph in the subsection, preceding the immunogenicity data based on the reference product labeling:

As with all therapeutic proteins, there is potential for immunogenicity. The detection of antibody formation is highly dependent on the sensitivity and specificity of the assay. Additionally, the observed incidence of antibody (including neutralizing antibody) positivity in an assay may be influenced by several factors, including assay methodology, sample handling, timing of sample collection, concomitant medications, and underlying disease. For these reasons, comparison of the incidence of antibodies in the studies described below with the incidence of antibodies in other studies or to other [core name] products may be misleading.

9

V. FDA-APPROVED PATIENT LABELING

If a Medication Guide is required, applicants must follow existing Medication Guide regulations for biosimilar product labeling.[17] If the FDA-approved patient labeling for the reference product includes Patient Information, applicants should develop Patient Information for the biosimilar product, incorporating relevant information from the Patient Information for the reference product, with appropriate modifications.

If the FDA-approved patient labeling for the reference product includes Instructions for Use (IFU), the IFU for the proposed biosimilar product should incorporate relevant information from the IFU for the reference product and present the information in a similar manner. The proposed IFU may differ from the IFU for the reference product where, for example, modified language or images are needed to describe the biosimilar product accurately. If other changes are proposed beyond those necessary to describe the biosimilar product accurately, applicants should discuss proposed changes with the Agency, including whether such changes are appropriate and whether additional data to support such changes are warranted. Additionally, if there are plans to conduct a human factors study and the applicant intends to submit a protocol for FDA's review, the applicant should seek FDA input on the proposed IFU when the human factors study protocol is submitted for FDA review. A full and final review of proposed product labeling, including the IFU, will occur in the context of the planned 351(k) application and may be informed by any human factors study findings submitted or other relevant data included in the application.

VI. REVISING BIOSIMILAR PRODUCT LABELING

A. Updating Safety Information

During the lifecycle of a biological product, changes in the labeling may be necessary to provide updated information needed for the safe and effective use of the product. As the reference product and biosimilar product are used more widely or under diverse conditions, new information may become available. This may include new risks or new information about known risks. A biosimilar product application holder must comply with applicable requirements regarding adverse experience review, reporting, and recordkeeping (see 21 CFR 600.80).

When new information becomes available that causes information in labeling to be inaccurate, false, or misleading, the application holder must take steps to change the content of its product labeling, in accordance with 21 CFR 601.12.[18] All holders of marketing applications for biological products have an ongoing obligation to ensure their labeling is accurate and up to date.[19] A biological product is misbranded, in violation of the Federal Food, Drug, and Cosmetic

---

[17] See 21 CFR part 208.

[18] See, e.g., 21 CFR 201.56(a)(2): "In accordance with . . . [21 CFR 601.12], the labeling must be updated when new information becomes available that causes the labeling to become inaccurate, false, or misleading."

[19] Ibid.

10

Contains Nonbinding Recommendations

Act (FD&C Act), when its labeling is false or misleading; does not provide adequate directions for use and adequate warnings; or prescribes, recommends, or suggests a dosage, manner, frequency, or duration of use of the drug that is dangerous to health (see 21 U.S.C. 331(a) through (b) and 352(a), (f), and (j)).

B.   Additional Conditions of Use

FDA recognizes that a biosimilar product application holder may be interested in seeking licensure for an additional condition(s) of use after product licensure in the following scenarios:

- The biosimilar product applicant originally obtained licensure for fewer than all of the conditions of use for which the reference product is licensed and is seeking licensure for one or more of the remaining licensed conditions of use of the reference product.

- The biologics license application (BLA) holder for the reference product received licensure for a new condition of use for the reference product after the original licensure of the biosimilar product.

The biosimilar product applicant may seek licensure for an additional condition(s) of use of the reference product in these scenarios by submitting a prior approval supplement(s) to the 351(k) application that contains the necessary data and information, including draft labeling revised to include the additional condition(s) of use sought. For more information on how to support licensure of the biosimilar product for an additional condition(s) of use for which the reference product is licensed, refer to the guidance documents on biosimilar product development on FDA's website.[20]

VII.   HOW TO SUBMIT INITIAL AND REVISED LABELING

New BLAs and supplement submissions for biosimilar product labeling should include the following:

- A clean version of reference product labeling that was used to develop the biosimilar product labeling

- A tracked changes and annotated version of proposed biosimilar product labeling explaining the differences from the reference product labeling

- A clean version of the proposed biosimilar product labeling

---

[20] https://www.fda.gov/Drugs/GuidanceComplianceRegulatoryInformation/Guidances/ucm290967.htm

11

VIII. INTERCHANGEABLE PRODUCTS

Any specific recommendations for labeling for interchangeable products, including any interchangeability statement similar to the biosimilarity statement described in section IV.C.1.b of this guidance, will be provided in future guidance.

12

APPENDIX C5

Interpretation of the "Deemed to be a License" Provision of the Biologics Price Competition and Innovation Act of 2009

Interpretation of the "Deemed to be a License" Provision of the Biologics Price Competition and Innovation Act of 2009

Guidance for Industry

U.S. Department of Health and Human Services
Food and Drug Administration
Center for Drug Evaluation and Research (CDER)
Center for Biologics Evaluation and Research (CBER)

December 2018
Procedural

Interpretation of the "Deemed to be a License" Provision of the Biologics Price Competition and Innovation Act of 2009

Guidance for Industry

Additional copies are available from:

Office of Communications, Division of Drug Information
Center for Drug Evaluation and Research
Food and Drug Administration
10001 New Hampshire Ave., Hillandale Bldg., 4th Floor
Silver Spring, MD 20993-0002
Phone: 855-543-3784 or 301-796-3400; Fax: 301-431-6353
Email: druginfo@fda.hhs.gov
http://www.fda.gov/Drugs/GuidanceComplianceRegulatoryInformation/Guidances/default.htm

and/or

Office of Communication, Outreach and Development
Center for Biologics Evaluation and Research
Food and Drug Administration
10903 New Hampshire Ave., Bldg. 71, Room 3128
Silver Spring, MD 20993-0002
Phone: 800-835-4709 or 240-402-8010
Email: ocod@fda.hhs.gov
http://www.fda.gov/BiologicsBloodVaccines/GuidanceComplianceRegulatoryInformation/Guidances/default.htm

U.S. Department of Health and Human Services
Food and Drug Administration
Center for Drug Evaluation and Research (CDER)
Center for Biologics Evaluation and Research (CBER)

December 2018
Procedural

Contains Nonbinding Recommendations

TABLE OF CONTENTS

I.   INTRODUCTION.. 1

II.   BACKGROUND 2

   A. BPCI Act.. 2

   B. Transition Period for Certain Biological Products.. 4

III.   INTERPRETATION OF THE "DEEMED TO BE A LICENSE" PROVISION 4

   A. FDA's Interpretation of Section 7002(e) of the BPCI Act............................. 4

      1. FDA Interprets section 7002(e)(4) to be Limited to Approved Applications...................... 5
      2. Removal of Biological Products from the Orange Book on March 23, 2020.................... 8
      3. Exclusivity.. 9

   B. Recommendations for Sponsors of Proposed Protein Products Intended for
Submission in an Application Under Section 505 of the FD&C Act 10

      1. "Stand-Alone" New Drug Applications 10
      2. 505(b)(2) Applications.. 11

APPENDIX... 14

Interpretation of the "Deemed to be a License" Provision of the Biologics Price Competition and Innovation Act of 2009

Guidance for Industry[1]

> This guidance represents the current thinking of the Food and Drug Administration (FDA or Agency) on this topic. It does not establish any rights for any person and is not binding on FDA or the public. You can use an alternative approach if it satisfies the requirements of the applicable statutes and regulations. To discuss an alternative approach, contact the FDA staff responsible for this guidance as listed on the title page.

I.   INTRODUCTION

This guidance describes FDA's interpretation of the provision of the Biologics Price Competition and Innovation Act of 2009 (BPCI Act) under which an application for a biological product approved under section 505 of the Federal Food, Drug, and Cosmetic Act (FD&C Act) (21 U.S.C. 355) as of March 23, 2020, will be deemed to be a license for the biological product under section 351 of the Public Health Service Act (PHS Act) (42 U.S.C. 262) on March 23, 2020. Specifically, this guidance describes FDA's interpretation of the "deemed to be a license" provision in section 7002(e) of the BPCI Act for biological products that are approved under section 505 of the FD&C Act as of March 23, 2020 (the transition date). This guidance also provides recommendations to sponsors of proposed protein products intended for submission in an application that may not receive final approval under section 505 of the FD&C Act on or before March 23, 2020, to facilitate alignment of product development plans with FDA's interpretation of section 7002(e) of the BPCI Act.

Although the majority of therapeutic biological products have been licensed under section 351 of the PHS Act, some protein products historically have been approved under section 505 of the FD&C Act (see the Appendix to this guidance for examples of such products). On March 23, 2010, the BPCI Act was enacted as part of the Patient Protection and Affordable Care Act (Public Law 111-148). The BPCI Act clarified the statutory authority under which certain protein products will be regulated by amending the definition of a "biological product"[2] in section 351(i) of the PHS Act to include a "protein (except any chemically synthesized

---

[1] This guidance has been prepared by the Center for Drug Evaluation and Research (CDER) and the Center for Biologics Evaluation and Research (CBER) at the Food and Drug Administration.

[2] As amended by the BPCI Act, a "biological product" is defined, in relevant part, as "a virus, therapeutic serum, toxin, antitoxin, vaccine, blood, blood component or derivative, allergenic product, protein (except any chemically synthesized polypeptide), or analogous product . . . applicable to the prevention, treatment, or cure of a disease or condition of human beings" (see section 351(i) of the PHS Act, see also 21 CFR 600.3(h)).

1

polypeptide),"[3] and describing procedures for submission of a marketing application for certain biological products.

The BPCI Act requires that a marketing application for a "biological product" (that previously could have been submitted under section 505 of the FD&C Act) must be submitted under section 351 of the PHS Act; this requirement is subject to certain exceptions during a 10-year transition period ending on March 23, 2020 (see section 7002(e)(1)-(3) and (e)(5) of the BPCI Act and section II of this guidance). On March 23, 2020 (i.e., the transition date), an approved application for a biological product under section 505 of the FD&C Act shall be deemed to be a license for the biological product under section 351 of the PHS Act (see section 7002(e)(4) of the BPCI Act). This guidance sets forth FDA's current interpretation of section 7002(e) of the BPCI Act.

In general, FDA's guidance documents do not establish legally enforceable responsibilities. Instead, guidances describe the Agency's current thinking on a topic and should be viewed only as recommendations, unless specific regulatory or statutory requirements are cited. The use of the word *should* in Agency guidances means that something is suggested or recommended, but not required.

II.   BACKGROUND

A.   BPCI Act

The BPCI Act amended the PHS Act and other statutes to create an abbreviated licensure pathway in section 351(k) of the PHS Act for biological products shown to be biosimilar to, or interchangeable with, an FDA-licensed biological reference product (see sections 7001 through 7003 of the BPCI Act). The objectives of the BPCI Act are conceptually similar to those of the Drug Price Competition and Patent Term Restoration Act of 1984 (Public Law 98-417) (commonly referred to as the "Hatch-Waxman Amendments"), which established abbreviated pathways for the approval of drug products under section 505(b)(2) and 505(j) of the FD&C Act. An abbreviated licensure pathway for biological products can present challenges given the scientific and technical complexities that may be associated with the generally larger and typically more complex structure of biological products, as well as the processes by which such

---

[3] FDA has described its interpretation of the statutory terms "protein" and "chemically synthesized polypeptide" in the amended definition of "biological product" in guidance. *See* draft guidance for industry *New and Revised Draft Questions and Answers on Biosimilar Development and the BPCI Act (Revision 2).* When final, this guidance will represent FDA's current thinking on this topic. FDA's guidances for industry are available on the FDA Drugs guidance web page at
http://www.fda.gov/Drugs/GuidanceComplianceRegulatoryInformation/Guidances/default.htm. We update guidances periodically. To make sure you have the most recent version of a guidance, check the FDA Drugs web guidance page. In addition, in the *Federal Register* of December 12, 2018, FDA also has issued a proposed rule to amend its regulation that defines "biological product" to incorporate changes made by the BPCI Act, and to provide its interpretation of the statutory terms "protein" and "chemically synthesized polypeptide." When final, this regulation will codify FDA's interpretation of these terms.

2

products are manufactured. Most biological products are produced in a living system such as a microorganism, or plant or animal cells, whereas small molecule drugs are typically manufactured through chemical synthesis.

Section 351(k) of the PHS Act, added by the BPCI Act, sets forth, among other things, the requirements for an application for a proposed biosimilar product and an application or a supplement for a proposed interchangeable product. Section 351(i) defines "biosimilarity" to mean that "the biological product is highly similar to the reference product notwithstanding minor differences in clinically inactive components" and that "there are no clinically meaningful differences between the biological product and the reference product in terms of the safety, purity, and potency of the product" (section 351(i)(2) of the PHS Act). A 351(k) application must contain, among other things, information demonstrating that the biological product is biosimilar to a reference product based upon data derived from analytical studies, animal studies, and a clinical study or studies, unless FDA determines, in its discretion, that certain studies are unnecessary in a 351(k) application (see section 351(k)(2) of the PHS Act). To meet the standard for "interchangeability," an applicant must provide sufficient information to demonstrate biosimilarity, and also to demonstrate that the biological product can be expected to produce the same clinical result as the reference product in any given patient and, if the biological product is administered more than once to an individual, the risk in terms of safety or diminished efficacy of alternating or switching between the use of the biological product and the reference product is not greater than the risk of using the reference product without such alternation or switch (see section 351(k)(4) of the PHS Act). Interchangeable products may be substituted for the reference product without the intervention of the prescribing health care provider (see section 351(i)(3) of the PHS Act).

The BPCI Act also includes, among other provisions:

- A 12-year exclusivity period from the date of first licensure of certain reference products, during which approval of a 351(k) application referencing that product may not be made effective (see section 351(k)(7) of the PHS Act)

- A 4-year exclusivity period from the date of first licensure of certain reference products, during which a 351(k) application referencing that product may not be submitted (see section 351(k)(7) of the PHS Act)

- An exclusivity period for the first biological product determined to be interchangeable with the reference product for any condition of use, during which a second or subsequent biological product may not be determined interchangeable with that reference product (see section 351(k)(6) of the PHS Act)

- Procedures for identifying and resolving patent disputes involving applications submitted under section 351(k) of the PHS Act (see section 351(l) of the PHS Act)

3

B.   Transition Period for Certain Biological Products

Section 7002(e) of the BPCI Act provides that a marketing application for a "biological product" (that previously would have been submitted under section 505 of the FD&C Act) *must* be submitted under section 351 of the PHS Act, subject to the following exception during the transition period described below:

- An application for a biological product *may* be submitted under section 505 of the FD&C Act not later than March 23, 2020, if the biological product is in a product class[4] for which a biological product in such product class was approved under section 505 of the FD&C Act not later than March 23, 2010.

  - ➤ However, an application for a biological product *may not* be submitted under section 505 of the FD&C Act if there is another biological product approved under section 351(a) of the PHS Act that could be a "reference product"[5] if such application were submitted under section 351(k) of the PHS Act.

An approved application for a biological product under section 505 of the FD&C Act shall be deemed to be a license for the biological product under section 351 of the PHS Act (a "deemed Biologics License Application (BLA)") on March 23, 2020.

III.   INTERPRETATION OF THE "DEEMED TO BE A LICENSE" PROVISION

A.   FDA's Interpretation of Section 7002(e) of the BPCI Act

Section 7002(e) of the BPCI Act is directed primarily to the submission of an application for a biological product during the transition period ending on March 23, 2020.[6] Though the transition scheme described in section 7002(e) of the BPCI Act culminates with the "deemed to be a license" provision in section 7002(e)(4), the statute is silent regarding the process for

---

[4] FDA has interpreted the statutory term "product class" for purposes of determining whether an application for a biological product may be submitted under section 505 of the FD&C Act during the transition period (see guidance for industry *Questions and Answers on Biosimilar Development and the BPCI Act*, at Q&A II.2).

[5] The term "reference product" means the single biological product licensed under section 351(a) of the PHS Act against which a biological product is evaluated in an application submitted under section 351(k) (see section 351(i)(4) of the PHS Act).

[6] General references in this guidance to "applications" submitted or approved under section 505 of the FD&C Act also may include abbreviated new drug applications (ANDAs), to the extent applicable. An ANDA generally must contain information to demonstrate, among other things, that the proposed generic drug has the same active ingredient(s), conditions of use, dosage form, route of administration, strength, and (with certain permissible differences) labeling as the reference listed drug (section 505(j)(2)(A) of the FD&C Act). Given the complexity of protein molecules and limitations of current analytical methods, it may be difficult for manufacturers of proposed protein products to demonstrate that the active ingredient in their proposed product is the same as the active ingredient in an already approved product, and thus ANDAs are not a focus of this guidance. There are no currently marketed biological products that were approved through the ANDA pathway.

accomplishing the transition of approved new drug applications (NDAs) to deemed BLAs, or the implications of the deeming process on pending applications.[7]

> *1.   FDA Interprets section 7002(e)(4) to be Limited to Approved Applications*

Section 7002(e)(4) of the BPCI Act provides:

> An approved application for a biological product under section 505 of the Federal Food, Drug, and Cosmetic Act (21 U.S.C. 355) shall be deemed to be a license for the biological product under such section 351 [of the PHS Act] on the date that is 10 years after the date of enactment of [the BPCI Act].

Section 7002(e)(4) is explicitly limited to an ***approved*** application under section 505 of the FD&C Act. Moreover, while this provision explicitly provides that an approved application under section 505 of the FD&C Act shall be deemed to be a BLA ***on*** the transition date, the statute does not provide a means for deeming an approved NDA to be an approved BLA prior to, or after, the transition date.[8] Finally, section 7002(e) of the BPCI Act does not provide a basis for the Agency to treat approved NDAs for biological products as both NDAs and BLAs after such applications are deemed to be BLAs. Therefore, FDA interprets section 7002(e) of the BPCI Act to plainly mean that, on March 23, 2020, only approved NDAs will be deemed to be BLAs. After March 23, 2020, the Agency will not approve any application submitted under section 505 of the FD&C Act for a biological product subject to the transition provision that is pending or tentatively approved.[9,10] As a corollary, applications for biological products approved

---

[7] In other legislation, Congress has described the implications of transitioning applications for drug products from one statutory scheme to another, while also describing the process that would be used in effecting the transition. See, e.g., section 107(c) of the Drug Amendments of 1962 (Pub. L. 87-781) (providing that all NDAs effective on the day immediately preceding the date of enactment of the Drug Amendments of 1962 shall be deemed approved as of the enactment date, and that the provision for withdrawal of approval of an application for lack of effectiveness generally would not apply to such deemed NDAs for a period of 2 years after the enactment date); section 125 of the Food and Drug Administration Modernization Act of 1997 (FDAMA) (Pub. L. 105-115) (repealing section 507 of the FD&C Act and providing that an application for an antibiotic drug approved under section 507 of the FD&C Act on the day before enactment of FDAMA shall, on and after the date of enactment, be considered to be an NDA submitted and filed under section 505(b) and approved under section 505(c) or an ANDA filed and approved under 505(j)).

[8] Compare section 7002(e)(4) of the BPCI Act with section 125 of FDAMA (providing that an approved application for the marketing of an antibiotic drug under section 507 of the FD&C Act "shall, *on and after such date of enactment*, be considered to be an application that was submitted and filed under section 505(b) . . . and approved for safety and effectiveness under section 505(c)" (emphasis added)) and FDA's guidance for industry *Repeal of Section 507 of the Federal Food, Drug, and Cosmetic Act* ("All action letters must use the 505(b) or 505(j) templates, even for drugs that originally were submitted under section 507, but are the subject of Agency action on or after November 21, 1997.").

[9] Tentative approval means that an NDA or ANDA otherwise meets the requirements for approval under the FD&C Act but cannot be approved until the expiration of an applicable period of patent and/or exclusivity protection. A drug product that is granted tentative approval is not an approved drug and will not be approved until FDA issues an approval letter after any necessary additional review of the NDA or ANDA (see 21 CFR 314.105; see also 21 CFR 314.107).

[10] The fact that section 7002(e)(2) of the BPCI Act permits submission of an application under section 505 of the FD&C Act "not later than" the transition date does not change this conclusion. Section 7002(e)(2) is not

5

under section 505 of the FD&C Act will no longer exist as NDAs and will be replaced by approved BLAs under section 351 of the PHS Act.[11]

Accordingly, an original 505(b)(2) application (including a resubmission) for a biological product that relies, at least in part, on FDA's finding of safety and/or effectiveness for a listed drug that is a biological product will receive a complete response if the application is pending at the end of the day (11:59 pm Eastern Daylight Time (EDT)) on Friday, March 20, 2020, because the NDA for the listed drug relied upon will no longer exist at midnight on Monday, March 23, 2020. An original application (including a resubmission) for a biological product that has been submitted as a 505(b)(1) application (i.e., a "stand-alone" NDA) or a 505(b)(2) application that does not rely, to any extent, on FDA's finding of safety and/or effectiveness for a listed drug that is a biological product (e.g., a 505(b)(2) application that relies on non-product-specific published literature) and is pending at the end of the day (11:59 pm EDT) on March 23, 2020, will receive a complete response.[12] Such applications may, for example, be withdrawn and submitted under section 351(a) or 351(k) of the PHS Act, as appropriate. We provide an overview of key dates/times below and recommendations to minimize the impact on development programs for any proposed biological products intended for submission under section 505 of the FD&C Act that may not be able to receive final approval by March 23, 2020.

---

inconsistent with the interpretation set forth here because, among other things, Congress presumably is aware that approval decisions can take a variable amount of time, and thus did not settle on a date by which such submissions would no longer be permitted. Moreover, if Congress meant to allow for pending applications submitted under section 505 of the FD&C Act to be deemed BLAs after the transition, it knew how to do so explicitly. See section 125 of FDAMA, *supra* note 8.

[11] See FDA's draft guidance for industry *The "Deemed to be a License" Provision of the BPCI Act: Questions and Answers* (Transition Q&A Draft Guidance) for additional information, including whether an approved application for a biological product under section 505 of the FD&C Act will be deemed a license for the biological product under section 351(a) or 351(k) of the PHS Act and administrative issues associated with the transition (including BLA numbers and user fee questions). When final, that guidance will represent FDA's current thinking on this topic.

[12] An applicant who seeks to obtain final approval of a tentatively approved NDA for a biological product on or before March 23, 2020, would need to submit an amendment requesting final approval. FDA recommends that the amendment should be submitted by a date that allows adequate time for FDA review and approval before March 23, 2020. Please refer to the recommended timeframes provided in the tentative approval letter and any applicable guidance for further information and contact the relevant review division with any questions (including questions about whether an inspection may be needed). An amendment requesting final approval of a tentatively approved application should provide the legal/regulatory basis for the request for final approval and should include a copy of any relevant court action, written consent to approval by the patent owner or exclusive patent licensee, or waiver of exclusivity by the relevant NDA holder, as appropriate, that has not been submitted previously to FDA under 21 CFR 314.107(e). In addition to a safety update, the amendment should identify whether there are any changes in the conditions under which the product was tentatively approved, i.e., updated labeling; chemistry, manufacturing, and controls data; and, as applicable, Risk Evaluation and Mitigation Strategy (REMS). Any changes require FDA review before final approval and the goal date for FDA review will be set accordingly.

6

Contains Nonbinding Recommendations

Table: Overview of Key Dates/Times Related to the Statutory Transition Provision

Date/Time	Relevant Application Type	Event
Friday, March 20, 2020, 11:59 pm (EDT)	Pending 505(b)(2) applications that rely, at least in part, on FDA's finding of safety and/or effectiveness for a listed drug that is a biological product	Deadline for any pending 505(b)(2) application of this type to be approved under the FD&C Act.
Monday, March 23, 2020, 12:00 am (EDT)	Approved NDAs for biological products	Approved NDAs for biological products are deemed to be BLAs, and cease to exist as NDAs.
Monday, March 23, 2020, 12:01 am (EDT)	351(k) BLA that relies on a deemed BLA for its reference product	A 351(k) BLA can be submitted for a proposed biosimilar or a proposed interchangeable to a biological reference product that is the subject of a deemed BLA.
Monday, March 23, 2020, during hours in which FDA is open for business	Approved NDAs for biological products	FDA intends to send a letter to each holder of an approved NDA for a biological product that advises that the approved NDA has been deemed to be a BLA by operation of the statute, and no longer exists as an NDA. FDA intends to update the Orange Book to remove biological product listings.
Monday, March 23, 2020, 11:59 pm (EDT)	Pending 505(b)(1) applications and pending 505(b)(2) applications that do not rely, to any extent, on FDA's finding of safety and/or effectiveness for a listed drug that is a biological product	Deadline for any pending 505(b)(1) application or any pending 505(b)(2) application of this type to be approved under the FD&C Act. An NDA approved on March 23, 2020, will be deemed to be a BLA immediately after approval under the FD&C Act.

FDA intends to assist applicants who may be affected by section 7002(e) of the BPCI Act, where feasible and appropriate. For example, during the review of a BLA submitted after the transition date under section 351(a) or 351(k) of the PHS Act for a proposed biological product that was previously submitted, but not approved, in an application under section 505 of the FD&C Act, FDA intends to consider any previously conducted scientific review by the Agency of such previous application under the FD&C Act, to the extent that such review is relevant to, and consistent with, applicable requirements of section 351 of the PHS Act.

An application generally includes all amendments and supplements to the application.[13] We recognize that there may be one or more supplements submitted to an approved NDA for a biological product before March 23, 2020, that is pending on March 23, 2020. Such supplements may include a prior approval supplement (e.g., an efficacy supplement,[14] a labeling supplement,

---

[13] See 21 CFR 314.3(b) (definition of *application*).

[14] An efficacy supplement is a supplement to an approved NDA proposing to make one or more related changes from among the following changes to product labeling: (1) Add or modify an indication or claim; (2) Revise the dose or dose regimen; (3) Provide for a new route of administration; (4) Make a comparative efficacy claim naming

7

or a manufacturing supplement), a supplement for changes being effected (CBE) in 30 days (for certain chemistry, manufacturing, and controls changes), or a supplement for changes being effected upon receipt by the Agency of the supplement (for certain safety-related labeling changes or any other labeling change that FDA specifically requests to be submitted in a CBE supplement).[15] At the time that FDA deems the approved NDA for a biological product to be a BLA on the transition date, FDA intends to also administratively convert any pending supplement to such approved NDA to a pending supplement to the deemed BLA, and to review such supplements under applicable standards for BLAs. For example, a pending "stand-alone" efficacy supplement to a "stand-alone" NDA[16] (e.g., a supplement intended to address a post-approval requirement or post-approval commitment) will be administratively converted to a pending efficacy supplement to the corresponding deemed 351(a) BLA on the transition date and reviewed under applicable standards for 351(a) BLAs. Similarly, a pending CBE supplement to an application submitted under the FD&C Act will be administratively converted to a pending CBE supplement to the deemed BLA on the transition date, irrespective of whether the change described in the CBE supplement has been implemented before or after the transition date. The Agency also intends to maintain the same goal date, where applicable, for completion of its review of such supplements.

> 2. *Removal of Biological Products from the Orange Book on March 23, 2020*

FDA intends to remove biological products that have been approved in NDAs from FDA's *Approved Drug Products With Therapeutic Equivalence Evaluations* (the Orange Book)[17] on March 23, 2020, based on the Agency's position that these products are no longer "listed drugs" and such NDAs may not be relied upon by a 505(b)(2) applicant (or ANDA applicant) for approval. After March 23, 2020, FDA will not approve any NDA (or ANDA), including those that are pending or tentatively approved, for a biological product.

Moreover, with the exception of orphan drug exclusivity and pediatric exclusivity, the exclusivity provisions of the FD&C Act serve to limit the submission or approval of applications under section 505 of the FD&C Act, but not under section 351 of the PHS Act. Section 7002(e) of the BPCI Act provides that no applications for biological products may be submitted under section 505 of the FD&C Act after the transition date. Accordingly, on March 23, 2020, any unexpired period of exclusivity associated with an approved NDA for a biological product subject to section 7002(e) of the BPCI Act (e.g., 5-year exclusivity or 3-year exclusivity) would

---

another drug product; (5) Significantly alter the intended patient population; (6) Change the marketing status from prescription to over-the-counter use; (7) Provide for, or provide evidence of effectiveness necessary for, the traditional approval of a product originally approved under subpart H of part 314; or (8) Incorporate other information based on at least one adequate and well-controlled clinical study (21 CFR 314.3(b)).

[15] See generally 21 CFR 314.70.

[16] See section III.B.1 of this guidance for information on "stand-alone" NDAs. There may be additional considerations for a pending 505(b)(2) efficacy supplement to a stand-alone NDA and a pending 505(b)(2) efficacy supplement to a 505(b)(2) application.

[17] Biological products approved in NDAs that are deemed to be BLAs will be listed in FDA's *Lists of Licensed Biological Products with Reference Product Exclusivity and Biosimilarity or Interchangeability Evaluations* (the Purple Book) on or shortly after the March 23, 2020, transition date.

cease to have any effect, and any patents listed in the Orange Book would no longer be relevant for purposes of determining the timing of approval of a 505(b)(2) application (or ANDA). However, any unexpired period of orphan drug exclusivity would continue to apply to the biological product for the protected use after the transition date, because orphan drug exclusivity can block the approval of a drug approved under section 505 of the FD&C Act or a biological product licensed under section 351 of the PHS Act (see section 527 of the FD&C Act (21 U.S.C. 360cc)). Similarly, any unexpired period of pediatric exclusivity associated with an approved NDA for a biological product would continue to apply to a deemed 351(a) BLA on and after March 23, 2020, provided that the conditions in section 351(m) of the PHS Act are met. Any post-approval requirements or post-approval commitments, including any pediatric assessments necessary to comply with the Pediatric Research Equity Act (PREA) (Public Law 108-155), also would transfer to the deemed BLA.

      3.   *Exclusivity*

FDA interprets section 7002(e) of the BPCI Act and section 351 of the PHS Act to mean that an approved NDA for a biological product that will be *deemed* to be "licensed" under section 351(a) of the PHS Act on March 23, 2020, can be a reference product for a proposed biosimilar product or a proposed interchangeable product (see section 351(i)(4) of the PHS Act). However, a biological product that was first approved in an NDA under section 505 of the FD&C Act and deemed "licensed" under section 351(a) of the PHS Act on March 23, 2020, will not have been "first licensed under subsection (a)" for purposes of section 351(k)(7) of the PHS Act. Thus, such a biological product will not be eligible for exclusivity under section 351(k)(7)(A) and (B) of the PHS Act.

Section 351(k)(7)(A) and (B) of the PHS Act describe a 12-year exclusivity period during which FDA may not approve a 351(k) application and a 4-year exclusivity period during which an applicant may not submit a 351(k) application ("reference product exclusivity"). Except as provided in section 351(k)(7)(C) of the PHS Act, these periods begin on "the date on which the reference product was first licensed under subsection (a) [referring to section 351(a) of the PHS Act]." However, section 351(k)(7)(C) of the PHS Act provides that reference product exclusivity shall not apply to a license for or approval of:

- A supplement for the biological product that is the reference product; or

- A subsequent application filed by the same sponsor or manufacturer of the biological product that is the reference product (or a licensor, predecessor in interest, or other related entity) under the conditions set forth in section 351(k)(7)(C) of the PHS Act.[18]

Nothing in the Biologics Price Competition and Innovation Act suggests that Congress intended for biological products approved under section 505 of the FD&C Act — some of which were approved decades ago — to obtain a 12-year period of reference product exclusivity upon being

---

[18] See section 351(k)(7)(C) of the PHS Act and FDA's guidance for industry *Reference Product Exclusivity for Biological Products Filed Under Section 351(a) of the PHS Act.* When final, this guidance will represent FDA's current thinking on this topic.

9

deemed to be licensed under section 351(a) of the PHS Act. Reference product exclusivity recognizes the fact that the sponsor of an eligible reference product generated (and submitted for review) the data and information required to obtain a license under section 351(a) of the PHS Act and limits competition from biosimilar and interchangeable products for a limited period of time. The biological products that will be deemed to have BLAs on the transition date, however, have already obtained marketing approval under a different statutory authority. Allowing such products to obtain a separate 12-year period of reference product exclusivity would inappropriately impede biosimilar or interchangeable product competition in several product classes.

Recognizing these principles, FDA interprets section 7002(e) of the BPCI Act together with section 351(k)(7) of the PHS Act such that section 351(k)(7)(A)-(B) of the PHS Act applies only to products that have undergone review and licensing under section 351(a), and not to biological products that will be deemed licensed under section 351(a) of the PHS Act on the transition date. At the same time, FDA interprets the limitations on eligibility for reference product exclusivity in section 351(k)(7)(C) of the PHS Act to apply to any "reference product," without regard to whether such product was "first licensed under subsection (a)" or instead deemed to be a license under section 7002(e) of the BPCI Act. Nothing in the BPCI Act suggests that Congress intended holders of deemed BLAs to be able to circumvent the statutory limitations on eligibility for a 12-year period of reference product exclusivity through subsequent submissions simply because the previous reference product was deemed to be licensed under section 7002(e). Therefore, FDA interprets section 351(k)(7) of the PHS Act together with section 7002(e) of the BPCI Act such that section 351(k)(7)(C) will operate to bar supplements to deemed BLAs and, where applicable, subsequent BLAs from being eligible for their own periods of reference product exclusivity.

B.   **Recommendations for Sponsors of Proposed Protein Products Intended for Submission in an Application Under Section 505 of the FD&C Act**

Sponsors of development programs for proposed protein products should evaluate whether a planned submission under section 505 of the FD&C Act would allow adequate time for approval of the application prior to March 23, 2020, considering, among other things, whether the submission may require a second cycle of review and, for certain types of applications, whether unexpired patents or exclusivity may delay final approval. FDA's recommendations for sponsors are based on whether a "stand-alone" or abbreviated development program is planned.

1.   "Stand-Alone" New Drug Applications

An application submitted under section 505(b)(1) of the FD&C Act (i.e., a "stand-alone" NDA) contains full reports of investigations of safety and effectiveness that were conducted by or for the applicant or for which the applicant has a right of reference or use. Sponsors of a proposed protein product intended for submission in an NDA under section 505(b)(1) of the FD&C Act should consider submitting a BLA under section 351(a) of the PHS Act. A 351(a) BLA for a biological product can be submitted before, on, or after March 23, 2020. Sponsors can contact

10

the relevant review division within the Office of New Drugs in FDA's CDER with any questions about a BLA submission.[19]

2. 505(b)(2) Applications

A 505(b)(2) application is an NDA that contains full reports of investigations of safety and effectiveness, where at least some of the information required for approval comes from studies not conducted by or for the applicant and for which the applicant has not obtained a right of reference or use (e.g., FDA's finding of safety and/or effectiveness for a listed drug or published literature). A 505(b)(2) application that seeks to rely on a listed drug must contain adequate data and information to demonstrate that the proposed product is sufficiently similar to the listed drug to justify reliance, in part, on FDA's finding of safety and/or effectiveness for the listed drug. Any aspects of the proposed product that differ from the listed drug must be supported by adequate data and information to support the safety and effectiveness of the proposed product.

Congress did not provide an approval pathway under the PHS Act that directly corresponds to section 505(b)(2) of the FD&C Act. Accordingly, there are additional considerations for sponsors of proposed protein products intended for submission in a 505(b)(2) application or a 505(b)(2) efficacy supplement, and sponsors may contact the relevant review division with any questions. If a sponsor anticipates that a planned 505(b)(2) application or 505(b)(2) efficacy supplement may not receive final approval before the transition date (e.g., due to the need for a second cycle of review, applicable unexpired exclusivity or listed patents, or a stay of approval due to patent infringement litigation), the sponsor should consider the following options:

- Modifying the development program to support submission of an application or efficacy supplement under section 351(a) of the PHS Act (i.e., a "stand-alone" BLA) before or after March 23, 2020. This may involve, for example, obtaining a right of reference from the application holder for the listed drug on which the proposed 505(b)(2) application or 505(b)(2) efficacy supplement would have relied or conducting studies with the proposed product to provide the scientific data that otherwise would have been relied upon to support approval of the application or the change proposed in the supplement, as applicable.[20]

- Modifying the development program to support submission of a 351(k) BLA for a proposed biosimilar product or a proposed interchangeable product at such time as there is a biological product licensed under section 351(a) of the PHS Act that could be a reference product.

---

[19] FDA has taken measures to minimize differences in the review and approval of products required to have approved BLAs under section 351 of the PHS Act and products required to have approved NDAs under section 505(b)(1) of the FD&C Act (see section 123(f) of FDAMA). However, certain differences continue to exist. For additional information on how FDA intends to address these issues, see the Transition Q&A Draft Guidance or contact the relevant review division. When final, this guidance will represent FDA's current thinking on this topic.

[20] FDA has issued guidance for industry on *Exocrine Pancreatic Insufficiency Drug Products – Submitting NDAs* and is considering how the concepts described in the guidance would apply to proposed pancreatic enzyme products submitted under the PHS Act.

11

Sponsors evaluating whether a proposed product could be submitted under section 351(k) of the PHS Act should consider whether they would be able to provide information demonstrating that, among other things, the proposed product:

- Is "highly similar" to a single reference product licensed under section 351(a) of the PHS Act, and that there are "no clinically meaningful differences" between the proposed product and the reference product in terms of safety, purity, and potency;

- Has the same route of administration, dosage form, and strength as the reference product;

- Utilizes the same mechanism(s) of action as the reference product for the proposed condition(s) of use (but only to the extent that the mechanism(s) of action are known); and

- Seeks licensure for a condition(s) of use (e.g., indication, dosing regimen) previously approved for the reference product.[21]

A sponsor of a proposed biological product that could meet the requirements for a proposed biosimilar and other applicable requirements would be able to submit a 351(k) BLA that cites the listed drug as its reference product after the NDA for the listed drug is deemed to be a BLA (or after another product that could be a reference product for the proposed product is licensed under section 351(a) of the PHS Act). Sponsors that intend to adapt their development programs to meet the requirements for a submission under section 351(k) of the PHS Act can request meetings with FDA, including a Biosimilar Biological Product Development (BPD) Type 3 meeting, before March 23, 2020, to support the development and review of a proposed biosimilar product or a proposed interchangeable product. Such meetings may be based on relevant comparative data with a listed drug that is the "intended reference product" (i.e., the listed drug that is intended to be the reference product after the NDA for such drug is deemed to be licensed under section 351(a) of the PHS Act).

Proposed products that are intended to differ in certain respects (e.g., different dosage forms, routes of administration, strengths, or conditions of use) from a previously approved product likely would need to be submitted under section 351(a) of the PHS Act and meet applicable statutory and regulatory requirements for a 351(a) BLA. Such products likely would be unable to use the 351(k) pathway to abbreviate their development program due to lack of a reference product or the inability to meet the statutory requirements for a proposed biosimilar product.

A sponsor may contact the relevant review division within the Office of New Drugs in FDA's CDER to request advice on a product-specific basis regarding the development of a protein product intended for submission in an application under the FD&C Act (during the transition

---

[21] See section 351(k) of the PHS Act; see also, generally, FDA's guidance documents on biosimilar products.

12

Contains Nonbinding Recommendations

period described in section 7002(e) of the BPCI Act) or under section 351(a) or 351(k) of the PHS Act, as appropriate.[22]

---

[22] For information on requesting a formal meeting regarding the development of a proposed biosimilar product intended for submission under section 351(k) of the PHS Act, see FDA's draft guidance for industry *Formal Meetings Between the FDA and Sponsors or Applicants of BsUFA Products.* For information on requesting a formal meeting regarding the development of a biological product intended for submission in an NDA before March 23, 2020, or in a 351(a) BLA, see FDA's draft guidance for industry *Formal Meetings Between the FDA and Sponsors or Applicants of PDUFA Products.* When final, these guidances will represent FDA's current thinking on these topics.

13

Contains Nonbinding Recommendations

APPENDIX

Examples of Biological Products That Have Been Approved Under the FD&C Act

chorionic gonadotropin products
desirudin products
follitropin products, urofollitropin products, and menotropins products
hyaluronidase products
imiglucerase products
insulin products, insulin mix products, and insulin analog products (e.g., insulin aspart, insulin detemir, insulin glargine, insulin glulisine, and insulin lispro products)
mecasermin products
pancrelipase products
pegademase products
pegvisomant products
sacrosidase products
somatropin products
taliglucerase alfa products and velaglucerase alfa products
thyrotropin alfa products

14

APPENDIX C6

Questions and Answers on Biosimilar Development and the BPCI Act

---

Questions and Answers on Biosimilar Development and the BPCI Act

Guidance for Industry

U.S. Department of Health and Human Services
Food and Drug Administration
Center for Drug Evaluation and Research (CDER)
Center for Biologics Evaluation and Research (CBER)

December 2018
Biosimilars

Revision 1

Questions and Answers on Biosimilar Development and the BPCI Act

Guidance for Industry

Additional copies are available from:

Office of Communications, Division of Drug Information
Center for Drug Evaluation and Research
Food and Drug Administration
10001 New Hampshire Ave., Hillandale Bldg., 4th Floor
Silver Spring, MD 20993-0002
Phone: 855-543-3784 or 301-796-3400; Fax: 301-431-6353
Email: druginfo@fda.hhs.gov
https://www.fda.gov/Drugs/GuidanceComplianceRegulatoryInformation/Guidances/default.htm

and/or

Office of Communication, Outreach and Development
Center for Biologics Evaluation and Research
Food and Drug Administration
10903 New Hampshire Ave., Bldg. 71, Room 3128
Silver Spring, MD 20993-0002
Phone: 800-835-4709 or 240-402-8010
Email: ocod@fda.hhs.gov
https://www.fda.gov/BiologicsBloodVaccines/GuidanceComplianceRegulatoryInformation/Guidances/default.htm

U.S. Department of Health and Human Services
Food and Drug Administration
Center for Drug Evaluation and Research (CDER)
Center for Biologics Evaluation and Research (CBER)

December 2018
Biosimilars

Revision 1

Contains Nonbinding Recommendations

TABLE OF CONTENTS

INTRODUCTION.. 1
BACKGROUND 3
QUESTIONS AND ANSWERS.. 5
    I.   BIOSIMILARITY OR INTERCHANGEABILITY... 5
    II.   PROVISIONS RELATED TO REQUIREMENT TO SUBMIT A BLA FOR A
          "BIOLOGICAL PRODUCT".. 17
    III. EXCLUSIVITY 19

Contains Nonbinding Recommendations

Questions and Answers on Biosimilar Development
and the BPCI Act
Guidance for Industry[1]

INTRODUCTION

This guidance document provides answers to common questions from prospective applicants and other interested parties regarding the Biologics Price Competition and Innovation Act of 2009 (BPCI Act). The question and answer (Q&A) format is intended to inform prospective applicants and facilitate the development of proposed *biosimilars* and *interchangeable biosimilars*,[2] as well as to describe FDA's interpretation of certain statutory requirements added by the BPCI Act.

The BPCI Act amended the Public Health Service Act (PHS Act) and other statutes to create an abbreviated licensure pathway in section 351(k) of the PHS Act for biological products shown to be biosimilar to, or interchangeable with, an FDA-licensed biological reference product (see sections 7001 through 7003 of the Patient Protection and Affordable Care Act (Pub. L. 111–148) (ACA)). FDA believes that guidance for industry that provides answers to commonly asked questions regarding FDA's interpretation of the BPCI Act will enhance transparency and facilitate the development and approval of biosimilar and interchangeable products. In addition, these Q&As respond to questions the Agency has received from prospective applicants regarding the appropriate statutory authority under which certain products will be regulated. FDA intends to update this guidance document to include additional Q&As as appropriate.

---

[1] This guidance has been prepared by the Center for Drug Evaluation and Research (CDER) and the Center for Biologics Evaluation and Research (CBER) at the Food and Drug Administration (FDA or the Agency).

We update guidances periodically. To make sure you have the most recent version of a guidance, check the FDA Drugs guidance web page at
https://www.fda.gov/Drugs/GuidanceComplianceRegulatoryInformation/Guidances/default.htm.

[2] In this guidance, the following terms are used to describe biological products licensed under section 351(k) of the PHS Act: (1) *biosimilar* or *biosimilar product* refers to a product that FDA has determined to be biosimilar to the reference product (see sections 351(i)(2) and 351(k)(2) of the PHS Act) and (2) *interchangeable biosimilar* or *interchangeable product* refers to a biosimilar product that FDA has determined to be interchangeable with the reference product (see sections 351(i)(3) and 351(k)(4) of the PHS Act). Biosimilarity, interchangeability, and related issues are discussed in more detail in the Background section of this guidance.

This guidance document revises the final guidance document entitled *Biosimilars: Questions and Answers Regarding Implementation of the Biologics Price Competition and Innovation Act of 2009,* to clarify and update certain Q&As and to add new Q&As. For certain Q&As, FDA has updated the Q&A by abbreviating the answer and, where appropriate, referring the reader to a separate guidance document that provides additional information on the topic. Alternatively, FDA may have withdrawn a Q&A if the topic is addressed in a separate guidance document or if FDA determined that the Q&A should be revised in some respect and reissued. Additional information about the Q&A format for this guidance document is provided in the Background section.

FDA is also issuing a draft guidance document entitled *New and Revised Draft Q&As on Biosimilar Development and the BPCI Act (Revision 2).* When finalized, this draft guidance document will be part of a series of guidance documents that FDA has developed to facilitate development of biosimilar and interchangeable products. The final guidance documents issued to date address a broad range of issues, including:

- Quality Considerations in Demonstrating Biosimilarity of a Therapeutic Protein Product to a Reference Product (April 2015)

- Scientific Considerations in Demonstrating Biosimilarity to a Reference Product (April 2015)

- Clinical Pharmacology Data to Support a Demonstration of Biosimilarity to a Reference Product (December 2016)

- Labeling for Biosimilar Products (July 2018)

In addition, FDA has published draft guidance documents related to the BPCI Act, which, when finalized, will represent FDA's current thinking. These draft guidance documents include:

- New and Revised Draft Q&As on Biosimilar Development and the BPCI Act (Revision 2) (December 2018)

- Considerations in Demonstrating Interchangeability With a Reference Product (January 2017)

- Formal Meetings Between the FDA and Sponsors or Applicants of BsUFA Products (June 2018)

- Reference Product Exclusivity for Biological Products Filed Under Section 351(a) of the PHS Act (August 2014)

2

Contains Nonbinding Recommendations

In general, FDA's guidance documents do not establish legally enforceable responsibilities. Instead, guidances describe the Agency's current thinking on a topic and should be viewed only as recommendations, unless specific regulatory or statutory requirements are cited. The use of the word *should* in Agency guidances means that something is suggested or recommended, but not required.

BACKGROUND

The BPCI Act

The BPCI Act was enacted as part of the ACA on March 23, 2010. The BPCI Act amended the PHS Act and other statutes to create an abbreviated licensure pathway for biological products shown to be biosimilar to, or interchangeable with, an FDA-licensed biological reference product (see sections 7001 through 7003 of the ACA). Section 351(k) of the PHS Act (42 U.S.C. 262(k)), added by the BPCI Act, sets forth the requirements for an application for a proposed biosimilar or interchangeable product.

Section 351(i) defines the term *biosimilar* or *biosimilarity* "in reference to a biological product that is the subject of an application under [section 351(k)]" to mean "that the biological product is highly similar to the reference product[3] notwithstanding minor differences in clinically inactive components" and that "there are no clinically meaningful differences between the biological product and the reference product in terms of the safety, purity, and potency of the product" (see section 351(i)(2) of the PHS Act).

Section 351(k)(4) of the PHS Act provides that upon review of an application submitted under section 351(k) or any supplement to such application, FDA will determine the biological product to be interchangeable with the reference product if FDA determines that the information submitted in the application (or a supplement to such application) is sufficient to show that the biological product "is biosimilar to the reference product" and "can be expected to produce the same clinical result as the reference product in any given patient"[4] and that "for a biological product that is administered more than once to an individual, the risk in terms of safety or diminished efficacy of alternating or switching between use of the biological product and the reference product is not greater than the risk of using the reference product without such alternation or switch."[5]

Section 351(i) of the PHS Act states that the term *interchangeable* or *interchangeability*, in reference to a biological product that is shown to meet the standards described in section 351(k)(4) of the PHS Act, means that "the biological product may be substituted for the reference product without the intervention of the health care provider who prescribed the reference product."

---

[3] *Reference product* means the single biological product licensed under section 351(a) of the PHS Act against which a biological product is evaluated in a 351(k) application (section 351(i)(4) of the PHS Act).
[4] Section 351(k)(4)(A) of the PHS Act.
[5] Section 351(k)(4)(B) of the PHS Act.

3

In this guidance document, the terms *proposed biosimilar product* and *proposed interchangeable product* are used to describe products that are under development or are the subject of a pending 351(k) biologics license application (BLA).

Certain other provisions of the BPCI Act are discussed in the context of the relevant Q&A.

"Question and Answer" Guidance Format

This final guidance document is a companion to the draft guidance document entitled *New and Revised Draft Q&As on Biosimilar Development and the BPCI Act (Revision 2)*. In this pair of guidance documents, FDA issues each Q&A in draft form in the draft guidance document, receives comments on the draft Q&A, and, as appropriate, moves the Q&A to this final guidance document after reviewing comments and incorporating suggested changes to the Q&A, when appropriate. A Q&A that was previously in the final guidance document may be withdrawn and moved to the draft guidance document if FDA determines that the Q&A should be revised in some respect and reissued in the draft Q&A guidance document. A Q&A also may be withdrawn and removed from the Q&A guidance documents if, for instance, the issue addressed in the Q&A is addressed in another FDA guidance document.

A reference will follow each question in this final guidance document describing the publication date of the current version of the Q&A, and whether the Q&A has been added to or modified in this final guidance document. FDA has maintained the original numbering of the Q&As used in the April 2015 final guidance document (*Biosimilars: Questions and Answers Regarding Implementation of the Biologics Price Competition and Innovation Act of 2009*) and May 2015 draft guidance document (*Biosimilars: Additional Questions and Answers Regarding Implementation of the Biologics Price Competition and Innovation Act of 2009*). For ease of reference, a Q&A retains the same number when it moves from the draft guidance document to the final guidance document and, where appropriate, when a Q&A is withdrawn from the final guidance document and moved to the draft guidance document.

Where a Q&A has been withdrawn from the final guidance document, this is marked in the final guidance document by several asterisks between nonconsecutively numbered Q&As and, where appropriate, explanatory text.

4

479

Contains Nonbinding Recommendations

QUESTIONS AND ANSWERS

I.   BIOSIMILARITY OR INTERCHANGEABILITY

Q. I.1.   ***Whom should a sponsor contact with questions about its proposed development program for a proposed biosimilar product or a proposed interchangeable product?***
[Updated/Retained in Final December 2018]

A. I.1.   FDA provides current contact information on its website. See FDA's website, "Biosimilars," available at https://www.fda.gov/biosimilars and click on the link, "Industry Information and Guidance" listed in the left column.

Q. I.2.   ***When should a sponsor request a meeting with FDA to discuss its development program for a proposed biosimilar product or a proposed interchangeable product, and what data and information should a sponsor provide to FDA as background for this meeting?***
[Updated/Retained in Final December 2018]

A. I.2.   See FDA's draft guidance for industry, *Formal Meetings Between the FDA and Sponsors or Applicants of BsUFA Products*[6] for a description of the different meeting types intended to facilitate biosimilar development programs in accordance with the Biosimilar User Fee Act of 2012 (BsUFA), as reauthorized by the Biosimilar User Fee Amendments of 2017 (BsUFA II) and the criteria/data needed to support the request. The type of meeting granted will depend on the stage of product development and whether the information submitted in the meeting package meets the criteria for the type of meeting.

Q. I.3.   ***Can a proposed biosimilar product have a formulation that is different from the reference product?***
[Updated/Retained in Final December 2018]

A. I.3.   Differences between the formulation of a proposed biosimilar product and the reference product may be acceptable. A 351(k) application must contain information demonstrating that the biological product is highly similar to the reference product notwithstanding minor differences in clinically inactive components. In addition, an applicant would need to demonstrate that there are no clinically meaningful differences between the biological product and the reference product in terms of safety, purity, and potency. It may be possible, for example, for a proposed biosimilar product formulated without human serum albumin to demonstrate biosimilarity to a reference product formulated with human serum albumin. For more information about FDA's current thinking on

---

[6] This draft guidance, when finalized, will represent FDA's current thinking on this topic.

Contains Nonbinding Recommendations

the interpretation of the statutory standard for biosimilarity, see FDA's guidances for industry on *Quality Considerations in Demonstrating Biosimilarity of a Therapeutic Protein Product to a Reference Product* and *Scientific Considerations in Demonstrating Biosimilarity to a Reference Product.*

Q. I.4. ***Can a proposed biosimilar product have a delivery device or container closure system that is different from its reference product?*** *[Updated/Retained in Final December 2018]*

A. I.4.   Some design differences in the delivery device or container closure system used with the proposed biosimilar product may be acceptable. It may be possible, for example, for an applicant to obtain licensure of a proposed biosimilar product in a pre-filled syringe or in an auto-injector device (which are considered the same dosage form), even if the reference product is licensed in a vial presentation, provided that the proposed biosimilar product meets the statutory standard for biosimilarity and adequate performance data for the delivery device or container closure system are provided. For a proposed biosimilar product in a different delivery device or container closure system, the delivery device or container closure system must be shown to be compatible for use with the final formulation of the biological product through appropriate studies, including, for example, extractable/leachable studies and stability studies. Also, for design differences in the delivery device or container closure system, performance testing and a human factors study may be needed.

However, an applicant will not be able to obtain licensure of a proposed biosimilar product when a design difference in the delivery device or container closure system results in any of the following:
- A clinically meaningful difference between the proposed biosimilar product and the reference product in terms of safety, purity, and potency;
- A different route of administration or dosage form; or
- A condition of use (e.g., indication, dosing regimen) for which the reference product has not been previously approved;

or otherwise does not meet the standard for biosimilarity.

A proposed biosimilar product in a delivery device will be considered a combination product and may, in some instances, require a separate application for the device.

For information about a delivery device or container closure system for a proposed interchangeable product, see FDA's draft guidance for industry, *Considerations in Demonstrating Interchangeability With a Reference Product.*[7]

---

[7] This draft guidance, when finalized, will represent FDA's current thinking on this topic.

6

481

Contains Nonbinding Recommendations

Q. I.5. ***Can an applicant obtain licensure of a proposed biosimilar product for fewer than all routes of administration for which an injectable reference product is licensed?***
[Issued April 2015]

A. I.5. Yes, an applicant may obtain licensure of a proposed biosimilar product for fewer than all routes of administration for which an injectable reference product is licensed. An applicant must demonstrate that there are no clinically meaningful differences between the proposed biosimilar product and the reference product in terms of safety, purity, and potency. In a limited number of circumstances, this may include providing information from one or more studies using a route of administration for which licensure is not requested (e.g., a study using subcutaneous administration may provide a more sensitive comparative assessment of immunogenicity of the reference product and a proposed biosimilar product, even though licensure of the proposed biosimilar product is requested only for the intravenous route of administration).

Q. I.6. ***Can an applicant obtain licensure of a proposed biosimilar product for fewer than all presentations (e.g., strengths or delivery device or container closure systems) for which a reference product is licensed?***
[Updated/Retained in Final December 2018]

A. I.6. An applicant is not required to obtain licensure of a proposed biosimilar product for all presentations for which the reference product is licensed. However, if an applicant seeks licensure for a particular indication or other condition of use for which the reference product is licensed and that indication or condition of use corresponds to a certain presentation of the reference product, the applicant may need to seek licensure for that particular presentation (see also questions and answers I.4 and I.5).

Q. I.7. ***Can an applicant obtain licensure of a proposed biosimilar product for fewer than all conditions of use for which the reference product is licensed?***
[Updated/Retained in Final December 2018]

A. I.7. An applicant generally may obtain licensure of a proposed biosimilar product for fewer than all conditions of use for which the reference product is licensed. The 351(k) application must include information demonstrating that the condition or conditions of use prescribed, recommended, or suggested in the proposed labeling submitted for the proposed biosimilar product have been previously approved for the reference product (see section 351(k)(2)(A)(i)(III) of the PHS Act).

7

Contains Nonbinding Recommendations

For information about the licensure of a proposed interchangeable product, see FDA's draft guidance for industry, *Considerations in Demonstrating Interchangeability With a Reference Product.*[8]

Q. I.8.   *Can a sponsor use comparative animal or clinical data with a non-U.S.-licensed product to support a demonstration that the proposed product is biosimilar to the reference product?*
[Updated/Retained in Final December 2018]

A. I.8.   A sponsor may use a non-U.S.-licensed comparator product in certain studies to support a demonstration that the proposed biological product is *biosimilar* to the U.S.-licensed reference product. However, as a scientific matter, analytical studies and at least one clinical pharmacokinetic (PK) study and, if appropriate, at least one pharmacodynamic (PD) study, intended to support a demonstration of biosimilarity must include an adequate comparison of the proposed biosimilar product directly with the U.S.-licensed reference product unless it can be scientifically justified that such a study is not needed.

If a sponsor seeks to use data from an animal study or a clinical study comparing its proposed biosimilar product to a non-U.S.-licensed product to address, in part, the requirements under section 351(k)(2)(A) of the PHS Act, the sponsor should provide adequate data or information to scientifically justify the relevance of these comparative data to an assessment of biosimilarity and establish an acceptable bridge to the U.S.-licensed reference product. As a scientific matter, the type of bridging data needed will always include data from analytical studies (e.g., structural and functional data) that directly compare all three products (i.e., the proposed biosimilar product, the U.S.-licensed reference product, and the non-U.S.-licensed comparator product), and is likely to also include bridging clinical PK and/or PD study data for all three products. All three pairwise comparisons should meet the pre-specified acceptance criteria for analytical and PK and/or PD similarity. The acceptability of such an approach will be evaluated on a case-by-case basis, and should be discussed in advance with the Agency. For certain complex biological products, a modified approach may be needed. A final determination about the adequacy of the scientific justification and bridge will be made during the review of the application.

Issues that a sponsor may need to address to use a non-U.S.-licensed comparator product in a biosimilar development program include, but are not limited to, the following:

- The relevance of the design of the clinical program to support a demonstration of biosimilarity to the U.S.-licensed reference product for the condition(s) of use and patient population(s) for which licensure is sought;

---

[8] This draft guidance, when finalized, will represent FDA's current thinking on this topic.

8

Contains Nonbinding Recommendations

- The relationship between the license holder for the non-U.S.-licensed comparator product and BLA holder for the U.S.-licensed reference product;

- Whether the non-U.S.-licensed comparator product was manufactured in a facility(ies) licensed and inspected by a regulatory authority that has similar scientific and regulatory standards as FDA (e.g., International Conference on Harmonisation (ICH) countries);

- Whether the non-U.S.-licensed comparator product was licensed by a regulatory authority that has similar scientific and regulatory standards as FDA (e.g., ICH countries) and the duration and extent to which the product has been marketed; and

- The scientific bridge between the non-U.S.-licensed comparator product and the U.S.-licensed reference product, including comparative physicochemical characterization, biological assays/functional assays, degradation profiles under stressed conditions, and comparative clinical PK and, when appropriate, PD data, to address the impact of any differences in formulation or primary packaging on product performance.

A sponsor should also address any other factors that may affect the relevance of comparative data with the non-U.S.-licensed comparator product to an assessment of biosimilarity with the U.S.-licensed reference product.

A sponsor may submit publicly available information regarding the non-U.S.-licensed comparator product to justify the extent of comparative data needed to establish a bridge to the U.S.-licensed reference product. The complexity of the products, particularly with respect to higher order structure, post-translational modifications (e.g., glycosylation), and the degree of heterogeneity associated with the product may affect the considerations for the scientific justification regarding the extent of bridging data. Additional factors that FDA may consider regarding the extent of bridging data include, but are not limited to, the following:

- Whether the formulation, dosage form, and strength of the U.S.-licensed reference product and non-U.S.-licensed comparator products are the same;

- The route of administration of the U.S.-licensed reference product and non-U.S.-licensed comparator products;

- The design of the physicochemical and biological/functional assessments and the use of multiple orthogonal methods with adequate sensitivity to detect differences among the products;

9

Contains Nonbinding Recommendations

- The scientific justification for the selection of the non-U.S.-licensed comparator lots used to establish the scientific bridge and how the selected lots relate to the material used in the nonclinical and clinical studies. The scientific bridge should include a sufficient number of lots of non-U.S.-licensed comparator product to adequately capture the variability in product quality attributes. When possible, the non-U.S.-licensed comparator lots used in the nonclinical or clinical studies should be included in the assessment performed to establish the analytical bridge.

Sponsors are encouraged to discuss with FDA during the development program the adequacy of the scientific justification and bridge to the U.S.-licensed reference product. A final decision about the adequacy of this scientific justification and bridge will be made by FDA during review of the 351(k) application.

For more information about whether a non-U.S.-licensed comparator can be used in studies intended to support the additional criteria required for a determination of interchangeability with the reference product, see FDA's draft guidance for industry, *Considerations in Demonstrating Interchangeability With a Reference Product.*[9]

Q. I.9.   *Is a clinical study to assess the potential of the biological product to delay cardiac repolarization (a QT/QTc study) or a drug-drug interaction study generally needed for licensure of a proposed biosimilar product? [Moved to Final from Draft December 2018]*

A. I.9.   In general, a 351(k) application for a proposed biosimilar product may rely upon the Agency's previous determination of safety, purity, and potency for the reference product, including any clinical QT/QTc interval prolongation and proarrhythmic potential and drug-drug interactions. If such studies were not required for the reference product, then these data generally would not be needed for licensure of a proposed biosimilar product under section 351(k) of the PHS Act. However, if the BLA holder for the reference product has been required to conduct postmarket studies or clinical trials under section 505(o)(3) of the Federal Food, Drug and Cosmetic Act (FD&C Act) to assess or identify a certain risk related to a QT/QTc study or a drug-drug interaction study and those studies have not yet been completed, then FDA may impose similar postmarket requirements on the 351(k) applicant in appropriate circumstances.

---

[9] This draft guidance, when finalized, will represent FDA's current thinking on this topic.

10

Q. I.10. ***How long and in what manner should sponsors retain reserve samples of the biological products used in comparative clinical PK and/or PD studies intended to support a 351(k) application?***
[Moved to Final from Draft December 2018]

A. I.10. Reserve samples establish the identity of the products tested in the actual study, allow for confirmation of the validity and reliability of the results of the study, and facilitate investigation of further follow-up questions that arise after the studies are completed. FDA recommends that the sponsor of a proposed biosimilar product retain reserve samples for at least 5 years following the date on which the 351(k) application is licensed, or, if such application is not licensed, at least 5 years following the date of completion of a comparative clinical PK and/or PD study of the reference product and the proposed biosimilar product (or other clinical study in which PK or PD samples are collected with the primary objective of assessing PK or PD similarity) that is intended to support a submission under section 351(k) of the PHS Act. Contact the FDA for specific advice if an alternative approach is being considered. For a 3-way PK similarity study, FDA recommends that samples of both comparator products be retained, in addition to samples of the proposed biosimilar product.

For most protein therapeutics, FDA recommends that a sponsor retain the following quantities of product and dosage units, which are expected to be sufficient for evaluation by state of the art analytical methods:

- A minimum of 10 dosage units each of the proposed biosimilar product, reference product and, if applicable, non-U.S.-licensed comparator product, depending on the amount of product within each unit. In general, this should provide for a total product mass of equal to or greater than 200 mg in a volume equal to or greater than 10 mL.

FDA recommends that the sponsor contact the review division to discuss the appropriate quantities of reserve samples in the following situations:

- A product mass of equal to or greater than 200 mg in a volume equal to or greater than 10 mL requires a large number of dosage units.
- Biological products other than protein therapeutics.

Q. I.11. This question and answer have been withdrawn. For information on extrapolation, see FDA's guidance for industry on *Scientific Considerations in Demonstrating Biosimilarity to a Reference Product.*

* * * * *

11

Q.I.12.   This question and answer have been withdrawn and moved to FDA's draft guidance for industry, *New and Revised Draft Q&As on Biosimilar Development and the BPCI Act (Revision 2).*

* * * * *

Q. I.13.   ***What constitutes "publicly-available information" regarding FDA's previous determination that the reference product is safe, pure, and potent to include in a 351(k) application?***
[Moved to Final from Draft December 2018]

A. I.13.   "Publicly-available information" in this context generally includes the current FDA-approved labeling for the reference product and the types of information found in the "action package" for a BLA (see section 505(l)(2)(C) of the FD&C Act). However, FDA notes that submission of publicly available information composed of less than the current FDA-approved labeling for the reference product and the action package for the reference product BLA will generally not be considered a bar to submission or approval of an acceptable 351(k) application.

FDA intends to post on the Agency's Web site publicly available information regarding FDA's previous determination of safety, purity, and potency for certain biological products to facilitate biosimilar development programs and submission of 351(k) applications. We note, however, that the publicly available information posted by FDA in this context does not necessarily include all information that would otherwise be disclosable in response to a Freedom of Information Act request.

Q. I.14.   ***Can an applicant obtain a determination of interchangeability between its proposed product and the reference product in an original 351(k) application?***
[Moved to Final from Draft December 2018]

A. I.14.   Yes. For more information, see FDA's draft guidance for industry, *Considerations in Demonstrating Interchangeability With a Reference Product.*[10]

Q. I.15.   ***Is a pediatric assessment under the Pediatric Research Equity Act (PREA) required for a proposed biosimilar product?***
[Updated/Retained in Final December 2018]

A. I.15.   Under the Pediatric Research Equity Act (PREA) (section 505B of the FD&C Act), all applications for new active ingredients, new indications, new dosage forms, new dosing regimens, or new routes of administration are required to contain a pediatric assessment to support dosing, safety, and effectiveness of the

---

[10] This draft guidance, when finalized, will represent FDA's current thinking on this topic.

12

Contains Nonbinding Recommendations

product for the claimed indication unless this requirement is waived, deferred, or inapplicable. [11]

Section 505B(l) of the FD&C Act[12] provides that a biosimilar product that has not been determined to be interchangeable with the reference product is considered to have a "new active ingredient" for purposes of PREA, and a pediatric assessment is generally required unless waived or deferred or inapplicable. Under the statute, an interchangeable product is not considered to have a "new active ingredient" for purposes of PREA. However, if an applicant first seeks licensure of its proposed product as a biosimilar product, the applicant must address applicable PREA requirements for its non-interchangeable biosimilar product even if it ultimately intends to subsequently seek licensure of the product as an interchangeable product.

See question and answer I.16 in the draft guidance for industry, *New and Revised Draft Q&As on Biosimilar Development and the BPCI Act (Revision 2),* for information on how a proposed biosimilar product applicant may fulfill the requirement for pediatric assessments under PREA.

FDA encourages prospective biosimilar applicants to submit plans for pediatric studies as early as practicable during product development. If there is no active investigational new drug application (IND) for the proposed biosimilar product and the sponsor intends to conduct a comparative clinical study as part of its development program, the initial pediatric study plan (PSP) should be submitted as a pre-IND submission. In this scenario, FDA encourages the sponsor to meet with FDA before submission of the initial PSP to discuss the details of the planned development program. It is expected that the sponsor will submit the initial PSP before initiating any comparative clinical study in its biosimilar development program. For more information see question and answer I.17 of this guidance. See also the draft guidance for industry, *Pediatric Study Plans: Content of and Process for Submitting Initial Pediatric Study Plans and Amended Pediatric Study Plans (March 2016).*[13]

* * * * *

---

[11] Section 505B(a)(1) was amended in 2017 by section 504 of the Food and Drug Administration Reauthorization Act (FDARA) (**Public Law 115-52**) (August 18, 2017) to include requirements for the submission of molecularly targeted pediatric cancer investigations for certain applications submitted on or after August 18, 2020, under section 505 of the FD&C Act or section 351 of the PHS Act. These requirements are not specifically addressed in this guidance.

[12] The statutory provision that appears in section 505(l) of the FD&C Act was originally enacted as section 505(n) of the FD&C Act (as amended by the BPCI Act on March 23, 2010). The provision was subsequently redesignated as 505(m) of the FD&C Act. See section 501(b) of the Food and Drug Administration Safety and Innovation Act (**Public Law 112-144**) (July 9, 2012). The provision was redesignated again as section 505(l). See section 3102(3) of the 21st Century Cures Act (**Public Law 114-255**) (December 13, 2016).

[13] This guidance, when finalized, will provide FDA's current thinking on issues related to pediatric study plans.

13

Q. I.17. *When should a proposed biosimilar product applicant submit an initial*
pediatric study plan (PSP)?
[Moved to Final from Draft December 2018]

A. I.17. Section 505B(e) of the Federal Food, Drug, and Cosmetic Act (FD&C Act)
requires applicants subject to the Pediatric Research Equity Act (PREA) to submit
an initial pediatric study plan (PSP) no later than 60 calendar days after the date
of an end-of-Phase 2 (EOP2) meeting, or at another time agreed upon by FDA
and the applicant. FDA has issued draft guidance on the PSP process, including
the timing of PSP submission.[14]

Sections 505B(e)(2)(C) and 505B(e)(3) of the FD&C Act set forth a process for
reaching agreement between an applicant and FDA on an initial PSP that
generally lasts up to 210 days. Given the potential length of this process, and in
the absence of an EOP2 meeting for a proposed biosimilar product, FDA
recommends that if a sponsor has not already initiated a comparative clinical
study intended to address the requirements under section 351(k)(2)(A)(i)(I)(cc) of
the Public Health Service (PHS) Act, the sponsor should submit an initial PSP as
soon as feasible, but no later than 210 days before initiating such a study. This is
intended to provide adequate time to reach agreement with FDA on the initial PSP
before the study is initiated. Depending on the details of the clinical program, it
may be appropriate to submit an initial PSP earlier in development. FDA
encourages the sponsor to meet with FDA to discuss the details of the planned
development program before submission of the initial PSP.

For additional guidance on submission of the PSP, including a PSP Template,
please refer to:
https://www.fda.gov/Drugs/DevelopmentApprovalProcess/DevelopmentResource
s/ucm049867.htm. After the initial PSP is submitted, a sponsor must work with
FDA to reach timely agreement on the plan, as required by section 505B(e)(2)-(3)
of the FD&C Act. It should be noted that requested deferrals or waivers in the
initial PSP will not be formally granted or denied until the product is licensed.

Q. I.18 *For biological products intended to be injected, how can an applicant*
demonstrate that its proposed biosimilar product has the same "dosage form" as
the reference product?
[Moved to Final from Draft December 2018]

A. I.18. Under section 351(k)(2)(A)(i)(IV) of the PHS Act, an applicant must demonstrate
that the *dosage form* of the proposed biosimilar or interchangeable product is the
same as that of the reference product. For purposes of implementing this statutory

---

[14] See the draft guidance for industry, *Pediatric Study Plans: Content of and Process for Submitting Initial
Pediatric Study Plans and Amended Pediatric Study Plans (March 2016).* This draft guidance, when finalized, will
provide FDA's current thinking on this topic.

14

provision, FDA considers the *dosage form* to be the physical manifestation containing the active and inactive ingredients that delivers a dose of the drug product. In the context of proposed biosimilar products intended to be injected, FDA considers, for example, "injection" (e.g., a solution) to be a different dosage form from "for injection" (e.g., a lyophilized powder). Thus, if the dosage form of the reference product is "injection," an applicant could not obtain licensure of a proposed biosimilar product with a dosage form of "for injection" even if the applicant demonstrated that the proposed biosimilar product, when constituted or reconstituted, could meet the other requirements for an application for a proposed biosimilar product.

For purposes of section 351(k)(2)(A)(i)(IV) of the PHS Act, FDA also considers emulsions and suspensions of products intended to be injected to be distinct dosage forms. Liposomes, lipid complexes, and products with extended-release characteristics present special scenarios due to their unique composition, and prospective applicants seeking further information should contact FDA.

It should be noted, however, that this interpretation regarding the same dosage form is for purposes of section 351(k)(2)(A)(i)(IV) of the PHS Act only. For example, this interpretation should not be cited by applicants seeking approval of a new drug application under section 505(c) of the FD&C Act, approval of an abbreviated new drug application under section 505(j) of the FD&C Act, or licensure of a BLA under section 351(a) of the PHS Act for purposes of determining whether separate applications should be submitted and assessed separate fees for different dosage forms.

Q. I.19. *If a non-U.S.-licensed product is proposed for importation and use in the U.S. in a clinical investigation intended to support licensure of a proposed product under section 351(k) (e.g., a bridging clinical PK and/or PD study), is a separate IND required for the non-U.S.-licensed product?*
[Moved to Final from Draft December 2018]

A. I.19. A sponsor may submit a single IND for a development program that is intended to support licensure of a proposed product under section 351(k) of the PHS Act and includes use of a non-U.S.-licensed product. The sponsor should submit information supporting the proposed clinical investigation with the non-U.S.-licensed comparator product under the IND. This scenario may occur, for example, if a sponsor seeks to use data from a clinical study comparing its proposed biosimilar product to a non-U.S.-licensed product to address, in part, the requirements under section 351(k)(2)(A) of the PHS Act, and proposes to conduct a clinical PK and/or PD study in the U.S. with all three products (i.e., the proposed biosimilar product, the U.S.-licensed reference product, and the non-U.S.-licensed product) to support establishment of a bridge between all three products and scientific justification for the relevance of these comparative data to an assessment of biosimilarity to the U.S.-licensed reference product.

15

A non-U.S.-licensed comparator product is considered an investigational new drug in the United States, and thus would require an IND for importation and use in the United States (see 21 CFR 312.110(a)). If a sponsor intends to conduct a clinical investigation in the United States using a non-U.S.-licensed comparator product, the IND requirements in 21 CFR part 312 also would apply to this product (see, e.g., 21 CFR 312.2).

With respect to chemistry, manufacturing, and controls (CMC) information, a sponsor should submit to the IND as much of the CMC information required by 21 CFR 312.23(a)(7) as is available. However, FDA recognizes that a sponsor may not be able to obtain all of the CMC information required by 21 CFR 312.23(a)(7) for a non-U.S.-licensed comparator product for which it is not the manufacturer. In these circumstances, the sponsor can request in an IND submission that FDA waive the regulatory requirements related to CMC information on the non-U.S.-licensed comparator product (21 CFR 312.10). The waiver request must include at least one of the following:

- An explanation why compliance with the requirements of 21 CFR 312.23(a)(7) is unnecessary or cannot be achieved;
- Information that will satisfy the purpose of the requirement by helping to ensure that the investigational drug will have the proper identity, strength, quality, and purity; or
- Other information justifying a waiver.[15]

Information that is relevant to whether the investigational drug will have the proper identity, strength, quality, and purity may include, for example, information indicating whether the investigational drug has been licensed by a regulatory authority that has similar scientific and regulatory standards as FDA (e.g., International Conference on Harmonisation (ICH) countries). This should include, to the extent possible, summary approval information and current product labeling made public by the foreign regulatory authority. In addition, a sponsor should also provide information on the conditions and containers that will be used to transport the drug product to the US clinical site(s) and information on the relabeling and repackaging operations that will be used to relabel the drug product vials for investigational use. This should include information on how exposure of the product to light and temperature conditions outside of the recommended storage conditions will be prevented. A risk assessment on the impact the relabeling operations may have on drug product stability should also be included.

The sponsor should consult with the appropriate FDA review division regarding the CMC information necessary to support the proposed clinical study.

---

[15] See 21 CFR 312.10(a).

16

As would be applicable to all investigational drugs, FDA reminds sponsors that the investigator brochure (IB) for studies to be conducted under the IND should be carefully prepared to ensure that it is not misleading, erroneous, or materially incomplete, which can be a basis for a clinical hold (see 21 CFR 312.42(b)(1)(iii) and (b)(2)(i)). For example, the term *reference product* should be used in the IB only to refer to the single biological product licensed under section 351(a) of the PHS Act against which the proposed product is evaluated for purposes of submitting a 351(k) application. The IB and study protocol(s) should use consistent nomenclature that clearly differentiates the proposed product from the reference product. The IB and study protocol(s) also should clearly describe whether the comparator used in each study is the US-licensed reference product or a non-U.S.-licensed comparator product, and use consistent nomenclature that clearly differentiates these products. If a non-U.S.-licensed comparator product is being used in a study conducted in the United States, the IB and study protocol(s) should clearly convey that the product is not FDA-approved and is considered an investigational new drug in the United States. The IB and study protocol(s) also should avoid conclusory statements regarding regulatory determinations (e.g., "comparable," "biosimilar," "interchangeable," "highly similar") that have not been made.

II. PROVISIONS RELATED TO REQUIREMENT TO SUBMIT A BLA FOR A "BIOLOGICAL PRODUCT"

Q.II.1. [This question and answer have been withdrawn and moved to FDA's draft guidance for industry, *New and Revised Draft Q&As on Biosimilar Development and the BPCI Act (Revision 2)*.]

Q. II.2. *How is "product class" defined for purposes of determining whether an application for a biological product may be submitted under section 505 of the FD&C Act during the transition period?*
[Issued April 2015]

A. II.2. For purposes of section 7002(e)(2) of the Affordable Care Act, a proposed biological product will be considered to be in the same "product class" as a protein product previously approved under section 505 of the FD&C Act on or before March 23, 2010, if both products are homologous to the same gene-coded sequence (e.g., the INS gene for insulin and insulin glargine) with allowance for additional novel flanking sequences (including sequences from other genes). Products with discrete changes in gene-coded sequence or discrete changes in post-translational modifications may be in the same product class as the previously approved product even if the result may be a change in product pharmacokinetics.

17

For naturally derived protein products that do not have identified sequences linked to specific genes and that were approved under section 505 of the FD&C Act on or before March 23, 2010, a proposed biological product is in the same product class as the naturally derived protein product if both products share a primary biological activity (e.g., the 4-number Enzyme Commission code for enzyme activity).

However, for any protein product (whether naturally derived or otherwise), if the difference between the proposed product and the protein product previously approved under section 505 of the FD&C Act alters a biological target or effect, the products are not in the same product class for purposes of section 7002(e)(2) of the Affordable Care Act.

Q. II.3. *What type of marketing application should be submitted for a proposed antibody-drug conjugate?*
[Moved to Final from Draft December 2018]

A. II.3.   A BLA should be submitted for a proposed monoclonal antibody that is linked to a drug (antibody-drug conjugate). FDA considers an antibody-drug conjugate to be a combination product composed of a biological product constituent part and a drug constituent part (see 21 CFR 3.2(e)(1); 70 FR 49848, 49857-49858 (August 25, 2005)).

CDER is the FDA center assigned to regulate antibody-drug conjugates, irrespective of whether the biological product constituent part or the drug constituent part is determined to have the primary mode of action. For more information see section 503(g) of the FD&C Act; see also, e.g., Transfer of Therapeutic Biological Products to the Center for Drug Evaluation and Research (June 30, 2003), available at https://www.fda.gov/CombinationProducts/JurisdictionalInformation/ucm136265.htm; Intercenter Agreement Between the Center for Drug Evaluation and Research and the Center for Biologics Evaluation and Research (October 31, 1991), available at https://www.fda.gov/CombinationProducts/JurisdictionalInformation/ucm121179.htm.

To enhance regulatory clarity and promote consistency, CDER considered several factors to determine the appropriate marketing application type for antibody-drug conjugates, including the relative significance of the safety and effectiveness questions raised by the constituent parts, particularly the highly specific molecular targeting by the antibody to a cell type, cellular compartment, or other marker at the site of action (as distinguished from mere alteration of systemic pharmacokinetics).

18

In light of such factors, CDER considers submission of a BLA under section 351 of the PHS Act to provide the more appropriate application type for antibody-drug conjugates.

Sponsors seeking to submit a BLA for a proposed antibody-drug conjugate may contact CDER's Office of New Drugs at 301-796-0700 for further information.

III. EXCLUSIVITY

Q. III.1. Can an applicant include in its 351(a) BLA submission a request for reference product exclusivity under section 351(k)(7) of the PHS Act?
[Moved to Final from Draft December 2018]

A. III.1. Yes. An applicant may include in its BLA submission a request for reference product exclusivity under section 351(k)(7) of the PHS Act, and FDA will consider the applicant's assertions regarding the eligibility of its proposed product for exclusivity. For more information, see FDA's draft guidance for industry on *Reference Product Exclusivity for Biological Products Filed Under Section 351(a) of the PHS Act.*[16] The draft guidance describes the types of information that reference product sponsors should provide to facilitate FDA's determination of the date of first licensure for their products.

Q. III.2. How can a prospective biosimilar applicant determine whether there is unexpired orphan exclusivity for an indication for which the reference product is licensed?
[Issued April 2015]

A. III.2. A searchable database for Orphan Designated and/or Approved Products and indications is available on FDA's Web site, and is updated on a monthly basis (see https://www.accessdata.fda.gov/scripts/opdlisting/oopd/index.cfm). FDA will not approve a subsequent application for the "same drug" for the same indication during the 7-year period of orphan exclusivity, except as otherwise provided in the FD&C Act and 21 CFR part 316.

---

[16] This draft guidance, when finalized, will provide FDA's current thinking on this topic.

19

APPENDIX C7

Considerations in Demonstrating Interchangeability With a Reference Product

---

Considerations in Demonstrating Interchangeability With a Reference Product

Guidance for Industry

U.S. Department of Health and Human Services
Food and Drug Administration
Center for Drug Evaluation and Research (CDER)
Center for Biologics Evaluation and Research (CBER)

May 2019
Biosimilars

Considerations in Demonstrating Interchangeability With a Reference Product

Guidance for Industry

Additional copies are available from:

Office of Communications, Division of Drug Information
Center for Drug Evaluation and Research
Food and Drug Administration
10001 New Hampshire Ave., Hillandale Bldg., 4ʰ Floor
Silver Spring, MD 20993-0002
Phone: 855-543-3784 or 301-796-3400; Fax: 301-431-6353
Email: druginfo@fda.hhs.gov
https://www.fda.gov/Drugs/GuidanceComplianceRegulatoryInformation/Guidances/default.htm

and/or

Office of Communication, Outreach and Development
Center for Biologics Evaluation and Research
Food and Drug Administration
10903 New Hampshire Ave., Bldg. 71, Room 3128
Silver Spring, MD 20993-0002
Phone: 800-835-4709 or 240-402-8010
Email: ocod@fda.hhs.gov
https://www.fda.gov/BiologicsBloodVaccines/GuidanceComplianceRegulatoryInformation/Guidances/default.htm

U.S. Department of Health and Human Services
Food and Drug Administration
Center for Drug Evaluation and Research (CDER)
Center for Biologics Evaluation and Research (CBER)

May 2019
Biosimilars

Contains Nonbinding Recommendations

TABLE OF CONTENTS

I.   INTRODUCTION 1

II.   BACKGROUND 2

III.   SCOPE 2

IV.   GENERAL PRINCIPLES 3

V.   FACTORS IMPACTING THE TYPE AND AMOUNT OF DATA AND
INFORMATION NEEDED TO SUPPORT A DEMONSTRATION OF
INTERCHANGEABILITY 5

    A.   Product-Dependent Factors That May Impact the Data Needed to Support a Demonstration
        of Interchangeability 6

        1. Product Complexity and the Extent of Comparative and Functional Characterization 6

        2. Product-Specific Immunogenicity Risk 7

        *3. Totality of Factors to Consider in Assessing the Data and Information Needed to Support a
        Demonstration of Interchangeability* 7

    B.   Biosimilar Product Postmarketing Data That May Impact the Data Needed to Support a
        Demonstration of Interchangeability 8

VI.   DATA AND INFORMATION NEEDED TO SUPPORT A DEMONSTRATION OF
INTERCHANGEABILITY 9

    A.   Considerations for the Design and Analysis of a Switching Study or Studies Needed to
        Support a Demonstration of Interchangeability 9

        1. Study Endpoints 10

        2. Study Design and Analysis 11

        3. Study Population 13

        4. Condition(s) of Use to Be Studied 14

        5. Route of Administration 14

    B.   Extrapolation of Data 14

VII. CONSIDERATIONS REGARDING THE COMPARATOR PRODUCT IN A
SWITCHING STUDY OR STUDIES 16

VIII. CONSIDERATIONS FOR DEVELOPING PRESENTATIONS FOR PROPOSED
INTERCHANGEABLE PRODUCTS 17

IX.   POSTMARKETING SAFETY MONITORING CONSIDERATIONS 18

ATTACHMENT I 20

Contains Nonbinding Recommendations

Considerations in Demonstrating Interchangeability
With a Reference Product
Guidance for Industry[1]

This guidance represents the current thinking of the Food and Drug Administration (FDA or Agency) on this topic. It does not establish any rights for any person and is not binding on FDA or the public. You can use an alternative approach if it satisfies the requirements of the applicable statutes and regulations. To discuss an alternative approach, contact the FDA office responsible for this guidance as listed on the title page.

I.   INTRODUCTION

This guidance is intended to assist sponsors in demonstrating that a proposed therapeutic protein product is interchangeable with a reference product for the purposes of submitting a marketing application or supplement under section 351(k) of the Public Health Service Act (PHS Act) (42 U.S.C. 262(k)). The Biologics Price Competition and Innovation Act of 2009 (BPCI Act) amends the PHS Act and other statutes to create an abbreviated licensure pathway in section 351(k) of the PHS Act for biological products shown to be biosimilar[2] to or interchangeable with an FDA-licensed biological reference product[3] (see sections 7001 through 7003 of the Patient Protection and Affordable Care Act (Affordable Care Act) (Public Law 111-148)). Although the 351(k) pathway applies generally to biological products, this guidance focuses on therapeutic protein products and gives an overview of important scientific considerations in demonstrating interchangeability of a proposed therapeutic protein product (*proposed interchangeable biosimilar[4]* or *proposed interchangeable product*) with a reference product.

---

[1] This guidance has been prepared by the Office of New Drugs in the Center for Drug Evaluation and Research (CDER) in cooperation with the Center for Biologics Evaluation and Research (CBER) at the Food and Drug Administration.

[2] Section 351(i)(2) of the PHS Act defines *biosimilar* or *biosimilarity* to mean that "the biological product is highly similar to the reference product notwithstanding minor differences in clinically inactive components" (highly similar provision) and that "there are no clinically meaningful differences between the biological product and the reference product in terms of the safety, purity, and potency of the product" (no clinically meaningful differences provision).

[3] Section 351(i)(4) defines *reference product* to mean "the single biological product licensed under subsection (a) against which a biological product is evaluated in an application submitted under subsection (k)."

[4] In this guidance, the following terms are used to describe biological products licensed under section 351(k) of the PHS Act: (1) "biosimilar" or "biosimilar product" refers to a product that FDA has determined to be biosimilar to the reference product (see sections 351(i)(2) and 351(k)(2) of the PHS Act) and (2) "interchangeable biosimilar" or "interchangeable product" refers to a biosimilar product that FDA has determined to be interchangeable with the reference product (see sections 351(i)(3) and 351(k)(4) of the PHS Act).

1

This guidance is one in a series of guidances that FDA is developing to implement the BPCI Act and includes references to information from other FDA guidances, where appropriate.

In general, FDA's guidance documents do not establish legally enforceable responsibilities. Instead, guidances describe the Agency's current thinking on a topic and should be viewed only as recommendations, unless specific regulatory or statutory requirements are cited. The use of the word *should* in Agency guidances means that something is suggested or recommended, but not required.

II.   BACKGROUND

Section 351(k) of the PHS Act, as amended by the BPCI Act, sets forth the requirements for an application for a proposed biosimilar product and an application or a supplement for a proposed interchangeable product. Section 351(k)(4) of the PHS Act further provides that upon review of an application submitted under section 351(k) or any supplement to such application, FDA will determine the biological product to be interchangeable with the reference product if FDA determines that the information submitted in the application or the supplement is sufficient to show that the biological product "is biosimilar to the reference product" and "can be expected to produce the same clinical result as the reference product in any given patient"[5] and that "for a biological product that is administered more than once to an individual, the risk in terms of safety or diminished efficacy of alternating or switching between use of the biological product and the reference product is not greater than the risk of using the reference product without such alternation or switch."[6]

Section 351(i) of the PHS Act states that the term *interchangeable* or *interchangeability*, in reference to a biological product that is shown to meet the standards described in section 351(k)(4) of the PHS Act, means that "the biological product may be substituted for the reference product without the intervention of the health care provider who prescribed the reference product."[7]

III.   SCOPE

This guidance provides an overview of important scientific considerations in demonstrating interchangeability with a reference product, including the following:

- Data and information needed to support a demonstration of interchangeability

---

[5] Section 351(k)(4)(A) of the PHS Act.

[6] Section 351(k)(4)(B) of the PHS Act.

[7] The terms *interchangeable* or *interchangeability* in this guidance have the same meaning as defined in section 351(i)(3) of the PHS Act.

2

- Considerations for the design and analysis of a switching study or studies to support a demonstration of interchangeability

- Considerations regarding the comparator product in a switching study or studies

- Abbreviated considerations for developing presentations, container closure systems, and delivery device constituent parts for proposed interchangeable products[8,9]

IV.   GENERAL PRINCIPLES

FDA intends to consider the totality of the evidence provided by a sponsor when the Agency evaluates the sponsor's demonstration of interchangeability according to the criteria set forth in section 351(k).

To support a demonstration of interchangeability, section 351(k)(4)(A) of the PHS Act provides, among other things, that a sponsor must show that the proposed interchangeable product "is biosimilar to the reference product." Where a product is first licensed as a biosimilar, that licensure may be referenced to support a showing for this statutory criterion for demonstrating interchangeability.

In addition, section 351(k)(4)(A) of the PHS Act provides that an application for an interchangeable product must include information sufficient to show that the proposed interchangeable product "can be expected to produce the same clinical result as the reference product in any given patient." FDA expects that sponsors will submit data and information to support a showing that the proposed interchangeable product can be expected to produce the same clinical result as the reference product in all of the reference product's licensed conditions of use.

---

[8] Products that include both a biological product and a device constituent part to deliver the biological product are combination products (see 21 CFR parts 3 and 4). For example, the delivery device constituent part and the biological product constituent part may be a single entity (e.g., a prefilled syringe) or the two constituent parts may be co-packaged (e.g., a biologic in a vial packaged in the same box with a syringe). The primary mode of action of these combination products is provided by the biological product constituent part, which is regulated by CDER or CBER. CDER or CBER, therefore, will have primary jurisdiction for these combination products; and these Centers and the Center for Devices and Radiological Health (CDRH) will coordinate as appropriate.

[9] Considerations specific to demonstrating interchangeability under section 351(k)(4) of the PHS Act with respect to container closure systems and delivery device constituent parts are addressed in section VIII of this guidance. This guidance does not address other information generally necessary to support the proposed container closure system and/or the delivery device constituent part of a proposed interchangeable product. Sponsors should also refer to relevant FDA guidance documents and resources from CBER, CDRH, CDER, and the Office of Combination Products (OCP) to assess what other data and information should be included to support the proposed container closure system(s) and/or delivery device constituent part(s). (Some of the FDA guidances and other resources that address these topics are referenced at appropriate places in section VIII of this guidance.)

3

The data and information necessary to meet the section 351(k)(4)(A) standard may vary depending on the nature of the proposed interchangeable product[10] and may include the following:

- The identification and analysis of the critical quality attributes[11]

- The identification of analytical differences between the reference product and the proposed interchangeable product, and, in addition, an analysis of the potential clinical impact of the differences

- An analysis of mechanism or mechanisms of action in each condition of use for which the reference product is licensed, which may include the following:

    - The target receptor or receptors for each relevant activity/function of the product

    - The binding, dose/concentration response, and pattern of molecular signaling upon engagement of target receptor or receptors

    - The relationship between product structure and target/receptor interactions

    - The location and expression of target receptor or receptors

- An analysis of any differences in the expected pharmacokinetics and biodistribution of the product in different patient populations for which the reference product is licensed

- An analysis of any differences in the expected immunogenicity risk of the product in different patient populations for which the reference product is licensed

- An analysis of any differences in expected toxicities of the product in each condition of use and patient population (including whether the expected toxicities are related to the pharmacological activity of the product or to off-target activities) for which the reference product is licensed

- Information on any other factor that may affect the safety or efficacy of the product in each condition of use and patient population for which the reference product is licensed

Where applicable, the data and information should include a scientific justification as to why any differences that exist between the reference product and the proposed interchangeable product, with respect to the factors described, do not preclude a showing that the proposed interchangeable product can be expected to produce the same clinical result as the reference product in any given patient. As previously noted, the data and information may vary depending

---

[10] Some of this data and information may have been generated previously by the sponsor to support a demonstration that the biological product is biosimilar to the reference product. If the applicant has previously submitted this data or information to FDA, (e.g., in an application for a biosimilar product) the applicant should consult with FDA as to how to reference or submit these data for purposes of seeking licensure as an interchangeable product.

[11] Critical quality attributes include those attributes that define a product's identity, quantity, safety, purity and potency. See the ICH guidance for industry *Q8(R2) Pharmaceutical Development* (November 2009).

4

on the nature of the proposed interchangeable product, and not all factors will necessarily be relevant to a given scientific justification. The data and information may also include a scientific rationale for extrapolation of data and information to support a demonstration of interchangeability. Extrapolation is further described in section VI.B of this guidance.

Generally, the data and information to support a showing under the "can be expected to produce the same clinical result as the reference product in any given patient" standard will likely not involve additional clinical studies other than those necessary to support other elements of demonstrating interchangeability, which are described in section VI. We note that although a sponsor may seek licensure for a proposed interchangeable product for fewer than all conditions of use for which the reference product is licensed, we recommend that a sponsor seek licensure for all of the reference product's licensed conditions of use when possible.

Further, for biological products administered more than once to a patient, section 351(k)(4)(B) of the PHS Act provides that another of the criteria for FDA to make a determination of interchangeability is a finding that information in the application is sufficient to show that "the risk in terms of safety or diminished efficacy of alternating or switching between use of the biological product and the reference product is not greater than the risk of using the reference product without such alternation or switch." FDA expects that applications generally will include data from a switching study or studies[12] in one or more appropriate conditions of use. FDA anticipates that data and information acquired from a switching study or studies will be useful in assessing the risk, in terms of safety and diminished efficacy, of alternating or switching between the products. Considerations for the design of a switching study, including study endpoints, study design and analysis, study population, condition(s) of use, and routes of administration to be studied, are discussed in detail in section VI.A of this guidance.

V.   FACTORS IMPACTING THE TYPE AND AMOUNT OF DATA AND INFORMATION NEEDED TO SUPPORT A DEMONSTRATION OF INTERCHANGEABILITY

The data and information needed to support a demonstration of interchangeability, beyond that needed to demonstrate biosimilarity,[13] may be dependent on and influenced by multiple factors, which are discussed in this section.

---

[12] The term *switching study or studies* as used throughout this guidance refers to a clinical study or studies used to determine the impact of alternating or switching between the proposed interchangeable product and the reference product.

[13] Data and information needed to demonstrate biosimilarity are discussed in section VII of the guidance for industry *Scientific Considerations in Demonstrating Biosimilarity to a Reference Product* (April 2015). We update guidances periodically. For the most recent version of a guidance, check the FDA guidance web page at https://www.fda.gov/RegulatoryInformation/Guidances/default.htm.

5

A.   **Product-Dependent Factors That May Impact the Data Needed to Support a Demonstration of Interchangeability**

    1.   *Product Complexity and the Extent of Comparative and Functional Characterization*

This section provides general, prospective considerations for evaluating the types and extent of data needed to support a demonstration of interchangeability. These considerations may affect the study design and aid in the justification of a development program for a proposed interchangeable product. Consistent with the guidance for industry *Scientific Considerations in Demonstrating Biosimilarity to a Reference Product* (April 2015),[14] the Agency recommends that sponsors use a stepwise approach to generating data and information, which may allow the sponsor to address any uncertainty about demonstrating interchangeability that may arise at each stage of product development. At each stage, the sponsor should evaluate the extent to which there is uncertainty about the interchangeability of the proposed product with the reference product and identify a strategy to address that uncertainty.

Section 351(k)(4)(A)(i) of the PHS Act provides that one of the criteria for FDA to make a determination of interchangeability is a finding that information in the application is sufficient to show that the proposed interchangeable product is biosimilar to the reference product. Such information would include, in part, a showing that the proposed interchangeable product meets the *highly similar* standard for demonstrating biosimilarity.[15] The "highly similar" standard applies to both interchangeable and biosimilar products.

The product's degree of structural and functional complexity may influence the extent of clinical data needed to support a demonstration of interchangeability. For example, clinical data needed to support a demonstration of interchangeability of a product expected to have a single target (e.g., a receptor) may be more limited than the clinical data that may be needed for a product acting on multiple targets or less-defined biological pathways. In addition, the extent of clinical data needed may be affected by the presence of structural features that specifically impact interchangeability (e.g., features that influence patient response to one product after exposure to another product).

FDA acknowledges that there is a range of comparative analytical data that may be submitted to support licensure under section 351(k) of the PHS Act.[16] Data sets that include highly sensitive analytics and/or sequential analytical methods that can identify molecules with different combinations of attributes (e.g., charge variants and glycoforms), as well as a comprehensive assessment of the relationships between attributes, may provide information that reduces the

---

[14] We update guidances periodically. For the most recent version of a guidance, check the FDA guidance web page at https://www.fda.gov/RegulatoryInformation/Guidances/default.htm.

[15] Section 351(i)(2) of the PHS Act defines *biosimilarity*, in part, to mean "that the biological product is highly similar to the reference product notwithstanding minor differences in clinically inactive components."

[16] See the guidance for industry *Quality Considerations in Demonstrating Biosimilarity of a Therapeutic Protein Product to a Reference Product* (April 2015) for the Agency's current thinking on factors to consider to support a demonstration that a proposed therapeutic protein product is *highly similar* to a reference product.

6

uncertainty about interchangeability. These approaches could be of greater importance for more complex products because these products would have a larger number of attributes and thus a potential for greater uncertainty regarding interchangeability. Advances in analytics may allow for extended analytical characterization that affect the extent of other data and information needed to support a demonstration of interchangeability and may in certain circumstances lead to a more selective and targeted approach to clinical studies intended to support a demonstration of interchangeability.

> 2. *Product-Specific Immunogenicity Risk*

Clinical experience with the reference product and comprehensive product risk assessments (e.g., regarding immunogenicity)[17] may also affect the data and information needed to support a demonstration of interchangeability. For example, products with a documented history of inducing detrimental immune responses may require more data to support a demonstration of interchangeability than products with an extensive documented history that immunogenicity does not impact clinical outcomes.

> 3. *Totality of Factors to Consider in Assessing the Data and Information Needed to Support a Demonstration of Interchangeability*

The factors discussed in sections V.A.1 and V.A.2 of this guidance need to be considered together to inform the data and information needed to support a demonstration of interchangeability in a particular context. Consider the following illustrative examples:

- Product A and its associated reference product have relatively low structural complexity and the reference product has no history of inducing severe immune responses related to immunogenicity. Product A also has a low incidence of serious adverse events related to immunogenicity, similar in nature and frequency to those observed with the reference product, as demonstrated in clinical studies conducted as part of the development program for Product A. Here, sufficiently extensive comparative analytical data supporting a demonstration that the proposed interchangeable product (Product A) is highly similar to the reference product, in addition to data derived from an appropriately designed dedicated switching or integrated study (see section VI.A), may be sufficient to support a demonstration of interchangeability.

- Product B and its associated reference product have high structural complexity and the reference product has a history of rare, life-threatening adverse events related to immunogenicity. Here, postmarketing data for the product as a licensed biosimilar, in addition to an appropriately designed switching study (see section VI.A), may provide additional data and information necessary to support a demonstration of interchangeability. The collection of biosimilar postmarketing data is described further in section V.B of this guidance.

Based on the factors discussed in sections V.A.1 and V.A.2, the uncertainty regarding the interchangeability of the respective proposed interchangeable products (described in the

---

[17] Section VII.D.2 in the guidance for industry *Scientific Considerations in Demonstrating Biosimilarity to a Reference Product* (April 2015) provides a discussion on clinical immunogenicity assessment.

7

preceding examples) would likely be different. Therefore, the data and information necessary to support a demonstration of interchangeability need to be considered on a case-by-case basis.

B. Biosimilar Product Postmarketing Data That May Impact the Data Needed to Support a Demonstration of Interchangeability

New tools and improved epidemiological approaches to evaluating postmarketing exposures and outcomes lend promise to the continued improvement of the capabilities of postmarketing surveillance and the collection of data related to the actual use of drug products in general However, our current thinking is that postmarketing data collected from products first licensed and marketed as a biosimilar, without corresponding data derived from an appropriately designed, prospective, controlled switching study or studies, generally would not be sufficient to support a demonstration of interchangeability. For example, we generally would not expect postmarketing data to provide sufficient information related to the impact on clinical pharmacokinetics (PK) and pharmacodynamics (PD) of switching or alternating between the use of the proposed interchangeable product and the reference product, which we think are important study endpoint considerations in the switching studies for the reasons described in section VI.A.1 of this guidance.

Notwithstanding these limitations, we recognize that in certain circumstances, postmarketing data from a licensed biosimilar product may be helpful as a factor when considering what data is necessary to support a demonstration of interchangeability. For example, some sponsors may wish to submit postmarketing data describing the real-world use of the biosimilar product, including certain safety data related to patient experience with some switching scenarios. Such data may reduce uncertainty about interchangeability and thus the data needed to support a demonstration of interchangeability. FDA will evaluate proposals to include postmarketing data in applications to support demonstrations of interchangeability on a case-by-case basis.

In certain situations, postmarketing surveillance data from the licensed biosimilar product in addition to data from an appropriately designed switching study may be needed to address uncertainty regarding a demonstration of interchangeability and add to the totality of the evidence to support a demonstration of interchangeability. Further, there may be situations where a postmarketing study, in addition to postmarketing surveillance data, from the licensed biosimilar product may be needed to address uncertainty regarding a demonstration of interchangeability. For example, as a scientific matter, for a reference product with a history of severe immunogenicity-related adverse events, additional data and information may be needed to support a demonstration of interchangeability. Such additional data may be able to be obtained through collection of postmarketing information if the product has been licensed as a biosimilar. Sponsors are encouraged to discuss with FDA their plans for the use of postmarketing data to address any uncertainty about interchangeability and add to the totality of the evidence to support a demonstration of interchangeability.

8

Contains Nonbinding Recommendations

VI.   DATA AND INFORMATION NEEDED TO SUPPORT A DEMONSTRATION OF INTERCHANGEABILITY

FDA recommends sponsors intending to develop a proposed interchangeable product to meet with FDA to discuss their proposed product development plan. Early discussions with FDA about product development plans, including adequate scientific justification for the proposed development program, will facilitate development of interchangeable products.[18]

A.   Considerations for the Design and Analysis of a Switching Study or Studies Needed to Support a Demonstration of Interchangeability

A switching study or studies will generally be expected to demonstrate that "for a biological product that is administered more than once to an individual, the risk in terms of safety or diminished efficacy of alternating or switching between use of the biological product and the reference product is not greater than the risk of using the reference product without such alternation or switch" set forth in section 351(k)(4)(B) of the PHS Act. The main purpose of a switching study or studies is to demonstrate that the risk in terms of safety or diminished efficacy of alternating or switching between use of the proposed interchangeable product and the reference product is not greater than the risk of using the reference product without such alternation or switch. A switching study or studies should evaluate changes in treatment that result in two or more alternating exposures (switch intervals) to the proposed interchangeable product and to the reference product.

If a sponsor of a proposed interchangeable product believes that data from a switching study is not necessary, FDA expects the sponsor to provide a justification for not needing such data as a part of the demonstration of interchangeability. For biological products that are not intended to be administered to an individual more than once, FDA expects that switching studies would generally not be needed. For products intended to be administered more than once, sponsors are encouraged to meet with FDA to discuss the planned development approach, including any proposed justification of why data from a switching study is not needed.

Design of switching studies may be informed by how the proposed interchangeable product will be used in clinical practice, taking into consideration scenarios where alternating or switching products might cause the most clinical concern. For treatments that have a long course of therapy, sponsors should anticipate dropouts in the study and should use a scientifically justifiable method to address the increased possibility of missing data.

As described in more detail in this section, a switching study is typically designed to assess whether switching between the reference product and the proposed interchangeable product will present risk in terms of safety or diminished efficacy that is greater than using the reference product without such switching. A switching study should generally evaluate whether switching between the reference product and the proposed interchangeable product will affect clinical

---

[18] See the draft guidance for industry *Formal Meetings Between the FDA and Sponsors or Applicants of BsUFA Products* (June 2018), which provides recommendations to industry on all formal meetings between the FDA and sponsors or applicants for proposed biosimilar products or proposed interchangeable products intended to be submitted under 351(k) of the PHS Act. This draft guidance, when finalized, will represent FDA's current thinking on this topic.

9

response in terms of safety or diminished efficacy reflected, in part, through an assessment of whether switching results in differences in immunogenicity and PK and/or PD (if available), as compared to not switching. If an apparent difference in clinical response in terms of safety or diminished efficacy is noticed between the switching and non-switching arms of the study (see section VI.A.2.a of this guidance), it would raise concerns as to whether the proposed interchangeable product is interchangeable.

FDA has outlined a flexible approach regarding the design of a switching study. FDA will address program-specific scientific matters (e.g., the impact of small patient populations) on a case-by-case basis in interactions with sponsors. To facilitate development of interchangeable products, FDA encourages sponsors to have early discussions with FDA about their product development plans.

1. Study Endpoints

The primary endpoint in a switching study or studies should assess the impact of switching or alternating between use of the proposed interchangeable product and the reference product on clinical PK and PD (if available). The PK and PD (if available) endpoints, as distinguished from clinical efficacy endpoints, are generally more likely to be sensitive to detect changes in exposure and/or activity that may arise as a result of alternating or switching. In addition to PK and/or PD parameters, a switching study would also be expected to descriptively assess immunogenicity and safety. A switching study may also incorporate the evaluation of efficacy endpoints. Although assessments of efficacy endpoints can be supportive, at therapeutic doses many clinical efficacy endpoints would generally be less sensitive to detect changes in exposure and/or activity that may arise as a result of alternating or switching.

Biologically relevant PD measures, if available, may be useful as shorter term, more sensitive indicators of the potential impact of alternating or switching on the risk of diminished efficacy as compared to efficacy endpoints. Relevant PD measures may also be useful to reflect multiple domains of activity, which could reduce residual uncertainty about interchangeability. Selection of PD endpoints should be scientifically justified for the intended purpose.[19] When PD endpoints that are sensitive to changes in drug concentration can be identified, PD analysis, in addition to PK analysis, may be useful to assess the impact of switching or alternating between the proposed interchangeable product and the reference product.

Study samples from the switching arm and non-switching arm should be assessed with the same PK, PD, or immunogenicity assay. FDA recommends that clinical PK, PD, and immunogenicity assays be developed and validated early in product development.[20,21] Sponsors are expected to demonstrate that the developed PK and/or PD assays are suitable for detecting changes on the selected PK and/or PD endpoint(s) as a result of alternating or switching between products. The

---

[19] See the guidance for industry, *Clinical Pharmacology Data to Support a Demonstration of Biosimilarity to a Reference Product* (December 2016).

[20] See guidance for industry, *Immunogenicity Testing of Therapeutic Protein Products—Developing and Validating Assays for Anti-Drug Antibody Detection* (January 2019).

[21] See guidance for industry, *Bioanalytical Method Validation* (May 2018).

10

validation study should demonstrate that the assay performs similarly for both the proposed interchangeable product and the reference product.

In summary, the primary endpoint(s) in a switching study or studies are recommended to be, in most cases, a comparison of PK and/or PD (if available) parameter(s) between the switching arm and non-switching arm following the final switch. In cases where PK and/or PD are not adequately sensitive endpoints (e.g., products with limited systemic exposure, or for which PD effects are not measurable), sponsors are expected to propose and justify selected endpoints other than PK or PD measures.

    2.   *Study Design and Analysis*

This section provides general recommendations and considerations related to study design and analysis. Sponsors may propose alternative approaches and are encouraged to discuss the proposed design and analysis of a switching study with FDA.

    a.   Dedicated Switching Study Design

A study with a lead-in period of treatment with the reference product, followed by a randomized two-arm period—with one arm incorporating switching between the proposed interchangeable product and the reference product (switching arm) and the other remaining as a non-switching arm receiving only the reference product (non-switching arm)—may be appropriate when designing a switching study. An illustrative example of switching study design is described in Attachment I. Considerations for the design and analysis of such a study are discussed as follows:

- Sample size: The sample size of the switching study should generally be based on PK considerations. Inter-subject variability in AUC_{tau} or C_{max} as described for the reference product should be primary considerations; however, prior information on product immunogenicity incidence and consequences should also be considered, and the sample size should be appropriately justified. When appropriate, inter-subject variability in PD endpoints may need to be considered. Study designers should anticipate the possibility of a considerable dropout rate for reasons unrelated to the study treatment arms. An anticipated high dropout rate due solely to an influence affecting all treatment arms could be assumed to be random. The negative impact on the statistical power of such a random influence could be precluded by factoring such influences into the sample size calculation. It should be noted that dropout rates or missing data rates that differentially affect the study treatment arms could represent treatment arm differences, and sponsors should provide adequate justification to FDA about any such differences and their possible causes. In addition, FDA will investigate possible causes of the noted differences in treatment arms.

- Number and duration of switches: The number and duration of switches between the reference product and the proposed interchangeable product should take into consideration the clinical condition to be treated, the therapeutic dosing of the product, and the duration of the exposure period to each product that would be expected to cause

11

the greatest concern in terms of immune response and resulting impact on safety and efficacy, if any.

- The lead-in period should be of sufficient duration to ensure an adequate baseline with respect to the study objectives before randomization to the switching period of the study.

- The switching arm is generally expected to incorporate at least two separate exposure periods (switch intervals) to each of the two products (i.e., at least three switches with each switch crossing over to the alternate product).

- In the switching arm, the final switch should be from the reference product to the proposed interchangeable product.

- The comparative assessment should occur during the final exposure period after a sufficient time (i.e., an adequate washout period of at least three or more half-lives) has elapsed following the last administration of the reference product in the switching arm. The number of doses of the proposed interchangeable product or reference product administered in the final exposure period will depend on the half-life and clinical dosing regimen.

- PK, PD, and immunogenicity sampling: To capture the full PK profile, intensive PK sampling should be performed during the final exposure period after at least three half-lives have elapsed following the last administration of the reference product in the switching arm. Trough PK sampling should be conducted at an appropriate time point during each exposure period to ensure that steady state is attained, when appropriate. The timing of PD[22] and immunogenicity[23] sampling should be appropriately justified.

- Study Analysis:

  - Primary analysis: For intravenous (IV) studies, AUC_{tau} will be considered a primary study endpoint. For subcutaneous (SC) studies, C_{max} and AUC_{tau} will be considered as co-primary study endpoints. The log-transformed AUC_{tau} and C_{max} data should be statistically analyzed using an average equivalence statistical approach.[24] The 90% confidence interval for the geometric mean ratio of AUC_{tau} (IV and SC data) and C_{max} (SC data) between the proposed interchangeable product and the reference product should be within 80% to 125%. C_{trough} and T_{max}

---

[22] See Section IV.H. Defining the Appropriate Pharmacodynamic Time Profile in the guidance for industry *Clinical Pharmacology Data to Support a Demonstration of Biosimilarity to a Reference Product* (December 2016).

[23] See Section VII.A. Obtaining Subject Samples in the guidance for industry *Immunogenicity Testing of Therapeutic Protein Products —Developing and Validating Assays for Anti-Drug Antibody Detection* (January 2019). Also see Section IV. Recommendations for Mitigating Immunogenicity Risk in the Clinical Phase of Development of Therapeutic Protein Products in the guidance for industry *Immunogenicity Assessment of Therapeutic Protein Product* (August 2014).

[24] See FDA's guidance for industry *Statistical Approaches to Establishing Bioequivalence* (February 2001).

Contains Nonbinding Recommendations

should also be analyzed as secondary endpoints. The sponsor should propose margins and statistical analyses appropriate for the evaluation of the PD endpoints.

– Safety, immunogenicity, and efficacy should be descriptively assessed as secondary endpoints. Regarding safety, it could be reasonable for a sponsor to focus on an evaluation of all serious adverse events, immune-related safety events, and adverse events of interest (e.g., known cardinal adverse events previously described with use of the reference product). The immunogenicity assessment should include, but not necessarily be limited to, an assessment of anti-drug antibody (ADA) and neutralizing antibody (NAb) incidence, ADA and NAb titer, and an evaluation of the impact of the development of ADA and NAb on PK, PD, safety, and efficacy.[25] Immunogenicity assays should be adequately sensitive to detect ADA and NAb in the presence of drug concentrations in study samples. Sponsors should discuss with FDA their planned evaluation of safety and immunogenicity.

b. Integrated Study Design

If a sponsor is considering a single study to (1) support a demonstration of no clinically meaningful differences between the reference product and the proposed product for biosimilarity[26] and (2) evaluate the impact of switching or alternating between the reference product and the proposed product for interchangeability, then an integrated, two-part study design may be appropriate. Following the time point(s) for evaluation of the appropriate endpoint(s) to support the demonstration of no clinically meaningful differences for biosimilarity between the proposed product and the reference product in the first part of the study, the subjects in the reference product arm should be re-randomized in the second part of the study to continue to receive the reference product (non-switching arm) or to switch to the proposed interchangeable product (switching arm) as described in section VI.A.2.a of this guidance.

An integrated study needs to be adequately powered to evaluate the appropriate endpoint(s) to support the demonstration of no clinically meaningful differences for biosimilarity, where the primary comparison is between the proposed product arm and the reference product arm. In addition, the study needs to be adequately powered to evaluate PK and PD (if available) following the final switch to support a demonstration of interchangeability, where the primary comparison is between the switching arm and the non-switching arm.

3. *Study Population*

The study population for switching studies should be adequately sensitive to allow for detection of differences as a result of switching between the reference product and proposed interchangeable product in PK and/or PD, common adverse events, and immunogenicity between

---

[25] Refer to recommendations for immunogenicity assessments discussed in section VII of the guidance for industry *Scientific Considerations in Demonstrating Biosimilarity to a Reference Product* (April 2015).

[26] Data and information needed to demonstrate biosimilarity are discussed in section VII of the guidance for industry *Scientific Considerations in Demonstrating Biosimilarity to a Reference Product* (April 2015).

13

the switching and non-switching arms. FDA generally recommends that sponsors use patients in switching studies because these studies are designed to assess the impact of switching and to mimic how the proposed interchangeable product will be used in clinical practice. With adequate scientific justification, however, sponsors may conduct switching studies in a patient population that is different from that used to support licensure of the reference product, or in healthy subjects. Sponsors should also provide adequate scientific justification to support that the study population is adequately sensitive to detect the impact of switching (e.g., differences in clinical PK and/or PD, common adverse events, and immunogenicity).

In a circumstance where a sponsor considers using healthy subjects, the sponsor should weigh the benefit of exposing healthy subjects to a proposed interchangeable product and/or the reference product during a clinical study against the risk of having them develop antibodies to the product, which in turn may preclude them from being able to receive the treatment in the future. However, there may be some limited situations where it is clinically and ethically appropriate to use healthy subjects in switching studies. Sponsors are strongly encouraged to discuss with FDA their rationale for conducting switching studies in healthy subjects before initiating studies, preferably before submitting a proposed protocol or protocol amendment.

4. Condition(s) of Use to Be Studied

A sponsor may obtain licensure only for a condition(s) of use for which the reference product is licensed. As described in section VI.B of this guidance, sponsors should consider choosing a condition of use to study that would support subsequent extrapolation of data to other conditions of use.

For example, if a reference product is licensed for multiple indications, one of which was approved under section 506(c) of the Federal Food, Drug, and Cosmetic Act and 21 CFR part 601, subpart E (accelerated approval), but the anticipated clinical benefit in that indication has not yet been verified in postmarketing studies, then sponsors should consider studying another indication for which the reference product is licensed, to avoid complications in the event that postmarketing studies of the reference product fail to verify the anticipated clinical benefit in the indication approved under accelerated approval.

5. Route of Administration

If a product is approved for more than one route of administration, sponsors should study the route of administration that will best assess how a patient's immune response will impact the clinical performance of the proposed interchangeable product, including changes in safety risk and efficacy. Choosing a more immunogenic route of administration (e.g., subcutaneous rather than intravenous) for use in switching studies may help sponsors anticipate the clinical implications of real-world use in clinical practice.

B. Extrapolation of Data

If the proposed product meets the statutory requirements for licensure as an interchangeable product under section 351(k) of the PHS Act based on, among other things, data and information sufficient to demonstrate interchangeability in an appropriate condition of use, the sponsor may seek licensure of the proposed product as an interchangeable product for one or more additional

14

conditions of use for which the reference product is licensed. The sponsor would need to provide sufficient scientific justification for extrapolating data and information to support a determination of interchangeability for each condition of use for which licensure as an interchangeable product is sought. The scientific justification for extrapolation should address, for example, the following issues for the tested and extrapolated conditions of use:

- The mechanism(s) of action in each condition of use for which the reference product is licensed, which may include the following:

    - The target receptor(s) for each relevant activity/function of the product

    - The binding, dose/concentration response, and pattern of molecular signaling upon engagement of target receptor(s)

    - The relationship between product structure and target/receptor interactions

    - The location and expression of target receptor(s)

- Differences, if any, in the expected PK and biodistribution of the product in different patient populations (relevant PD measures may also provide important information on the mechanism(s) of action)

- Differences, if any, in the expected immunogenicity risk of the product in different patient populations

- Differences, if any, in expected toxicities in each condition of use and patient population (including whether the expected toxicities are related to the pharmacological activity of the product or to off-target activities)

- Any other factor that may affect the safety or efficacy of the product in each condition of use and patient population for which the reference product is licensed[27]

Differences between conditions of use with respect to the factors described above do not necessarily preclude extrapolation. A scientific justification should address these differences in the context of the totality of the evidence supporting a demonstration of interchangeability. Advanced structural and functional characterization may provide additional support for the justification for extrapolation.

In choosing a condition of use to study that would permit subsequent extrapolation of data to other conditions of use, FDA recommends that a sponsor consider a condition of use that would be adequately sensitive to assess the risk of alternating or switching between the products, in terms of safety or diminished efficacy, in a switching study.

---

[27] These factors are also discussed in section VII.D.4. Extrapolation of Clinical Data Across Indications in the guidance for industry *Scientific Considerations in Demonstrating Biosimilarity to a Reference Product* (April 2015).

15

VII. CONSIDERATIONS REGARDING THE COMPARATOR PRODUCT IN A SWITCHING STUDY OR STUDIES

As defined in section 351(i)(3) of the PHS Act, an interchangeable product may be substituted for the reference product without the prescribing health care provider's intervention. As described above, sponsors will generally be expected to conduct a switching study or studies to address section 351(k)(4)(B) of the PHS Act: "for a biological product that is administered more than once to an individual, the risk in terms of safety or diminished efficacy of alternating or switching between use of the biological product and the reference product is not greater than the risk of using the reference product without such alternation or switch." The goal of a switching study or studies is to support a determination that a biosimilar product is interchangeable with a reference product that is licensed for use in the United States.

If a sponsor seeks to use data derived from a switching study or studies comparing a proposed interchangeable product with a non-U.S.-licensed comparator product as part of the demonstration that the proposed interchangeable product meets the standard described in section 351(k)(4)(B) of the PHS Act, the sponsor should provide adequate data and information to establish a "bridge" between the non-U.S.-licensed comparator and the U.S.-licensed reference product and thereby justify the relevance of the data obtained using the non-U.S.-licensed comparator to an evaluation of whether the requirements of section 351(k)(4)(B) have been met. This section describes considerations for the type and extent of data needed to establish an adequate bridge in this context.

In the context of demonstrating biosimilarity to a reference product, FDA has stated that "sponsors may seek to use data derived from animal or clinical studies comparing a proposed product with a non-U.S.-licensed comparator product to address, in part, the requirements under section 351(k)(2)(A) of the PHS Act."[28,29] In clinical studies used to support a demonstration of no clinically meaningful differences as a part of demonstrating biosimilarity, the comparator product (whether it is a non-U.S.-licensed product or a U.S.-licensed reference product) serves as a control against which the proposed product is evaluated. However, in a switching study that is designed to evaluate the impact of switching or alternating to support a determination of interchangeability, the comparator product plays a different role.

As described in section VI.A., a switching study is typically designed to assess whether switching between the reference product and the proposed interchangeable product will present risk in terms of safety or diminished efficacy that is greater than using the reference product without such switching. A switching study should generally evaluate whether switching between the reference product and the proposed interchangeable product will affect clinical response in terms of safety or diminished efficacy reflected, in part, through an assessment of whether switching results in differences in immunogenicity and PK and/or PD (if available), as compared

---

[28] See section V on U.S.-licensed reference product and other comparators in the guidance for industry *Scientific Considerations in Demonstrating Biosimilarity to a Reference Product* (April 2015).

[29] See Q.I.8 in the guidance for industry *Questions and Answers on Biosimilar Development and the BPCI Act* (December 2018), which discusses use of a non-U.S.-licensed product to support a demonstration that the proposed product is biosimilar to the reference product.

16

to not switching. Hence, rather than being used only as a control, the comparator product is used in a switching study in both the active switching arm and the control non-switching arm. Therefore, the type and extent of bridging data needed to justify the use of a non-U.S.-licensed comparator in a switching study may be different or more extensive than is needed in other contexts.

It is possible that the reference product and the non-U.S.-licensed comparator product have, for example, subtle differences in levels of specific structural features (e.g., acidic variants, deamidations), process related impurities, or formulation. These subtle differences may not preclude use of the non-U.S.-licensed product as a comparator in certain studies to support a demonstration of biosimilarity because the comparator is being used as a control in an evaluation that does not involve switching back and forth. However, in the context of switching between the products, multiple exposures to each product may potentially prime the immune system to recognize subtle differences in structural features between products. The overall immune response could be increased under these conditions. This immunologic response is highly dependent on the structural differences between the proposed interchangeable product and the comparator product used in the switching study, in addition to other potential differences between the products such as impurities and formulation.

For the reasons described above, the type and extent of data needed to justify the use of a non-U.S.-licensed comparator in a switching study may be different or more extensive than is needed in other contexts in which a non-U.S.-licensed comparator is used. However, FDA believes that when supported by adequate data and information, it may be reasonable to use a non-U.S.-licensed comparator in a switching study. Sponsors are encouraged to contact FDA early in the product development process to discuss the design of a switching study, including any proposal to provide adequate scientific justification to support the use of data generated in a switching study using a non-U.S.-licensed comparator product to support a demonstration of interchangeability.

VIII. CONSIDERATIONS FOR DEVELOPING PRESENTATIONS FOR PROPOSED INTERCHANGEABLE PRODUCTS

The data and information needed to support a demonstration of interchangeability, beyond that needed to demonstrate biosimilarity,[30] may also be influenced by the proposed product's presentation.[31] Sponsors are encouraged to contact FDA early during product development to discuss the proposed presentation and specific considerations related to licensure of the proposed product as an interchangeable under section 351(k) of the PHS Act.

---

[30] Data and information needed to demonstrate biosimilarity are discussed in section VII of the guidance for industry *Scientific Considerations in Demonstrating Biosimilarity to a Reference Product* (April 2015).

[31] For the purposes of this guidance, the term *presentation* means the container closure system and any delivery device constituent part of the product.

When developing a product for licensure as an interchangeable product under section 351(k) of the PHS Act, it is important that sponsors carefully consider the presentation of the proposed interchangeable product relative to the reference product.[32] A sponsor developing an interchangeable product generally should not seek licensure for a presentation for which the reference product is not licensed. For example, if the reference product is only marketed in a vial and a prefilled syringe, a sponsor should not seek licensure for the proposed interchangeable product for a different presentation, such as an auto-injector. However, if a sponsor is considering the development of a presentation for which the reference product is not licensed, this should be discussed with FDA. In such cases, FDA will evaluate whether the proposed presentation could support a demonstration of interchangeability.

As applicable, a general description of the presentation should be provided in the chemistry, manufacturing, and controls section of the application. There should be complete chemistry, manufacturing, and controls information for the proposed interchangeable product, including, if applicable, delivery device constituent part design, and development information. The presentation should be shown to be compatible for use with the final formulation of the proposed interchangeable product through appropriate studies, including, for example, extractable/leachable studies, performance testing, and stability studies. Data and information supporting the appropriate use and performance testing of the delivery device constituent part of the proposed interchangeable product should be submitted.

IX.   POSTMARKETING SAFETY MONITORING CONSIDERATIONS

Robust postmarketing safety monitoring is an important component in ensuring the safety and effectiveness of biological products, including biosimilar and interchangeable products.

Postmarketing safety monitoring for interchangeable products should first take into consideration any particular safety or effectiveness concerns associated with the use of the reference product and its class, the proposed interchangeable product in its development and clinical use (if marketed outside the United States), the specific condition of use and patient population, and patient exposure in the interchangeability development program. Postmarketing safety monitoring for an interchangeable product should also have adequate pharmacovigilance mechanisms in place.[33] Rare but potentially serious safety risks may not be detected during preapproval clinical testing because the size of the population exposed likely will not be large enough to assess rare events. In particular cases, such risks may need to be evaluated through

---

[32] See Q.I.4 and Q.I.6 in the guidance for industry *Questions and Answers on Biosimilar Development and the BPCI Act* (December 2018).

[33] For general pharmacovigilance considerations, see the guidance for industry *Good Pharmacovigilance Practices and Pharmacoepidemiologic Assessment* (March 2005) and the guidance for industry *Postmarketing Adverse Experience Reporting for Human Drug and Licensed Biological Products: Clarification of What to Report* (August 1997).

18

postmarketing surveillance or studies. In addition, as with any other biological product, FDA may require a postmarketing study or a clinical trial to evaluate certain safety risks.[34]

Because some aspects of postmarketing safety monitoring are product-specific and dependent upon the risk that is the focus of monitoring, FDA encourages sponsors to consult with appropriate FDA divisions to discuss the sponsor's proposed approach to postmarketing safety monitoring.

---

[34] See section 505(o)(3) and 505(p)(1)(A)(ii) of the Federal Food, Drug, and Cosmetic Act.

19

Contains Nonbinding Recommendations

ATTACHMENT I

Example of a **Switching Study Design**

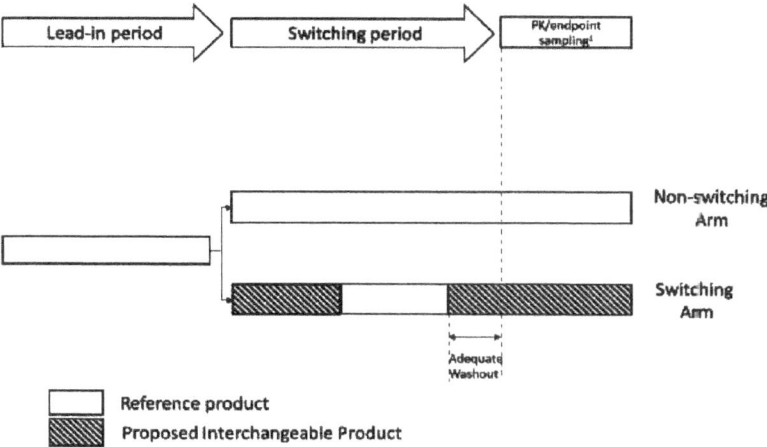

Reference product

Proposed Interchangeable Product

[1]Appropriate PK parameters and other endpoints (e.g., PD) also collected and analyzed in previous switch intervals.

Figure is not drawn to scale.

20

517

APPENDIX D1

Guidance for Industry Reference Product Exclusivity for Biological Products Filed Under Section 351(a) of the PHS Act

---

Guidance for Industry
Reference Product Exclusivity for Biological Products Filed Under Section 351(a) of the PHS Act

DRAFT GUIDANCE

This guidance document is being distributed for comment purposes only.

Comments and suggestions regarding this draft document should be submitted within 60 days of publication in the *Federal Register* of the notice announcing the availability of the draft guidance. Submit electronic comments to http://www.regulations.gov. Submit written comments to the Division of Dockets Management (HFA-305), Food and Drug Administration, 5630 Fishers Lane, rm. 1061, Rockville, MD 20852. All comments should be identified with the docket number listed in the notice of availability that publishes in the *Federal Register*.

For questions regarding this draft document contact (CDER) Sandra Benton at 301-796-2500 or (CBER) Office of Communication, Outreach and Development at 1-800-835-4709 or 240-402-7800.

U.S. Department of Health and Human Services
Food and Drug Administration
Center for Drug Evaluation and Research (CDER)
Center for Biologics Evaluation and Research (CBER)

August 2014
Procedural

Guidance for Industry
Reference Product Exclusivity for Biological Products Filed Under Section 351(a) of the PHS Act

Additional copies are available from:

Office of Communications
Division of Drug Information, Bldg. 51, Room 2201
Center for Drug Evaluation and Research
Food and Drug Administration
10903 New Hampshire Ave., Silver Spring, MD 20993
Phone: 301-796-3400; Fax: 301-847-8714
druginfo@fda.hhs.gov
http://www.fda.gov/Drugs/GuidanceComplianceRegulatoryInformation/Guidances/default.htm
and/or
Office of Communication, Outreach and
Development
Center for Biologics Evaluation and Research
Food and Drug Administration
10903 New Hampshire Ave., Bldg. 71, Room 3128
Silver Spring, MD 20993
ocod@fda.hhs.gov
http://www.fda.gov/BiologicsBloodVaccines/GuidanceComplianceRegulatoryInformation/Guidances/default.htm
(Tel) 800-835-4709 or 301-827-1800

U.S. Department of Health and Human Services
Food and Drug Administration
Center for Drug Evaluation and Research (CDER)
Center for Biologics Evaluation and Research (CBER)

August 2014
Procedural

Contains Nonbinding Recommendations

Draft — Not for Implementation

TABLE OF CONTENTS

I.   INTRODUCTION 1

II.   BACKGROUND 2

III.   DISCUSSION 3

    A.   "Licensor, Predecessor in Interest, or Other Related Entity" 4

    B.   "Modification to the Structure of the Biological Product" 5

    C.   "Result[s] in Change in Safety, Purity, or Potency" 6

IV.   SUGGESTED INFORMATION FOR 351(a) APPLICANTS TO PROVIDE TO FDA 7

V.   PUBLICATION OF DECISION 8

1   **Guidance for Industry[1]**
2   **Reference Product Exclusivity for Biological Products**
3   **Filed Under 351(a) of the PHS Act**
4

5
6   This draft guidance, when finalized, will represent the Food and Drug Administration's (FDA's or the
7   Agency's) current thinking on this topic. It does not create or confer any rights for or on any person and
8   does not operate to bind FDA or the public. You can use an alternative approach if the approach satisfies
9   the requirements of the applicable statutes and regulations. If you want to discuss an alternative approach,
10   contact the FDA staff responsible for implementing this guidance. If you cannot identify the appropriate
11   FDA staff, call the appropriate number listed on the title page of this guidance.
12

13
14   **I.   INTRODUCTION**
15
16   This guidance is intended to assist sponsors who are developing biological products, sponsors of
17   biologics license applications (BLAs), and other interested parties in providing information that
18   will help the Agency determine the date of first licensure for a reference product under
19   351(k)(7)(C) of the Public Health Service Act (PHS Act), as added by the Biologics Price
20   Competition and Innovation Act of 2009 (BPCI Act). Under 351(k)(7), licensure of an
21   application for a biosimilar or interchangeable product under 351(k) of the PHS Act (also known
22   as a 351(k) application) may not be made effective by FDA until the date that is 12 years after
23   the date on which the reference product referred to in the 351(k) application was first licensed
24   under section 351(a) of the PHS Act. In addition, a 351(k) application may not be submitted to
25   FDA for review until 4 years after the date of first licensure of the reference product. This
26   period of time in which a 351(k) application may not be licensed (or submitted for review) is
27   known as the reference product exclusivity[2] period. Thus, a decision under 351(k)(7)(C)
28   regarding the date of first licensure of a reference product submitted under 351(a) is, in effect, a
29   decision on eligibility for reference product exclusivity and on the date on which such
30   exclusivity begins to run.
31
32   Not every licensure of a biological product under 351(a) is considered a "first licensure" that
33   gives rise to its own exclusivity period. Under the terms of 351(k)(7), the dates of licensure of
34   applications for certain changes to previously licensed biological products from the same or
35   certain related sponsors are explicitly not considered the dates of first licensure for purposes of
36   giving rise to a period of reference product exclusivity. As discussed further in this guidance,
37   reference product sponsors generally have superior information about changes to previously

---

[1] This guidance has been prepared by the Office of Medical Policy in the Center for Drug Evaluation and Research
(CDER) in cooperation with the Center for Biologics Evaluation and Research (CBER) at the Food and Drug
Administration.
[2] The term *exclusivity* as applied to a particular product generally refers to a statutory limitation on FDA's ability to
accept for review or to license or approve certain competing products for a specified period of time. Exclusivity
provisions can be found in the Federal Food, Drug, and Cosmetic Act (FD&C Act) at, among others, 505(c)(3)(E),
505(j)(5)(F), 505A(b) and (c), 527(a), and in the PHS Act at 351(k)(7).

1

38   licensed products and corporate relationships to other sponsors that are relevant to a
39   determination of the date of first licensure under 351(k)(7)(C). In this guidance, we describe the
40   types of information that reference product sponsors should provide to facilitate FDA's
41   determination of the date of first licensure for their products.
42
43   FDA's guidance documents, including this guidance, do not establish legally enforceable
44   responsibilities. Instead, guidances describe the Agency's current thinking on a topic and should
45   be viewed only as recommendations, unless specific regulatory or statutory requirements are
46   cited. The use of the word *should* in Agency guidances means that something is suggested or
47   recommended, but not required.
48
49   **II.   BACKGROUND**
50
51   The BPCI Act was enacted as part of the Patient Protection and Affordable Care Act (Affordable
52   Care Act) (Public Law 111–148) on March 23, 2010. The BPCI Act amends the PHS Act and
53   other statutes to create an abbreviated licensure pathway for biological products shown to be
54   biosimilar to or interchangeable with an FDA-licensed biological reference product (see sections
55   7001 through 7003 of the Affordable Care Act). Section 351(k) of the PHS Act (42 U.S.C.
56   262(k)), added by the BPCI Act, sets forth the requirements for an application for a proposed
57   biosimilar product and an application or a supplement for a proposed interchangeable product.
58
59   Section 351(k)(7) of the PHS Act, entitled "Exclusivity for Reference Product," describes
60   reference product exclusivity, the period of time in which a 351(k) sponsor is not permitted to
61   submit and FDA is not permitted to license a 351(k) application that references a reference
62   product, the single biological product licensed under section 351(a) of the PHS Act against
63   which a biological product is evaluated in a 351(k) application.[3] Under this section, exclusivity
64   for the reference product is described in terms of a prohibition on acceptance or approval of an
65   application for a biosimilar or interchangeable product for a period of time starting from the date
66   of first licensure. Specifically, approval of a 351(k) application may not be made effective until
67   12 years after the date of first licensure of the reference product, which under the statute
68   excludes the date of licensure of supplements and certain other applications.[4] A 351(k)
69   application for a biosimilar or interchangeable biological product cannot be submitted for review
70   until 4 years after the date on which the reference product was first licensed under section 351(a)
71   of the PHS Act.[5] As provided by section 351(m) of the PHS Act, an additional six-month period
72   of exclusivity (in which a biosimilar or interchangeable biological product cannot be licensed or
73   accepted for review) will attach to the 12- and 4-year periods, respectively, if the sponsor
74   conducts pediatric studies that meet the requirements for pediatric exclusivity pursuant to section
75   505A of the Federal Food, Drug, and Cosmetic Act (FD&C Act).[6] Furthermore, a biological
76   product seeking licensure as biosimilar to or interchangeable with a reference product indicated

---

[3] Section 7002(b)(3) of the Affordable Care Act, adding section 351(i)(4) of the PHS Act.
[4] Sections 7002(a)(7)(A) and 7002(a)(7)(C) of the Affordable Care Act, adding sections 351(k)(7)(A) and 351(k)(7)(C) of the PHS Act.
[5] Section 7002(a)(7)(B) of the Affordable Care Act, adding section 351(k)(7)(B) of the PHS Act.
[6] Section 7002(g) of the Affordable Care Act, adding section 351(m) of the PHS Act. This period is referred to as the pediatric exclusivity period.

77 for a rare disease or condition and granted 7 years of "orphan drug exclusivity" under section
78 527(a) of the FD&C Act, may not be licensed by FDA for the protected orphan indication until
79 after the expiration of the 7-year orphan drug exclusivity period or the 12-year reference product
80 exclusivity period granted under section 351(k)(7) of the PHS Act, whichever is later.[7]
81
82 Determining the date of first licensure for a reference product, in turn, determines whether a
83 particular biological product qualifies for a period of exclusivity under 351(k)(7) of the PHS Act
84 and the date on which such exclusivity, if any, will expire. Making this determination can
85 present unique challenges given the requirements of section 351(k)(7) of the PHS Act. These are
86 made more acute because of the scientific and technical complexities that may be associated with
87 the larger and typically more complex structures of biological products as compared with small
88 molecule drugs, as well as the processes by which such biological products are made. Therefore,
89 the 351(a) applicant may provide information to FDA, such as that described in this guidance or
90 other relevant information, to assist FDA with its analysis of the date of first licensure for a
91 biological product under section 351(k)(7) of the PHS Act.[8]
92
93 **III. DISCUSSION**
94
95 A biological product submitted for licensure under section 351(a) of the PHS Act (a 351(a)
96 application) may be eligible for a period of exclusivity that commences on the date of its
97 licensure unless its date of licensure is not considered a date of first licensure because it falls
98 within an exclusion under 351(k)(7)(C). In most instances, the date of first licensure will be the
99 initial date the particular product at issue was licensed in the United States.
100
101 Under section 351(k)(7)(C) of the PHS Act, however, the date of first licensure does not include
102 the date of licensure of (and a new period of exclusivity shall not be available for) a biological
103 product licensed under section 351(a) of the PHS Act if the licensure is for:
104
105 - a supplement for the biological product that is the reference product; or
106 - a subsequent application filed by the same sponsor or manufacturer of the
107   biological product (or a licensor, predecessor in interest, or other related
108   entity) for:
109   - a change (not including a modification to the structure of the
110   biological product) that results in a new indication, route of
111   administration, dosing schedule, dosage form, delivery system,
112   delivery device, or strength; or
113   - a modification to the structure of the biological product that does not
114   result in a change in safety, purity, or potency.[9]
115

---

[7] Section 7002(h) of the Affordable Care Act.
[8] This guidance document does not include an exhaustive list of information that a sponsor may submit to assist FDA in determining the date of first licensure. FDA recommends that sponsors submit any additional information regarding the date of first licensure that they think supports eligibility for exclusivity and include an explanation of its relevance.
[9] Section 7002(a)(7)(C) of the Affordable Care Act, adding section 351(k)(7)(C) of the PHS Act.

3

Contains Nonbinding Recommendations

Draft — Not for Implementation

116 The exclusions noted above indicate that Congress did not intend for every biological product
117 licensed under section 351(a) of the PHS Act to be eligible for a separate period of reference
118 product exclusivity. Because of these exclusions, for each product licensed under section 351(a)
119 of the PHS Act that may serve as a reference product for a biosimilar application, FDA must
120 make a determination regarding the date of first licensure.
121
122 Thus, for instance, FDA must determine whether an application is considered a "subsequent
123 application filed by the same sponsor or manufacturer of the biological product (or a licensor,
124 predecessor in interest, or other related entity)." For such applications, FDA must determine
125 whether a particular application is for a "modification to the structure" of a biological product
126 previously licensed by such an entity. If FDA concludes that a particular application filed by a
127 relevant entity includes a "modification to the structure" of a previously licensed biological
128 product that was the subject of a 351(a) application filed by the same sponsor or manufacturer, or
129 its licensor, predecessor in interest, or other related entity, FDA must also determine whether
130 such a structural modification would result in a "change in safety, purity, or potency."
131
132 A sponsor may submit the information described in section IV of this guidance document to
133 assist FDA in determining the date of first licensure for a biological product to determine
134 whether the product is eligible for its own period of exclusivity or is subject to an exclusion
135 described in 351(k)(7)(C). If the sponsor cannot adequately characterize the biological product,
136 FDA recommends that the sponsor consult FDA for additional guidance.
137
138   A.   **"Licensor, Predecessor in Interest, or Other Related Entity"**
139
140 Section 351(k)(7)(C) of the PHS Act excludes from the date of first licensure the date of
141 approval of supplements and certain subsequent applications filed by the same sponsor or a
142 licensor, predecessor in interest, or other entity that is "related" to the sponsor of a previously
143 licensed biological product. The Agency has experience in construing other provisions that
144 require examination of the relationships between business entities to determine eligibility of a
145 new drug application for exclusivity.[10] For example, in the context of 3-year new drug product
146 exclusivity, the Agency has included studies conducted or funded by the applicant's predecessor
147 in interest in any assessment of eligibility for exclusivity. It has construed the term "predecessor
148 in interest" to mean an entity (e.g., a corporation) that the sponsor has taken over, merged with,
149 or purchased, or from which the sponsor has purchased all rights to the drug [reference
150 product].[11] Also, the Agency has construed a predecessor in interest to include an entity which
151 has granted to the applicant exclusive rights to a new drug application or the data upon which
152 exclusivity is based, which may include licensors, assignors, and joint venture partners,
153 depending on the circumstances of the case.[12]
154

---

[10] Sections 505(c)(3)(E)(iii) and 505(j)(5)(F)(iii) of the FD&C Act (requiring that a study be "conducted or sponsored by the applicant" to qualify for 3-year new drug product exclusivity).

[11] 21 CFR 314.108(a); see also 21 CFR 314.50(j)(4)(iii).

[12] See the final rule entitled "Abbreviated New Drug Application Regulations; Patent and Exclusivity Provisions" (patent and exclusivity final rule), published in the Federal Register of October 3, 1994 (59 FR 50338 at 50359 and 50362). Sections 21 CFR 314.108(a) and 314.50(j)(4)(iii) also state that the purchase of nonexclusive rights to a clinical investigation after it is completed is not sufficient to satisfy this definition of predecessor in interest.

4

155 With respect to 351(k)(7)(C), the Agency intends to interpret the term "predecessor in interest"
156 as it does in the 3-year new drug product exclusivity context.[13] It will consider any entity that
157 the sponsor has taken over, merged with, or purchased, or that has granted the sponsor exclusive
158 rights to market the biological product under the 351(a) application, or had exclusive rights to the
159 data underlying that application to be a predecessor in interest for purposes of the first licensure
160 provisions at section 351(k)(7)(C) of the PHS Act.
161
162 The Agency intends to consider a "licensor" under the BPCI Act to be any entity that has granted
163 the sponsor a license to market the biological product, regardless of whether such license is
164 exclusive. This term would include, for instance, entities that continue to retain rights to
165 develop, manufacture, or market the biological product, and/or rights to intellectual property that
166 covers the biological product.
167
168 Although the BPCI Act does not define the term "other related entity," the Agency generally will
169 consider an applicant to be a "related entity" in this context if (1) either entity owns, controls, or
170 has the power to own or control the other entity (either directly or through one or more other
171 entities) or (2) the entities are under common ownership or control. The Agency also may find
172 that two parties are related entities for purposes of the BPCI Act if the entities are or were
173 engaged in certain commercial collaborations relating to the development of the biological
174 product(s) at issue.[14] In analyzing whether the relationship between the parties would result in a
175 finding that they were "other related entities," the Agency expects to consider not only
176 ownership and control of the investigational new drug application (IND) and the BLA, but also
177 the level of collaboration between the entities during the development program as a whole.
178
179 **B.   "Modification to the Structure of the Biological Product"**
180
181 The statute specifies that the date of first licensure excludes (and, therefore, a new period of
182 exclusivity will not run from) the date of approval of an application for a change that results in a
183 new indication, route of administration, dosing schedule, dosage form, delivery system, delivery
184 device, or strength unless that change includes a "modification to the structure of the biological
185 product" and such modification results in a change in safety, purity, or potency. It is thus
186 essential to first determine whether a new product includes a modification to the structure of a
187 previously licensed product to assess whether the licensure of the new product is a first licensure
188 that triggers its own period of exclusivity.
189
190 Therefore, a sponsor seeking to assist FDA in determining the date of first licensure for a
191 reference product licensed under 351(a), should describe the structural similarities and
192 differences between its proposed product and any previously licensed biological product that was
193 the subject of a 351(a) application filed by the same sponsor or manufacturer (or its licensor,
194 predecessor in interest, or other related entity). For protein products, described structural
195 differences should include, as appropriate, any differences in amino acid sequence, glycosylation
196 patterns, tertiary structures, post-translational events (including any chemical modifications of

---

[13] Patent and exclusivity final rule (59 FR 50338 at 50362).
[14] This generally would not include service contracts, unless such contracts reflect common ownership or
development of the product(s) at issue.

5

197   the molecular structure such as pegylation), and infidelity of translation or transcription, among
198   others. In determining whether a biological product includes a modification to the structure of a
199   previously licensed biological product, FDA also will consider the principal structural molecular
200   features of both products and whether the modified product affects the same molecular target as
201   the previously licensed product. If a sponsor employs a cell line modified from that used to
202   manufacture the previously licensed product (for example, one employing a modified gene
203   construct) to manufacture a new product, modification of the structure will not simply be
204   presumed. Instead, a sponsor seeking to demonstrate that this new product is nevertheless
205   eligible for its own period of exclusivity should first demonstrate that the product has been
206   structurally modified. Any demonstration that the structure has been modified should be
207   followed by a demonstration that the change has resulted in a change in safety, purity, or
208   potency, as explained in section III.C below.
209
210   **C.**   **"Result[s] in Change in Safety, Purity, or Potency"**
211
212   Section 351(k)(7)(C)(ii)(II) of the PHS Act excludes from the date of first licensure the dates of
213   approval of those modifications to the structure of the previously licensed product that do not
214   "result in a change in safety, purity, or potency."[15] The determination of whether a structural
215   modification results in a change in safety, purity, or potency will be made case-by-case and will
216   generally need to be based on data submitted by the sponsor. The supporting information
217   provided should include measurable effects (typically demonstrated in preclinical or clinical
218   studies and shown by relevant methods such as bioassays) clearly describing how the
219   modification resulted in a change in safety, purity, or potency compared to the previously
220   licensed product. Supporting information can include references to the data and information
221   submitted in the 351(a) application of the previously licensed product. Evidence that a change
222   resulted in a change in safety, purity, or potency may include evidence that the change will result
223   in a meaningful benefit to public health, such as a therapeutic advantage or other substantial
224   benefit when compared to the previously licensed biological product.
225
226   In cases where FDA determines that a proposed biological product includes a modification to the
227   structure of a previously licensed biological product, FDA generally will presume that the
228   modification has resulted in a change to the proposed product's safety, purity, or potency if the
229   sponsor of the proposed product demonstrates that it affects a different molecular target than the
230   original product. A molecular target can be any molecule in the body whose activity is modified
231   by the product, resulting in a desirable therapeutic effect. Such molecular targets can include
232   receptors, enzymes, ion channels, structural or membrane transport proteins, nucleic acids, and
233   pathogens, among others.
234

---

[15] The standard for licensure of a biological product as "potent" under section 351(a) of the PHS Act has long been interpreted to include effectiveness (see 21 CFR 600.3(s) and the guidance for industry *Providing Clinical Evidence of Effectiveness for Human Drug and Biological Products*). In that guidance, we use the terms "safety and effectiveness" and "safety, purity, and potency" interchangeably in the discussions pertaining to biosimilar products. We update guidances periodically. To make sure you have the most recent version of a guidance, check the FDA Drugs guidance Web page at
http://www.fda.gov/Drugs/GuidanceComplianceRegulatoryInformation/Guidances/default.htm.

235 If the modified product affects the same molecular target as the previously licensed product, its
236 sponsor should provide data to show that the changes in structure result in a change in safety,
237 purity, or potency of the modified product when compared to the previously licensed product. If
238 a sponsor can provide such data, FDA may determine that the date of licensure of the modified
239 product is the date of first licensure as set forth in section 351(k)(7)(C) of the PHS Act.
240
241 If the sponsor does not demonstrate that a modification in the structure results in a change in
242 safety, purity, or potency compared to the previously licensed product, or that the modified
243 product affects a different molecular target than the previously licensed product (resulting in a
244 presumption that there is a change in safety purity or potency), the date of licensure of the
245 modified product generally would not be the date of first licensure, and that product would
246 therefore not be eligible for its own period of exclusivity.
247
248 Under 351(k)(7)(C)(ii)(I) of the PHS Act, the date of approval of a change to a previously
249 licensed product from the same sponsor (or a licensor, predecessor in interest, or other related
250 entity) that does not include a modification to the structure of the sponsor's original product but
251 which results in a new indication, route of administration, dosing schedule, dosage form,
252 delivery system, delivery device, or strength is excluded from the date of first licensure; and an
253 application for such a change is not eligible for its own period of exclusivity.
254

255 **IV.   SUGGESTED INFORMATION FOR 351(a) APPLICANTS TO PROVIDE TO**
256 **FDA**
257
258 FDA recommends that a sponsor include information such as that described in this guidance at
259 the time the 351(a) application is submitted or, in the case of an already licensed 351(a)
260 application, as correspondence to the application.[16] Alternatively, this information can be
261 submitted as an amendment to the 351(a) application. However, the determination of the date of
262 first licensure and of eligibility for exclusivity may not always be made at the time of licensure,
263 particularly if the determination presents complicated scientific, legal, or factual issues; if the
264 information to support such a determination is submitted late in the review cycle; if such
265 information is incomplete; or if FDA requests additional information to make its determination.
266
267 To assist FDA in evaluating the date of first licensure as described in section 351(k)(7)(C) of the
268 PHS Act, FDA suggests that sponsors provide the following information:
269
270   1. A list of all licensed biological products that are structurally related to the biological
271   product that is the subject of the 351(a) application being considered. This list should
272   include products that share some of the same principal molecular structural features of
273   the product being considered, but generally can be limited to products that affect the

---

[16] The Agency recommends, however, that any exclusivity request be placed specifically in the electronic common technical document (eCTD) Module 1.3.5.3 (the Exclusivity Claim section of Module 1, Administrative Information) of the application.

7

274   same molecular target.[17] Products that target different epitopes of the same molecular
275   target should be included. Where specific molecular targets have not been defined, this
276   list should include products that share the narrowest target that can be characterized.
277   This may be a pathway, cell type, tissue, or organ system. If this assessment results in
278   the conclusion that no product that has the same molecular target or shares some of the
279   same principal molecular structural features has been licensed, a sponsor should provide
280   an adequate justification to support the assertion that there are no previously licensed
281   products that are relevant for purposes of determining the date of first licensure.
282

283   2. Of those licensed biological products identified in item 1 above, a list of those for which
284   the sponsor or one of its affiliates, including any licensors, predecessors in interest, or
285   related entities,[18] are the current or previous license holder.
286

287   3. Description of the structural differences between the proposed product and any products
288   identified in item 2 above. For protein products, this should include, but is not limited to,
289   changes in amino acid sequence, differences due to post-translational events, infidelity of
290   translation or transcription, differences in glycosylation patterns or tertiary structure, and
291   differences in biological activities.[19]
292

293   4. Evidence of the change in safety, purity, and/or potency between the proposed product
294   and any products identified in item 2 above. This should include, but is not limited to, a
295   description of how the structural differences identified in item 3 above relate to changes
296   in safety, purity, and/or potency.
297

298   Any other information and data that would assist the FDA in making a determination regarding
299   the date of first licensure for a 351(a) application should also be included.
300

301   **V.   PUBLICATION OF DECISION**
302

303   FDA is reviewing options for making information publicly available regarding reference product
304   exclusivity and dates of first licensure. Once a method is determined, plans to communicate this
305   information will be provided on FDA's Web site.

---

[17] See, for example, 21 CFR 316.3(b)(13) and its definition of "same drug" as it relates to orphan drug products and the description of structural differences of large molecule drug products.

[18] In compiling this list, "predecessor in interest," "licensor," and "other related entity" should be defined as described in section III.A of this guidance.

[19] Biological activities can be an important measure of structural changes.

8

APPENDIX D2

Citizen Petitions and Petitions for Stay of Action Subject to Section 505(q) of the Federal Food, Drug, and Cosmetic Act

Citizen Petitions and Petitions for Stay of Action Subject to Section 505(q) of the Federal Food, Drug, and Cosmetic Act
Guidance for Industry

DRAFT GUIDANCE

This guidance document is being distributed for comment purposes only.

Comments and suggestions regarding this draft document should be submitted within 60 days of publication in the *Federal Register* of the notice announcing the availability of the draft guidance. Submit electronic comments to https://www.regulations.gov. Submit written comments to the Dockets Management Staff (HFA-305), Food and Drug Administration, 5630 Fishers Lane, Rm. 1061, Rockville, MD 20852. All comments should be identified with the docket number listed in the notice of availability that publishes in the *Federal Register*.

For questions regarding this draft document, contact (CDER) Kim Thomas 301-796-3601.

U.S. Department of Health and Human Services
Food and Drug Administration
Center for Drug Evaluation and Research (CDER)

October 2018
Procedural

Revision 2

Citizen Petitions and Petitions for Stay of Action Subject to Section 505(q) of the Federal Food, Drug, and Cosmetic Act
Guidance for Industry

Additional copies are available from:
Office of Communications, Division of Drug Information
Center for Drug Evaluation and Research
Food and Drug Administration
10001 New Hampshire Ave., Hillandale Bldg., 4th Floor
Silver Spring, MD 20993-0002
Phone: 855-543-3784 or 301-796-3400; Fax: 301-431-6353
Email: druginfo@fda.hhs.gov
http://www.fda.gov/Drugs/GuidanceComplianceRegulatoryInformation/Guidances/default.htm

U.S. Department of Health and Human Services
Food and Drug Administration
Center for Drug Evaluation and Research (CDER)

October 2018
Procedural

Revision 2

Contains Nonbinding Recommendations
Draft — Not for Implementation
TABLE OF CONTENTS

I. INTRODUCTION 1

II. BACKGROUND 2

 A. Scope of Section 505(q) 2

 B. Determination of Delay Necessary To Protect the Public Health 3

 C. Certification and Verification 3

 D. Final Agency Action 3

 E. Judicial Review 4

 F. Exceptions and Reporting 4

III. DISCUSSION 4

 A. How Does FDA Determine if Section 505(q) Applies to a Particular Petition? 5

  1. Petition Submitted on or After September 27, 2007, or July 9, 2012 5

  2. Petition Submitted in Writing and Pursuant to § 10.30 or 10.35 6

  3. ANDA, 505(b)(2) Application, or 351(k) Application Is Pending at the Time the Petition Is
   Submitted and the Application's User Fee Goal Date Is On or Before the 150-day Deadline for
   Final Agency Action on the Petition 7

  4. Petition Requests an Action That Could Delay Approval of a Pending ANDA, 505(b)(2)
   Application, or 351(k) Application 8

  5. Petition Does Not Fall Within Any of the Exceptions Described in Section 505(q)(4) 8

 B. How Does FDA Determine if a Petition Would Delay Approval of an ANDA, 505(b)(2)

  Application, or 351(k) Application? 8

 C. How Does FDA Apply the Certification Requirements in Section 505(q)(1)(H)? 10

  1. Determination of Whether a Certification Is Complete 11

  2. What a Petitioner Should Do if a Certification Is Deficient 12

 D. How Does FDA Apply the Verification Requirements in Section 505(q)(1)(I)? 13

 E. What Is the Relationship Between the Review of Petitions Under Section 505(q) and the

  Review of ANDAs, 505(b)(2) Applications, and 351(k) Applications for Which the Agency

  Has Not Yet Made a Final Decision on Approvability? 14

 F. What Considerations May Suggest That a Petition Was Submitted for the Primary Purpose

  of Delaying Approval of an Application? 15

i

1 **Citizen Petitions and Petitions for Stay of Action Subject to**
2 **Section 505(q) of the Federal Food, Drug, and Cosmetic Act**
3 **Guidance for Industry[1]**
4
5

6
7 This draft guidance, when finalized, will represent the current thinking of the Food and Drug
8 Administration (FDA or Agency) on this topic. It does not establish any rights for any person and is not
9 binding on FDA or the public. You can use an alternative approach if it satisfies the requirements of the
10 applicable statutes and regulations. To discuss an alternative approach, contact the FDA staff responsible
11 for this guidance as listed on the title page.
12

13
14
15 **I. INTRODUCTION**
16
17 This guidance provides information regarding FDA's current thinking on interpreting section
18 505(q) of the Federal Food, Drug, and Cosmetic Act (FD&C Act). Section 505(q) of the FD&C
19 Act[2] governs certain citizen petitions and petitions for stay of Agency action that request that
20 FDA take any form of action related to a pending application described in section 505(b)(2) or
21 505(j) of the FD&C Act[3] or a pending application for licensure of a biological product as
22 biosimilar or interchangeable that is submitted under section 351(k) of the Public Health Service
23 Act (PHS Act).[4]
24
25 This guidance describes FDA's interpretation of section 505(q) regarding how the Agency
26 determines if (1) the provisions of section 505(q) addressing the treatment of citizen petitions
27 and petitions for stay of Agency action (collectively, petitions) apply to a particular petition and
28 (2) a petition would delay approval of a pending abbreviated new drug application (ANDA),
29 505(b)(2) application, or 351(k) application. This guidance also describes how FDA interprets
30 the provisions of section 505(q) requiring that (1) a petition include a certification and (2)
31 supplemental information or comments to a petition include a verification. It also addresses the
32 relationship between the review of petitions and pending ANDAs, 505(b)(2) applications, and
33 351(k) applications for which the Agency has not yet made a decision on approvability.
34
35 This guidance revises the guidance for industry *Citizen Petitions and Petitions for Stay of Action*
36 *Subject to Section 505(q) of the Federal Food, Drug, and Cosmetic Act* issued in November

---

[1] This guidance has been prepared by the Office of Regulatory Policy in the Center for Drug Evaluation and Research (CDER) at the Food and Drug Administration.
[2] 21 U.S.C. 355(q). For brevity, in this guidance, references to section 505(q) of the FD&C Act are cited as section 505(q).
[3] 21 U.S.C. 355(b)(2) and (j). In this guidance, an application described in section 505(b)(2) of the FD&C Act is referred to as a 505(b)(2) application and an application submitted under section 505(j) of the FD&C Act is referred to as an abbreviated new drug application (ANDA).
[4] 42 U.S.C. 262(k). In this guidance, an application submitted under section 351(k) of the PHS Act is referred to as a 351(k) application.

1

37   2014. This revision updates the November 2014 guidance to account for recent regulatory
38   changes to add 21 CFR 10.31[5] to FDA's regulations and modify 10.30 and 10.35. The revision
39   also describes a change in FDA's current thinking on what constitutes a 505(q) petition. In
40   addition, FDA is revising this guidance to describe some of the considerations that FDA will take
41   into account in determining whether a petition is submitted with the primary purpose of delaying
42   the approval of an application under section 505(q)(1)(E).
43
44   In general, FDA's guidance documents do not establish legally enforceable responsibilities.
45   Instead, guidances describe the Agency's current thinking on a topic and should be viewed only
46   as recommendations, unless specific regulatory or statutory requirements are cited. The use of
47   the word *should* in Agency guidances means that something is suggested or recommended, but
48   not required.
49
50
51   **II.   BACKGROUND**
52
53   The Food and Drug Administration Amendments Act of 2007 (FDAAA) was enacted on
54   September 27, 2007. Section 914 of Title IX of FDAAA took effect on the date of enactment
55   and amended section 505 of the FD&C Act by adding a new subsection (q).[6]
56
57   Section 505(q), as enacted by FDAAA, applied to certain petitions that request that FDA take
58   any form of action related to a pending ANDA or 505(b)(2) application and governs the manner
59   in which these petitions are treated.
60
61   The Food and Drug Administration Safety and Innovation Act (FDASIA) was enacted on July 9,
62   2012.[7] Section 1135 of FDASIA amended section 505(q) of the FD&C Act in two ways. First,
63   it shortened from 180 days to 150 days FDA's deadline for final Agency action on the petitions
64   subject to section 505(q). Second, with the exceptions noted below, it expanded the scope of
65   section 505(q) to include certain petitions related to 351(k) applications.
66
67   The provisions of section 505(q) are described in greater detail below.
68
69   **A.   Scope of Section 505(q)**
70
71   Section 505(q)(1)(A), together with section 505(q)(5), describes the general scope of section
72   505(q). Section 505(q)(1)(A) provides:
73
74   The Secretary shall not delay approval of a pending application submitted under
75   subsection (b)(2) or (j) of this section or section 351(k) of the Public Health Service Act
76   because of any request to take any form of action relating to the application, either before
77   or during consideration of the request, unless–
78

---

[5] On Nov. 8, 2016, FDA issued a final rule amending certain regulations relating to citizen petitions, petitions for
stay of action, and the submission of documents to FDA (81 FR 78500).
[6] Pub.L. 110-85, 121 Stat. 823 (as amended by Pub.L. 110-316, 122 Stat. 3509).
[7] Pub.L. 112-144, 126 Stat. 993.

79   (i) the request is in writing and is a petition submitted to the Secretary pursuant
80   to section 10.30 or 10.35 of title 21, Code of Federal Regulations (or any
81   successor regulations); and
82   (ii) the Secretary determines, upon reviewing the petition, that a delay is
83   necessary to protect the public health.
84
85   In section 505(q)(5), the term *application* is defined as an application submitted under section
86   505(b)(2) or 505(j) of the FD&C Act or 351(k) of the PHS Act and the term *petition* is defined as
87   a request described in 505(q)(1)(A)(i).
88
89   **B.**   **Determination of Delay Necessary To Protect the Public Health**
90
91   If FDA determines that a delay of approval of an ANDA, 505(b)(2) application, or 351(k)
92   application is necessary to protect the public health, FDA is required to provide to the applicant
93   not later than 30 days after making the determination:
94
95   • Notification that the determination has been made,
96   • If applicable, any clarification or additional data that the applicant should submit to
97   the petition docket to allow FDA to review the petition promptly, and
98   • A brief summary of the specific substantive issues raised in the petition which form
99   the basis of the determination.[8]
100
101   At FDA's discretion, the information is to be conveyed by either a document or a meeting with
102   the applicant.[9] The information conveyed as part of the notification is to be considered part of
103   the application and subject to the disclosure requirements applicable to information in such
104   application.[10]
105
106   **C.**   **Certification and Verification**
107
108   Under section 505(q)(1)(H), FDA may not consider a petition for review unless the petition is in
109   writing and signed and contains a certification that is specified in that section. In addition, FDA
110   may not accept for review any supplemental information or comments on a petition unless the
111   submission is in writing and signed and contains a specific verification.[11]
112
113   **D.**   **Final Agency Action**
114
115   Section 505(q)(1)(F) governs the timeframe for final Agency action on a petition. Under this
116   provision, FDA shall take final Agency action on a petition not later than 150 days after the date
117   on which the petition is submitted. The 150-day period is not to be extended for any reason,
118   including any determination made under section 505(q)(1)(A) regarding delay of approval of an
119   application, the submission of comments or supplemental information, or the consent of the
120   petitioner.

---

[8] Section 505(q)(1)(B).
[9] Section 505(q)(1)(C).
[10] Section 505(q)(1)(D).
[11] Section 505(q)(1)(I).

Contains Nonbinding Recommendations

Draft — Not for Implementation

121
122 Under section 505(q)(1)(E), FDA may deny a petition at any point if the Agency determines that
123 a petition or a supplement to the petition was submitted with the primary purpose of delaying the
124 approval of an application and the petition does not on its face raise valid scientific or regulatory
125 issues.[12] As discussed further in section III.F of this guidance, section 505(q)(1)(E) also
126 provides that FDA may issue guidance to describe the factors that will be used to determine
127 whether a petition is submitted with the primary purpose of delaying the approval of an
128 application.
129
130 **E.   Judicial Review**
131
132 Section 505(q)(2) governs judicial review of final Agency action. Section 505(q)(2) does not
133 apply to a petition addressing issues concerning a 351(k) application.[13]
134
135 Under section 505(q)(2)(A), FDA shall be considered to have taken final Agency action on a
136 petition if FDA makes a final decision within the meaning of 21 CFR 10.45(d) during the 150-
137 day period or the 150-day period expires without FDA having made a final decision. Under
138 section 505(q)(2)(B), if a civil action is filed against the Secretary with respect to any issues
139 raised in the petition before final Agency action, a court shall dismiss the action without
140 prejudice for failure to exhaust administrative remedies. Section 505(q)(2)(C) describes the
141 information to be included in the administrative record.
142
143 **F.   Exceptions and Reporting**
144
145 Section 505(q)(4) exempts certain categories of petitions from the provisions of section 505(q)
146 — in particular, petitions relating to 180-day generic drug exclusivity under section
147 505(j)(5)(B)(iv) and petitions from a 505(b)(2), ANDA, or 351(k) applicant regarding FDA
148 actions with respect to that application. Section 505(q)(3) and section 914(b) of FDAAA also
149 provide for certain reporting requirements from FDA to Congress.
150
151
152 **III.   DISCUSSION**
153
154 As described in section II of this guidance, the provisions of section 505(q) addressing the
155 treatment of petitions apply only to certain petitions. These provisions include, for example, the
156 requirements that approval of an ANDA, 505(b)(2) application, or 351(k) application not be
157 delayed by a petition absent an Agency determination that a delay is necessary to protect the
158 public health, the provisions requiring final Agency action on the petition within 150 days of
159 submission, and the provisions requiring a certification or a verification.
160
161 We describe below how we determine:
162   • if the provisions of section 505(q) apply to a particular petition

---

[12] Section 505(q)(1)(E).
[13] Section 505(q)(4)(B).

4

163   •   if a petition would delay approval of a pending ANDA, 505(b)(2) application, or
164   351(k) application
165
166   We also describe how we interpret:
167   •   section 505(q)(1)(H) requiring that a petition include a certification
168   •   section 505(q)(1)(I) requiring that supplemental information or comments on a
169   petition include a verification
170   •   section 505(q)(1)(E) stating that the Agency may deny a petition or a supplement to a
171   petition that was submitted with the primary purpose of delaying approval of an
172   application and that does not on its face raise valid scientific or regulatory issues
173
174   We also describe the relationship between the review of petitions under section 505(q) and the
175   review of ANDAs, 505(b)(2) applications, and 351(k) applications for which the Agency has not
176   yet made a final decision on approvability.
177
178   **A.**   **How Does FDA Determine if Section 505(q) Applies to a Particular Petition?**
179
180   We interpret section 505(q) to apply to a petition only if the petition meets all of the
181   following:
182
183   •   The petition is submitted to FDA on or after September 27, 2007, (if the subject
184   matter of the petition relates to approval of an ANDA or 505(b)(2) application) or on
185   or after July 9, 2012, (if the subject matter of the petition relates to approval of a
186   351(k) application)
187   •   The petition is submitted in writing and pursuant to 21 CFR 10.30 or 10.35
188   •   An ANDA, 505(b)(2) application, or 351(k) application is pending at the time the
189   petition is submitted to FDA and the application's user fee goal date is on or before
190   the 150-day deadline for final Agency action on the petition
191   •   The petitioner requests an action that could delay approval of a pending ANDA,
192   505(b)(2) application, or 351(k) application
193   •   The petition does not fall within any of the exceptions described in section 505(q)(4)
194
195   We discuss each criterion in greater detail below.
196
197   *1.*   *Petition Submitted on or After September 27, 2007, or July 9, 2012*
198
199   Because section 914 of FDAAA became effective on September 27, 2007, we believe that the
200   provisions of section 505(q) only apply to petitions that are submitted on or after September 27,
201   2007 (if the subject matter of the petition relates to approval of an ANDA or 505(b)(2)
202   application). We do not believe that section 505(q) applies to any petitions that were submitted
203   before September 27, 2007, because section 505(q) does not state that it applies retroactively to
204   petitions submitted before the effective date. Likewise, we do not believe that section 505(q)
205   applies to any petitions whose subject matter relates to the approval of a 351(k) application if
206   those petitions were submitted before July 9, 2012, because section 505(q) does not state that it
207   applies retroactively to those petitions. In addition, either of these interpretations might impose a

5

208 statutory-day deadline for final Agency action on a petition after the deadline has already
209 passed.[14]
210
211 Even if section 505(q) were interpreted to apply retroactively, FDA would not be able to review
212 any petition submitted before the applicable date because those petitions would not contain the
213 required certification and, as explained in section III.C of this guidance, the statute does not
214 permit a petitioner to cure the deficiency by supplementing a petition to add the certification to
215 the petition.
216
217   2.   *Petition Submitted in Writing and Pursuant to § 10.30 or 10.35*
218
219 Under section 505(q) of the FD&C Act, a petition must be submitted in writing and pursuant to
220 § 10.30 or 10.35. Section 10.30 of our regulations describes FDA's general requirements for
221 submitting a citizen petition, and § 10.35 describes our requirements for submitting a request for
222 administrative stay of action. If these requirements are not met, we will not consider section
223 505(q) to apply to the petition.
224
225 We note that communications with the Agency regarding any issues with the potential to delay
226 the approval of an ANDA, 505(b)(2) application, or 351(k) application (regardless of whether
227 the communications are considered to be petitions subject to section 505(q)) are appropriately
228 submitted through the petition process pursuant to § 10.30 or 10.35 rather than as
229 correspondence to the new drug application (NDA), ANDA, 505(b)(2) application, 351(k)
230 application, or another process.[15] Similarly, any communications regarding a citizen petition
231 should be filed as comments in the appropriate docket, not to the NDA, ANDA, 505(b)(2)
232 application, or 351(k) application.
233
234 We also remind persons that they may not cross-reference or rely upon information that is not
235 included in the petition. Under §§ 10.30(b) and 10.35(b), petitions must be submitted in
236 accordance with 21 CFR 10.20. Section 10.20(c) requires that "[i]nformation referred to or
237 relied upon in a submission is to be included in full and may not be incorporated by reference,
238 unless previously submitted in the same proceeding." In addition, the certification required for
239 petitions subject to section 505(q) (described in section III.C of this guidance) and the
240 certification required for citizen petitions under § 10.30(b) require the petitioner to certify that
241 "this petition includes all information and views upon which the petition relies." A petition
242 therefore is required to include all information referred to or relied upon by the petitioner. In
243 addition, the petition should contain all information, both favorable and unfavorable, regarding
244 the petitioner's claims.
245

---

[14] A petition subject to 505(q) that was submitted on or after September 27, 2007, but before July 9, 2012, is subject to the 180-day deadline. A petition subject to section 505(q) that was submitted on or after July 9, 2012, is subject to the 150-day deadline.

[15] As discussed below, interested persons can express their views on issues related to bioequivalence for a drug product by submitting comments in response to a *Federal Register* notice regarding draft product-specific bioequivalence recommendations, instead of by submitting a petition concerning bioequivalence standards for a drug product.

246   3.   *ANDA, 505(b)(2) Application, or 351(k) Application Is Pending at the Time the*
247   *Petition Is Submitted and the Application's User Fee Goal Date Is On or Before*
248   *the 150-day Deadline for Final Agency Action on the Petition*

249

250   Section 505(q)(1)(A) describes the scope of section 505(q) (see section II of this guidance).
251   Section 505(q)(1)(A) specifically references pending applications and contemplates the
252   possibility that approval could be delayed by issues raised in a petition. Therefore, we are
253   implementing section 505(q) to apply only to petitions for which, at the time the petition is
254   submitted, at least one ANDA, 505(b)(2) application, or 351(k) application related to the subject
255   matter of the petition is pending[16] and at least one such application's user fee goal date is on or
256   before the 150-day deadline for final Agency action on the petition.[17]

257

258   If there is no related ANDA, 505(b)(2) application, or 351(k) application pending at the time that
259   the petition is submitted, then we will not consider the provisions of section 505(q) to apply to
260   the petition. Likewise, if there is a related ANDA, 505(b)(2) application, or 351(k) application
261   pending at the time that the petition is submitted but the applicable user fee goal date is after the
262   150-day deadline for final Agency action on the petition, then we will not consider the provisions
263   of section 505(q) to apply to the petition.[18] FDA has determined that this way of implementing
264   section 505(q) aligns with the public health mission of the new drug and generic drug review
265   programs and FDA's commitments under the Prescription Drug User Fee Act, the Generic Drug
266   User Fee Amendments, and the Biosimilar User Fee Act. In particular, the Agency believes that
267   implementation of the processes described in this guidance will align the timelines to review and
268   respond to petitions with the timelines for review of the applications themselves, which will
269   provide greater efficiency for both efforts while still ensuring that scientific and regulatory issues
270   raised in a petition are considered prior to ANDA, 505(b)(2) application, or 351(k) application

---

[16] Although the existence of a pending application generally is not made public by FDA, a potential petitioner may be aware of the existence of a pending ANDA or 505(b)(2) application because of (1) a paragraph IV patent notification, from the applicant to the NDA holder and the patent owner, stating that the application has been submitted and explaining the factual and legal bases for the applicant's opinion that the patent is invalid or not infringed (see section 505(b)(2)(B) and (j)(2)(B) of the FD&C Act); (2) a public announcement by the applicant disclosing the submission of the application; or (3) the tentative approval of an ANDA or 505(b)(2) application made public by FDA or the applicant. In addition, FDA's website identifies drug products for which the Agency has received an ANDA with a paragraph IV certification. A potential petitioner may be aware of the existence of a pending 351(k) application because of (1) patent information exchanged under provisions of section 351(l) of the PHS Act, (2) information made available from patent infringement proceedings between a biologics license application holder and 351(k) applicant, (3) a public announcement by the applicant disclosing the submission of the application, or (4) the tentative approval of a 351(k) application made public by FDA or the applicant.

[17] User fee goal dates reflect commitments made with respect to the Prescription Drug User Fee Act, Pub. L. 102-571 (as amended by Pub. L. 115-52, Tit. I) for 505(b)(2) applications; the Generic Drug User Fee Amendments, Pub. L. 112-144, Tit. III (as amended by Pub. L. 115-52, Tit. III) for ANDAs; and the Biosimilar User Fee Act, Pub. L. 112-144, Tit. IV (as amended by Pub. L. 115-52, Tit. IV) for 351(k) applications.

[18] If we determine that the provisions of section 505(q) do not apply to a particular petition (e.g., if an application is pending but the applicable user fee goal is after the 150-day deadline for final Agency action on the petition), we intend to address the issues raised in the petition in a timely manner so that we are not delayed in taking action on pending applications. See the Generic Drug User Fee Amendments Reauthorization Performance Goals and Program Enhancements Fiscal Years 2018-2022, available at http://www.fda.gov/downloads/ForIndustry/UserFees/GenericDrugUserFees/UCM525234.pdf.

7

271   approval. This will help ensure Agency experts do not have to consider petitions separately from
272   application review and therefore prematurely.
273
274   We also believe our approach is appropriate to ensure the fair and orderly implementation of
275   section 505(q). The evaluation of whether a related ANDA, 505(b)(2) application, or 351(k)
276   application is pending (and thus the evaluation of whether a petition is subject to the provisions
277   of section 505(q)) will be made at the time that the petition is submitted. If we were to take a
278   "rolling" evaluation approach, the status of the petition could change at any time from (1) a
279   petition that is not subject to section 505(q) to one that is subject to section 505(q) should a
280   related ANDA, 505(b)(2) application, or 351(k) application be submitted before we have taken
281   final Agency action on the petition or (2) a petition that is subject to section 505(q) to one that is
282   not subject to section 505(q) if the related ANDA(s), 505(b)(2) application(s), or 351(k)
283   application(s) are subsequently withdrawn or approved and there are no longer any related
284   applications pending. Such a change in the status of the petition would disrupt the orderly
285   application of the provisions of section 505(q) and the Agency's processing of the petition and
286   also could prejudice petitioners and commenters.
287
288   4.   *Petition Requests an Action That Could Delay Approval of a Pending ANDA,*
289   *505(b)(2) Application, or 351(k) Application*
290
291   As noted, section 505(q)(1)(A) contemplates the possibility that approval of a pending ANDA,
292   505(b)(2) application, or 351(k) application could be delayed by issues raised in the petition.
293   Therefore, we are implementing section 505(q) by applying it only to petitions that request an
294   action that could delay approval of a pending ANDA, 505(b)(2) application, or 351(k)
295   application. If the action requested by the petition does not have the potential to delay approval
296   of the pending application under any reasonable theory, we will not consider the provisions of
297   section 505(q) to apply to the petition.
298
299   5.   *Petition Does Not Fall Within Any of the Exceptions Described in Section*
300   *505(q)(4)*
301
302   Section 505(q)(4) provides that section 505(q) will not apply to any petitions that:
303
304   •   relate solely to the timing of approval of an application pursuant to the 180-day
305   exclusivity provision at section 505(j)(5)(B)(iv) of the FD&C Act, or
306   •   are from the applicant of the ANDA, 505(b)(2) application, or 351(k) application and
307   seek only to have FDA take or refrain from taking any action with respect to that
308   application.
309
310   If either of these exceptions applies, we will not consider the provisions of section 505(q) to
311   apply to the petition.
312
313   **B.   How Does FDA Determine if a Petition Would Delay Approval of an ANDA,**
314   **505(b)(2) Application, or 351(k) Application?**
315
316   Under section 505(q)(1)(A), FDA shall not delay approval of an ANDA, 505(b)(2) application,
317   or 351(k) application because of a petition unless the Agency determines that a delay is

318   necessary to protect the public health. To implement this provision, first we determine if the
319   provisions of section 505(q) apply to the petition based on the considerations described in
320   section III.A of this guidance. If the provisions apply, we then determine if the petition may be
321   summarily denied as described in section 505(q)(1)(E) (which allows denial of a petition that
322   was submitted with the primary purpose of delaying approval of an application and does not on
323   its face raise valid scientific or regulatory issues).[19]
324
325   If we do not find that the petition may be summarily denied, we will determine if the petition
326   would be the cause of a delay in an approval of an ANDA, 505(b)(2) application, or 351(k)
327   application by using a *but for* test. In other words, would the ANDA, 505(b)(2) application, or
328   351(k) application be ready for approval but for the issues raised by the petition?
329

330   •   If, regardless of the petition, the ANDA, 505(b)(2) application, or 351(k) application
331   would not be ready for approval within the 150-day period for final Agency action on
332   the petition (e.g., because the applicant receives a complete response letter during the
333   150-day period), then the petition would not delay the approval, and section
334   505(q)(1)(A) would not be implicated.
335

336   •   If the ANDA, 505(b)(2) application, or 351(k) application would be ready for
337   approval but for the resolution of the issues raised in the petition within the 150-day
338   period for final Agency action on the petition, then section 505(q)(1)(A) would be
339   implicated, and we would next determine if a delay of approval is necessary to protect
340   the public health.
341

342   We determine if a delay of approval is necessary to protect the public health based on our
343   preliminary evaluation of the issues raised in the petition. The Agency considers the following
344   scenario:
345

346   If the application were to be approved before the Agency completed the
347   substantive review of the issues in the petition and, after further review, the
348   Agency concluded that the petitioner's arguments against approval were
349   meritorious, could the presence on the market of drug products that did not meet
350   the requirements for approval identified by the petitioner negatively affect the
351   public health?
352

353   If, after undertaking this analysis, we conclude that the public health could be negatively affected
354   under these circumstances, the Agency will conclude that a delay "is necessary to protect the
355   public health" and will delay approval of the pending application until the issues raised in the
356   petition are resolved. Issues that could implicate the public health include, for example, (1)
357   whether a proposed generic drug product is bioequivalent to the reference listed drug or (2)
358   whether an indication can be safely omitted from the labeling because that indication is protected
359   by a patent.
360

---

[19] See section III.F of this guidance.

9

361 If we determine that a delay of approval of an application is necessary to protect the public
362 health, we will notify the applicant as required by section 505(q)(1)(B) and (C) of the FD&C
363 Act. Under these provisions, we are required to provide the following information to the
364 applicant not later than 30 days after making the determination:

365 • Notification that the determination has been made,
366 • If applicable, any clarification or additional data that the applicant should submit to
367   the petition docket to allow FDA to review the petition promptly, and
368 • A brief summary of the specific substantive issues raised in the petition which form
369   the basis of the determination.
370

371 We will convey this information to the applicant by either a letter or a meeting with the
372 applicant.[20] As provided in section 505(q)(1)(D), we will consider the information conveyed in
373 the notification to be part of the application and subject to the disclosure requirements applicable
374 to information in such application. We do not intend to notify the petitioner if a determination
375 has been made that a delay in approval of an application is necessary to protect the public health
376 because the provisions of section 505(q) do not require such a notification to the petitioner. We
377 will resolve any public health issues before approving the application. If we, in the course of
378 considering the petition, later determine that a delay of approval is no longer necessary to protect
379 the public health, we will proceed with approving the application.
380

381 Regardless of whether we determine that a delay of approval of an application is or is not
382 necessary to protect the public health, we will continue to consider the 150-day period for final
383 Agency action under section 505(q)(1)(F) to apply to the petition.
384

385 **C.   How Does FDA Apply the Certification Requirements in Section 505(q)(1)(H)?**
386

387 Section 505(q)(1)(H) of the FD&C Act provides that FDA shall not consider a petition for
388 review unless the petition is in writing and signed and contains the following certification:
389

390 I certify that, to my best knowledge and belief: (a) this petition includes all information
391 and views upon which the petition relies; (b) this petition includes representative data
392 and/or information known to the petitioner which are unfavorable to the petition; and (c) I
393 have taken reasonable steps to ensure that any representative data and/or information
394 which are unfavorable to the petition were disclosed to me. I further certify that the
395 information upon which I have based the action requested herein first became known to
396 the party on whose behalf this petition is submitted on or about the following date:
397 _____[in the blank space, provide the date on which such information first became
398 known to such party]. If I received or expect to receive payments, including cash and
399 other forms of consideration, to file this information or its contents, I received or expect
400 to receive those payments from the following persons or organizations: _____ [in the
401 blank space, provide the names of such persons or organizations]. I verify under penalty
402 of perjury that the foregoing is true and correct as of the date of the submission of this
403 petition.
404

---

[20] See section 505(q)(1)(C).

405 In addition, 21 CFR 10.31 requires certain citizen petitions and petitions for stay of action,
406 including those petitions subject to section 505(q), to contain this certification. Therefore, all
407 petitions that fall within the scope of section 505(q) must be in writing and signed and contain
408 the complete 505(q) certification to be considered for review by FDA.[21] If, based on the
409 considerations described in section II.A of this guidance, section 505(q) applies to the petition,
410 but the petition is not in writing or signed, or does not contain the complete certification, we will
411 not review the petition.
412
413   *1. Determination of Whether a Certification Is Complete*
414
415 As part of our determination of whether a petition contains the complete 505(q) certification, we
416 will evaluate whether (1) the language of the certification in the petition exactly mirrors the
417 language provided in section 505(q) and (2) the petitioner provided a date on which the
418 information first became known to the party on whose behalf the petition is submitted.[22]
419 Because section 505(q) sets forth the exact words to be used in the certification, we will consider
420 a certification to be deficient if every word in the petitioner's certification does not match every
421 word of the certification provided in section 505(q). In other words, the petitioner's certification
422 must correspond verbatim to the certification in section 505(q). For example, if, rather than
423 using the phrase "first became known to the party on whose behalf this petition is submitted," the
424 petitioner substitutes the phrase "first became known to me," we will consider the certification to
425 be deficient. We believe this interpretation is mandated by the statutory language because
426 section 505(q) specifies the exact text of the certification.
427
428 Section 505(q) also requires that the petitioner provide in the certification the date on or about
429 which the information first became known to the party. Section 505(q) includes a blank space in
430 the certification for that information. We consider a "date" to include a month, day, and year.
431 Therefore, we will consider a certification to be deficient if the petitioner has not provided the
432 month, day, and year on or about which the information first became known to the party on
433 whose behalf the petition is submitted. For example, if the petitioner provides "May 2010" as
434 the date in the certification, we would consider the certification to be deficient. The text of the
435 certification provided in section 505(q) includes a qualification that the petitioner learned of the
436 information "on or about the following date." Therefore, we believe the certification would
437 accommodate instances in which a petitioner may not know the exact date on which it became
438 aware of the information. To the extent that a petitioner believes further explanation of the date
439 is needed, we believe that the blank space in the certification allows for the insertion of
440 additional information. In addition, there may be instances in which different types of
441 information became known to the petitioner over a period of time. In that case, the petitioner
442 should provide each estimated relevant date and identify the information associated with the
443 particular date. We caution that when adding information, the petitioner should ensure that the
444 words of the certification (except for what is provided in the blank space) continue to exactly
445 match the words of the certification as provided by section 505(q).

---

[21] See section 505(q)(1)(H) and 21 CFR 10.31. Please note that under section 10.31(a)(1), certification is required for every petition that requests any form of action that could, if taken, delay approval of one of the types of applications described therein, regardless of whether that petition is ultimately found to be subject to the statutory deadline in section 505(q)(1)(F).
[22] See also 21 CFR 10.31.

11

446
447 For example, a certification that we would consider to be complete and acceptable could include
448 additional information explaining the petitioner's specified date or dates as follows:
449
450   I certify that, to my best knowledge and belief: (a) this petition includes all information
451   and views upon which the petition relies; (b) this petition includes representative data
452   and/or information known to the petitioner which are unfavorable to the petition; and (c) I
453   have taken reasonable steps to ensure that any representative data and/or information
454   which are unfavorable to the petition were disclosed to me. I further certify that the
455   information upon which I have based the action requested herein first became known to
456   the party on whose behalf this petition is submitted on or about the following date:
457   September 21, 1995 (information about bioavailability issues with the innovator drug);
458   November 12, 2009 (publication of a draft bioequivalence guidance for the drug); March
459   30, 2010 (information that an ANDA had been submitted). If I received or expect to
460   receive payments, including cash and other forms of consideration, to file this
461   information or its contents, I received or expect to receive those payments from the
462   following persons or organizations: Company A. I verify under penalty of perjury that
463   the foregoing is true and correct as of the date of the submission of this petition.
464
465   2.   *What a Petitioner Should Do if a Certification Is Deficient*
466
467 We also interpret section 505(q)(1)(H) to require that the certification be included in the original
468 petition. Section 505(q)(1)(H) refers to the "petition" as the subject document that must contain
469 the certification. Because sections 505(q)(1)(E) and 505(q)(1)(I) distinguish between petitions
470 and supplements to petitions,[23] the reference to a petition in section 505(q)(1)(H) refers only to
471 the original petition and not to a supplement. Therefore, if a petition is missing the complete
472 certification, we will not permit a petitioner to cure the deficiency by submitting a supplement to
473 add the certification to the petition.
474
475 If a petitioner has submitted a petition that is missing the required certification but is otherwise
476 within the scope of section 505(q) and the petitioner would like FDA to review the petition, the
477 petitioner should (1) submit a letter withdrawing the deficient petition pursuant to § 10.30(g) and
478 (2) submit a new petition that contains the certification. In this case, the provisions of section
479 505(q) governing the treatment of petitions will apply only to the new petition that includes the
480 required certification because we cannot review the deficient petition under section
481 505(q)(1)(H). In particular, we consider the 150-day timeframe for FDA to take final Agency
482 action on the petition to begin from the date of submission of the new, complete petition and not
483 the original, deficient petition.
484
485 FDA will not review a petition that is subject to section 505(q) but is missing the required
486 certification. Under 21 CFR 10.31(c), all petitioners raising issues that could delay the approval
487 of a possible ANDA, 505(b)(2) application, or 351(k) application must include the
488 certification in their petitions to ensure FDA consideration. Although we may contact a
489 petitioner to notify him or her of a missing or deficient certification, we note that it is the

---

[23] Section 505(q)(1)(I) requires that supplemental information include a verification as described in section III.D of this guidance.

490   responsibility of the petitioner to ensure that its petition complies with the applicable
491   requirements of section 505(q), as well as all other applicable statutory and regulatory
492   requirements.
493
494   **D.   How Does FDA Apply the Verification Requirements in Section 505(q)(1)(I)?**
495
496   Section 505(q)(1)(I) provides that FDA shall not accept for review any supplemental information
497   or comments on a petition unless the supplemental information or comments are in writing,
498   signed, and contain the following verification:
499
500   I certify that, to my best knowledge and belief: (a) I have not intentionally delayed
501   submission of this document or its contents; and (b) the information upon which I have
502   based the action requested herein first became known to me on or about _____ [in
503   the blank space, provide the date on which such information first became known to such
504   party]. If I received or expect to receive payments, including cash and other forms of
505   consideration, to file this information or its contents, I received or expect to receive those
506   payments from the following persons or organizations: _____ [in the blank space,
507   provide the names of such persons or organizations]. I verify under penalty of perjury
508   that the foregoing is true and correct as of the date of the submission of this petition.
509
510   Section 505(q)(1)(I) applies to any supplemental information or comments that are submitted to
511   a petition that is subject to section 505(q). If any such supplemental information or comments
512   do not include the required verification, FDA will not review the submission.
513
514   In addition, 21 CFR 10.31 requires supplemental information or comments to certain citizen
515   petitions and petitions for stay of action, including those petitions subject to section 505(q), to
516   contain this verification. However, as explained in the preamble to the final rule enacting 21
517   CFR 10.31 (81 FR 78500, Nov. 8, 2016), the language of the verification included in the
518   regulation contains one minor technical correction to the language of the verification set out in
519   the statute. We changed "I verify under penalty of perjury that the foregoing is true and correct
520   as of the date of the submission of this *petition*" to "I verify under penalty of perjury that the
521   foregoing is true and correct as of the date of the submission of this *document*" (emphasis
522   added).
523
524   We will consider a verification to be deficient if it does not exactly mirror the words of the
525   verification either in section 505(q)(1)(I) of the FD&C Act or 21 CFR 10.31(d). Because the
526   statute specifies the word "petition" and the regulation specifies the word "document," we will
527   accept either "petition" or "document" in the last sentence of the verification.
528
529   As with our approach to the certification as explained in section III.C of this guidance, we also
530   will consider a verification to be deficient if the petitioner or commenter does not provide a
531   month, day, and year for the "date" in the verification.
532
533   If a petitioner or commenter has submitted supplemental information or comments without the
534   required verification or with an incomplete verification and the petitioner or commenter would
535   like FDA to review the submission, the petitioner or commenter should resubmit the
536   supplemental information or comments with the required verification to FDA.
537

13

538 FDA will not review any supplemental information or comments to petitions that are subject to
539 section 505(q) if the supplemental information or comments are missing the required
540 verification.[24] All of these petitioners or commenters must include the verification in their
541 supplemental information or comments to a petition to ensure FDA consideration. Petitioners
542 and commenters should not rely on FDA reviewers to notify them that their supplements or
543 comments will not be reviewed because of a missing or deficient verification. In some instances,
544 FDA receives numerous supplements and comments in a docket, and it would be
545 administratively burdensome to monitor all the dockets for 505(q) petitions and notify
546 commenters about the statutory requirement. It is the responsibility of petitioners and
547 commenters to ensure that their supplemental information or comments comply with the
548 applicable requirements of section 505(q), as well as all other applicable statutory and regulatory
549 requirements.
550
551 E. **What Is the Relationship Between the Review of Petitions Under Section 505(q) and**
552 **the Review of ANDAs, 505(b)(2) Applications, and 351(k) Applications for Which**
553 **the Agency Has Not Yet Made a Final Decision on Approvability?**
554
555 A petition may request that FDA take an action related to a specific aspect of a pending ANDA,
556 505(b)(2) application, or 351(k) application for which the Agency will not have made a final
557 decision regarding approvability by the date that the petition response is due. As described in
558 section II.D of this guidance, section 505(q)(1)(F) requires FDA to take final Agency action on a
559 petition within 150 days of submission. The review of applications that may be affected by the
560 petition is governed by a separate review process, which will not necessarily be completed by the
561 date the petition response is due.[25] If a petition requests that the Agency take an action related to
562 a specific aspect of a pending application, we will consider the review status of the affected
563 application(s) in determining how it would be appropriate for the Agency to respond to the
564 request to take the action requested in the petition within the 150-day timeframe.
565
566 The provisions in section 505 of the FD&C Act and FDA's regulations at 21 CFR part 314
567 establish certain procedures by which the Agency reviews an NDA or ANDA and notifies an
568 applicant if it determines that an application is approved (§ 314.105) or may not be approved
569 (section 505(c) and 505(j); §§ 314.125 and 314.127), or identifies the deficiencies in the
570 application and the steps an applicant may take to respond to the deficiencies (§ 314.110). In
571 addition, the statute and regulations describe a specific process through which an applicant
572 whose application the Agency has found not to meet the requirements for approval may
573 challenge the Agency's determination (section 505(c)(1)(B) and (d), 505(j)(5)(E); § 314.200).
574 Under this process, the Agency must give the applicant notice of an opportunity for a hearing on
575 whether the application is approvable, with a specific timeframe and process should the applicant
576 request such a hearing. These procedures ensure that applicants have an adequate opportunity to
577 challenge a finding by the Agency that a product does not meet the requirements for approval.
578

---

[24] See section 505(q)(1)(I) and 21 CFR 10.31(d).
[25] Even though the application will have a user fee goal date that falls on or before the 150 days for FDA to take
final Agency action on the related petition, the action on the user fee goal date may be a complete response rather
than an approval.

14

579   By contrast, responses to petitions, including petitions subject to section 505(q), constitute final
580   Agency action and are subject to immediate review by the courts, subject to the exception stated
581   in section II.E of this guidance. They therefore carry with them none of the procedural rights for
582   the affected applicants that attach to a decision to deny approval of an application. If we were to
583   respond substantively to a petitioner's request regarding the approvability of a certain aspect of a
584   pending application before we have taken a final action on the approvability of the application as
585   a whole, such response could interfere with the statutory and regulatory scheme governing the
586   review of applications and related procedural rights of applicants.[26] There is no evidence that in
587   enacting section 505(q), Congress intended to limit applicants' procedural rights by requiring
588   that the Agency make decisions that constitute final Agency action on the approvability of
589   specific aspects of a pending application (e.g., the acceptability of a proposed trade name,
590   specific claims proposed in a drug product's labeling) on a piecemeal basis outside of the process
591   established under the FD&C Act and regulations.[27]
592
593   In light of these considerations, we do not interpret section 505(q) to require a substantive final
594   Agency decision within 150 days on the approvability of a specific aspect of a pending
595   application. In particular, we do not interpret section 505(q) to require such a decision when a
596   final decision on the approvability of the application as a whole has not yet been made and when
597   rendering such a decision could deprive an applicant of procedural rights established by statute
598   and regulations. In such a situation, as described in the preceding sentence we would expect in
599   the ordinary course to deny a petition without comment on the substantive approval issue.
600
601   **F.   What Considerations May Suggest That a Petition Was Submitted for the Primary**
602   **Purpose of Delaying Approval of an Application?**
603
604   Section 505(q)(1)(E) provides that FDA may issue guidance to describe the considerations that
605   will be used to determine whether a petition is submitted with the primary purpose of delaying
606   the approval of an application. Although each case is unique, the following are some of the
607   considerations that FDA expects to take into account in determining whether a petition has been
608   submitted with the primary purpose of delaying an application as contemplated by section
609   505(q)(1)(E) (this list is not intended to be exhaustive and in any given case no single factor may
610   be outcome determinative):
611

---

[26] We also note that under applicable statutory and regulatory provisions, we are generally prohibited from disclosing information regarding applications that have not yet been approved. Depending upon the nature and specificity of a petition, these limitations on disclosure also may circumscribe the Agency's ability to respond substantively to issues raised in a petition that affect a pending application.

[27] In the past, we have responded to requests related to general standards for approval (e.g., bioequivalence criteria for generic drug products) that may pertain to one or more pending drug applications, without commenting on the approvability of any particular aspect of a specific pending application. We distinguish our approach of responding to petitions that involve general policies or standards for approval of a drug application from our approach described above, which applies to petitions that involve narrow issues of approvability of a specific aspect or aspects of a pending application or those in which our review of a given application would inform our decisions regarding the sufficiency of the specific data and information needed for approval. We will continue to evaluate each citizen petition on a case-by-case basis with respect to the appropriateness of responding to the petitioner's requests vis-à-vis any pending applications.

612 • Submission of a petition where it appears, based on the date that relevant information
613   relied upon in the petition became known to the petitioner (or reasonably should have
614   been known to the petitioner), that the petitioner has taken an unreasonable length of time
615   to submit the petition
616 • Submission of multiple and/or serial petitions raising issues that reasonably could have
617   been known to the petitioner at the time of submission of the earlier petition or petitions
618 • Submission of a petition close in time to a known, first date upon which an ANDA,
619   505(b)(2) application, or 351(k) application could be approved (e.g., submission close in
620   time to the expiration of a blocking patent or exclusivity)
621 • Submission of a petition without any data or information in support of the scientific
622   positions set forth in the petition
623 • Submission of a petition raising the same or substantially similar issues as a prior petition
624   to which FDA has already substantively responded, particularly where the subsequent
625   submission closely follows in time the earlier response
626 • Submission of a petition concerning standards for approval of a drug product for which
627   FDA has provided an opportunity for public input (such as when FDA has issued draft or
628   final product-specific guidance applicable to the drug product) and the petitioner has not
629   provided comment other than through the petition.[28]
630 • Submission of a petition requesting that other applicants must meet standards for testing,
631   data, or labeling for their products that are more onerous or rigorous than the standards
632   applicable to the applicable listed drug and/or petitioner's version of the same product
633 • Other relevant considerations including the history of the petitioner with the Agency
634   (such as whether the petitioner has a history of submitting petitions that we have
635   determined were submitted with the primary purpose of delay)
636
637   If FDA determines that a petition has been submitted with the primary purpose of delaying an
638   application, we will then determine if the petition may be summarily denied as described in
639   section 505(q)(1)(E) (which allows denial of a petition that was submitted with the primary
640   purpose of delay and does not on its face raise valid scientific or regulatory issues). We will
641   determine, on a case-by-case basis, whether a petition that was submitted with the primary
642   purpose of delay also does not on its face raise valid scientific or regulatory issues and therefore
643   may be summarily denied.
644
645   We may note our determination regarding the primary purpose of delaying an application and
646   our basis for that determination in our petition response. In addition, if we determine that a
647   petition has been submitted with the primary purpose of delaying an application, we intend to
648   refer the matter to the Federal Trade Commission. Finally, we will highlight our determinations

---

[28] We note that there are means other than submission of a petition by which interested persons can express their views on issues related to bioequivalence. FDA has been posting draft product-specific bioequivalence recommendations on its website at
http://www.fda.gov/Drugs/GuidanceComplianceRegulatoryInformation/Guidances/ucm075207.htm and announcing in a *Federal Register* notice the availability of these recommendations and the opportunity for the public to consider and comment on the recommendations. We encourage interested persons to submit any comments related to bioequivalence issues in response to a *Federal Register* notice announcing the recommendations.

16

649   regarding petitions submitted with the primary purpose of delaying application approvals in our
650   annual report to Congress.[29]
651

---

[29] See section 505(q)(3).

APPENDIX D3

Formal Meetings Between the FDA and Sponsors or Applicants of BsUFA Products

Formal Meetings Between the FDA and Sponsors or Applicants of BsUFA Products
Guidance for Industry

DRAFT GUIDANCE

This guidance document is being distributed for comment purposes only.

Comments and suggestions regarding this draft document should be submitted within 90 days of publication in the *Federal Register* of the notice announcing the availability of the draft guidance. Submit electronic comments to https://www.regulations.gov. Submit written comments to the Dockets Management Staff (HFA-305), Food and Drug Administration, 5630 Fishers Lane, Rm. 1061, Rockville, MD 20852. All comments should be identified with the docket number listed in the notice of availability that publishes in the *Federal Register*.

For questions regarding this draft document, contact (CDER) Neel Patel at 301-796-0970 or (CBER) the Office of Communication, Outreach, and Development at 800-835-4709 or 240-402-8010.

U.S. Department of Health and Human Services
Food and Drug Administration
Center for Drug Evaluation and Research (CDER)
Center for Biologics Evaluation and Research (CBER)

June 2018
Procedural

18958449dft.docx
5/31/2018

Formal Meetings Between the FDA and Sponsors or Applicants of BsUFA Products

Guidance for Industry

Additional copies are available from:

Office of Communications, Division of Drug Information
Center for Drug Evaluation and Research
Food and Drug Administration
10001 New Hampshire Ave., Hillandale Bldg., 4th Floor
Silver Spring, MD 20993-0002
Phone: 855-543-3784 or 301-796-3400; Fax: 301-431-6353; Email: druginfo@fda.hhs.gov
https://www.fda.gov/Drugs/GuidanceComplianceRegulatoryInformation/Guidances/default.htm

and/or

Office of Communication, Outreach, and Development
Center for Biologics Evaluation and Research
Food and Drug Administration
10903 New Hampshire Ave., Bldg. 71, rm. 3128
Silver Spring, MD 20993-0002
Phone: 800-835-4709 or 240-402-8010; Email: ocod@fda.hhs.gov
https://www.fda.gov/BiologicsBloodVaccines/GuidanceComplianceRegulatoryInformation/Guidances/default.htm

U.S. Department of Health and Human Services
Food and Drug Administration
Center for Drug Evaluation and Research (CDER)
Center for Biologics Evaluation and Research (CBER)

June 2018
Procedural

TABLE OF CONTENTS

I.   INTRODUCTION... 1
II.   BACKGROUND 2
III.   MEETING TYPES 2
        A.   BIA Meeting 3
        B.   BPD Type 1 Meeting... 3
        C.   BPD Type 2 Meeting... 4
        D.   BPD Type 3 Meeting... 4
        E.   BPD Type 4 Meeting... 5
IV.   BSUFA FEES ASSOCIATED WITH THE BPD PROGRAM................. 5
V.   MEETING FORMATS 5
VI.   MEETING REQUESTS 6
VII.   ASSESSING AND RESPONDING TO MEETING REQUESTS............. 8
        A.   Meeting Denied 9
        B.   Meeting Granted 9
VIII.   MEETING PACKAGE 10
        A.   Timing of Meeting Package Submission 10
        B.   Where and How Many Copies of Meeting Packages to Send 10
        C.   Meeting Package Content.. 11
IX.   PRELIMINARY RESPONSES 12
X.   RESCHEDULING MEETINGS.. 13
XI.   CANCELING MEETINGS 14
XII.   MEETING CONDUCT 14
XIII.   MEETING MINUTES... 15
REFERENCES... 17

1 **Formal Meetings Between the FDA and**
2 **Sponsors or Applicants of BsUFA Products**
3 **Guidance for Industry[1]**
4
5
6

7
8   This draft guidance, when finalized, will represent the current thinking of the Food and Drug
9   Administration (FDA or Agency) on this topic. It does not establish any rights for any person and is not
10 binding on FDA or the public. You can use an alternative approach if it satisfies the requirements of the
11 applicable statutes and regulations. To discuss an alternative approach, contact the FDA staff responsible
12 for this guidance as listed on the title page.
13

14
15
16
17 **I.   INTRODUCTION**
18
19 This guidance provides recommendations to industry on formal meetings between the Food and
20 Drug Administration (FDA) and sponsors or applicants relating to the development and review
21 of biosimilar or interchangeable biological products regulated by the Center for Drug Evaluation
22 and Research (CDER) or the Center for Biologics Evaluation and Research (CBER). This
23 guidance does not apply to meetings associated with the development of products intended for
24 submission in, or with the review of, new drug applications or abbreviated new drug applications
25 under section 505 of the Federal Food, Drug and Cosmetic Act (FD&C Act), biologics license
26 applications (BLAs) under section 351(a) of the Public Health Service Act (PHS Act), or
27 submissions for devices under the FD&C Act.[2] For the purposes of this guidance, *formal*
28 *meeting* includes any meeting that is requested by a sponsor or applicant (hereafter referred to as
29 *requester(s)*) following the procedures provided in this guidance and includes meetings
30 conducted in any format (i.e., face to face, teleconference/videoconference, or written response
31 only (WRO)).
32

---

[1] This guidance has been prepared by the Center for Drug Evaluation and Research (CDER) in cooperation with the Center for Biologics Evaluation and Research (CBER) at the Food and Drug Administration.

[2] For information on meetings for new drug applications and 351(a) BLAs, see the draft guidance for industry *Formal Meetings Between the FDA and Sponsors or Applicants of PDUFA Products.* When final, this guidance will represent the FDA's current thinking on this topic. For the most recent version of a guidance, check the FDA Drugs or Biologics guidance web pages at
https://www.fda.gov/Drugs/GuidanceComplianceRegulatoryInformation/Guidances/default.htm and
https://www.fda.gov/BiologicsBloodVaccines/GuidanceComplianceRegulatoryInformation/Guidances/default.htm.

1

33 This guidance discusses the principles of good meeting management practices (GMMPs) and
34 describes standardized procedures for requesting, preparing, scheduling, conducting, and
35 documenting such formal meetings.[3]
36
37 In general, FDA's guidance documents do not establish legally enforceable responsibilities.
38 Instead, guidances describe the Agency's current thinking on a topic and should be viewed only
39 as recommendations, unless specific regulatory or statutory requirements are cited. The use of
40 the word *should* in Agency guidances means that something is suggested or recommended, but
41 not required.
42
43
44 **II.   BACKGROUND**
45
46 Each year, FDA review staff participate in many meetings with requesters who seek advice
47 relating to the development and review of a biosimilar or interchangeable product. Because
48 these meetings often represent critical points in the regulatory and development process, it is
49 important that there are efficient, consistent procedures for the timely and effective conduct of
50 such meetings. The GMMPs in this guidance are intended to provide consistent procedures that
51 will promote well-managed meetings and to ensure that such meetings are scheduled within a
52 reasonable time, conducted efficiently, and documented appropriately.
53
54 As part of the reauthorization of the Biosimilar User Fee Act (BsUFA),[4] the FDA has committed
55 to specific performance goals that include meeting management goals for formal meetings that
56 occur between the FDA and requesters.[5]
57
58
59 **III.   MEETING TYPES[6]**
60
61 There are five types of formal meetings that occur between requesters and FDA staff to discuss
62 development and review of a biosimilar or interchangeable product: Biosimilar Initial Advisory
63 (BIA), Biosimilar Biological Product Development (BPD) Type 1, BPD Type 2, BPD Type 3,
64 and BPD Type 4.
65

---

[3] The previous guidance for industry *Formal Meetings Between the FDA and Biosimilar Biological Product Sponsors or Applicants* published November 18, 2015, has been withdrawn.

[4] The Biosimilar User Fee Act of 2012 (BsUFA I) added sections 744G and 744H to the FD&C Act, authorizing FDA to collect user fees for a 5-year period from persons that develop biosimilar biological products. BsUFA was reauthorized for a 5-year period in 2017 under Title IV of the FDA Reauthorization Act of 2017 (BsUFA II), enacted on August 18, 2017.

[5] See the BsUFA II goals letter titled "BsUFA Reauthorization Performance Goals and Procedures Fiscal Years 2018 Through 2022" available on the FDA website at https://www.fda.gov/downloads/ForIndustry/UserFees/BiosimilarUserFeeActBsUFA/UCM521121.pdf.

[6] The meeting types and goal dates are described in the BsUFA II goals letter and apply to formal meetings between FDA staff and requesters of BsUFA meetings; they do not apply to meetings with CDER Office of Generic Drugs, CDER Office of Compliance, or CDER Office of Prescription Drug Promotion.

2

66 Requesters are not required to request meetings in sequential order (i.e., BIA, BPD Type 2, BPD
67 Type 3, then BPD Type 4). The meeting type requested depends on the stage of the development
68 program and/or the advice being sought. Although the FDA would, in general, grant one BIA
69 meeting and one BPD Type 4 meeting for a particular biosimilar or interchangeable product,
70 requesters can request, as appropriate, as many BPD Type 2 and Type 3 meetings as needed to
71 support the development and review of a biosimilar or interchangeable product.
72
73 ### A.   BIA Meeting
74
75 A BIA meeting is an initial assessment limited to a general discussion regarding whether
76 licensure under section 351(k) of the PHS Act may be feasible for a particular product, and if so,
77 general advice on the expected content of the development program. This meeting type does not
78 include any meeting that involves substantive review of summary data or full study reports.
79 However, preliminary comparative analytical similarity data from at least one lot of the proposed
80 biosimilar or interchangeable product compared to the U.S.-licensed reference product should be
81 provided in the meeting package. The analytical similarity data should be sufficient to enable the
82 FDA to make a preliminary determination as to whether licensure under section 351(k) of the
83 PHS Act may be feasible for a particular product and to provide meaningful advice. A general
84 overview of the development program, including synopses of results and findings from all
85 completed studies and information about planned studies, also should be provided.
86
87 Extensive analytical, nonclinical, and/or clinical data are not expected to be provided based on
88 the expected stage of development of the proposed biosimilar or interchangeable product. If the
89 requester is seeking targeted advice on the adequacy of any comparative data or extensive advice
90 for any aspect of a planned or ongoing biosimilar or interchangeable development program, a
91 different meeting type should be requested.
92
93 ### B.   BPD Type 1 Meeting
94
95 A BPD Type 1 meeting is a meeting that is necessary for an otherwise stalled development
96 program to proceed or a meeting to address an important safety issue. Examples of a BPD Type
97 1 meeting include the following:
98
99 - Meetings to discuss clinical holds: (1) in which the requester seeks input on how to
100   address the hold issues; or (2) in which a response to hold issues has been submitted, and
101   reviewed by the FDA, but the FDA and the requester agree that the development is
102   stalled and a new path forward should be discussed.
103
104 - Meetings that are requested after receipt of an FDA nonagreement Special Protocol
105   Assessment letter in response to protocols submitted under the special protocol
106   assessment procedures as described in the guidance for industry *Special Protocol*
107   *Assessment.*[7]
108

---

[7] We update guidances periodically. To make sure you have the most recent version of a guidance, check the FDA
guidance web page at https://www.fda.gov/RegulatoryInformation/Guidances/default.htm.

109   • Meetings to discuss an important safety issue, when such an issue is identified and the
110   FDA and requester agree that the issue should be discussed.
111

112   • Dispute resolution meetings as described in 21 CFR 10.75 and 312.48 and in the
113   guidance for industry and review staff *Formal Dispute Resolution: Sponsor Appeals*
114   *Above the Division Level.*
115

116   • Post-action meetings requested after an FDA regulatory action other than an approval
117   (i.e., issuance of a complete response letter).
118

119   • Meetings requested within 30 days of FDA issuance of a refuse-to-file letter to discuss
120   whether the FDA should file the application.
121

122   **C.   BPD Type 2 Meeting**
123

124 A BPD Type 2 meeting is a meeting to discuss a specific issue (e.g., ranking of quality attributes;
125 chemistry, manufacturing, and controls such as control strategy; study design or endpoints; post-
126 approval changes) or questions for which the FDA will provide targeted advice regarding an
127 ongoing development program. This meeting type may include substantive review of summary
128 data but does not include review of full study reports.
129

130   **D.   BPD Type 3 Meeting**
131

132 A BPD Type 3 meeting is an in-depth data review and advice meeting regarding an ongoing
133 development program. This meeting type includes substantive review of full study reports or an
134 extensive data package (e.g., detailed and robust analytical similarity data), FDA advice
135 regarding the similarity between the proposed biosimilar or interchangeable product and the
136 reference product based on a comprehensive data package, and FDA advice regarding the need
137 for additional studies, including design and analysis, based on a comprehensive data package.
138

139   • Examples of a BPD Type 3 meeting submission include the following:
140

141   − Comprehensive analytical similarity data that permit the FDA to make a preliminary
142   evaluation of analytical similarity during development. The level of analytical data
143   provided should be similar to what the requester intends to submit in a 351(k) BLA
144   (e.g., full study reports and/or datasets that support the full study reports).
145

146   − Full study report(s) for a clinical study or clinical studies.
147

148   • Based on the data and/or datasets and results reported in the full study reports, the FDA
149   encourages the requester to provide an update on the development plan of the proposed
150   biosimilar or interchangeable product. Examples of topics the requester can address as
151   part of a BPD Type 3 meeting in addition to the in-depth data submitted include the
152   following:
153

154   − Proposal for any planned additional studies

4

155
156   – Proposal for extrapolation
157
158   **E.   BPD Type 4 Meeting**
159
160   A BPD Type 4 meeting is a presubmission meeting to discuss the format and content of a
161   complete application for an original biosimilar or interchangeable product application or
162   supplement submitted under 351(k) of the PHS Act. The purpose of this meeting is to discuss
163   the format and content of the planned submission and other items, including the following:
164
165   • Identification of those studies that the sponsor is relying on to support a demonstration of
166   biosimilarity or interchangeability
167
168   • Discussion of any potential review issues identified based on the information provided
169
170   • Identification of the status of ongoing or needed studies to adequately address the
171   Pediatric Research Equity Act
172
173   • Acquainting FDA reviewers with the general information to be submitted in the
174   marketing application (including technical information)
175
176   • Discussion of the best approach to the presentation and formatting of data in the
177   marketing application
178
179
180   **IV.   BSUFA FEES ASSOCIATED WITH THE BPD PROGRAM**
181
182   Under the BsUFA user fee provisions of the FD&C Act, BPD fees are assessed for products in
183   the BPD program. BPD fees include the initial BPD fee, the annual BPD fee, and the
184   reactivation fee. No fee is associated with a BIA meeting. For more information about BsUFA
185   fees, including the assessment of BPD fees and the consequences for failure to pay any required
186   BPD fees, refer to the draft guidance for industry *Assessing User Fees Under the Biosimilar*
187   *User Fee Amendments of 2017.*[8]
188
189
190   **V.   MEETING FORMATS**
191
192   There are three formats for formal meetings: face to face, teleconference/videoconference, and
193   WRO as follows:
194
195   1. **Face to face** — Traditional face-to-face meetings are those in which the majority of
196   attendees participate in person at the FDA.
197

---

[8] When finalized, this guidance will represent the FDA's current thinking on this topic.

5

198   2. **Teleconference/Videoconference** — Teleconferences/videoconferences are meetings in
199   which the attendees participate from various remote locations via an audio (e.g.,
200   telephone) and/or video connection.
201
202   3. **Written response only (WRO)** — WRO responses are sent to requesters in lieu of
203   meetings conducted in one of the other two formats described above. Requesters may
204   request this meeting format for BIA and BPD Type 2 meetings.
205
206
207 **VI.   MEETING REQUESTS**
208
209 To make the most efficient use of FDA resources, before seeking a meeting, requesters should
210 consult the information publicly available from the FDA that relates to biosimilar or
211 interchangeable product development.[9]
212
213 To promote efficient meeting management, requesters should try to anticipate future needs and,
214 to the extent practical, combine related product development issues into the fewest possible
215 meetings.
216
217 To request a meeting, submit a written request to the FDA via the respective center's document
218 room (paper submissions) or via the electronic gateway, as appropriate. Written meeting
219 requests must be made in accordance with any applicable electronic submission requirements.[10]
220 Requests should be addressed to the appropriate review division or office and, if previously
221 assigned, submitted to the pre-investigational new drug application (pre-IND) file or application
222 (e.g., investigational new drug application (IND), BLA). Meeting requests sent by fax or email
223 are considered courtesy copies only and are not a substitute for a formal submission.
224
225 A meeting request for the development of a proposed biosimilar or interchangeable product with
226 multiple indications that span multiple review divisions should be submitted to the division that
227 has regulatory oversight of the reference product.
228
229 The meeting request should include adequate information for the FDA to assess the potential
230 utility of the meeting and to identify FDA staff necessary to discuss proposed agenda items.
231
232 The meeting request should include the following information:
233
234   1. The application number (if previously assigned).
235
236   2. The development-phase code name of product (if pre-licensure).
237

---

[9] See the guidance for industry *Best Practices for Communication Between IND Sponsors and FDA During Drug Development.*

[10] See the guidances for industry *Providing Regulatory Submissions in Electronic Format — Submissions Under Section 745A(a) of the Federal Food, Drug, and Cosmetic Act* and *Providing Regulatory Submissions in Electronic Format — Certain Human Pharmaceutical Product Applications and Related Submissions Using the eCTD Specifications.*

238   3. The proper name (if post-licensure).
239
240   4. The structure (if applicable).
241
242   5. The reference product proper and proprietary names.
243
244   6. The proposed indication(s) or context of product development.
245
246   7. Pediatric study plans, if applicable.
247
248   8. Human factors engineering plan, if applicable.
249
250   9. Combination product information (e.g., constituent parts, including details of the device
251   constituent part, intended packaging, planned human factors studies), if applicable.
252
253   The meeting request must include the following information for the performance goals described
254   in section I.I., Meeting Management Goals, of the commitment letter to apply:[11]
255
256   1. The meeting type being requested (i.e., BIA meeting, BPD Type 1, 2, 3, or 4 meeting).
257   The rationale for requesting the meeting type should also be included.
258
259   2. The proposed format of the meeting (i.e., face to face, teleconference/videoconference or
260   WRO).
261
262   3. A brief statement of the purpose of the meeting. This statement should include a brief
263   background of the issues underlying the agenda. It also can include a brief summary of
264   completed or planned studies or data that the requester intends to discuss at the meeting,
265   the general nature of the critical questions to be asked, and where the meeting fits in
266   overall development plans. Although the statement should not provide the details of
267   study designs or completed studies, it should provide enough information to facilitate
268   understanding of the issues, such as a small table that summarizes major results.
269
270   4. A list of the specific objectives or outcomes the requester expects from the meeting.
271
272   5. A proposed agenda, including estimated times needed for discussion of each agenda item.
273
274   6. A list of questions, grouped by FDA discipline. For each question there should be a brief
275   explanation of the context and purpose of the question.
276
277   7. A list of planned attendees from the requester's organization, which should include their
278   names and titles. The list should also include the names, titles, and affiliations of
279   consultants and interpreters, if applicable.
280
281   8. A list of requested FDA attendees and/or discipline representative(s). Note that requests
282   for attendance by FDA staff who are not otherwise essential to the application's review

---

[11] See BsUFA II goals letter.

7

283   may affect the ability to hold the meeting within the specified time frame of the meeting
284   type being requested. Therefore, when attendance by nonessential FDA staff is
285   requested, the meeting request should provide a justification for such attendees and state
286   whether or not a later meeting date is acceptable to the requester to accommodate the
287   nonessential FDA attendees.
288
289   9. Suggested dates and times (e.g., morning or afternoon) for the meeting that are within or
290   beyond the appropriate scheduling time frame of the meeting type being requested (see
291   Table 2 in section VII.B., Meeting Granted). Dates and times when the requester is not
292   available should also be included.
293
294   When submitting a meeting request, the requester should define the specific areas of input
295   needed from the FDA. A well-written meeting request that includes the above components can
296   help the FDA understand and assess the utility and timing of the meeting related to product
297   development or review. The list of requester attendees and the list of requested FDA attendees
298   can be useful in providing or preparing for the input needed at the meeting. However, during the
299   time between the request and the meeting, the planned attendees can change. If there are
300   changes, an updated list of attendees with their titles and affiliations should be provided to the
301   appropriate FDA contact at least 1 week before the meeting.
302
303   The objectives and agenda provide overall context for the meeting topics, but it is the list of
304   questions that is most critical to understanding the kind of information or input needed by the
305   requester and to focus the discussion should the meeting be granted. Each question should be
306   precise and include a brief explanation of the context and purpose of the question. The questions
307   submitted within a single meeting request should be limited to those that can be reasonably
308   answered within the allotted meeting time, taking into consideration the complexity of the
309   questions submitted. Similar considerations regarding the complexity of questions submitted
310   within a WRO should be applied.
311
312
313   **VII.   ASSESSING AND RESPONDING TO MEETING REQUESTS**
314
315   Although requesters should request a specific meeting type and format, the FDA assesses each
316   meeting request, including WRO requests for BIA and BPD Type 2 meetings, and determines
317   whether or not the request should be granted, the appropriate meeting type, and the appropriate
318   meeting format. Requests for BPD Type 2, 3, and 4 meetings will be honored except in the most
319   unusual circumstances. However, if the FDA determines that WRO format is not appropriate for
320   a requested WRO meeting or that in-person format (i.e., face to face or
321   teleconference/videoconference) is not appropriate for a requested in-person meeting, we will
322   notify the requester that the meeting has been denied, as described in section VII.A., Meeting
323   Denied.
324
325   The meeting request should be accompanied by the meeting package (see section VIII.C.,
326   Meeting Package Content, for additional information regarding the content of the meeting
327   package). This ensures that the FDA has adequate information to assess the potential utility of
328   the meeting and prepare for the meeting. If the meeting package is not submitted to the review

8

329   division with the meeting request, the FDA will consider the meeting request incomplete and
330   generally will deny the meeting request.
331
332   **A.   Meeting Denied**
333
334   If a meeting request is denied, the FDA will notify the requester in writing according to the
335   timelines described in Table 1. The notification will include an explanation of the reason for the
336   denial. Denials will be based on a substantive reason, not merely on the absence of a minor
337   element of the meeting request or a minor element of the meeting package. For example, a
338   meeting request can be denied because it is premature for the stage of product development, is
339   clearly unnecessary, or is not appropriate for the format requested (e.g., face to
340   face/videoconference/teleconference versus WRO) or the meeting package does not provide an
341   adequate basis for the meeting discussion.
342
343   The FDA may also deny requests for meetings that do not have substantive information related
344   to the elements described in section VI., Meeting Requests. A subsequent request to schedule
345   the meeting will be considered as a new request (i.e., a request that is assigned a new set of time
346   frames described below in section VII. B., Meeting Granted).
347
348   **B.   Meeting Granted**
349
350   If a meeting request is granted, the FDA will notify the requester in writing according to the
351   timelines described in Table 1. For face-to-face and teleconference/videoconference meetings,
352   the notification will include the date, time, conferencing arrangements and/or location of the
353   meeting, and expected FDA participants. For BIA and BPD Type 2 WRO meetings, the
354   notification will include the date the FDA intends to send the written response (see Table 3 for
355   FDA WRO response timelines).
356
357   For face-to-face and teleconference/videoconference meetings, the FDA will schedule the
358   meeting on the next available date at which all expected FDA staff are available to attend;
359   however, the meeting should be scheduled consistent with the type of meeting requested (see
360   Table 2 for FDA meeting scheduling time frames). If the requested date for any meeting type is
361   greater than the specified time frame, the meeting date should be within 14 calendar days of the
362   requested date.
363
364   **Table 1: FDA Meeting Request Response Timelines**

Meeting Type	Response Time (calendar days from receipt of meeting request and meeting package)
BIA	21 days
BPD 1	14 days
BPD 2	21 days
BPD 3	21 days
BPD 4	21 days

365
366

9

367   Table 2: FDA Meeting Scheduling Time Frames

Meeting Type	Meeting Scheduling (calendar days from receipt of meeting request and meeting package)
BIA	75 days
BPD 1	30 days
BPD 2	90 days
BPD 3	120 days
BPD 4	60 days

368
369
370   Table 3: FDA WRO Response Timelines

Meeting Type	WRO Response Time (calendar days from receipt of WRO meeting request and meeting package)
BIA	75 days
BPD 2	90 days

371
372
373   **VIII.   MEETING PACKAGE**
374
375   Premeeting preparation is critical for achieving a productive discussion or exchange of
376   information. Preparing the meeting background package should help the requester focus on
377   describing its principal areas of interest. The meeting package should provide information
378   relevant to the discussion topics and enable the FDA to prepare adequately for the meeting.
379
380   **A.   Timing of Meeting Package Submission**
381
382   As discussed in section VII., Assessing and Responding to Meeting Requests, if the meeting
383   package is not submitted with the meeting request for each meeting type, the meeting request
384   will be considered incomplete and the FDA generally will deny the meeting.
385
386   **B.   Where and How Many Copies of Meeting Packages to Send**
387
388   Requesters should submit an archival meeting package to the appropriate review division or
389   office or, if previously assigned, to the relevant pre-IND file or application(s) (e.g., IND, BLA)
390   via the appropriate center's document room (paper submission) or via the electronic gateway, as
391   applicable. Submissions must be made in accordance with any applicable electronic submission
392   requirements.[12]
393

---

[12] See the guidances for industry *Providing Regulatory Submissions in Electronic Format — Submissions Under Section 745A(a) of the Federal Food, Drug, and Cosmetic Act* and *Providing Regulatory Submissions in Electronic Format — Certain Human Pharmaceutical Product Applications and Related Submissions Using the eCTD Specifications.*

10

394   To facilitate the meeting process, CDER strongly suggests that copies of meeting packages
395   provided in electronic format also be provided in paper (desk copies). The number of desk
396   copies of a meeting package will vary based on the meeting. The CDER project manager will
397   advise on the number of desk copies needed for the meeting attendees. CBER neither requests
398   nor accepts paper copies (desk copies) of meeting packages that have been submitted in
399   electronic format.
400
401   **C.   Meeting Package Content**
402
403   The meeting package should provide information relevant to the product, stage of development,
404   and meeting type requested (see section III., Meeting Types), in addition to any supplementary
405   information needed to develop responses to issues raised by the requester or review division.
406   The meeting package should contain sufficient detail to meet the intended meeting objectives.
407   For example, inclusion of raw data in addition to the derived conclusions may be appropriate in
408   some situations. Similarly, merely describing a result as *significant* does not provide the review
409   division with enough information to give good advice or identify important problems the
410   requester may have missed. FDA guidances identify and address many issues related to
411   biosimilar or interchangeable product development and should be considered when planning,
412   developing, and providing information needed to support a meeting with the FDA.[13] If a product
413   development plan deviates from current guidances, or from current practices, the deviation
414   should be recognized and explained. Known or expected difficult design and evidence issues
415   should be raised for discussion (e.g., selection of study populations, doses, or endpoints different
416   from those studied for the reference product's licensure; extrapolation of indications).
417
418   To facilitate FDA review, the meeting package content should be organized according to the
419   proposed agenda. The meeting package should be a sequentially paginated document with a
420   table of contents, appropriate indices, appendices, and cross references. It should be tabbed or
421   bookmarked to enhance reviewers' navigation across different sections within the package, both
422   in preparation for and during the meeting. Meeting packages generally should include the
423   following information in the order listed below:
424
425   1.   The application number (if previously assigned).
426
427   2.   The development-phase code name of product (if pre-licensure).
428
429   3.   The proper name (if post-licensure).
430
431   4.   The structure (if applicable).
432
433   5.   The reference product proprietary and proper names.
434
435   6.   The proposed indication(s) or context of product development.
436

---

[13] See the FDA Biosimilars guidance web page, available at
https://www.fda.gov/Drugs/GuidanceComplianceRegulatoryInformation/Guidances/ucm290967.htm.

11

437 7. The dosage form, route of administration, dosing regimen (frequency and duration), and
438 presentation(s).
439
440 8. Pediatric study plans, if applicable.
441
442 9. Human factors engineering plan, if applicable.
443
444 10. Combination product information (e.g., constituent parts, including details of the device
445 constituent part, intended packaging, planned human factors studies), if applicable.
446
447 11. A list of all individuals, with their titles and affiliations, who will attend the requested
448 meeting from the requester's organization, including consultants and interpreters, if
449 applicable.
450
451 12. A background section that includes the following:
452
453 a. A brief history of the development program and relevant communications with the
454 FDA before the meeting
455
456 b. Substantive changes in product development plans (e.g., manufacturing changes, new
457 study population or endpoint), when applicable
458
459 c. The current status of product development (e.g., chemistry, manufacturing, and
460 controls; nonclinical; and clinical, including any development outside the United
461 States, as applicable)
462
463 13. A brief statement summarizing the purpose of the meeting.
464
465 14. A proposed agenda, including estimated times needed for discussion of each agenda item.
466
467 15. A list of questions for discussion grouped by FDA discipline and with a brief summary
468 for each question to explain the need or context for the question. Questions regarding
469 combination product issues should be grouped together.
470
471 16. Data to support discussion organized by FDA discipline and question. The level of detail
472 of the data should be appropriate to the meeting type requested and the stage of product
473 development.
474
475
476 **IX. PRELIMINARY RESPONSES**
477
478 Communications before the meeting between requesters and the FDA, including preliminary
479 responses, can serve as a foundation for discussion or as the final meeting responses.
480 Nevertheless, preliminary responses should not be construed as *final* unless there is agreement
481 between the requester and the FDA that additional discussion is not necessary for any question
482 (i.e., when the meeting is canceled because the requester is satisfied with the FDA's preliminary

12

565

483   responses), or a particular question is considered resolved allowing time for discussion of the
484   other questions during the meeting. Preliminary responses communicated by the FDA are not
485   intended to generate the submission of new information or new questions. If a requester
486   nonetheless provides new data or a revised or new proposal, the FDA may not be able to provide
487   comments on the new information, and the requester may need to submit a new meeting request
488   for the FDA to provide feedback on the new information.
489
490   The FDA holds internal meetings, including meetings with the CDER or CBER Biosimilar
491   Review Committee, to discuss the content of meeting packages and to gain internal alignment on
492   the preliminary responses. The FDA will send the requester its preliminary responses to the
493   questions in the meeting package no later than 5 calendar days before the face-to-face,
494   videoconference, or teleconference meeting date for BPD Type 2 and BPD Type 3 meetings.
495   For all other meeting types, the FDA intends to send the requester its preliminary responses no
496   later than 2 calendar days before the face-to-face, videoconference, or teleconference meeting.
497
498

499   **X.   RESCHEDULING MEETINGS**
500
501   Occasionally, circumstances arise that necessitate the rescheduling of a meeting. If a meeting
502   needs to be rescheduled, it should be rescheduled as soon as possible after the original date. A
503   new meeting request should not be submitted. Requesters and the FDA should take reasonable
504   steps to avoid rescheduling meetings. For example, if an attendee becomes unavailable, a
505   substitute can be identified, or comments on the topic that the attendee would have addressed can
506   be forwarded to the requester following the meeting. It will be at the discretion of the review
507   division whether the meeting should be rescheduled depending on the specific circumstances.
508
509   The following situations are examples of when a meeting may be rescheduled by FDA. This list
510   includes representative examples and is not intended to be an exhaustive list.
511
512   ● The review team determines that additional information is needed to address the
513   requester's questions or other important issues, and it is possible to identify the additional
514   information needed and arrange for its timely submission.
515
516   ● Essential attendees are no longer available for the scheduled date and time because of an
517   unexpected or unavoidable conflict or an emergency situation.
518
519   ● Before preliminary responses are sent by the FDA, the requester sends the FDA
520   additional questions or data that are intended for discussion at the meeting and require
521   additional review time.
522
523   ● It is determined that attendance by additional FDA personnel not originally anticipated or
524   requested is critical and their unavailability precludes holding the meeting on the original
525   date.
526
527

13

528 **XI. CANCELING MEETINGS**
529
530 Failure to pay required BPD fees for a product, within the required time frame, may result in the
531 cancellation by FDA of a previously scheduled BPD meeting.[14] For more information or BPD
532 fees, refer to the draft guidance for industry *Assessing User Fees Under the Biosimilar User Fee*
533 *Amendments of 2017.*[15] If the requester pays the required BPD fee after the meeting has been
534 canceled because of nonpayment, the goal time frame for FDA's response to a meeting request
535 will be calculated from the date on which FDA received the payment, not the date on which the
536 sponsor originally submitted the meeting request.[16]
537
538 Occasionally, other circumstances arise that necessitate the cancellation of a meeting. If a
539 meeting is canceled for reasons other than nonpayment of a required BPD fee, the FDA will
540 consider a subsequent request to schedule a meeting to be a new request and the goal time frame
541 for FDA's response will be calculated from the date of the subsequent request. Requesters and
542 the FDA should take reasonable steps to avoid canceling meetings (unless the meeting is no
543 longer necessary). Cancellation will be at the discretion of the review division and will depend
544 on the specific circumstances.
545
546 The following situations are examples of when a meeting may be canceled. This list includes
547 representative examples and is not intended to be an exhaustive list.
548
549 • The requester determines that preliminary responses to its questions are sufficient for its
550 needs and additional discussion is not necessary (see section IX., Preliminary Responses).
551 In this case, the requester should contact the FDA regulatory project manager to request
552 cancellation of the meeting. The FDA will consider whether it agrees that the meeting
553 should be canceled. Some meetings can be valuable because of the discussion they
554 generate and the opportunity for the division to ask about relevant matters, even if the
555 preliminary responses seem sufficient to answer the requester's questions. If the FDA
556 agrees that the meeting can be canceled, the reason for cancellation will be documented
557 and the preliminary responses will represent the final responses and the official record.
558
559 • The FDA determines that the meeting package is inadequate. Meetings are scheduled on
560 the condition that the requester has submitted appropriate information to support the
561 discussion. Adequate planning by the requester should avoid this problem.
562
563
564 **XII. MEETING CONDUCT**
565
566 Meetings will be chaired by an FDA staff member and begin with introductions and an overview
567 of the agenda. Attendees should not make audio or visual recordings of discussions at meetings
568 described in this guidance.

---

[14] See section 744H(a)(1)(E)(i) of the FD&C Act.

[15] When finalized, this guidance will represent the FDA's current thinking on this topic.

[16] See BsUFA II goals letter.

Contains Nonbinding Recommendations
Draft — Not for Implementation

569
570 Presentations by requesters generally are not needed because the information necessary for
571 review and discussion should be part of the meeting package. If a requester plans to make a
572 presentation, the presentation should be discussed ahead of time with the FDA project manager
573 to determine if a presentation is warranted and to ensure that the FDA has the presentation
574 materials ahead of the meeting, if possible. All presentations should be kept brief to maximize
575 the time available for discussion. The length of the meeting will not be increased to
576 accommodate a presentation. If a presentation contains more than a small amount of content,
577 distinct from clarifications or explanations of previous data, that was not included in the original
578 meeting package submitted for review, FDA staff may not be able to provide commentary.
579
580 Either a representative of the FDA or the requester should summarize the important discussion
581 points, agreements, clarifications, and action items. Summation can be done at the end of the
582 meeting or after the discussion of each question. Generally, the requester will be asked to
583 present the summary to ensure that there is mutual understanding of meeting outcomes and
584 action items. FDA staff can add or further clarify any important points not covered in the
585 summary and these items can be added to the meeting minutes.
586
587 At BPD Type 4 meetings for original applications reviewed under the BsUFA Program for
588 Enhanced Review Transparency and Communication for Original 351(k) BLAs (also known as
589 *the Program*),[17] the requester and the FDA should also summarize agreements regarding the
590 content of a complete application and any agreements reached on delayed submission of certain
591 minor application components.
592
593
594 **XIII. MEETING MINUTES**
595
596 Because the FDA's minutes are the official records of meetings, the FDA's documentation of
597 meeting outcomes, agreements, disagreements, and action items is critical to ensuring that this
598 information is preserved for meeting attendees and future reference. The FDA will issue the
599 official, finalized minutes to the requester within 30 calendar days after the meeting.
600
601 The following are general considerations regarding meeting minutes:
602
603 • FDA minutes will outline the important agreements, disagreements, issues for further
604   discussion, and action items from the meeting in bulleted format. This information does
605   not need to be in great detail. The minutes are not intended to represent a transcript of
606   the meeting.
607
608 • FDA project managers will use established templates to ensure that all important meeting
609   information is captured.
610
611 • The FDA may communicate additional information in the final minutes that was not
612   explicitly communicated during the meeting (e.g., pediatric requirements, data standards)

---

[17] See BsUFA II goals letter.

15

613   or that provides further explanation of discussion topics. The FDA's final minutes will
614   distinguish this additional information from the discussion that occurred during the
615   meeting.
616
617 The following steps should be taken when a requester disagrees that the minutes are an accurate
618 account of the meeting:
619
620   •   The requester should contact the FDA project manager and describe the concern
621
622   •   If, after contacting the FDA project manager, the requester still disagrees with the content
623   of the minutes, the requester should submit a description of the specific disagreements
624   either:
625
626   −   To the application; or
627
628   −   If there is no application, in a letter to the division director, with a copy to the FDA
629   project manager
630
631   •   The review division and the office director, if the office director was present at the
632   meeting, will take the concerns under consideration
633
634   −   If the minutes are deemed to accurately and sufficiently reflect the meeting
635   discussion, the FDA project manager will convey this decision to the requester and
636   the minutes will stand as the official documentation of the meeting.
637
638   −   If the FDA deems it necessary, changes will be documented in an addendum to the
639   official minutes. The addendum will also document any remaining requester
640   objections.
641
642 To request information on additional issues that were not addressed at the meeting, the requester
643 should submit a new meeting request or a submission containing specific questions for FDA
644 feedback.
645

16

646 **REFERENCES**
647
648 **Related guidances**[1]
649
650 Draft guidance for industry *Assessing User Fees Under the Biosimilar User Fee Amendments of*
651 *2017*[2]
652
653 Guidance for industry and review staff *Best Practices for Communication Between IND*
654 *Sponsors and FDA During Drug Development*
655
656 Guidance for review staff and industry *Good Review Management Principles and Practices for*
657 *PDUFA Products*
658
659 **Related CBER SOPPs**[3]
660
661 SOPP 8101.1: *Regulatory Meetings With Sponsors and Applicants for Drugs and Biological*
662 *Products*
663
664 SOPP 8404.1: *Procedures for Filing an Application When the Applicant Protests a Refusal to*
665 *File Action (File Over Protest)*
666
667 **Other guidances**
668
669 Draft guidance for industry *Formal Meetings Between the FDA and Sponsors or Applicants of*
670 *PDUFA Products*[4]
671
672 Guidance for industry *Providing Regulatory Submissions in Electronic Format — Certain*
673 *Human Pharmaceutical Product Applications and Related Submissions Using the eCTD*
674 *Specifications*
675
676 Guidance for industry *Providing Regulatory Submissions in Electronic Format — Submissions*
677 *Under Section 745A(a) of the Federal Food, Drug, and Cosmetic Act*
678

---

[1] We update guidances periodically. To make sure you have the most recent version of a guidance, check the FDA Drugs or Biologics guidance web pages at
https://www.fda.gov/Drugs/GuidanceComplianceRegulatoryInformation/Guidances/default.htm and
https://www.fda.gov/BiologicsBloodVaccines/GuidanceComplianceRegulatoryInformation/Guidances/default.htm.

[2] When final, this guidance will represent the FDA's current thinking on this topic. For the most recent version of a guidance, check the FDA Drugs or Biologics guidance web pages at
https://www.fda.gov/Drugs/GuidanceComplianceRegulatoryInformation/Guidances/default.htm and
https://www.fda.gov/BiologicsBloodVaccines/GuidanceComplianceRegulatoryInformation/Guidances/default.htm.

[3] SOPPs can be found on the Biologics Procedures (SOPPs) web page at
https://www.fda.gov/BiologicsBloodVaccines/GuidanceComplianceRegulatoryInformation/ProceduresSOPPs/default.htm.

[4] When final, this guidance will represent the FDA's current thinking on this topic.

17

Contains Nonbinding Recommendations
Draft — Not for Implementation

679   Guidance for industry *Special Protocol Assessment*
680
681   Guidance for industry and review staff *Formal Dispute Resolution: Sponsor Appeals Above the*
682   *Division Level*
683

18

APPENDIX D4

New and Revised Draft Q&As on Biosimilar Development and the BPCI Act (Revision 2)

New and Revised Draft Q&As on Biosimilar Development and the BPCI Act (Revision 2)

Guidance for Industry

DRAFT GUIDANCE

This guidance document is being distributed for comment purposes only.

Comments and suggestions regarding this draft document should be submitted within 60 days of publication in the *Federal Register* of the notice announcing the availability of the draft guidance. Submit electronic comments to https://www.regulations.gov. Submit written comments to the Division of Dockets Management (HFA-305), Food and Drug Administration, 5630 Fishers Lane, rm. 1061, Rockville, MD 20852. All comments should be identified with the docket number listed in the notice of availability that publishes in the *Federal Register*.

For questions regarding this draft document contact (CDER) Sandra Benton at 301-796-1042 or (CBER) Office of Communication, Outreach and Development at 1-800-835-4709 or 240-402-8010.

U.S. Department of Health and Human Services
Food and Drug Administration
Center for Drug Evaluation and Research (CDER)
Center for Biologics Evaluation and Research (CBER)

December 2018
Biosimilars

Revision 2

New and Revised Draft Q&As on Biosimilar Development and the BPCI Act (Revision 2)

Guidance for Industry

Additional copies are available from:

Office of Communications, Division of Drug Information
Center for Drug Evaluation and Research
Food and Drug Administration
10001 New Hampshire Ave., Hillandale Bldg., 4th Floor
Silver Spring, MD 20993-0002
Phone: 855-543-3784 or 301-796-3400; Fax: 301-431-6353
Email: druginfo@fda.hhs.gov
https://www.fda.gov/Drugs/GuidanceComplianceRegulatoryInformation/Guidances/default.htm

and/or

Office of Communication, Outreach and Development
Center for Biologics Evaluation and Research
Food and Drug Administration
10903 New Hampshire Ave., Bldg. 71, Room 3128
Silver Spring, MD 20993-0002
Phone: 800-835-4709 or 240-402-8010
Email: ocod@fda.hhs.gov
https://www.fda.gov/BiologicsBloodVaccines/GuidanceComplianceRegulatoryInformation/Guidances/default.htm

U.S. Department of Health and Human Services
Food and Drug Administration
Center for Drug Evaluation and Research (CDER)
Center for Biologics Evaluation and Research (CBER)

December 2018
Biosimilars

Revision 2

Contains Nonbinding Recommendations

Draft — Not for Implementation

TABLE OF CONTENTS

INTRODUCTION.. 1

BACKGROUND 3

QUESTIONS AND ANSWERS... 5

   I.   BIOSIMILARITY OR INTERCHANGEABILITY.................................... 5

   II.   PROVISIONS RELATED TO REQUIREMENTS TO SUBMIT A BLA FOR A
        "BIOLOGICAL PRODUCT" 12

   III. EXCLUSIVITY 14

1 **New and Revised Draft Q&As on Biosimilar Development and the**
2 **BPCI Act (Revision 2)**
3 **Guidance for Industry[1]**
4
5

6
7 This draft guidance, when finalized, will represent the current thinking of the Food and Drug
8 Administration (FDA or Agency) on this topic. It does not establish any rights for any person and is not
9 binding on FDA or the public. You can use an alternative approach if it satisfies the requirements of the
10 applicable statutes and regulations. To discuss an alternative approach, contact the FDA staff responsible
11 for this guidance as listed on the title page.
12

13
14 **INTRODUCTION**
15
16 This draft guidance document provides answers to common questions from prospective
17 applicants and other interested parties regarding the Biologics Price Competition and Innovation
18 Act of 2009 (BPCI Act). The question and answer (Q&A) format is intended to inform
19 prospective applicants and facilitate the development of proposed *biosimilars* and
20 *interchangeable biosimilars*,[2] as well as to describe FDA's interpretation of certain statutory
21 requirements added by the BPCI Act.
22
23 The BPCI Act amended the Public Health Service Act (PHS Act) and other statutes to create an
24 abbreviated licensure pathway in section 351(k) of the PHS Act for biological products shown to
25 be biosimilar to, or interchangeable with, an FDA-licensed biological reference product (see
26 sections 7001 through 7003 of the Patient Protection and Affordable Care Act (Pub. L. 111–148)
27 (ACA)). FDA believes that guidance for industry that provides answers to commonly asked
28 questions regarding FDA's interpretation of the BPCI Act will enhance transparency and
29 facilitate the development and approval of biosimilar and interchangeable products. In addition,
30 these Q&As respond to questions the Agency has received from prospective applicants regarding

---

[1] This draft guidance has been prepared by the Center for Drug Evaluation and Research (CDER) and the Center for
Biologics Evaluation and Research (CBER) at the Food and Drug Administration (FDA or the Agency).

We update guidances periodically. To make sure you have the most recent version of a guidance, check the FDA
Drugs guidance web page at
https://www.fda.gov/Drugs/GuidanceComplianceRegulatoryInformation/Guidances/default.htm.

[2] In this draft guidance, the following terms are used to describe biological products licensed under section 351(k) of
the PHS Act: (1) *biosimilar* or *biosimilar product* refers to a product that FDA has determined to be biosimilar to
the reference product (see sections 351(i)(2) and 351(k)(2) of the PHS Act) and (2) *interchangeable biosimilar* or
interchangeable product refers to a biosimilar product that FDA has also determined to be interchangeable with the
reference product (see sections 351(i)(3) and 351(k)(4) of the PHS Act). Biosimilarity, interchangeability, and
related issues are discussed in more detail in the Background section of this draft guidance.

Draft — Not for Implementation

31   the appropriate statutory authority under which certain products will be regulated. FDA intends
32   to update this draft guidance document to include additional Q&As as appropriate.
33
34   This draft guidance document revises the draft guidance document, *Biosimilars: Additional*
35   *Questions and Answers Regarding Implementation of the Biologics Price Competition and*
36   *Innovation Act of 2009.*[3] The draft guidance document contains Q&As distributed for comment
37   purposes only and includes new Q&As, as well as revisions to Q&As that appeared in previous
38   versions of the draft or final guidance documents. Additional information about the Q&A format
39   for this draft guidance document is provided in the Background section.
40
41   FDA is also issuing a final guidance document entitled *Questions and Answers on Biosimilar*
42   *Development and the BPCI Act.* This final guidance document is part of a series of guidance
43   documents that FDA has developed to facilitate development of biosimilar and interchangeable
44   products. The final guidance documents issued to date address a broad range of issues,
45   including:
46
47   •   Quality Considerations in Demonstrating Biosimilarity of a Therapeutic Protein
48   Product to a Reference Product (April 2015)

49   •   Scientific Considerations in Demonstrating Biosimilarity to a Reference Product
50   (April 2015)

51   •   Questions and Answers on Biosimilar Development and the BPCI Act (December
52   2018)

53   •   Clinical Pharmacology Data to Support a Demonstration of Biosimilarity to a
54   Reference Product (December 2016)

55   •   Labeling for Biosimilar Products (July 2018)

56
57   In addition, FDA has published draft guidance documents related to the BPCI Act, which, when
58   finalized, will represent FDA's current thinking. These draft guidance documents include:
59
60   •   Considerations in Demonstrating Interchangeability With a Reference Product
61   (January 2017)

62   •   Formal Meetings Between the FDA and Sponsors or Applicants of BsUFA
63   Products (June 2018)

64   •   Reference Product Exclusivity for Biological Products Filed Under Section 351(a)
65   of the PHS Act (August 2014)

66

---

[3] FDA has adjusted the title of this draft guidance to more clearly communicate that this draft guidance contains *draft* questions and answers.

2

67 In general, FDA's guidance documents do not establish legally enforceable responsibilities.
68 Instead, guidances describe the Agency's current thinking on a topic and should be viewed only
69 as recommendations, unless specific regulatory or statutory requirements are cited. The use of
70 the word *should* in Agency guidances means that something is suggested or recommended, but
71 not required.
72
73 **BACKGROUND**
74
75 *The BPCI Act*
76
77 The BPCI Act was enacted as part of the ACA on March 23, 2010. The BPCI Act amended the
78 PHS Act and other statutes to create an abbreviated licensure pathway for biological products
79 shown to be biosimilar to, or interchangeable with, an FDA-licensed biological reference product
80 (see sections 7001 through 7003 of the ACA). Section 351(k) of the PHS Act (42 U.S.C.
81 262(k)), added by the BPCI Act, sets forth the requirements for an application for a proposed
82 biosimilar or interchangeable product.
83
84 Section 351(i) defines the term *biosimilar* or *biosimilarity* "in reference to a biological product
85 that is the subject of an application under [section 351(k)]" to mean "that the biological product
86 is highly similar to the reference product[4] notwithstanding minor differences in clinically
87 inactive components" and that "there are no clinically meaningful differences between the
88 biological product and the reference product in terms of the safety, purity, and potency of the
89 product" (see section 351(i)(2) of the PHS Act).
90
91 Section 351(k)(4) of the PHS Act provides that upon review of an application submitted under
92 section 351(k) or any supplement to such application, FDA will determine the biological product
93 to be interchangeable with the reference product if FDA determines that the information
94 submitted in the application (or a supplement to such application) is sufficient to show that the
95 biological product "is biosimilar to the reference product" and "can be expected to produce the
96 same clinical result as the reference product in any given patient"[5] and that "for a biological
97 product that is administered more than once to an individual, the risk in terms of safety or
98 diminished efficacy of alternating or switching between use of the biological product and the
99 reference product is not greater than the risk of using the reference product without such
100 alternation or switch."[6]
101
102

---

[4] *Reference product* means the single biological product licensed under section 351(a) of the PHS Act against which
a biological product is evaluated in a 351(k) application (section 351(i)(4) of the PHS Act).
[5] Section 351(k)(4)(A) of the PHS Act.
[6] Section 351(k)(4)(B) of the PHS Act.

3

Draft — Not for Implementation

103   Section 351(i) of the PHS Act states that the term *interchangeable* or *interchangeability*, in
104   reference to a biological product that is shown to meet the standards described in section
105   351(k)(4) of the PHS Act, means that "the biological product may be substituted for the
106   reference product without the intervention of the health care provider who prescribed the
107   reference product."
108
109   In this draft guidance document, the terms *proposed biosimilar product* and *proposed*
110   *interchangeable product* are used to describe products that are under development or are the
111   subject of a pending 351(k) biologics license application (BLA).
112
113   Certain other provisions of the BPCI Act are discussed in the context of the relevant Q&A.
114
115   *"Question and Answer" Guidance Format*
116
117   This draft guidance document is a companion to the final guidance document, *Questions and*
118   *Answers on Biosimilar Development and the BPCI Act.* In this pair of guidance documents,
119   FDA issues each Q&A in draft form in this draft guidance document, receives comments on the
120   draft Q&A, and, as appropriate, moves the Q&A to the final guidance document, after reviewing
121   comments and incorporating suggested changes to the Q&A, when appropriate. A Q&A that
122   was previously in the final guidance document may be withdrawn and moved to the draft
123   guidance document if FDA determines that the Q&A should be revised in some respect and
124   reissued in a revised draft Q&A for comment. A Q&A also may be withdrawn and removed
125   from the Q&A guidance documents if, for instance, the issue addressed in the Q&A is addressed
126   in another FDA guidance document.
127
128   A reference will follow each question in this draft guidance document describing the publication
129   date of the current version of the Q&A, and whether the Q&A has been added to or modified in
130   this draft guidance document. FDA has maintained the original numbering of the guidance
131   Q&As used in the April 2015 final guidance document (*Biosimilars: Questions and Answers*
132   *Regarding Implementation of the Biologics Price Competition and Innovation Act of 2009*) and
133   May 2015 draft guidance document (*Biosimilars: Additional Questions and Answers Regarding*
134   *Implementation of the Biologics Price Competition and Innovation Act of 2009*). For ease of
135   reference, a Q&A retains the same number when it moves from the draft guidance document to
136   the final guidance document and, where appropriate, when a Q&A is withdrawn from the final
137   guidance document and moved to the draft guidance document.
138
139   Where a Q&A has been withdrawn from the final guidance document, this is marked in the final
140   guidance document by several asterisks between nonconsecutively numbered Q&As and, where
141   appropriate, explanatory text.
142

4

143   **QUESTIONS AND ANSWERS**

144   **I.**   **BIOSIMILARITY OR INTERCHANGEABILITY**

145

146   * * * * *

147   *Q. I.12.* *How can an applicant demonstrate that its proposed injectable biosimilar*
148   *product or proposed injectable interchangeable product has the same*
149   *"strength" as the reference product?*
150   *[Moved to Draft from Final December 2018]*

151

152   A. I.12. Under section 351(k)(2)(A)(i)(IV) of the PHS Act, an applicant must demonstrate
153   that the "strength" of the proposed biosimilar product or proposed interchangeable
154   product is the same as that of the reference product. Data and information
155   generated as part of the analytical similarity assessment may inform the
156   determination that a proposed biosimilar product or proposed interchangeable
157   product has the same strength as its reference product. As a scientific matter,
158   there may be a need to take into account different factors and approaches in
159   determining the "strength" of different biological products. Sponsors should
160   discuss their proposed approach with FDA and provide an adequate scientific
161   basis for their approach to demonstrating same strength.

162

163   In general, a sponsor of a proposed biosimilar product or proposed
164   interchangeable product with an "injection" dosage form (e.g., a solution) can
165   demonstrate that its product has the same strength as the reference product by
166   demonstrating that both products have the same total content of drug substance (in
167   mass or units of activity) and the same concentration of drug substance (in mass
168   or units of activity per unit volume). In general, for a proposed biosimilar product
169   or proposed interchangeable product that is a dry solid (e.g., a lyophilized
170   powder) from which a constituted or reconstituted solution is prepared, a sponsor
171   can demonstrate that the product has the same strength as the reference product by
172   demonstrating that both products have the same total content of drug substance (in
173   mass or units of activity).

174

175   Although not a part of demonstrating same "strength," if the proposed biosimilar
176   product or proposed interchangeable product is a dry solid (e.g., a lyophilized
177   powder) from which a constituted or reconstituted solution is prepared, the 351(k)
178   application generally should contain information that the concentration of the
179   proposed biosimilar product or proposed interchangeable product, when
180   constituted or reconstituted, is the same as that of the reference product, when
181   constituted or reconstituted.

182

183   A sponsor should determine the content of drug substance for both the reference
184   product and the proposed biosimilar product or proposed interchangeable product

5

185	using the same method. The strength of the proposed product generally should be
186	expressed using the same units of measure as the reference product.
187	
188	**Q. I.16.** ***How can a proposed biosimilar product applicant fulfill the requirement for***
189	***pediatric assessments or investigations under the Pediatric Research Equity Act***
190	***(PREA)?***
191	**[Updated/Retained in Draft December 2018]**
192	
193	A. I.16. Applicants for proposed biosimilar products should address PREA requirements
194	based upon the nature and extent of pediatric information in the reference product
195	labeling. PREA requirements are applicable to proposed biosimilar products that
196	have not been determined to be interchangeable with a reference product only to
197	the extent that compliance with PREA would not result in: (1) a condition of use
198	that has not been previously approved for the reference product; or (2) a dosage
199	form, strength, or route of administration that differs from that of the reference
200	product.
201	
202	As a preliminary matter, we note that there are differences in the use of the term
203	"extrapolation" in the context of a proposed biosimilar product under the PHS Act
204	and in the context of PREA.
205	
206	• An applicant may provide scientific justification for "extrapolation" to
207	support approval of a biosimilar product under section 351(k) of the PHS
208	Act for one or more conditions of use. For more information on
209	extrapolation in this context, see FDA's guidance for industry on *Scientific*
210	*Considerations in Demonstrating Biosimilarity to a Reference Product.*
211	
212	• "Pediatric extrapolation" refers to establishing the effectiveness of a drug
213	in a pediatric population without requiring a separate study in that
214	population when the course of the disease and the effects of the drug are
215	sufficiently similar in the pediatric population and the adult population (or
216	another pediatric population) in which the drug has been studied and
217	shown to be effective (see section 505B(a)(2)(B) and (a)(3)(B) of the
218	Federal Food Drug and Cosmetic Act (FD&C Act).
219	
220	In the discussion that follows, the term "extrapolation" generally will be used to
221	refer to extrapolation to support approval of a biosimilar product under section
222	351(k) of the PHS Act for one or more conditions of use, and not to pediatric
223	extrapolation.
224	
225	• Adequate pediatric information in reference product labeling
226	
227	If the labeling for the reference product contains adequate pediatric
228	information (e.g., information reflecting an adequate pediatric assessment)

6

229 with respect to an indication for which a biosimilar applicant seeks
230 licensure in adults, the biosimilar applicant may fulfill PREA requirements
231 for that indication by satisfying the statutory requirements for showing
232 biosimilarity and providing an adequate scientific justification under the
233 BPCI Act for extrapolating the pediatric information from the reference
234 product to the proposed biosimilar product.
235
236 If the submitted scientific justification for extrapolation under section
237 351(k) of the PHS Act is inadequate, a biosimilar applicant must submit
238 appropriate data to fulfill applicable PREA requirements.
239
240 • Lack of adequate pediatric information in reference product labeling
241
242 If the labeling for the reference product does not contain adequate
243 pediatric information for one or more pediatric age groups for an
244 indication for which a biosimilar applicant seeks licensure in adults, and
245 applicable PREA requirements were deferred for the reference product for
246 those pediatric age groups, a biosimilar applicant should request a deferral
247 of PREA requirements for those pediatric age groups. The biosimilar
248 applicant should amend or supplement its 351(k) BLA, as appropriate, to
249 seek approval for updated labeling, supported by biosimilar extrapolation
250 or appropriate data, that includes relevant pediatric information after the
251 reference product labeling is updated with that information.
252
253 If the labeling for the reference product does not contain adequate
254 pediatric information for one or more pediatric age groups for an
255 indication for which a biosimilar applicant seeks licensure in adults, and
256 PREA requirements were waived for, or inapplicable to, the reference
257 product for those pediatric age groups, a biosimilar applicant should note
258 this information in its initial pediatric study plan (iPSP), if any, but does
259 not need to request a waiver of PREA requirements for those age groups.
260 For proposed biosimilars, obligations under PREA are circumscribed by
261 the BPCI Act to require an assessment only for indications and age groups
262 or other conditions of use in which the reference product has been or will
263 be assessed. In other words, the Agency has determined that PREA
264 requirements are applicable to a proposed biosimilar product that has not
265 been determined to be interchangeable with a reference product only to the
266 extent that compliance with PREA would not result in: (1) a condition of
267 use that has not been previously approved for the reference product, or (2)
268 a dosage form, strength, or route of administration that differs from that of
269 the reference product.
270
271 FDA's recommendations to biosimilar applicants with respect to the PREA
272 requirements reflect a clarification based on the Agency's interpretation of the

7

273 interaction between section 505B of the FD&C Act (PREA) and section 351(k) of
274 the PHS Act. Biosimilar applicants previously requested, and the Agency
275 granted, waivers in instances where PREA requirements were waived for or
276 determined to be inapplicable to the reference product. However, upon further
277 consideration, waivers for biosimilars applicants under those circumstances were
278 not necessary, and the practice is more accurately described in terms of the
279 Agency's interpretation of the BPCI Act and PREA. The BPCI Act added section
280 351(k) of the PHS Act and amended section 505B of the FD&C Act to specify
281 that PREA is applicable to a biosimilar product that has not been determined to be
282 interchangeable with a reference product (see section 7002(a), (d)(2) of the BPCI
283 Act). FDA reads section 351(k) of the PHS Act and PREA together with respect
284 to the need to conduct assessments of and seek licensure for certain pediatric uses
285 and pediatric formulations. An application submitted under section 351(k) of the
286 PHS Act must include, among other things, information demonstrating that "the
287 condition or conditions of use prescribed, recommended, or suggested in the
288 labeling proposed for the biological product have been previously approved for
289 the reference product" and "the route of administration, the dosage form, and the
290 strength of the biological product are the same as those of the reference product"
291 (section 351(k)(2)(A)(i)(III)-(IV) of the PHS Act). FDA has determined that,
292 when the reference product does not have adequate pediatric use information in its
293 labeling or an age-appropriate formulation for a relevant pediatric population, the
294 obligations for the biosimilar applicant under PREA are circumscribed by section
295 351(k) of the PHS Act insofar as the biosimilar applicant would not be expected
296 to obtain licensure for a pediatric use (or describe that use in product labeling)
297 that has not been licensed for the reference product and would not be expected to
298 obtain licensure of a product that would result in a dosage form, strength, or route
299 of administration that differs from that of the reference product.
300
301 By establishing an abbreviated licensure pathway for biosimilar and
302 interchangeable products, the BPCI Act reflects the strong public health interest in
303 the licensure and availability of those products. Such licensure could result in
304 increased competition, as well as greater access to biological products. The
305 Agency's interpretation of section 351(k) and PREA assures that biosimilar
306 applicants are not subject to greater regulatory burdens than those faced by
307 reference product sponsors with respect to the study of pediatric uses.
308
309 This approach preserves the intent and availability of an abbreviated licensure
310 pathway for biosimilars, while helping to ensure that a biosimilar product is
311 labeled and formulated for relevant pediatric conditions of use that have been
312 approved for the reference product. FDA also recognizes the important interests
313 furthered by PREA and appreciates the need to study pediatric uses of biological
314 products and to include pediatric use information in product labeling.
315 Consequently, in appropriate cases, FDA may take additional steps within its
316 authority to assure that pediatric use information is included in biological product

8

317 labeling.[7] Such actions may include invoking the "marketed drugs" provision
318 under PREA, in certain circumstances, to require sponsors to conduct pediatric
319 assessments, or take other appropriate steps, to support pediatric labeling for both
320 the biosimilar product and the reference product.[8]
321
322 If a biosimilar applicant believes that none of the situations described above
323 applies to its proposed product, the applicant should contact FDA for further
324 information.
325
326 *Q. I.20.* *What is the nature and type of information that a sponsor should provide to*
327 *support a post-approval manufacturing change for a licensed biosimilar*
328 *product?*
329 *[New December 2018]*
330
331 A. I.20 In general, a sponsor who intends to make a manufacturing change to a licensed
332 biosimilar product should follow the principles outlined in the International
333 Council for Harmonisation (ICH) guidance for industry *Q5E Comparability of*
334 *Biotechnological/Biological Products Subject to Changes in their Manufacturing*
335 *Process (June 2005)*. Accordingly, the sponsor should provide sufficient data and
336 information to demonstrate the comparability of the biosimilar product before and
337 after the manufacturing change. The comparability assessment should include: a)
338 side-by-side analytical comparison of a sufficient number of lots of pre-change
339 and post-change material, including an assessment of stability; and b) a
340 comparison of analytical data from the post-change material to historical
341 analytical data from lots used in the analytical similarity assessment, including
342 data from lots used in clinical studies that supported licensure of the biosimilar
343 product. A well-qualified, in-house reference standard should also be included in
344 the comparability exercise. In certain cases, additional reference materials may
345 be included in the comparability study. The extent of data and information
346 necessary to establish comparability would be commensurate with the type of
347 manufacturing change and its potential impact on product quality, safety, and
348 efficacy.
349
350 In addition, FDA continues to consider the nature and type of information a
351 sponsor should provide to support a post-approval manufacturing change to a
352 biological product determined by FDA to be interchangeable with the reference
353 product under section 351(k)(4) of the PHS Act. FDA intends to provide specific
354 recommendations for post-approval manufacturing changes to interchangeable
355 biological products in future guidance.

---

[7] For instance, if the Agency determines that the basis for the reference product's waiver under PREA no longer applies to a particular age group (e.g., because it is now feasible to study a younger pediatric age group), FDA may, as appropriate, contact the 351(k) biosimilar product sponsor, as well as the reference product sponsor, and require further action by both parties to comply with PREA. *See* § 505B(a)(5) of the FD&C Act.

[8] *See* § 505B(b) of the FD&C Act.

9

356
357   A sponsor may seek approval, in a supplement to an approved 351(k) BLA, of a
358   route of administration, a dosage form, or a strength that is the same as that of the
359   reference product, but that has not previously been licensed under the 351(k)
360   BLA.[9] FDA intends to provide specific recommendations on this topic in future
361   guidance.
362
363   *Q. I.21.*   *May a sponsor seek approval, in a 351(k) application or a supplement to an*
364   *approved 351(k) application, of a route of administration, a dosage form, or a*
365   *strength that is not the same as that of the reference product?*
366   *[New December 2018]*
367
368   A. I.21.   No. Under section 351(k)(2)(A)(i)(IV) of the PHS Act, a 351(k) application must
369   include information demonstrating that "the route of administration, the dosage
370   form, and the strength" of the proposed biosimilar or interchangeable product "are
371   the same as those of the reference product." An applicant may not seek approval,
372   in a 351(k) application or a supplement to an approved 351(k) application, for a
373   route of administration, a dosage form, or a strength that is not the same as that of
374   the reference product.
375
376   *Q. I.22.*   *May a sponsor seek approval, in a 351(k) application or a supplement to an*
377   *approved 351(k) application, for a condition of use that has not previously been*
378   *approved for the reference product?*
379   *[New December 2018]*
380
381   A. I.22   No. Under section 351(k)(2)(A)(i)(III) of the PHS Act, the 351(k) application
382   must include information demonstrating that the condition or conditions of use
383   prescribed, recommended, or suggested in the labeling proposed for the proposed
384   biosimilar or interchangeable product have been previously approved for the
385   reference product. A 351(k) applicant may not seek approval, in a 351(k)
386   application or a supplement to an approved 351(k) application, of a condition of
387   use (e.g., indication, dosing regimen) that has not been previously approved for
388   the reference product.
389
390   *Q.I.23*   *May a prospective 351(k) BLA applicant request a letter from FDA stating that*
391   *study protocols intended to support a 351(k) application contain safety*
392   *protections comparable to an applicable Risk Evaluation and Mitigation*
393   *Strategy (REMS) for the reference product?*
394   *[New December 2018]*
395

---

[9] As described elsewhere in this draft guidance (Q&A I.21), a 351(k) applicant may not seek approval of a route of administration, a dosage form, or a strength that is not the same as the reference product, including in a supplement to an approved 351(k) application. This draft guidance, when finalized, will represent FDA's current thinking on this topic. See Q&A I.21 for additional information.

10

396   A.I.23   Yes. There have been reports of instances in which a reference product holder
397   has refused to sell product to a prospective applicant for a competing product that
398   is seeking to conduct studies to support approval, and the reference product holder
399   cites the risk evaluation and mitigation strategy (REMS) with elements to assure
400   safe use (ETASU) for the reference product as justification.

401
402   In the interest of facilitating a prospective biosimilar applicant's access to
403   supplies of the reference product to conduct the testing necessary to support
404   351(k) BLA approval, FDA will, on request, review (one or more) study protocols
405   submitted by a prospective 351(k) BLA applicant to assess whether they provide
406   safety protections comparable to those in the applicable REMS with ETASU. If
407   the Agency determines that comparable protections exist, FDA will notify the
408   prospective 351(k) BLA applicant. If requested to do so by the prospective
409   351(k) BLA applicant, FDA will then issue a separate letter to the reference
410   product holder stating that comparable protections exist and indicating that FDA
411   will not consider it to be a violation of the REMS for the reference product holder
412   to provide the prospective 351(k) BLA applicant with a sufficient quantity of the
413   reference product to allow it to perform testing necessary to support its 351(k)
414   BLA.

415
416   Requesting such a protocol review or letter is not a legal requirement. If a
417   prospective 351(k) BLA applicant wishes to request such a letter or protocol
418   review, however, it should (1) confirm that the product at issue is subject to a
419   REMS with ETASU by checking the Agency's online listing of approved
420   REMS[10], and (2) contact FDA for more information. For contact information, see
421   FDA's website, "Biosimilars," available at https://www.fda.gov/biosimilars and
422   click on the link, "Industry Information and Guidance" listed in the left column.

423
424   *Q.I.24 May an applicant submit data and information to support approval of a*
425   *proposed biosimilar or interchangeable product for an indication for which the*
426   *reference product has unexpired orphan exclusivity?*
427   *[New December 2018]*

428
429   A.I.24   Yes. An applicant may submit data and information to support approval of a
430   proposed biosimilar or interchangeable product for one or more indications for
431   which the reference product has unexpired orphan exclusivity. For example, an
432   applicant may submit data and information intended to provide sufficient
433   scientific justification for extrapolation to support approval of a proposed
434   biosimilar or interchangeable product for one or more indications for which the
435   reference product has unexpired orphan exclusivity. However, FDA will not be
436   able to approve the proposed biosimilar or interchangeable product for the
437   protected indication(s) until the orphan exclusivity expires.

---

[10] See Approved Risk Evaluation and Mitigation Strategies (REMS):
https://www.accessdata.fda.gov/scripts/cder/rems/index.cfm

11

438
439

440 **II. PROVISIONS RELATED TO REQUIREMENTS TO SUBMIT A BLA FOR A**
441 **"BIOLOGICAL PRODUCT"**
442
443 *Q. II.1. How does FDA interpret the category of "protein (except any chemically*
444 *synthesized polypeptide)" in the amended definition of "biological product" in*
445 *section 351(i)(1) of the PHS Act?*
446 *[Moved to Draft from Final December 2018]*
447
448 A. II.1. The BPCI Act amends the definition of "biological product" in section 351(i) of
449 the PHS Act to include a "protein (except any chemically synthesized
450 polypeptide)" and provides that an application for a biological product must be
451 submitted under section 351 of the PHS Act, subject to certain exceptions during
452 the 10-year transition period ending on March 23, 2020, described in section
453 7002(e) of the Affordable Care Act.
454
455 FDA has developed the following interpretations of the statutory terms "protein"
456 and "chemically synthesized polypeptide" to implement the amended definition of
457 "biological product" and provide clarity to prospective applicants regarding the
458 statutory authority under which such products are regulated.
459
460 *Protein* — FDA interprets the term "protein" to mean any alpha amino acid
461 polymer with a specific defined sequence that is greater than 40 amino acids in
462 size.
463
464 Where a single amino acid polymer is greater than 40 amino acids in size and is
465 related to a naturally occurring peptide, such polymer would be reviewed to
466 determine whether the additional amino acids that cause the peptide to exceed 40
467 amino acids in size raise any concerns about the risk/benefit profile of the
468 product.
469
470 Some amino acid polymers are composed of multiple amino acid chains that are
471 associated with each other. When two or more amino acid chains are associated
472 with each other in a manner that occurs in nature, the size of the amino acid
473 polymer for purposes of our interpretation of the statutory terms "protein" and
474 "chemically synthesized polypeptide" is based on the total number of amino acids
475 in those chains, and is not limited to the number of amino acids in a contiguous
476 sequence. In other words, the amino acids in each such amino acid chain will be
477 added together to determine whether the product meets the numerical threshold in
478 FDA's interpretation of the terms "protein" and "chemically synthesized
479 polypeptide." However, for products with amino acid chains that are associated
480 with each other in a manner that is not found in nature (i.e., amino acid chains that

12

481   are associated with each other in a novel manner that is not found in naturally
482   occurring proteins), FDA intends to conduct a fact-specific, case-by-case analysis
483   to determine whether the size of the amino acid polymer, for purposes of our
484   interpretation of the statutory terms "protein" and "chemically synthesized
485   polypeptide," should be based on adding each of the amino acids in the amino
486   acid chains together or should be based on separate consideration of the amino
487   acid chains (e.g., the number of amino acids in the largest chain). In such cases,
488   FDA may consider in its analysis, among other things, any structural or functional
489   characteristics of the product.
490
491   *Chemically synthesized polypeptide* — The term "chemically synthesized
492   polypeptide" means any alpha amino acid polymer that (1) is made entirely by
493   chemical synthesis; and (2) is greater than 40 amino acids but less than 100 amino
494   acids in size.
495
496   A chemically synthesized polypeptide, as described, is not a "biological product"
497   and will be regulated as a drug under the FD&C Act unless the polypeptide
498   otherwise meets the statutory definition of a "biological product."
499
500   Where a single amino acid polymer is greater than 99 amino acids in size and is
501   related to a naturally occurring peptide or polypeptide of shorter length, such
502   polymer would be reviewed to determine whether the additional amino acids that
503   cause the polymer to exceed 99 amino acids in size raise any concerns about the
504   risk/benefit profile of the product.
505
506   FDA's interpretation of these statutory terms is informed by several factors. The
507   scientific literature describes a "protein" as a defined sequence of alpha amino
508   acid polymers linked by peptide bonds, and generally excludes "peptides" from
509   the category of "protein." A "peptide" generally refers to polymers that are
510   smaller, perform fewer functions, contain less three-dimensional structure, are
511   less likely to be post-translationally modified, and thus are generally characterized
512   more easily than proteins. Consistent with the scientific literature, FDA interprets
513   the term "protein" in the statutory definition of biological product in a manner
514   that does not include peptides. To enhance regulatory clarity and minimize
515   administrative complexity, FDA has decided to distinguish proteins from peptides
516   based solely on size (i.e., number of amino acids).
517
518   In the absence of clear scientific consensus on the criteria that distinguish proteins
519   from peptides, including the exact size at which a chain(s) of amino acids
520   becomes a protein, FDA reviewed the pertinent literature and concluded that a
521   threshold of 40 amino acids is appropriate for defining the upper size boundary of
522   a peptide. Accordingly, FDA interprets the BPCI Act such that any polymer
523   composed of 40 or fewer amino acids is a peptide and not a protein. Therefore,

13

Draft — Not for Implementation

524 unless a peptide otherwise meets the statutory definition of a "biological product"
525 (e.g., a peptide vaccine), it will be regulated as a drug under the FD&C Act.
526
527 The statutory category of "protein" parenthetically excludes "any chemically
528 synthesized polypeptide." There are several definitions of "polypeptide" in the
529 scientific literature. Some are broad (e.g., polypeptide means any amino acid
530 polymer), while others are more narrow (e.g., polypeptide means any amino acid
531 polymer composed of fewer than 100 amino acids). FDA believes that a narrow
532 interpretation of polypeptide is most appropriate in this context because, among
533 other reasons, this avoids describing an exception to the category of "protein" that
534 includes a broader category of molecules. Therefore, FDA interprets the statutory
535 exclusion for "chemically synthesized polypeptide" to mean any molecule that is
536 made entirely by chemical synthesis and that is composed of greater than 40
537 amino acids but less than 100 amino acids in size. Such molecules will be
538 regulated as drugs under the FD&C Act, unless the chemically synthesized
539 polypeptide otherwise meets the statutory definition of a "biological product."
540
541 There may be additional considerations for proposed products that are
542 combination products or meet the statutory definition of both a "device" and a
543 "biological product." We encourage prospective sponsors to contact FDA for
544 further information on a product-specific basis.
545
546   * * * * *
547
548 **III.**   **EXCLUSIVITY**
549
550   * * * * *
551
552

14

APPENDIX D5

Development of Therapeutic Protein Biosimilars: Comparative Analytical Assessment and Other Quality-Related Considerations

Development of Therapeutic Protein Biosimilars: Comparative Analytical Assessment and Other Quality-Related Considerations

Guidance for Industry

DRAFT GUIDANCE

This guidance document is being distributed for comment purposes only.

Comments and suggestions regarding this draft document should be submitted within 60 days of publication in the *Federal Register* of the notice announcing the availability of the draft guidance. Submit electronic comments to https://www.regulations.gov. Submit written comments to the Dockets Management Staff (HFA-305), Food and Drug Administration, 5630 Fishers Lane, Rm. 1061, Rockville, MD 20852. All comments should be identified with the docket number listed in the notice of availability that publishes in the *Federal Register*.

For questions regarding this draft document, contact (CDER) Sandra Benton, 301-796-1042, or (CBER) Office of Communication, Outreach and Development, 800-835-4709 or 240-402-80 0.

U.S. Department of Health and Human Services
Food and Drug Administration
Center for Drug Evaluation and Research (CDER)
Center for Biologics Evaluation and Research (CBER)

May 2019
Biosimilars

Development of Therapeutic Protein Biosimilars: Comparative Analytical Assessment and Other Quality-Related Considerations

Guidance for Industry

Additional copies are available from:

Office of Communications, Division of Drug Information
Center for Drug Evaluation and Research
Food and Drug Administration
10001 New Hampshire Ave., Hillandale Bldg., 4th Floor
Silver Spring, MD 20993-0002
Phone: 855-543-3784 or 301-796-3400; Fax: 301-431-6353
Email: druginfo@fda.hhs.gov
https://www.fda.gov/drugs/guidance-compliance-regulatory-information/guidances-drugs

and/or

Office of Communication, Outreach and Development
Center for Biologics Evaluation and Research
Food and Drug Administration
10903 New Hampshire Ave., Bldg. 71, Room 3128
Silver Spring, MD 20993-0002
Phone: 800-835-4709 or 240-402-7800
Email: ocod@fda.hhs.gov
https://www.fda.gov/vaccines-blood-biologics/guidance-compliance-regulatory-information-biologics/biologics-guidances

U.S. Department of Health and Human Services
Food and Drug Administration
Center for Drug Evaluation and Research (CDER)
Center for Biologics Evaluation and Research (CBER)

May 2019
Biosimilars

Contains Nonbinding Recommendations
Draft — Not for Implementation

TABLE OF CONTENTS

I.   INTRODUCTION 1

II.   BACKGROUND 3

III.   SCOPE 6

IV.   GENERAL PRINCIPLES 6

V.   FACTORS FOR CONSIDERATION IN PERFORMING THE COMPARATIVE
ANALYTICAL ASSESSMENT 10

    A.   Expression System 11

    B.   Manufacturing Process 11

    C.   Physicochemical Properties 12

    D.   Functional Activities 13

    E.   Target Binding 14

    F.   Impurities 14

    G.   Reference Product and Reference Standards 15

    H.   Finished Drug Product 17

    I.   Stability 18

VI.   COMPARATIVE ANALYTICAL ASSESSMENT 18

    A.   Considerations for Reference and Biosimilar Products 19

      1. Reference Product 19

      2. Proposed Product 19

      3. Accounting for Reference Product and Proposed Product Lots 20

      4. Reference Product and Non-U.S.-Licensed Comparator Products ... 20

    B.   Considerations for Data Analysis 21

      1. Risk Assessment 21

      2. Quantitative and Qualitative Data Analysis 22

    C.   Comparative Analytical Assessment Conclusions 24

VII.   CONCLUSION 24

VIII.   RELEVANT GUIDANCES 25

    GLOSSARY 28

i

1   **Development of Therapeutic Protein Biosimilars: Comparative**
2   **Analytical Assessment and Other Quality-Related Considerations**
3
4   **Guidance for Industry[1]**
5

6
7   This draft guidance, when finalized, will represent the current thinking of the Food and Drug
8   Administration (FDA or Agency) on this topic. It does not establish any rights for any person and is not
9   binding on FDA or the public. You can use an alternative approach if it satisfies the requirements of the
10   applicable statutes and regulations. To discuss an alternative approach, contact the FDA staff responsible
11   for this guidance as listed on the title page.
12

13
14
15
16   **I.**   **INTRODUCTION**
17
18   This guidance describes the Agency's recommendations on the design and evaluation of
19   comparative analytical studies intended to support a demonstration that a proposed therapeutic
20   protein product is biosimilar to a reference product licensed under section 351(a) of the Public
21   Health Service Act (PHS Act). Additionally, this guidance is intended to provide
22   recommendations to sponsors on the scientific and technical information for the chemistry,
23   manufacturing, and controls (CMC) portion of a marketing application for a proposed product
24   submitted under section 351(k) of the PHS Act.
25
26   The Biologics Price Competition and Innovation Act of 2009 (BPCI Act) amends the PHS Act
27   and other statutes to create an abbreviated licensure pathway in section 351(k) of the PHS Act
28   for biological products shown to be biosimilar to, or interchangeable with, an FDA-licensed
29   reference product (see sections 7001 through 7003 of the Patient Protection and Affordable Care
30   Act (ACA) (Public Law 111-148). Although the 351(k) pathway applies generally to biological
31   products, this guidance focuses on therapeutic protein products and provides an overview of
32   recommendations for the comparative analytical assessment and other important scientific
33   considerations to support a demonstration of biosimilarity between a proposed therapeutic

---

[1] This draft guidance has been prepared by the Center for Drug Evaluation and Research (CDER) and the Center for Biologics Evaluation and Research (CBER) at the Food and Drug Administration.

1

34 protein product (referred to as a *proposed biosimilar*[2] or *proposed biosimilar product*) and the
35 reference product.[3]
36
37 This guidance is one in a series of guidances that FDA is developing to facilitate implementation
38 of the BPCI Act.
39
40 Relevant final guidance documents[4] issued to date address a broad range of issues, including:
41
42 • *Scientific Considerations in Demonstrating Biosimilarity to a Reference Product*
43 (April 2015)

44 • *Questions and Answers on Biosimilar Development and the BPCI Act* (December
45 2018)

46 • *Clinical Pharmacology Data to Support a Demonstration of Biosimilarity to a*
47 *Reference Product* (December 2016)

48 • *Labeling for Biosimilar Products* (July 2018)

49 • *Considerations in Demonstrating Interchangeability With a Reference Product*
50 (May 2019)

51
52 In addition, FDA has published draft guidance documents related to the BPCI Act, which, when
53 finalized, will represent FDA's current thinking. These draft guidance documents include:
54
55 • *Formal Meetings Between the FDA and Sponsors or Applicants of BsUFA*
56 *Products* (June 2018)

57 • *Reference Product Exclusivity for Biological Products Filed Under Section*
58 *351(a) of the PHS Act* (August 2014)

59 • *New and Revised Draft Q&As on Biosimilar Development and the BPCI Act*
60 *(Revision 2)* (December 2018)

61

---

[2] In this guidance, the following terms are used to describe biological products licensed under section 351(k) of the PHS Act: (1) "biosimilar" or "biosimilar product" refers to a product that FDA has determined to be biosimilar to the reference product (see sections 351(i)(2) and 351(k)(2) of the PHS Act) and (2) "interchangeable biosimilar" or "interchangeable product" refers to a biosimilar product that FDA has determined to be interchangeable with the reference product (see sections 351(i)(3) and 351(k)(4) of the PHS Act).

[3] A 351(k) application for a proposed biosimilar product must include information demonstrating biosimilarity based on data derived from, among other things, "analytical studies that demonstrate that the biological product is highly similar to the reference product notwithstanding minor differences in clinically inactive components." Section 351(k)(2)(A)(i)(I)(aa) of the PHS Act.

[4] We update guidances periodically. For the most recent version of a guidance, check the FDA guidance web page at https://www.fda.gov/regulatory-information/search-fda-guidance-documents.

2

62 When applicable, references to information in these final and draft guidances are included in this
63 guidance.
64
65 In general, FDA's guidance documents do not establish legally enforceable responsibilities.
66 Instead, guidances describe the Agency's current thinking on a topic and should be viewed only
67 as recommendations, unless specific regulatory or statutory requirements are cited. The use of
68 the word *should* in Agency guidances means that something is suggested or recommended, but
69 not required.
70
71
72 **II.   BACKGROUND**
73
74 In the 1980s, FDA began to receive marketing applications for biotechnology-derived protein
75 products, mostly for recombinant DNA-derived versions of naturally sourced products.
76 Consequently, FDA established a regulatory approach for the approval of recombinant DNA-
77 derived protein products, which was announced in the *Federal Register* (51 FR 23302, June 26,
78 1986), in conjunction with a 1985 document titled *Points to Consider in the Production and*
79 *Testing of New Drugs and Biologicals Produced by Recombinant DNA Technology.*[5] This
80 approach addresses the submission of an investigational new drug application (IND) to FDA for
81 evaluation before initiation of clinical investigations in human subjects and submission and
82 potential approval of a new drug application (NDA) or biologics license application (BLA)
83 before marketing products made with recombinant DNA technology, even if the active
84 ingredient in the product is thought to be identical to a naturally occurring substance or a
85 previously approved product. The policy set forth in those documents was developed in part
86 because of the challenges in evaluating protein products solely by physicochemical and
87 functional testing and because the biological system in which such a protein product is produced
88 can have a significant effect on the structure and function of the product itself.
89
90 Improvements in manufacturing processes, process controls, materials, and product testing, as
91 well as characterization tests and studies, have led to a gradual evolution in the regulation of
92 protein products. For example, in 1996, FDA provided recommendations in the *FDA Guidance*
93 *Concerning Demonstration of Comparability of Human Biological Products, Including*
94 *Therapeutic Biotechnology-derived Products*, which explains how a sponsor may demonstrate,
95 through a combination of analytical testing, functional assays (in vitro and/or in vivo),
96 assessment of pharmacokinetics (PK) and/or pharmacodynamics (PD) and toxicity in animals,
97 and clinical testing (clinical pharmacology, safety, and/or efficacy), that a manufacturing change
98 does not adversely affect the safety, identity, purity, or potency of its FDA-approved product.
99

---

[5] For more information, this document is available on FDA's Other Recommendations for Biologics Manufacturers web page at https://www.fda.gov/vaccines-blood-biologics/guidance-compliance-regulatory-information-biologics/other-recommendations-biologics-manufacturers.

3

100   Since 1996, FDA has approved many manufacturing process changes for licensed biological
101   products based on a demonstration of product comparability before and after the process change,
102   as supported by quality criteria and analytical testing and without the need for additional
103   nonclinical data and clinical safety and/or efficacy studies. In some cases, uncertainty about the
104   effect of the change and/or the results of the biochemical/functional comparability studies has
105   necessitated collection and assessment of additional data, including nonclinical and/or clinical
106   testing, to demonstrate product comparability. These concepts were further developed in the
107   International Conference on Harmonisation of Technical Requirements for Registration of
108   Pharmaceuticals for Human Use (ICH) and resulted in the ICH guidance for industry *Q5E*
109   *Comparability of Biotechnological/Biological Products Subject to Changes in Their*
110   *Manufacturing Process* (June 2005).
111
112   Although the scope of ICH Q5E is limited to an assessment of the comparability of a biological
113   product before and after a manufacturing process change made by the same manufacturer, certain
114   general scientific principles described in ICH Q5E are applicable to an assessment of
115   biosimilarity between a proposed product and its reference product. However, demonstrating
116   that a proposed product is biosimilar to an FDA-licensed reference product manufactured by a
117   different manufacturer typically will be more complex and will likely require more extensive and
118   comprehensive data than assessing the comparability of a product before and after a
119   manufacturing process change made by the product's sponsor. A manufacturer that modifies its
120   own manufacturing process has extensive knowledge and information about the product and the
121   existing process, including established controls and acceptance parameters. By contrast, the
122   manufacturer of a proposed biosimilar will have no direct knowledge of the manufacturing
123   process for the reference product and will have its own manufacturing process (e.g., different cell
124   line, raw materials, equipment, processes, process controls, acceptance criteria).
125
126   Therefore, comprehensive comparative analytical data are necessary to build the foundation for a
127   development program for a proposed biosimilar product intended for submission under section
128   351(k) of the PHS Act.
129
130   *The BPCI Act*
131
132   The BPCI Act, enacted as part of the (ACA) on March 23, 2010, amends the PHS Act and other
133   statutes to create an abbreviated licensure pathway for biological products shown to be
134   biosimilar to, or interchangeable with, an FDA-licensed biological reference product (see
135   sections 7001 through 7003 of the ACA). Section 351(k) of the PHS Act (42 U.S.C. 262(k)),
136   added by the BPCI Act, sets forth the requirements for an application for a proposed biosimilar
137   product or a proposed interchangeable product. An application submitted under section 351(k)

4

138   must contain, among other things, information demonstrating that "the biological product is
139   biosimilar to a reference product" based upon data derived from:
140
141   •   Analytical studies that demonstrate that the biological product is highly similar to the
142   reference product notwithstanding minor differences in clinically inactive components;
143   •   Animal studies (including the assessment of toxicity); and
144   •   A clinical study or studies (including the assessment of immunogenicity and PK or PD)
145   that are sufficient to demonstrate safety, purity, and potency in one or more appropriate
146   conditions of use for which the reference product is licensed and intended to be used and
147   for which licensure is sought for the biological product.[6]
148
149   FDA has the discretion to determine that an element above is unnecessary in a 351(k)
150   application.[7]
151
152   The term *biosimilar* or *biosimilarity* is defined in the PHS Act "in reference to a biological
153   product that is the subject of an application under [section 351(k)]" to mean "that the biological
154   product is highly similar to the reference product notwithstanding minor differences in clinically
155   inactive components" and that "there are no clinically meaningful differences between the
156   biological product and the reference product in terms of the safety, purity, and potency of the
157   product" (section 351(i)(2) of the PHS Act). The term *reference product* is defined in the PHS
158   Act as the single biological product licensed under section 351(a) of the PHS Act against which a
159   biological product is evaluated in a 351(k) application (section 351(i)(4) of the PHS Act).
160
161   Section 351(k)(4) of the PHS Act provides that upon review of an application submitted under
162   section 351(k) or any supplement to such application, FDA will determine the biological product
163   to be interchangeable with the reference product if FDA determines that the information
164   submitted in the application (or a supplement to such application) is sufficient to show that the
165   biological product "is biosimilar to the reference product" and "can be expected to produce the
166   same clinical result as the reference product in any given patient"[8] and that "for a biological
167   product that is administered more than once to an individual, the risk in terms of safety or
168   diminished efficacy of alternating or switching between use of the biological product and the
169   reference product is not greater than the risk of using the reference product without such
170   alternation or switch."[9]
171
172   The term *interchangeable* or *interchangeability* is defined in the PHS Act, in reference to a
173   biological product that is shown to meet the standards described in section 351(k)(4) of the PHS

---

[6] Section 351(k)(2)(A)(i)(I) of the PHS Act.

[7] Section 351(k)(2)(A)(ii) of the PHS Act.

[8] Section 351(k)(4)(A) of the PHS Act.

[9] Section 351(k)(4)(B) of the PHS Act.

174   Act, to mean that "the biological product may be substituted for the reference product without
175   the intervention of the health care provider who prescribed the reference product" (section
176   351(i)(3) of the PHS Act).
177
178
179   **III.   SCOPE**
180
181   This document provides guidance on the use of comparative analytical studies that are relevant to
182   assessing whether the proposed product is biosimilar to a reference product for purposes of
183   submission of a marketing application under section 351(k) of the PHS Act. This document is
184   not intended to provide an overview of FDA's approach to determining interchangeability, which
185   is addressed in a separate guidance document.[10] Although this guidance applies specifically to
186   therapeutic protein products, the general scientific principles may be informative for the
187   development of proposed biosimilars to other protein products, such as in vivo protein diagnostic
188   products. If the reference product cannot be adequately characterized for the purpose of
189   demonstrating that a proposed product is biosimilar to the reference product as recommended in
190   this guidance, the application may not be appropriate for submission under section 351(k) of the
191   PHS Act.
192
193   This guidance also describes considerations for CMC information that is relevant to assessing
194   whether the proposed product is biosimilar to the reference product. It is critical that all product
195   applications contain a complete and thorough CMC section that provides the necessary and
196   appropriate information (e.g., characterization, adventitious agent safety, process controls, and
197   specifications) to support that the manufacturing process consistently delivers a product with the
198   intended quality characteristics. This guidance should be used as a companion to other
199   guidances available from FDA that describe the CMC information appropriate for evaluation of
200   protein products.[11] We encourage early interaction with FDA to discuss specific CMC issues
201   that may arise for a sponsor's proposed product.
202
203
204   **IV.   GENERAL PRINCIPLES**
205
206   Advances in analytical sciences (both physicochemical and biological) enable some protein
207   products to be characterized extensively in terms of their physicochemical and biological
208   properties. These analytical procedures have improved the ability to identify and characterize

---

[10] See FDA's guidance for industry, *Considerations in Demonstrating Interchangeability With a Reference Product* (May 2019).

[11] For CMC requirements for submission of a marketing application, sponsors should consult current regulations and see the guidance for industry *Submission on Chemistry, Manufacturing, and Controls Information for a Therapeutic Recombinant DNA-Derived Product or a Monoclonal Antibody Product for In-vivo Use* (August 1996), as well as other applicable FDA guidance documents.

6

209 not only the desired product but also product-related substances and product- and process-related
210 impurities.[12] Advances in manufacturing science and production methods may enhance the
211 likelihood that a proposed product can be demonstrated to be highly similar to a reference
212 product by better targeting the reference product's physiochemical and functional properties. In
213 addition, advances in analytical sciences may enable detection and characterization of
214 differences between the protein products. These differences should be further assessed to
215 understand the impact on the biosimilar product clinical performance relative to the reference
216 product.
217
218 Despite improvements in analytical techniques, current analytical methodology may not be able
219 to detect or characterize all relevant structural and functional differences between the two protein
220 products. A thorough understanding of each analytical method's limitations will be critical to a
221 sponsor's successful identification of residual uncertainties and, in turn, to the design of
222 subsequent testing. In addition, there may be incomplete understanding of the relationship
223 between a product's structural attributes and its clinical performance. FDA encourages the use of
224 available state-of-the-art technology. Sponsors should use appropriate analytical methodologies
225 that have adequate sensitivity and specificity to detect and characterize differences between the
226 proposed product and the reference product.
227
228 As part of a complete CMC data submission, an application submitted under section 351(k) of
229 the PHS Act is required to include analytical studies that demonstrate that the biological product
230 is highly similar to the reference product.[13] The rationale for the approach to the comparative
231 analytical assessment should be clearly described, with consideration of the characteristics,
232 known mechanism of action(s), and function of the reference product.
233
234 Comparative analytical data provide the foundation for the development of a proposed product
235 for submission in an application under section 351(k) of the PHS Act and can influence decisions
236 about the type and amount of animal and clinical data needed to support a demonstration of
237 biosimilarity. Such analytical data should be available early in product development and will
238 permit more detailed discussion with the Agency because known quality attributes can be used to
239 shape biosimilar development and justify certain development decisions. Thus, in addition to the
240 preliminary comparative analytical data that should be submitted to support an initial advisory
241 meeting,[14] FDA encourages sponsors to submit comprehensive comparative analytical data early

---

[12] The use of the terms *product-related substances* and *product- and process-related impurities* is consistent with their use and meaning in the ICH guidance for industry *Q6B Specifications: Test Procedures and Acceptance Criteria for Biotechnological/Biological Products* (August 1999).

[13] See section 351(k)(2)(A)(i)(I)(aa) of the PHS Act.

[14] See the draft guidance for industry *Formal Meetings Between the FDA and Sponsors or Applicants of BsUFA Products* (June 2018), which provides recommendations to industry on all formal meetings between the FDA and sponsors or applicants for proposed biosimilar products or proposed interchangeable products intended to be submitted under 351(k) of the PHS Act. When final, this guidance will represent FDA's current thinking on this topic.

7

242 in the development process: at the pre-IND stage; with the original IND submission; or with the
243 submission of data from the initial clinical studies, such as PK and PD studies. FDA will best be
244 able to provide meaningful input on the extent and scope of animal and additional clinical studies
245 for a proposed biosimilar development program once the Agency has considered the comparative
246 analytical data.
247
248 Comprehensive, robust comparative physicochemical and functional studies (these may include
249 biological assays, binding assays, and enzyme kinetics) should be performed to evaluate the
250 proposed product and the reference product. A meaningful comparative analytical assessment
251 depends on, among other things, the capabilities of available state-of-the-art analytical assays to
252 assess, for example, the molecular weight of the protein, complexity of the protein (higher order
253 structure and posttranslational modifications), degree of heterogeneity, functional properties,
254 impurity profiles, and degradation profiles denoting stability. The capability of the methods used
255 in these analytical assessments, as well as their limitations, should be described by the sponsor.
256 Physicochemical and functional characterization studies should be sufficient to establish relevant
257 quality attributes, including those that define a product's identity, quantity, safety, purity, and
258 potency. The product-related impurities and product-related substances should be identified,
259 characterized as appropriate, quantified, and compared using multiple lots of the proposed
260 product and multiple lots of the reference product, to the extent feasible and relevant, as part of
261 an assessment of the potential impact on the safety, purity, and potency of the product.
262
263 Because therapeutic proteins are made in living systems, there may be heterogeneity in certain
264 quality attributes of these products. Heterogeneity in therapeutic proteins may arise in a number
265 of ways and may affect the expected clinical performance of a protein product. Replication
266 errors in the DNA encoding the protein sequence and amino acid misincorporation may occur
267 during translation, although the level of these errors is typically low. In addition, most protein
268 products undergo posttranslational modifications that can alter the functions of the protein by
269 attaching other biochemical groups such as phosphate and various lipids and carbohydrates; by
270 proteolytic cleavage following translation; by changing the chemical nature of an amino acid
271 (e.g., formylation); or by many other mechanisms. Such modifications can result from
272 intracellular activities during cell culture or by deliberate modification of the protein (e.g.,
273 PEGylation). Other posttranslational modifications can be a consequence of manufacturing
274 process operations; for example, glycation may occur with exposure of the product to reducing
275 sugars. Also, certain storage conditions may be more or less permissive for certain degradation
276 pathways such as oxidation, deamidation, or aggregation. All of these product-related variants
277 may alter the biological properties of the expressed recombinant protein. Therefore,
278 identification and determination of the relative levels of these variants should be included in the
279 comparative analytical characterization studies.
280
281 The three-dimensional conformation of a protein is an important factor in its biological function.
282 Proteins generally exhibit complex three-dimensional conformations (tertiary structure and, in
283 some cases, quaternary structure) because of their large size and the rotational characteristics of
284 protein alpha carbons, among other things. The resulting flexibility enables dynamic, but subtle,
285 changes in protein conformation over time, some of which may be required for functional

8

286 activity. These rotations are often dependent on low-energy interactions, such as hydrogen
287 bonds and van der Waals forces, which may be very sensitive to environmental conditions.
288 Current analytical technology is capable of evaluating the three-dimensional structure of many
289 proteins. Using multiple, relevant, state-of-the-art methods can help define tertiary protein
290 structure and, to varying extent, quaternary structure, and can add to the body of information
291 supporting biosimilarity. At the same time, a protein's three-dimensional conformation can often
292 be difficult to define precisely using current physicochemical analytical technology. Any
293 differences in higher order structure between a proposed product and a reference product should
294 be evaluated in terms of a potential effect on protein function and stability. Thus, functional
295 assays are also critical tools for evaluating the integrity of the higher order structures.
296
297 A scientifically sound characterization that provides a comprehensive understanding of the
298 chemical, physical, and biological characteristics of the proposed product is essential to the
299 design of the manufacturing process and to the conduct of development studies for all biological
300 products. The body of knowledge that emerges will serve to support a demonstration of product
301 quality and the effectiveness of a suitable control system during development, and support
302 approval of the product.
303
304 Proposed biosimilar product, manufacturers should perform in-depth chemical, physical, and
305 bioactivity comparisons with side-by-side analyses of an appropriate number of lots of the
306 proposed product and the reference product and, where available and appropriate, a comparison
307 with a reference standard for suitable attributes (e.g., potency). For a discussion of reference
308 standards, see section V.G of this guidance. Evaluation of multiple lots of a reference product
309 and multiple lots of a proposed product enables estimation of product variability across lots. The
310 number of lots needed to understand the lot-to-lot variability of both the reference and proposed
311 products may differ on a case-by-case basis and should be scientifically justified by the sponsor.
312
313 FDA encourages sponsors to consult with the Agency to ensure that an appropriate number of
314 lots are evaluated. Identification of specific lots of a reference product used in comparative
315 analytical studies, together with expiration dates and time frames and when the lots were
316 analyzed and used in other types of studies (nonclinical or clinical studies), should be provided.
317 This information will be useful in justifying acceptance criteria to ensure product consistency, as
318 well as to support the comparative analytical assessment of the proposed product and the
319 reference product. However, acceptance criteria should be based on the totality of the analytical
320 data and not simply on the observed range of product attributes of the reference product. This is
321 because some product attributes act in combination to affect a product's safety, purity, and
322 potency profile; therefore, their potential interaction should be considered when conducting the
323 comparative analytical assessment and setting specifications. For example, for some
324 glycoproteins, the content and distribution of tetra-antennary and N-acetyllactosamine repeats
325 can affect in vivo potency and should not be evaluated independently of each other.
326

9

327   Additionally, data obtained for lots used in nonclinical and clinical studies and relevant
328   information on the relationship between an attribute and the performance of the drug product
329   (see ICH Q8(R2))[15] can also be used to help establish acceptance criteria.
330
331   An extensive analytical characterization may reveal differences between the reference product
332   and the proposed product, especially when using analytical techniques capable of discriminating
333   qualitative or quantitative differences in product attributes. Emphasis should be placed on
334   developing orthogonal quantitative methods to definitively identify any differences in product
335   attributes. Based on the results of analytical studies assessing functional and physicochemical
336   characteristics, including, for example, higher order structure, posttranslational modifications,
337   and impurity and degradation profiles, the sponsor may have an appropriate scientific basis for a
338   selective and targeted approach to subsequent animal and/or clinical studies to support a
339   demonstration of biosimilarity. It may be useful to compare differences in the quality attributes
340   of the proposed product with those of the reference product using a meaningful fingerprint-like
341   analysis algorithm[16] that covers a large number of additional product attributes and their
342   combinations with high sensitivity using orthogonal methods. Enhanced approaches in
343   manufacturing science, as discussed in ICH Q8(R2), may facilitate production processes that can
344   better match a reference product's fingerprint.[17] Such a strategy could further quantify the
345   overall similarity between two molecules and may lead to additional bases for a more selective
346   and targeted approach to subsequent animal and/or clinical studies.
347
348   The type, nature, and extent of any differences between the proposed product and the reference
349   product, introduced by design or observed from comprehensive analytical characterization of
350   multiple manufacturing lots, should be clearly described and discussed. The discussion should
351   include identification and comparison of relevant quality attributes from product
352   characterization. The potential clinical effects of observed structural and functional differences
353   between the two products should be assessed and supported by animal or clinical studies, if
354   necessary.
355
356
357   **V.   FACTORS FOR CONSIDERATION IN PERFORMING THE COMPARATIVE**
358   **ANALYTICAL ASSESSMENT**
359
360   When performing the comparative analytical assessment to support a demonstration of
361   biosimilarity, manufacturers should consider a number of factors, including the following:

---

[15] See the ICH guidance for industry *Q8(R2) Pharmaceutical Development* (November 2009).

[16] For more information on fingerprint-like analysis, refer to Kozlowski S, J Woodcock, K Midthun, R3 Sherman, 2011, Developing the Nation's Biosimilars Program, N Engl J Med; 365:385-388.

[17] See the ICH guidances for industry *Q8(R2) Pharmaceutical Development* (November 2009), *Q9 Quality Risk Management* (June 2006), *Q10 Pharmaceutical Quality System* (April 2009), and *Q11 Development and Manufacture of Drug Substances* (November 2012) for guidance on enhanced approaches in manufacturing science.

362
363   **A.**   **Expression System**
364
365 Therapeutic protein products can be produced in microbial cells (prokaryotic or eukaryotic), cell
366 lines (e.g., mammalian, avian, insect, plant), or tissues derived from animals or plants. It is
367 expected that the expression construct for a proposed product will encode the same primary
368 amino acid sequence as its reference product. However, minor modifications, such as N- or C-
369 terminal truncations (e.g., the heterogeneity of C-terminal lysine of a monoclonal antibody) that
370 are not expected to change the product performance, may be justified and should be explained by
371 the sponsor. Possible differences between the chosen expression system (i.e., host cell and the
372 expression construct) of the proposed product and that of the reference product should be
373 carefully considered because the type of expression system will affect the types of process- and
374 product-related substances, impurities, and contaminants (including potential adventitious
375 agents) that may be present in the protein product. For example, the expression system can have
376 a significant effect on the types and extent of translational and posttranslational modifications
377 that are imparted to the proposed product, which may introduce additional uncertainty into the
378 demonstration that the proposed product is biosimilar to the reference product.
379
380 Minimizing differences between the proposed product and reference product expression systems
381 to the extent possible can enhance the likelihood of producing a biosimilar protein product. Use
382 of different expression systems will be evaluated on a case-by-case basis.
383
384   **B.**   **Manufacturing Process**
385
386 A comprehensive understanding of all steps in the manufacturing process for the proposed
387 product should be established during product development. As a scientific matter,
388 characterization tests, process controls, and specifications that will emerge from information
389 gained during process development must be specific for the proposed product and manufacturing
390 process. The use of enhanced approaches[18] to pharmaceutical development, along with quality
391 risk management and effective quality systems, will facilitate the consistent manufacturing of a
392 high-quality product. As a scientific matter, as with biological products originally licensed under
393 section 351(a) of the PHS Act, an application for a biological product submitted for licensure
394 under section 351(k) of the PHS Act may not incorporate by reference drug substance, drug
395 substance intermediate, or drug product information contained in a Master File (MF) because a
396 license holder is generally expected to have knowledge of and control over the manufacturing
397 process for the biological product for which it has a license.[19] Other types of contract

---

[18] See the ICH guidances for industry *Q8(R2) Pharmaceutical Development* (November 2009), *Q9 Quality Risk Management* (June 2006), *Q10 Pharmaceutical Quality System* (April 2009), and *Q11 Development and Manufacture of Drug Substances* (November 2012) for guidance on enhanced approaches in manufacturing science.

[19] A MF for drug substance, drug substance intermediate, or drug product information for a biological product may be referenced to support an investigational new drug application (IND) for a proposed biosimilar product. Assurance of product quality should be provided on each lot of material produced by the MF holder. Procedures

11

398   manufacturing arrangements can be considered if the sponsor does not intend to manufacture the
399   product for licensure.[20]
400
401   A sponsor considering manufacturing changes after completing the initial comparative analytical
402   assessment or after completing clinical studies intended to support a 351(k) application will need
403   to demonstrate comparability between the pre- and post-change proposed product and may need
404   to conduct additional studies. The nature and extent of the changes may determine the extent of
405   these additional studies. The comparative analytical studies should include a sufficient number
406   of lots of the proposed biosimilar product used in clinical studies as well as from the proposed
407   commercial process if the process used to produce the material used in the clinical studies is
408   different.
409
410   **C.   Physicochemical Properties**
411
412   Physicochemical assessment of the proposed product and the reference product should consider
413   all relevant characteristics of the protein product (e.g., the primary, secondary, tertiary, and
414   quaternary structure; posttranslational modifications; and functional activity(ies)). The objective
415   of this assessment is to maximize the potential for detecting differences in quality attributes
416   between the proposed product and the reference product.
417
418   The sponsor should address the concept of the desired product (and its variants) as discussed in
419   ICH Q6B[21] when designing and conducting the characterization studies. Thus, it will be
420   important to understand the heterogeneity of the proposed product and the reference product
421   (e.g., the nature, location, and levels of glycosylation) and the ranges of variability of different
422   isoforms, including those that result from posttranslational modifications.
423
424   Particular analytical methodologies can be used to assess specific physicochemical
425   characteristics of proteins. These methodologies are described in published documents,
426   including scientific literature, regulatory guidelines, and pharmacopeial compendia. Some
427   techniques provide information on multiple characteristics. It is expected that appropriate
428   analytical test methods will be selected based on the nature of the protein being characterized
429   and knowledge regarding the structure and heterogeneity of the reference product and the
430   proposed product, as well as characteristics critical to product performance.
431

---

should also be in place to ensure that the IND sponsor is notified by the MF holder of significant changes to the MF potentially affecting product quality. The sponsor is expected to provide notification to the Agency of any relevant change in the IND in order to initiate a reevaluation of the MF.

[20] See the guidance for industry *Cooperative Manufacturing Arrangements for Licensed Biologics* (November 2008).

[21] See the ICH guidance for industry *Q6B Specifications: Test Procedures and Acceptance Criteria for Biotechnological/Biological Products* (August 1999).

12

432   To address the full range of physicochemical properties or biological activities adequately, it is
433   often necessary to apply more than one analytical procedure to evaluate the same quality
434   attribute. Methods that use different physicochemical or biological principles to assess the same
435   attribute are especially valuable because they provide independent data to support the quality of
436   that attribute (e.g., orthogonal methods to assess aggregation). In addition, the use of
437   complementary analytical techniques in series, such as peptide mapping or capillary
438   electrophoresis combined with mass spectrometry of the separated molecules, should provide a
439   meaningful and sensitive method for comparing products.
440
441   Unlike routine quality control assays, tests used to characterize the product do not necessarily
442   need to be validated; however, the tests used to characterize the product should be scientifically
443   sound, fit for their intended use, and provide results that are reproducible and reliable. In
444   selecting these tests, it is important to consider the characteristics of the protein product,
445   including known and potential impurities. Information regarding the ability of a method to
446   discern relevant differences between a proposed product and a reference product should be
447   submitted as part of the comparison. The methods should be demonstrated to be of appropriate
448   sensitivity and specificity to provide meaningful information as to whether the proposed product
449   and the reference product are highly similar.
450
451   **D.   Functional Activities**
452
453   Functional assays serve multiple purposes in the characterization of protein products. These tests
454   act to complement physicochemical analyses and are a quantitative measure of the function of
455   the protein product.
456
457   Depending on the structural complexity of the protein and available analytical technology, the
458   physicochemical analysis may be unable to confirm the integrity of the higher order structures.
459   Instead, the integrity of such structures can usually be inferred from the product's biological
460   activity. If the clinically relevant mechanism(s) of action are known for the reference product or
461   can reasonably be determined, the functional assays should reflect such mechanism(s) of action
462   to the extent possible. Multiple functional assays should, in general, be performed as part of the
463   comparative analytical assessments. The assessment of functional activity is also useful in
464   providing an estimate of the specific activity of a product as an indicator of manufacturing
465   process consistency, as well as product purity, potency, and stability.
466
467   If a reference product exhibits multiple functional activities, sponsors should perform a set of
468   appropriate assays designed to evaluate the range of relevant activities for that product. For
469   example, with proteins that possess multiple functional domains expressing enzymatic and
470   receptor-mediated activities, sponsors should evaluate both activities to the extent that these
471   activities are relevant to product performance. For products where functional activity can be
472   measured by more than one parameter (e.g., enzyme kinetics or interactions with blood clotting
473   factors), the comparative characterization of each parameter between products should be
474   assessed.

13

475
476 The sponsor should recognize the potential limitations of some types of functional assays, such
477 as high variability, that might preclude detection of small but significant differences between the
478 proposed product and the reference product. Because a highly variable assay may not provide a
479 meaningful assessment as to whether the proposed product is highly similar to the reference
480 product, sponsors are encouraged to develop assays that are less variable and are sensitive to
481 changes in the functional activities of the product. In addition, in vitro bioactivity assays may
482 not fully reflect the clinical activity of the protein. For example, these assays generally do not
483 predict the bioavailability (PK and biodistribution) of the product, which can affect PD and
484 clinical performance. Also, bioavailability can be dramatically altered by subtle differences in
485 glycoform distribution or other posttranslational modifications. Thus, these limitations should be
486 taken into account when assessing the robustness of the quality of data supporting biosimilarity
487 and the need for additional information that may address residual uncertainties. Finally,
488 functional assays are important in assessing the occurrence of neutralizing antibodies in
489 nonclinical and clinical studies.
490
491   **E.   Target Binding**
492
493 When binding is part of the activity attributed to the protein product, analytical tests should be
494 performed to characterize the proposed product in terms of its specific binding properties (e.g., if
495 binding to a receptor is inherent to protein function, this property should be measured and used
496 in comparative studies) (see ICH Q6B for additional details). Various methods such as surface
497 plasmon resonance, microcalorimetry, or classical Scatchard analysis can provide information on
498 the kinetics and thermodynamics of binding. Such information can be related to the functional
499 activity and characterization of the proposed product's higher order structure.
500
501   **F.   Impurities**
502
503 The sponsor should characterize, identify, and quantify product-related impurities in the
504 proposed product and the reference product, to the extent feasible.[22] If a comparative
505 physicochemical analysis reveals comparable product-related impurities at similar levels
506 between the two products, pharmacological/toxicological studies to characterize potential
507 biological effects of specific impurities may not be necessary. However, if the manufacturing
508 process used to produce the proposed product introduces different impurities or higher levels of
509 impurities than those present in the reference product, additional pharmacological/toxicological
510 or other studies may be necessary. As discussed in the ICH guidance for industry *S6(R1)*
511 *Preclinical Safety Evaluation of Biotechnology-Derived Pharmaceuticals* (May 2012), "[i]t is

---

[22] The use of the terms *product-* and *process-related impurities* is consistent with their use and meaning in
ICH Q6B.

512 preferable to rely on purification processes to remove impurities . . . rather than to establish a
513 preclinical testing program for their qualification."[23]
514
515 Process-related impurities arising from cell substrates (e.g., host cell DNA, host cell proteins),
516 cell culture components (e.g., antibiotics, media components), and downstream processing steps
517 (e.g., reagents, residual solvents, leachables, endotoxin, bioburden) should be evaluated. The
518 process-related impurities in the proposed product are not expected to match those observed in
519 the reference product and are not included in the comparative analytical assessment. The chosen
520 analytical procedures should be adequate to detect, identify, and accurately quantify biologically
521 significant levels of impurities. [24] In particular, results of immunological methods used to detect
522 host cell proteins depend on the assay reagents and the cell substrate used. Such assays should
523 be validated using the product cell substrate and orthogonal methodologies to ensure accuracy
524 and sensitivity.
525
526 As with any biological product, the safety of the proposed product with regard to adventitious
527 agents or endogenous viral contamination, should be ensured by screening critical raw materials
528 and confirmation of robust virus removal and inactivation achieved by the manufacturing
529 process. [25]
530
531 **G.   Reference Product and Reference Standards**
532
533 A thorough physicochemical and biological assessment of the reference product should provide a
534 base of information from which to develop the proposed product and justify reliance on certain
535 existing scientific knowledge about the reference product. Sufficient evidence that the proposed
536 product is highly similar to the reference product must be provided to support a selective and
537 targeted approach in early product development (e.g., selected animal studies and/or additional
538 clinical studies).[26]
539
540 The comparative analytical assessment submitted with the marketing application to support the
541 demonstration of biosimilarity of the proposed product to the reference product should include
542 lots of the proposed product used in principal clinical study(ies), as well as the proposed
543 commercial product. As stated earlier in section V.B, a sponsor considering manufacturing
544 changes after completing the initial comparative analytical assessment or after completing
545 clinical studies intended to support a 351(k) application may need to conduct additional

---

[23] See the ICH guidance for industry *S6(R1) Preclinical Safety Evaluation of Biotechnology-Derived Pharmaceuticals* (May 2012), page 2.

[24] See the ICH guidance for industry *Q2B Validation of Analytical Procedures: Methodology* (May 1997).

[25] See the ICH guidance for industry *Q5A Viral Safety Evaluation of Biotechnology Products Derived From Cell Lines of Human or Animal Origin* (September 1998).

[26] See 21 CFR 312.23 for IND application content and format.

15

546 comparative analytical studies of the proposed product and the reference product. The nature
547 and extent of the changes may determine the extent of these additional analytical studies.
548
549 If the drug substance has been extracted from the reference product to conduct analytical studies,
550 the sponsor should describe the extraction procedure and provide support that the procedure
551 itself does not alter relevant product quality attributes. This undertaking would include
552 consideration of alteration or loss of the desired products and impurities and relevant product-
553 related substances, and it should include appropriate controls to ensure that relevant
554 characteristics of the protein are not significantly altered by the extraction procedure.
555
556 If there is a suitable, publicly available, and well-established reference standard for the protein, a
557 physicochemical and/or functional comparison of the proposed product with this standard may
558 also provide useful information.[27] For example, if an international standard for calibration of
559 potency is available, a comparison of the relative potency of the proposed product with this
560 potency standard should be performed. As recommended in ICH Q6B, an in-house reference
561 standard(s) should always be qualified and used for control of the manufacturing process and
562 product.
563
564 An in-house reference standard is typically developed from early development lots or lots used in
565 a clinical study(ies). Additional reference standards may be qualified later in development and
566 for a BLA submission. Ideally, a sponsor will have established and properly qualified primary
567 and working reference standards that are representative of proposed product lots used in clinical
568 studies that support the application.
569
570 For the development of a proposed product, a reference product lot or a lot of a non-U.S.-
571 licensed comparator product (see section VI.A.4 of this guidance) is typically qualified as an
572 initial reference standard. Once clinical lots of the proposed product have been manufactured, it
573 is expected that one of these lots will be properly qualified (including bridging to previous
574 reference standards) for use as a reference standard for release and stability, as well as
575 comparative analytical testing. If possible, once an in-house reference standard is properly
576 qualified, there should be sufficient quantities to use throughout the development of the proposed
577 product. All lots of reference standards used during the development of a proposed product
578 should be properly qualified. In addition to release testing methods, the qualification protocol
579 for reference standards should include all analytical methods that report the result relative to the
580 reference standard.
581
582 For all methods where the result is reported relative to the reference standard, the assignment of
583 a potency of 100% should include a narrow acceptable potency range and ensure control over
584 product drift. For example, a sponsor should consider the use of a pre-determined two-sided
585 confidence interval (CI) of the mean of the replicates, where the mean relative potency and the
586 95% CI are included within a sufficiently narrow range (e.g., 90-110%). There should be an

---

[27] Although studies with such a reference standard may be useful, they are not sufficient to satisfy the BPCI Act's requirement to demonstrate the biosimilarity of the proposed product to the U.S.-licensed reference product.

16

587   evaluation across the history of multiple reference standard qualifications to address potential
588   drift.
589
590   A sponsor generally should not use a correction factor to account for any differences in, for
591   example, potency or biological activity between reference standards.
592
593   Use of reference standards inadequately qualified for analytical methods that report results
594   relative to the reference standard is likely to raise concerns regarding the comparative analytical
595   assessment. One approach to address these concerns, if applicable, may be to store the reference
596   product and non-U.S.-licensed comparator product lots under conditions that maintain stability
597   long term, if feasible. Prior to submission of a 351(k) application, the prospective applicant
598   should conduct a reevaluation of all proposed product, reference product, and non-U.S.-licensed
599   comparator product lots using the same reference standard for those methods that report the
600   result relative to the reference standard. Data supporting the stability of the reference product
601   and non-U.S.-licensed comparator product beyond the expiration date under these conditions
602   should be included in the submission.
603
604   In summary, analytical studies carried out to support the approval of a proposed product should
605   not focus solely on the characterization of the proposed product in isolation. Rather, these
606   studies should be part of a broad comparison that includes, but is not limited to, the proposed
607   product, the reference product, and, where applicable, a non-U.S.-licensed comparator,
608   applicable reference standards, and consideration of relevant publicly available information.
609
610   **H.   Finished Drug Product**
611
612   Product characterization studies of a proposed product should be performed on the most
613   downstream intermediate best suited for the analytical procedures used. The attributes evaluated
614   should be stable through any further processing steps. For these reasons, characterization studies
615   are often performed on the drug substance. However, if a drug substance is reformulated and/or
616   exposed to new materials in the finished dosage form, the impact of these changes should be
617   considered. Whenever possible, if the finished drug product is best suited for a particular
618   analysis, the sponsors should analyze the finished drug product. If an analytical method more
619   sensitively detects specific attributes in the drug substance but the attributes it measures are
620   critical and/or may change during manufacture of the finished drug product, comparative
621   characterization may be called for on both the extracted protein and the finished drug product.
622
623   Proteins are very sensitive to their environment. Therefore, differences in excipients or primary
624   packaging may affect product stability and/or clinical performance. Differences in formulation
625   and primary packaging[28] between the proposed product and the reference product are among the
626   factors that may affect whether or how subsequent clinical studies may take a selective and

---

[28] See the ICH guidance for industry *Q8(R2) Pharmaceutical Development* (November 2009).

627   targeted approach.[29] Sponsors should clearly identify excipients used in the proposed product
628   that differ from those in the reference product. The acceptability of the type, nature, and extent
629   of any differences between the finished proposed product and the finished reference product
630   should be evaluated and supported by appropriate data and rationale. Additionally, different
631   excipients in the proposed product should be supported by existing toxicology data for the
632   excipient or by additional toxicity studies with the formulation of the proposed product.
633   Excipient interactions as well as direct toxicities should be considered.
634
635   **I.**   **Stability**
636
637   As part of an appropriate physicochemical and functional comparison of the stability profile of
638   the proposed product with that of the reference product, accelerated and stress stability studies,
639   as well as forced degradation studies, should be used to establish degradation profiles and to
640   provide a direct stability comparison of the proposed product with the reference product. These
641   comparative studies should be conducted under multiple stress conditions (e.g., high
642   temperature, freeze thaw, light exposure, and agitation) that can cause incremental product
643   degradation over a defined time period. Results of these studies may reveal product differences
644   that warrant additional evaluations and also identify conditions under which additional controls
645   should be employed in manufacturing and storage.[30] Sufficient real time, real-condition stability
646   data from the proposed product should be provided to support the proposed shelf life.
647
648   **VI.**   **COMPARATIVE ANALYTICAL ASSESSMENT**
649
650   A thorough understanding of the reference product is critical for a successful biosimilar
651   development program. The Agency recommends that sponsors approach the comparative
652   analytical assessment by first understanding the physicochemical and biological characteristics
653   of the reference product. A full characterization of the reference product, in addition to
654   consideration of publicly available information, will form the basis of product understanding. As
655   described previously, protein products are complex molecules that generally are manufactured in
656   living cells and purified using a variety of technologies; therefore, they have a certain degree of
657   inherent lot-to-lot variability in terms of quality characteristics. The observed lot-to-lot
658   variability may derive from manufacturing conditions and from analytical assay variability.
659   Factors that contribute to lot-to-lot variability in the manufacture of a protein product include the
660   source of certain raw materials (e.g., growth medium, resins, or separation materials) and
661   different manufacturing sites. Therefore, the comparative analytical assessment, it is important
662   to adequately characterize the lot-to-lot variability of the reference product and the proposed
663   biosimilar product.

---

[29] For more discussion on *selective and targeted approaches*, please refer to the guidance for industry *Scientific Considerations in Demonstrating Biosimilarity to a Reference Product* (April 2015).

[30] See ICH guidances for industry *Q5C Quality of Biotechnological Products: Stability Testing of Biotechnological/Biological Products* (July 1996) and *Q1A(R2) Stability Testing of New Drug Substances and Products* (November 2003).

18

664
665   **A.   Considerations for Reference and Biosimilar Products**
666
667   *1.   Reference Product*
668
669   To ensure that the full range of product variability is accurately captured, sponsors should
670   acquire multiple reference product lots throughout the development program of a proposed
671   biosimilar in sufficient quantity to conduct multiple physiochemical and functional assays.
672   Considering the inherent heterogeneity present in protein products and the expected lot-to-lot
673   variability stemming from manufacturing processes, the Agency recommends that a sponsor
674   include at least 10 reference product lots (acquired over a time frame that spans expiration dates
675   of several years), in the analytical assessment to ensure that the variability of the reference
676   product is captured adequately. The final number of lots should be sufficient to provide adequate
677   information regarding the variability of the reference product. In cases where limited numbers of
678   reference product lots are available (e.g., for certain orphan drugs), alternate flexible comparative
679   analytical assessments plans should be proposed and discussed with the Agency.
680
681   *2.   Proposed Product*
682
683   The Agency recommends that a sponsor include at least 6 to 10 lots of the proposed product in
684   the comparative analytical assessment, to ensure 1) adequate characterization of the proposed
685   product and understanding of manufacturing variability, and 2) adequate comparison to the
686   reference product. These should include lots manufactured with the investigational- and
687   commercial-scale processes, and may include validation lots, as well as product lots
688   manufactured at different scales, including engineering lots. These lots should be representative
689   of the intended commercial manufacturing process. If there is a manufacturing process change
690   during development, it may be possible, with adequate scientific justification, to use data
691   generated from lots manufactured with a different process. However, data should be provided in
692   the 351(k) BLA to support comparability of drug substance and drug product manufactured with
693   the different processes and/or scales. The extent of process development design (as described in
694   guidelines *ICH Q8 (R2) Pharmaceutical Development* and *ICH Q11 Development and*
695   *Manufacture of Drug Substances*) and process understanding should be used in support of the
696   number of proposed biosimilar product lots proposed for inclusion in the comparative analytical
697   assessment in the 351(k) application.
698
699   To the extent possible, proposed biosimilar lots included in the comparative analytical
700   assessment described in section VI.B, Considerations for Data Analysis, should be derived from
701   different drug substance batches to adequately represent the variability of attributes inherent to
702   the drug substance manufacturing process. Drug product lots derived from the same drug
703   substance batch(es) are not considered sufficiently representative of such variability, except for
704   use in testing certain drug product attributes for which variability is mostly dependent on the
705   drug product manufacturing process (e.g., protein concentration). Although it may be preferable
706   to compare the proposed product lots to the reference product lots, it may be acceptable to also

19

707   include independent drug substance batches (if the drug substance was not used to make drug
708   product), if needed, to attain a sufficient number of lots for the comparative analytical
709   assessment.
710
711   3.   *Accounting for Reference Product and Proposed Product Lots*
712
713   Sponsors should account for all the reference product lots acquired and characterized. The
714   351(k) BLA should include data and information from all reference product and proposed
715   product lots that were evaluated in any manner, including the specific physicochemical,
716   functional, animal, and clinical studies for which a lot was used. When a lot is specifically
717   selected to be included in or excluded from certain analytical studies, a justification should be
718   provided. The date of the analytical testing as well as the product expiration date should be
719   provided in the application. In general, expired reference product lots should not be included in
720   the comparative analytical assessment because lots analyzed beyond their expiration date could
721   lead to results outside the range that would normally be observed in unexpired lots, which may
722   result in overestimated reference product variability. Testing of lots past expiry may be
723   acceptable if samples are stored under long term conditions (e.g., frozen at -80°C) provided that
724   sponsors submit data and information demonstrating that storage does not impact the quality of
725   the product (see section V.G).
726
727   The same type of information and data described above to be collected for reference product lots
728   should also be provided on every manufactured drug substance and drug product lot of the
729   proposed product.
730
731   Reference product and proposed product lots used in the clinical studies (e.g., PK and PD, if
732   applicable, similarity, and comparative clinical study) should be included in the comparative
733   analytical assessment.
734
735   4.   *Reference Product and Non-U.S.-Licensed Comparator Products*
736
737   As described in other guidances, a sponsor that intends to use a non-U.S.-licensed comparator in
738   certain studies should provide comparative analytical data and analysis for all pairwise
739   comparisons (i.e., U.S.-licensed product versus proposed biosimilar product, non-U.S.-licensed
740   comparator product versus proposed biosimilar product, and U.S.-licensed product versus non-
741   U.S.-licensed comparator product).
742
743   The acceptance criteria used to support a demonstration that a proposed biosimilar product is
744   highly similar to the reference product should be derived from data generated from a sponsor's
745   analysis of the reference product. The comparative analytical assessment should be based on a
746   direct comparison of the proposed product to the reference product. As a scientific matter,
747   combining data from the reference product and non-U.S.-licensed comparator product to
748   determine the acceptance criteria or to perform the comparative analytical assessment to the
749   proposed product would not be acceptable to support a demonstration that the proposed product

750   is biosimilar to the reference product. For example, combining data from the reference product
751   and non-U.S.-licensed products may result in a larger range and broader similarity acceptance
752   criteria than would be obtained by relying solely on data from reference product lots. Sponsors
753   are encouraged to discuss with FDA, during product development, any plans to submit data
754   derived from products approved outside of the U.S. in support of a 351(k) application.
755
756   **B.   Considerations for Data Analysis**
757
758   Sponsors should develop a comparative analytical assessment plan and discuss the approach with
759   the Agency as early as practicable. A final comparative analytical assessment report should be
760   available at the time a 351(k) BLA is submitted.
761
762   The Agency recommends development of a comparative analytical assessment plan using a
763   stepwise approach. The first step is a determination of the quality attributes that characterize the
764   reference product in terms of its structural/physicochemical and functional properties. These
765   quality attributes are then ranked according to their risk to potentially impact activity, PK/PD,
766   safety, efficacy, and immunogenicity. Finally, the attributes are evaluated using quantitative
767   analysis, considering the risk ranking of the quality attributes, as well as other factors. It should
768   be noted, however, that some attributes may be highly critical (e.g., primary sequence) but not
769   amenable to quantitative analysis.
770
771   *1.   Risk Assessment*
772
773   FDA recommends that sponsors develop a risk assessment tool to evaluate and rank the reference
774   product quality attributes in terms of potential impact on the mechanism(s) of action and function
775   of the product. Certain quality evaluations of the reference product (e.g., its degradation rates,
776   which are determined from stability or forced degradation studies) generally should not be
777   included in the risk ranking. However, these evaluations should still factor into the comparative
778   analytical assessment of the proposed biosimilar and reference product.

779   Development of the risk assessment tool should be informed by relevant factors, including:
780
781   • Potential impact of an attribute on clinical performance: Specifically, FDA recommends
782   that sponsors consider the potential impact of an attribute on activity, PK/PD, safety,
783   efficacy, and immunogenicity. Sponsors should consider publicly available information,
784   as well as the sponsor's own characterization of the reference product, in determining the
785   potential impact of an attribute on clinical performance.
786
787   • The degree of uncertainty surrounding a certain quality attribute: For example, when
788   there is limited understanding of the relationship between the degree of change in an
789   attribute and the resulting clinical impact, FDA recommends that that attribute be ranked
790   as having higher risk because of the uncertainty raised.
791

21

614

792   FDA recommends that an attribute that is a high risk for any one of the performance categories
793   (i.e., activity, PK/PD, safety, efficacy, and immunogenicity) be classified as high risk. Ideally,
794   the risk assessment tool should result in a list of attributes ordered by the risk to the patient. The
795   risk scores for attributes should, therefore, be proportional to patient risk. The scoring criteria
796   used in the risk assessment should be clearly defined and justified, and the risk ranking for each
797   attribute should be justified with appropriate citations to the literature and data provided.
798
799   2.   *Quantitative and Qualitative Data Analysis*
800
801   Appropriate analyses of the comparative analytical data are necessary to support a demonstration
802   that the proposed product is highly similar to the reference product notwithstanding minor
803   differences in clinically inactive components. One approach to data analysis would be the use of
804   descriptive quality ranges for assessing quantitative quality attributes of high and moderate risk,
805   and the use of raw data/graphical comparisons for quality attributes with the lowest risk ranking
806   or for those quality attributes that cannot be quantitatively measured (e.g., primary sequence).
807   The acceptance criteria for the quality ranges (QR) method in the comparative analytical
808   assessment should be based on the results of the sponsor's own analysis of the reference product
809   for a specific quality attribute. The QR should be defined as $(\hat{\mu}_R - X\hat{\sigma}_R, \hat{\mu}_R + X\hat{\sigma}_R)$, where $\hat{\mu}_R$ is
810   the sample mean, and $\hat{\sigma}_R$ is the sample standard deviation based on the reference product lots.
811   The multiplier (X) should be scientifically justified for that attribute and discussed with the
812   Agency. Based on our experience to date, methods such as tolerance intervals are not
813   recommended for establishing the similarity acceptance criteria because a very large number of
814   lots would be required to establish meaningful intervals. The sponsor can propose other methods
815   of data analysis, including equivalence testing.
816
817   The objective of the comparative analytical assessment is to verify that each attribute, as
818   observed in the proposed biosimilar and the reference product, has a similar population mean and
819   similar population standard deviation. Comparative analysis of a quality attribute would
820   generally support a finding that the proposed product is highly similar to the reference product
821   when a sufficient percentage of biosimilar lot values (e.g., 90%) fall within the QR defined for
822   that attribute. The Agency recommends that narrower acceptance criteria of the QR method in
823   the comparative analytical assessment (e.g., a lower X value) be applied to higher risk quality
824   attributes.
825
826   In addition to risk ranking, other factors should be considered in determining which type of
827   quantitative data analysis should be applied to a particular attribute or assay. Some additional
828   factors that should be considered when determining the appropriate type of data evaluation and
829   analysis of results include:
830
831   •   Nature of the attribute: Attributes that are known to be of high risk should be prioritized
832   over attributes with unknown but potentially high risk (i.e., attributes with a high-risk
833   ranking due to uncertainty).
834

22

835   •   <u>Distribution of the attribute</u>: In general, the Agency recommends that sponsors develop
836   the manufacturing process to target the centers of distribution of the quality attributes of
837   the reference product as closely as possible. Therefore, the QR, which assumes that the
838   population mean and standard deviation are similar, is an appropriate approach to
839   demonstrate that the proposed product is highly similar to the reference product. If there
840   are concerns with the distribution, additional information or analyses may be needed to
841   support the QR method or to support a different analysis approach. For example, the
842   distribution of an attribute in the proposed biosimilar product that is biased towards one
843   side of the reference product distribution may raise concerns depending on the nature of
844   the attribute and the role the attribute plays in, for example, the mechanism of action of
845   the product. If such a distribution is observed, appropriate justification may be needed,
846   as a scientific matter, to support the comparative analytical assessment of the products.
847   In cases where an attribute in the reference product is not normally distributed, sponsors
848   should consult with the Agency.
849
850   •   <u>Abundance of the attribute</u>: Because of the inherent heterogeneity present in protein
851   products, an attribute of the reference product that may pose a high risk when the
852   attribute is present in high abundance (e.g., percent aggregation or percent oxidation)
853   may pose a significantly lower risk (or negligible risk) if the attribute is low-abundance.
854   The abundance of the attribute should be confirmed in both the reference product (as
855   determined by the proposed product sponsor's analysis of the reference product) and the
856   proposed product. Limit assays do not necessarily need to be evaluated using QR;
857   however, the selected limits regarding the amount of an attribute should be defined and
858   justified. The justification should also include consideration of how the amount of the
859   attribute changes over time.
860
861   •   <u>Sensitivity of assay used for assessing an attribute</u>: Although multiple, orthogonal assays
862   are encouraged for assessing an attribute, not all assays assessing the attribute need to be
863   evaluated in the same manner. While the most sensitive assay for detecting product
864   differences should be evaluated using QR, it may be appropriate to evaluate the results of
865   other assays for the same attribute using a graphical comparison. A justification should
866   be provided for the method of evaluation used for each type of assay.
867
868   •   <u>Types of attributes/assays</u>: Quantitative analyses may not be applicable to some
869   attributes, (e.g., protein sequence or certain assays used for higher order structure
870   evaluation, or to assays that are only qualitative). The comparative analytical assessment
871   plan should clearly define specific assays where quantitative data analyses would not be
872   applied, and the rationale for that decision.
873
874   •   <u>Publicly available information</u>: Publicly available information may be relevant to the
875   appropriate type of data analysis and acceptance criteria in the comparative analytical
876   assessment. A sponsor should seek additional advice from the Agency on the inclusion
877   of any publicly available information in the comparative analytical assessment.

23

878
879   For qualitative analyses of lower risk attributes, FDA recommends side-by-side data presentation
880   (e.g., spectra, thermograms, graphical representation of data), to allow for a visual comparison of
881   the proposed product to the reference product.
882
883   The final comparative analytical assessment plan should include the risk ranking of attributes,
884   the type of data evaluation to be used for each attribute/assay, and the final data analysis plan.
885   The plan should specify the anticipated availability of both proposed biosimilar and reference
886   product lots for evaluation of each attribute/assay and should include a rationale for why the
887   proposed number of lots should be considered sufficient for the evaluation. The comparative
888   analytical assessment plan should be discussed with the Agency as early in the biosimilar
889   development program as possible so that agreement can be reached on which attributes/assays
890   should be evaluated. The final comparative analytical assessment plan should be submitted to
891   the Agency prior to initiating the final analytical assessments; typically, this occurs in a meeting
892   with the Agency.
893
894   **C.   Comparative Analytical Assessment Conclusions**
895
896   In the comparative analytical assessment, risk ranking and data analysis are used to evaluate a
897   large number of attributes, often using multiple orthogonal assays. FDA evaluates the totality of
898   the analytical data; if the results of a particular assay do not meet pre-specified criteria, this alone
899   does not preclude a demonstration of high similarity. For example, if differences between
900   products are observed as part of the comparative analytical assessment (including the
901   components of the assessment that were not included in the risk ranking), the sponsor may
902   provide additional scientific information (risk assessment and additional data) and a justification
903   for why these differences do not preclude a demonstration that the products are highly similar.
904
905   In certain situations, changes to the manufacturing process of the biosimilar product may be
906   needed to resolve differences observed in the comparative analytical assessment. Data should be
907   provided demonstrating that the observed differences were resolved by any manufacturing
908   changes, and that other quality attributes were not substantially affected. If other attributes were
909   affected by the manufacturing change, data should be provided to demonstrate that the impact of
910   the change has been evaluated and addressed.
911
912   **VII.   CONCLUSION**
913
914   The foundation for an assessment and a demonstration of biosimilarity between a proposed
915   product and its reference product includes analytical studies that demonstrate that the proposed
916   product is highly similar to the reference product notwithstanding minor differences in clinically
917   inactive components. The demonstration that the proposed product is biosimilar to the reference
918   product thus involves robust characterization of the proposed product, including comparative
919   physicochemical and functional studies with the reference product. The information gained from
920   these studies is necessary for the development of a proposed product as a biosimilar. In addition,

24

921   a 351(k) application for a proposed product must contain, among other things, information
922   demonstrating biosimilarity based on data derived from animal studies (including the assessment
923   of toxicity) and a clinical study or studies (including the assessment of immunogenicity and PK
924   or PD), unless the Agency determines that an element is unnecessary in a particular 351(k)
925   application.[31] A sponsor's ability to discern and understand the impact of relevant analytical
926   differences between the proposed product and its reference product is critical to determine
927   whether the statutory standard for biosimilarity can be met.
928
929
930   **VIII. RELEVANT GUIDANCES**
931
932   The following draft and final guidance documents may be relevant to sponsors developing or
933   considering development of a proposed biosimilar product. All Agency guidance documents are
934   available on FDA's web page
935   (https://www.fda.gov/regulatory-information/search-fda-guidance-documents).
936

937   *1.* Guidance for industry *Scientific Considerations in Demonstrating Biosimilarity to a*
938   *Reference Product* (April 2015)
939

940   *2.* Guidance for industry *Questions and Answers on Biosimilar Development and the BPCI*
941   *Act* (December 2018)
942

943   *3.* Draft guidance for industry *New and Revised Draft Q&As on Biosimilar Development*
944   *and the BPCI Act (Revision 2)* (December 2018)
945

946   *4.* Draft guidance for industry *Formal Meetings Between the FDA and Sponsors or*
947   *Applicants of BsUFA Products* (June 2018)
948

949   *5.* Guidance for industry *Clinical Pharmacology Data to Support a Demonstration of*
950   *Biosimilarity to a Reference Product* (December 2016)
951

952   *6. Demonstration of Comparability of Human Biological Products, Including Therapeutic*
953   *Biotechnology-derived Products* (April 1996)
954

955   *7. Points to Consider in the Manufacture and Testing of Monoclonal Antibody Products for*
956   *Human Use* (February 1997)
957

958   *8.* Guidance for industry for the *Submission of Chemistry, Manufacturing, and Controls*
959   *Information for a Therapeutic Recombinant DNA-Derived Product or a Monoclonal*
960   *Antibody Product for In Vivo Use* (August 1996)
961

---

[31] Section 351(k)(2)(A)(i)(I) of the PHS Act.

25

962	9. Guidance for industry *Cooperative Manufacturing Arrangements for Licensed Biologics*
963	(November 2008)
964	
965	10. ICH guidance for industry *M4: The CTD —Quality* (ICH M4Q) (August 2001)
966	
967	11. ICH guidance for industry *Q1A(R2) Stability Testing of New Drug Substances and*
968	*Products* (ICH Q1A(R2)) (November 2003)
969	
970	12. ICH guidance for industry *Q2(R1) Validation of Analytical Procedures: Text and*
971	*Methodology* (ICH Q2(R1) (November 2005)
972	
973	13. ICH guidance for industry *Q2B Validation of Analytical Procedures: Methodology* (ICH
974	Q2B) (May 1997)
975	
976	14. ICH guidance for industry *Q3A(R) Impurities in New Drug Substances* (ICH Q3A(R))
977	(June 2008)
978	
979	15. ICH guidance for industry *Q5A Viral Safety Evaluation of Biotechnology Products*
980	*Derived from Cell Lines of Human or Animal Origin* (ICH Q5A) (September 1998)
981	
982	16. ICH guidance for industry *Q5B Quality of Biotechnological Products: Analysis of the*
983	*Expression Construct in Cells Used for Production of r-DNA Derived Protein Products*
984	(ICH Q5B) (February 1996)
985	
986	17. ICH guidance for industry *Q5C Quality of Biotechnological Products: Stability Testing*
987	*of Biotechnological/Biological Products* (ICH Q5C) (July 1996)
988	
989	18. ICH guidance for industry *Q5D Quality of Biotechnological/Biological Products:*
990	*Derivation and Characterization of Cell Substrates Used for Production of*
991	*Biotechnological/Biological Products* (ICH Q5D) (September 1998)
992	
993	19. ICH guidance for industry *Q5E Comparability of Biotechnological/Biological Products*
994	*Subject to Changes in Their Manufacturing Process* (ICH Q5E) (June 2005)
995	
996	20. ICH guidance for industry *Q6B Specifications: Test Procedures and Acceptance Criteria*
997	*for Biotechnological/Biological Products* (ICH Q6B) (August 1999)
998	
999	21. ICH guidance for industry *Q7 Good Manufacturing Practice Guidance for Active*
1000	*Pharmaceutical Ingredients* (ICH Q7) (September 2016)
1001	
1002	22. ICH guidance for industry *Q8(R2) Pharmaceutical Development* (ICH Q8(R2))
1003	(November 2009)
1004	

26

1005   *23*. ICH guidance for industry *Q9 Quality Risk Management* (ICH Q9) (June 2006)
1006
1007   *24*. ICH guidance for industry *Q10 Pharmaceutical Quality System* (ICH Q10) (April 2009)
1008
1009   *25*. ICH guidance for industry *Q11 Development and Manufacture of Drug Substances* (ICH
1010   Q11) (November 2012)
1011
1012   *26*. ICH guidance for industry *S6(R1) Preclinical Safety Evaluation of Biotechnology-*
1013   *Derived Pharmaceuticals* (ICH S6(R1)) (May 2012)
1014

27

1015
1016   **GLOSSARY**[32]
1017   For the purpose of this document, the following definitions apply:
1018
1019   *Biosimilar or biosimilarity* means "the biological product is highly similar to the
1020   reference product notwithstanding minor differences in clinically inactive components,"
1021   and "there are no clinically meaningful differences between the biological product and
1022   the reference product in terms of the safety, purity, and potency of the product."[33]
1023
1024   *Chemically synthesized polypeptide* means any alpha amino acid polymer that (a) is made
1025   entirely by chemical synthesis and (b) is less than 100 amino acids in size.
1026
1027   *Product*, when used without modifiers, is intended to refer to the intermediates, drug
1028   substance, and/or drug product, as appropriate. The use of the term *product* is consistent
1029   with the use of the term in ICH Q5E.
1030
1031   *Protein* means any alpha amino acid polymer with a specific defined sequence that is
1032   greater than 40 amino acids in size.
1033
1034   *Reference product* means the single biological product licensed under section 351(a) of
1035   the PHS Act against which a biological product is evaluated in a 351(k) application.[34]
1036
1037

---

[32] For additional information on the Agency's interpretation of certain terms relevant to implementation of the BPCI Act, see the draft guidance for industry *New and Revised Draft Q&As on Biosimilar Development and the BPCI Act (Revision 2)* (December 2018). When final, this guidance will represent FDA's current thinking on this topic.

[33] Section 351(i)(2) of the PHS Act.

[34] Section 351(i)(4) of the PHS Act.

28

APPENDIX E

FDA Approvals and U.S. Launches of Biosimilars

The table below lists, in chronological order, the 23 biosimilar products that have received FDA-approval as of the writing of this appendix (September 17, 2019).

Biosimilar—Applicant	Reference Product	aBLA Approval Date	U.S. Launch Date (if applicable)
ZARXIO (filgrastim-sndz) *Sandoz*	NEUPOGEN [biosimilar #1]	Mar. 6, 2015	Sept. 3, 2015
INFLECTRA (infliximab-dyyb) *Celltrion*	REMICADE [biosimilar #1]	Apr. 5, 2016	Nov. 21, 2016
ERELZI (etanercept-szzs) *Sandoz*	ENBREL [biosimilar #1]	Aug. 30, 2016	
AMJEVITA (adalimumab-atto) *Amgen*	HUMIRA [biosimilar #1]	Sept. 23, 2016	
RENFLEXIS (infliximab-abda) *Samsung Bioepis*	REMICADE [biosimilar #2]	Apr. 21, 2017	July 24, 2017
CYLTEZO (adalimumab-adbm) *Boehringer Ingelheim*	HUMIRA [biosimilar #2]	Aug. 26, 2017	
MVASI (bevacizumab-awwb) *Amgen*	AVASTIN [biosimilar #1]	Sept. 14, 2017	July 18 2019
OGIVRI (trastuzumab-dkst) *Mylan*	HERCEPTIN [biosimilar #1]	Dec. 1, 2017	
IXIFI (infliximab-qbtx) *Pfizer*	REMICADE [biosimilar #3]	Dec. 13, 2017	
RETACRIT (epoetin alfa-epbx) *Hospira*	EPOGEN/PROCRIT [biosimilar #1]	May 15, 2018	Nov. 12, 2018
FULPHILA (pegfilgrastim-jmdb) *Mylan*	NEULASTA [biosimilar #1]	June 4, 2018	July 30, 2018
NIVESTYM (filgrastim-aafi) *Pfizer*	NEUPOGEN [biosimilar #2]	July 20, 2018	Oct. 1, 2018
HYRIMOZ (adalimumab-adaz) *Sandoz*	HUMIRA [biosimilar #3]	Oct. 31, 2018	
UDENYCA (pegfilgrastim-cbqv) *Coherus*	NEULASTA [biosimilar #2]	Nov. 2, 2018	Jan. 3, 2019

Biosimilar—Applicant	Reference Product	aBLA Approval Date	U.S. Launch Date (if applicable)
TRUXIMA (rituximab-abbs) *Celltrion*	RITUXAN [biosimilar #1]	Nov. 28, 2018	
HERZUMA (trastuzumab-pkrb) *Celltrion*	HERCEPTIN [biosimilar #2]	Dec. 14, 2018	
ONTRUZANT (trastuzumab-dttb) *Samsung Bioepis*	HERCEPTIN [biosimilar #3]	Jan. 18, 2019	
TRAZIMERA (trastuzumab-qyyp) *Pfizer*	HERCEPTIN [biosimilar #4]	Mar. 11, 2019	
ETICOVO (etanercept-ykro) *Samsung Bioepis*	ENBREL [biosimilar #2]	Apr. 25, 2019	
KANJINTI (trastuzumab-anns) *Amgen*	HERCEPTIN [biosimilar #5]	June 13, 2019	July 18, 2019
ZIRABEV (bevacizumab-bvzr) *Pfizer*	AVASTIN [biosimilar #2]	June 28, 2019	
RUXIENCE (rituximab-pvvr) *Pfizer*	RITUXAN [biosimilar #2]	July 23, 2019	
HADLIMA (adalimumab-bwwd) *Samsung Bioepis*	HUMIRA [biosimilar #4]	July 23, 2019	

APPENDIX F

BPCIA Litigations

The tables below summarize the history, status and, if applicable, outcome of each of the patent litigations under the BPCIA (as of September 17, 2019). As listed below, the litigations are organized by reference product, which are organized in chronological order, based upon the date of the first BPCIA litigation concerning that product:

1) Biosimilars of NEUPOGEN (filgrastim) or NEULASTA (pegfilgrastim)
2) Biosimilars of REMICADE (infliximab)
3) Biosimilars of EPOGEN/PROCRIT (epoetin alfa)
4) Biosimilars of ENBREL (etanercept)
5) Biosimilars of HUMIRA (adalimumab)
6) Biosimilars of AVASTIN (bevacizumab)
7) Biosimilars of HERCEPTIN (trastuzumab)
8) Biosimilars of RITUXAN (rituximab)

The filgrastim and pegfilgrastim litigations are grouped together because, in some instances, a single defendant's filgrastim and pegfilgrastim litigations were coordinated or consolidated for trial, or litigated in a single action.

1) Biosimilars of NEUPOGEN (Filgrastim) or NEULASTA (Pegfilgrastim)

REFERENCE PRODUCT INFORMATION
Filgrastim
Tradename: NEUPOGEN
Applicant: Amgen
BLA No.: 103353
Original FDA-Approval: February 20, 1991
Current FDA-Approved Indications: *(see approved label for further information)* • Decrease the incidence of infection, as manifested by febrile neutropenia, in patients with nonmyeloid malignancies receiving myelosuppressive anti-cancer drugs associated with a significant incidence of severe neutropenia with

fever.

- Reduce the time to neutrophil recovery and the duration of fever, following induction or consolidation chemotherapy treatment of patients with acute myeloid leukemia (AML).
- Reduce the duration of neutropenia and neutropenia-related clinical sequelae, e.g., febrile neutropenia, in patients with nonmyeloid malignancies undergoing myeloablative chemotherapy followed by bone marrow transplantation (BMT).
- Mobilize autologous hematopoietic progenitor cells into the peripheral blood for collection by leukapheresis.
- Reduce the incidence and duration of sequelae of severe neutropenia (e.g., fever, infections, oropharyngeal ulcers) in symptomatic patients with congenital neutropenia, cyclic neutropenia, or idiopathic neutropenia.
- Increase survival in patients acutely exposed to myelosuppressive doses of radiation (Hematopoietic Syndrome of Acute Radiation Syndrome).

Current FDA-Approved Dosage Forms: *(see approved label for further information)*

- Vials for subcutaneous injection or intravenous infusion: 300 mcg/mL or 480 mcg/1.6 mL in a single-dose vial.
- Prefilled syringes for subcutaneous injection: 300 mcg/0.5 mL or 480 mcg/0.8 mL in a single-dose prefilled syringe.

Pegfilgrastim

Tradename: NEULASTA
Applicant: Amgen
BLA No.: 125031
Original FDA-Approval: January 31, 2002

Current FDA-Approved Indications: *(see approved label for further information)*

- Decrease the incidence of infection, as manifested by febrile neutropenia, in patients with non-myeloid malignancies receiving myelosuppressive anti-cancer drugs associated with a clinically significant incidence of febrile neutropenia; and
- Increase survival in patients acutely exposed to myelosuppressive doses of radiation (Hematopoietic Subsyndrome of Acute Radiation Syndrome).

Current FDA-Approved Dosage Forms: *(see approved label for further information)*

- Prefilled syringes for subcutaneous injection: 6 mg/0.6 mL in a single-dose prefilled syringe for manual use only; or 6 mg/ 0.6 mL in a single-dose prefilled syringe co-packaged with the on-body injector (OBI) for Neulasta (Neulasta Onpro kit).

FILGRASTIM AND/OR PEGFILGRASTIM BPCIA LITIGA-TIONS

1. _Amgen v. Sandoz_   **Concerned Molecule(s): filgrastim & pegfilgrastim**

Case Name: _Amgen Inc. and Amgen Manufacturing, Limited v. Sandoz Inc., Sandoz International GmbH, and Sandoz GmbH_, Civil Action Nos. 3:14-cv-04741-RS, and 3:16-cv-02581-RS (N.D. Cal.). Related: _Amgen Inc. v. Sandoz Inc._, Civil Action No. 2:16-cv-1276-SRC-CLW (D.N.J.); _Sandoz Inc. v. Amgen Inc. et al._, Civil Action No. 3:19-cv-977-RS (N.D. Cal.).

Biosimilar Application Information:
- _Filgrastim_
  - **Applicant:** Sandoz
  - **Subsection (k) BLA No.:** 125553
  - **Original FDA-Submission Date:** May 8, 2014
  - **Original FDA-Acceptance Date:** July 24, 2014
  - **Original FDA-Approval Date:** March 6, 2015
  - **Approved Name:** ZARXIO (filgrastim-sndz)
  - **U.S. Commercial Launch Date**: September 3, 2015
- _Pegfilgrastim_
  - **Applicant:** Sandoz
  - **Subsection (k) BLA No.:** 761045
  - **Original FDA-Submission Date:** _Est._ Sept. 2015
  - **Original FDA-Acceptance Date:** November 18, 2015 (not approved)

Patent Dance:
- _Filgrastim_: N/A. Sandoz elected not to participate in the patent dance. On July 8, 2014, Sandoz provided Amgen with notice of FDA acceptance of its aBLA and notice of commercial marketing.
- _Pegfilgrastim_
  - **BSA's (_l_)(2) disclosure:** The parties began exchanging information pursuant to the BPCIA's patent dance provisions on November 13, 2015. The specifics of this initial disclosure have not been publicly disclosed, nor have any violations been alleged.
  - **RPS's (_l_)(3)(A) list:** Amgen provided Sandoz with a list of patents that included the '878 and '784 patents. The specifics of this disclosure have not been publicly

disclosed, nor have any violations been alleged.

- **BSA's (*l*)(3)(B) detailed statement:** Sandoz provided Amgen with a detailed statement and represented that it did not intend to commercially market its biosimilar before the '784 patent expired. The specifics of this disclosure have not been publicly disclosed, nor have any violations been alleged.

- **RPS's (*l*)(3)(C) detailed statement and (*l*)(4)/(5) negotiations:** Amgen provided Sandoz with a responsive detailed statement. The parties engaged in negotiations and agreed on April 12, 2016 to immediately litigate only the '878 and '784 patents.

- **BSA's (*l*)(8)(A) notice of commercial marketing:** unknown

Litigation:
- **Complaints:**
  - *Filgrastim*: Filed on October 24, 2014, alleging infringement of one patent, as well as state-law claims arising out of alleged violations of the BPCIA.
  - *Pegfilgrastim*: Filed on May 12, 2016, alleging infringement of two patents.
- **District Court Disposition:** While co-pending, the cases were coordinated for discovery and trial.
  - *Injunctive relief*: Early on in the filgrastim case, the district court denied Amgen's request for an injunction under federal and state law to enjoin Sandoz from commercially launching its filgrastim biosimilar, based on Sandoz's alleged violations of the BPCIA. Amgen filed an interlocutory appeal that eventually made its way to the U.S. Supreme Court, which held that the requested injunction was not available under federal law; on remand, the Federal Circuit held that the requested injunction was also not available under state law, thus upholding the district court's denial of the injunction.
  - *Merits*: Ultimately, the parties litigated the '427 and '878 patents to final judgment. On August 4, 2016, the district court construed certain claim terms of the '427 patent in a manner contrary to Amgen's position, after which Amgen stipulated to Sandoz's non-infringement of that patent contingent upon Amgen's right to appeal from the district court's claim construction order. On December 19, 2017, the district court granted summary judgment of non-infringement of the '878 patent in favor of Sandoz. Amgen appealed.
- **Appeal(s):**
  - *Injunctive relief*:
    - **Fed. Cir. No. 15-1499:** On July 21, 2015, the Federal Circuit issued a split decision (a) holding that participa-

tion in the patent dance is not mandatory, (b) holding that notice of commercial marketing can be provided *only after FDA-approval*, and (c) affirming the district court's dismissal of Amgen's state-law claims. *See* 794 F.3d 1347 (Fed. Cir. 2015). Both sides filed petitions for writs of *certiorari*, which the Supreme Court granted.

- **S. Ct. Nos. 15-1039, -1195:** On June 12, 2017, the Supreme Court issued a unanimous opinion (a) holding that a biosimilar applicant's compliance with patent dance provision (*l*)(2)(A) cannot be compelled under federal law; (b) holding that a biosimilar applicant may provide notice of commercial marketing even *prior to FDA-approval*, and (3) vacating judgment on the state-law claim and remanding for further consideration. *See* 137 S. Ct. 1664 (2017).

- **Fed. Cir. No. 15-1499, on remand:** On December 15, 2017, the Federal Circuit held that Amgen's state-law claims, which were based on Sandoz's alleged failure to follow the BPCIA's patent dance procedures, were preempted by federal law on both field and conflict grounds. *See* 877 F.3d 1315 (Fed. Cir. 2017).

- *Merits*: **Fed. Cir. No. 18-1551:** On May 8, 2019, a Federal Circuit panel affirmed the district court's judgment of non-infringement of the '427 and '878 patents in Sandoz's favor. On June 7, 2019, Amgen filed a petition for rehearing *en banc* regarding the panel's doctrine of equivalents analysis for the '878 patent. On September 3, 2019, the Federal Circuit denied en banc rehearing, but granted panel rehearing through which the panel modified certain language in its May 8, 2019 opinion.

2. *Amgen v. Apotex*	Concerned Molecule(s): pegfilgrastim & filgrastim

Case Name: *Amgen Inc. and Amgen Manufacturing, Limited v. Apotex Inc. and Apotex Corp.*, Civil Action Nos. 0:15-61631-JIC and 0:15-62081-JIC (S.D. Fla.) (consolidated); Follow-on Case: *Amgen Inc. and Amgen Manufacturing, Limited v. Apotex Inc. and Apotex Corp.*, Civil Action No. 0:18-61828-JIC (S.D. Fla.).

Biosimilar Application Information:
- *Pegfilgrastim*
  - **Applicant:** Apotex
  - **Subsection (k) BLA No.:** 761026
  - **Original FDA-Submission Date:** October 16, 2014
  - **Original FDA-Acceptance Date:** December 16, 2014 (not approved)
- *Filgrastim*:
  - **Applicant:** Sandoz

- **Subsection (k) BLA No.:** 761045
- **Original FDA-Submission Date:** December 12, 2014
- **Original FDA-Acceptance Date:** February 13, 2015 (not approved)

Patent Dance:
- *Pegfilgrastim*:
  - **BSA's (*l*)(2) disclosure:** On December 31, 2014, Apotex provided a copy of its aBLA to Amgen.
  - **RPS's (*l*)(3)(A) list:** On February 27, 2015, Amgen provided Apotex with a list of patents that included the '138 and '784 patents.
  - **BSA's (*l*)(3)(B) detailed statement:** On April 17, 2015, Apotex provided a detailed statement regarding the listed patents.
  - **RPS's (*l*)(3)(C) detailed statement and (*l*)(4)/(5) negotiations:** On June 16, 2015, Amgen provided Apotex with a responsive detailed statement. The parties negotiated beginning on June 22, 2015, and agreed on July 7, 2015 to immediately litigate only the '138 and '784 patents.
  - **BSA's (*l*)(8)(A) notice of commercial marketing:** April 17, 2015
- *Filgrastim*:
  - **BSA's (*l*)(2) disclosure:** On March 4, 2015, Apotex provided a copy of its aBLA to Amgen.
  - **RPS's (*l*)(3)(A) list:** On May 1, 2015, Amgen provided Apotex with a list of patents that included the '138 and '427 patents.
  - **BSA's (*l*)(3)(B) detailed statement:** On June 29, 2015, Apotex provided a detailed statement regarding the listed patents.
  - **RPS's (*l*)(3)(C) detailed statement and (*l*)(4)/(5) negotiations:** On August 28, 2015, Amgen provided Apotex with a responsive detailed statement. The parties negotiated beginning on August 29, 2015, and agreed on September 4, 2015 to immediately litigate only the '138 and '427 patents.
  - **BSA's (*l*)(8)(A) notice of commercial marketing:** April 17, 2015

Litigation:
- **Complaints:**
  - *Pegfilgrastim*: Filed on August 6, 2015, alleging infringement of two patents (the '138 and '784) and alleged violations of the BPCIA. (C.A. No. 15-61631)
  - *Filgrastim*: Filed on October 2, 2015, alleging infringe-

ment of two patents (the '138 and '427) and alleged violations of the BPCIA. (C.A. No. 15-62081)

- *Follow-on pegfilgrastim and filgrastim litigation*: Filed on
  August 7, 2018, alleging infringement of a newly issued,
  related patent. (C.A. No. 18-61828)

● **District Court Disposition:**

- **First round of litigation:** The original two cases were
  consolidated.

  - *Injunctive relief*: On December 10, 2015, the district
    court granted Amgen a preliminary injunction enjoining
    Apotex from marketing its biosimilar pegfilgrastim
    product until 180 days after Apotex notifies Amgen that
    its biosimilar application has received FDA approva_
    and that Apotex intends to begin commercial
    marketing. In granting the injunction, the district
    relied on the Federal Circuit's July 21, 2015 holding in
    Amgen v. Sandoz that notice of commercial marketing
    can be provided *only after FDA-approval*—a holding
    which was ultimately overturned by the Supreme Court
    in 2017. The injunction against Apotex, however, was
    affirmed on appeal.

  - *Merits*: Ultimately, the parties litigated the '138 patent
    to final judgment. On September 6, 2016, following a
    July 2016 bench trial, the district court ruled that nei-
    ther of Apotex's proposed biosimilar products would
    infringe the '138 patent. The district court also ruled
    that Apotex had failed to prove that the patent was
    invalid. Amgen appealed.

- **Second round of litigation:** Amgen initiated a second
  round of litigation after the first round of litigation had
  already concluded. On August 26, 2019, the district court
  granted a stipulation and unopposed motion of the parties
  to substitute the Apotex defendants with Accord
  BioPharma. As of September 17, 2019, this case is pending in early discovery, with a jury trial set for May 11,
  2020.

● **Appeal(s):**

- *Injunctive relief*:

  - **Fed. Cir. No. 16-1308:** On July 5, 2016, the Federal
    Circuit affirmed the district court's grant of a pre_imi-
    nary injunction. *See* 827 F.3d 1052 (Fed. Cir. 2016).
    Apotex filed a petition for writ of *certiorari*.

  - **S. Ct. No. 16-332:** On December 12, 2016, the Supreme
    Court denied Apotex's *certiorari* petition. *See* 137 S. Ct.
    591 (2016).

- *Merits*: **Fed. Cir. No. 17-1010:** On November 13, 2017,
  the Federal Circuit affirmed the district court's judgment
  of non-infringement of the '138 patent in Apotex's favor.
  See 712 F. App'x 985 (Fed. Cir. 2017).

3. *Amgen v. Coherus*	**Concerned Molecule(s): pegfilgrastim**

Case Name: *Amgen Inc. and Amgen Manufacturing, Limited v. Coherus Biosciences Inc.*, Civil Action No. 1:17-cv-00546-LPS (D. Del.).

Biosimilar Application Information:
- **Applicant:** Coherus
- **Subsection (k) BLA No.:** 761039
- **Original FDA-Submission Date:** August 9, 2016
- **Original FDA-Acceptance Date:** October 6, 2016
- **Original FDA-Approval Date:** November 2, 2018
- **Approved Name:** UDENYCA (pegfilgrastim-cbqv)
- **U.S. Commercial Launch Date**: January 3, 2019

Patent Dance:
- **BSA's (l)(2) disclosure:** The parties began exchanging information pursuant to the BPCIA's patent dance provisions on October 11, 2016. The specifics of this initial disclosure have not been publicly disclosed, nor have any violations been alleged.
- **RPS's (l)(3)(A) list:** Amgen provided Coherus with a list of patents that included the '707 patent. The specifics of this disclosure have not been publicly disclosed, nor have any violations been alleged.
- **BSA's (l)(3)(B) detailed statement:** Coherus provided Amgen with its own list of patent and a detailed statement regarding the listed patents. The specifics of this disclosure have not been publicly disclosed, nor have any violations been alleged.
- **RPS's (l)(3)(C) detailed statement and (l)(4)/(5) negotiations:** Amgen provided Coherus with a responsive detailed statement. The parties negotiated under (l)(4) and agreed that the '707 patent would be included in the action for patent infringement. The specifics of these disclosures and negotiations have not been publicly disclosed, nor have any violations been alleged.
- **BSA's (l)(8)(A) notice of commercial marketing:** Unknown

Litigation:
- **Complaint:** Filed on May 10, 2017, alleging infringement of one patent (the '707).
- **District Court Disposition:** On March 27, 2018, the district court granted Coherus's motion to dismiss Amgen's

complaint for failure to state a claim upon which relief may be granted, and also denied Amgen leave to amend its complaint. Amgen had only alleged infringement by Coherus under the doctrine of equivalents, and the district court found that Amgen's claim was barred on grounds of prosecution history estoppel and the dedication-disclosure doctrine. Amgen appealed.

- **Appeal: Fed. Cir. No. 18-1993:** On July 29, 2019, a Federal Circuit panel affirmed the district court's dismissal of Amgen's complaint in Coherus's favor.

4. *Amgen v. Mylan*	Concerned Molecule(s): pegfilgrastim

Case Name: *Amgen Inc. and Amgen Manufacturing, Limited v. Mylan Inc., Mylan Pharmaceuticals Inc., Mylan GmbH, and Mylan N.V.*, Civil Action No. 2:17-cv-01235-MRH (W.D. Pa.).

Biosimilar Application Information:
- **Applicant:** Mylan
- **Subsection (k) BLA No.:** 761075
- **Original FDA-Submission Date:** December 9, 2016
- **Original FDA-Acceptance Date:** February 7, 2017
- **Original FDA-Approval Date:** June 4, 2018
- **Approved Name:** FULPHILA (pegfilgrastim-jmdb)
- **U.S. Commercial Launch Date**: July 30, 2018

Patent Dance:
- **BSA's (*l*)(2) disclosure:** On March 2, 2017, Mylan previded Amgen's counsel with access to Mylan's aBLA, but did not provide manufacturing process information beyond that included in the aBLA.
- **RPS's (*l*)(3)(A) list:** On May 1, 2017, Amgen listed provided Coherus with a list of patents that include the '707 patent. On June 7, 2017, Amgen supplemented its list, adding at least the '997 patent.
- **BSA's (*l*)(3)(B) detailed statement:** On June 5, 2017, Mylan provided a detailed statement regarding the listed patents. On June 9, 2017, Mylan provided a detailed statement regarding the newly listed '997 patent.
- **RPS's (*l*)(3)(C) detailed statement and (*l*)(4)/(5) negotiations:** On August 4, 2017, Amgen provided Coherus with a responsive detailed statement regarding the '707 patent and another patent. On August 8, 2017, Amgen provided Coherus with a responsive detailed statement regarding the '997 patent. The parties negotiated but failed to reach agreement on which patents would be included in an immediate patent infringement action. Pursuant to (*l*)(5),

the parties identified the '707 and '997 patents for inclusion in an infringement action.
- **BSA's (*l*)(8)(A) notice of commercial marketing:** June 12, 2017

Litigation:
- **Complaint:** Filed on September 22, 2017, alleging infringement of two patents (the '707 and '997).
- **District Court Disposition:** On September 13, 2019, the parties submitted a joint stipulation of non-infringement in favor of Mylan, thereby resolving all disputes in the case, subject to the court's approval.

5. *Amgen v. Kashiv*	**Concerned Molecule(s): filgrastim**

Case Name: *Amgen Inc. and Amgen Manufacturing, Limited v. Kashiv Biosciences, LLC, Amneal Pharmaceuticals LLC, and Amneal Pharmaceuticals, Inc.*, Civil Action No. 2:18-cv-03347-CCC-MF (D.N.J.).

Biosimilar Application Information:
- **Applicant:** Kashiv (previously Adello Biologics, LLC)
- **Subsection (k) BLA No.:** 761082
- **Original FDA-Submission Date:** December 9, 2016
- **Original FDA-Acceptance Date:** September 8, 2017 (not approved)

Patent Dance: N/A: Adello elected not to participate in the patent dance. On September 11, 2017, Adello provided its notice of commercial marketing to Amgen.

Litigation:
- **Complaint:** Filed on March 8, 2018, alleging infringement of 17 patents. Amended complaint filed on October 3, 2018, alleging infringement of a subset of four patents.
- **District Court Disposition:** The case is currently pending in discovery. As of September 17, 2019, expert discovery is scheduled to close on January 20, 2020, but the court has not yet scheduled trial or a final pretrial conference.

6. *Amgen v. Hospira*	**Concerned Molecule(s): filgrastim**

Case Name: *Amgen Inc. and Amgen Manufacturing, Limited v. Hospira, Inc. and Pfizer Inc.*, Civil Action No. 1:18-cv-01064-CFC (D. Del.).

Biosimilar Application Information:
- **Applicant:** Hospira
- **Subsection (k) BLA No.:** 761080
- **Original FDA-Submission Date:** September 21, 2017
- **Original FDA-Acceptance Date:** November 20, 2017
- **Original FDA-Approval Date:** July 20, 2018
- **Approved Name:** NIVESTYM (filgrastim-aafi)
- **U.S. Commercial Launch Date**: October 1, 2018

Patent Dance:
- **BSA's (*l*)(2) disclosure:** On December 11, 2017, Hospira produced portions of its aBLA to Amgen and produced the remaining portions of the aBLA to Amgen by February 13, 2018.
- **RPS's (*l*)(3)(A) list:** On February 8, 2018, Amgen listed six patents (including the '997).
- **BSA's (*l*)(3)(B) detailed statement:** On April 4, 2018, Hospira provided a detailed statement regarding the listed patents.
- **RPS's (*l*)(3)(C) detailed statement and (*l*)(4)/(5) negotiations:** On June 1, 2018, Amgen provided Hospira with a responsive detailed statement regarding listed patents. The parties negotiated beginning on June 7, 2018, and agreed on June 22, 2018 to immediately litigate only the '997 patent.
- **BSA's (*l*)(8)(A) notice of commercial marketing:** Unknown

Litigation:
- **Complaint:** Filed on July 18, 2018, alleging infringement of one patent (the '997).
- **District Court Disposition:** The case is currently pending in discovery. As of September 17, 2019, a jury trial is scheduled to begin on June 15, 2020.

7. *Amgen v. Tanvex*	Concerned Molecule(s): filgrastim

Case Name: *Amgen Inc. and Amgen Manufacturing, Limited v. Tanvex BioPharma USA, Inc., Tanvex BioPharma, Inc., and Tanvex Biologics Corp.*, Civil Action No. 3:19-cv-01374-H-MSB (S.D. Cal.).

Biosimilar Application Information:
- **Applicant:** Tanvex
- **Subsection (k) BLA No.:** 761126

- **Original FDA-Submission Date:** September 30, 2018
- **Original FDA-Acceptance Date:** November 27, 2018 (not approved)

Patent Dance:
- **BSA's (*l*)(2) disclosure:** On December 17, 2018, Tanvex produced its aBLA to Amgen, and produced additional batch records on February 1, 2019.
- **RPS's (*l*)(3)(A) list:** On February 15, 2019, Amgen provided a list of patents that included the '287 patent.
- **BSA's (*l*)(3)(B) detailed statement:** On April 12, 2019, provided a detailed statement regarding the listed patents.
- **RPS's (*l*)(3)(C) detailed statement and (*l*)(4)/(5) negotiations:** On June 11, 2010, Amgen provided Tanvex with a responsive detailed statement regarding listed patents. The parties negotiated beginning on June 24, 2019, and within 15 days agreed to immediately litigate only the '287 patent.
- **BSA's (*l*)(8)(A) notice of commercial marketing:** April 1, 2019

Litigation:
- **Complaint:** Filed on July 23, 2019, alleging infringement of one patent (the '287).
- **District Court Disposition:** As of September 17, 2019, Tanvex has not yet answered Amgen's complaint.

2) Biosimilars of REMICADE (Infliximab)

REFERENCE PRODUCT INFORMATION

Tradename: REMICADE
Applicant: Janssen
BLA No.: 103772
Original FDA-Approval: August 24, 1998
 	
Current FDA-Approved Indications: *(see approved label for further information)*
  • Crohn's Disease:
    • reducing signs and symptoms and inducing and maintaining clinical remission in adult patients with moderately to severely active disease who have had an inadequate response to conventional therapy.
    • reducing the number of draining enterocutaneous and rectovaginal fistulas and maintaining fistula closure in adult patients with fistulizing disease.

- Pediatric Crohn's Disease: reducing signs and symptoms and inducing and maintaining clinical remission in pediatric patients with moderately to severely active disease who have had an inadequate response to conventional therapy.

- Ulcerative Colitis: reducing signs and symptoms, inducing and maintaining clinical remission and mucosal healing, and eliminating corticosteroid use in adult patients with moderately to severely active disease who have had an inadequate response to conventional therapy.

- Pediatric Ulcerative Colitis: reducing signs and symptoms and inducing and maintaining clinical remission in pediatric patients with moderately to severely active disease who have had an inadequate response to conventional therapy.

- Rheumatoid Arthritis in combination with methotrexate: reducing signs and symptoms, inhibiting the progression of structural damage, and improving physical function in patients with moderately to severely active disease.

- Ankylosing Spondylitis: reducing signs and symptoms in patients with active disease.

- Psoriatic Arthritis: reducing signs and symptoms of active arthritis, inhibiting the progression of structural damage, and improving physical function.

- Plaque Psoriasis: treatment of adult patients with chronic severe (i.e., extensive and/or disabling) plaque psoriasis who are candidates for systemic therapy and when other systemic therapies are medically less appropriate.

Current FDA-Approved Dosage Forms: *(see approved label for further information)*
- 100 mg lyophilized infliximab in a 20 mL vial for intravenous infusion.

INFLIXIMAB BPCIA LITIGATIONS

1. *Janssen v. Celltrion*   **Concerned Molecule(s): infliximab**

Case Name(s): *Janssen Biotech, Inc. v. Celltrion Healthcare Co., Ltd., Celltrion, Inc., and Hospira, Inc.*, Civil Action No. 1:17-cv-11008-MLW, 1:15-cv-10698-MLW, and 1:16-cv-11117 (D. Mass) (consolidated). Related: *Janssen Biotech, Inc. v. Hyclone Laboratories, Inc.*, Civil Action No. 1-16-cv-71-BCW (D. Utah); *Celltrion Healthcare Co., Ltd., and Celltrion, Inc. v. Janssen Biotech, Inc.*, 1:14-cv-11613-MLW (D. Mass.).

Biosimilar Application Information:
- **Applicant:** Celltrion
- **Subsection (k) BLA No.:** 125544

- **Original FDA-Submission Date:** August 8, 2014
- **Original FDA-Acceptance Date:** October 7, 2014
- **Original FDA-Approval Date:** April 5, 2016
- **Approved Name:** INFLECTRA (infliximab-dyyb)
- **U.S. Commercial Launch Date:** November 21, 2016

Patent Dance:
- **BSA's (*l*)(2) disclosure:** On October 27, 2014, Celltrion produced a copy of its aBLA, but no other manufacturing process information, to Janssen.
- **RPS's (*l*)(3)(A) list:** On December 26, 2014, Janssen listed six patents, including the '471 and '083 patents.
- **BSA's (*l*)(3)(B) detailed statement:** On February 5, 2015, Celltrion provided a detailed statement regarding the listed patents and indicated that Celltrion "consented to Janssen's patent list" for the litigation and that further exchanges and negotiations were therefore not necessary.
- **RPS's (*l*)(3)(C) detailed statement and (*l*)(4)/(5) negotiations:** In response to Celltrion's position about further exchanges and negotiations, Janssen filed its first complaint on March 6, 2015, without providing a responsive detailed statement or engaging negotiations. In April 2017, Celltrion attempted to re-engage in negotiations and trigger another period during which Janssen must file a complaint; although Janssen contended that the attempt was legally ineffective, Janssen filed another complaint on May 31, 2017.
- **BSA's (*l*)(8)(A) notice of commercial marketing:** February 5, 2015

Litigation:
- **Complaints:**
  - Originally filed on March 6, 2015, alleging infringement of six patents (including the '471 and '083) and violations of the BPCIA. (C.A. No. 15-10698)
  - Janssen filed a second complaint on June 14, 2016, alleging actual (as opposed to artificial) acts of infringement of the '083 patent. (C.A. No. 16-11117)
  - Janssen filed a third complaint on May 31, 2017, alleging infringement of the '083 patent, in response to Celltrion's attempt to re-engage in good-faith negotiations pursuant to (*l*)(4). (C.A. No. 17-11008)
- **District Court Disposition:** The three cases were consolidated. Ultimately, the parties litigated the '471 and '083 patents to final judgment.
  - *'471 patent*: On August 18, 2016, the district court granted summary judgment in favor of Celltrion that all claims of

the '471 patent are invalid on the ground of obviousness-type double patenting. Janssen appealed the ruling, while the district court case continued regarding the '083 patent.

- *'083 patent*: On October 31, 2018, the district court denied Celltrion's motion to dismiss the complaint for lack of standing. On July 30, 2018, the district court granted summary judgment of non-infringement in Celltrion's favor. Janssen had only alleged infringement of the '083 patent under the doctrine of equivalents, and the district court found that Janssen's claim was barred under the doctrine of ensnarement. Janssen appealed the grant of summary judgment, and Celltrion cross-appealed the denial of its motion to dismiss for lack of standing.

- **Appeal(s):**
  - *'471 patent*: **Fed. Cir. No. 17-1120:** On January 23, 2018, the Federal Circuit dismissed Janssen's appeal as moot. *See* 2018 WL 2072723 (Fed. Cir. Jan. 23, 2018). The Federal Circuit based the dismissal upon its simultaneous affirmance of an obviousness-type double patenting rejection of the patent's claims in an *ex parte* reexamination that was concurrently on appeal (No. 17-1257). *See In re Janssen Biotech, Inc.*, 880 F.3d 1315 (Fed. Cir. 2018)
  - *'083 patent*: **Fed. Cir. No. 18-2321:** The parties completed briefing the summary judgment and standing issues on June 18, 2019. As of September 17, 2019, oral argument has not yet been scheduled.

2. *Janssen v. Samsung Bioepis*	Concerned Molecule(s): infliximab

Case Name(s): *Janssen Biotech, Inc. v. Samsung Bioepis Co., Ltd.*, Civil Action No. 2:17-cv-3524-MCA-SCM (D.N.J.).

Biosimilar Application Information:
- **Applicant:** Samsung Bioepis
- **Subsection (k) BLA No.:** 761054
- **Original FDA-Submission Date:** March 21, 2016
- **Original FDA-Acceptance Date:** May 20, 2016
- **Original FDA-Approval Date:** April 21, 2017
- **Approved Name:** RENFLEXIS (infliximab-abda)
- **U.S. Commercial Launch Date**: July 24, 2017

Patent Dance: N/A: Samsung Bioepis elected not to participate in the patent dance. On May 26, 2016, Samsung Bioepis provided its notice of commercial marketing to Janssen.

Litigation:

- **Complaint:** Complaint filed on May 17, 2017, alleging infringement of three patents and violations of the BPCIA, including early notice of commercial marketing.
- **District Court Disposition:** On November 10, 2017, the parties filed a stipulation of voluntary dismissal, disposing of all remaining claims in the case.
- **Appeal:** N/A

3) Biosimilars of EPOGEN/PROCRIT (Epoetin Alfa)

REFERENCE PRODUCT INFORMATION

Tradename: EPOGEN®/PROCRIT®
 Applicant: Amgen
 BLA No.: 103234
 Original FDA-Approval: June 1, 1989
 	
 Current FDA-Approved Indications: *(see approved label for further information)*
 • Treatment of anemia due to:
   • Chronic Kidney Disease (CKD) in patients on dialysis and not on dialysis.
   • Zidovudine in patients with HIV-infection.
   • The effects of concomitant myelosuppressive chemotherapy, and upon initiation, there is a minimum of two additional months of planned chemotherapy.
 • Reduction of allogeneic RBC transfusions in patients undergoing elective, noncardiac, nonvascular surgery.
 	
 Current FDA-Approved Dosage Forms: *(see approved label for further information)*
 • 2,000 Units/mL, 3,000 Units/mL, 4,000 Units/mL, and 10,000 Units/mL in single-dose vials
 • 20,000 Units/2 mL (10,000 Units/mL) and 20,000 Units/mL in multiple-dose vials (contains benzyl alcohol)

EPOETIN ALFA BPCIA LITIGATIONS
1. *Amgen v. Hospira*   **Concerned Molecule(s): epoetin alfa**   **Case Name(s):** *Amgen Inc. and Amgen Manufacturing, Limited, v. Hospira, Inc.*, Civil Action No. 1:15-cv-00839-RGA (D. Del.).   **Biosimilar Application Information:**   • **Applicant:** Hospira

- **Subsection (k) BLA No.:** 125545
- **Original FDA-Submission Date:** December 16, 2014
- **Original FDA-Acceptance Date:** February 23, 2015
- **Original FDA-Approval Date:** May 15, 2018
- **Approved Name:** RETACRIT (epoetin alfa-epbx)
- **U.S. Commercial Launch Date**: Nov. 12, 2018

Patent Dance:

- **BSA's (*l*)(2) disclosure:** On March 3, 2015, Hospira produced a copy of its aBLA to Amgen, but did not produce any manufacturing process information beyond that included in the aBLA.
- **RPS's (*l*)(3)(A) list:** On May 1, 2015, Amgen listed three patents (the '349, '298 and '637 patents)
- **BSA's (*l*)(3)(B) detailed statement:** On June 19, 2015, Hospira provided a detailed statement regarding the '298 and '637 patents, and represented that it did not intend to commercially market its biosimilar before the '349 patent expired.
- **RPS's (*l*)(3)(C) detailed statement and RPS's (*l*)(4)/(5) negotiations:** On August 18, 2015, Amgen provided a responsive detailed statement regarding all three listed patents. On August 19, 2015, Hospira notified Amgen that it agreed that all three listed patents could be subject to a patent infringement action. Amgen characterized Hospira's unilateral acceptance of that list as a refusal to engage in good-faith negotiations, in violation of (*l*)(4).
- **BSA's (*l*)(8)(A) notice of commercial marketing:** April 8, 2015

Litigation:

- **Complaint:** Filed on September 18, 2015, alleging infringement of two patents (the '349 and '298 patents) and violations of the BPCIA.
- **Notable Discovery Issue:** On May 4, 2016, the district court denied Amgen's motion to compel discovery from Hospira related to patents that Amgen did not include on its (*l*)(3)(A) list. Amgen filed an interlocutory appeal, which was eventually dismissed by the Federal Circuit for lack of jurisdiction.
- **District Court Disposition:** The district court held a jury trial in September 2017 concerning the issues of infringement and validity of the '298 and '349 patents, both of which had since expired. The jury reached the following verdict: (1) Hospira's manufacture of 14 of 21 accused batches of drug substance in 2013-2015 was not protected activity under the safe harbor of 35 U.S.C. § 271(e)(1) and infringed the asserted claims of the '298 patent; (2) Hospira

did not infringe the asserted claims of the '349 patent; (3) Hospira had not proven that the asserted claims of the '298 and '349 patents were invalid; and (4) Amgen was entitled to a damages award of $70 million for Hospira's infringement. On August 27, 2018, the district court upheld the jury's verdict and denied the parties' respectively motions for judgment as a matter of law and alternative motions for a new trial or for remittitur. The district court entered final judgment that tacked on over $10 million in pre- and post-judgment interest to Amgen's damages award. Hospira appealed the adverse infringement, validity and damages rulings regarding the '298 patent, and Amgen cross-appealed the district court's judgment of non-infringement of the '349 patent.

- **Appeals:**
  - *Discovery issue:* **Fed. Cir. No. 16-2179:** On August 10, 2017, the Federal Circuit dismissed Amgen's interlocutory appeal for lack of jurisdiction under the collateral order doctrine. *See Amgen Inc. v. Hospira, Inc.*, 866 F.3d 1355 (Fed. Cir. 2017).
  - *Merits:* **Fed. Cir. No. 19-1067:** The parties completed appellate briefing in April 2019. Oral argument is scheduled for September 30, 2019.

4) Biosimilars of ENBREL (Etanercept)

REFERENCE PRODUCT INFORMATION
Tradename: ENBREL®
Applicant: Amgen
BLA No.: 103795
Original FDA-Approval: Nov. 2, 1998
Current FDA-Approved Indications: *(see approved label for further information)*   • Rheumatoid Arthritis (RA)   • Polyarticular Juvenile Idiopathic Arthritis (JIA) in patients aged 2 years or older   • Psoriatic Arthritis (PsA)   • Ankylosing Spondylitis (AS)   • Plaque Psoriasis (PsO) in patients 4 years or older
Current FDA-Approved Dosage Forms: *(see approved label for further information)*   • Subcutaneous injection: 25 mg/0.5 mL and 50 mg/mL clear,

colorless solution in a single-dose prefilled syringe

- Subcutaneous injection: 50 mg/mL clear, colorless solution in a single-dose prefilled SureClick autoinjector
- Subcutaneous injection: 25 mg lyophilized powder in a multiple-dose vial for reconstitution
- Subcutaneous injection: 50 mg/mL clear, colorless solution in Enbrel Mini single-dose prefilled cartridge for use with the AutoTouch reusable autoinjector only

ETANERCEPT ALFA BPCIA LITIGATIONS

1. *Immunex v. Sandoz* **Concerned Molecule(s): etanercept**

Case Name(s): *Immunex Corporation, Amgen Manufacturing, Limited, and Hoffman-La Roche Inc. v. Sandoz Inc., Sandoz International Gmbh, Sandoz Gmbh*, Civil Action No. 2:16-cv-1118-CCC-MF (D.N.J.).

Biosimilar Application Information:
- **Applicant:** Sandoz
- **Subsection (k) BLA No.:** 761042
- **Original FDA-Submission Date:** July 30, 2015
- **Original FDA-Acceptance Date:** September 29, 2015
- **Original FDA-Approval Date:** August 30, 2016
- **Approved Name:** ERELZI (etanercept-szzs)

Patent Dance:
- **BSA's (*l*)(2) disclosure:** On October 19, 2015, Sandoz provided Immunex's counsel with access to its aBLA. On November 16, 2015, Sandoz provided, at Immunex's request, additional documents related to Sandoz's manufacturing process.
- **RPS's (*l*)(3)(A) list:** On December 18, 2015, Immunex listed at least seven patents.
- **BSA's (*l*)(3)(B) detailed statement:** On January 27, 2016, Sandoz provided a detailed statement regarding the listed patents.
- **RPS's (*l*)(3)(C) detailed statement and (*l*)(4)/(5) negotiations:** Also on January 27, 2016, Sandoz notified Immunex that Sandoz agreed that all listed patents could be subject to a patent infringement action and that Sandoz waived its right to receive an (*l*)(3)(C) detailed statement from Immunex. Immunex characterized Sandoz's unilateral acceptance of that list as a refusal to engage in good-faith negotiations, in violation of (*l*)(4).

- **BSA's (*l*)(8)(A) notice of commercial marketing:** Unknown

Litigation:
- **Complaint:** Filed on February 26, 2016, alleging infringement of five patents.
- **District Court Disposition:** Ultimately, the parties proceeded to trial on two patents (the '522 and '182 patents). Prior to trial, Sandoz stipulated to infringement. On August 9, 2019, the district court ruled in favor of Amgen, holding that the asserted claims of the two patents were not invalid due to lack of written description and enablement, obviousness, and obviousness-type double patenting. On September 6, 2019, the parties filed their proposed final judgments under seal. Sandoz has publicly stated that it intends to appeal the district court's judgment, once it is entered.

2. Immunex v. Samsung Bioepis	**Concerned Molecule(s): etanercept**

Case Name(s): *Immunex Corporation, Amgen Manufacturing, Limited, and Hoffman-La Roche Inc. v. Samsung Bioepis Co., Ltd.*, Civil Action No. 19-11755 (D. N. J.).

Biosimilar Application Information:
- **Applicant:** Samsung Bioepis
- **Subsection (k) BLA No.:** 761066
- **Original FDA-Submission Date:** May 25, 2017
- **Original FDA-Acceptance Date:** October 25, 2018
- **Approved Name:** ETICOVO (etanercept-ykro)
- **Original FDA-Approval Date:** April 25, 2019

Patent Dance: N/A: Samsung Bioepis elected not to participate in the patent dance. According to Samsung Bioepis' August 5, 2019 answer to the complaint, it had not yet provided its notice of commercial marketing.

Litigation:
- **Complaint:** Filed on April 29, 2019, alleging infringement of 5 patents.
- **District Court Disposition:** Case pending in pleadings phase.

5) Biosimilars of HUMIRA (Adalimumab)

REFERENCE PRODUCT INFORMATION

Tradename: HUMIRA
Applicant: AbbVie
BLA No.: 125057
Original FDA-Approval: December 31, 2002

Current FDA-Approved Indications: (see approved label for further information)

- Rheumatoid Arthritis (RA): Reducing signs and symptoms, inducing major clinical response, inhibiting the progression of structural damage, and improving physical function in adult patients with moderately to severely active RA.
- Juvenile Idiopathic Arthritis (JIA): Reducing signs and symptoms of moderately to severely active polyarticular JIA in patients 2 years of age and older.
- Psoriatic Arthritis (PsA): Reducing signs and symptoms, inhibiting the progression of structural damage, and improving physical function in adult patients with active PsA.
- Ankylosing Spondylitis (AS): Reducing signs and symptoms in adult patients with active AS.
- Adult Crohn's Disease (CD): Reducing signs and symptoms and inducing and maintaining clinical remission in adult patients with moderately to severely active Crohn's disease who have had an inadequate response to conventional therapy. Reducing signs and symptoms and inducing clinical remission in these patients if they have also lost response to or are intolerant to infliximab.
- Pediatric Crohn's Disease: Reducing signs and symptoms and inducing and maintaining clinical remission in patients 6 years of age and older with moderately to severely active Crohn's disease who have had an inadequate response to corticosteroids or immunomodulators such as azathioprine, 6-mercaptopurine, or methotrexate.
- Ulcerative Colitis (UC): Inducing and sustaining clinical remission in adult patients with moderately to severely active ulcerative colitis who have had an inadequate response to immunosuppressants such as corticosteroids, azathioprine or 6-mercaptopurine (6-MP). The effectiveness of HUMIRA has not been established in patients who have lost response to or were intolerant to TNF blockers.
- Plaque Psoriasis (Ps): The treatment of adult patients with moderate to severe chronic plaque psoriasis who are candidates for systemic therapy or phototherapy, and when other systemic therapies are medically less appropriate.
- Hidradenitis Suppurativa (HS): The treatment of moderate

to severe hidradenitis suppurativa in patients 12 years of age and older.
- Uveitis (UV): The treatment of non-infectious intermediate, posterior, and panuveitis in adults and pediatric patients 2 years of age and older.

Current FDA-Approved Dosage Forms: (see approved label for further information)
- Injection: 80 mg/0.8 mL in a single-use prefilled pen (HUMIRA Pen)
- Injection: 80 mg/0.8 mL in a single-use prefilled glass syringe
- Injection: 40 mg/0.8 mL in a single-use prefilled pen (HUMIRA Pen)
- Injection: 40 mg/0.4 mL in a single-use prefilled pen (HUMIRA Pen)
- Injection: 40 mg/0.8 mL in a single-use prefilled glass syringe
- Injection: 40 mg/0.4 mL in a single-use prefilled glass syringe
- Injection: 20 mg/0.4 mL in a single-use prefilled glass syringe
- Injection: 20 mg/0.2 mL in a single-use prefilled glass syringe
- Injection: 10 mg/0.2 mL in a single-use prefilled glass syringe
- Injection: 10 mg/0.1 mL in a single-use prefilled glass syringe
- Injection: 40 mg/0.8 mL in a single-use glass vial for institutional use only

ADALIMUMAB BPCIA LITIGATIONS

1. *AbbVie v. Amgen*   **Concerned Molecule(s): adalimumab**

Case Name(s): *AbbVie Inc. and AbbVie Biotechnology Ltd. v. Amgen Inc. and Amgen Manufacturing Ltd.*, Civil Action No. 1:16-cv-666-MSG (D. Del).

Biosimilar Application Information:
- **Applicant:** Amgen
- **Subsection (k) BLA No.:** 761024
- **Original FDA-Submission Date:** November 24, 2015
- **Original FDA-Acceptance Date:** January 22, 2016
- **Original FDA-Approval Date:** September 23, 2016

- **Approved Name:** AMJEVITA (adalimumab-atto)
- **Settlement-Authorized U.S. Commercial Launch Date:** January 31, 2023

Patent Dance:
- **BSA's (*l*)(2) disclosure:** On February 10, 2016, Amgen produced a copy of its aBLA to AbbVie.
- **RPS's (*l*)(3)(A) list:** On April 11, 2016, AbbVie listed 61 patents. Over the course of April through June 2016, AbbVie supplemented its list to add a total of six newly issued patents, pursuant to (*l*)(7).
- **BSA's (*l*)(3)(B) detailed statement:** On June 10, 2016 Amgen provided AbbVie with a detailed statement regarding the listed patents.
- **RPS's (*l*)(3)(C) detailed statement and RPS's (*l*)(4)/(5) negotiations:** On June 21, 2016, AbbVie provided a responsive detailed statement regarding 60 of the 66 then-listed patents. The parties were unable to reach an agreement on a set of patents to immediately litigate during negotiations. On August 4, 2016, each side exchanged a list of six patents pursuant, resulting in a total of ten that could be the subject of a first-wave litigation, given the overlap of two patents identified in the exchange.
- **BSA's (*l*)(8)(A) notice of commercial marketing:** Not provided before or during litigation.

Litigation:
- **Complaint:** Filed on August 4, 2016, alleging infringement of ten patents.
- **District Court Disposition:** On September 28, 2017, the parties filed a joint stipulation of dismissal, mutually agreeing to dismiss all claims and counterclaims in view of a settlement agreement.
- **Appeal:** N/A

2. *AbbVie v. Boehringer Ingelheim*	Concerned Molecule(s): adalimumab

Case Name(s): *AbbVie Inc. and AbbVie Biotechnology Ltd. v. Boehringer Ingelheim International Gmbh, Boehringer Ingelheim Pharmaceuticals, Inc., and Boehringer Ingelheim Fremont, Inc.*, Civil Action No. 1:17-cv-1065-MSG-RL (D. Del).

Biosimilar Application Information:
- **Applicant:** Boehringer Ingelheim
- **Subsection (k) BLA No.:** 761058
- **Original FDA-Submission Date:** October 27, 2016

- **Original FDA-Acceptance Date:** January 9, 2017
- **Original FDA-Approval Date:** August 26, 2017
- **Approved Name:** CYLTEZO (adalimumab-adbm)
- **Settlement-Authorized U.S. Commercial Launch Date:** July 1, 2023

Patent Dance:
- **BSA's (*l*)(2) disclosure:** On January 13, 2017, Boehringer Ingelheim provided AbbVie with access to its aBLA.
- **RPS's (*l*)(3)(A) list:** On March 13, 2017, AbbVie listed 71 patents. Over the course of April through June 2017, AbbVie supplemented its list to add a total of three newly issued patents, pursuant to (*l*)(7).
- **BSA's (*l*)(3)(B) detailed statement:** On May 12, 2017, Boehringer Ingelheim provided AbbVie with a detailed statement regarding the listed patents. Boehringer Ingelheim supplemented its detailed statement on May 18, 2017 and July 6, 2017.
- **RPS's (*l*)(3)(C) detailed statement and RPS's (*l*)(4)/(5) negotiations:** On July 11, 2017, AbbVie provided a responsive detailed statement. On July 31, 2017, the parties exchanged lists of five patents pursuant to (*l*)(5), resulting in a total of eight patents that could be the subject of a first-wave litigation, given the overlap of two patents identified in the exchange.
- **BSA's (*l*)(8)(A) notice of commercial marketing:** Not provided before or during litigation.

Litigation:
- **Complaint:** Filed on August 2, 2017, alleging infringement of eight patents.
- **District Court Disposition:** On May 15, 2019, the parties filed a joint stipulation of dismissal, mutually agreeing to dismiss all claims and counterclaims in view of a settlement agreement.
- **Appeal:** N/A

3. *AbbVie v. Sandoz*	Concerned Molecule(s): adalimumab

Case Name(s): *AbbVie Inc. and AbbVie Biotechnology Ltd. v. Sandoz Inc., Sandoz Gmbh, and Sandoz International Gmbh*, Civil Action No. 3:18-cv-12668 (D.N.J.).

Biosimilar Application Information:
- **Applicant:** Sandoz
- **Subsection (k) BLA No.:** 761071

- **Original FDA-Submission Date:** October 30, 2017
- **Original FDA-Acceptance Date:** January 16, 2018
- **Original FDA-Approval Date:** October 31, 2018
- **Approved Name:** HYRIMOZ (adalimumab-adaz)
- **Settlement-Authorized U.S. Commercial Launch Date:** September 30, 2023

Patent Dance:
- **BSA's (*l*)(2) disclosure:** On January 17, 2018, Sandoz provided AbbVie with access to its aBLA.
- **RPS's (*l*)(3)(A) list:** On March 18, 2018, AbbVie listed 84 patents. Over the course of April and May 2018, AbbVie supplemented its list to add a total of two newly issued patents, pursuant to (*l*)(7).
- **BSA's (*l*)(3)(B) detailed statement:** On May 16, 2018, Sandoz provided a detailed statement regarding the listed patents.
- **RPS's (*l*)(3)(C) detailed statement and RPS's (*l*)(4)/(5) negotiations:** On July 15, 2018, AbbVie provided a responsive detailed statement concerning 84 listed patents. On August 10, 2018, each side identified one patent pursuant to (*l*)(5), resulting in a total of two patents that could be the subject of a first-wave litigation.
- **BSA's (*l*)(8)(A) notice of commercial marketing:** Not provided before or during litigation.

Litigation:
- **Complaint:** Filed on August 10, 2018, alleging infringement of two patents.
- **District Court Disposition:** On October 12, 2018, the parties filed a joint stipulation of dismissal, mutually agreeing to dismiss all claims and counterclaims in view of a settlement agreement
- **Appeal:** N/A

6) Biosimilars of AVASTIN (Bevacizumab)

REFERENCE PRODUCT INFORMATION
Tradename: AVASTIN
Applicant: Genentech
BLA No.: 125085
Original FDA-Approval: February 26, 2004
Current FDA-Approved Indications: • Metastatic colorectal cancer:

- in combination with intravenous 5-fluorouracil-based chemotherapy for first- or second-line treatment; or
- in combination with fluoropyrimidine-irinotecan or fluoropyrimidine-oxaliplatin-based chemotherapy for second-line treatment in patients who have progressed on a first-line Avastin-containing regimen;

but not for adjuvant treatment of colon cancer.

- Unresectable, locally advanced, recurrent or metastatic non-squamous non-small cell lung cancer, in combination with carboplatin and paclitaxel for first-line treatment.
- Recurrent glioblastoma in adults.
- Metastatic renal cell carcinoma in combination with interferon alfa.
- Persistent, recurrent, or metastatic cervical cancer, in combination with paclitaxel and cisplatin, or paclitaxel and topotecan.
- Epithelial ovarian, fallopian tube, or primary peritoneal cancer:
  - in combination with carboplatin and paclitaxel, followed by Avastin as a single agent, for stage III or IV disease following initial surgical resection;
  - in combination with paclitaxel, pegylated liposomal doxorubicin, or topotecan for platinum-resistant recurrent disease who received no more than 2 prior chemotherapy regimens; or
  - in combination with carboplatin and paclitaxel or carboplatin and gemcitabine, followed by Avastin as a single agent, for platinum-sensitive recurrent disease

Current FDA-Approved Dosage Forms: (see approved label for further information)

- Injection, for intravenous use: 100 mg/4 mL (25 mg/mL) or 400 mg/16 mL (25 mg/mL) clear to slightly opalescent, color-less to pale brown solution in single-dose vial.

BEVACIZUMAB BPCIA LITIGATIONS
1. *Genentech v. Amgen* **Concerned Molecule(s): bevacizumab**
Case Name(s): *Genentech, Inc. and City of Hope v. Amgen Inc.*, Civil Action Nos. 1:17-cv-1407-CFC, and 1:17-cv-1471-CFC (D. Del.) (consolidated); and *Genentech, Inc. and City of Hope v. Immunex Rhode Island Corp. and Amgen Inc.*, 1:19-cv-602-CFC (D. Del.). Related: *Genentech, Inc. v. Amgen Inc.*, Civil Action No. 1:17-cv-165-GMS (D. Del.), and *Amgen Inc. v. Genentech, Inc.*, 2:17-cv-7349-GW-AGR (C.D. Cal.).

Biosimilar Application Information:
• **Applicant:** Amgen
• **Subsection (k) BLA No.:** 761028
• **Original FDA-Submission Date:** November 14, 2016
• **Original FDA-Acceptance Date:** January 4, 2017
• **Original FDA-Approval Date:** September 14, 2017
• **Approved Name:** MVASI (bevacizumab-awwb)
• **U.S. Commercial Launch Date:** July 18, 2019
Patent Dance:
• **BSA's (*l*)(2) disclosure:** On January 23, 2017, Amgen produced a copy of its aBLA, but no additional manufacturing process information. On February 15, 2017, Genentech filed a complaint in D. Del., seeking a declaratory judgement that Amgen failed to comply with (*l*)(2) and an extension of Genentech's date to provide its (*l*)(3)(A) patent list, but the district court dismissed Genentech's complaint on March 1, 2017. (C.A. No. 17-165)
• **RPS's (*l*)(3)(A) list:** On March 24, 2017, Genentech listed 27 patents.
• **BSA's (*l*)(3)(B) detailed statement:** On May 23, 2017, Amgen provided a detailed statement with respect to patents on Genentech's (*l*)(3)(A) list.
• **RPS's (*l*)(3)(C) detailed statement and RPS's (*l*)(4)/(5) negotiations:** On July 22, 2017, Genentech provided its responsive detailed statement regarding 25 of its listed patents. The parties' negotiations took place over the course of September and early October 2017.
• **BSA's (*l*)(8)(A) notice of commercial marketing:** On October 6, 2017, Amgen provided its notice of commercial marketing to Genentech.
Litigation:
• **Complaints:** On October 6, 2017 (the same day on which Amgen provided notice of commercial marketing), Amgen filed a complaint for declaratory judgment against Genentech in N.D. Cal., but that case was subsequently dismissed for lack of jurisdiction. (C.A. No. 17-7349) On October 6 and 18, 2017, Genentech filed patent infringement and declaratory judgment complaints against Amgen, alleging infringement of a combined 25 patents. (C.A. Nos. 17-1407, 17-1471) On March 29, 2019, Genentech filed a third complaint against Amgen, alleging infringement of 14 patents (including two previously unasserted patents) based on supplements that Amgen filed to its aBLA. (C.A. No. 19-602)
• **District Court Disposition:** The 17-1407 and -1471 cases

are pending in discovery, with a jury trial scheduled for July 13, 2020. As of September 17, 2019, the 19-602 case is subject to a pending motion to dismiss by Amgen. On July 18, 2019, in the 19-602 case, the district court denied Genentech's motion to enforce subsection $(l)(8)(A)$ of the BPCIA to enjoin Amgen's launch until at least 180 days after it provides a new notice of commercial marketing, in view of Amgen's supplements to its aBLA; Genentech has appealed. The district court also denied Genentech's motion for an injunction pending appeal.

- **Appeal: Fed. Cir. No. 19-2155:** As of September 17, 2019, the parties are in the midst of appellate briefing regarding Genentech's appeal from the denial of its motion to enforce subsection $(l)(8)(A)$. On August 16, 2019, the Federal Circuit denied Genentech's motion for an injunction pending appeal.

2. _Genentech v. Pfizer_	**Concerned Molecule(s): bevacizumab**

Case Name(s): _Genentech, Inc. and City of Hope v. Pfizer Inc.,_ Civil Action No. 1:19-cv-638-CFC.

Biosimilar Application Information:
- **Applicant:** Pfizer
- **Subsection (k) BLA No.:** 761099
- **Original FDA-Submission Date:** June 29, 2018
- **Original FDA-Acceptance Date:** August 28, 2018
- **Original FDA-Approval Date:** June 28, 2019
- **Approved Name:** ZIRABEV (bevacizumab-bvzr)

Patent Dance:
- **BSA's $(l)(2)$ disclosure:** On September 14, 2018, Pfizer produced a copy of a portion of its aBLA, but no additional manufacturing process information.
- **RPS's $(l)(3)(A)$ list:** On November 13, 2018, Genentech listed 31 patents.
- **BSA's $(l)(3)(B)$ detailed statement:** On December 21, 2018, Pfizer provided a detailed statement with respect to patents on Genentech's $(l)(3)(A)$ list. On January 18, 2019, before Genentech's response was due, Pfizer served its notice of commercial marketing.
- **RPS's $(l)(3)(C)$ detailed statement and RPS's $(l)(4)/(5)$ negotiations:** On February 19, 2019, Genentech provided its responsive detailed statement regarding 23 of its listed patents, which included infringement contentions for 17 of those patents. On March 6, 2019, Pfizer indicated that it agreed to litigate those 17 patents.

- **BSA's (*l*)(8)(A) notice of commercial marketing:** On January 18, 2019, Pfizer provided its notice of commercial marketing to Genentech.

Litigation:
- **Complaint:** On April 5, 2019, Genentech filed a patent infringement and declaratory judgment complaint against Pfizer, alleging infringement of 22 patents.
- **District Court Disposition:** As of September 17, 2019, the case is pending in early discovery.

7) Biosimilars of HERCEPTIN (Trastuzumab)

REFERENCE PRODUCT INFORMATION

Tradename: HERCEPTIN
Applicant: Genentech
BLA No.: 103792
Original FDA-Approval: September 25, 1998

Current FDA-Approved Indications: *(see approved label for further information)*
- The treatment of HER2-overexpressing breast cancer.
- The treatment of HER2-overexpressing metastatic gastric or gastroesophageal junction adenocarcinoma.

Current FDA-Approved Dosage Forms: *(see approved label for further information)*
- Injection, for intravenous use: 100 mg/4 mL (25 mg/mL) or 400 mg/16 mL (25 mg/mL) clear to slightly opalescent, colorless to pale brown solution in single-dose vial.

TRASTUZUMAB BPCIA LITIGATIONS

1. *Genentech v. Pfizer*   **Concerned Molecule(s): trastuzumab**

Case Name(s): *Genentech, Inc. and City of Hope, v. Pfizer, Inc.*, Civil Action No. 1:17-cv-1672-GMS (D. Del.).

Biosimilar Application Information:
- **Applicant:** Pfizer
- **Subsection (k) BLA No.:** 761081
- **Original FDA-Submission Date:** June 22, 2017
- **Original FDA-Acceptance Date:** August 21, 2017

- **Original FDA-Approval Date:** March 11, 2019
- **Approved Name:** TRAZIMERA (trastuzumab-qyyp)

Patent Dance:
- **BSA's (*l*)(2) disclosure:** On September 5, 2017, Pfizer provided a copy of its aBLA and additional manufacturing process information to Genentech.
- **RPS's (*l*)(3)(A) list:** Disclosed on November 3, 2017, listing 40 patents.
- **BSA's (*l*)(3)(B) detailed statement:** N/A: Genentech filed suit immediately after Pfizer provided notice of commercial marketing on November 17, 2017, which was before Pfizer's detailed statement was due.
- **RPS's (*l*)(3)(C) detailed statement and (*l*)(4)/(5) negotiations:** N/A.
- **BSA's (*l*)(8)(A) notice of commercial marketing:** On November 17, 2017, Pfizer provided its notice of commercial marketing to Genentech.

Litigation:
- **Complaint:** Filed November 17, 2017, alleging infringement of 40 patents. Amended complaint filed on March 23, 2018, listing 20 patents.
- **District Court Disposition:** On December 4, 2018, the parties filed a joint stipulation of dismissal, mutually agreeing to dismiss all claims and counterclaims in view of a settlement agreement.
- **Appeal:** N/A

2. *Genentech v. Celltrion*	**Concerned Molecule(s): trastuzumab**

Case Name(s): *Genentech, Inc., City of Hope, and Hoffman-La Roche, Inc. v. Celltrion, Inc., Celltrion Healthcare Co., Ltd., Teva Pharmaceuticals USA, Inc.,* and *Teva Pharmaceuticals International GmbH*, Civil Action Nos. 1:18-cv-95-GMS (D. Del.) and 1:18-cv-1025-GMS (D. Del.) (consolidated). Related: *Celltrion, Inc. v. Genentech, Inc.*, 4:18-cv-274-JSW (N.D. Cal.).

Biosimilar Application Information:
- **Applicant:** Celltrion
- **Subsection (k) BLA No.:** 761091
- **Original FDA-Submission Date:** May 30, 2017
- **Original FDA-Acceptance Date:** July 28, 2017
- **Original FDA-Approval Date:** December 14, 2018
- **Approved Name:** HERZUMA (trastuzumab-pkrb)

Patent Dance:

- **BSA's (*l*)(2) disclosure:** On September 25, 2017, Celltrion provided a copy of its aBLA to Genentech.
- **RPS's (*l*)(3)(A) list:** Disclosed on October 10, 2017, listing 40 patents.
- **BSA's (*l*)(3)(B) detailed statement:** On November 7, 2017 Celltrion provided a detailed statement alleging non-infringement and invalidity for 38 of the 40 patents on Genentech's (*l*)(3)(A) list.
- **RPS's (*l*)(3)(C) detailed statement and RPS's (*l*)(4)/(5) negotiations:** On January 5, 2018 Genentech provided its response to the non-infringement and invalidity statements for 18 of the 38 patents addressed in Celltrion's (*l*)(3)(B) statement. Genentech proposed that Celltrion agree that all patents addressed in its (*l*)(3)(C) statement be included in an infringement action. Celltrion responded on January 11, 2018, seeking a declaratory judgment of non-infringement, invalidity, and/or unenforceability for all 38 patents addressed in their (*l*)(3)(B) statement and indicating that they wished to litigate all of the patents on Genentech's (*l*)(3)(A) list.
- **BSA's (*l*)(8)(A) notice of commercial marketing:** On January 11, 2018, Celltrion provided its notice of commercial marketing to Genentech.

Litigation:

- **Complaints:** On January 11, 2018, Celltrion and Teva filed a complaint for declaratory judgment against Genentech in N.D. Cal., but that case was subsequently dismissed for lack of jurisdiction. On January 12, 2018, Genentech filed a complaint against Celltrion and Teva in D. Del.
- **District Court Disposition:** On December 20, 2018, the parties filed a joint stipulation of dismissal, mutually agreeing to dismiss all claims and counterclaims in view of a settlement agreement.
- **Appeal (Fed. Cir. No. 18-2160):** Celltrion and Teva appealed the C.D. Cal. decision dismissing their declaratory judgment complaint. The appeal was dismissed, pursuant to an unopposed motion.

3. *Genentech v. Amgen*   **Concerned Molecule(s): trastuzumab**

Case Name(s): *Genentech, Inc. and City of Hope v. Amgen Inc.*, Civil Action No. 1:18-cv-924-CFC (D. Del.).

Biosimilar Application Information:

- **Applicant:** Amgen

- **Subsection (k) BLA No.:** Not disclosed
- **Original FDA-Submission Date:** July 28, 2017
- **Original FDA-Acceptance Date:** September 26, 2017
- **Original FDA-Approval Date:** June 13, 2019
- **Approved Name:** KANJINTI (trastuzumab-anns)

Patent Dance:

- **BSA's (*l*)(2) disclosure:** On October 16, 2017, Amgen produced a copy of its aBLA tp Genentech.
- **RPS's (*l*)(3)(A) list:** On December 15, 2017, Genentech listed 36 patents. On February 6, 2018, Genentech supplemented its list to add a newly issued patent.
- **BSA's (*l*)(3)(B) detailed statement:** On February 13, 2018, Amgen provided a detailed statement regarding the listed patents.
- **RPS's (*l*)(3)(C) detailed statement and RPS's (*l*)(4)/(5) negotiations:** On April 13, 2018, Genentech provided a responsive detailed statement regarding 18 listed patents. On May 23, 2018, the parties agreed that all 37 patents addressed in Genentech's (*l*)(3)(C) statement could be the subject of an immediate action for patent infringement.
- **BSA's (*l*)(8)(A) notice of commercial marketing:** On May 15, 2018, Amgen provided its notice of commercial marketing to Genentech.

Litigation:

- **Complaint:** Filed on June 21, 2018, alleging infringement of 37 patents.
- **District Court Disposition:** The case is pending in discovery. A bench trial is scheduled for December 9, 2019.

4. *Genentech v. Samsung Bioepis*	**Concerned Molecule(s): trastuzumab**

Case Name(s): *Genentech, Inc. and City of Hope v. Samsung Bioepis Co., Ltd.*, Civil Action No. 1:18-cv-1363 (D. Del.).

Biosimilar Application Information:

- **Applicant:** Samsung Bioepis
- **Subsection (k) BLA No.:** 761100
- **Original FDA-Submission Date:** October 20, 2017
- **Original FDA-Acceptance Date:** December 19, 2017
- **Original FDA-Approval Date:** January 18, 2019
- **Approved Name:** ONTRUZANT (trastuzumab-dttb)

Patent Dance:

- **BSA's (*l*)(2) disclosure:** On January 8, 2018, Bioepis producted a copy of its aBLA to Genentech.
- **RPS's (*l*)(3)(A) list:** On April 23, 2018, Genentech listed 38 patents.
- **BSA's (*l*)(3)(B) detailed statement:** On June 22, 2018, Samsung Bioepis provided a detailed statement regarding the listed patents.
- **RPS's (*l*)(3)(C) detailed statement and RPS's (*l*)(4)/(5) negotiations:** On August 17, 2018, Genentech provided its responsive detailed statement regarding 21 listed patents. The parties negotiated beginning on August 23, 2018, and agreed on September 3, 2018 to immediately litigate these 21 patents.
- **BSA's (*l*)(8)(A) notice of commercial marketing:** On September 5, 2018, Samsung Bioepis provided its notice of commercial marketing to Genentech.

Litigation:
- **Complaint:** Filed on September 4, 2018, alleging infringement of 21 patents.
- **District Court Disposition:** On June 28, 2019, the parties filed a joint stipulation of dismissal, mutually agreeing to dismiss all claims and counterclaims in view of a settlement agreement.

8) Biosimilars of RITUXAN (Rituximab)

REFERENCE PRODUCT INFORMATION

Tradename: RITUXAN
Applicant: Genentech
BLA No.: 103705
Original FDA-Approval: November 26, 1997

Current FDA-Approved Indications: *(see approved label for further information)*
- Non-Hodgkin's Lymphoma (NHL):
  - Relapsed or refractory, low grade or follicular, CD20-positive B-cell NHL as a single agent.
  - Previously untreated follicular, CD20-positive, B-cell NHL in combination with first line chemotherapy and, in patients achieving a complete or partial response to a rituximab product in combination with chemotherapy, as single-agent maintenance therapy.
  - Non-progressing (including stable disease), low-grade, CD20-positive, B-cell NHL as a single agent after first-line cyclophosphamide, vincristine, and prednisone (CVP)

chemotherapy.

- Previously untreated diffuse large B-cell, CD20-positive NHL in combination with (cyclophosphamide, doxorubicin, vincristine, and prednisone) (CHOP) or other anthracycline-based chemotherapy regimens.
- Chronic Lymphocytic Leukemia (CLL): Previously untreated and previously treated CD20-positive CLL in combination with fludarabine and cyclophosphamide (FC).
- Rheumatoid Arthritis (RA) in combination with methotrexate in adult patients with moderately-to severely-active RA who have inadequate response to one or more TNF antagonist therapies.
- Granulomatosis with Polyangiitis (GPA) (Wegener's Granulomatosis) and Microscopic Polyangiitis (MPA) in adult patients in combination with glucocorticoids.
- Moderate to severe Pemphigus Vulgaris (PV) in adult patients.

Current FDA-Approved Dosage Forms: *(see approved label for further information)*
- Injection: 100 mg/10 mL (10 mg/mL) and 500 mg/50 mL (10 mg/mL) solution in single-dose vials.

RITUXIMAB BPCIA LITIGATIONS

1. *Genentech v. Sandoz*   **Concerned Molecule(s): rituximab**

Case Name(s): *Genentech, Inc., Biogen, Inc., and City of Hope v. Sandoz, Inc., Sandoz International GmbH, and Sandoz GmbH*, Civil Action No. 1:17-cv-13507-RMB-KMW (D.N.J.).

Biosimilar Application Information:
- **Applicant:** Sandoz
- **Subsection (k) BLA No.:** 761093
- **Original FDA-Submission Date:** *Est.* July 2017
- **Original FDA-Acceptance Date:** September 12, 2017

Patent Dance:
- **BSA's (*l*)(2) disclosure:** Sandoz elected not to participate in the patent dance. On September 28, 2017, Sandoz informed Genentech that it would instead allow Genentech to access its aBLA and related documents for a period of 60 days and invite litigation on any patent that Genentech believed would be infringed by its proposed product. Sandoz provided these documents beginning on October 24, 2017.
- **RPS's (*l*)(3)(A) list:** N/A

- **BSA's (*l*)(3)(B) detailed statement:** N/A
- **RPS's (*l*)(3)(C) detailed statement and RPS's (*l*)(4)/(5) negotiations:** N/A
- **BSA's (*l*)(8)(A) notice of commercial marketing:** Unknown

Litigation:
- **Complaint:** Filed on December 21, 2017, alleging infringement of 24 patents.
- **District Court Disposition:** On December 7, 2018, the case was dismissed without prejudice pursuant to a joint stipulation wherein Sandoz indicated its intent no longer to pursue the subject aBLA.
- **Appeal:** N/A

2. *Genentech v. Celltrion*	**Concerned Molecule(s): rituximab**

Case Name(s): *Genentech, Inc., Biogen, Inc., Hoffman-La Roche Inc., and City of Hope v. Celltrion, Inc., Celltrion Healthcare Co., Ltd., Teva Pharmaceuticals USA, Inc., Teva Pharmaceuticals International Gmbh*, Civil Action Nos. 1:18-cv-574-RMB-KMW (D.N.J.) and 1:18-cv-11553-RMB-KMW (D.N.J.) (consolidated). Related: *Celltrion, Inc. v. Genentech, Inc.*, 4:18-cv-276-JSW (N.D. Cal.).

Biosimilar Application Information:
- **Applicant:** Celltrion
- **Subsection (k) BLA No.:** 761088
- **Original FDA-Submission Date:** April 28, 2017
- **Original FDA-Acceptance Date:** June 27, 2017
- **Original FDA-Approval Date:** November 28, 2018
- **Approved Name:** TRUXIMA (rituximab-abbs)

Patent Dance:
- **BSA's (*l*)(2) disclosure:** On July 17, 2017, Celltrion provided a copy of its aBLA to Genentech.
- **RPS's (*l*)(3)(A) list:** On September 14, 2017, Genentech listed 40 patents.
- **BSA's (*l*)(3)(B) detailed statement:** On November 9, 2017, Celltrion provided a detailed statement to Genentech indicating that 37 patents on the list were invalid, unenforceable and/or not infringed.
- **RPS's (*l*)(3)(C) detailed statement and RPS's (*l*)(4)/(5) negotiations:** On January 5, 2018, Genentech provided a responsive detailed statement regarding a subset of the patents addressed in Celltrion's statement. On January 11,

2018, Celltrion indicated that it wished to litigate all of the patents on Genentech's original list and filed a declaratory judgment complaint. Genentech alleged that this response violated the BPCIA and filed its own complaint the next day. On June 6, 2018, Celltrion indicated that it would identify 40 patents to litigate. The parties exchanged lists of patents on June 11, 2018. On July 11, 2018, Genentech filed a second complaint based on that subsequent exchange.

- **BSA's (l)(8)(A) notice of commercial marketing:** On January 11, 2018, Celltrion provided its notice of commercial marketing to Genentech.

Litigation:

- **Complaints:** On January 11, 2018, Celltrion and Teva filed a complaint for declaratory judgment against Genentech in N.D. Cal., but that case was subsequently dismissed for lack of jurisdiction. On January 12, 2018, Genentech filed a complaint against Celltrion and Teva in D.N.J., alleging infringement of 40 patents. On July 11, 2018, Genentech filed a second complaint against Celltrion and Teva in D.N.J., alleging infringement of 18 of those patents.

- **District Court Disposition:** On December 20, 2018, the parties filed a joint stipulation of dismissal, mutually agreeing to dismiss all claims and counterclaims in view of a settlement agreement.

- **Appeal (Fed. Cir. No. 18-2161):** Celltrion and Teva appealed the C.D. Cal. decision dismissing their declaratory judgment complaint. The appeal was dismissed before decision, pursuant to an unopposed motion.

Table of Laws and Rules

UNITED STATES CONSTITUTION

	Sec.		Sec.
Art. III	4:1	Amend VII	4:55
Art. III, § 2	4:42		

FEDERAL FOOD, DRUG AND COSMETIC ACT

Sec.	Sec.	Sec.	Sec.
505(q)	3:22	505A	3:19

PATENT ACT

Sec.	Sec.
271	4:60

PUBLIC HEALTH SERVICE ACT

Sec.	Sec.	Sec.	Sec.
351	3:2	351(k)(7)(B)	3:18
351(a)	3:15, 3:18	351(k)(7)(C)	3:18
351(i)(1)	3:2	351(l)(3)(A)	4:14
351(k)	3:6	351(l)(4)	4:98
351(k)(6)	4:97	351(m)(4)	3:19
351(k)(7)(A)	3:18		

UNITED STATES CODE ANNOTATED

U.S.C.A. Sec.	Sec.	19 U.S.C.A. Sec.	Sec.
271(e)(4)	4:91	1337(a)(1)(A)	6:2
Ch 42, § 262(l)	4:2	1337(a)(2)	6:2
		1337(a)(3)	6:2
19 U.S.C.A. Sec.	**Sec.**	1337(b)(1)	6:3
1337(a)	6:2, 6:4	1337(b)(2)	6:3

UNITED STATES CODE ANNOTATED—Continued

19 U.S.C.A. Sec.   **Sec.**

1337(d)	6:3, 6:4
1337(d)(1)	6:3
1337(e)	6:3, 6:4
1337(f)	6:4
1337(f)(1)	6:3
1337(j)	6:3
2191	6:2

21 U.S.C.A. Sec.   **Sec.**

355	8:3
355(b)(2)(A)(iii)	4:17
355(b)(2)(iv)	4:17
355(b)(3)(D)(ii)	4:17
355(j)(2)(A)(v)	9:1
355(j)(2)(A)(vii)(IV)	4:56
355(q)	3:22
355a(b)(1)(A)(ii)	3:20
355a(c)(1)(A)(ii)	3:20
355c	3:6
360(h)(3)	3:24
360(h)(4)	3:24
360aa to 360ee	3:20
360cc(b)	3:20
360ee(b)(2)	3:20
374	3:24
374(b)	3:24
301 et. seq.	3:14

28 U.S.C.A. Sec.   **Sec.**

1319(c)(3)	4:36
1331	4:40
1332(c)(1)	4:34
1338(a)	4:40
1391(b)(1) to (2)	4:39
1391(c)(2)	4:39
1391(c)(3)	4:36
1400(b)	4:33, 4:37
1782	7:1
1782(a)	7:1, 7:3
2201	4:38
2201(a)	4:40
2202	4:40

35 U.S.C.A. Sec.   **Sec.**

100(d)	4:42
101 to 103	4:73

35 U.S.C.A. Sec.   **Sec.**

101	4:80, 4:81
102	4:80, 4:82, 5:2
102(a)(1)	4:82
103	4:80, 4:81, 4:83, 5:2
103(a)	4:83
112	4:70, 4:73, 4:80, 4:84, 5:6
141(c)	5:2
262(l)(3)(B)(ii)(II)	4:17
271	4:14, 4:69
271(a) to (c)	4:57
271(a)	4:42, 4:57, 4:71, 4:92
271(b)	4:76, 4:92
271(c)	4:77, 4:92
271(e)	4:3
271(e)(1)	4:53, 4:56, 4:60, 4:79, 4:93
271(e)(2)	4:41, 4:56
271(e)(2)(A)	4:41, 4:42, 4:56
271(e)(2)(C)	4:33, 4:38, 4:40, 4:41, 4:42, 4:45, 4:56, 4:57, 4:76
271(e)(2)(C)(i)	4:69
271(e)(2)(C)(ii)	4:44, 4:69
271(e)(4)	4:90, 4:91, 4:93
271(e)(4)(A)	4:92
271(e)(4)(D)	4:97
271(e)(6)	4:98
271(e)(6)(A), (B)	4:20
271(e)(6)(C)	4:14
271(g)	4:57, 4:78, 6:2
271(g)(1)	4:78
271(g)(2)	4:78
281	4:42
282	4:84, 4:86
283	4:90, 4:97
284	4:92
285	4:17, 4:93
311(b)	5:2, 5:15
311(c)(1)	5:2
314(a)	5:2, 5:19
314(b)	5:2
315	5:20
315(a)(1)	5:3
315(b)	5:3, 5:8
315(c)	5:18
315(e)	5:15
315(e)(2)	5:13

UNITED STATES CODE ANNOTATED—Continued

35 U.S.C.A. Sec.	Sec.
316(a)(5)	5:2
316(a)(11)	5:19
316(e)	5:2
319	5:20
321(c)	5:2
322(a)(2)	5:14
324(a)	5:2
325(a)(1)	5:3
325(e)	5:15, 5:18
325(e)(2)	5:13
326(a)(5)	5:2
326(e)	5:2
329	5:20

42 U.S.C.A. Sec.	Sec.
262	3:1, 4:17
262(c)	3:24
262(i)(1)	3:2
262(i)(2)	3:6, 3:10, 9:4
262(i)(2)(B)	9:4
262(i)(4)	3:3
262(k)(2)	9:4
262(k)(2)(A)(i)(I) to (cc)	3:6, 3:9
262(k)(2)(A)(i)(II)	3:6
262(k)(2)(A)(i)(III) to (IV)	3:6
262(k)(2)(A)(i)(V)	3:6
262(k)(4)(A)(i)	3:12
262(k)(6)	3:13, 4:97, 4:98
262(k)(6)(A) to (C)	3:13
262(k)(7)	4:97
262(k)(7)(A)	3:18
262(k)(7)(B)	3:18
262(k)(7)(C)	3:18
262(l)(1)	4:2, 4:65
262(l)(1)(A)	4:8
262(l)(1)(B)(i)	4:8
262(l)(1)(B)(ii)	4:9, 4:10, 4:65, 4:68
262(l)(1)(B)(iii)	4:9
262(l)(1)(C)	4:9
262(l)(1)(D)	4:12, 4:65
262(l)(1)(F)	4:12

42 U.S.C.A. Sec.	Sec.
262(l)(1)(H)	4:13
262(l)(2)	4:3, 4:52
262(l)(2)(A)	4:2, 4:3, 4:5, 4:17
262(l)(2)(B)	4:2
262(l)(3)(A)	4:2, 4:44, 4:53
262(l)(3)(A)(i) to (ii)	4:14
262(l)(3)(B)	4:2
262(l)(3)(B)(i)	4:16, 4:89
262(l)(3)(B)(ii)	4:45
262(l)(3)(C)	4:2, 4:89
262(l)(4) to (5)	4:2, 4:53
262(l)(4)	4:19
262(l)(4)(A)	4:2
262(l)(4)(B) to (5)(B)(i)	4:2
262(l)(5)	4:20, 4:45
262(l)(5)(A)	4:19
262(l)(5)(B)(i)	4:2, 4:19
262(l)(5)(B)(i)(I)	4:53
262(l)(5)(B)(ii)	4:2, 4:19
262(l)(5)(B)(ii)(II)	4:53
262(l)(6)	4:42, 4:97
262(l)(6)(A) to (B)	4:2
262(l)(6)(B)	4:53
262(l)(6)(C)(i)	4:20, 4:45
262(l)(6)(C)(ii)	4:20
262(l)(7)	4:14, 4:21, 4:45, 4:58
262(l)(7)(A) to (B)	4:2
262(l)(8)	4:21
262(l)(8)(A)	4:45
262(l)(8)(B)	4:2, 4:35, 4:43, 4:54, 4:58
262(l)(8)(B)(i)	4:2
262(l)(8)(C)	4:58
262(l)(9)	4:40, 4:42
262(l)(9)(A)	4:46, 4:47, 4:54
262(l)(9)(B)	4:2, 4:19, 4:20, 4:26, 4:38, 4:45
262(l)(9)(C)	4:2, 4:3, 4:6, 4:14, 4:38, 4:44, 4:52
262(m)(4)	3:19

UNITED STATES PUBLIC LAWS

Pub. L. No.	Sec.	Pub. L. No.	Sec.
97-414	3:20	111-148	3:1
98-417 (1984)	3:14	115-52	3:16
108-155	3:6		

CODE OF FEDERAL REGULATIONS

21 C.F.R. Sec.	Sec.	21 C.F.R. Sec.	Sec.
10.115	3:1	601.3(a)(1) to (2)	3:23
201.57(a)	9:2	601.3(a)(3)	3:23
Part 202	3:25	601.3(b)	3:23
Part 203	3:25	601.3(c)	3:23
Part 207	3:25	601.12	9:2
Part 211	3:25		
314.3	9:4	**37 C.F.R. Sec.**	**Sec.**
314.94(a)(7)	9:4	42.20(c)	5:18
Part 600, Subpart D	3:25	42.71(d)(2)	5:2
600.3	3:2	42.73(d)(3)	5:16
600.3(h)	3:2	42.100(c)	5:2, 5:18
600.3(k)	3:21	42.120(b)	5:2
601.3(a)	3:23	42.122(b)	5:18

FEDERAL RULES OF CIVIL PROCEDURE

Rule	Sec.	Rule	Sec.
3	4:59	26(a)(1)	4:59
4(c) to (d)	4:59	26(a)(1)(A)	4:59
12(a)(1)(a)	4:59	26(a)(1)(C)	4:59
12(b)(6)	4:73	26(f)(1)	4:59
12(g)(2)	4:33	26(f)(2)	4:59
12(h)(1)	4:33	30(b)(6)	4:61
16(b)(2)	4:59	38(a)	4:55
16(b)(3)(A)	4:59	65(a)	4:60
16(b)(3)(B)	4:59		

FEDERAL REGISTER

83 Fed. Reg.	Sec.
63817	3:2

SENATE BILLS

No.	Sec.
659, 116 Cong...................	8:5

LOUISIANA REVISED STATUTES ANNOTATED

Sec.	Sec.
9:2800.55	9:3

MISSISSIPPI CODE ANNOTATED

Sec.	Sec.
11-1-63	9:3

RESTATEMENT THIRD, TORTS (PRODUCTS LIABILITY)

Sec.	Sec.
2..............................	9:4

Table of Cases

A

Abbott Laboratories v. Baxter Pharmaceutical Products, Inc., 471 F.3d 1363 (Fed. Cir. 2006)—4:82

Abbott Laboratories v. Teva Pharmaceuticals USA, Inc., 432 F. Supp. 2d 408 (D. Del. 2006)—8:4

Abbott Laboratories v. Tor-Pharm, Inc., 300 F.3d 1367 (Fed. Cir. 2002)—4:69

AbbVie Deutschland GmbH & Co., KG v. Janssen Biotech, Inc., 759 F.3d 1285 (Fed. Cir. 2014)—4:84

AbbVie Inc. v. Boehringer Ingelheim International GmbH, 2019 WL 1571666 (D. Del. 2019)—8:5

AbbVie Inc. v. Boehringer Ingelheim International GmbH, 2019 WL 917990 (D. Del. 2019)—4:58

Abbvie Inc. v. Mathilda and Terence Kennedy Institute of Rheumatology Trust, 764 F.3d 1366 (Fed. Cir. 2014)—4:85

Abtox, Inc. v. Exitron Corp., 122 F.3d 1019 (Fed. Cir. 1997)—4:79

Acorda Therapeutics Inc. v. Mylan Pharmaceuticals Inc., 817 F.3d 755 (Fed. Cir. 2016)—4:41

ACQIS, LLC v. EMC Corp., 109 F. Supp. 3d 352 (D. Mass. 2015)—5:8

Actos End Payor Antitrust Litigation, In re, 2015-2 Trade Cas. (CCH) ¶ 79309, 2015 WL 5610752 (S.D. N.Y. 2015)—8:2

Agfa Corp. v. Creo Products Inc., 451 F.3d 1366 (Fed. Cir. 2006)—4:55

Aggrenox Antitrust Litigation, In re, 94 F. Supp. 3d 224 (D. Conn. 2015)—8:2

AGIS Software Development, LLC v. ZTE Corporation, 2018 WL 4854023 (E.D. Tex. 2018)—4:33

Aguayo v. Crompton & Knowles Corp., 183 Cal. App. 3d 1032, 228 Cal. Rptr. 768 (2d Dist. 1986)—9:1

AIA America, Inc. v. Avid Radiopharmaceuticals, 866 F.3d 1369 (Fed. Cir. 2017)—4:55

Air Vent, Inc. v. Owens Corning Corp., 2012 WL 1607145 (W.D. Pa. 2012)—5:11

Ajinomoto Co., Inc. v. Archer-Daniels-Midland Co., 228 F.3d 1338 (Fed. Cir. 2000)—4:78

Akebia Therapeutics, Inc. v. FibroGen, Inc., 793 F.3d 1108 (9th Cir. 2015)—7:3

Alcon, Inc. v. Teva Pharmaceuticals USA, Inc., 2010 WL 3081327 (D. Del. 2010)—4:97

Alice Corp. Pty. Ltd. v. CLS Bank Intern., 573 U.S. 208, 134 S. Ct. 2347, 189 L. Ed. 2d 296 (2014)—4:81

Allergan, Inc. v. Teva Pharmaceuticals USA, Inc., 2017 WL 132265 (E.D. Tex. 2017)—4:63

Amerigen Pharmaceuticals Limited v. UCB Pharma GmBH, 913 F.3d 1076 (Fed. Cir. 2019)—5:20

Ameritox, Ltd. v. Millennium Health, LLC, 88 F. Supp. 3d 885 (W.D. Wis. 2015)—4:81

Amgen Inc. v. Apotex Inc., 712 Fed. Appx. 985 (Fed. Cir. 2017)—4:17, 4:18, 4:69, 4:70

Amgen Inc. v. Apotex Inc., 827 F.3d 1052 (Fed. Cir. 2016)—4:14, 4:19, 4:26, 4:51, 4:58

Amgen, Inc. v. Chugai Pharmaceutical Co., Ltd., 927 F.2d 1200 (Fed. Cir. 1991)—4:84

Amgen Inc. v. Coherus BioSciences Inc., 931 F.3d 1154 (Fed. Cir. 2019)—4:69, 4:73

Amgen Inc. v. F. Hoffman-La Roche Ltd, 580 F.3d 1340 (Fed. Cir. 2009)—4:78

Amgen, Inc. v. Genentech, Inc., 2018 WL 910198 (C.D. Cal. 2018)—4:29, 4:47

Amgen Inc. v. Hoechst Marion Roussel, Inc., 314 F.3d 1313 (Fed. Cir. 2003)—4:82

Amgen Inc. v. Hospira, Inc., 336 F. Supp. 3d 333 (D. Del. 2018)—4:56, 4:69, 4:79, 4:82

Amgen Inc. v. Hospira, Inc., 866 F.3d 1355 (Fed. Cir. 2017)—4:2, 4:5, 4:6, 4:14, 4:44, 4:62

Amgen Inc. v. Hospira, Inc., 2016 Markman 7013483, 2016 WL 7013483 (D. Del. 2016)—4:70

Amgen Inc. v. International Trade Com'n, 565 F.3d 846 (Fed. Cir. 2009)—6:2

Amgen, Inc. v. Roche Holding Ltd., 519 F.3d 1343 (Fed. Cir. 2008)—6:2

Amgen Inc. v. Sandoz Inc., 923 F.3d 1023 (Fed. Cir. 2019)—4:69, 4:70, 4:71, 4:72

Amgen Inc. v. Sandoz Inc., 877 F.3d 1315 (Fed. Cir. 2017)—4:3, 4:6, 4:17, 4:56, 4:58

Amgen Inc. v. Sandoz Inc., 2015 WL 1264756 (N.D. Cal. 2015)—4:3, 4:6, 4:24, 4:49

Amgen Inc. v. Sandoz Inc., 794 F.3d 1347 (Fed. Cir. 2015)—4:3, 4:5, 4:6, 4:24

Amgen Inc. v. Sanofi, 872 F.3d 1367 (Fed. Cir. 2017)—4:84

Anglin, In re, 2009 WL 4739481 (D. Neb. 2009)—7:2

Anton/Bauer, Inc. v. PAG, Ltd., 329 F.3d 1343 (Fed. Cir. 2003)—4:58

Apicore US LLC v. Beloteca, Inc., 2019 WL 1746079 (E.D. Tex. 2019)—4:38

Apotex, Inc., In re, 49 Fed. Appx. 902 (Fed. Cir. 2002)—4:56

Ariad Pharmaceuticals, Inc. v. Eli Lilly and Co., 598 F.3d 1336 (Fed. Cir. 2010)—4:84

Ariosa Diagnostics, Inc. v. Sequenom, Inc., 788 F.3d 1371 (Fed. Cir. 2015)—4:81

Arthrex, Inc. v. Smith & Nephew, Inc., 880 F.3d 1345 (Fed. Cir. 2018)—5:16

Association for Molecular Pathology v. Myriad Genetics, Inc., 569 U.S. 576, 133 S. Ct. 2107, 186 L. Ed. 2d 124 (2013)—4:81

AstraZeneca AB v. Apotex Corp., 782 F.3d 1324 (Fed. Cir. 2015)—4:92

Astrazeneca AB v. Dr. Reddy's Laboratories, Ltd., 2010 WL 1375176 (S.D. N.Y. 2010)—4:96

AstraZeneca LP v. Apotex, Inc., 633 F.3d 1042 (Fed. Cir. 2010)—4:76

Athena Diagnostics, Inc. v.

Mayo Collaborative Services, LLC, 927 F.3d 1333 (Fed. Cir. 2019)—4:81

Athena Diagnostics, Inc. v. Mayo Collaborative Services, LLC, 915 F.3d 743 (Fed. Cir. 2019)—4:81

B

Back v. Wickes Corp., 375 Mass. 633, 378 N.E.2d 964, 24 U.C.C. Rep. Serv. 1164 (1978)—9:3

Bai v. L & L Wings, Inc., 160 F.3d 1350 (Fed. Cir. 1998)—4:69

Banks v. ICI Americas, Inc., 264 Ga. 732, 450 S.E.2d 671 (1994)—9:3

Barker v. Lull Engineering Co., 20 Cal. 3d 413, 143 Cal. Rptr. 225, 573 P.2d 443, 96 A.L.R.3d 1 (1978)—9:3

Bascom Global Internet Services, Inc. v. AT&T Mobility LLC, 827 F.3d 1341 (Fed. Cir. 2016)—4:81

Bayer Pharma AG v. Watson Laboratories, Inc., 2016 WL 7468172 (D. Del. 2016)—4:97

Beacon Theatres, Inc. v. Westover, 359 U.S. 500, 79 S. Ct. 948, 3 L. Ed. 2d 988, 2 Fed. R. Serv. 2d 650 (1959)—4:55

Bell & Howell Document Management Products Co. v. Altek Systems, 132 F.3d 701 (Fed. Cir. 1997)—4:70

Berkheimer v. HP Inc., 881 F.3d 1360 (Fed. Cir. 2018)—4:81

BigCommerce, Inc., In re, 890 F.3d 978 (Fed. Cir. 2018)—4:34

Billiar v. Minnesota Min. and Mfg. Co., 623 F.2d 240 (2d Cir. 1980)—9:1

Bio-Technology General Corp. v. Genentech, Inc., 80 F.3d 1553 (Fed. Cir. 1996)—4:78, 6:4

Bloxom v. Bloxom, 512 So. 2d 839, 72 A.L.R.4th 43 (La. 1987)—9:1

Boston Scientific Corp. v. Cordis Corp., 777 F. Supp. 2d 783 (D. Del. 2011)—5:7, 5:11

Bowman v. Wyeth, LLC, 2012 WL 684116 (D. Minn. 2012)—9:1

BRCA1- and BRCA2-Based Hereditary Cancer Test Patent Litigation, In re, 774 F.3d 755 (Fed. Cir. 2014)—4:81

Bristol-Myers Squibb Co. v. Teva Pharmaceuticals USA, Inc., 752 F.3d 967 (Fed. Cir. 2014)—4:83

Bristol-Myers Squibb Company v. Mylan Pharmaceuticals Inc., 2017 WL 3980155 (D. Del. 2017)—4:35, 4:38

Bruesewitz v. Wyeth LLC, 562 U.S. 223, 131 S. Ct. 1068, 179 L. Ed. 2d 1 (2011)—9:3

Brunette Mach. Works, Limited v. Kockum Industries, Inc., 406 U.S. 706, 92 S. Ct. 1936, 32 L. Ed. 2d 428 (1972)—4:36

Butamax Advanced Biofuels LLC v. Gevo, Inc., 117 F. Supp. 3d 632 (D. Del. 2015)—4:84

Byrd v. Blue Ridge Rural Elec. Co-op., Inc., 356 U.S. 525, 78 S. Ct. 893, 2 L. Ed. 2d 953 (1958)—4:55

C

Camp v. Gress, 250 U.S. 308, 39 S. Ct. 478, 63 L. Ed. 997 (1919)—4:33

Campos v. Firestone Tire & Rubber Co., 98 N.J. 198, 485 A.2d 305 (1984)—9:1

Cannarella v. Volvo Car USA LLC, 2016 WL 9450451 (C.D. Cal. 2016)—5:5

Canton Bio Medical, Inc. v. Integrated Liner Technologies, Inc., 216 F.3d 1367 (Fed. Cir. 2000)—4:71, 4:73

Carroll Touch, Inc. v. Electro Mechanical Systems, Inc., 15 F.3d 1573 (Fed. Cir. 1993)—4:71

Caterpillar Tractor Co. v. Beck, 593 P.2d 871 (Alaska 1979)—9:3

Celeritas Technologies, Ltd. v. Rockwell Intern. Corp., 150 F.3d 1354 (Fed. Cir. 1998)—4:82

Celgene Corporation v. Hetero Labs Limited, 2018 WL 1135334 (D.N.J. 2018)—4:35

Celltrion Healthcare Co., Ltd. v. Kennedy Trust for Rheumatology Research, 2014 WL 6765996 (S.D. N.Y. 2014)—4:1

Celltrion, Inc. v. Genentech, Inc., 2018 WL 2448254 (N.D. Cal. 2018)—4:29, 4:47

Centocor Ortho Biotech, Inc. v. Abbott Laboratories, 636 F.3d 1341 (Fed. Cir. 2011)—4:84

Cephalon, Inc. v. Watson Pharmaceuticals, Inc., 707 F.3d 1330 (Fed. Cir. 2013)—4:84

Chatman v. Pfizer, Inc., 960 F. Supp. 2d 641 (S.D. Miss. 2013)—9:1

Chauffeurs, Teamsters and Helpers, Local No. 391 v. Terry, 494 U.S. 558, 110 S. Ct. 1339, 108 L. Ed. 2d 519 (1990)—4:55

Ciprofloxacin Hydrochloride Antitrust Litigation, In re, 544 F.3d 1323 (Fed. Cir. 2008)—8:2

Clearlamp, LLC v. LKQ Corporation, 2016 WL 4734389 (N.D. Ill. 2016)—5:13, 5:15

Clerici, In re, 481 F.3d 1324 (11th Cir. 2007)—7:3

Cleveland Clinic Foundation v. True Health Diagnostics LLC, 760 Fed. Appx. 1013 (Fed. Cir. 2019)—4:81

Click-To-Call Technologies, LP v. Ingenio, Inc., YellowPages.com, LLC, 899 F.3d 1321 (Fed. Cir. 2018)—5:3

CollegeNet, Inc. v. ApplyYourself, Inc., 418 F.3d 1225 (Fed. Cir. 2005)—4:70

Connell v. Sears, Roebuck & Co., 722 F.2d 1542 (Fed. Cir. 1983)—4:82

Conoco, Inc. v. Energy & Environmental Intern., L.C., 460 F.3d 1349 (Fed. Cir. 2006)—4:73

Consumer Watchdog v. Wisconsin Alumni Research Foundation, 753 F.3d 1258 (Fed. Cir. 2014)—5:20

Continental Can Co. USA, Inc. v. Monsanto Co., 948 F.2d 1264 (Fed. Cir. 1991)—4:82

Cooper Notification, Inc. v. Twitter, Inc., 2010 WL 5149351 (D. Del. 2010)—5:11

Cray Inc., In re, 871 F.3d 1355 (Fed. Cir. 2017)—4:35

C.R. Bard, Inc. v. Advanced Cardiovascular Systems, Inc., 911 F.2d 670 (Fed. Cir. 1990)—4:76

Cruciferous Sprout Litigation, In re, 301 F.3d 1343 (Fed. Cir. 2002)—4:82

Cubist Pharmaceuticals, Inc. v. Hospira, Inc., 75 F. Supp. 3d 641 (D. Del. 2014)—4:82

Cuozzo Speed Technologies, LLC v. Lee, 136 S. Ct. 2131,

195 L. Ed. 2d 423 (2016)—
5:2

Curtis v. Loether, 415 U.S. 189, 94 S. Ct. 1005, 39 L. Ed. 2d 260, 18 Fed. R. Serv. 2d 189 (1974)—4:55

Cybor Corp. v. FAS Technologies, Inc., 138 F.3d 1448 (Fed. Cir. 1998)—4:73

Cyclobenzaprine Hydrochloride Extended-Release Capsule Patent Litigation, In re, 676 F.3d 1063 (Fed. Cir. 2012)—4:83

D

Daimler AG v. Bauman, 571 U.S. 117, 134 S. Ct. 746, 187 L. Ed. 2d 624 (2014)—4:41

Davol, Inc. v. Atrium Medical Corp., 2013 WL 3013343 (D. Del. 2013)—5:10

DDR Holdings, LLC v. Hotels.com, L.P., 773 F.3d 1245 (Fed. Cir. 2014)—4:81

Deering Precision Instruments, L.L.C. v. Vector Distribution Systems, Inc., 347 F.3d 1314 (Fed. Cir. 2003)—4:73

Denver & R. G. W. R. Co. v. Brotherhood of R. R. Trainmen, 387 U.S. 556, 87 S. Ct. 1746, 18 L. Ed. 2d 954, 11 Fed. R. Serv. 2d 361 (1967)—4:34

DePuy Spine, Inc. v. Medtronic Sofamor Danek, Inc., 567 F.3d 1314 (Fed. Cir. 2009)—4:74

Deutsche Bank Trust Co. Americas, In re, 605 F.3d 1373 (Fed. Cir. 2010)—4:10

Diamond v. Charles, 476 U.S. 54, 106 S. Ct. 1697, 90 L. Ed. 2d 48 (1986)—4:42

Digital Biometrics, Inc. v. Identix, Inc., 149 F.3d 1335 (Fed. Cir. 1998)—4:70

D.L. Auld Co. v. Chroma Graphics Corp., 714 F.2d 1144 (Fed. Cir. 1983)—4:82

Dow Chemical Co. v. Nova Chemicals Corp. (Canada), 803 F.3d 620 (Fed. Cir. 2015)—4:84

DSU Medical Corp. v. JMS Co., Ltd., 471 F.3d 1293 (Fed. Cir. 2006)—4:76

E

Eagle Comtronics, Inc. v. Arrow Communication Laboratories, Inc., 305 F.3d 1303 (Fed. Cir. 2002)—4:72

Eastern R. R. Presidents Conference v. Noerr Motor Freight, Inc., 365 U.S. 127, 81 S. Ct. 523, 5 L. Ed. 2d 464 (1961)—8:4

Eastman Kodak Co. v. Goodyear Tire & Rubber Co., 114 F.3d 1547 (Fed. Cir. 1997)—4:72

eBay Inc. v. MercExchange, L.L.C., 547 U.S. 388, 126 S. Ct. 1837, 164 L. Ed. 2d 641, 27 A.L.R. Fed. 2d 685 (2006)—4:97

Eisai Co. Ltd. v. Dr. Reddy's Laboratories, Ltd., 533 F.3d 1353 (Fed. Cir. 2008)—4:83

Eli Lilly and Co. v. Actavis Elizabeth LLC, 435 Fed. Appx. 917 (Fed. Cir. 2011)—4:77

Eli Lilly and Co. v. American Cyanamid Co., 82 F.3d 1568 (Fed. Cir. 1996)—4:78

Eli Lilly and Co. v. Barr Laboratories, Inc., 251 F.3d 955 (Fed. Cir. 2001)—4:82

Ellis v. Tribune Television Co., 443 F.3d 71 (2d Cir. 2006)—9:5

Endo Pharmaceuticals Inc. v. Teva Pharmaceuticals USA, Inc., 919 F.3d 1347 (Fed. Cir. 2019)—4:81

Ethicon, Inc. v. U.S. Surgical Corp., 135 F.3d 1456, 48 Fed. R. Evid. Serv. 1226 (Fed. Cir. 1998)—4:42

Ever Win Intern. Corp. v. Radioshack Corp., 902 F. Supp. 2d 503 (D. Del. 2012)—5:7, 5:18

Evolutionary Intelligence, LLC v. Apple, Inc., 2014 WL 93954 (N.D. Cal. 2014)—5:4, 5:5, 5:6

Evolutionary Intelligence, LLC v. Sprint Nextel Corporation, 2014 WL 819277 (N.D. Cal. 2014)—5:6

Evridge v. American Honda Motor Co., 685 S.W.2d 632 (Tenn. 1985)—9:1

Exergen Corporation v. Kaz USA, Inc., 725 Fed. Appx. 959 (Fed. Cir. 2018)—4:81

F

Federal Trade Commission v. AbbVie Inc., 329 F. Supp. 3d 98 (E.D. Pa. 2018)—8:4

Felix v. Hoffmann-LaRoche, Inc., 540 So. 2d 102 (Fla. 1989)—9:1

Ferring B.V. v. Watson Laboratories, Inc.-Florida, 764 F.3d 1401 (Fed. Cir. 2014)—4:69

Festo Corp. v. Shoketsu Kinzoku Kogyo Kabushiki Co., Ltd., 344 F.3d 1359 (Fed. Cir. 2003)—4:73

Festo Corp. v. Shoketsu Kinzoku Kogyo Kabushiki Co., Ltd., 535 U.S. 722, 122 S. Ct. 1831, 152 L. Ed. 2d 944 (2002)—4:73, 4:84

Finjan, Inc. v. Symantec Corp., 139 F. Supp. 3d 1032 (N.D. Cal. 2015)—5:5, 5:8

Finnigan Corp. v. International Trade Com'n, 180 F.3d 1354 (Fed. Cir. 1999)—4:82

Fisher-Price, Inc. v. Dynacraft BSC, Inc., 2017 WL 5153588 (N.D. Cal. 2017)—5:6

Flexible Technologies, Inc. v. SharkNinja Operating LLC, 2018 WL 1175043 (D.S.C. 2018)—4:33

Ford Motor Co. v. U.S., 811 F.3d 1371 (Fed. Cir. 2016)—4:50

F.T.C. v. Actavis, Inc., 570 U.S. 136, 133 S. Ct. 2223, 186 L. Ed. 2d 343 (2013)—8:2

G

Gabapentin Patent Litigation, In re, 2011 WL 1807448 (D.N.J. 2011)—4:95

Gabapentin Patent Litigation, In re, 503 F.3d 1254 (Fed. Cir. 2007)—4:56

Galderma Laboratories, L.P. v. Teva Pharmaceuticals USA, Inc., 290 F. Supp. 3d 599 (N.D. Tex. 2017)—4:35

Genentech, Inc. v. Amgen Inc., 2019 WL 4058929 (D. Del. 2019)—4:17

Genentech, Inc. v. Amgen Inc., 2018 WL 503253 (D. Del. 2018)—4:19

Genentech, Inc., In re, 367 F. Supp. 3d 1274 (N.D. Okla. 2019)—9:3, 9:4

General Electric Company v. Vibrant Media, Inc., 2013 WL 6328063 (D. Del. 2013)—5:5

General Motors Corp. v. California Research Corp., 9 F.R.D. 565 (D. Del. 1949)—4:55

Genetic Technologies Ltd. v. Merial L.L.C., 818 F.3d 1369 (Fed. Cir. 2016)—4:81

Georgia-Pacific Corp. v. U.S. Plywood Corp., 318 F. Supp. 1116 (S.D. N.Y. 1970)—4:93

Gilead Sciences, Inc. v. Merck &

Co., Inc., 888 F.3d 1231 (Fed. Cir. 2018)—4:86

Glaxo Group Ltd. v. Apotex, Inc., 2001 WL 1246628 (N.D. Ill. 2001)—4:56

Glaxo, Inc. v. Novopharm, Ltd., 110 F.3d 1562 (Fed. Cir. 1997)—4:42

Global-Tech Appliances, Inc. v. SEB S.A., 563 U.S. 754, 131 S. Ct. 2060, 179 L. Ed. 2d 1167 (2011)—4:76

Grain Processing Corp. v. American Maize-Products Co., 185 F.3d 1341 (Fed. Cir. 1999)—4:93, 4:95

Graver Tank & Mfg. Co. v. Linde Air Products Co., 339 U.S. 605, 70 S. Ct. 854, 94 L. Ed. 1097 (1950)—4:72

Guarino v. Wyeth LLC, 823 F. Supp. 2d 1289 (M.D. Fla. 2011)—9:1

Gurley By and Through Gurley v. American Honda Motor Co., Inc., 505 So. 2d 358 (Ala. 1987)—9:1

H

Halo Electronics, Inc. v. Pulse Electronics, Inc., 136 S. Ct. 1923, 195 L. Ed. 2d 278 (2016)—4:93

Harbour Victoria Inv. Holdings Ltd. Section 1782 Petitions, In re, 2015 WL 4040420 (S.D. N.Y. 2015)—7:2

Helicopteros Nacionales de Colombia, S.A. v. Hall, 466 U.S. 408, 104 S. Ct. 1868, 80 L. Ed. 2d 404 (1984)—4:41

Hertz Corp. v. Friend, 559 U.S. 77, 130 S. Ct. 1181, 175 L. Ed. 2d 1029 (2010)—4:34

Hockerson-Halberstadt, Inc. v. Avia Group Intern., Inc., 222 F.3d 951 (Fed. Cir. 2000)—4:70

Hollingsworth v. Perry, 570 U.S. 693, 133 S. Ct. 2652, 186 L. Ed. 2d 768 (2013)—4:42

HTC Corporation, In re, 889 F.3d 1349 (Fed. Cir. 2018)—4:36

I

ImageVision.Net, Inc. v. Internet Payment Exchange, Inc., 2013 WL 663535 (D. Del. 2013)—5:7, 5:9, 5:11

Immunex Corp. v. Sandoz Inc., 395 F. Supp. 3d 366 (D.N.J. 2019)—4:83

Immunex Corp. v. Sanofi, 2018 WL 2717852 (C.D. Cal. 2018)—5:5, 5:7

Immunex Corporation v. Sanofi, 2018 WL 6252460 (C.D. Cal. 2018)—4:84

Immunomedics, Inc. v. Roger Williams Medical Center, 2017 Markman 788122, 2017 WL 788122 (D.N.J. 2017)—4:84

Infogation Corp. v. ZTE Corporation, 2017 WL 2123625 (S.D. Cal. 2017)—5:6

In re Application of Masters for an Order Pursuant to 28 U.S.C. § 1782 to Conduct Discovery for Use in a Foreign Proceeding, 315 F. Supp. 3d 269 (D.D.C. 2018)—7:2

Intel Corp. v. Advanced Micro Devices, Inc., 542 U.S. 241, 124 S. Ct. 2466, 159 L. Ed. 2d 355, 64 Fed. R. Evid. Serv. 742, 58 Fed. R. Serv. 3d 696 (2004)—7:3, 7:4

Intellectual Ventures II LLC v. FedEx Corporation, 2017 WL 4812434 (E.D. Tex. 2017)—5:5

IPCom GMBH & Co. KG v. Apple Inc., 61 F. Supp. 3d 919 (N.D. Cal. 2014)—7:2

J

Jack Guttman, Inc. v. Kopykake Enterprises, Inc., 302 F.3d 1352 (Fed. Cir. 2002)—4:70

Janssen Biotech, Inc. v. Celltrion Healthcare Co. Inc., 239 F. Supp. 3d 328 (D. Mass. 2017)—4:19, 4:98

Janssen Biotech, Inc. v. Celltrion Healthcare Co. Inc., 210 F. Supp. 3d 244 (D. Mass. 2016)—4:85

Janssen Biotech, Inc. v. Celltrion Healthcare Co., Ltd., 296 F. Supp. 3d 336 (D. Mass. 2017)—4:42

Janssen Biotech, Inc., In re, 880 F.3d 1315 (Fed. Cir. 2018)—4:85

Jones v. Rath Packing Co., 430 U.S. 519, 97 S. Ct. 1305, 51 L. Ed. 2d 604 (1977)—9:4

Jonsson v. Stanley Works, 903 F.2d 812 (Fed. Cir. 1990)—4:73

Joy Technologies, Inc. v. Flakt, Inc., 6 F.3d 770 (Fed. Cir. 1993)—4:75

K

Key Mfg. Group, Inc. v. Microdot, Inc., 925 F.2d 1444 (Fed. Cir. 1991)—4:74

Key Pharmaceuticals v. Hercon Laboratories Corp., 161 F.3d 709 (Fed. Cir. 1998)—4:70

Keystone Driller Co. v. General Excavator Co., 290 U.S. 240, 54 S. Ct. 146, 78 L. Ed. 293 (1933)—4:87

King Drug Co. of Florence, Inc. v. Smithkline Beecham Corp., 791 F.3d 388 (3d Cir. 2015)—8:2

Knowles Electronics LLC v. Iancu, 886 F.3d 1369 (Fed. Cir. 2018)—5:17

Kozlowski v. John E. Smith's Sons Co., 87 Wis. 2d 882, 275 N.W.2d 915 (1979)—9:1

KSR Intern. Co. v. Teleflex Inc., 550 U.S. 398, 127 S. Ct. 1727, 167 L. Ed. 2d 705 (2007)—4:83

L

Lang v. Pacific Marine and Supply Co., Ltd., 895 F.2d 761 (Fed. Cir. 1990)—4:35

Lantech, Inc. v. Keip Mach. Co., 32 F.3d 542 (Fed. Cir. 1994)—4:71

Lashley v. Pfizer, Inc., 750 F.3d 470 (5th Cir. 2014)—9:1

Letters Rogatory from Tokyo Dist., Tokyo, Japan, In re, 539 F.2d 1216, 46 A.L.R. Fed. 950 (9th Cir. 1976)—7:2

Libbey-Owens Ford Glass Co. v. L & M Paper Co., 189 Neb. 792, 205 N.W.2d 523 (1973)—9:1

Limelight Networks, Inc. v. Akamai Technologies, Inc., 572 U.S. 915, 134 S. Ct. 2111, 189 L. Ed. 2d 52 (2014)—4:76

Lipitor Antitrust Litigation, In re, 868 F.3d 231 (3d Cir. 2017)—8:2, 8:4

Lockwood, In re, 50 F.3d 966 (Fed. Cir. 1995)—4:55

Loestrin 24 Fe Antitrust Litigation, In re, 261 F. Supp. 3d 307 (D.R.I. 2017)—8:2

London v. Carson Pirie Scott & Co., 946 F.2d 1534 (Fed. Cir. 1991)—4:72

Lujan v. Defenders of Wildlife, 504 U.S. 555, 112 S. Ct. 2130, 119 L. Ed. 2d 351 (1992)—4:42

M

Manville Sales Corp. v. Paramount Systems, Inc., 917

F.2d 544 (Fed. Cir. 1990)—4:76

Markman v. Westview Instruments, Inc., 517 U.S. 370, 116 S. Ct. 1384, 134 L. Ed. 2d 577 (1996)—4:55, 4:84

Markman v. Westview Instruments, Inc., 52 F.3d 967 (Fed. Cir. 1995)—4:70

Maxchief Investments Limited v. Plastic Development Group, LLC, 2017 WL 3479504 (E.D. Tenn. 2017)—4:34

Mayo Collaborative Services v. Prometheus Laboratories, Inc., 566 U.S. 66, 132 S. Ct. 1289, 182 L. Ed. 2d 321, 90 A.L.R. Fed. 2d 685 (2012)—4:81

McClain v. Ortmayer, 141 U.S. 419, 12 S. Ct. 76, 35 L. Ed. 800 (1891)—4:84

MedImmune, Inc. v. Genentech, Inc., 549 U.S. 118, 127 S. Ct. 764, 166 L. Ed. 2d 604 (2007)—4:50

MEMC Electronic Materials, Inc. v. Mitsubishi Materials Silicon Corp., 420 F.3d 1369 (Fed. Cir. 2005)—4:76

Merck & Co., Inc. v. Teva Pharmaceuticals USA, Inc., 347 F.3d 1367 (Fed. Cir. 2003)—4:82

Merck & Co., Inc., In re, 197 F.R.D. 267 (M.D. N.C. 2000)—7:2

Merck KGaA v. Integra Lifesciences I, Ltd., 545 U.S. 193, 125 S. Ct. 2372, 162 L. Ed. 2d 160 (2005)—4:56, 4:79

Metallizing Engineering Co. v. Kenyon Bearing & Auto Parts Co., 153 F.2d 516 (C.C.A. 2d Cir. 1946)—4:82

Metro-Goldwyn-Mayer Studios Inc. v. Grokster, Ltd., 545 U.S. 913, 125 S. Ct. 2764, 162 L. Ed. 2d 781 (2005)—4:76

Micron Technology, Inc., In re, 875 F.3d 1091, 99 Fed. R. Serv. 3d 210 (Fed. Cir. 2017)—4:33

Microsoft Corp. v. International Trade Com'n, 731 F.3d 1354 (Fed. Cir. 2013)—6:2

Milwaukee Electric Tool Corporation v. Snap-On Incorporated, 271 F. Supp. 3d 990 (E.D. Wis. 2017)—5:15

Minnesota Mining and Mfg. Co. v. Alphapharm Pty. Ltd., 2002 WL 1352426 (D. Minn. 2002)—4:56

Mission Abstract Data L.L.C. v. Beasley Broadcast Group, Inc., 2011 WL 5523315 (D. Del. 2011)—5:11

Momenta Pharmaceuticals, Inc. v. Amphastar Pharmaceuticals, Inc., 686 F.3d 1348 (Fed. Cir. 2012)—4:79

Momenta Pharmaceuticals, Inc. v. Bristol-Myers Squibb Company, 915 F.3d 764 (Fed. Cir. 2019)—5:20

Momenta Pharmaceuticals, Inc. v. Teva Pharmaceuticals USA Inc., 809 F.3d 610 (Fed. Cir. 2015)—4:78, 4:79

MorphoSys AG v. Janssen Biotech, Inc., 358 F. Supp. 3d 354 (D. Del. 2019)—4:84

Morris v. Wyeth, Inc., 2011 WL 4973839 (W.D. La. 2011)—9:1

Multiform Desiccants, Inc. v. Medzam, Ltd., 133 F.3d 1473 (Fed. Cir. 1998)—4:72

Mutual Pharmaceutical Co., Inc. v. Bartlett, 570 U.S. 472, 133 S. Ct. 2466, 186 L. Ed. 2d 607 (2013)—9:2, 9:4

Mylan Pharmaceuticals Inc. v. Research Corporation Technologies, Inc., 914 F.3d 1366 (Fed. Cir. 2019)—5:20

Mytee Products, Inc. v. Harris Research, Inc., 439 Fed. Appx. 882 (Fed. Cir. 2011)—4:97

N

Natural Alternatives International, Inc. v. Creative Compounds, LLC, 918 F.3d 1338 (Fed. Cir. 2019)—4:81

Nautilus, Inc. v. Biosig Instruments, Inc., 572 U.S. 898, 134 S. Ct. 2120, 189 L. Ed. 2d 37 (2014)—4:84

Neste Oil Oyj v. Dynamic Fuels, LLC, 2013 WL 424754 (D. Del. 2013)—5:11

New York ex rel. Schneiderman v. Actavis PLC, 787 F.3d 638 (2d Cir. 2015)—8:1

Nexium (Esomeprazole) Antitrust Litigation, In re, 842 F.3d 34 (1st Cir. 2016)—8:2

NFC Technology LLC v. HTC America, Inc., 2015 WL 1069111 (E.D. Tex. 2015)—5:6, 5:8

Niaspan Antitrust Litigation, In re, 42 F. Supp. 3d 735 (E.D. Pa. 2014)—8:2

Nobelpharma AB v. Implant Innovations, Inc., 141 F.3d 1059 (Fed. Cir. 1998)—8:4

Nolan v. Dillon, 261 Md. 516, 276 A.2d 36 (1971)—9:1

Novartis Pharmaceuticals Corp. v. Roxane Laboratories, Inc., 2009 WL 1140440 (D.N.J. 2009)—4:56

Novo Nordisk of North America, Inc. v. Genentech, Inc., 77 F.3d 1364 (Fed. Cir. 1996)—4:78

Nutrition 21 v. U.S., 930 F.2d 867 (Fed. Cir. 1991)—4:58

O

Octane Fitness, LLC v. ICON Health & Fitness, Inc., 572 U.S. 545, 134 S. Ct. 1749, 188 L. Ed. 2d 816 (2014)—4:93, 4:96

Oil-Dri Corporation of America v. Nestle Purina Petcare Company, 2019 WL 861394 (N.D. Ill. 2019)—5:15

O'Keeffe, In re, 650 Fed. Appx. 83 (2d Cir. 2016)—7:2

Oncology Foundation v. Avanza Development Services, LLC, 2017 WL 2376769 (D. Md. 2017)—7:3

Ortho-McNeil Pharmaceutical, Inc. v. Mylan Laboratories, Inc., 520 F.3d 1358 (Fed. Cir. 2008)—4:92

Ortho-McNeil Pharmaceutical, Inc. v. Mylan Laboratories Inc., 2007 WL 869545 (D.N.J. 2007)—4:97

Otsuka Pharmaceutical Co., Ltd. v. Sandoz, Inc., 678 F.3d 1280 (Fed. Cir. 2012)—4:83

Otsuka Pharmaceutical Co., Ltd. v. Torrent Pharmaceuticals Ltd., Inc., 118 F. Supp. 3d 646 (D.N.J. 2015)—8:4

Otsuka Pharmaceutical Co., Ltd. v. Torrent Pharmaceuticals Ltd., Inc., 99 F. Supp. 3d 461 (D.N.J. 2015)—4:58

O2 Micro Intern. Ltd. v. Beyond Innovation Technology Co., Ltd., 521 F.3d 1351 (Fed. Cir. 2008)—4:70

P

Pa., Com. of v. Nelson, 350 U.S. 497, 76 S. Ct. 477, 100 L. Ed. 640 (1956)—9:5

Pall Corp. v. Micron Separations, Inc., 66 F.3d 1211, 43

Fed. R. Evid. Serv. 97 (Fed. Cir. 1995)—4:95

Penner, In re, 2017 WL 5632658 (D. Mass. 2017)—7:2

Pfizer Inc. v. Johnson & Johnson, 333 F. Supp. 3d 494 (E.D. Pa. 2018)—8:6

Phigenix, Inc. v. Genentech Inc., 238 F. Supp. 3d 1177 (N.D. Cal. 2017)—4:84

Phigenix, Inc. v. Immunogen, Inc., 845 F.3d 1168 (Fed. Cir. 2017)—5:20

Phillips v. AWH Corp., 415 F.3d 1303 (Fed. Cir. 2005)—4:70

Pitney Bowes, Inc. v. Hewlett-Packard Co., 182 F.3d 1298 (Fed. Cir. 1999)—4:70

PLIVA, Inc. v. Mensing, 564 U.S. 604, 131 S. Ct. 2567, 180 L. Ed. 2d 580 (2011)—9:1, 9:2

Precision Instrument Mfg. Co. v. Automotive Maintenance Machinery Co., 324 U.S. 806, 65 S. Ct. 993, 89 L. Ed. 1381 (1945)—4:87

Prentis v. Yale Mfg. Co., 421 Mich. 670, 365 N.W.2d 176 (1984)—9:3

Procter & Gamble Co. v. Kraft Foods Global, Inc., 549 F.3d 842 (Fed. Cir. 2008)—5:4

Procter & Gamble Co. v. Teva Pharmaceuticals USA, Inc., 566 F.3d 989 (Fed. Cir. 2009)—4:83

Professional Real Estate Investors, Inc. v. Columbia Pictures Industries, Inc., 508 U.S. 49, 113 S. Ct. 1920, 123 L. Ed. 2d 611 (1993)—8:4

R

Realtime Data LLC v. Actian Coporation, 2016 WL 3277259 (E.D. Tex. 2016)—5:8

Remicade Antitrust Litigation, In re, 345 F. Supp. 3d 566 (E.D. Pa. 2018)—8:4, 8:6

Renishaw PLC v. Marposs Societa' per Azioni, 158 F.3d 1243 (Fed. Cir. 1998)—4:70

Rite-Hite Corp. v. Kelley Co., Inc., 56 F.3d 1538 (Fed. Cir. 1995)—4:42, 4:93

Rix v. General Motors Corp., 222 Mont. 318, 723 P.2d 195 (1986)—9:3

Roche Molecular Systems, Inc. v. CEPHEID, 905 F.3d 1363 (Fed. Cir. 2018)—4:81

Rochester Drug Co-op., Inc. v. Braintree Laboratories, 712 F. Supp. 2d 308 (D. Del. 2010)—8:4

Rutgers v. Qiagen N.V., 2016 WL 828101 (D.N.J. 2016)—4:81

S

Sandoz Inc. v. Amgen Inc., 137 S. Ct. 1664, 198 L. Ed. 2d 114 (2017)—4:2, 4:3, 4·6, 4:17, 4:18, 4:19, 4:24, 4:26, 4:41, 4:51, 4:69, 4:71, 6:2

Sandoz Inc. v. Amgen Inc., 773 F.3d 1274 (Fed. Cir. 2014)—4:1

Sanofi-Aventis Deutschland GmbH v. Glenmark Pharmaceuticals Inc., 821 F. Supp. 2d 681 (D.N.J. 2011)—4:92

SAS Institute, Inc. v. Iancu, 138 S. Ct. 1348, 200 L. Ed. 2d 695 (2018)—5:15

Scaltech, Inc. v. Retec/Tetra, LLC, 269 F.3d 1321, 45 U.C.C. Rep. Serv. 2d 1036 (Fed. Cir. 2001)—4:82

Schering Corp. v. Geneva Pharmaceuticals, 339 F.3d 1373 (Fed. Cir. 2003)—4:82

Schlich, In re, 893 F.3d 40 (1st Cir. 2018)—7:3

Schreiber Foods, Inc. v. Beatrice Cheese, Inc., 402 F.3d 1198, 61 Fed. R. Serv. 3d 174 (Fed. Cir. 2005)—4:42

Scott v. Neely, 140 U.S. 106, 11 S. Ct. 712, 35 L. Ed. 358 (1891)—4:55

SenoRx, Inc. v. Hologic, Inc., 2013 WL 144255 (D. Del. 2013)—5:11

Sergeants Benevolent Association Health & Welfare Fund v. Acta Vis, PLC, 2016 WL 4992690 (S.D. N.Y. 2016)—8:2

Shaw Industries Group, Inc. v. Automated Creel Systems, Inc., 817 F.3d 1293 (Fed. Cir. 2016)—5:15

Shire US, Inc. v. Allergan, Inc., 375 F. Supp. 3d 538 (D.N.J. 2019)—8:6

Singleton v. International Harvester Co., 685 F.2d 112 (4th Cir. 1981)—9:3

SmithKline Corp. v. Eli Lilly & Co., 575 F.2d 1056 (3d Cir. 1978)—8:6

SmithKline Diagnostics, Inc. v. Helena Laboratories Corp., 859 F.2d 878 (Fed. Cir. 1988)—4:69

Soundscriber Corp. v. U. S., 175 Ct. Cl. 644, 360 F.2d 954 (1966)—4:82

Southwall Technologies, Inc. v. Cardinal IG Co., 54 F.3d 1570 (Fed. Cir. 1995)—4:70, 4:73

Spansion, Inc. v. International Trade Com'n, 629 F.3d 1331 (Fed. Cir. 2010)—6:3

SRI Intern. Inc. v. Internet Sec. Systems, Inc., 2011 WL 5166436 (D. Del. 2011)—4:95

Stonite Products Co. v. Melvin Lloyd Co., 315 U.S. 561, 62 S. Ct. 780, 86 L. Ed. 1026 (1942)—4:33

Strayhorn v. Wyeth Pharmaceuticals, Inc., 887 F. Supp. 2d 799 (W.D. Tenn. 2012)—9:1

Sunovion Pharmaceuticals, Inc. v. Teva Pharmaceuticals USA, Inc., 731 F.3d 1271 (Fed. Cir. 2013)—4:69

T

Takeda Chemical Industries, Ltd. v. Mylan Laboratories, Inc., 549 F.3d 1381 (Fed. Cir. 2008)—4:96

Takeda Chemical Industries, Ltd. v. Mylan Laboratories, Inc., 459 F. Supp. 2d 227 (S.D. N.Y. 2006)—4:17

Takeda Pharmaceuticals U.S.A., Inc. v. West-Ward Pharmaceutical Corp., 785 F.3d 625 (Fed. Cir. 2015)—4:76

Tamoxifen Citrate Antitrust Litigation, In re, 466 F.3d 187 (2d Cir. 2006)—8:2

Tanabe Seiyaku Co., Ltd. v. U.S. Intern. Trade Com'n, 109 F.3d 726 (Fed. Cir. 1997)—4:70, 4:72

TAS Energy, Inc. v. San Diego Gas & Elec. Co., 2014 WL 794215 (S.D. Cal. 2014)—5:5, 5:6

TC Heartland LLC v. Kraft Foods Group Brands LLC, 137 S. Ct. 1514, 197 L. Ed. 2d 816 (2017)—4:34

Technology Licensing Corp., In re, 423 F.3d 1286 (Fed. Cir. 2005)—4:55

Tegal Corp. v. Tokyo Electron America, Inc., 257 F.3d 1331 (Fed. Cir. 2001)—4:55

Teva Pharmaceuticals USA, Inc. v. Sandoz, Inc., 574 U.S. 318, 135 S. Ct. 831, 190 L. Ed. 2d 719 (2015)—4:70

Texas v. U.S., 523 U.S. 296, 118 S. Ct. 1257, 140 L. Ed. 2d 406, 124 Ed. Law Rep. 28 (1998)—4:1

Textron Innovations Inc. v. Toro Co., 2007 WL 7772169 (D. Del. 2007)—5:11

Therasense, Inc. v. Becton, Dickinson and Co., 649 F.3d 1276 (Fed. Cir. 2011)—4:86, 4:88

Thibault v. Sears, Roebuck & Co., 118 N.H. 802, 395 A.2d 843 (1978)—9:3

TianRui Group Co. Ltd. v. International Trade Com'n, 661 F.3d 1322 (Fed. Cir. 2011)—6:2

Titan Tire Corp. v. Case New Holland, Inc., 566 F.3d 1372 (Fed. Cir. 2009)—4:58

Toshiba Corp. v. Imation Corp., 681 F.3d 1358 (Fed. Cir. 2012)—4:77

Trover Group, Inc. v. Dedicated Micros USA, 2015 WL 1069179 (E.D. Tex. 2015)—5:6, 5:9

TruePosition, Inc., v. Polaris Wireless, Inc.,, 2013 WL 5701529 (D. Del. 2013)—5:8

Tull v. U.S., 481 U.S. 412, 107 S. Ct. 1831, 95 L. Ed. 2d 365, 7 Fed. R. Serv. 3d 673 (1987)—4:55

Tyco Healthcare Group LP v. Ethicon Endo-Surgery, Inc., 587 F.3d 1375 (Fed. Cir. 2009)—4:42

U

United Mine Workers of America v. Pennington, 381 U.S. 657, 85 S. Ct. 1585, 14 L. Ed. 2d 626 (1965)—8:4

U.S. v. Western Pac. R. Co., 352 U.S. 59, 77 S. Ct. 161, 1 L. Ed. 2d 126 (1956)—9:5

V

Vanda Pharmaceuticals Inc. v. West-Ward Pharmaceuticals International Limited, 887 F.3d 1117 (Fed. Cir. 2018)—4:81

VE Holding Corp. v. Johnson Gas Appliance Co., 917 F.2d 1574 (Fed. Cir. 1990)—4:38

Vita-Mix Corp. v. Basic Holding, Inc., 581 F.3d 1317 (Fed. Cir. 2009)—4:77

Vitronics Corp. v. Conceptronic, Inc., 90 F.3d 1576 (Fed. Cir. 1996)—4:70

W

Walker Process Equipment, Inc. v. Food Machinery & Chemical Corp., 382 U.S. 172, 86 S. Ct. 347, 15 L. Ed. 2d 247 (1965)—8:4

Wands, In re, 858 F.2d 731 (Fed. Cir. 1988)—4:84

Wang Laboratories, Inc. v. Mitsubishi Electronics America, Inc., 103 F.3d 1571 (Fed. Cir. 1997)—4:73

Wang Laboratories, Inc. v. Toshiba Corp., 993 F.2d 858 (Fed. Cir. 1993)—4:93

Warner-Jenkinson Co., Inc. v. Hilton Davis Chemical Co., 520 U.S. 17, 117 S. Ct. 1040, 137 L. Ed. 2d 146 (1997)—4:72

Warner-Lambert Co. v. Teva Pharmaceuticals USA, Inc., 418 F.3d 1326 (Fed. Cir. 2005)—4:84

Wellbutrin XL Antitrust Litigation Indirect Purchaser Class, In re, 868 F.3d 132 (3d Cir. 2017)—8:4

Wi-Fi One, LLC v. Broadcom Corporation, 887 F.3d 1329 (Fed. Cir. 2018)—5:14

Wilson Sporting Goods Co. v.

David Geoffrey & Associates, 904 F.2d 677 (Fed. Cir. 1990)—4:74

Wilton v. Seven Falls Co., 515 U.S. 277, 115 S. Ct. 2137, 132 L. Ed. 2d 214 (1995)—4:50

Winter v. Natural Resources Defense Council, Inc., 555 U.S. 7, 129 S. Ct. 365, 172 L. Ed. 2d 249 (2008)—4:58

W.L. Gore & Associates, Inc. v. Garlock, Inc., 721 F.2d 1540 (Fed. Cir. 1983)—4:82

Wyeth v. Levine, 555 U.S. 555, 129 S. Ct. 1187, 173 L. Ed. 2d 51 (2009)—9:1, 9:4

Y

Yamanouchi Pharmaceutical Co. v. Danbury Pharmacal, Inc., 21 F. Supp. 2d 366 (S.D. N.Y. 1998)—4:96

Yamanouchi Pharmaceutical Co., Ltd. v. Danbury Pharmacal, Inc., 231 F.3d 1339, 180 A.L.R. Fed. 743 (Fed. Cir. 2000)—4:17

Z

ZTE (USA) Inc., In re, 890 F.3d 1008 (Fed. Cir. 2018)—4:33

Index

ABBREVIATED BIOLOGICS LICENSE APPLICATIONS (aBLAs)
Generally, § 3:3, 3:6 to 3:14
Better than reference product, consequences, § 3:10
BPCIA, jurisdiction before submission of aBLA, § 4:1
Clinical trials, § 3:8
Demonstrating biosimilarity requirements, § 3:6 to 3:11
Exclusivity, interchangeable product, § 3:13
Interchangeability, demonstrating, § 3:12, 3:13
Labeling requirements, § 3:11
Manufacturing information, § 3:7
NDAs to BLAs, conversion, § 3:5
No patent linkage, § 3:14
Proving biosimilarity, § 3:9
Reference product, consequences of comparison, § 3:10
Worse than reference product, consequences, § 3:10

ANTICIPATION
Validity, ineligible subject matter, § 4:82

ANTITRUST ACTIONS
Generally, § 8:1 to 8:6
Acquisition and enforcement of intellectual property
patent thickets, § 8:5
sham litigation, § 8:4
walker process fraud, § 8:4
Challenges to patent settlement agreements, § 8:2
Enforcement. Acquisition and enforcement of intellectual property, above

ANTITRUST ACTIONS—Cont'd
Exclusionary contracting and rebating strategies, § 8:6
Filing agreements with government, § 8:3

APPEALS
Post-grant proceedings, § 5:20

APPLICATION TYPES
Abbreviated Biologics License Applications (aBLAs), § 3:3
Biologics License Applications (BLAs), § 3:2
Drug products not regulated as biological products, § 3:4
NDAs to BLAs, conversion, § 3:5

APPROVAL
FDA Approval (this index)

ATTORNEYS' FEES
Remedies, enforceability of patent, § 4:96

BIOBETTERS
Generally, § 3:15

BIOLOGICS LICENSE APPLICATIONS (BLAs)
Generally, § 3:2

BIOLOGICS PRICE COMPETITION AND INNOVATION ACT (BPCIA)
Generally, § 2:1, 4:1 to 4:98
Discovery
generally, § 4:61 to 4:68
confidentiality tiers, § 4:68
expedited discovery, § 4:64
manufacturing information, § 4:62
overlapping patents-in-suit, § 4:63

BIOLOGICS PRICE COMPETITION AND INNOVATION ACT (BPCIA) —Cont'd
Discovery—Cont'd
  preliminary injunction, § **4:64**
  prosecution bars, § **4:66**
  protective orders, § **4:65 to 4:68**
  regulatory bars, § **4:67**
  same biological product, § **4:63**
Newly issued or licensed patents, § **4:21**
Notice of Commercial Marketing (NCM) (this index)
Patent Dance (this index)
Patent Infringement Liability (this index)
Post-Grant Proceedings (this index)
Preliminary injunctions, § **4:58, 4:64**
Remedies (this index)
Scheduling and staging, § **4:59, 4:60**

CITIZEN PETITIONS
FDA approval process, § **3:22**

COMMENCEMENT OF SUIT
Generally, § **4:32 to 4:57**
Declaratory Judgment Action (this index)
Jurisdiction (this index)
Jury Trial (this index)
Limitation on claims
  generally, § **4:51 to 4:54**
  failure of applicant to provide notice, § **4:52**
  first wave litigation, § **4:53**
  scope-limiting ability of applicant, § **4:53**
  second wave litigation, § **4:54**
Standing, § **4:42**
Venue (this index)

CONFIDENTIAL INFORMATION
Patent Dance (this index)

CONFIDENTIAL INFORMATION—Cont'd
Protective orders, confidentiality tiers, § **4:68**

CONSTRUCTION
Patent infringement liability, claim construction, § **4:70**

COUNTERCLAIMS
Reference product sponsor (RPS), right to bring declaratory judgment action, § **4:49**

DECLARATORY JUDGMENT ACTION
Reference product sponsor (RPS), right to bring
  262(l)(9)(A), § **4:46**
  262(l)(9)(B), § **4:45**
  262(l)(9)(C), § **4:44 to 4:46**
  generally, § **4:43 to 4:50**
  counterclaims, application to, § **4:49**
  discretionary exercise of declaratory judgment jurisdiction, § **4:50**
  limits on ability of applicants to seek declaratory relief, § **4:47**
  non-jurisdictional treatment by courts, § **4:48**
  timing of suit, § **4:46**
  Venue, § **4:37 to 4:39**

DISCOVERY
Biologics Price Competition and Innovation Act (BPCIA) (this index)
Foreign litigation
  generally, § **7:1 to 7:4**
  discretion, § **7:4**
  ex parte application, § **7:3**
  Section 1782 Action, § **7:2 to 7:4**

DOCTRINE OF EQUIVALENTS
Patent infringement liability, direct infringement, § **4:76**

DOUBLE PATENTING
Obviousness-type, § **4:85**

ENFORCEMENT AND ENFORCEABILITY
Antitrust Actions (this index)
Intellectual property acquisition and enforcement. **Antitrust Actions** (this index)
NCM provisions, § **4:26**
Patent dance, confidential information, § **4:13**
Patent Infringement Liability (this index)
Remedies (this index)

ENSNAREMENT
Patent infringement liability, direct infringement, § **4:78**

ESTOPPEL
Generally, § **5:13 to 5:16**
Patent infringement liability, prosecution history estoppel, § **4:77**
Patent owner estoppel, § **5:16**
Real parties in interest and privity, § **5:14**
Scope of estoppel, § **5:15**

EXCLUSIVITY
FDA approval process, provisions impacting biosimilars, § **3:17 to 3:20**

EX PARTE APPLICATION
Discovery, foreign litigation, § **7:3**

FDA APPROVAL
Generally, § **3:1**
Application Types (this index)
Process
generally, § **3:16 to 3:23**
citizen petitions, § **3:22**
complete response letters, § **3:23**
exclusivity provisions impacting biosimilars, § **3:17 to 3:20**
naming, § **3:21**

FDA APPROVAL—Cont'd
Process—Cont'd
orphan drug exclusivity, § **3:20**
pediatric exclusivity, § **3:19**
reference product exclusivity, § **3:18**
review timeline, § **3:16 to 3:20**

FIRST WAVE LITIGATION
Commencement of suit, limitation on claims, § **4:53**
Patent dance, § **4:19, 4:20**

FOREIGN MATTERS
Discovery in the US for use in foreign litigation. **Discovery** (this index)
International Trade Commission (ITC) (this index)
Patent infringement liability, products manufactured abroad using domestically patented process, § **4:75**
Venue, foreign defendants, § **4:36**

FRAUD
Antitrust actions, intellectual property acquisition and enforcement, walker process, § **8:4**

INJUNCTIONS
Permanent injunctive relief, § **4:97**
Preliminary Injunctions (this index)

INSPECTIONS
Post-licensure requirements, establishment inspection, § **3:24**

INTERCHANGEABILITY
Abbreviated biologics license applications (aBLAs), § **3:12, 3:13**

INTERNATIONAL TRADE COMMISSION (ITC)
Comparison between Section 337 investigations and district court litigations, § **6:4**

**INTERNATIONAL TRADE
COMMISSION (ITC)
—Cont'd**
Elements of Section 337 violation,
§ 6:2
Remedies, § 6:3
Section 337 actions, § 6:1 to 6:4

JOINDER
Post-grant proceedings, § 5:18

JURISDICTION
Discretionary exercise of declara-
tory judgment jurisdiction,
§ 4:50
Personal, § 4:41
Product liability claims, primary
jurisdiction, § 9:5
Subject matter, § 4:40

JURY TRIAL
Generally, § 4:55 to 4:57
Biosimilar v. biosimilar patent
cases, § 4:57
BPCIA cases, § 4:56
Right to, § 4:55 to 4:57

LABELING
Biologics license applications
(BLAs), abbreviated applica-
tions, § 3:11
Product liability claims, FDA
biosimilar labeling, § 9:2

MANUFACTURING
Abbreviated biologics license
applications (aBLAs),
manufacturing information,
§ 3:7
BPCIA, discovery, manufacturing
information, § 4:62
Product liability claims,
manufacturing defect claims,
§ 9:3

MOTIONS
Stay, § 5:12

NAMES AND NAMING
FDA approval process, § 3:21

NEGOTIATION
Patent dance, § 4:19, 4:20

**NOTICE OF COMMERCIAL
MARKETING (NCM)**
Generally, § 4:22 to 4:31
Second wave litigation
generally, § 4:28 to 4:31
appearance of, § 4:31
factors impacting bringing suit
after NCM provided,
§ 4:30
who can bring suit after
applicant provides NCM,
§ 4:29
Statute governing NCM
generally, § 4:23 to 4:27
enforcement of NCM provi-
sions, § 4:26
open NCM-related questions,
§ 4:27
requirements for providing
NCM, § 4:25
timing of NCM, § 4:24
Timing of NCM, § 4:24

OBVIOUSNESS
Double patenting, obviousness-
type, § 4:85
Ineligible subject matter, § 4:83
Validity, § 4:83, 4:85

ORPHAN DRUGS
FDA approval process, orphan
drug exclusivity, § 3:20

PATENT DANCE
3A statement, § 4:14
3B statement by biosimilar
applicant
generally, § 4:15 to 4:17
detailed statement, § 4:17
list, § 4:16
3C statement by RPS, § 4:18
Generally, § 4:2 to 4:20
Confidential information, protection
generally, § 4:8 to 4:13

PATENT DANCE—Cont'd
Confidential information, protection—Cont'd
  enforceability, § **4:13**
  prosecution bar, § **4:10**
  recipients of confidential information, § **4:9 to 4:11**
  regulatory bar, § **4:11**
  use during and after patent dance, § **4:12**
Disclosure of product information to RPS
  generally, § **4:3 to 4:7**
  additional requested information, § **4:7**
  consequences of failure to provide, § **4:6**
  copy of aBLA, § **4:4**
  "such other information," § **4:5**
First wave of litigation, § **4:19, 4:20**
Negotiation, § **4:19, 4:20**
Reference product sponsor (RPS)
  disclosure of product information to RPS, above
  statements, § **4:14, 4:18**
Unenforceability allegations, § **4:88, 4:89**

PATENT INFRINGEMENT LIABILITY
Generally, § **4:69 to 4:79**
Claim construction, § **4:70**
Direct infringement, literal, § **4:71**
Doctrine of equivalents, § **4:76**
Enforceability
  generally, § **4:86 to 4:89**
  inequitable conduct, § **4:88**
  unclean hands, § **4:87**
  unenforceability allegations in BPCIA patent dance, § **4:89**
Ensnarement, § **4:78**
Indirect infringement
  generally, § **4:72 to 4:78**
  contributory infringement, § **4:74**

PATENT INFRINGEMENT LIABILITY—Cont'd
Indirect infringement—Cont'd
  doctrine of equivalents, § **4:76**
  ensnarement, § **4:78**
  induced infringement, § **4:73**
  products manufactured abroad using domestically patented process, § **4:75**
  prosecution history estoppel, § **4:77**
  safe harbor, § **4:79**
Literal direct infringement, § **4:71**
Safe harbor, § **4:79**
Validity of patent. **Validity** (this index)

PEDIATRICS
FDA approval process, pediatric exclusivity, § **3:19**

POST-GRANT PROCEEDINGS
Generally, § **5:1 to 5:20**
Appeals, § **5:20**
Estoppel (this index)
Joinder, § **5:18**
Parallel post-grant proceedings and BPCIA litigations, § **5:3**
Serial petitions, § **5:19**
Settlement, § **5:17**
Stays (this index)

POST-LICENSURE REQUIREMENTS
Additional requirements, § **3:25**
Establishment inspection, § **3:24**

PREEMPTION
Product liability claims, field preemption, § **9:5**

PRELIMINARY INJUNCTIONS
Generally, § **4:58**
Expedited discovery, § **4:64**

PRODUCT LIABILITY CLAIMS
Generally, § **9:1 to 9:5**
Failure to warn claims, § **9:1**
Field preemption, § **9:5**

PRODUCT LIABILITY CLAIMS
—Cont'd
Labeling, FDA biosimilar label-
ing, § 9:2
Manufacturing defect claims,
§ 9:3
Primary jurisdiction, § 9:5
Product design defect claims,
§ 9:4

PROTECTIVE ORDERS
Generally, § 4:65 to 4:68
Confidentiality tiers, § 4:68
Prosecution bars, § 4:66
Regulatory bars, § 4:67

REFERENCE PRODUCTS
Abbreviated biologics license
applications (aBLAs), consequences of comparison,
§ 3:10
FDA approval process, reference
product exclusivity, § 3:18
Reference product sponsor (RPS)
Declaratory Judgment Action
(this index)
Patent Dance (this index)

REMEDIES
Generally, § 4:90 to 4:98
Conforming amendments of
BPCIA, § 4:91
Delaying effective date of FDA
approval, § 4:92
Enforceability of patent
at-risk launch, § 4:95
attorneys' fees, § 4:96
monetary damages, § 4:94, 4:95
pre-market activity, § 4:94
safe harbor, § 4:94
Injunctions (this index)
ITC remedies, § 6:3
Limitations on remedies, § 4:98
Monetary damages, enforceability
of patent, § 4:94, 4:95
Monetary relief, § 4:93 to 4:95

SAFE HARBOR
Patent infringement liability,
§ 4:79
Remedies, enforceability of
patent, § 4:94

SECOND WAVE LITIGATION
Commencement of suit, limitation
on claims, § 4:54
Notice of Commercial Market-
ing (NCM) (this index)

SERIAL PETITIONS
Post-grant proceedings, § 5:19

SETTLEMENT
Antitrust actions, challenges to
patent settlement agreements,
§ 8:2
Post-grant proceedings, § 5:17

STANDING
Commencement of suit, § 4:42

STAYS
Generally, § 5:4 to 5:11
Motions to stay, § 5:12
Simplification of issues, § 5:6
Stage of litigation, § 5:5
Undue prejudice
generally, § 5:7 to 5:11
relationship of parties, § 5:11
review request, timing, § 5:8
status of review proceedings,
§ 5:10
stay request, timing, § 5:9

TIME AND TIMING
Declaratory judgment action, right
of RPS to bring, § 4:46
FDA approval process, review
timeline, § 3:16 to 3:20
Notice of commercial marketing
(NCM), timing of, § 4:24
Remedies, delaying effective date
of FDA approval, § 4:92
Review request, timing, § 5:8
Scheduling and staging, § 4:60

TIME AND TIMING—Cont'd
Scheduling and staging, BPCIA, § **4:59**
Stay request, timing, § **5:9**

TRIALS
Biologics license applications (BLAs), abbreviated applications, § **3:8**

UNCLEAN HANDS
Patent infringement liability, enforceability, § **4:87**

VALIDITY
Generally, § **4:80 to 4:85**
Enablement, lack of, § **4:84**
Indefiniteness, § **4:84**
Ineligible subject matter
generally, § **4:81 to 4:83**
anticipation, § **4:82**
obviousness, § **4:83**

VALIDITY—Cont'd
Obviousness-type double patenting, § **4:85**
Written description, lack of, § **4:84**

VENUE
Generally, § **4:32 to 4:39**
Declaratory judgment, § **4:37 to 4:39**
Patent infringement actions
generally, § **4:33 to 4:36**
declaratory judgment, § **4:38, 4:39**
defendant's residence, § **4:34**
foreign defendants, § **4:36**
infringement, § **4:35**
place of business, § **4:35**

WRITTEN DESCRIPTION
Validity, lack of written description, § **4:84**